Third BlackboxNLP Workshop on Analyzing and Interpreting Neural Networks for NLP (BlackboxNLP2020)

Online
20 November 2020

ISBN: 978-1-7138-1988-2

BlackboxNLP2020

**Proceedings of the Third BlackboxNLP Workshop on
Analyzing and Interpreting Neural Networks for NLP**

Introduction

BlackboxNLP is the workshop on analyzing and interpreting neural networks for NLP.

In the last few years, neural networks have rapidly become a central component in NLP systems. The improvement in accuracy and performance brought by the introduction of neural networks has typically come at the cost of our understanding of the system: How do we assess what the representations and computations are that the network learns? The goal of this workshop is to bring together people who are attempting to peek inside the neural network black box, taking inspiration from machine learning, psychology, linguistics, and neuroscience.

In this third edition of the workshop, hosted by the 2020 conference on Empirical Methods in Natural Language Processing (EMNLP), we accepted 31 archival papers and 9 extended abstracts. The workshop also provided a platform for authors of EMNLP-Findings papers to present their work as a poster at the workshop. Lastly, for the first time, BlackboxNLP included a shared interpretation mission. One paper submitted to this mission has a *demo* presentation, of the interpretability library `diagnnose`, and is included as the last paper in these proceedings (submission number 70).

BlackboxNLP would not have been possible without the dedication of its program committee. We would like to thank them for their invaluable effort in providing timely and high-quality reviews on a short notice. We are also grateful to our invited speakers for contributing to our program.

Afra Alishahi, Yonatan Belinkov, Grzegorz Chrupała, Dieuwke Hupkes, Yuval Pinter and Hassan Sajjad

Organizers:

Afra Alishahi, Tilburg University
Yonatan Belinkov, Technion - Israel Institute of Technology
Grzegorz Chrupała, Tilburg University
Dieuwke Hupkes, University of Amsterdam
Yuval Pinter, Georgia Institute of Technology
Hassan Sajjad, Qatar Computing Research Institute

Program Committee:

Samira Abnar, University of Amsterdam
Željko Agić, Unity Technologies Copenhagen
Antonios Anastasopoulos
Leila Arras - Fraunhofer Heinrich Hertz Institute
Jasmijn Bastings - Google
Lisa Beinborn - University of Amsterdam
Laurent Besacier - Laboratoire d'Informatique de Grenoble
Stergios Chatzikyriakidis - University of Gotheburg
Barry Devereux - Queen's University
Ewan Dunbar - Université Paris Diderot
Allyson Ettinger - University of Chicago
Antske Fokkens - Vrije Universiteit Amsterdam
Robert Frank - Yale University
Alexander Fraser - LMU Munich
Richard Futrell - University of California, Irvine
Sebastian Gehrmann - Harvard University
David Harwath - MIT
John Hewitt - Stanford University
Cassandra Jacobs - University of Wisconsin
Yair Lakretz - NeuroSpin
Shalom Lappin - University of Gothenburg
Miryam de Lhoneux - Uppsala University
Tal Linzen - Johns Hopkins University
Nelson F. Liu - University of Washington
Pranava Madhyastha - Imperial College London
Arya McCarthy - Johns Hopkins University
Paola Merlo - University of Geneva
Raymond Mooney - UT AUstin Joakim Nivre - Uppsala University
Sebastian Padó - University of Stuttgart
Ellie Pavlick - Brown University
Rudolf Rosa - Charles University
Carolyn Rose - CMU Sebastian Ruder - DeepMind
Wojciech Samek - Fraunhofer Heinrich Hertz Institute
Naomi Saphra - University of Edinburgh
Sabine Schulte im Walde - University of Stuttgart
Rico Sennrich - University of Zurich
Pia Sommerauer - Vrije Universiteit Amsterdam

Ivan Titov - University of Edinburgh
Francesca Toni - Imperial College London
Reut Tsarfaty - Open University
Sarah Wiegreffe - Georgia Tech
Adina Williams - New York University
Diyi Yang - Georgia Tech
Fabio Massimo Zanzotto - University of Rome

Invited Speakers:

Idan Blank, UCLA
Roger Levy, MIT
Anna Rogers, University of Copenhagen

Table of Contents

Conference Program

The programme of BlackboxNLP2020 consists of three keynote presentations, six selected oral presentations, one demo paper and two poster sessions. Due to the virtual nature of the conference, these activities are distributed over three blocks, such that every activity occurs twice and is accessible for any time zone. The full programme of the workshop can be found at https://blackboxnlp.github.io.

The three keynotes at BlackboxNLP2020 are:

Roger Levy, MIT
Evaluating and calibrating neural language models for human-like language processing

Anna Rogers, University of Copenhagen
When BERT plays the lottery, all tickets are winning!

Idan Blank, UCLA
Understanding NLP's blackbox with the brain's blackbox and vice versa

The six papers selected for oral presentation are:

What Happens To BERT Embeddings During Fine-tuning?
Amil Merchant, Elahe Rahimtoroghi, Ellie Pavlick and Ian Tenney

Dissecting Lottery Ticket Transformers: Structural and Behavioral Study of Sparse Neural Machine Translation
Rajiv Movva and Jason Zhao

Evaluating Attribution Methods using White-Box LSTMs
Yiding Hao

The EOS Decision and Length Extrapolation
Benjamin Newman, John Hewitt, Percy Liang and Christopher D. Manning

BERTs of a feather do not generalize together: Large variability in generalization across models with similar test set performance
R. Thomas Mccoy, Junghyun Min and Tal Linzen

The elephant in the interpretability room: Why use attention as explanation when we have saliency methods?
Jasmijn Bastings and Katja Filippova

The shared task paper selected to give a demo presentation is:

diagNNose: A Library for Neural Activation Analysis
Jaap Jumelet

All other papers in these proceedings, as well as the nine accepted abstracts, are presented at the poster sessions of the conference. Also a selection of related EMNLP-findings papers are present at the poster sessions.

BERTering RAMS: What and How Much does BERT Already Know About Event Arguments? — A Study on the RAMS Dataset

Varun Gangal, Eduard Hovy
Language Technologies Institute
Carnegie Mellon University
{vgangal,hovy}@cs.cmu.edu

Abstract

Using the attention map based probing framework from (Clark et al., 2019), we observe that, on the RAMS dataset (Ebner et al., 2020)[1], BERT's attention heads[2] have modest but well above-chance ability to spot event arguments sans *any training or domain finetuning*, varying from a low of 17.77% for *Place* to a high of 51.61% for *Artifact*. Next, we find that linear combinations of these heads, estimated with ≈11% of available total event argument detection supervision, can push performance well-higher for some roles — highest two being *Victim* (68.29% Accuracy) and *Artifact* (58.82% Accuracy). Furthermore, we investigate how well our methods do for cross-sentence event arguments. We propose a procedure to isolate "best heads" for cross-sentence argument detection separately of those for intra-sentence arguments. The heads thus estimated have superior cross-sentence performance compared to their jointly estimated equivalents, albeit only under the unrealistic assumption that we already know the argument is present in another sentence. Lastly, we seek to isolate to what extent our numbers stem from lexical frequency based associations between gold arguments and roles. We propose NONCE, a scheme to create adversarial test examples by replacing gold arguments with randomly generated "nonce" words. We find that learnt linear combinations are robust to NONCE, though individual best heads can be more sensitive.

1 Introduction

The NLP representation paradigm has undergone a drastic change in this decade — moving from lin-

---

[1]Refer to Figure 1 of that paper for an example illustrating four role names. Since these role names are human readable and intuitively named, we refer to them without elaboration.

[2]We use *map* to refer to the per-example word-word activations at a particular layer-head, while *head* refers either to the identity of the particular layer-head. We ground these terms more clearly in §2.1

guistic/task motivated 0-1 feature families to per-word-type pretrained vectors (Pennington et al., 2014) to contextual embeddings (Peters et al., 2018).

Contextual embeddings (CEs) produce in-context representations for each token - the representation framework being a large, pretrained encoder with per-token outputs. The typical procedure to use CEs for a downstream task is to add one or more task layers atop each token, or for a designated token per-sentence, depending on the nature of the task.

The task layers (and optionally, the representation) are then "*finetuned*" using a task specific loss, albeit with a slower training rate than would be used for from-scratch training. ELMo (Peters et al., 2018) was an early CE. The three-fold recipe of a transformer based architecture, masked language modelling objective and large pre-training corpora, starting with BERT (Devlin et al., 2018) led to CEs which were vastly effective for most tasks.

The strong performance of contextual representations with just shallow task layers and minimal finetuning drove the urge to understand what and how much these models *already knew* about aspects of syntax and semantics. The study of methods and analysis to do this has come to be called *probing*. Besides "explaining" CE featurization, probing can aid in finding lacunae to be addressed by future representations.

Linzen et al. (2016), one of the early works on probing, evaluated whether language models could predict the correct verb form agreeing with the noun. Marvin and Linzen (2018) generalized this approach beyond single-word gaps with a larger suite of "minimal pairs". They also control for lexical confounding and expand the probing to new aspects such as reflexive anaphora and NPIs. Gulordava et al. (2018) evaluate subject-verb agreement but only through "nonce" sentences to con-

Proceedings of the Third BlackboxNLP Workshop on Analyzing and Interpreting Neural Networks for NLP, pages 1–10
Online, November 20, 2020. ©2020 Association for Computational Linguistics

trol for both lexical confounding and memorization[3]. Lakretz et al. (2019) isolate units of LSTM language models whose activations closely track verb-noun number agreement, particularly for hard, long-distance cases. Clark et al. (2019), whose probing methods we adopt, examine if BERT attention heads capture dependency structure.

In this work, we probe what and how much a pretrained BERT representation already knows about event roles and their arguments. Understanding how well event arguments are represented can be a first foray into understanding other aspects about events. Extraction of event arguments is often a prerequisite for more complex event tasks. Some examples are event coreference (Lu and Ng, 2018), detecting event-event temporal (Vashishtha et al., 2019) and causal relations (Dunietz et al., 2017), sub-event structure (Araki et al., 2014) and generating approximate causal paths (Kang et al., 2017). Tuples of event-type and arguments are one way of inducing script like-structures (Chambers and Jurafsky, 2008). In summary, our work makes the following contributions:

1. We show that there always exists a BERT attention head (BESTHEAD) with above-chance ability to detect arguments, for a given event role. We also show that this ability is even stronger through learnt linear combinations (LINEAR) of heads.
2. We notice a relative weakness at detecting cross sentence arguments (§3.3). Motivated by this, we devise a procedure to isolate only the cross-sentence argument detection ability of heads w.r.t a role (§3.3.1). Our procedure considerably improves cross-sentence performance for some roles (§3.4), especially for INSTRUMENT and PLACE.
3. Lastly, we seek to isolate how much of the zero-shot argument detection ability originates solely from the model's world knowledge and lexical frequency based associations. To do this, we propose NONCE, a method to perturb test examples to dampen such associations (§2.5.3). We find that the LINEAR approach is robust to NONCE perturbation, while BESTHEAD is more sensitive.

---
[3]A motivation for our ablation in §2.5.3

2 Methodology

2.1 Background

2.1.1 Transformers

The Transformer architecture (Vaswani et al., 2017) consists of $|L|$ layers, each comprised of $|H| > 1$ "self-attention" heads. Here, we describe the architecture just enough to ground terminology - we defer to the original work for detailed exposition.

In a given layer l^4, a single self-attention head h consists of three steps - First, query, key and value projections $q_i^h = Q_h^T e_i, k_i^h = K_h^T e_i, v_i^h = V_h^T e_i$ are computed from the previous layer's token embedding e_i. Then, softmax normalized dot products $\alpha_{ij}^h = \frac{(q_i^h)^T k_j^h}{\sum_m (q_i^h)^T k_m^h}$ are computed between the current token's query projection and other token's key projections. These dot products a.k.a *attention values* are then used as weights to combine all token value projections - $o_i^h = \sum_j \alpha_{ij}^h v_j^h$ gives the current head's token output o_i^h. Finally, the outputs from all heads are concatenated and projected to get the per-token embeddings for the current layer $o_i = W^T Concat(\{o_i^0, o_i^1 \ldots o_i^{|H|-1}\})$

Henceforth, we refer to the parameter tuple $\{Q_{h,l}, K_{h,l}, V_{h,l}\}$, uniquely identified by $h \in \{0, 1, \ldots |H| - 1\}, l \in \{0, 1, \ldots |L| - 1\}$ as the "*attention head*" or simply "*head*", while values $\alpha_{ij}^{h,l}$ are collectively referred to as the "*attention map*".

2.1.2 BERT

BERT uses a Transformer architecture with 12 heads and 12 layers[5]. It comes with an associated BPE tokenizer (Sennrich et al., 2015) which tokenizes raw inputs to subwords. Its vocabulary contains three special tokens - [CLS], [SEP] and [MASK]. While [CLS] and [SEP] serve as start and end (or sequence-separator) tokens, [MASK] is used in pretraining as described next.

BERT follows a two-stage pretraining process. In the first stage, also known as masked language modelling (MLM), randomly selected token positions are replaced with [MASK]. The task is to predict the true identities of words at these positions, given the sequence. This stage uses single sentences as training examples. In the second stage, also known as next sentence prediction (NSP), the

---
[4]We omit layer index l in the rest of the passage to declutter our notation.

[5]For *bert-base*. *bert-large* uses 24 heads and 24 layers.

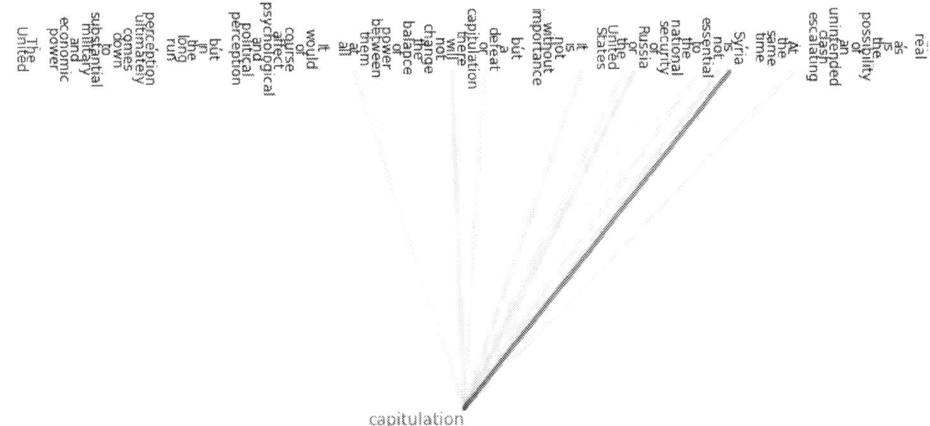

Figure 1: In this example, the head chosen by BESTHEAD for the PLACE role, correctly picks out the argument "*Syria*" for the trigger "*capitulation*". Attention probabilities are shown as blue lines from trigger token to other tokens, with boldness indicating magnitude. It manages to evade distractor pronouns (*there*) and other geographical entity names (*Russia* and *United States*). The text above flows in right to left direction. The full text reads: "*Chances of intentional conflict are real as is the possibility of an unintended clash escalating . At the same time, Syria is not essential to the national security of Russia or the United States. It is not without importance but a defeat or **capitulation** there will not change the balance of power between them at all . . .*"

model is given a pair of sentences (separated by [SEP]), with the task being to predict whether these were truly consecutive or not.

Unless otherwise mentioned, we use the *bert-base-uncased* model. We use the implementation of BERT from HuggingFace. [6] (Wolf et al., 2019)

2.2 Dataset

We use the recently released RAMS dataset (Ebner et al., 2020) for all our experiments. The reasons for using this particular dataset for our analysis are

- It has a wide mix of reasonably frequent roles (represented well across splits) from different kinds of frames . Discussion on non-frequent roles can be found in §3.6.

- For many roles, it has examples with the gold arguments being in a different sentence from the event trigger. This makes it easy to probe for intra-sentence and cross-sentence argument extraction in the same set of experiments. Analysis of cross-sentence performance can be found in §3.3 and §3.4

We note that the dataset is in English (Bender and Friedman, 2018) and observations made may not generalize to other languages.

2.2.1 Setup

For example x, we refer to the event, role, gold argument and document as e, r, a and D. D is an ordered sequence of tokens $\{w_0, w_1 \ldots w_{|D|-1}\}$. i_e denotes the event trigger index[7].

We use the layer index l and head indices 0 to $|H| - 1$ to index the respective head's attention distribution *from* token i to all other tokens $j \in D$ at index i_e.

$$P^*_{l,h}(j|i_e) = \alpha^{i_e j}_{l,h}, 0 \leq l < |L|, 0 \leq h < |H| \quad (1)$$

Note, however that there exist a complementary set of attention values from each token j *to* the token i_e. To use a unified indexing scheme to refer to these values, we use negative indices from -1 to $-|H|$ as their head indices. Since these values come from attention-head activations of different positions, they need to be renormalized to use them as probabilities.

$$P^*_{l,-h}(j|i_e) = \frac{\alpha^{j i_e}_{l,h-1}}{\sum_{k \in D} \alpha^{k i_e}_{l,h-1}}, 0 < h \leq |H| \quad (2)$$

2.2.2 Words and Subwords

Our above framework assumed that the attention maps are between whole word tokens. However, BERT represents a sentence as a sequence of BPE-subwords at every level, including for the attention maps.

We use the quite intuitive approach described in Section 4.1 of (Clark et al., 2019) - incoming attentions to constituent subwords of a word are added to get the attention to that word. Outgoing attention

---

[7]To simplify our analysis, we do not include multi-word triggers. These form only $\approx 1.6\%$ of the cases in the dataset.

3

values from constituent subwords are averaged to get the outgoing attention value from the word.

Note that the above operations precede the probability computations in Equations 1 and 2.

2.2.3 Dataset Splits

We follow the practice of earlier probing works such as (Sorodoc et al., 2020) and (Linzen et al., 2016) of using one of the smaller splits for training. Specifically, we use the original dev split of RAMS (924 examples in total) as our training split. Note that each example could contain multiple role-argument pairs.

Splits	Examples	Tokens
Train (Original Dev)	924	0.12M
Dev (Original Test)	871	0.11M
Test (Original Train)	7329	0.98M

Table 1: Split example counts and token sizes from the RAMS. Note that we use different splits since our work is a probing exercise.

2.3 Evaluation Measure

For a given event e and role r, we define a predicted argument token index $\widehat{a}$ to be accurate if it corresponds to any of the tokens in the gold argument span $[a_{r,e}^{beg}, a_{r,e}^{end}]$. This is described formally in Equation 3. I stands for the 0-1 indicator function.

$$Acc_{e,r,a}(\widehat{a}) = I(a_{r,e}^{beg} \leq \widehat{a} < a_{r,e}^{end}) \qquad (3)$$

Typical measures of argument extraction differ from the one we use, being span-based. Given the limitations of our probing approaches, we lack a clear mechanism of predicting multi-word spans, and can only predict likely single tokens for the argument, which led us to choose this measure[8].

2.4 Approaches

2.4.1 BestHead

Let $X = \{e_m, r_m, a_m\}_{m=1}^{m=M}$ be the training set. X_r is the subset of training examples with $r_m = r$. For each role r, BestHead selects the head $\{l, h\}_{best}(r)$ with best aggregate accuracy on X_r. Other than one pass over the training set for comparing aggregate accuracies of heads for each role, there is no learning required for this method. At test-time, based on the test role, the respective best head is used to predict the argument token.

---

[8]We will interchangeably refer to Acc as just *"accuracy"* in plain-text in the rest of the paper

$$Acc_{l,h}^{X_r} = \sum_{m=1}^{m=M_r} Acc_{e_m,r,a_m}(\arg\max_j \widehat{P}_{l,h}(j|i_{e_m}))$$

$$\{l,h\}_{best}(r) = \arg\max_{l,h} Acc_{l,h}^{X_r}$$

2.4.2 LINEAR

The LINEAR model learns a weighted linear combination of all $|L| \times |H| \times 2$ head distributions (twice for the *"from"* and *"to"* heads).

$$\phi(j|i) = \sum_{l=0}^{l=|L|-1} \sum_{h=-|H|}^{h=|H|-1} w_{l,h}\widehat{P}_{l,h}(j|i) + B$$

$$\widehat{P}(j|i) = \frac{\phi(j|i)}{\sum_{k=0}^{k=|D|-1} \phi(k|i)}$$

Note that gradients are not backpropagated into BERT - only the linear layer parameters $w_{l,h}, B$ are updated during backpropagation. This formulation is the same as the one in (Clark et al., 2019).

For our loss function, we use the KL Divergence $KL(\widehat{P}||P)$ between the predicted distribution over document tokens $\widehat{P}$ and the gold distribution over document tokens P. For the gold distribution over arg tokens, the probability mass is equally distributed tokens in the argument span, with zero mass on the other tokens.

$$KL(\widehat{P}||P) = \sum_{k=0}^{k=|D|-1} \widehat{P}(k|i) \log \frac{\widehat{P}(k|i)}{P(k|i)}$$

2.5 Baselines

2.5.1 RAND

The expected accuracy of following the strategy of randomly picking any token i from the document D as the argument (other than the trigger word i_e itself). For a given role r with a gold argument $a_{r,e}$ of length $|a_{r,e}|$, this equals $\frac{|a_{r,e}|}{|D|-1}$.

2.5.2 SentOnly

The expected accuracy of following the strategy of randomly picking any token from the same sentence S_e as the argument, save the event trigger itself. This is motivated by the intuition that event arguments mostly lie in-sentence. This equals $\frac{|a_{r,e}|}{|S_e|-1}$

2.5.3 NONCE procedure

We wish to isolate how much of the heads performance is due to memorized "world knowledge" and typical lexical associations e.g *Russia* would typically always be a PLACE or TARGET. Recent works have shown that BERT does retain such associations, including for first names (Shwartz et al., 2020), and enough so that it can act as a reasonable knowledge base (Petroni et al., 2019).

One way of implementing this is to create perturbed test examples where gold arguments are replaced with synthetically created "nonce" words not necessarily related to the context. This is similar to the approach of (Gulordava et al., 2018).

- Each gold argument token is replaced by a randomly generated token with the same number of characters as the original string.

- Stop words such as determiners, pronouns, and conjunctions are left unaltered, though they might be a part of the argument span.

- We also ensure that the shape of the original argument, i.e the profile of case, digit vs letter is maintained[9]. e.g *Russia-15* can be randomly replaced by *Vanjia-24*, which has the same shape *Xxxx-dd*.

- Note that we do not take pronounceability of the nonce word into account. Though this could arguably be a relevant invariant to maintain, we were not sure of an apt way to enforce it automatically.

- We also note that BERT may end up using a likely larger number of subword tokens to replace the nonce words than it would use for the gold argument token. Since these are essentially randomly composed tokens, they can contain subwords which are rarely seen in vocabulary tokens.

We refer to this procedure as NONCE, and overloading the term, the test set so created as the NONCE test set.

3 Experiments

3.1 Spotting the Best Head

In Table 2, we record the accuracies and layer positions of best heads for the 15 most frequent roles.

1. BESTHEAD always has higher accuracy than the RAND and SENT baselines.
2. 5 of the 15 roles can be identified with 40%+ accuracy - the highest being COMMUNICATOR , at 51.61%.

Role	$\{l,h\}_{best}$	%Accuracy
DEFENDANT	8,10	35.90
DESTINATION	0,8	21.43
ORIGIN	7,-1	31.82
TRANSPORTER	8,10	31.58
INSTRUMENT	9,7	31.37
BENEFICIARY	8,10	26.56
ATTACKER	7,-8	33.93
TARGET	9,1	**44.61**
GIVER	8,10	25.55
VICTIM	9,1	**46.34**
ARTIFACT	4,-6	**50.42**
COMMUNICATOR	8,10	**51.61**
PARTICIPANT	8,10	28.57
RECIPIENT	7,10	**40.78**
PLACE	9,1	17.77

Table 2: Best layer-head pair , $\{l,h\}_{best}$ and % Accuracy for the 15 most frequent roles in RAMS, using *bert-base-uncased*. +ve h indices denote "from" heads, while -ve indices denote "to" heads, as explained in §2.2.1

3. The best head for arguments which are not together present in frames is often the same. For instance, Layer 8, Head 10 is the best head for TRANSPORTER, ATTACKER, COMMUNICATOR and BENEFICIARY.
4. Most best heads are located in the higher layers, specifically the 7th, 8th or 9th layers. An exception are the best head for DESTINATION and ARTIFACT roles, located in the 0th layer and 4th layers respectively.
5. *Place* roles are the hardest to identify, with an accuracy of 17.77%.
6. Layer 8, Head 10 seems to be doing a lot of the heavylifting. For 7 out of 15 roles, this is the best head. This shows that it is quite "overworked" in terms of the number of roles it tracks. Furthermore, though some of these role pairs are from different frames (e.g see Point 3 above), some aren't, e.g GIVER and BENEFICIARY. In such cases, atleast one of the two arguments predicted for these two roles is sure to be inaccurate - e.g the head would point to either the GIVER or BENEFICIARY, but not both. [10]
7. Most of the best heads for roles are "from" heads rather than "to" heads, apart from those for ORIGIN, ATTACKER and ARTIFACT.

3.2 LINEAR Performance

Table 3 shows test accuracies for both LINEAR and BESTHEAD approaches, and also the baselines.

For 12 of the 15 roles, LINEAR has higher accuracy than BESTHEAD. There are three exceptions - ORIGIN and INSTRUMENT, which suffer a decline

---

[9]We are aware that case mostly doesn't matter since we use bert-*-uncased in most experiments

[10]It is quite non-intuitive for GIVER and BENEFICIARY spans to overlap — we don't see any examples with the same.

Role	Rand	SentOnly	BestHead	Linear
Defendant	1.75	6.98	35.90	56.41
Destination	1.91	7.67	21.43	39.28
Origin	1.36	7.27	31.82	28.79
Transporter	1.63	6.57	31.58	43.42
Instrument	1.88	6.29	31.37	25.49
Beneficiary	1.34	6.28	26.56	34.37
Attacker	2.07	8.52	33.93	46.43
Target	1.78	7.30	44.61	44.61
Giver	1.58	6.29	25.55	32.22
Victim	1.50	6.42	46.34	68.29
Artifact	1.86	7.62	50.42	58.82
Communicator	1.58	6.55	51.61	63.71
Participant	1.49	6.19	28.57	30.72
Recipient	1.83	8.57	40.78	44.69
Place	1.67	6.84	17.77	31.93

Table 3: Test accuracies using all the baselines and probe approaches described in §§2.4 for the 15 most frequent roles in RAMS. Both BestHead and Linear probes outdo the baselines. Linear usually does better, but not for all roles (e.g Origin). Refer to §3.2 for a longer discussion.

Role	BestHead+CSO	Linear+CSO
Origin	4.76 ($31.82 \rightarrow 0.00$)	4.76 ($56.41 \rightarrow 16.34$)
Instrument	47.37 ($31.37 \rightarrow 21.22$)	52.63 ($25.49 \rightarrow 31.51$)
Participant	24.99 ($28.57 \rightarrow 6.37$)	29.16 ($30.72 \rightarrow 6.37$)
Place	15.31 ($17.77 \rightarrow 10.18$)	30.61 ($31.93 \rightarrow 9.30$)

Table 4: Accuracies on cross-sentence test examples using BestHead+CSO and Linear+CSO. The values $Acc_{Total} \rightarrow Acc_{Cross}$ in parentheses are the total test accuracy and cross-sentence test accuracy respectively, using the simple version of the same approach i.e BestHead and Linear. The % of cross-sentence examples for each role are: {Origin:31.82 Instrument:37.26 Participant:17.14 Place:29.52}

and Target, which remains the same. A possible reason could be the higher fraction of cross-sentence gold arguments for these roles. The five roles with lowest number of intra-sentence arguments are Destination (58.92%), Instrument (62.74%), Origin (68.18%), Place (70.48%) and Target (81.53%).

While Destination and Place do see increases in Linear compared to BestHead, it could be the case that none of the individual heads are particularly good at capturing cross-sentence arguments for the other three roles, while the best head is already good enough to capture the intra-sentence case. This would make Linear not any more rich as a hypothesis space compared to BestHead - causing the similar or slightly worse accuracy. In §3.3 we dig deeper into the aspect of cross-sentence performance.

3.3 Cross-Sentence Performance

From Table 4, we observe that both BestHead and Linear performance degrades in the cross-sentence case i.e when "trigger sentence" and "gold argument sentence" differ. Three potential reasons:

1. There are too few instances of cross-sentence event arguments in the small supervised set we use. Furthermore, even if there are a sufficient quantum of cross-sentence event arguments, these form a much smaller proportion of the total instances in comparison to the intra-sentence instances.
2. Because the limited number of attention heads are already dominated by intra-sentence aspects such as dependency relations, punctuation and subject-verb agreement (Clark et al.,

2019), it is difficult for a single attention head to have a higher value for outside sentence tokens compared to in-sentence ones.
3. Different heads might be best for intra and cross-sentence performance, and finding one best head for both could be sub-optimal.

3.3.1 Cross Sentence Occlusion (CSO)

Motivated by the above reasons, we devise a procedure which we refer to as cross-sentence occlusion (CSO). Since Reason 1 is a property of the data distribution, we attempt to alleviate Reasons 2 and 3. To address Reason 3, we try to learn a different head (combination) for the cross-sentence case. To address Reason 2, while finding the best cross-sentence head, we zero-mask out the attention values corresponding to in-sentence[11] tokens and re-normalize the probability distribution.

In practice, one would not be able to use two separate argument detectors for the intra and cross-sentence cases for the same role, since ground-truth information of whether the argument is cross-sentence would be unavailable. We assume this contrived setting only to allow easy analysis[12], and to gloss over the lack of an intuitive zero-shot mechanism of switching between the two cases, when predicting arguments using just attention heads.

3.4 +CSO Results

From Table 4, we can observe the improvement in cross-sentence test accuracy when using the +CSO approach over its simple counterpart, both for BestHead and Linear. The only exception to this is the Origin role, where Linear betters Linear-CSO.

For the Instrument role, both Best-Head+CSO and Linear+CSO get close to 50%

---

[11] RAMS comes with a given sentence segmentation.

[12] And also so that we can validate our diagnosis for poor cross-sentence performance in §3.3

accuracy. In part, their relatively stronger performance can be explained by BESTHEAD and LINEAR already being relatively better at detecting cross-sentence INSTRUMENT (just above 20%, but higher than the sub-15 accuracies on the other roles). Nevertheless, CSO still leads to a doubling of accuracies for both approaches.

We highlight here again that these numbers are only on that subset of the test set where we know that the gold arguments are located in other sentences - though this setting is useful for analysis, a model actually solving this task won't have access to this information.

Even in our case, there is no obvious way to have a consolidated probe which uses a LINEAR+CSO and LINEAR component together, since this would require learning an additional component which predicts whether the gold arguments lie intra-sentence or across-sentence.

3.5 Effect of NONCE

In Figures 2a and 2b, we compare the performances of our methods on perturbations of the test set created using the NONCE procedure outlined in §2.5.3 with their normal test performance. Since NONCE is stochaistic, corresponding results are averaged over NONCE sets created with 5 different seeds.

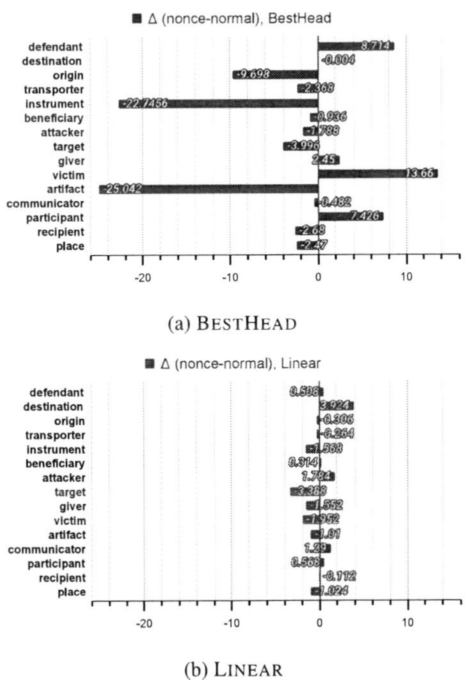

(a) BESTHEAD

(b) LINEAR

Figure 2: Difference in a) BESTHEAD and b) LINEAR accuracies over normal and NONCE test sets

BESTHEAD test performance is more sensitive to NONCE than LINEAR. Especially for INSTRUMENT, ARTIFACT and ORIGIN, the decrease in accuracy is quite drastic. Surprisingly, we also see increases for 4 of the 15 roles - DEFENDANT, GIVER, VICTIM and PARTICIPANT. All other roles see small decreases. For LINEAR, however, most roles are largely unmoved by NONCE, showing that LINEAR relies less on lexical associations.

3.6 Non-Frequent Roles

So far, we've focussed on analyzing the 15 most frequent roles. In this subsection, we also evaluate our approaches for some non-frequent roles outside this set, such as PREVENTER and PROSECUTOR. The results are presented in Table 5. Note that, owing to high sparsity for these roles, these results should be taken with "a pinch of salt" (which is why we chose to separate them out from the frequent roles).

For the frequent roles, we had seen that LINEAR was mostly better than, or equally good as BESTHEAD. For the non-frequent roles, we see that the comparative performance of LINEAR vs BESTHEAD varies a lot more - LINEAR is better for 6 of the 11 roles, and worse for the other 5. The fall in LINEAR performance is largest for PROSECUTOR $(58.33 \rightarrow 16.67)$.

We conjecture that this drop is due to poor generalization as a result of learning from lesser supervision as a result of the roles being non-frequent. Since BESTHEAD has only two parameters (identity of the best head) compared to the 289 parameters of LINEAR, the latter is more sensitive to this problem.

Secondly, we notice that the gap between BESTHEAD and the RAND and SENTONLY baselines is much narrower. For VEHICLE and MONEY, SENTONLY even outdoes BESTHEAD. For VEHICLE, the BESTHEAD accuracy even drops to 0. However, in all these cases, we find that LINEAR still manages to outdo both baselines. We conjecture that these cases could be due to the best head predicted not being very generalizable due to small training set size (for that role). Though LINEAR would also suffer from poor generalization in this case, it might stand its ground better since it relies on multiple heads rather than just one.

3.7 Cased vs Uncased

In our analysis so far, we have been using the same contextual embedding mechanism through-

Role	RAND	SENTONLY	BESTHEAD	LINEAR
PREVENTER	1.51	7.30	15.00	43.14
PASSENGER	1.46	6.79	57.45	45.45
CRIME	3.06	12.62	25.81	57.99
INJURER	1.52	6.51	29.03	16.13
EMPLOYEE	1.47	6.87	53.85	50.00
KILLER	1.75	10.63	14.29	47.62
MONEY	1.51	7.77	4.17	25.00
DETAINEE	1.60	8.39	62.50	50.00
PROSECUTOR	1.55	6.34	58.33	16.67
JUDGECOURT	1.33	6.78	22.22	41.67
VEHICLE	1.47	6.15	0	18.18

Table 5: Test accuracies using all the baselines and probe approaches described in §§2.4 for some non frequent roles. Both BESTHEAD and LINEAR probes still outdo the baselines in most cases, but not as convincingly as for frequent roles. Unlike the frequent roles case, LINEAR actually does worse than BESTHEAD for many roles.

out, namely *bert-base-uncased*. In Figure 3a, we plot the difference of BESTHEAD test accuracies when using *bert-base-cased* vs *bert-base-uncased*.

We can see that *bert-base-uncased* is better for most roles - except for *Attacker*, *Victim* and *Artifact*. We also notice that the best layer-head configuration $\{l_{best}, h_{best}\}$ is mostly not preserved between the *bert-base-cased* and *bert-base-uncased* scenarios. The difference between *bert-base-uncased* and *bert-base-cased* is even more drastic in the cross sentence only experiment , for instance, while there exists a single head which can find cross-sentence *Instrument* args with 37% accuracy, the best such head of *bert-base-cased* has only 17% accuracy.

3.8 Qualitative Examples

In Figure 3.8, we illustrate some examples of BESTHEAD identifying arguments. We defer further discussion to Appendix §A owing to lack of space.

4 Related Work

A complete description of the large body of work on probing is beyond the scope of this paper. Besides those discussed earlier, other aspects studied include filler-gap dependencies (Wilcox et al., 2018), function word comprehension (Kim et al., 2019), sentence-level properties (Adi et al., 2016) and negative polarity items (Warstadt et al., 2019).

Probing is not limited to examining pairwise word relations or sentence properties. Hewitt and Manning (2019) find that BERT token representations are linearly projectable into a space where they embed constituency structure. Recently, Sorodoc et al. (2020) probed transformer based language models for coreference. However, they restrict themselves to entity coreference. Further-

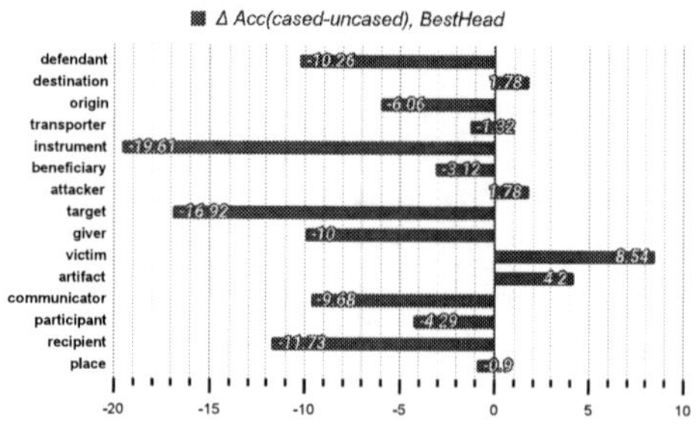

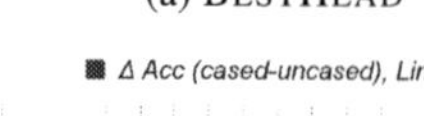

(a) BESTHEAD

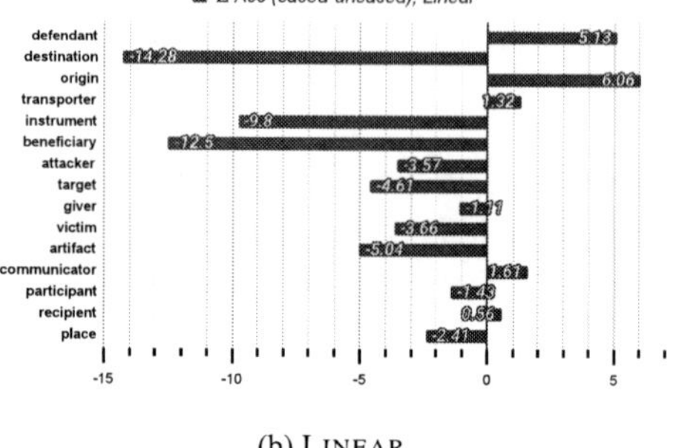

(b) LINEAR

Figure 3: Δ in Test accuracy of a) BESTHEAD b) LINEAR using *bert-base-uncased* vs *bert-base-cased*

more, they exclude MLMs like BERT from their analysis.

Hewitt and Liang (2019) raised a note of caution about classifier based probes, pointing out that probes themselves could be rich enough to learn certain phenomena even with random representations. We avoid direct classifier-based probing, thus avoiding the mentioned pitfalls.

5 Conclusion

We showed how BERT's attention heads have modest but well above chance ability to detect arguments for event roles. This ability is achievable either with only i) 2 parameters per role (BESTHEAD) ii) 289 parameters per role (LINEAR). Furthermore, the supervision required to reach this is just $\approx 11\%$ of full training set size. Secondly, we propose a method to learning separate heads (combinations) for cross-sentence argument detection. Our experiments show that the heads so learnt have higher cross-sentence accuracy. Thirdly, we show that LINEAR performance is robust to a perturbed NONCE test setting with weakened lexical associations. In future, we plan to extend our probing to other event aspects like coreference and subevents.

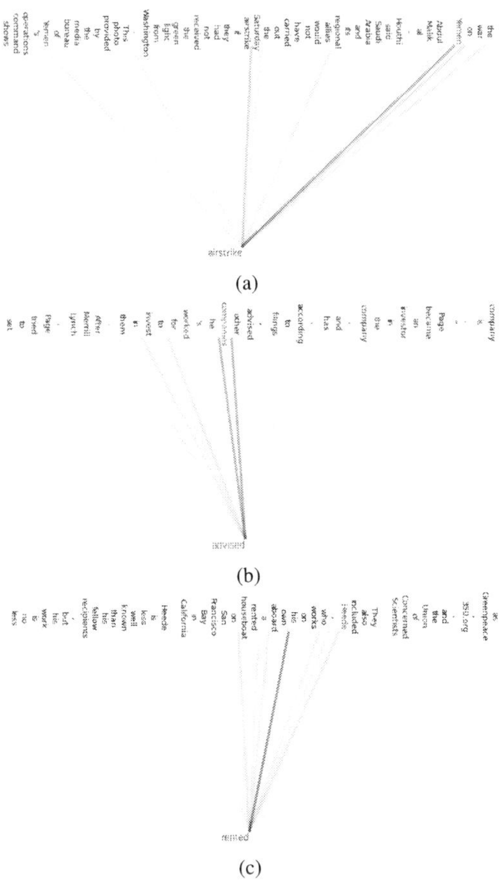

Figure 4: In (a), BESTHEAD correctly picks out the TARGET of *"airstrike"* as *"Yemen"*. In (b), BESTHEAD correctly picks out the RECIPIENT of *"advised"* as *"companies"*. In (c), the token picked is coreferent but not identical to the gold argument. Attentions are shown as blue lines from trigger token, with lineweight ∝ value. Gold arguments are shaded green .

Acknowledgments

We thank Nikita Moghe and Hiroaki Hayashi as well as the three anonymous reviewers for their valuable feedback.

References

Yossi Adi, Einat Kermany, Yonatan Belinkov, Ofer Lavi, and Yoav Goldberg. 2016. Fine-grained analysis of sentence embeddings using auxiliary prediction tasks. *arXiv preprint arXiv:1608.04207*.

Jun Araki, Zhengzhong Liu, Eduard H Hovy, and Teruko Mitamura. 2014. Detecting Subevent Structure for Event Coreference Resolution. In *LREC*, pages 4553–4558.

Emily M Bender and Batya Friedman. 2018. Data statements for natural language processing: Toward mitigating system bias and enabling better science.

Transactions of the Association for Computational Linguistics, 6:587–604.

Nathanael Chambers and Dan Jurafsky. 2008. Unsupervised learning of narrative event chains. In *Proceedings of ACL-08: HLT*, pages 789–797.

Kevin Clark, Urvashi Khandelwal, Omer Levy, and Christopher D Manning. 2019. What does BERT look at? an analysis of BERT's attention. *arXiv preprint arXiv:1906.04341*.

Jacob Devlin, Ming-Wei Chang, Kenton Lee, and Kristina Toutanova. 2018. Bert: Pre-training of deep bidirectional transformers for language understanding. *arXiv preprint arXiv:1810.04805*.

Jesse Dunietz, Lori Levin, and Jaime G Carbonell. 2017. The BECauSE corpus 2.0: Annotating causality and overlapping relations. In *Proceedings of the 11th Linguistic Annotation Workshop*, pages 95–104.

Seth Ebner, Patrick Xia, Ryan Culkin, Kyle Rawlins, and Benjamin Van Durme. 2020. Multi-sentence argument linking. In *Proceedings of the 58th Annual Meeting of the Association for Computational Linguistics*, pages 8057–8077, Online. Association for Computational Linguistics.

Kristina Gulordava, Piotr Bojanowski, Edouard Grave, Tal Linzen, and Marco Baroni. 2018. Colorless green recurrent networks dream hierarchically. *arXiv preprint arXiv:1803.11138*.

John Hewitt and Percy Liang. 2019. Designing and interpreting probes with control tasks. *arXiv preprint arXiv:1909.03368*.

John Hewitt and Christopher D Manning. 2019. A structural probe for finding syntax in word representations. In *Proceedings of the 2019 Conference of the North American Chapter of the Association for Computational Linguistics: Human Language Technologies, Volume 1 (Long and Short Papers)*, pages 4129–4138.

Dongyeop Kang, Varun Gangal, Ang Lu, Zheng Chen, and Eduard Hovy. 2017. Detecting and explaining causes from text for a time series event. In *Proceedings of the 2017 Conference on Empirical Methods in Natural Language Processing*, pages 2758–2767.

Najoung Kim, Roma Patel, Adam Poliak, Alex Wang, Patrick Xia, R Thomas McCoy, Ian Tenney, Alexis Ross, Tal Linzen, Benjamin Van Durme, et al. 2019. Probing what different NLP tasks teach machines about function word comprehension. *arXiv preprint arXiv:1904.11544*.

Yair Lakretz, German Kruszewski, Theo Desbordes, Dieuwke Hupkes, Stanislas Dehaene, and Marco Baroni. 2019. The emergence of number and syntax units in LSTM language models. *arXiv preprint arXiv:1903.07435*.

Tal Linzen, Emmanuel Dupoux, and Yoav Goldberg. 2016. Assessing the ability of LSTMs to learn syntax-sensitive dependencies. *Transactions of the Association for Computational Linguistics*, 4:521–535.

Jing Lu and Vincent Ng. 2018. Event Coreference Resolution: A Survey of Two Decades of Research. In *IJCAI*, pages 5479–5486.

Rebecca Marvin and Tal Linzen. 2018. Targeted syntactic evaluation of language models. *arXiv preprint arXiv:1808.09031*.

Jeffrey Pennington, Richard Socher, and Christopher D Manning. 2014. Glove: Global vectors for word representation. In *Proceedings of the 2014 conference on empirical methods in natural language processing (EMNLP)*, pages 1532–1543.

Matthew E Peters, Mark Neumann, Mohit Iyyer, Matt Gardner, Christopher Clark, Kenton Lee, and Luke Zettlemoyer. 2018. Deep contextualized word representations. *arXiv preprint arXiv:1802.05365*.

Fabio Petroni, Tim Rocktäschel, Patrick Lewis, Anton Bakhtin, Yuxiang Wu, Alexander H Miller, and Sebastian Riedel. 2019. Language models as knowledge bases? *arXiv preprint arXiv:1909.01066*.

Rico Sennrich, Barry Haddow, and Alexandra Birch. 2015. Neural machine translation of rare words with subword units. *arXiv preprint arXiv:1508.07909*.

Vered Shwartz, Rachel Rudinger, and Oyvind Tafjord. 2020. ” you are grounded!”: Latent Name Artifacts in Pre-trained Language Models. *arXiv preprint arXiv:2004.03012*.

Ionut Sorodoc, Kristina Gulordava, and Gemma Boleda. 2020. Probing for Referential information in Language Models. In *Proceedings of the 58th Annual Meeting of the Association for Computational Linguistics*, pages 4177–4189.

Siddharth Vashishtha, Benjamin Van Durme, and Aaron Steven White. 2019. Fine-grained temporal relation extraction. *arXiv preprint arXiv:1902.01390*.

Ashish Vaswani, Noam Shazeer, Niki Parmar, Jakob Uszkoreit, Llion Jones, Aidan N Gomez, Łukasz Kaiser, and Illia Polosukhin. 2017. Attention is all you need. In *Advances in Neural Information Processing Systems*, pages 5998–6008.

Alex Warstadt, Yu Cao, Ioana Grosu, Wei Peng, Hagen Blix, Yining Nie, Anna Alsop, Shikha Bordia, Haokun Liu, Alicia Parrish, et al. 2019. Investigating Bert's knowledge of Language: Five Analysis Methods with NPIs. *arXiv preprint arXiv:1909.02597*.

Ethan Wilcox, Roger Levy, Takashi Morita, and Richard Futrell. 2018. What do RNN Language models learn about Filler-Gap Dependencies? *arXiv preprint arXiv:1809.00042*.

Thomas Wolf, Lysandre Debut, Victor Sanh, Julien Chaumond, Clement Delangue, Anthony Moi, Pierric Cistac, Tim Rault, R'emi Louf, Morgan Funtowicz, and Jamie Brew. 2019. Huggingface's transformers: State-of-the-art natural language processing. *ArXiv*, abs/1910.03771.

Emergent Language Generalization and Acquisition Speed are not tied to Compositionality

Eugene Kharitonov
Facebook AI
kharitinov@fb.com

Marco Baroni
Facebook AI, ICREA
mbaroni@fb.com

Abstract

Studies of discrete languages emerging when neural agents communicate to solve a joint task often look for evidence of compositional structure. This stems for the expectation that such a structure would allow languages to be acquired faster by the agents and enable them to generalize better. We argue that these beneficial properties are only loosely connected to compositionality. In two experiments, we demonstrate that, depending on the task, non-compositional languages might show equal, or better, generalization performance and acquisition speed than compositional ones. Further research in the area should be clearer about what benefits are expected from compositionality, and how the latter would lead to them.

1 Introduction

There is a recent spike of interest in studying the languages that emerge when artificial neural agents communicate to solve a common task (Foerster et al., 2016; Lazaridou et al., 2016; Havrylov and Titov, 2017). A good portion of such studies looks for traces of *compositional* structure in those languages, or even tries to inject such structure into them (Kottur et al., 2017; Choi et al., 2018; Lazaridou et al., 2018; Mordatch and Abbeel, 2018; Andreas, 2019; Cogswell et al., 2019; Li and Bowling, 2019; Resnick et al., 2019; Chaabouni et al., 2020). Besides possibly providing insights on how compositionality emerged in natural language (Townsend et al., 2018), this emphasis is justified by the idea that a compositional language has various *desirable* properties. In particular, compositional languages are expected to help agents to better *generalize* to new (composite) inputs (Kottur et al., 2017; Lazaridou et al., 2018), and to be faster to acquire (Cogswell et al., 2019; Li and Bowling, 2019; Ren et al., 2019).

We engage here with this ongoing research pursuit. We step back and reflect on the benefits that compositionality can bring to the emergent languages: if there is none, then it is unlikely that agents will develop compositional languages on their own. Indeed, several studies have shown that compositionality does not emerge naturally among neural agents (e.g. Kottur et al., 2017; Lazaridou et al., 2018; Andreas, 2019). On the other hand, understanding what benefits compositionality could bring to a language would help us in establishing the conditions for its emergence.

Compositionality is typically seen as a property of a language, independent of the task being considered. However, the task will likely influence properties such as generalization and ease of acquisition, that compositionality is expected to correlate with. Our experiments show that it is easy to construct tasks for which a compositional language is equally hard, or harder, to acquire and does not generalize better than a non-compositional one. Hence, language emergence researchers need to be clear about i) which benefits they expect from compositionality and ii) in which way compositionality would lead to those benefits in their setups. Otherwise, the agents will likely develop perfectly adequate communication systems that are not compositional.

2 Operationalizing compositionality

Before we proceed, let us clarify our definition of compositionality. Linguists and philosophers have extensively studied the topic for centuries (see Pagin and Westerståhl, 2010a,b, for a thorough review). However, the standard definition that a language is compositional if the meaning of each expression in it is a function of the meaning of its parts and the rules to combine them is so general as to be vacuous for our purposes (under such definition, even the highly opaque languages

Proceedings of the Third BlackboxNLP Workshop on Analyzing and Interpreting Neural Networks for NLP, pages 11–15
Online, November 20, 2020. ©2020 Association for Computational Linguistics

we will introduce below are compositional, *contra* our intuitions).

In most current language emergence research, the input to language is composite in the sense that it consists of ensembles of elements. In this context, intuitively, a language is compositional if its symbols denote input elements in a *disentangled* way, so that they can be freely juxtaposed to refer to arbitrary combinations of them. More precisely, the following property might suffice for a limited but practical characterization of compositionality. Given a set of atomic input elements (for example, a set of independent attribute values), each atomic symbol should refer to one and only one input element, *independently of the other symbols it co-occurs with.*[1] A language where all symbols respect this property is compositional in the intuitive sense that, if we know the symbols that denote a set of input elements, we can assemble them (possibly, following some syntactic rules of the language) to refer to the ensemble of those input elements, irrespective of whether we have ever observed the relevant ensemble. Consider for example a world where inputs consist of two attributes, each taking a number of values. A language licensing only two-character sequences, where the character in the first position refers to the value of the first attribute, and that in the second position independently refers to the value of the second, would be compositional in our sense. On the other hand, a language that also licenses two-character sequences, but where both characters in a sequence are needed to decode the values of both the first and the second input attribute, would not be compositional. We will refer to the lack of symbol interdependence in denoting distinct input elements as *naïve compositionality.*[2]

We believe that naïve compositionality captures the intuition behind explicit and implicit definitions of compositionality in emergent language research. For example, Kottur et al. (2017) deem non-compositional those languages that either use single symbols to refer to ensembles of input elements, or where the meaning of a symbol depends on the context in which it occurs. Havrylov and Titov (2017) looked for symbol-position combinations that encode a single concept in an image, as a sign of a compositional behavior. A naïvely compositional language will maximize the two recently proposed compositionality measures of residual entropy (Resnick et al., 2019) and positional disentanglement (Chaabouni et al., 2020).

Naïve compositionality is also closely related to the notion of *disentanglement* in representation learning (Bengio et al., 2013). Interestingly, Locatello et al. (2018) reported that disentanglement is not necessarily helpful for sample efficiency in downstream tasks, as had been previously argued. This resonates with our results below.

3 Communication Game

We base our experimental study on a one-episode one-direction communication game, as commonly done in the relevant literature (Lazaridou et al., 2016, 2018; Havrylov and Titov, 2017; Chaabouni et al., 2019). In this setup, we have two agents, Sender and Receiver. An input i is fed into Sender, in turn Sender produces a message m, which is consumed by Receiver. Receiver produces its output $\hat{o}$. Comparing the output $\hat{o}$ with the ground-truth output o provides a loss. We used EGG (Kharitonov et al., 2019) to implement the experiments.[3]

In contrast to the language emergence scenario, we use a hard-coded Sender agent that produces a fixed, pre-defined language. This allows us to easily control the (naïve) compositionality of the language and measure how it affects Receiver's performance. This setup is akin to the motivating example of Li and Bowling (2019).

We study two Receiver's characteristics: (i) acquisition speed, measured as the number of epoch needed to achieve a fixed level of performance on training set, and (ii) generalization performance on held-out data.

4 Experimental setup

To demonstrate that compositionality of a language alone, detached from the task at hand, does not necessarily lead to higher generalization or faster acquisition speed, we design two experiments.

The first experiment (*attval*) operates in an attribute-value world, similar to those of Kottur et al. (2017); Chaabouni et al. (2019). We fix two languages, one compositional and one not,

---

[1] We leave the definition of what counts as an atomic symbol open: it could be a single character, a character bound to a certain position in a message string, a character sequence, etc.

[2] Naïve in the sense that it is only appropriate when complex meanings are ensembles of atomic meanings. The definition breaks down when complex meanings result from functions that merge their components in different ways than simple ensembling, as is often the case in natural language.

[3] The code is available at https://github.com/facebookresearch/EGG/tree/master/egg/zoo/compositional_efficiency.

| **Acquisition speed** | | |
task-identity	task-linear	task-entangled
LSTM		
lang-identity $\quad$ $5.3_{\pm 0.1}$	$30.0_{\pm 1.4}$	$20.1_{\pm 0.6}$
lang-entangled $\quad$ $20.1_{\pm 0.5}$	$26.6_{\pm 0.8}$	$5.5_{\pm 0.2}$
GRU		
lang-identity $\quad$ $5.6_{\pm 0.2}$	$94.0_{\pm 7.7}$	$57.4_{\pm 13.9}$
lang-entangled $\quad$ $37.2_{\pm 2.7}$	$91.5_{\pm 4.7}$	$5.7_{\pm 0.2}$
Test accuracy		
task-identity	task-linear	task-entangled
LSTM		
lang-identity $\quad$ $0.97_{\pm 0.00}$	$0.0_{\pm 0.0}$	$0.06_{\pm 0.01}$
lang-entangled $\quad$ $0.08_{\pm 0.01}$	$0.0_{\pm 0.0}$	$0.97_{\pm 0.00}$
GRU		
lang-identity $\quad$ $0.97_{\pm 0.00}$	$0.0_{\pm 0.0}$	$0.06_{\pm 0.01}$
lang-entangled $\quad$ $0.10_{\pm 0.02}$	$0.0_{\pm 0.0}$	$0.97_{\pm 0.00}$

Table 1: Attval experiment. Top: epochs to achieve perfect accuracy on training set. Bottom: test accuracy after convergence. $\pm$ marks 1 standard error of the mean.

and build three tasks: (i) "easy" for compositional language and "hard" for non-compositional; (ii) equally "hard" for both; (iii) "hard" for compositional language and "easy" for non-compositional language. Informally, we control the amount of computation needed by Receiver to perform a task starting from a language, where it can be equally hard to rely on compositional or non-compositional languages, or the answers could even be readily available in a non-compositional language.

In the second experiment (*coordinates*), we design a single task that is equally "easy" for an entire family of languages (parameterized by a continuous value), including compositional and non-compositional ones. The task is to transmit points on the 2D plane (thus, the input ensembles here are pairs of point coordinates). Here, we leverage the observation that a typical neural model has a linear output layer, for which it is equally easy to learn any rotation of the ground-truth outputs. Such rotation-group-invariance could play role in games where continuous image embeddings are used as input (Lazaridou et al., 2016; Havrylov and Titov, 2017).

4.1 Attval experiment

Input Sender's input i is a two-dimensional vector; each dimension encodes one of two attributes, each having n_v values: $i \in \{1..n_v\} \times \{1..n_v\}$.

Languages We consider two languages, with messages of length two and vocabulary size n_v. The first language, *lang-identity*, represents the in-

puts as-is, by putting the value of the first (second) attribute in the first (second) position: $(m_1, m_2) \leftarrow (i_1, i_2)$. In the second language, *lang-entangled*, the first and the second positions are obtained as follows:

$$m_j \leftarrow (i_1 + (-1)^j \cdot i_2) \mod n_v, \quad j \in \{1, 2\} \tag{1}$$

Lang-identity and *lang-entangled* have exactly the same n_v^2 utterances. While *lang-identity* is naïvely compositional (one symbol encodes one attribute only), *lang-entangled* is not: each symbol of an utterance encodes equal amount of information about both attributes and both symbols are equally needed for decoding each attribute.[4]

Tasks We consider three tasks. In all of them, Receiver outputs two discrete values, $o \in \{1..n_v\} \times \{1..n_v\}$. In *task-identity*, Receiver has to recover the original input of Sender, i. In the second task, *task-linear*, Receiver needs to output two values that are obtained as integer linear-modulo operations of the original input values: $o \leftarrow A \cdot i + b \mod n_v$. In the third task, *task-entangled*, we require Receiver to output $o_j \leftarrow (i_1 + (-1)^j \cdot i_2) \mod n_v$. In this task, the output values derive from the same attribute transform applied in the *lang-entangled* language (Eq. 1). This language-task pair mirrors the *lang-identity/task-identity* pair: each symbol encodes one *output* value.

Architecture and hyperparameters Receiver is implemented as an LSTM (Hochreiter and Schmidhuber, 1997) or a GRU cell (Cho et al., 2014). Its output layer specifies two categorical distributions over n_v values, encoding two output values. As a loss, we use the sum of per-output negative log-likelihoods. We used the following hyperparameters: $n_v = 31$; hidden layer size 100; embedding size 50; batch size 32; 500 epochs training with Adam (learning rate 10^{-2}). Each configuration was run 20 times with different random seeds. A random $1/5$ of the data is used as test set.

4.2 Coordinates experiment

Input We sample points uniformly from the unit circle, centered at the origin: $i \in \mathbb{R}^2$, $i^T i \leq 1$. We sample 10^3 points for training, 10^3 for testing.

---

[4] Note that *lang-entangled* is still (non-naïvely) compositional, in the sense that its messages can be predictably derived by applying Eq. 1 to the input pairs.

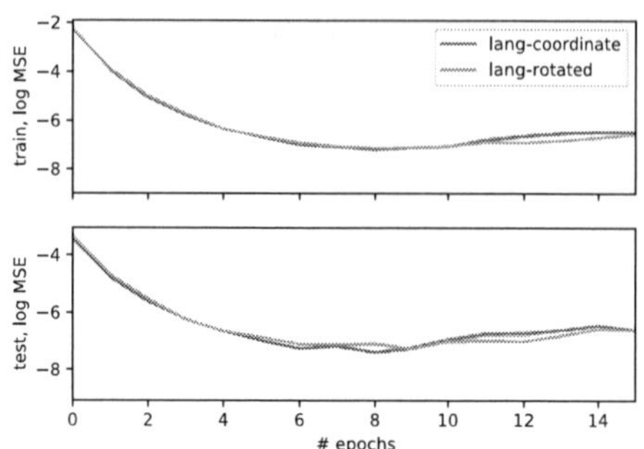

Figure 1: Coordinates experiment: log MSE vs. training epoch.

Languages We consider two languages with utterances of length two. In the first language, *lang-coordinate*, Sender sequentially transmits both coordinates of a point: $m_j \leftarrow i_j$. More precisely, the symbols refer to discretized coordinates from a $n_v \times n_v$ square grid, covering $[-1, 1] \times [-1, 1]$. This language is naïvely compositional w.r.t. the coordinate-wise representation of the inputs.

We construct the second language, *lang-rotated*, in the following way. We start with *lang-coordinate*, but apply a rotation of the plane by $\pi/4$ before feeding a point into Sender.[5] Effectively, this makes Sender "use" a rotated coordinate grid for encoding the coordinates. As a result of the rotation, *lang-rotated* ceases to be naïvely compositional in the original (non-rotated) world. Each symbol of *lang-rotated* carries equal amounts of information about both coordinates of i.

Task Receiver has to recover the original (non-rotated) coordinates i of a point.

Architecture and loss Receiver is an LSTM with hidden size 100 and embedding size 50; n_v is 100; batch size is 32; we use Adam with learning rate 10^{-3}. As a loss, we use MSE. We run each configuration with 10 random seeds.

5   Results

Attval experiment In Table 1 we provide the results of the *attrval* experiment, depending on language, task, and Receiver architecture. We report the number of epochs to achieve perfect accuracy on training set (top) and the accuracy on the hold-out set after training (bottom).

Consider the convergence speed first. For both Receiver architectures *lang-identity* converges considerably faster than *lang-entangled*. This agrees with the findings of Li and Bowling (2019). However, in *task-linear* both languages demonstrate roughly the same convergence speed (the difference is not stat. sig.). In *task-entangled*, *lang-entangled* becomes more efficient to acquire than the naïvely compositional *lang-identity*. Interestingly, the acquisition times of *task-identity/lang-identity* and *task-entangled/lang-entangled* are symmetrical.

Next, consider the test accuracy of the same runs as above, measuring generalization to new attval combinations. We observe the same patterns: *task-linear* is equally hard to generalize from both languages; *lang-identity* reaches high test accuracy in *task-identity*, while *lang-entangled* leads to equally high accuracy on *task-entangled*. In contrast, *lang-identity* performs very poorly on *task-entangled*, just as *lang-entangled* does on *task-identity*.

Coordinates experiment Figure 1 reports learning curves for train and test sets (cueing acquisition speed and generalization, respectively). There is little difference between the compositional and non-compositional languages, in either training or held-out loss trajectories. Note also that, evidently, the linear mapping required here to undo the non-naïvely compositional transformation is easier for the networks than the non-linear operation we applied in the Attval experiment, pointing to the importance of taking the intrinsic biases of neural networks into account when designing language emergence experiments.

6   Discussion and Conclusion

Our toy experiments with hand-coded languages make the possibly obvious but currently overlooked point that, in isolation from the target task, there is nothing special about a language being (naïvely) compositional. A non-compositional language can be equally or faster to acquire than a compositional one, and it can provide the same or better generalization capabilities. Thus, if our goal is to let compositional languages emerge, we should be very clear about which characteristics of our setup should lead to its emergence.

Our concern is illustrated by the recent findings of Chaabouni et al. (2020), who observed that the degree of compositionality of emergent languages is not correlated with the generalization capabilities of the agents that rely on them to solve a task.

---

[5] Rotating by any angle $(0, \pi/2)$ makes the language non-compositional; $\pi/4$ maximally entangles it.

Indeed, lacking any specific pressure towards developing a (naïvely) compositional language, their agents were perfectly capable of developing generalizable but non-compositional communication systems. Our experiments provide a plausible explanation of their findings.

A stronger conclusion is that perhaps we should altogether forget about compositionality as an end goal. The current emphasis on it might just be a misguided effect of our human-centric bias. We should instead directly concentrate on the properties we want agent languages to have, such as fast learning, transmission and generalization.

References

Jacob Andreas. 2019. Measuring compositionality in representation learning. *arXiv preprint arXiv:1902.07181*.

Yoshua Bengio, Aaron Courville, and Pascal Vincent. 2013. Representation learning: A review and new perspectives. *IEEE Transactions on Pattern Analysis and Machine Intelligence*, 35(8).

Rahma Chaabouni, Eugene Kharitonov, Diane Bouchacourt, Emmanuel Dupoux, and Marco Baroni. 2020. Compositionality and generalization in emergent languages. In *Proceedings of ACL*.

Rahma Chaabouni, Eugene Kharitonov, Emmanuel Dupoux, and Marco Baroni. 2019. Anti-efficient encoding in emergent communication. In *Advances in Neural Information Processing Systems*, pages 6290–6300.

Kyunghyun Cho, Bart Van Merriënboer, Caglar Gulcehre, Dzmitry Bahdanau, Fethi Bougares, Holger Schwenk, and Yoshua Bengio. 2014. Learning phrase representations using rnn encoder-decoder for statistical machine translation. *arXiv preprint arXiv:1406.1078*.

Edward Choi, Angeliki Lazaridou, and Nando de Freitas. 2018. Compositional obverter communication learning from raw visual input. In *ICLP*.

Michael Cogswell, Jiasen Lu, Stefan Lee, Devi Parikh, and Dhruv Batra. 2019. Emergence of compositional language with deep generational transmission. *arXiv preprint arXiv:1904.09067*.

Jakob Foerster, Ioannis Alexandros Assael, Nando de Freitas, and Shimon Whiteson. 2016. Learning to communicate with deep multi-agent reinforcement learning. In *NIPS*, Barcelona, Spain.

Serhii Havrylov and Ivan Titov. 2017. Emergence of language with multi-agent games: Learning to communicate with sequences of symbols. In *NeurIPS*.

Sepp Hochreiter and Jürgen Schmidhuber. 1997. Long short-term memory. *Neural computation*, 9(8):1735–1780.

Eugene Kharitonov, Rahma Chaabouni, Diane Bouchacourt, and Marco Baroni. 2019. EGG: a toolkit for research on emergence of lanGuage in games. In *EMNLP*.

Satwik Kottur, José Moura, Stefan Lee, and Dhruv Batra. 2017. Natural language does not emerge 'naturally' in multi-agent dialog. In *Proceedings of EMNLP*, pages 2962–2967, Copenhagen, Denmark.

Angeliki Lazaridou, Karl Moritz Hermann, Karl Tuyls, and Stephen Clark. 2018. Emergence of linguistic communication from referential games with symbolic and pixel input. In *ICLR*.

Angeliki Lazaridou, Alexander Peysakhovich, and Marco Baroni. 2016. Multi-agent cooperation and the emergence of (natural) language. *arXiv preprint arXiv:1612.07182*.

Fushan Li and Michael Bowling. 2019. Ease-of-teaching and language structure from emergent communication. *arXiv preprint arXiv:1906.02403*.

Francesco Locatello, Stefan Bauer, Mario Lucic, Gunnar Rätsch, Sylvain Gelly, Bernhard Schölkopf, and Olivier Bachem. 2018. Challenging common assumptions in the unsupervised learning of disentangled representations. *arXiv preprint arXiv:1811.12359*.

Igor Mordatch and Pieter Abbeel. 2018. Emergence of grounded compositional language in multi-agent populations. In *AAAI*.

Peter Pagin and Dag Westerståhl. 2010a. Compositionality I: Definitions and variants. *Philosophy Compass*, 5(3):250–264.

Peter Pagin and Dag Westerståhl. 2010b. Compositionality II: Arguments and problems. *Philosophy Compass*, 5(3):265–282.

Yi Ren, Shangmin Guo, Serhii Havrylov, Shay Cohen, and Simon Kirby. 2019. Enhance the compositionality of emergent language by iterated learning. In *Proceedings of the NeurIPS Emergent Communication Workshop*.

Cinjon Resnick, Abhinav Gupta, Jakob Foerster, Andrew M Dai, and Kyunghyun Cho. 2019. Capacity, bandwidth, and compositionality in emergent language learning. *arXiv preprint arXiv:1910.11424*.

Simon Townsend, Sabrina Engesser, Sabine Stoll, Klaus Zuberbühler, and Balthasar Bickel. 2018. Compositionality in animals and humans. *PLOS Biology*, 16(8):1–7.

Examining the rhetorical capacities of neural language models

Zining Zhu[1,2], Chuer Pan[1], Mohamed Abdalla[1,2], Frank Rudzicz[1,2,3,4]
1: University of Toronto; 2: Vector Institute
3: Li Ka Shing Knowledge Institute, St Michael's Hospital
4: Surgical Safety Technologies
`zining@cs.toronto.edu, chuer.pan@mail.utoronto.ca`
`{msa, frank}@cs.toronto.edu`

Abstract

Recently, neural language models (LMs) have demonstrated impressive abilities in generating high-quality discourse. While many recent papers have analyzed the syntactic aspects encoded in LMs, to date, there has been no analysis of the inter-sentential, rhetorical knowledge. In this paper, we propose a method that quantitatively evaluates the rhetorical capacities of neural LMs. We examine the capacities of neural LMs understanding the rhetoric of discourse by evaluating their abilities to encode a set of linguistic features derived from Rhetorical Structure Theory (RST). Our experiments show that BERT-based LMs outperform other Transformer LMs, revealing the richer discourse knowledge in their intermediate layer representations. In addition, GPT-2 and XLNet apparently encode less rhetorical knowledge, and we suggest an explanation drawing from linguistic philosophy. Our method presents an avenue towards quantifying the rhetorical capacities of neural LMs.

1 Introduction

In recent years, neural LMs (especially contextualized LMs) have shown profound abilities to generate texts that could be almost indistinguishable from human writings (Radford et al., 2019). Neural LMs could be used to generate concise summaries (Song et al., 2019), coherent stories (See et al., 2019), and complete documents given prompts (Keskar et al., 2019). It is natural to question their source and extent of rhetorical knowledge: What makes neural LMs articulate, and how? While some recent works query the linguistic knowledge (Hewitt and Manning, 2019; Liu et al., 2019a; Chen et al., 2019; Belinkov et al., 2017), this open question remain unanswered. We hypothesize that contextualized neural LMs encode rhetorical knowledge in their intermediate representations, and would like to quantify the extent they encode rhetorical knowledge.

To verify our hypothesis, we hand-craft a set of 24 rhetorical features including those used to examine rhetorical capacities of students (Mohsen and Alshahrani, 2019; Liu and Kunnan, 2016; Zhang, 2013; Powers et al., 2001), and evaluate how well neural LMs encode these rhetorical features in the representations while encoding texts.

Recent work has started to evaluate encoded features from hidden representations. Among them, probing (Alain and Bengio, 2017; Adi et al., 2017) has been a popular choice. Previous work probed morphological (Belinkov et al., 2017; Bisazza and Tump, 2018), agreement (Giulianelli et al., 2018), and syntactic features (Hewitt and Manning, 2019; Hewitt and Liang, 2019). Probing involves optimizing a simple projection model from representations to features. The loss of this optimization measures the difficulty to decode features from the representations.

In this work, we use a probe containing self attention mechanism. We first project the variable-length embeddings to a fixed-length latent representation per document. Then, we apply a simple diagnostic classifier to detect rhetorical features from this latent representation. This design of probe reduces the total number of parameters, and enable us to better understand each model's ability to encode rhetorical knowledge. We find that:

- The BERT-based LMs encode more rhetorical features, and in a more stable manner, than other models.
- The semantics of non-contextualized embeddings also pertain to some rhetorical features, but less than most layers of contextualized language models.

These observations allow us to investigate the mechanisms of neural LMs to better understand the

16

Proceedings of the Third BlackboxNLP Workshop on Analyzing and Interpreting Neural Networks for NLP, pages 16–32
Online, November 20, 2020. ©2020 Association for Computational Linguistics

degree to which they encode linguistic knowledge. We demonstrate how discourse-level features can be queried and analyzed from neural LMs. All of our code and parsed tree data will be available at github.

2 Structural analysis of discourse

Various frameworks exist for "good discourse" (Lawrence and Reed, 2019; Irish and Weiss, 2009; Toulmin, 1958), but most of them are inaccessible to quantitative analysis. In this work, we use Rhetorical Structure Theory (Mann and Thompson, 1988; Mann et al., 1989) since it represents the structures of discourse using trees, allowing straightforward quantitative analysis. There are two components in an RST parse-tree:

- Each leaf node represents an elementary discourse unit (EDU). The role of an EDU in an article is similar to that of a word in a sentence.
- Each non-leaf node denotes a relation involving its two children. Often, one of the children is more dependent on the other, and less essential to the writer's purpose. This child is referred to as "satellite", while the more central child is the "nucleus".

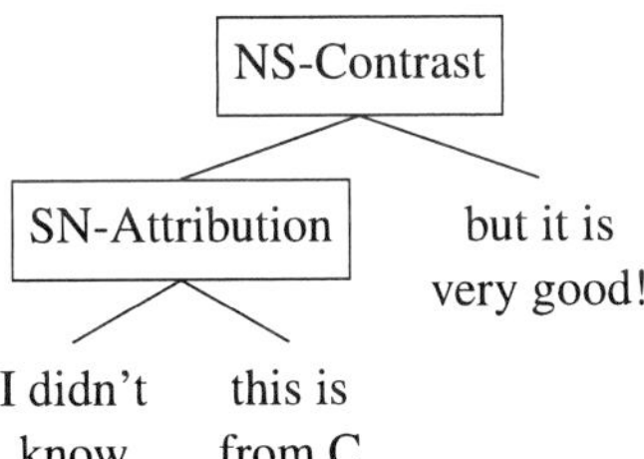

Figure 1: A portion of an RST tree, selected from IMDB (Maas et al., 2011) `train/pos/1_7.txt`, and parsed with Feng and Hirst (2014). Nodes with rectangle borders are discourse relations, and those without borders are individual EDUs. The "N" and "S" prefix for discourse relations stand for "nucleus" and "satellite" respectively.

Tree representations are clear, easy to understand, and allow us to compute features to numerically depict the rhetorical aspects of documents.

2.1 Rhetorical features

Previous work used RST features to analyze the quality of discourse, to assess writing abilities

(Wang et al., 2019; Zhang, 2013), examine linguistic coherence (Feng et al., 2014; Abdalla et al., 2017), and to analyze arguments (Chakrabarty et al., 2019). In this project, we extract similar RST features in the following three categories:

Discourse relation occurrences (`Sig`) We include the number of relations detected in each document. There are 18 relations in this category[1]. Unfortunately, the relations adopted by open-source RST parsers are not unified. To allow for comparison against other parsers, we do not differentiate subtle differences between relations, therefore grouping very similar relations, following the approach in (Feng and Hirst, 2012). (E.g., we consider both Topic-Shift and Topic-Drift to be a `Topic-Change`). Specifically, this approach does not differentiate between the sequence of nucleus and satellite (e.g., NS-Evaluation and SN-Evaluation are both considered as an `Evaluation`).

Tree property features (`Tree`) We compute the depth and the Yngve depth (the number of right-branching in the tree) (Yngve, 1960) of each tree node, and include their mean and variance as characteristic features, following previous work extracting tree linguistic features (Li et al., 2019; Zhu et al., 2019).

EDU related features (`EDU`) We include the mean and variance of EDU lengths of each document. We hypothesize the longer EDUs indicate higher levels of redundancy in discourse, hence extracting rhetorical features require memory across longer spans.

Overall, there are 24 features from three categories. We normalize them to zero mean and unit variance, and take these RST features for probing. The features are not independent of each other. Specifically, the features of each group tend to describe the same property from different aspects.[2]

---

[1] The 18 relations are: Attribution, Background, Cause, Comparison, Condition, Contrast, Elaboration, Enablement, Evaluation, Explanation, Joint, Manner-Means, Topic-Comment, Summary, Temporal, Topic-Change, Textual-organization, and Same-unit.

[2] For example, `Sig` features describe the composition of the document in a histogram. For the same document, if a relation is changed, e.g., from `Contrast` to `Attribution`, then the occurrence of both `Contrast` and `Attribution` are affected.

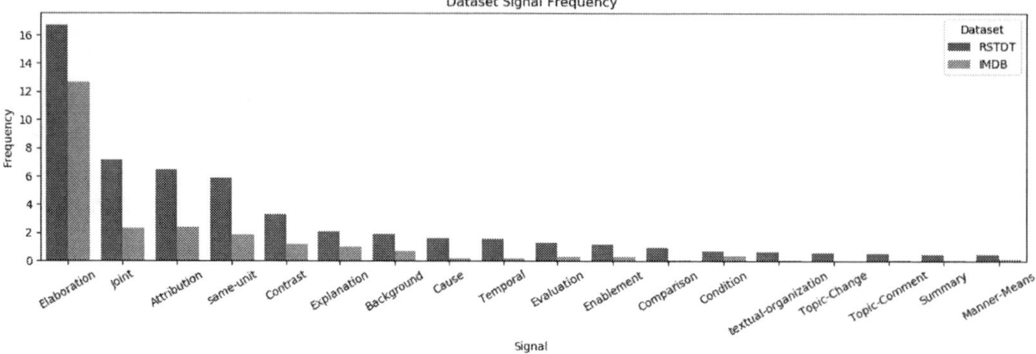

Figure 2: RST relation occurrences per document. RST-DT contain longer documents than IMDB on average. However, the distributions of frequencies between these two datasets are relatively consistent, with `Elaboration`, `Joint`, and `Attribution` the most frequent signals.

2.2 Probe

Our probing method contains two weight parameters, W_d and W_p. First, we embed a document with L tokens using a neural LM with D dimensions to get a raw representation matrix $X \in \mathbb{R}^{L \times D}$. We use a projection matrix $W_d \in \mathbb{R}^{D \times d}$ to reduce the embedding dimension from D (e.g., $D = 768$ for BERT and 2048 for XLM) to a much smaller one, d. Then, we use self attention similar to Lin et al. (2017) to collect the information spread across the document to a condensed form:

$$A = (XW_d)^T (XW_d) \in \mathbb{R}^{d \times d}$$

We flatten A into a vector with fixed size: $\tilde{A} = (d^2, 1)$. We use a probing matrix $W_p \in \mathbb{R}^{d^2 \times m}$ to extract RST features $v \in \mathbb{R}^m$ from attention, normalize them to zero mean and unit variance, and optimize based on the expected L_2 error:

$$\min_{W_d, W_p} \mathbb{E}||W_p^T \tilde{A} - v||^2$$

Note that the reduction from D to d using W_p is necessary, because it significantly lowers the number of parameters of the probing model. If there were no W_d (i.e., $d = 768$), then W_p alone would require $768^2 m$ parameters to probe m features. Now, we let $d = 10$, then W_d and W_p combined have $D \times d + d^2 m \approx 7680 + 100m$ parameters. Considering $m \in \mathcal{O}(10^1)$, the total parameter size is reduced from $\mathcal{O}(10^6)$ to $\mathcal{O}(10^3)$.

There is one more step before we can use this loss to measure the difficulty of probing rhetorical features. L_2 error scales linearly with the dimension of features m, so it is necessary to normalize the L_2 error by m, to ensure that the losses can be compared across linguistic feature sets. The *difficulty* of probing a group of m features $v \in \mathbb{R}^m$ therefore is:

$$\text{Difficulty} = \frac{1}{m}\mathbb{E}\left||W_p^T \tilde{A} - v\right||^2$$

3 Experiments

3.1 Data

Most state-of-the-art rhetorical parsers are trained on either Penn Discourse Treebank (Ji and Eisenstein, 2014; Feng and Hirst, 2012) or RST-DT (Feng and Hirst, 2014; Joty et al., 2015; Surdeanu et al., 2015; Heilman and Sagae, 2015; Li et al., 2016; Wang et al., 2017; Yu et al., 2018). Although the documents contain accurate discourse annotations, RST-DT (Carlson et al., 2001) only has 385 documents. The Penn Discourse Treebank (Prasad et al., 2008) has 2,159 documents but their annotations do not follow the RST framework. So in addition to RST-DT, we extend the analysis to a 100 times larger dataset, IMDB (Maas et al., 2011).

IMDB contains 50,000 movie reviews without discourse annotations. In these reviews, the authors explain and elaborate upon their opinions towards certain movies and give ratings. We removed html tags, and attempt to parse all of them (i.e., both train and test data) using a two-pass parser from Feng and Hirst (2014). We discarded 1,977 documents that the RST parser generate ill-formatted trees[3]. Of the remaining documents, we additionally filtered out those with sequence lengths greater than 512 tokens[4], resulting in 40,833 documents.

---

[3] As determined by `nltk.tree`.

[4] As determined by any one of the tokenizers, since these

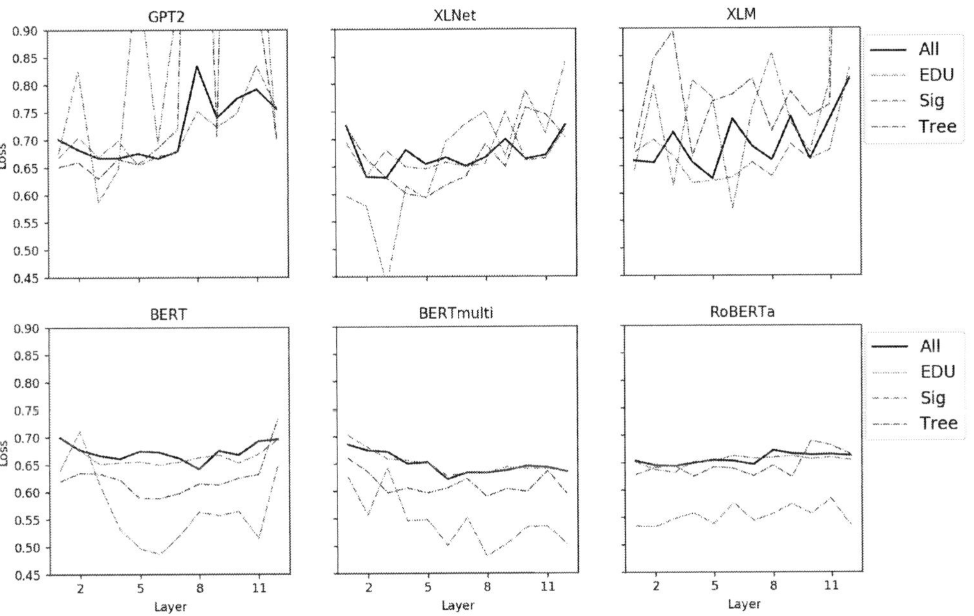

Figure 3: Loss vs layer plot of six neural LMs on four RST feature sets on IMDB. The solid lines represent all RST features combined, while each dash-dotted line denotes one component (EDU, Sig, or Tree feature group for red, green, and blue respectively). In general, BERT-based LMs (BERT, BERT-multi, RoBERTa) encode rhetorical features in a more stable and easy-to-probe manner than the rest.

After parsing each document into an "RST-tree", we extracted the features mentioned in Section 2.1 from these parsed trees. Figure 2 shows the occurrence of the 18 RST relations per document, and Table 1 shows the statistics of remaining 6 features. In addition, we include several examples of parsed RST trees in Appendix.

Feature name	Mean $\pm$ stdev
tree_depth_mean	3.9±1.4
tree_depth_var	4.6±4.2
tree_Yngve_mean	9.2±8.8
tree_Yngve_var	100.6±164.6
edu_len_mean	8.6±1.4
edu_len_var	21.8±16.0

Table 1: Statistics of the 6 non-occurrence-based RST features. The prefix "tree_" here refers to the parsed "RST-tree".

language models come with their own tokenizers. Note that RoBERTa adds two special tokens, so this threshold becomes 510 for RoBERTa.

3.2 Language models

We considered the following popular neural LMs:

- BERT$_{\text{BASE}}$ (Devlin et al., 2019) This LM with 110M parameters is built with 12-layer Transformer encoder (Vaswani et al., 2017) with 768 hidden dimensions. It is trained with masked LM (i.e., cloze) and next sentence prediction objectives using 16GB text.
- BERT-multi (Wolf et al., 2019) Same as BERT, BERT-multi is also a 12-layer Transformer encoder with 768 hidden dimensions and 110M parameters. Its difference from BERT is that, BERT-multi is trained on top 104 languages with the largest Wikipedia.
- RoBERTa (Liu et al., 2019b) is an enhanced version of BERT with the same architecture, similar masked LM objectives, and 10 times larger training corpus (over 160GB).
- GPT-2 (Radford et al., 2019) is a 12-layer Transformer decoder with 768 hidden dimensions. There are 117M parameters in total. GPT-2 is pretrained on 40GB of text. Unlike BERT, GPT-2 is a uni-directional LM.

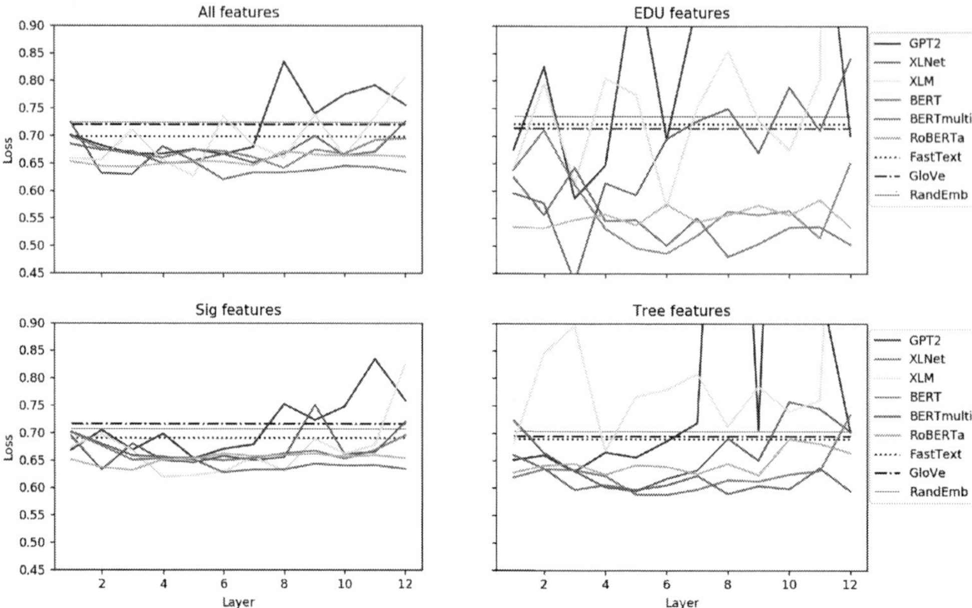

Figure 4: Probing loss, compared to those from non-contextualized baselines, for four feature groups, on IMDB. BERT-based neural LMs stably outperform the word embedding baselines in almost all layers.

- XLM (Lample and Conneau, 2019) is 12-layer Transformer with 2048-hidden dimensions. We use the English model trained with masked language model (MLM) objective. Different from BERT (taking sentence pairs as input), XLM takes continuous streams of tokens as input.
- XLNet (Yang et al., 2019) is a 12-layer Transformer-XL (Dai et al., 2019) with two streams of self attention and 768 hidden dimensions and 110M parameters. The XLNet we use is trained on 33GB texts using the "permutation language modeling" objective, with its LM factorization according to shuffled orders, but its positional encoding correspond to the original sequence order. The permutation LM objective introduces diversity and randomness to the context.

To make comparisons between models fair, we limit to 12-layer neural LMs. The models are pretrained by Huggingface (Wolf et al., 2019).

3.3 Implementation

We formulated probing as an optimization problem, and implemented our solution with PyTorch (Paszke et al., 2019) and the Adam optimizer (Kingma and Ba, 2014) for 40 epochs. If the training loss stalls (i.e., does not change by $\geq 10^{-3}$), or if the training loss rises by more than 10% from the previous epoch, we stop the optimization. All optimizations follow the same learning rate tuning schemas.

In our experiments, the representation dimension d is taken to be 10, while the LM dimensions D is 2048 for XLM and 768 for the rest.

4 Results and Discussion

4.1 Where do LMs encode RST features?

From Figure 3, neural LMs encode RST features in different manners, depending on their structures. In general, for BERT-based models, features seem to distribute evenly across layers. On GPT-2 and XLNet, lower layers seem to encode slightly more EDU and Sig features than higher levels, whereas Tree features seem to be more concentrated in layers 2-6. The results on XLM are relatively noisy, possibly because the uni-language version does not benefit from the performance boost of cross-language modeling.

Contrasting with previous work that suggested

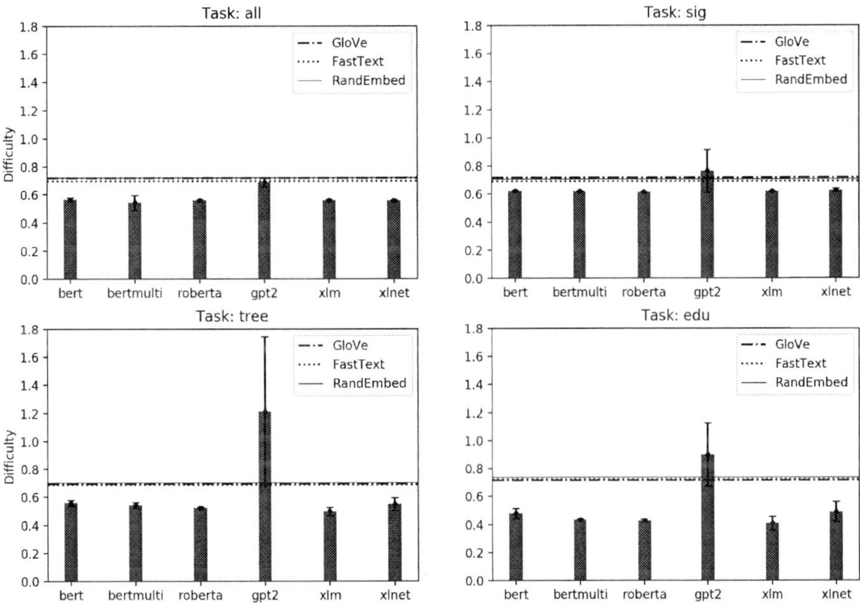

Figure 5: Probing performances of averaging 12 layers for 6 neural LMs on 4 tasks in IMDB, compared to the three non-contextual baselines. All LMs except GPT-2 outperform non-contextual LM baselines. Plots for RST-DT (Figure 6 in Appendix) reveal similar patterns.

that middle layers most contain syntactic features (Hewitt and Manning, 2019; Jawahar et al., 2019), our results indicate a less definitive localization for discourse features, except for the first and final layers. We suggest that the reason they encode less discourse information is that the first layer focuses on connections between "locations", while the final layer focuses on extracting representations most relevant to the final task.

Are RST features equally hard to probe? Figure 3 also shows the difficulty in probing features across feature sets. In BERT-based models, `EDU` and `Tree` features are comparably easier to probe, whereas the `Sig` feature groups is more challenging. However, GPT-2, XLNet, and XLM do not regard `EDU` or `Tree` features easier to probe than other groups. Nevertheless, the results on all features correlate more to the `Sig` features.

How about averaging layers? For comparison, we also used the mean of all 12 layers for each neural LM. Figure 5 shows the probing results. Except GPT-2, other LMs show similar performances when the representations of layers are averaged. In

addition, the performances show that `Sig` features are harder to probe than `Tree` and `EDU` features, whereas the aggregation task (using all features) appears harder than each of its three component feature groups.

4.2 Deconstructing the probe

We perform ablation studies to illustrate the effectiveness of probing, deconstructing the language model probe step-by-step. First, we get rid of the contextualization component in language modeling by using non-contextualized word embeddings, GloVe and FastText. Then, we discard the semantic component of word embedding by mapping tokens to randomly generated vectors (RandEmbed). Finally, we remove all information pertaining to the text, leading to a random predictor for RST features, RandGuess.

Non-contextualized word embeddings We consider two popular word embeddings here:

- GloVe (Pennington et al., 2014) contains 2.2M vocabulary items and produces 300-dimensional word vectors. The GloVe embedding we use is pretrained on Common Crawl.

- FastText (Bojanowski et al., 2017) is trained on Wikipedia 2017 + UMBC (16B tokens) including subword information, and produces 300-dimensional word vectors.

Word embeddings map each token into a D-dimensional semantic space. Therefore, for a document of length L, the embedded matrix also has shape $L \times D$. The difference from the contextualized neural LMs is that, the D-dimensional vectors of every word do not depend on their contexts.

Random embeddings In this step, we assign a non-trainable random embedding vector per token in the vocabulary. This removes the semantic information encoded by GloVe and FastText word embeddings.

As shown in Figure 4, 5: RandEmbed is worse than GloVe and FastText (except for GloVe in `Sig` features task). This verifies some semantic information is preserved in word embeddings.

Contextualized LMs against baseline First, the lack of context restrict the probing performance of non-contextualized baselines. They are worse than most layers in contextualized LMs (in Figure 4), and are worse than all except GPT-2 if we average the layers (in Figure 5).

Second, it is impossible for any LM to have a "negative" rhetorical capacity. If the probing loss is worse than RandEmbed baseline, that means the RST probe can not detect rhetorical features of the given category encoded in the representations. This is what happens in some layers of GPT-2, XLM, and XLNet, and the mean of all layers of GPT-2.

Random guesser To measure the capacity of baseline embeddings, we set up a random guesser as a "baseline-of-baseline". The random guesser outputs the arithmetic mean of RST features plus a small Gaussian noise (with s.d. $\sigma \in \{0, 0.01, 0.1, 1.0\}$) The output of RandGuess is completely independent of the discourse. As shown in Table 2, the best of the four random guessers is much worse than any of the three word embedding baselines, which is expected.

4.3 Why are some LMs better?

From probing experiments (Figure 3, 4, and 5) we can see that BERT-based LMs have slightly better rhetorical capacities than XLNet, and much better capacities than GPT-2. We present two hypotheses as following.

Config	RST Feature Set			
	All	EDU	Sig	Tree
FastText	.6987	.7215	.6911	.6889
GloVe	.7204	.7142	.7166	.6942
RandEmbed	.7238	.7365	.7077	.7034
RandGuess	1101.5	128.9	3.1	6799.0

Table 2: Comparison between RST probing losses of non-contextual word embeddings (FastText, GloVe), random embedding (RandEmbed), and a trivial guessor (RandGuess).

Rhetorics favor contexts from both directions BERT-based LMs use Transformer encoders, whereas GPT-2 use Transformer decoders. Their main difference is that a Transformer encoder considers contexts from both "past" and "future", while a Transformer decoder only conditions on the context from the "past" (Vaswani et al., 2017). GPT-2 attends to uni-directional contexts. Apparently both the "past" and "future" context would contribute to the rhetorical features of words. Without "future" contexts, GPT-2 would encode less rhetorical information.

Random permutation makes encoded rhetorics harder to decode The difference between XLNet and other LMs is the permutation in context. While permutation increases the diversity in discourse, they could also bring in new meaning to the texts. For example, the sentence in Figure 1 ("I didn't know this is from C, but it is very good!") has several syntactically plausible factorization sequences:

- I didn't know C ...
- ... this is C ...
- I know it is very good ...
- I didn't know this is good ...
- ... didn't this C good ...

Apparently such diversity in contexts makes the upper layers of XLNet contain harder-to-decode rhetorical features. If we average the representations of all layers, XLNet has larger variance than BERT-based LMs. We hypothesize that larger layer-wise difference is a factor of such instability for averaged representations.

4.4 Limitations

RST probing is not perfect. While we designed our comparisons to be rigorous, there are still several limitations to the RST probe, described below.

- RST signals are noisy. The RST relation classification task is less defined than established tasks like POS tagging. Humans tend to disagree with the annotators, resulting in a merely 65.8% accuracy in relation classification (i.e., the task introduced by Marcu (2000)). Regardless, state-of-the-art discourse parsers currently have performances slightly higher than 60% (Feng and Hirst, 2014; Ji and Eisenstein, 2014; Wang et al., 2017).
- Train / test corpus discrepancy of RST parsers. Most available RST parsers are trained on RST-DT consisting of Wall Street Journal articles. The results of parsers are affected by the corpus. As shown in some examples in Appendix, the IMDB movie review dataset contains less formal languages, introducing noise in segmentations and relation signals. To counteract noise of this type, we recommend evaluating LMs using a corpus similar to the scenario of applying the LM.
- Only 12-layer LMs are involved, to compare across various layers fairly. But our approach would be applicable to 3-layer ELMo and deeper LMs as well. Appropriate statistical controls would naturally need to be applied.
- Not all documents can be analyzed. First, documents longer than 512 tokens cannot be encoded into one vector in our probing model. Second, while RST provides elegant frameworks for analyzing rhetorical structures of discourse, in practice, the RST pipeline does not guarantee a successful analysis for an arbitrary document scraped online.

5   Related work

Recent work has considered the interpretability of contextualized representations. For example, Jain and Wallace (2019) found attention to be uncorrelated to gradient-based feature importance, while Wiegreffe and Pinter (2019) suggested such approaches allowed too much flexibility to give convincing results. Similarly, Serrano et al. (2019) considered attention representations to be noisy indicators of feature importance.

Many tasks in argument mining, similar to our task of examining neural LMs, require understanding the rhetorical aspects of discourse (Lawrence and Reed, 2019). This allows RST to be applied in relevant work. For example, RST enables understanding and analyzing argument structures of monologues (Peldszus and Stede, 2016) and, when used with other discourse features, RST can improve role-labelling in online arguments (Chakrabarty et al., 2019).

Probing neural LMs is an emergent diagnostic task on those models. Previous work probed morphological (Bisazza and Tump, 2018), agreement (Giulianelli et al., 2018), and syntactic features (Hewitt and Manning, 2019). Hewitt and Liang (2019) compared different probes, and recommended linear probes with as few parameters as possible, for the purpose of reducing overfitting. Recently, Pimentel et al. (2020) argued against this choice from an information-theoretic point of view. Voita and Titov (2020) presents an optimization goal for probes based on minimum description length.

Liu et al. (2019a) proposed 16 diverse probing tasks on top of contextualized LMs including token labeling (e.g., PoS), segmentation (e.g., NER, grammatical error detection) and pairwise relations. While LMs augmented with a probing layer could reach state-of-the-art performance on many tasks, they found that LMs still lacked fine-grained linguistic knowledge. DiscoEval (Chen et al., 2019) showed that BERT outperformed traditional pretrained sentence encoders in encoding discourse coherence features, which our results echo.

6   Conclusion

In this paper, we propose a method to quantitatively analyze the amount of rhetorical information encoded in neural language models. We compute features based on Rhetorical Structure Theory (RST) and probe the RST features from contextualized representations of neural LMs. Among six popular neural LMs, we find that contextualization helps to generally improve the rhetorical capacities of LMs, while individual models may vary in quality. In general, LMs attending to contexts from both directions (BERT-based) encode rhetorical knowledge in a more stable manner than those using unidirectional contexts (GPT-2) or permuted contexts (XLNet).

Our method presents an avenue towards quantitatively describing rhetorical capacities of neural language models based on unlabeled, target-domain corpus. This method may be used for selecting suitable LMs in tasks including rhetorical acts classifications, discourse modeling, and response generation.

Acknowledgement

We thank the anonymous reviewers for feedback. Rudzicz is supported by a CIFAR Chair in artificial intelligence. Abdalla is supported by a Vanier scholarship.

References

Mohamed Abdalla, Frank Rudzicz, and Graeme Hirst. 2017. Rhetorical structure and Alzheimer's disease. *Aphasiology*, 32(1):41–60.

Yossi Adi, Einat Kermany, Yonatan Belinkov, Ofer Lavi, and Yoav Goldberg. 2017. Fine-grained analysis of sentence embeddings using auxiliary prediction tasks. In *ICLR*, Toulon, France.

Guillaume Alain and Yoshua Bengio. 2017. Understanding intermediate layers using linear classifier probes. In *ICLR*, Toulon, France.

Yonatan Belinkov, Nadir Durrani, Fahim Dalvi, Hassan Sajjad, and James Glass. 2017. What do Neural Machine Translation Models Learn about Morphology? In *ACL*, pages 861–872, Vancouver, Canada. Association for Computational Linguistics.

Arianna Bisazza and Clara Tump. 2018. The lazy encoder: A fine-grained analysis of the role of morphology in neural machine translation. In *EMNLP*, pages 2871–2876, Brussels, Belgium. Association for Computational Linguistics.

Piotr Bojanowski, Edouard Grave, Armand Joulin, and Tomas Mikolov. 2017. Enriching word vectors with subword information. *TACL*, 5:135–146.

Lynn Carlson, Daniel Marcu, and Mary Ellen Okurowski. 2001. Building a Discourse-Tagged Corpus in the Framework of Rhetorical Structure Theory. In *SIGDIAL Workshop*.

Tuhin Chakrabarty, Christopher Hidey, Smaranda Muresan, Kathy McKeown, and Alyssa Hwang. 2019. AMPERSAND: Argument Mining for PERSuAsive oNline Discussions. In *EMNLP*, pages 2933–2943, Hong Kong, China. Association for Computational Linguistics.

Mingda Chen, Zewei Chu, and Kevin Gimpel. 2019. Evaluation Benchmarks and Learning Criteria for Discourse-Aware Sentence Representations. In *EMNLP*, pages 649–662, Hond Kong, China. Association for Computational Linguistics.

Zihang Dai, Zhilin Yang, Yiming Yang, Jaime Carbonell, Quoc Le, and Ruslan Salakhutdinov. 2019. Transformer-XL: Attentive Language Models beyond a Fixed-Length Context. In *ACL*, pages 2978–2988, Florence, Italy. Association for Computational Linguistics.

Jacob Devlin, Ming-Wei Chang, Kenton Lee, and Kristina Toutanova. 2019. BERT: Pre-training of Deep Bidirectional Transformers for Language Understanding. In *NAACL*. Association for Computational Linguistics.

Vanessa Wei Feng and Graeme Hirst. 2012. Text-level Discourse Parsing with Rich Linguistic Features. In *ACL*, pages 60–68, Jeju Island, Korea. Association for Computational Linguistics.

Vanessa Wei Feng and Graeme Hirst. 2014. A Linear-Time Bottom-Up Discourse Parser with Constraints and Post-Editing. In *ACL*, pages 511–521, Baltimore, Maryland. Association for Computational Linguistics.

Vanessa Wei Feng, Ziheng Lin, and Graeme Hirst. 2014. The Impact of Deep Hierarchical Discourse Structures in the Evaluation of Text Coherence. In *COLING*, pages 940–949, Dublin, Ireland. Dublin City University and Association for Computational Linguistics.

Mario Giulianelli, Jack Harding, Florian Mohnert, Dieuwke Hupkes, and Willem Zuidema. 2018. Under the hood: Using diagnostic classifiers to investigate and improve how language models track agreement information. In *EMNLP BlackBoxNLP*, pages 240–248, Brussels, Belgium. Association for Computational Linguistics.

Michael Heilman and Kenji Sagae. 2015. Fast rhetorical structure theory discourse parsing. *arXiv preprint 1505.02425*.

John Hewitt and Percy Liang. 2019. Designing and interpreting probes with control tasks. In *EMNLP*, pages 2733–2743, Hong Kong, China. Association for Computational Linguistics.

John Hewitt and Christopher D Manning. 2019. A Structural Probe for Finding Syntax in Word Representations. In *NAACL*, pages 4129–4138, Minneapolis, Minnesota. Association for Computational Linguistics.

Robert Irish and Peter Eliot Weiss. 2009. *Engineering communication: from principles to practice*. Oxford University Press Canada.

Sarthak Jain and Byron C. Wallace. 2019. Attention is not Explanation. In *NAACL*, pages 3543–3556, Minneapolis, Minnesota. Association for Computational Linguistics.

Ganesh Jawahar, Benoît Sagot, and Djamé Seddah. 2019. What Does BERT Learn about the Structure of Language? In *ACL*, pages 3651–3657, Florence, Italy. Association for Computational Linguistics.

Yangfeng Ji and Jacob Eisenstein. 2014. Representation learning for text-level discourse parsing. In *ACL*, pages 13–24, Baltimore, Maryland. Association for Computational Linguistics.

Shafiq Joty, Giuseppe Carenini, and Raymond T Ng. 2015. CODRA: A Novel Discriminative Framework for Rhetorical Analysis. *Computational Linguistics*, 41(3):385–435.

Nitish Shirish Keskar, Bryan McCann, Lav Varshney, Caiming Xiong, and Richard Socher. 2019. CTRL - A Conditional Transformer Language Model for Controllable Generation. *arXiv preprint 1909.05858*.

Diederik Kingma and Jimmy Ba. 2014. Adam: A method for stochastic optimization. In *ICLR*, Banff, Canada.

Guillaume Lample and Alexis Conneau. 2019. Cross-lingual Language Model Pretraining. *arXiv preprint arXiv:1901.07291*.

John Lawrence and Chris Reed. 2019. Argument Mining: A Survey. *Computational Linguistics*, pages 1–54.

Bai Li, Yi-Te Hsu, and Frank Rudzicz. 2019. Detecting dementia in Mandarin Chinese using transfer learning from a parallel corpus. In *NAACL*, pages 1991–1997, Minneapolis, Minnesota. Association for Computational Linguistics.

Qi Li, Tianshi Li, and Baobao Chang. 2016. Discourse Parsing with Attention-based Hierarchical Neural Networks. In *EMNLP*, pages 362–371, Austin, Texas. Association for Computational Linguistics.

Zhouhan Lin, Minwei Feng, Cicero Nogueira dos Santos, Mo Yu, Bing Xiang, Bowen Zhou, and Yoshua Bengio. 2017. A structured self-attentive sentence embedding. In *ICLR*, Toulon, France.

Nelson F. Liu, Matt Gardner, Yonatan Belinkov, Matthew E. Peters, and Noah A. Smith. 2019a. Linguistic Knowledge and Transferability of Contextual Representations. pages 1073–1094, Minneapolis, Minnesota. Association for Computational Linguistics.

Sha Liu and Antony Kunnan. 2016. Investigating the Application of Automated Writing Evaluation to Chinese Undergraduate English Majors: A Case Study of WriteToLearn. *CALICO*, 33(1):71–91.

Yinhan Liu, Myle Ott, Naman Goyal, Jingfei Du, Mandar Joshi, Danqi Chen, Omer Levy, Mike Lewis, Luke Zettlemoyer, and Veselin Stoyanov. 2019b. RoBERTa: A Robustly Optimized BERT Pretraining Approach. *arXiv preprint 1907.11692*.

Andrew L Maas, Raymond E Daly, Peter T Pham, Dan Huang, Andrew Y Ng, and Christopher Potts. 2011. Learning Word Vectors for Sentiment Analysis. In *ACL*, pages 142–150, Portland, Oregon, USA. Association for Computational Linguistics.

William C Mann, Christian M I M Matthiessen, and Sandra A Thompson. 1989. Rhetorical structure theory and text analysis. *ISI Research Report*.

William C. Mann and Sandra A. Thompson. 1988. Rhetorical Structure Theory: Toward a functional theory of text organization. *Interdisciplinary Journal for the Study of Discourse*, 8(3):243–281.

Daniel Marcu. 2000. *The Theory and Practice of Discourse Parsing and Summarization*. MIT Press, Cambridge, MA, USA.

Mohammed Ali Mohsen and Abdulaziz Alshahrani. 2019. The Effectiveness of Using a Hybrid Mode of Automated Writing Evaluation System on EFL Students' Writing. *Teaching English with Technology*, 19(1):118–131.

Adam Paszke, Sam Gross, Francisco Massa, Adam Lerer, James Bradbury, Gregory Chanan, Trevor Killeen, Zeming Lin, Natalia Gimelshein, Luca Antiga, Alban Desmaison, Andreas Köpf, Edward Yang, Zach DeVito, Martin Raison, Alykhan Tejani, Sasank Chilamkurthy, Benoit Steiner, Lu Fang, Junjie Bai, and Soumith Chintala. 2019. PyTorch: An Imperative Style, High-Performance Deep Learning Library. In *NeurIPS*.

Andreas Peldszus and Manfred Stede. 2016. Rhetorical structure and argumentation structure in monologue text. In *ArgMining Workshop*, pages 103–112, Berlin, Germany. Association for Computational Linguistics.

Jeffrey Pennington, Richard Socher, and Christopher D Manning. 2014. GloVe: Global Vectors for Word Representation. In *EMNLP*, pages 1532–1543, Doha, Qatar.

Tiago Pimentel, Josef Valvoda, Rowan Hall Maudslay, Ran Zmigrod, Adina Williams, and Ryan Cotterell. 2020. Information-Theoretic Probing for Linguistic Structure. Association of Computational Linguistics.

Donald E Powers, Jill C Burstein, Martin Chodorow, Mary E Fowles, and Karen Kukich. 2001. Stumping E-Rater: Challenging the Validity of Automated Essay Scoring. Technical report, Educational Testing Service, Princeton, New Jersey.

Rashmi Prasad, Nikhil Dinesh, Alan Lee, Eleni Miltsakaki, Livio Robaldo, Aravind Joshi, and Bonnie Webber. 2008. The Penn Discourse TreeBank 2.0. In *LREC*, Marrakech, Morocco. European Language Resources Association (ELRA).

Alec Radford, Jeffrey Wu, Rewon Child, David Luan, Dario Amodei, and Ilya Sutskever. 2019. Language models are unsupervised multitask learners. *OpenAI Blog*, 1(8).

Abigail See, Aneesh Pappu, Rohun Saxena, Akhila Yerukola, and Christopher D Manning. 2019. Do Massively Pretrained Language Models Make Better Storytellers? In *CoNLL*, pages 843–861, Hong Kong, China. Association for Computational Linguistics.

Sofia Serrano, Noah A Smith, and Paul G Allen. 2019. Is Attention Interpretable? In *ACL*, pages 2931–2951, Minneapolis, Minnesota. Association for Computational Linguistics.

Kaitao Song, Xu Tan, Tao Qin, Jianfeng Lu, and Tie-Yan Liu. 2019. MASS: Masked Sequence to Sequence Pre-training for Language Generation. In *ICML*, Long Beach, California.

Mihai Surdeanu, Thomas Hicks, and Marco A Valenzuela-Escárcega. 2015. Two Practical Rhetorical Structure Theory Parsers. In *NAACL*, Denver, Colorado.

Stephen Toulmin. 1958. *The Uses of Argument*. Cambridge University Press.

Ashish Vaswani, Noam Shazeer, Niki Parmar, Jakob Uszkoreit, Llion Jones, Aidan N. Gomez, Lukasz Kaiser, and Illia Polosukhin. 2017. Attention Is All You Need. In *NeurIPS*, Long Beach, California.

Elena Voita and Ivan Titov. 2020. Information-Theoretic Probing with Minimum Description Length. *arXiv preprint arXiv:2003.12298*.

Xinhao Wang, Binod Gyawali, James V Bruno, Hillary R Molloy, Keelan Evanini, and Klaus Zechner. 2019. Using Rhetorical Structure Theory to Assess Discourse Coherence for Non-native Spontaneous Speech. In *DisRPT*, pages 153–162, Minneapolis, Minnesota. Association for Computational Linguistics.

Yizhong Wang, Sujian Li, and Houfeng Wang. 2017. A Two-Stage Parsing Method for Text-Level Discourse Analysis. In *ACL*, pages 184–188, Vancouver, Canada. Association for Computational Linguistics.

Sarah Wiegreffe and Yuval Pinter. 2019. Attention is not not Explanation. In *EMNLP*, pages 11–20, Hong Kong, China. Association for Computational Linguistics.

Thomas Wolf, Lysandre Debut, Victor Sanh, Julien Chaumond, Clement Delangue, Anthony Moi, Pierric Cistac, Tim Rault, R'emi Louf, Morgan Funtowicz, and Jamie Brew. 2019. HuggingFace's Transformers: State-of-the-art Natural Language Processing. *arXiv preprint 1910.03771*.

Zhilin Yang, Zihang Dai, Yiming Yang, Jaime Carbonell, Ruslan Salakhutdinov, and Quoc V. Le. 2019. XLNet: Generalized Autoregressive Pretraining for Language Understanding.

Victor H Yngve. 1960. A model and an hypothesis for language structure. *Proceedings of the American philosophical society*, 104(5):444–466.

Nan Yu, Meishan Zhang, and Guohong Fu. 2018. Transition-based neural RST parsing with implicit syntax features. In *COLING*, pages 559–570, Santa Fe, New Mexico, USA. Association for Computational Linguistics.

Mo Zhang. 2013. Contrasting Automated and Human Scoring of Essays. Technical report, Educational Testing Service.

Zining Zhu, Jekaterina Novikova, and Frank Rudzicz. 2019. Detecting cognitive impairments by agreeing on interpretations on linguistic features. In *NAACL*, pages 1431–1441, Minnespolis, Minnesota. Association for Computational Linguistics.

A   Experiments on RST-DT

As a sanity check, we include experiments on RST-DT (Carlson et al., 2001) corpus with the same preprocessing and feature extraction procedures (i.e., perform feature extraction and embedding on the article level, and ignoring the overlength articles). As shown in Figure 6, BERT-family and XLM outperform GPT-2 and XLNet. Also, the noncontextualized embedding baselines show worse performances than contextualized embeddings in general, with some exceptions (e.g., GPT-2 on EDU features). These are similar to the IMDB results.

What are different is that the probing losses of RST-DT are lower than the IMDB experiments in general. We consider two possible explanations. First, the IMDB signals contain more noise, so that probing rhetorical features from IMDB would be naturally more difficult than probing from the RST-DT dataset. Second, it is possible that the probes overfit the much smaller RST-DT dataset.

B   Examples of parse trees

We include several examples of IMDB parse trees in Appendix here, including some examples where the RST parser makes mistakes on a new domain, movie review. For clarity of illustration, these examples are among the shorter movie reviews. More parse trees can be generated by our visualization code, which is contained in our submitted scripts.

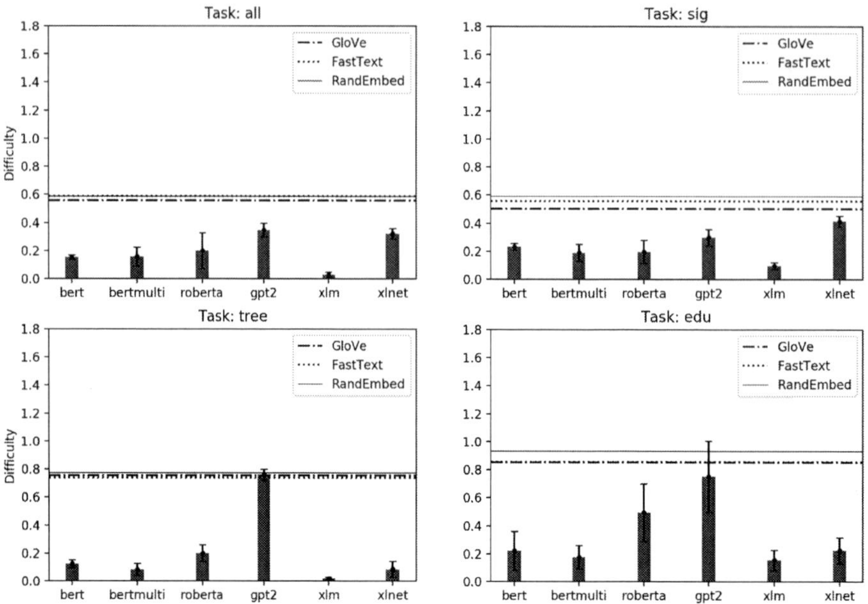

Figure 6: Probing performances of averaging 12 layers for 6 neural LMs on 4 tasks in RST-DT, compared to the three non-contextual baselines.

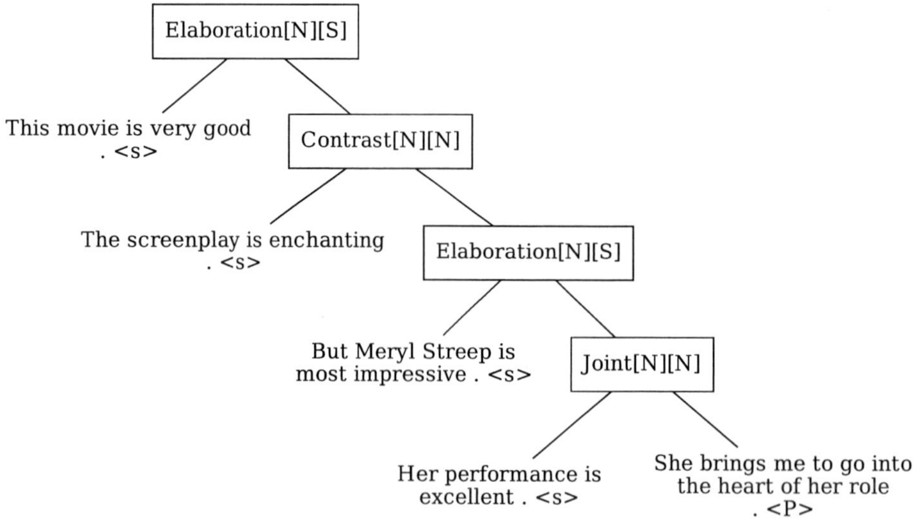

Figure 7: IMDB `train/pos/10348_8.txt`. The <s> and <P> are appended automatically by the parser, marking the end of sentences and paragraphs respectively.

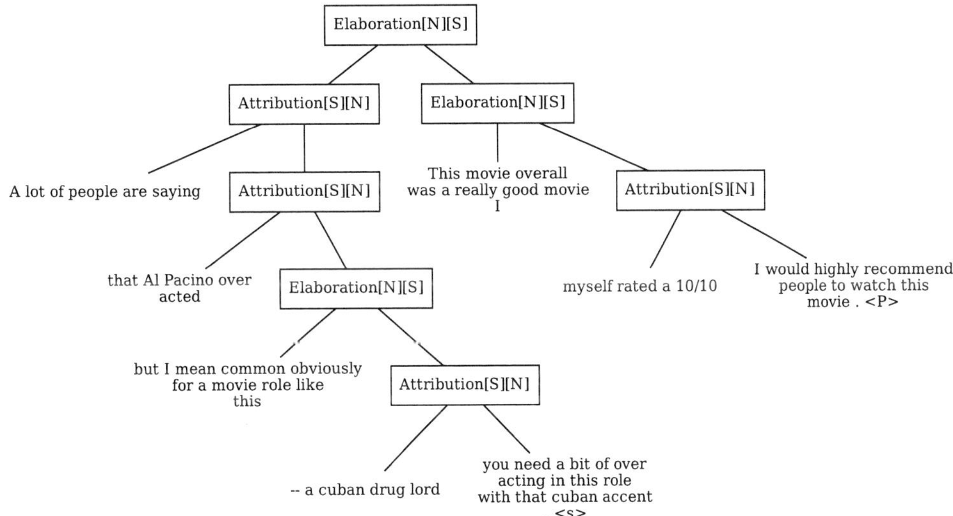

Figure 8: IMDB `train/pos/11857_10.txt`. There is an EDU segmentation error: the "I" is incorrectly assigned to the previous sentence "This movie overall was a really good movie". Apparently some lexical cues the EDU segmentator relies on (e.g., sentence finishes with a period sign) is not always followed in IMDB.

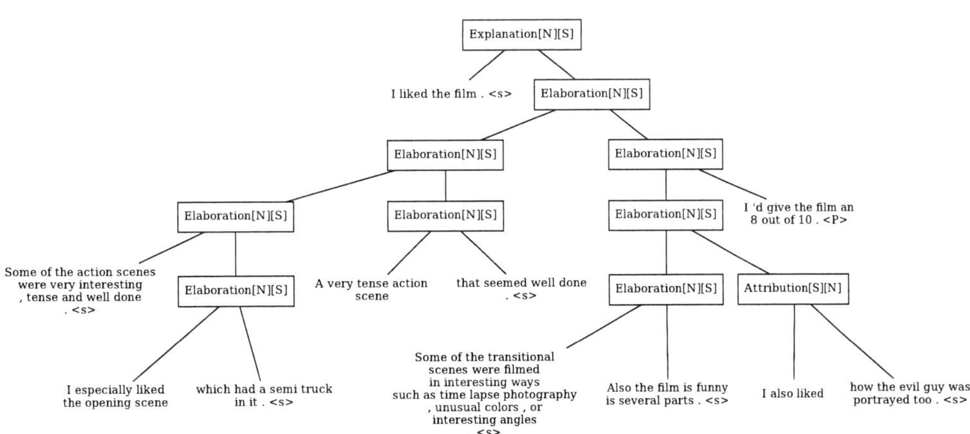

Figure 9: IMDB `train/pos/1000_8.txt`. The parser captures the key sentence of this review. All sentences following the first one act as reasons to explain how the reviewer liked the film.

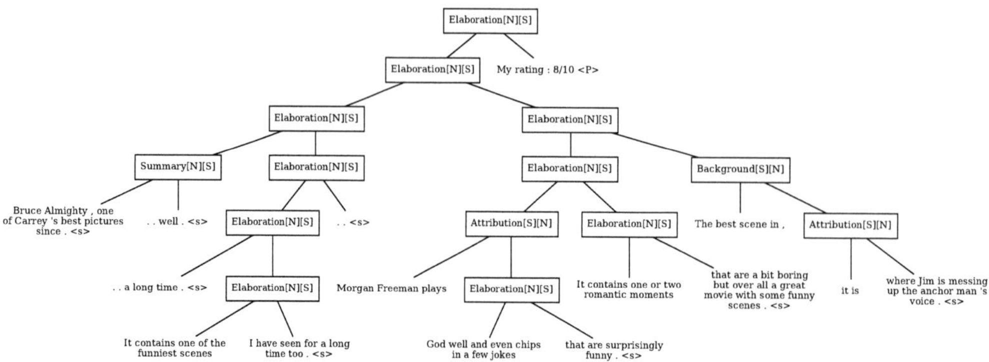

Figure 10: IMDB `train/pos/10301_8.txt`. The interjection, "well", is incorrectly identified as the satellite of the `summary` signal. This is likely caused by the discrepancy between the train (RST-DT) and test (IMDB) corpus discrepancy for the RST parser. The RST-DT dataset contains news articles, which are more formal than the online review in IMDB. The term "well" is therefore more likely to be identified as other senses.

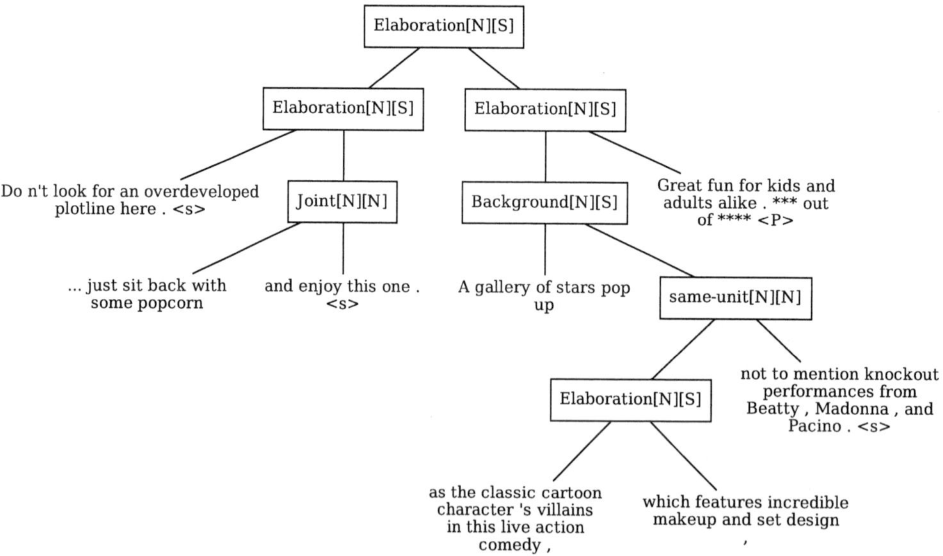

Figure 11: IMDB `train/pos/11825_8.txt`. One might suggest that the last EDU could be moved one level higher (so that it summarizes the whole review), but this parsing is also reasonable, since the mention of kids elaborates the descriptions of the makeup and the views.

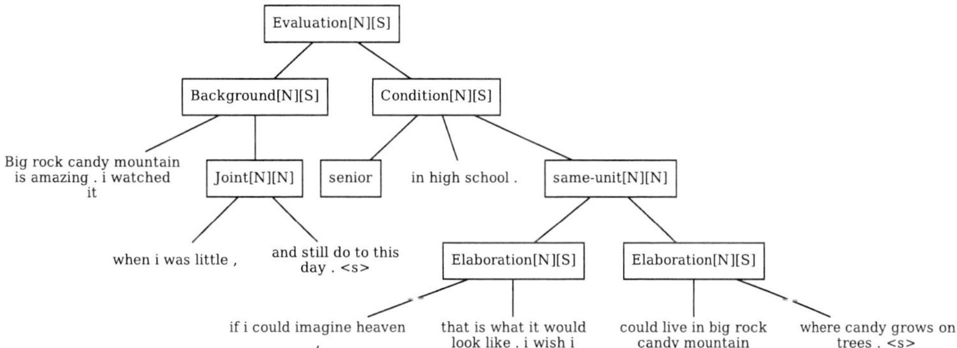

Figure 12: IMDB `train/pos/10788_10.txt`. This is an example of the EDU segmentation contains mistake. The "i wish i" should be merged with the subsequent EDU, "could live in big rock candy mountain". Note that the sentence starts with two lowercase "i" (which should be uppercase). The non-standard usages like these are unique for less formal texts like IMDB.

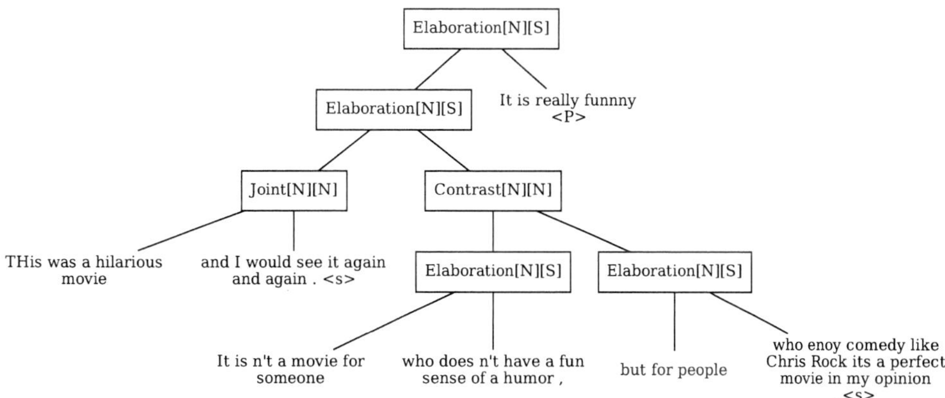

Figure 13: IMDB `train/pos/11686_10.txt`.

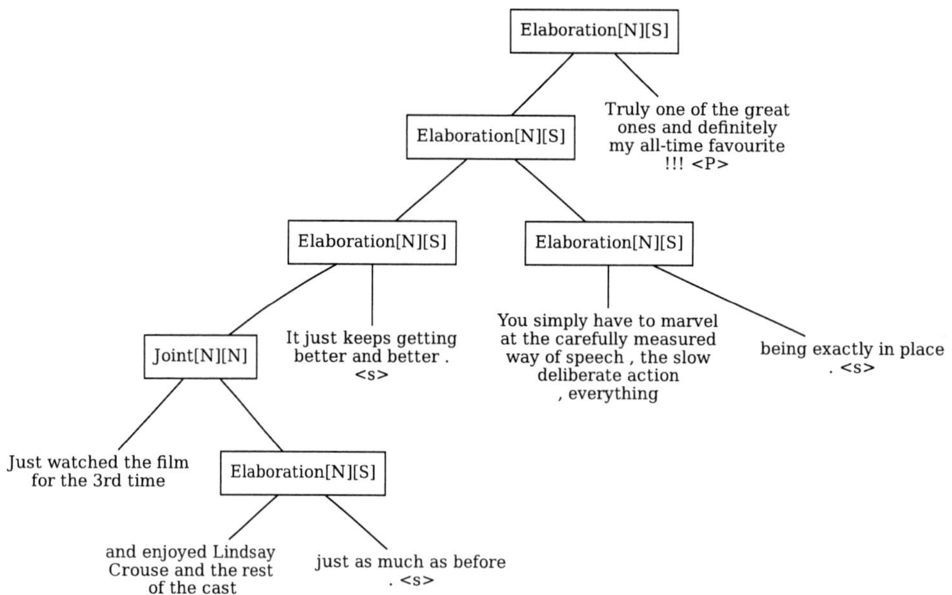

Figure 14: **IMDB** `train/pos/10264_10.txt`

What Happens To BERT Embeddings During Fine-tuning?

Amil Merchant[1] *   **Elahe Rahimtoroghi**[1]   **Ellie Pavlick**[1,2]   **Ian Tenney**[1]
[1] Google Research   [2] Brown University
{amilmerchant, elahe, epavlick, iftenney}@google.com

Abstract

While much recent work has examined how linguistic information is encoded in pre-trained sentence representations, comparatively little is understood about how these models change when adapted to solve downstream tasks. Using a suite of analysis techniques—supervised probing, unsupervised similarity analysis, and layer-based ablations—we investigate how fine-tuning affects the representations of the BERT model. We find that while fine-tuning necessarily makes some significant changes, there is no catastrophic forgetting of linguistic phenomena. We instead find that fine-tuning is a conservative process that primarily affects the top layers of BERT, albeit with noteworthy variation across tasks. In particular, dependency parsing reconfigures most of the model, whereas SQuAD and MNLI involve much shallower processing. Finally, we also find that fine-tuning has a weaker effect on representations of out-of-domain sentences, suggesting room for improvement in model generalization.

1   Introduction

Unsupervised pre-training of deep language models has led to significant advances on many NLP tasks, with the popular BERT model (Devlin et al., 2019) and successors (e.g. Lan et al., 2019; Raffel et al., 2020) dominating the GLUE leaderboard (Wang et al., 2019) and other benchmarks over the past year. Many recent works have attempted to better understand these models and explain what makes them so powerful. Particularly, behavioral studies (e.g. Marvin and Linzen, 2018; Goldberg, 2019), diagnostic probing classifiers (e.g. Veldhoen et al., 2016; Belinkov et al., 2017; Hupkes

et al., 2018), and unsupervised techniques (e.g. Saphra and Lopez, 2019; Voita et al., 2019a) have shed light on the representations from the pre-trained models and have shown that they encode a wide variety of linguistic phenomena (Tenney et al., 2019b; Liu et al., 2019).

However, in the standard recipe for models such as BERT (Devlin et al., 2019), after initializing with pre-trained weights, they are then trained for a few epochs on a supervised dataset. Considerably less is understood about what happens during this fine-tuning stage. Current understanding is based largely on the models' performance. While fine-tuned Transformers achieve state-of-the-art accuracy, they also can end up learning shallow heuristics (McCoy et al., 2019b; Gururangan et al., 2018; Poliak et al., 2018), suggesting a disconnect between the richness of features learned from pre-training and those used by fine-tuned models. Thus, in this work, we seek to understand how the internals of the model–the representation space–change when fine-tuned for downstream tasks. We focus on three widely-used NLP tasks: dependency parsing, natural language inference (MNLI), and reading comprehension (SQuAD), and ask:

- What happens to the encoding of linguistic features such as syntactic and semantic roles? Are these preserved, reinforced, or forgotten as the encoder learns a new task? Do different tasks change how shallowly this information is encoded? (Section 4)

- Where in the model are changes made? Are parameter updates concentrated in a small number of layers or are there changes throughout the model? (Section 5)

- Do these changes generalize or does the new behavior only apply to the specific domain on which fine-tuning occurred? (Section 6)

* Work done as member of the Google AI Residency program https://ai.google/research/join-us/ai-residency/

Proceedings of the Third BlackboxNLP Workshop on Analyzing and Interpreting Neural Networks for NLP, pages 33–44
Online, November 20, 2020. ©2020 Association for Computational Linguistics

We approach these questions with three complementary analysis techniques. Supervised probing classifiers (Tenney et al., 2019b; Hewitt and Manning, 2019; Voita and Titov, 2020) provide a means of explicitly testing for the presence of pre-specified linguistic phenomena, while Representational Similarity Analysis (RSA; Kriegeskorte et al., 2008) gives a task-agnostic measurement of the change in model activations. Finally, we corroborate our results with two types of layer-based ablations–truncation and partial freezing–and measure their effect on end-task performance.

Taken together, we conclude that fine-tuning involves primarily shallow model changes, evidenced by three specific observations. First, linguistic features are not lost during fine-tuning but tasks can differ in how they either surface or obfuscate different phenomena. Second, fine-tuning tends to affect only the top few layers of BERT, albeit with variation across tasks: SQuAD and MNLI have a relatively shallow effect, while dependency parsing involves deeper changes to the encoder. We confirm this by partial-freezing experiments which test how many layers *need* to change to do well on each task and relate this to an estimate of task *difficulty* (with respect to the pre-training regime) via layer ablations. Finally, we observe that fine-tuning induces large changes on in-domain examples, yet on out-of-domain sentences, the representations more closely resemble those of the pre-trained model.

2   Related Work

Base model   Many recent papers have focused on understanding sentence encoders such as ELMo (Peters et al., 2018a) and BERT (Devlin et al., 2019), focusing primarily on the "innate" abilities of the pre-trained ("Base") models. For example, analyses of attention weights have shown interpretable patterns (Coenen et al., 2019; Vig and Belinkov, 2019; Voita et al., 2019b; Hoover et al., 2019) and found strong correlations to syntax (Clark et al., 2019). Kovaleva et al. (2019) also saw that fine-tuning mainly changes the attention of the last few layers, consistent with our findings in Section 5.1. However, other studies have cast doubt on what conclusions can be drawn from attention patterns (Jain and Wallace, 2019; Serrano and Smith, 2019; Brunner et al., 2019).

More generally, supervised probing models and diagnostic classifiers make few assumptions beyond the existence of model activations and can test for the presence of a wide variety of phenomena. Tenney et al. (2019b); Liu et al. (2019); Peters et al. (2018b) introduced task suites that probe for high-level linguistic phenomena such as part-of-speech, entity types, and coreference, while Tenney et al. (2019a) showed that these phenomena are represented in a hierarchical order within the layers of BERT. Hewitt and Manning (2019) used a geometrically-motivated probe to explore syntactic structures, and Voita and Titov (2020) and Pimentel et al. (2020) designed information-theoretic techniques that can measure the model and data complexity.[1]

While probing models depend on labelled data, parallel work has studied the same encoders using unsupervised techniques. Voita et al. (2019a) used a form of canonical correlation analysis (PWCCA; Morcos et al., 2018) to study the layer-wise evolution of representations, while Saphra and Lopez (2019) explored how these representations evolve during training. Abnar et al. (2019) used Representational Similarity Analysis (RSA; Laakso and Cottrell, 2000; Kriegeskorte et al., 2008) to study the effect of context on encoder representations, while Chrupała and Alishahi (2019) correlated them with syntax.

Fine-tuning   Comparatively few analyses have focused on understanding the fine-tuning process. Initial studies of fine-tuned encoders have shown state-of-the-art performance on benchmark suites such as GLUE (Wang et al., 2019) and surprising sample efficiency (Peters et al., 2018a). However, behavioral studies with challenge sets (McCoy et al., 2019b; Poliak et al., 2018; Ettinger et al., 2018; Kim et al., 2018) have shown limited ability to generalize to out-of-domain data and across syntactic perturbations. van Aken et al. (2019) focused on question-answering models with task-specific probes. Peters et al. (2019) analyzed the effects of fine-tuning with respect to the performance of diagnostic classifiers. Gauthier and Levy (2019) studied fine-tuning via RSA, finding a significant divergence between the representations of models fine-tuned on different tasks. Concurrent work by Tamkin et al. (2020) investigated the transferability of pre-trained language models and performed an number of layer ablations. Consistent with our observations in Section 5.2, they find

---

[1]See Belinkov and Glass (2019) and Rogers et al. (2020) for a survey of probing methods.

differences in which layers are important for fine-tuning different tasks. However, none of the prior provides a comprehensive analysis of what happens to the internal representations of the BERT model. In our work, we find that by comparing the Base to the fine-tuned models either via probing, RSA, and layer ablations provides novel insights about this additional phase of training.

3 Experimental Setup

BERT We focus on the popular BERT model (Devlin et al., 2019), focusing on the 12-layer `base_uncased` variant.[2] We denote the pre-trained model as **Base** and refer to fine-tuned versions by the name of the task.

MNLI A common benchmark for natural language understanding, the MNLI dataset (Williams et al., 2018) contains over 433K sentence pairs annotated with textual entailment information. We fine-tune BERT using the architecture and parameters of Devlin et al. (2019), using a softmax layer on `[CLS]` representation to predict the output label. Across three trials, the evaluation accuracy of our BERT Base model is 83.3 ± 0.1, slightly lower but comparable to the published score of 84.6.

SQuAD The SQuADv1.1 dataset (Rajpurkar et al., 2016) contains over 100K crowd-sourced question-answer pairs, created from a set of Wikipedia articles. We fine-tune BERT using the architecture and parameters of Devlin et al. (2019), which uses two independent softmax layers to predict the start and end tokens of the answer span. Our average F1 score is 89.2 ± 0.2, slightly higher than the published 88.5.

Dependency Parsing We also introduce a BERT model fine-tuned on dependency parsing (Dep). We include this task to present a contrasting perspective from the prior two datasets, since prior research has suggested that much of the information needed to solve dependency parsing is already present after pre-training (Hewitt and Manning, 2019; Goldberg, 2019; Tenney et al., 2019b). Our model is trained on data from the CoNLL 2017 Shared Task (Zeman et al., 2017) and uses the features of BERT as input to a bi-affine classifier, similar to Dozat and Manning (2017). The model uses a learning rate of 3×10^{-5}

with a 10% warm-up portion, uses an Adam optimizer (Kingma and Ba, 2014), and is trained for 20 epochs. The Labeled Attachment Score (LAS) on the development set is 96.3 ± 0.1 for our model[3]

4 What happens to linguistic features?

Equipped with the models trained on these downstream tasks, we ask how the representation of linguistic features compare to those in the pre-trained model? Recent studies have shown that these robust features are not necessarily used to inform predictions on downstream tasks, with models appearing to use dataset heuristics such as lexical overlap (McCoy et al., 2019b) or word priors (Poliak et al., 2018), but it is an open question whether this is because these features are forgotten entirely or simply are not always used. We explore this with supervised probing techniques, using edge probing (Tenney et al., 2019b) and structural probes (Hewitt and Manning, 2019) to explore how well linguistic information can be recovered from the fine-tuned model.

Edge Probing Edge probing aims to measure how contextual representations encode various linguistic phenomena, including part-of-speech, entity typing, and coreference. We use the tasks and parameters of Tenney et al. (2019b), which uses a two-layer MLP to predict edge and span labels from frozen encoder representations.[4] As we are interested in whether the linguistic knowledge is retained by the model overall, we utilize the *mix* version of the edge probes, which takes as input a learned scalar mixing of the representations from every layer.[5] After training, we report the micro-averaged F1 scores on a held-out test set.

Structural Probe Complementary to the edge probes, the structural probes of Hewitt and Manning (2019) analyze how well representations encode syntactic structure. Specifically, the probe identifies whether the squared L2 distance of representations under some linear transformation en-

---

[2]We use the original TensorFlow (Abadi et al., 2015) implementation from `https://github.com/google-research/bert`.

[3] We provide additional details of the experiments and datasets in Appendix C for the purpose of reproducibility.

[4]The dependency labeling task is from the English Web Treebank (Silveira et al., 2014), SPR corresponds to SPR1 from Teichert et al. (2017), and relations is Task 8 from SemEval 2010 (Hendrickx et al., 2010). All of the other tasks are from OntoNotes 5.0 (Weischedel et al., 2013).

[5]We also explored the effects of fine-tuning on the *top* layer of BERT to provide additional insight into whether this linguistic information may be lost from the top layers even if still present elsewhere. For results, see Appendix A.

		Δ for Baselines		Δ for Fine-tuned Models		
Task	**BERT Base**	**Lexical**	**Randomized**	**MNLI**	**SQuAD**	**Dep**
POS	97.5	-9.0	-13.6	-0.2	**-1.5**	-0.2
Constituents	84.4	-12.9	-24.1	**-2.2**	0.1	**4.4**
Dependencies	95.5	-15.6	-18.2	-0.5	**-2.5**	0.2
Entities	96.2	-6.6	-10.0	-0.3	-0.9	-0.6
SRL	92.9	-13.6	-15.0	-0.4	**-2.9**	-0.5
Coreference	95.7	-5.8	-6.2	-0.5	-0.8	**-1.2**
SPR	84.6	-6.6	-12.2	-0.7	-0.4	**-1.2**
Relations	79.5	-20.7	-40.5	-0.8	-0.4	**-2.5**

Table 1: Comparison of F1 performance on the edge probing tasks before and after fine-tuning. The BERT Base performance is consistent with (Tenney et al., 2019b), and the results show that the fine-tuned models retain most of the linguistic concepts discovered during unsupervised pre-training. We report single numbers for clarity, but note that variation across runs is ±0.5 between probing runs, ±0.7 between fine-tuning runs from the same checkpoint, and ±1.0 point between different pre-training runs.

codes the dependency parse. The two versions of the structural probe either attempt to predict the tree depth for each word (distance from the root node) or pairwise distances for all words in the parse tree. For both, we measure the Spearman correlation between predicted and true values [6]

4.1 Results

The results from both probing tasks demonstrate that the linguistic features from pre-training are preserved in the fine-tuned models. This is first seen in the edge probing metrics presented in Table 1. For the sake of comparison, we provide baseline results on the output of the embedding layer (Lexical) and a randomly initialized BERT architecture (Randomized). These baselines are important as inspection-based analysis can often discover patterns that are not obviously present due to the high capacity of auxiliary classifiers. For example, Zhang and Bowman (2018); Hewitt and Liang (2019) found that expressive-enough probing methods can perform surprisingly well even when trained on randomized encoders.

Across the edge probing suite, we see only small changes in F1 score from the fine-tuned models compared to BERT base. In most cases, we observe a drop in performance of 0.5-2%, with some variation: MNLI and SQuAD lead to drops of 1.5-3% on syntactic tasks–constituents, and POS, dependencies, and SRL, respectively–while the dependency parsing model leads to signifi-

cantly improved syntactic performance (+4% on constituent labeling) while dropping performance on the more semantically-oriented coreference, SPR, and relation classification tasks. We hypothesize that these changes relate to the similarity between tasks: a task like constituent labels help improve dependency parsing, and is thus strengthened, whereas higher level semantic tasks such as SPR contribute less directly and such information may be lost during fine-tuning. Nonetheless, in most cases these effects are small: they are comparable to the variation between randomly-seeded fine-tuning runs (±0.7), and much smaller than the difference between the full model and the Lexical or Randomized baselines, suggesting that most linguistic information from BERT is still available within the model after fine-tuning.

Next, we turn to the structural probe, with results seen in Figure 1. First, the dependency parsing fine-tuned model shows improvements in the Spearman correlation, as early as layer 5. Since the structural probes are designed and trained to look for syntax, this result suggests that the fine-tuning improves the model's internal representation of such information. This makes intuitive sense as the fine-tuning task is aligned with the probing task. On the MNLI and SQuAD fine-tuned models, we observe minimal changes in performance, with small drops within the final layer. This artifact likely emerges from the fine-tuning setup where the last layer is only needed for classification or span prediction and therefore is unlikely to also retain all the linguistic information.[7]

---

[6]Note that Hall Maudslay et al. (2020) has recently raised concern about these metrics, but we follow the original method of Hewitt and Manning (2019) for the most comparable results.

[7]A similar story emerges when repeating the edge probing models on the last layer of BERT; see Appendix A.

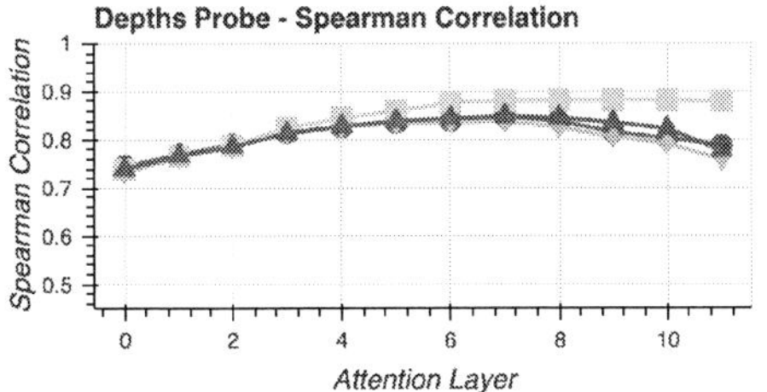
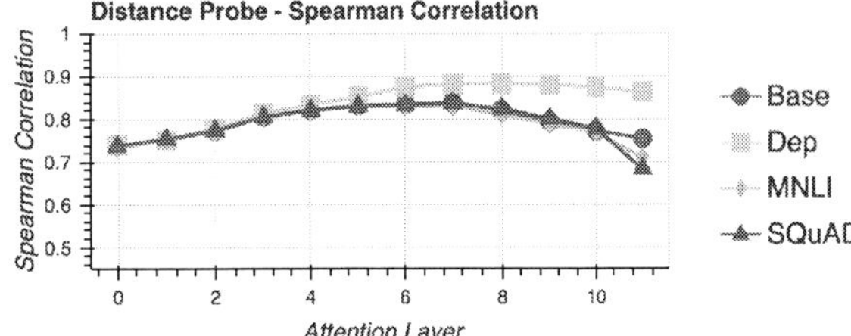

Figure 1: Comparison of the structural probe performance on BERT models before and after fine-tuning. The stability of the Spearman correlations between both the depths and distance probes suggest that the embeddings still retain significant information about the syntax of inputted sentences.

This result suggests that the actual magnitude of change within the "syntactic subspace" is quite small. This is consistent with observations by Gauthier and Levy (2019) and suggests that information about syntactic structure is well-preserved in models on downstream tasks.

One caveat of the experimentation above is that it uses complex diagnostic classifiers and only reports final model performance. Instead, what if the linguistic features were simply becoming more difficult to extract from the representations? Then, they could be not as readily "available" after fine-tuning. We explored this hypothesis using Minimum Description Length probes (Voita and Titov, 2020), with the results presented in Appendix B. We found minimal differences across most tasks, where the only significant result was that fine-tuning on dependency parsing made the corresponding edge probing task easier to learn as a function of the number of examples.

4.2 Conclusion

Overall, our results suggest that linguistic features are still available, and that the fine-tuning process does not lead to catastrophic forgetting. Nonetheless, behavioral analyses have shown that fine-tuned models can still fail to leverage even simple syntactic knowledge in their predictions (McCoy et al., 2019b,a; Min et al., 2020), and may instead rely on annotation artifacts (Gururangan et al., 2018) or pattern matching (Jia and Liang, 2017). This suggests that the changes from fine-tuning are conservative: rich features are still present even if the model ends up finding a naive, simple solution.

5 Where do the representations change?

The supervised probes from the previous section are highly targeted: as trained models, they are sensitive to particular linguistic phenomena, but they also can learn to ignore everything else. If the supervised probe is closely related to the fine-tuning task–such as for syntactic probes and dependency parsing–we observe significant changes in performance, but otherwise we see little effect. Nonetheless, we know that *something* must be changing during fine-tuning–at minimum because, as shown in Peters et al. (2019), performance degrades significantly if the encoder is completely frozen. To explore this change, we turn to an unsupervised technique, Representational Similarity Analysis (RSA; Laakso and Cottrell, 2000), which is sensitive to the global structure of the embedding space, and corroborate our findings with layer-based ablations. While these techniques are not targeted to specific linguistic phenomena, they do provide a powerful exploratory tool that can illuminate which parts of the model change and how they vary across datasets.

5.1 Representational Similarity Analysis

RSA is a technique for measuring the similarity between two different representation spaces for a given set of stimuli. Originally developed for neuroscience (Kriegeskorte et al., 2008), it has become increasingly used to analyze similarity between neural network activations (Abnar et al., 2019; Chrupała and Alishahi, 2019). The method works by using a common set of n examples, used to create two sets of representations. For each set, a kernel is used to define a pairwise similarity matrix in $\mathbb{R}^{n \times n}$. The final similarity score between the two representation spaces is calculated as the Pearson correlation between the flattened upper triangulars of the two similarity matrices.

In our application, we pass ordinary sentences (Wikipedia), sentence-pairs (MNLI), or question-answer pairs (SQuAD) as inputs to the BERT model, and select a random sample ($n = 5000$) of

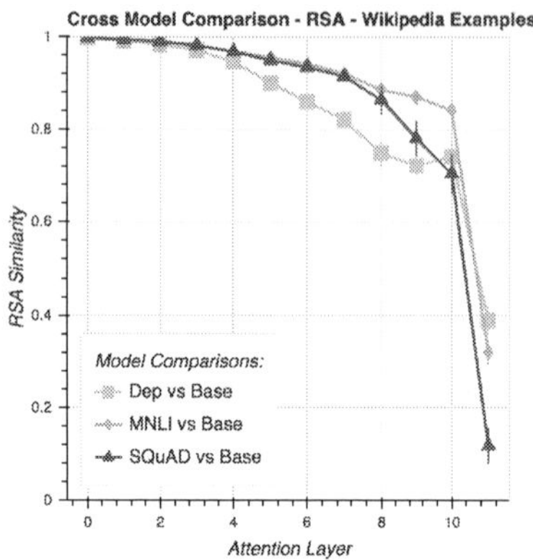

Figure 2: Comparison of the representations from BERT base and various fine-tuned models, when tested on Wikipedia examples. The dependency probing model starts to diverge from BERT Base around layer 5, matching previous results from edge probing. For the MNLI and SQuAD models, the differences from the Base model arise in the top layers of the network.

tokens as stimuli. This input is consistent with the masked language model pre-training, various fine-tuning tasks, and diagnostic classifiers in analyzing the contextual representations for every token. We extract the activations of corresponding layers from the two models to compare (e.g. Base vs. a fine-tuned model). Following previous applications of RSA to text representations (Abnar et al., 2019; Chrupała and Alishahi, 2019), we adopt the cosine similarity kernel.

While RSA does not require learning any parameters and is thus resistant to overfitting (Abdou et al., 2019), the metric can be sensitive to spurious signals in the representations that may not be relevant to model behavior.[8] To mitigate this, we repeat the BERT pre-training procedure (as described in Section 3 of Devlin et al., 2019) from scratch three times. For each pre-trained checkpoints, we fine-tune on the three downstream task and report the average for these independent runs.

Results Figure 2 shows the results of our RSA analysis comparing the three task models, Dep, MNLI, and SQuAD, to BERT Base at each layer. Note that in these figures, lower values imply greater change relative to the pre-trained model. Across all tasks, we observe that changes generally arise in the top layers of the network, with little change observed in the layers closest to the in-

put. To first order, this may be a result of optimization: vanishing gradients result in the most change in the layers closest to the loss. Yet we interestingly do observe significant differences between tasks. For dependency parsing, we observe the deepest changes, departing from the Base model as early as layers 4 and 5. This result likely arises as syntactic understanding of input is maximized in the early layers of the model, as measured by the edge probes of (Tenney et al., 2019a) and presented structural probes. Performing optimally on this task would require surfacing this information in all subsequent layers, leading to these changes.

Except for the last layer which is particularly sensitive to the form of the output (span-based for dependencies and SQuAD, or using the [CLS] token for MNLI), we see that MNLI involves the smallest changes to the model: the second-to-last attention layer still shows a very high similarity score of 0.84 ± 0.02 compared to the representations of the pre-trained encoder. The SQuAD model shows a slightly steeper change, behaving similarly to the Base model through layer 7 but dropping off afterwards - suggesting that fine-tuning on this task involves a deeper, yet still relatively shallow reconfiguration of the encoder. SQuAD likely shows deeper processing as choosing an answer span still requires satisfying a number of syntactic constraints and requires evolution across more than just two layers (van Aken et al., 2019), but overall, we see that for these benchmark tasks, fine-tuning is conservative and only changes a fraction of the model's representations.

5.2 Layer Ablations

As an unsupervised, metric-based technique, RSA tells us about broad changes in the representation space, but does not in itself say if these changes are important for the model's behavior–i.e. for the processing necessary to solve the downstream task. To measure our observations in terms of task performance, we turn to two layer ablation studies.

Partial Freezing can be thought of as a test for how many layers *need* to change for a downstream task. We freeze the bottom k layers (and the embeddings)–treating them as features–but allow the rest to adapt. Effectively, this clamps the first k layers to have RSA similarity of 1 with the Base model. Also, we perform **model truncation** as a rough estimate of difficulty for each task, and as an attempt to de-couple the results of partial

---

[8]We note that probing techniques are more robust to this, since they learn to focus on relevant features.

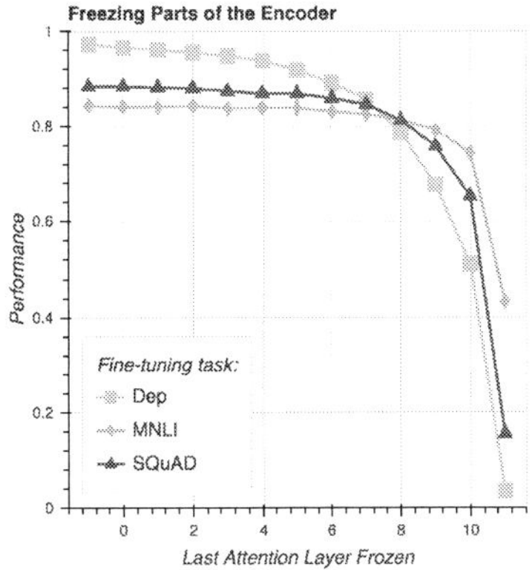

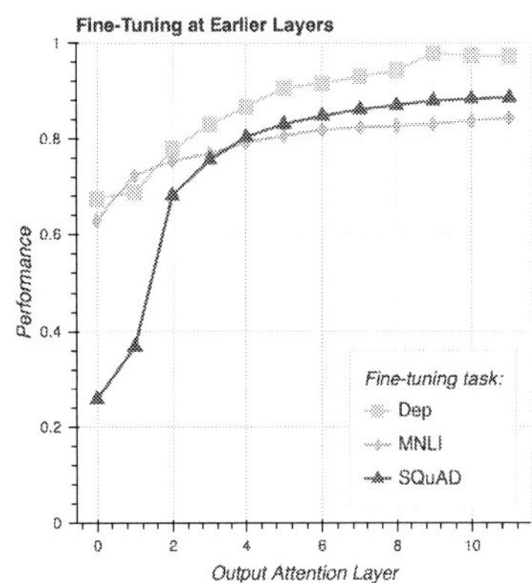

Figure 3: Effects of freezing an increasing number of layers during fine-tuning on performance (we report the evaluation accuracy for MNLI, F1 score for SQuAD, and LAS for Dep). The point at -1 corresponds to no frozen components. The graph shows that only a few unfrozen layers are needed to improve task performance, supporting the shallow processing conclusion.

Figure 4: Effects of fine-tuning at earlier layers of BERT. We note that the MNLI evaluation accuracy and SQuAD F1 score approach the full model performance by layer 6, whereas the dependency parsing LAS seems to require more layers.

freezing from helpful features that may be available in top layers of BERT Base (Tenney et al., 2019a). Figure 3 (partial freezing) and Figure 4 (truncation) show the effect on task performance.

The patterns we observe corroborate the findings of our RSA analysis. On MNLI, we find that performance does not drop significantly unless the last two layers are frozen, while the truncated models are able to achieve comparable performance with only three attention layers. This suggests that while natural language inference (Dagan et al., 2006) is known to be a complex task *in the limit*, most MNLI examples can be resolved with relatively shallow processing. SQuAD exhibits a similar trend: we see a significant performance drop when 3 or fewer layers are allowed to change (e.g. freezing through layer 8 or higher), consistent with where RSA finds the greatest change. From our truncation experiment, we similarly see that only five layers are needed to achieve comparable performance to the full model.

Dependency parsing performance drops even more rapidly–in both experiments–consistent with the results from RSA. This is surprising, since probing analysis (Goldberg, 2019; Marvin and Linzen, 2018) suggests that many syntactic phenomena are well-captured by the pre-trained model, and diagnostics for dependency parsing in particular (Tenney et al., 2019b,a; Hewitt and Manning, 2019; Clark et al., 2019) show strong performance from probes on frozen models. Yet

as observed with the structural probes (Figure 1) there is headroom available, and it appears that to capture it requires changing deeper parts of the model. We hypothesize that this effect may come from the hierarchical nature of parsing, which requires additional layers to determine the full tree structure. Fully reconciling these observations would be a promising direction for future work.

6 Out-of-Domain Behavior

Finally, we ask whether the effects of fine-tuning are general: do they apply only to inputs that look like the fine-tuning data, or do they lead to broader changes in behavior? This is usually explored by behavioral methods, in which a model is trained on one domain and evaluated on another– for example, the mismatched evaluation for MNLI (Williams et al., 2018)–but this analysis is limited by the availability of labeled data. By using RSA, we can test this in an unsupervised manner.

We use RSA to compare the fine-tuned model to Base and observe the degree of similarity when inputs are drawn from different corpora. We use random samples from the development sets for MNLI (as `premise [SEP] hypothesis`) and SQuAD (as `question [SEP] passage`) as in-domain for their respective models,[9] and as the out-of-domain control we use random Wikipedia sentences (which resemble the pre-training domain). As in Section 5.1, we use the

---

[9] Note that these are unseen during fine-tuning, although RSA scores do not change significantly if the MNLI or SQuAD training sets are used.

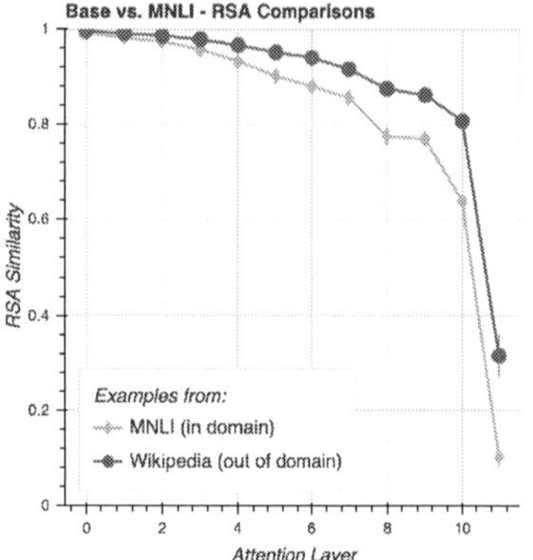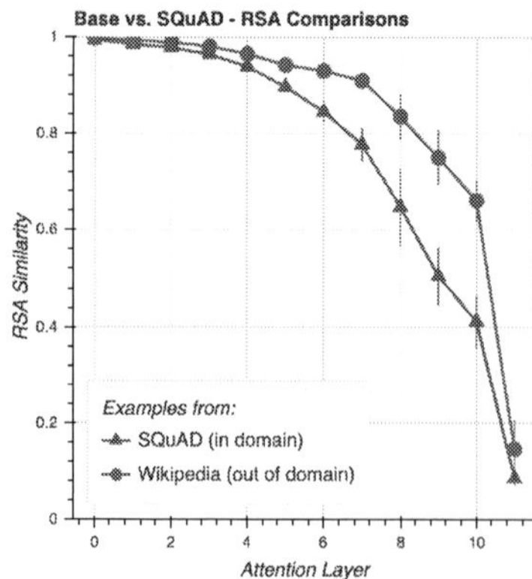

Figure 5: Comparison of the representations in the MNLI (left) and SQuAD (right) fine-tuned models and those of BERT Base, with the different lines corresponding to examples coming from various datasets. These graphs show that fine-tuning models only lead to shallow changes, consolidated to the last few layers. Also, we see that fine-tuning has a much greater impact on the token representations of in-domain data.

representations of $n = 5000$ tokens as our stimuli for each comparison.[10] Results for the MNLI and SQuAD fine-tuned models are shown in Figure 5.

Although we see that all models diverge from BERT Base in the top layers, there is a significantly larger change in the representations on in-domain examples. This suggests that fine-tuning is specific to the target domain. For other examples, such as the Wikipedia sentences which resemble the pre-training data, the similarity score with BERT Base is much higher. This suggests that fine-tuning leads the model to change its representations for the new domain but to continue to behave more like the Base model otherwise. This final result again shows that fine-tuning is conservative and suggests room for improvement in model generalization to out-of-domain sentences.

7 Conclusions

In this paper, we employ three complementary analysis methods to gain insight into effects of fine-tuning on the representations produced by BERT. From supervised probing analyses, we find that the linguistic structures discovered during pre-training remain available after fine-tuning, though this information is not strengthened by tuning on benchmark tasks such as MNLI and SQuAD. In light of prior studies (McCoy et al., 2019b; Jia and Liang, 2017) which have shown that end-task models often fall back on simple heuristics, our results are especially interesting: they suggest that the model has the option of using stronger features, but chooses to use heuristics instead.

Next, our results using RSA and layer ablations show that the changes from fine-tuning alter a fraction of the model capacity, specifically within the top few layers (up to some variation across tasks). Also, although fine-tuning has a significant effect on the representations of in-domain sentences, the representations of out-of-domain examples remain much closer to those of the pre-trained model.

Overall, these conclusions suggest that fine-tuning–as currently practiced–is a conservative process: preserving linguistic features, affecting only a few layers, and specific to in-domain examples. While the standard fine-tuning recipe undeniably leads to strong performance on many tasks, there appears to be room for improvement: an opportunity to refine this transfer step–potentially by utilizing more of the model capacity–to better the generalization and transferability.

Finally, in this work, we pulled from a range of analysis techniques to understand very fine-grained aspects of model representations (via probing classifiers) and coarse-grained ones (via RSA). An important direction for future work is the development of new techniques which allow for more exploration of the middle ground. Given available techniques, we can illuminate broadly that models are changing and test hypotheses about specific features (with probing tasks or attention analyses). New principled methods for discovering which features change will be invaluable for a deeper understanding of these models.

---

[10] We also tested single-sentence examples from MNLI and SQuAD by only taking the premise and question respectively; the trends were similar to Figure 5.

Acknowldgements

We thank our anonymous reviewers for their helpful feedback; Deepak Ramachandran, Kelvin Guu, and Slav Petrov for providing feedback on an early draft of this paper; and Tim Dozat for his help implementing the fine-tuning task for dependency parsing.

References

Martín Abadi, Ashish Agarwal, Paul Barham, Eugene Brevdo, Zhifeng Chen, Craig Citro, Greg S. Corrado, Andy Davis, Jeffrey Dean, Matthieu Devin, Sanjay Ghemawat, Ian Goodfellow, Andrew Harp, Geoffrey Irving, Michael Isard, Yangqing Jia, Rafal Jozefowicz, Lukasz Kaiser, Manjunath Kudlur, Josh Levenberg, Dandelion Mané, Rajat Monga, Sherry Moore, Derek Murray, Chris Olah, Mike Schuster, Jonathon Shlens, Benoit Steiner, Ilya Sutskever, Kunal Talwar, Paul Tucker, Vincent Vanhoucke, Vijay Vasudevan, Fernanda Viégas, Oriol Vinyals, Pete Warden, Martin Wattenberg, Martin Wicke, Yuan Yu, and Xiaoqiang Zheng. 2015. TensorFlow: Large-scale machine learning on heterogeneous systems. Software available from tensorflow.org.

Mostafa Abdou, Artur Kulmizev, Felix Hill, Daniel M. Low, and Anders Søgaard. 2019. Higher-order comparisons of sentence encoder representations. In *Proceedings of the 2019 Conference on Empirical Methods in Natural Language Processing and the 9th International Joint Conference on Natural Language Processing (EMNLP-IJCNLP)*, pages 5837–5844, Hong Kong, China. Association for Computational Linguistics.

Samira Abnar, Lisa Beinborn, Rochelle Choenni, and Willem Zuidema. 2019. Blackbox meets blackbox: Representational similarity & stability analysis of neural language models and brains. In *Proceedings of the 2019 ACL Workshop BlackboxNLP: Analyzing and Interpreting Neural Networks for NLP*, pages 191–203, Florence, Italy. Association for Computational Linguistics.

Betty van Aken, Benjamin Winter, Alexander Lser, and Felix A. Gers. 2019. How does bert answer questions? a layer-wise analysis of transformer representations.

Yonatan Belinkov, Nadir Durrani, Fahim Dalvi, Hassan Sajjad, and James Glass. 2017. What do neural machine translation models learn about morphology? In *Proceedings of the 55th Annual Meeting of the Association for Computational Linguistics (Volume 1: Long Papers)*, pages 861–872, Vancouver, Canada. Association for Computational Linguistics.

Yonatan Belinkov and James Glass. 2019. Analysis methods in neural language processing: A survey. *Transactions of the Association for Computational Linguistics*, 7:49–72.

Gino Brunner, Yang Liu, Damin Pascual, Oliver Richter, Massimiliano Ciaramita, and Roger Wattenhofer. 2019. On identifiability in transformers.

Grzegorz Chrupała and Afra Alishahi. 2019. Correlating neural and symbolic representations of language. In *Proceedings of the 57th Annual Meeting of the Association for Computational Linguistics*, pages 2952–2962, Florence, Italy. Association for Computational Linguistics.

Kevin Clark, Urvashi Khandelwal, Omer Levy, and Christopher D. Manning. 2019. What does BERT look at? an analysis of BERT's attention. In *Proceedings of the 2019 ACL Workshop BlackboxNLP: Analyzing and Interpreting Neural Networks for NLP*, pages 276–286, Florence, Italy. Association for Computational Linguistics.

Andy Coenen, Emily Reif, Ann Yuan, Been Kim, Adam Pearce, Fernanda B. Viégas, and Martin Wattenberg. 2019. Visualizing and measuring the geometry of BERT. *CoRR*, abs/1906.02715.

Ido Dagan, Oren Glickman, and Bernardo Magnini. 2006. The pascal recognising textual entailment challenge. In *Proceedings of the First International Conference on Machine Learning Challenges: Evaluating Predictive Uncertainty Visual Object Classification, and Recognizing Textual Entailment*, MLCW'05, pages 177–190, Berlin, Heidelberg. Springer-Verlag.

Jacob Devlin, Ming-Wei Chang, Kenton Lee, and Kristina Toutanova. 2019. BERT: Pre-training of deep bidirectional transformers for language understanding. In *Proceedings of the 2019 Conference of the North American Chapter of the Association for Computational Linguistics: Human Language Technologies, Volume 1 (Long and Short Papers)*, pages 4171–4186, Minneapolis, Minnesota. Association for Computational Linguistics.

Timothy Dozat and Christopher D. Manning. 2017. Deep biaffine attention for neural dependency parsing. In *ICLR (Poster)*. OpenReview.net.

Allyson Ettinger, Ahmed Elgohary, Colin Phillips, and Philip Resnik. 2018. Assessing composition in sentence vector representations. In *Proceedings of the 27th International Conference on Computational Linguistics*, pages 1790–1801, Santa Fe, New Mexico, USA. Association for Computational Linguistics.

Jon Gauthier and Roger Levy. 2019. Linking artificial and human neural representations of language. In *Proceedings of the 2019 Conference on Empirical Methods in Natural Language Processing and the 9th International Joint Conference on Natural Language Processing (EMNLP-IJCNLP)*, pages 529–539, Hong Kong, China. Association for Computational Linguistics.

Yoav Goldberg. 2019. Assessing bert's syntactic abilities. *CoRR*, abs/1901.05287.

Suchin Gururangan, Swabha Swayamdipta, Omer Levy, Roy Schwartz, Samuel Bowman, and Noah A. Smith. 2018. Annotation artifacts in natural language inference data. In *Proceedings of the 2018 Conference of the North American Chapter of the Association for Computational Linguistics: Human Language Technologies, Volume 2 (Short Papers)*, pages 107–112, New Orleans, Louisiana. Association for Computational Linguistics.

Rowan Hall Maudslay, Josef Valvoda, Tiago Pimentel, Adina Williams, and Ryan Cotterell. 2020. A tale of a probe and a parser. In *Proceedings of the 58th Annual Meeting of the Association for Computational Linguistics*, pages 7389–7395, Online. Association for Computational Linguistics.

Iris Hendrickx, Su Nam Kim, Zornitsa Kozareva, Preslav Nakov, Diarmuid Ó Séaghdha, Sebastian Padó, Marco Pennacchiotti, Lorenza Romano, and Stan Szpakowicz. 2010. SemEval-2010 task 8: Multi-way classification of semantic relations between pairs of nominals. In *Proceedings of the 5th International Workshop on Semantic Evaluation*, pages 33–38, Uppsala, Sweden. Association for Computational Linguistics.

John Hewitt and Percy Liang. 2019. Designing and interpreting probes with control tasks. In *Proceedings of the 2019 Conference on Empirical Methods in Natural Language Processing and the 9th International Joint Conference on Natural Language Processing (EMNLP-IJCNLP)*, pages 2733–2743, Hong Kong, China. Association for Computational Linguistics.

John Hewitt and Christopher D. Manning. 2019. A structural probe for finding syntax in word representations. In *Proceedings of the 2019 Conference of the North American Chapter of the Association for Computational Linguistics: Human Language Technologies, Volume 1 (Long and Short Papers)*, pages 4129–4138, Minneapolis, Minnesota. Association for Computational Linguistics.

Benjamin Hoover, Hendrik Strobelt, and Sebastian Gehrmann. 2019. exbert: A visual analysis tool to explore learned representations in transformers models. *arXiv preprint arXiv:1910.05276*.

Dieuwke Hupkes, Sara Veldhoen, and Willem Zuidema. 2018. Visualisation and'diagnostic classifiers' reveal how recurrent and recursive neural networks process hierarchical structure. *Journal of Artificial Intelligence Research*, 61:907–926.

Sarthak Jain and Byron C. Wallace. 2019. Attention is not Explanation. In *Proceedings of the 2019 Conference of the North American Chapter of the Association for Computational Linguistics: Human Language Technologies, Volume 1 (Long and Short Papers)*, pages 3543–3556, Minneapolis, Minnesota. Association for Computational Linguistics.

Robin Jia and Percy Liang. 2017. Adversarial examples for evaluating reading comprehension systems. In *Proceedings of the 2017 Conference on Empirical Methods in Natural Language Processing*, pages 2021–2031, Copenhagen, Denmark. Association for Computational Linguistics.

Juho Kim, Christopher Malon, and Asim Kadav. 2018. Teaching syntax by adversarial distraction. In *Proceedings of the First Workshop on Fact Extraction and VERification (FEVER)*, pages 79–84, Brussels, Belgium. Association for Computational Linguistics.

Diederik Kingma and Jimmy Ba. 2014. Adam: A method for stochastic optimization. *International Conference on Learning Representations*.

Olga Kovaleva, Alexey Romanov, Anna Rogers, and Anna Rumshisky. 2019. Revealing the dark secrets of bert. *arXiv preprint arXiv:1908.08593*.

N. Kriegeskorte, M. Mur, and P. Bandettini. 2008. Representational similarity analysis - connecting the branches of systems neuroscience. *Front Syst Neurosci*, 2:4.

Aarre Laakso and Garrison Cottrell. 2000. Content and cluster analysis: assessing representational similarity in neural systems. *Philosophical psychology*, 13(1):47–76.

Zhenzhong Lan, Mingda Chen, Sebastian Goodman, Kevin Gimpel, Piyush Sharma, and Radu Soricut. 2019. Albert: A lite bert for self-supervised learning of language representations.

Nelson F. Liu, Matt Gardner, Yonatan Belinkov, Matthew E. Peters, and Noah A. Smith. 2019. Linguistic knowledge and transferability of contextual representations. In *Proceedings of the 2019 Conference of the North American Chapter of the Association for Computational Linguistics: Human Language Technologies, Volume 1 (Long and Short Papers)*, pages 1073–1094, Minneapolis, Minnesota. Association for Computational Linguistics.

Rebecca Marvin and Tal Linzen. 2018. Targeted syntactic evaluation of language models. In *Proceedings of the 2018 Conference on Empirical Methods in Natural Language Processing*, pages 1192–1202, Brussels, Belgium. Association for Computational Linguistics.

R Thomas McCoy, Junghyun Min, and Tal Linzen. 2019a. Berts of a feather do not generalize together: Large variability in generalization across models with similar test set performance. *arXiv preprint arXiv:1911.02969*.

Tom McCoy, Ellie Pavlick, and Tal Linzen. 2019b. Right for the wrong reasons: Diagnosing syntactic heuristics in natural language inference. In *Proceedings of the 57th Annual Meeting of the Association for Computational Linguistics*, pages 3428–3448, Florence, Italy. Association for Computational Linguistics.

Junghyun Min, R Thomas McCoy, Dipanjan Das, Emily Pitler, and Tal Linzen. 2020. Syntactic data augmentation increases robustness to inference heuristics. *arXiv preprint arXiv:2004.11999*.

Ari Morcos, Maithra Raghu, and Samy Bengio. 2018. Insights on representational similarity in neural networks with canonical correlation. In S. Bengio, H. Wallach, H. Larochelle, K. Grauman, N. Cesa-Bianchi, and R. Garnett, editors, *Advances in Neural Information Processing Systems 31*, pages 5727–5736. Curran Associates, Inc.

Matthew Peters, Mark Neumann, Mohit Iyyer, Matt Gardner, Christopher Clark, Kenton Lee, and Luke Zettlemoyer. 2018a. Deep contextualized word representations. In *Proceedings of the 2018 Conference of the North American Chapter of the Association for Computational Linguistics: Human Language Technologies, Volume 1 (Long Papers)*, pages 2227–2237, New Orleans, Louisiana. Association for Computational Linguistics.

Matthew Peters, Mark Neumann, Luke Zettlemoyer, and Wen-tau Yih. 2018b. Dissecting contextual word embeddings: Architecture and representation. In *Proceedings of the 2018 Conference on Empirical Methods in Natural Language Processing*, pages 1499–1509, Brussels, Belgium. Association for Computational Linguistics.

Matthew E. Peters, Sebastian Ruder, and Noah A. Smith. 2019. To tune or not to tune? adapting pretrained representations to diverse tasks. In *Proceedings of the 4th Workshop on Representation Learning for NLP (RepL4NLP-2019)*, pages 7–14, Florence, Italy. Association for Computational Linguistics.

Tiago Pimentel, Josef Valvoda, Rowan Hall Maudslay, Ran Zmigrod, Adina Williams, and Ryan Cotterell. 2020. Information-theoretic probing for linguistic structure. *arXiv preprint arXiv:2004.03061*.

Adam Poliak, Jason Naradowsky, Aparajita Haldar, Rachel Rudinger, and Benjamin Van Durme. 2018. Hypothesis only baselines in natural language inference. In *Proceedings of the Seventh Joint Conference on Lexical and Computational Semantics*, pages 180–191, New Orleans, Louisiana. Association for Computational Linguistics.

Yada Pruksachatkun, Phil Yeres, Haokun Liu, Jason Phang, Phu Mon Htut, Alex Wang, Ian Tenney, and Samuel R Bowman. 2020. jiant: A software toolkit for research on general-purpose text understanding models. *arXiv preprint arXiv:2003.02249*.

Colin Raffel, Noam Shazeer, Adam Roberts, Katherine Lee, Sharan Narang, Michael Matena, Yanqi Zhou, Wei Li, and Peter J Liu. 2020. Exploring the limits of transfer learning with a unified text-to-text transformer. *Journal of Machine Learning Research*, 21(140):1–67.

Pranav Rajpurkar, Jian Zhang, Konstantin Lopyrev, and Percy Liang. 2016. SQuAD: 100,000+ questions for machine comprehension of text. In *Proceedings of the 2016 Conference on Empirical Methods in Natural Language Processing*, pages 2383–2392, Austin, Texas. Association for Computational Linguistics.

J. Rissanen. 1984. Universal coding, information, prediction, and estimation. *IEEE Transactions on Information Theory*, 30(4):629–636.

Anna Rogers, Olga Kovaleva, and Anna Rumshisky. 2020. A primer in bertology: What we know about how bert works. *arXiv preprint arXiv:2002.12327*.

Naomi Saphra and Adam Lopez. 2019. Understanding learning dynamics of language models with SVCCA. In *Proceedings of the 2019 Conference of the North American Chapter of the Association for Computational Linguistics: Human Language Technologies, Volume 1 (Long and Short Papers)*, pages 3257–3267, Minneapolis, Minnesota. Association for Computational Linguistics.

Sofia Serrano and Noah A. Smith. 2019. Is attention interpretable? In *Proceedings of the 57th Annual Meeting of the Association for Computational Linguistics*, pages 2931–2951, Florence, Italy. Association for Computational Linguistics.

Natalia Silveira, Timothy Dozat, Marie-Catherine de Marneffe, Samuel Bowman, Miriam Connor, John Bauer, and Christopher D. Manning. 2014. A gold standard dependency corpus for English. In *Proceedings of the Ninth International Conference on Language Resources and Evaluation (LREC-2014)*.

Alex Tamkin, Trisha Singh, Davide Giovanardi, and Noah Goodman. 2020. Investigating transferability in pretrained language models. *arXiv preprint arXiv:2004.14975*.

Adam Teichert, Adam Poliak, Benjamin Van Durme, and Matthew R Gormley. 2017. Semantic proto-role labeling. In *Thirty-First AAAI Conference on Artificial Intelligence (AAAI-17)*.

Ian Tenney, Dipanjan Das, and Ellie Pavlick. 2019a. BERT rediscovers the classical NLP pipeline. In *Proceedings of the 57th Annual Meeting of the Association for Computational Linguistics*, pages 4593–4601, Florence, Italy. Association for Computational Linguistics.

Ian Tenney, Patrick Xia, Berlin Chen, Alex Wang, Adam Poliak, R Thomas McCoy, Najoung Kim, Benjamin Van Durme, Sam Bowman, Dipanjan Das, and Ellie Pavlick. 2019b. What do you learn from context? probing for sentence structure in contextualized word representations. In *International Conference on Learning Representations*.

Sara Veldhoen, Dieuwke Hupkes, Willem H Zuidema, et al. 2016. Diagnostic classifiers revealing how neural networks process hierarchical structure. In *CoCo @ NIPS*, pages 69–77.

Jesse Vig and Yonatan Belinkov. 2019. Analyzing the structure of attention in a transformer language model. In *Proceedings of the 2019 ACL Workshop BlackboxNLP: Analyzing and Interpreting Neural Networks for NLP*, pages 63–76, Florence, Italy. Association for Computational Linguistics.

Elena Voita, Rico Sennrich, and Ivan Titov. 2019a. The bottom-up evolution of representations in the transformer: A study with machine translation and language modeling objectives. In *Proceedings of the 2019 Conference on Empirical Methods in Natural Language Processing and the 9th International Joint Conference on Natural Language Processing (EMNLP-IJCNLP)*, pages 4395–4405, Hong Kong, China. Association for Computational Linguistics.

Elena Voita, David Talbot, Fedor Moiseev, Rico Sennrich, and Ivan Titov. 2019b. Analyzing multi-head self-attention: Specialized heads do the heavy lifting, the rest can be pruned. In *Proceedings of the 57th Annual Meeting of the Association for Computational Linguistics*, pages 5797–5808, Florence, Italy. Association for Computational Linguistics.

Elena Voita and Ivan Titov. 2020. Information-theoretic probing with minimum description length. *arXiv preprint arXiv:2003.12298*.

Alex Wang, Amanpreet Singh, Julian Michael, Felix Hill, Omer Levy, and Samuel R. Bowman. 2019. GLUE: A multi-task benchmark and analysis platform for natural language understanding. In *International Conference on Learning Representations*.

Ralph Weischedel, Martha Palmer, Mitchell Marcus, Eduard Hovy, Sameer Pradhan, Lance Ramshaw, Nianwen Xue, Ann Taylor, Jeff Kaufman, Michelle Franchini, et al. 2013. Ontonotes release 5.0 ldc2013t19. *Linguistic Data Consortium, Philadelphia, PA*, 23.

Adina Williams, Nikita Nangia, and Samuel Bowman. 2018. A broad-coverage challenge corpus for sentence understanding through inference. In *Proceedings of the 2018 Conference of the North American Chapter of the Association for Computational Linguistics: Human Language Technologies, Volume 1 (Long Papers)*, pages 1112–1122. Association for Computational Linguistics.

Dani Yogatama, Cyprien de Masson d'Autume, Jerome Connor, Tomas Kocisky, Mike Chrzanowski, Lingpeng Kong, Angeliki Lazaridou, Wang Ling, Lei Yu, Chris Dyer, et al. 2019. Learning and evaluating general linguistic intelligence. *arXiv preprint arXiv:1901.11373*.

Daniel Zeman, Martin Popel, Milan Straka, Jan Hajic, Joakim Nivre, Filip Ginter, Juhani Luotolahti, Sampo Pyysalo, Slav Petrov, Martin Potthast, Francis Tyers, Elena Badmaeva, Memduh Gokirmak, Anna Nedoluzhko, Silvie Cinkova, Jan Hajic jr., Jaroslava Hlavacova, Václava Kettnerová, Zdenka Uresova, Jenna Kanerva, Stina Ojala, Anna Missilä, Christopher D. Manning, Sebastian Schuster, Siva Reddy, Dima Taji, Nizar Habash, Herman Leung, Marie-Catherine de Marneffe, Manuela Sanguinetti, Maria Simi, Hiroshi Kanayama, Valeria dePaiva, Kira Droganova, Héctor Martínez Alonso, Çağr Çöltekin, Umut Sulubacak, Hans Uszkoreit, Vivien Macketanz, Aljoscha Burchardt, Kim Harris, Katrin Marheinecke, Georg Rehm, Tolga Kayadelen, Mohammed Attia, Ali Elkahky, Zhuoran Yu, Emily Pitler, Saran Lertpradit, Michael Mandl, Jesse Kirchner, Hector Fernandez Alcalde, Jana Strnadová, Esha Banerjee, Ruli Manurung, Antonio Stella, Atsuko Shimada, Sookyoung Kwak, Gustavo Mendonca, Tatiana Lando, Rattima Nitisaroj, and Josie Li. 2017. Conll 2017 shared task: Multilingual parsing from raw text to universal dependencies. In *Proceedings of the CoNLL 2017 Shared Task: Multilingual Parsing from Raw Text to Universal Dependencies*, pages 1–19, Vancouver, Canada. Association for Computational Linguistics.

Kelly Zhang and Samuel Bowman. 2018. Language modeling teaches you more than translation does: Lessons learned through auxiliary syntactic task analysis. In *Proceedings of the 2018 EMNLP Workshop BlackboxNLP: Analyzing and Interpreting Neural Networks for NLP*, pages 359–361.

Y. Zhu, R. Kiros, R. Zemel, R. Salakhutdinov, R. Urtasun, A. Torralba, and S. Fidler. 2015. Aligning books and movies: Towards story-like visual explanations by watching movies and reading books. In *2015 IEEE International Conference on Computer Vision (ICCV)*, pages 19–27.

It's not Greek to mBERT:
Inducing Word-Level Translations from Multilingual BERT

Hila Gonen[1]   Shauli Ravfogel[1,2]   Yanai Elazar[1,2]   Yoav Goldberg[1,2]
[1]Computer Science Department, Bar Ilan University
[2]Allen Institute for Artificial Intelligence
{hilagnn, shauli.ravfogel, yanaiela, yoav.goldberg}@gmail.com

Abstract

Recent works have demonstrated that multilingual BERT (mBERT) learns rich cross-lingual representations, that allow for transfer across languages. We study the word-level translation information embedded in mBERT and present two simple methods that expose remarkable translation capabilities with no fine-tuning. The results suggest that most of this information is encoded in a non-linear way, while some of it can also be recovered with purely linear tools. As part of our analysis, we test the hypothesis that mBERT learns representations which contain both a language-encoding component and an abstract, cross-lingual component, and explicitly identify an empirical language-identity subspace within mBERT representations.

1 Introduction

Multilingual-BERT (mBERT) is a version of BERT (Devlin et al., 2019), trained on the concatenation of Wikipedia in 104 different languages. Recent works show that it excels in zero-shot transfer between languages, for a variety of tasks (Pires et al., 2019; Muller et al., 2020), despite being trained with no parallel supervision.

Previous work has mainly focused on what is needed for zero-shot transfer to work well (Muller et al., 2020; Karthikeyan et al., 2020; Wu and Dredze, 2019), and on characterizing the representations of mBERT (Singh et al., 2019). However, we still lack a proper understanding of this model.

In this work we study (1) how much word-level translation information is recoverable by mBERT; and (2) how this information is stored. We focus on the representations of the last layer, and on the embedding matrix that is shared between the input and output layers – which are together responsible for token prediction.

For our first goal, we start by presenting a simple and strong method to extract word-level translation information. Our method is based on explicit querying of mBERT: given a source word and a target language, we feed mBERT with a template such as *"The word 'SOURCE' in LANGUAGE is: [MASK]."* where LANGUAGE is the target language, and SOURCE is an English word to translate. Getting the correct translation as the prediction of the masked token exposes mBERT's ability to provide word-level translation. This template-based method is surprisingly successful, especially considering the fact that no parallel supervision was provided to the model while training, and that word translation is not part of the training objective.

This raises the possibility of easy disentanglement between language identity and lexical semantics in mBERT representations. We test this hypothesis by trying to explicitly disentangle language-identity from lexical semantics under linearity assumptions. We propose a method for disentangling a language-encoding component and a language-neutral component from both the embedding representations and word-in-context representations. Furthermore, we learn the emperical "langauge subspace" in mBERT, which is a linear subspace that is spanned by all directions that are linearly correlative to the language identity. We demonstrate that the representations are well-separated by language on that subspace.

We leverage these insights and empirical results to show that it is possible to perform analogies-based translation by taking advantage of this disentanglement: we can alter the language-encoding component, while keeping the lexical component intact. We compare between the template-based method and the analogies-based method and discuss their similarities and differences, as well as their limitations.

The two methods together show that mBERT

Proceedings of the Third BlackboxNLP Workshop on Analyzing and Interpreting Neural Networks for NLP, pages 45–56
Online, November 20, 2020. ©2020 Association for Computational Linguistics

acquired, to a large degree, the ability to perform word-level translation, despite the fact that it is not trained on any parallel data explicitly. The results suggest that most of the information is stored in a non-linear way, but with some linearly-recoverable components.

Our contribution in this work is two-fold: (a) we present two simple methods for word-level translation using mBERT, that require no training or finetuning of the model, which demonstrate that mBERT stores parallel information in different languages; (b) we show that mBERT representations are composed of language-encoding and language-neutral components and present a method for extracting those components. Our code is available at `https://github.com/gonenhila/mbert`.

2   Previous Work

Pires et al. (2019) begin a line of work that studies mBERT representations and capabilities. In their work, they inspect the model's zero-shot transfer abilities using different probing experiments, and propose a way to map sentence representations in different languages, with some success. Karthikeyan et al. (2020) further analyze the properties that affect zero shot transfer by experimenting with bilingual BERTs on RTE (recognizing textual entailment) and NER. They analyse performance with respect to linguistic properties and similarities of the source and the target languages, and some parameters of the model itself (e.g. network architecture and learning objective). In a closely related work, Wu and Dredze (2019) perform transfer learning from English to 38 languages, on 5 tasks (POS, parsing, NLI, NER, Document classification), and report good results. Additionally, they show that language-specific information is preserved in all layers. Wang et al. (2019) learn alignment between contextualized representations, and use it for zero shot transfer.

Beyond focusing on zero-shot transfer abilities, an additional line of work studies the representations of mBERT and the information it stores. Using hierarchical clustering based on the CCA similarity scores between languages, Singh et al. (2019) are able to construct a tree structure that faithfully describes relations between languages. Chi et al. (2020) learn a linear syntax-subspace in mBERT, and point out to syntactic regulartieis in the representations that transfer across languages. In the recent work of Cao et al. (2020), the authors define

the notion of *contextual* word alignment. They design a fine-tuning loss for improving alignments and show that they are able to improve zero-shot transfer after this alignment-based fine-tuning. One main difference from our work is that they fine-tune the model according to their new definition of contextual alignment, while we analyze and use the information already stored in the model. One of the closest works to ours is that of Libovický et al. (2019), where they assume that mBERT's representations have a language-neutral component, and a language-specific component. They remove the language specific component by subtracting the centroid of the language from the representations, and make an attempt to prove the assumption by using probing tasks on the original vs. new representations. They show that the new representations are more language-neutral to some extent, but lack experiments that show a complementary component. While those works demonstrate that mBERT representations in different languages can be aligned successfully with appropriate supervision, we propose an explicit *decomposition* of the representations to language-encoding and language-neutral components, and also demonstrate that implicit word-level translations can be easily distilled from the model when exposed to the proper stimuli.

3   Word-level Translation using Pre-defined Templates

We study the extent to which it is possible to extract word-level translation directly from mBERT.

3.1   Word-level Translation: You Just Have to Ask

We present a simple and overwhelmingly successful method for word-level translation with mBERT. This method is based on the idea of explicitly querying mBERT for a translation, similar to what has been done with LMs for other tasks (Petroni et al., 2019; Jiang et al., 2019; Talmor et al., 2019). We experimented with seven different templates and found the following to work best: *"The word* 'SOURCE' *in* LANGUAGE *is: [MASK]."*[1] The predictions from the [MASK] token induce a distribution over the vocabulary, and we take the most probable word as the translation.

---

[1] where SOURCE is the word we wish to translate and [MASK] is the special token that BERT uses as an indication for word prediction, see Section A in the Appendix for the other templates.

	@1	@10	@100	rank	log	win
Baseline	0.036	0.244	0.575	4303.4	4.58	–
Analogies	0.105	0.463	0.737	2458.1	3.19	89.8%
Template	**0.449**	**0.703**	**0.845**	**243.4**	**1.68**	**91.6%**

Table 1: Word-level translation results with the template-based method and the analogies-based method (introduced in Section 5). @1-100 stand for accuracy@k (higher is better), "rank" stands for the average rank of the correct translation, "log" stands for the log of the average rank, and "win" stands for the percentage of cases in which the tested method is strictly better than the baseline.

	@1	@5	@10	@50	@100
Noun	(0.044)	(0.189)	(0.279)	(0.520)	(0.593)
	0.113	0.379	0.494	0.696	0.741
Adjective	(0.037)	(0.102)	(0.183)	(0.474)	(0.567)
	0.105	0.310	0.418	0.666	0.706
Verb	(0.006)	(0.105)	(0.168)	(0.355)	(0.427)
	0.039	0.201	0.317	0.576	0.645

Table 2: Word-level translation results per POS with the template-based method. The numbers in parathesis relate to the baseline.

3.2 Evaluation

To evaluate lexical translation quality, we use NorthEuraLex[2] (Dellert et al., 2019), a lexical database providing translations of 1016 words into 107 languages. We use these parallel translations to evaluate our translation method when translating from English to other target languages.[3] We restrict our evaluation to a set of common languages from diverse language families: Russian, French, Italian, Dutch, Spanish, Hebrew, Turkish, Romanian, Korean, Arabic and Japanese. We omit cases in which the source word or the target word are tokenized using mBERT into more than a single token.[4] The words in the dataset are from different POS, with Nouns, Adjectives and Verbs being the most common ones.[5] For all our experiments with mBERT, we use the transformer library of HuggingFace (Wolf et al., 2019).

Results We report accuracy@k in translating the English source word into different languages (for $k \in \{1, 10, 100\}$): for each word pair, we check whether the target word was included in the first k retrieved words. Note that we remove the source word itself from the ranking.[6] We report three additional metrics: (a) **avg-rank**: the average rank of the target word (its position in the ranking of predictions); (b) **avg-log-rank**: the average of the log of the rank, to limit the effect of cases in which the rank is extremely low and skews the average; (c) **hard-win**: percent of cases in which the method results in a strictly better rank for the translated word compared to the baseline. We take the predictions we get for the masked token as the method's candidates for translation. As a baseline, we take the embedding representation of the source word and look for the closest words to it. Table 1 shows the results of the template-based method and the baseline. This method significantly improves over the baseline in all metrics and achieves impressive accuracy results: acc@1 of 0.449 and acc@10 of 0.703, beating the baseline in 91.6% of the cases.

Accuracy per POS To get a finer analysis of this method, we also evaluate the translations per POS. We report results on the 3 most common POS: nouns, adjectives and verbs.[7] As one might expect, nouns are the easiest to translate (both for the baseline and for our method), followed by adjectives, then verbs. See Table 2 for full results.

Note that the results for these common POS tags are lower than the average over the full dataset. We hypothesize that words belonging to closed-class POS tags, such as pronouns, are easier to translate.

3.3 Visualization of the Representation Space

To further understand the mechanism of the method, we turn to inspect the resulting representations. For each word pair, we feed mBERT with the full template and extract the last-layer representation of the masked token, right before the multiplication with the output embeddings. In Figure 1 we plot the t-SNE projection (Maaten and Hinton, 2008) of those representations, colored by language. The representations clearly cluster ac-

---

[2] http://northeuralex.org/

[3] We use this data also for experimenting with source languages other than English, in Section 5.

[4] Number of translated pairs we are left with in each language: Russian: 224, French: 429, Italian: 352, Dutch: 347, Spanish: 452, Hebrew: 158, Turkish: 199, Romanian: 243, Korean: 42, Arabic: 191, Japanese: 214.

[5] Number of words from each POS: 'N': 480, 'V': 340, 'A': 102, 'ADV': 47, 'NUM': 22, 'PRN': 9, 'PRP': 7, 'FADV': 4, 'FPRN': 2, 'CNJ': 2, 'FNUM': 1.

[6] This removal mainly affects acc@1, since in many cases, the first retrieved word is the source word. This is a common practice, especially for the analogies-based method (Mikolov et al., 2013a).

[7] We have 1765, 363, 323 instances, respectively. Other POS have less than 200 instances, and are thus omitted from the analysis.

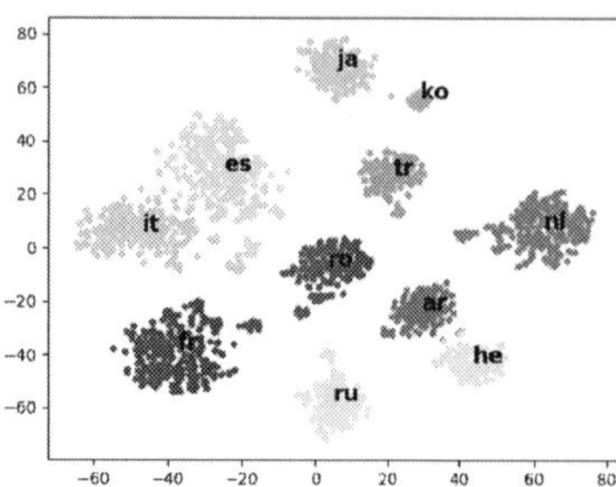

Figure 1: t-SNE projections of the representations of the template-based method.

cording to the target language. The ability of these representations to encode the target language may explain how this method successfully produces the translation into the correct language.

3.4 Predicting the Language

Due to the representations clustering based on the target language (rather than semantics), we hypothesize that mBERT is also capable of predicting the target language given the source word and its translation.

To verify that, we take the same template as before, this time masking the name of the language instead of the target word.[8] We then compute acc@1,5,10 for all languages and report that for the 20 languages with the most accurate results in Table 3 (the full results can be found in Table 8 in the Appendix). The results are impressive, suggesting that mBERT indeed encodes the target language identity in this setting. The languages on which mBERT is most accurate are either widely-spoken languages (e.g. German, French), or languages with a unique script (e.g. Greek, Russian, Arabic). Indeed, we get a Spearman correlation of 0.53 between acc@1 and the amount of training data in each language.[9]

We also compute a confusion matrix for the 20 most accurate languages, shown in Figure 2. In order to better identify the nuances, we use the square-root of the values, instead of the values themselves, and remove English (which is frequently predicted

Language	acc@1	acc@5	acc@10
greek	0.986	0.998	1.000
russian	0.943	0.994	0.998
arabic	0.794	0.963	0.984
hebrew	0.761	0.968	0.990
german	0.758	0.951	0.991
japanese	0.716	0.939	0.966
korean	0.664	0.905	0.949
french	0.637	0.976	0.992
latin	0.626	0.900	0.959
polish	0.576	0.728	0.803
italian	0.572	0.873	0.947
spanish	0.503	0.757	0.878
finnish	0.404	0.622	0.748
turkish	0.399	0.589	0.709
dutch	0.315	0.846	0.965
welsh	0.262	0.548	0.680
swedish	0.262	0.492	0.692
hungarian	0.254	0.395	0.493
portuguese	0.236	0.587	0.808
danish	0.231	0.388	0.567

Table 3: Prediction accuracy of the language, when the language is masked in the template (20 most accurate languages).

as the target language, probably since the template is in English). The confusion matrix reveals the expected behavior – mBERT confuses mainly between typologically related languages, specifically those of the same language family: Germanic languages (German, Dutch, Swedish, Danish), Romance languages (French, Latin, Italian, Spanish, Portuguese), and Semitic languages (Arabic, Hebrew). In addition, we can also identify some confusion between Germanic and Romance languages (which share much of the alphabet), as well as over-prediction of languages with a lot of training data (e.g. German, French).

4 Dissecting mBERT Representations

In the previous section, we saw that mBERT contains abundant word-level translation knowledge. How is this knowledge represented? We turn to analyze both the representations of words in context and those of the output embeddings.

It has been assumed in previous work that the representations are composed of a language-encoding component and a language-neutral component (Libovický et al., 2019). In what follows, we explicitly try to find such a decomposition: we decompose $v = v_{lang} + v_{lex}$, where v_{lang} and v_{lex} are orthogonal vectors, v_{lang} is the part in the representation that is indicative of language identity, and v_{lex} maintains lexical information, but is in-

---

[8] We use all languages in NortEuraLex that are a single token according to mBERT tokenization – there are 47 such languages except for English.

[9] We considered the number of articles per language from Wikipedia: `https://en.wikipedia.org/wiki/Wikipedia:Multilingual_statistics`, recorded in May 2020.

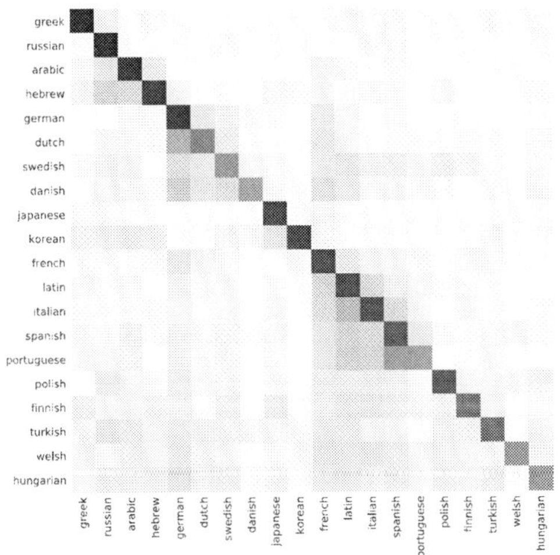

Figure 2: Confusion matrix of language prediction when the language is masked in the template. 20 most accurate languages are included, English is omitted.

variant to language identity. Specifically, we test the hypothesis using the following interventions:

- Measuring the degree to which removing v_{lang} results in language-neutral word representations.

- Measuring the degree to which removing v_{lex} results in word representations which are clustered by language identity (regardless of lexical semantics).

- Removing the v_{lang} component from word-in-context representations and from the output embeddings, to induce MLM prediction in other languages.

Splitting the representations into components is done using INLP (Ravfogel et al., 2020), an algorithm for removing information from vector representations.

4.1 mBERT Decomposition by Nullspace Projections

We formalize the decomposition objective defined earlier as finding two linear *subspaces* within the representation space, which contain language-independent and language-identity features. The recently proposed Iterative Null-space Projection (INLP) method (Ravfogel et al., 2020) allows to remove linearly-decodable information from vector representations. Given a dataset of representations X (in our case, mBERT word-in-context representations and output embeddings) and annotations Z for the information to be removed (language identity) the method renders Z linearly unpredictable from X. It does so by iteratively training linear predictors $w_1, \ldots, w_n$ of Z, calculating the projection matrix onto their nullspace $P_N := P_N(w_1), \ldots, P_N(w_n)$, and transforming $X \leftarrow P_N X$. Recall that by the nullsapce definition this guarantees $w_i P_N X = 0, \forall w_i$, i.e., the features w_i uses for language prediction are neutralized.

While the nullsapce $N(w_1, \ldots, w_n)$ is a subspace in which Z is not linearly predictable, the complement rowspace $R(w_1, \ldots, w_n)$ is a subspace of the representation space X that corresponds to the property Z. In our case, this subspace is *mBERT language-identity subspace*. In the following sections we utilize INLP in two complementary ways: (1) we use the null-space projection matrix P_N to zero out the language identity subspace, in order to render the representations *invariant* to language identity[10]; and (2) we use the *rowspace* projection matrix $P_R = I - P_N$ to project mBERT representations onto the language-identity subspace, keeping only the parts that are useful for language-identity prediction. We hypothesize that the first operation would render the representations more language-neutral, while the latter would discard the components that are shared across languages.

Setup We start by applying INLP on random representations and getting the two mentioned projection matrices: on the nullspace, and on the rowspace. We repeat this process twice: first, for representations in context, and second, for output embeddings. For each of these two cases, we sample random tokens from 5000 sentences[11] in 15 different languages, extract their respective representations (in context or simply output embeddings), and run INLP on those representations with the objective of identifying the language, for 20 iterations. We end up with 4 matrices: projection matrix on the null-space and on the rowspace for representations in context, and the same for output embeddings.

---

[10]to the extent that language identity is indeed encoded in a linear subspace, and that INLP finds this subspace.

[11]For the output embeddings, we exclude tokens that start with "##", for the last layer representations, sampled tokens may include "CLS" or "SEP".

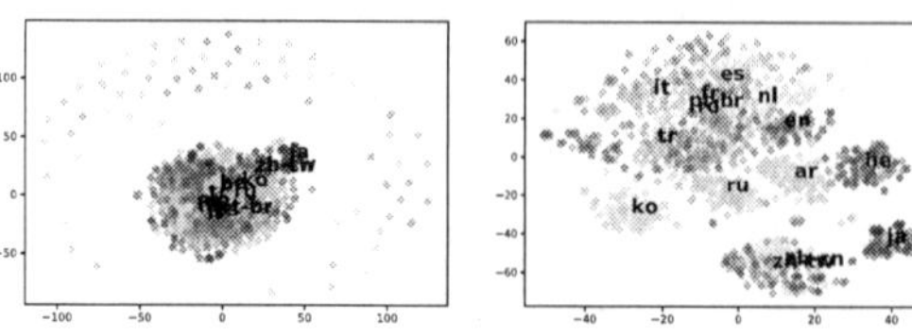 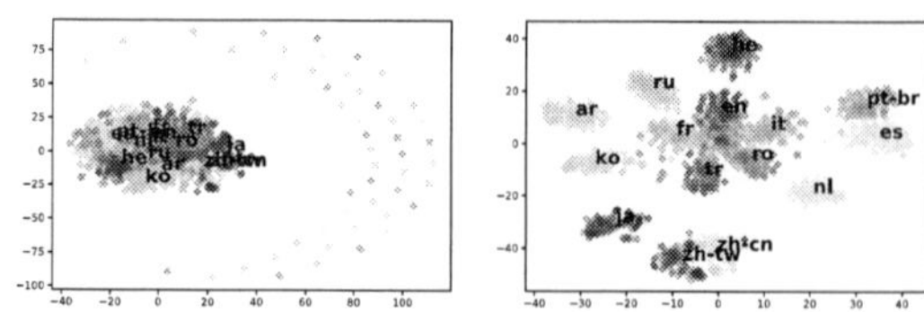

Figure 3: t-SNE projection of the output embeddings of random words from different languages, originally (left) and after projection onto the language-identity subspace (right).

Figure 4: t-SNE projection of last-hidden-layer representation of random words from different languages, originally (left) and after projection onto the language-identity subspace (right).

TED corpus   For the experiments depicted in Sections 4 and 5, we use a dataset of transcripts of TED talks in 60 languages, collected by Ye et al. (2018)[12]. For the INLP trainings, we use the 15 most frequent languages in the dataset after basic filtering, 12 of which are also included in NorthEuraLex.

4.2   Language-Neutral and Language-Encoding Representations

We aim to use INLP nullspace and rowspace projection matrices as an intervention that is designed to test the hypothesis on the exsitence of two independent subspaces in mBERT. Concretely, we perform two experiments: (a) a cluster analysis, using t-SNE (Maaten and Hinton, 2008) and a cluster-coherence measure, of representations projected on the null-space and the row-space from different languages. We expect to see decreased and increased separation by language identity, respectively; (b) we perform nullsapce projection intervention on both the last hidden state of mBERT, and on the output embeddings, and proceed to predict a distribution over all tokens. We expect that neutralizing the language-identity information this way will encourage mBERT to perform semantically-adequate word prediction, while decreasing its ability to choose the correct language in the context of the input sentence.

t-SNE and Clustering   To test the hypothesis on the existence of a "language-identity" subspace in mBERT, we project the representations of a random subset of words from TED dataset, from the embedding layer and the last layer, on the subspace that is spanned by all language classifiers, using INLP rowspace-projection matrix. Figures 3 and 4

[12]https://github.com/neulab/word-embeddings-for-nmt

present the results for the embedding layer and the last layer, respectively. In both cases, we witness a significant improvement in clustering according to language identity. At the same time, some different trends are observed across layers: the separability is better in the last layer. Romance languages, which share much of the script and some vocabulary, are well separated in the last layer, but less so in the embeddings layer. Taiwanese and mainland Chinese (zh-tw and zh-cn, respectively) are well separable in the last layer, but not in the embedding layer. These findings suggest that the way mBERT encodes language identity differs across layers: while lower layers focus on lexical dimensions – and thus cluster the two Chinese variants, and the Romance languages, together – higher layers separate them, possibly by subtler cues, such as topical differences or syntactic alternations. This aligns with Singh et al. (2019) who demonstrated that mBERT representations become more language-specific along the layers.

To quantify the influence of the projection to the language rowspace, we calculate V-measure (Rosenberg and Hirschberg, 2007), which assesses the degree of clustering according to language identity. Specifically, we perform K-means clustering with the number of languages as K, and then calculate V-measure to quantify alignment between the clusters and the language identity. On the embedding layer, this measure increases from 35.5% in the original space, to 61.8% on the language-identity subspace; and for the last layer, from 80.5% in the original space, to 90.35% in the language-identity subspace, both showing improved clustering by language identity.

When projecting the representations on the nullspace we get the opposite trend: less separation by language-identity. The full results of this complementary projection can be found in Section C in

	top-1	top-5	top-10	top-20	top-50
NONE	0.921	0.807	0.783	0.773	0.767
INLP $_{\text{EMBED}}$	0.906	0.584	0.520	0.477	0.437
INLP $_{\text{REPR}}$	0.908	0.550	0.484	0.441	0.403
INLP $_{\text{BOTH}}$	0.868	0.488	0.414	0.366	0.325

Table 4: Percentage of English words out of top-k predictions of the MLM, when performing INLP on the output embeddings, on the representations in context or on both.

	avg-cos-sim
NONE	0.471
INLP $_{\text{EMBED}}$	0.443
INLP $_{\text{REPR}}$	0.460
INLP $_{\text{BOTH}}$	0.438

Table 5: Average cosine-similarity between the original token and the top-10 MLM predictions for it, when performing INLP on the output embeddings, on the representations in context or on both.

the Appendix.

Inducing Language-Neutral Token Predictions
By the disentanglement hypothesis, removing the language-encoding part of the representations should render the prediction language-agnostic. To test that, we take contextualized representations of random tokens in English sentences, and look at the original masked language model (MLM) predictions over those representations. We then compare these predictions with three variations: (a) when projecting the representations themselves on the null-space of the language-identity subspace, (b) when projecting the output embedding matrix on that null-space, (c) when projecting both the representations and the output embedding matrix on the null-space.

In order to inspect the differences in predictions we get, we train a classifier[13] that given the embedding of a word, predicts whether it is in English or not. Then, we compute the percentage of English/non-English words in the top-k predictions for each of the variants. The results are depicted in Table 4, for $k \in 1, 5, 10, 20, 50$. As expected, when projecting both the representations and the embeddings, we get most predictions that are not in English (the results are the average over 6000 instances).

The decrease in English predictions can be the result of noise that is introduced by the projection operation. To verify that the influence of the projection is focused on the langauge-identity, and not on the lexical-semantics content of the vectors, we employ a second evaluation that focuses on the semantic coherence of the predictions. We look at the top-10 predictions in each case, and compute the cosine-similarity between the original word in the sentence, and each prediction. We expect the average cosine-similarity to drop significantly if the new predictions are mostly noise. However, if the

predictions are reasonably related to the original words, we expect to get a similar average. Since some of the predictions are not in English, we use MUSE cross-lingual embeddings for this evaluation (Conneau et al., 2017). The results are shown in Table 5. As expected, the average cosine similarity is almost the same in all cases (the average is taken across the same 6000 instances). To get a sense of the resulting predictions, we show four examples (of different POS) in Table 6. In all cases most words that were removed from the top-10 predictions are English words, while most new words are translations of the original word into other languages.

5 Analogies-based Translation

In the previous section we established the assumption that mBERT representations are composed of a language-neutral and a language-encoding components. In this section, we present another mechanism for word-translation with mBERT, which is based on manipulating the language-encoding component of the representation, in a similar way to how analogies in word embeddings work (Mikolov et al., 2013b). This new method has a clear mechanism behind it, and it serves as an additional validation for our assumption about the two independent components.

The idea is simple: we create a single vector representation for each language, as explained below. Then, in order to change the embedding of a word in language SOURCE to language TARGET, we simply subtract from it the vector representation of language SOURCE and add the vector representation of language TARGET. Finally, in order to get the translation of the source word into the target language, we multiply the resulting representation by the output embedding matrix to get the closest words to it out of the full vocabulary. Below is a detailed explanation of the implementation.

---

[13] SCIKIT-LEARN implementation (Pedregosa et al., 2011) with default parameters.

mother		sometimes		visited		beginning	
before	after	before	after	before	after	before	after
mother	mother	sometimes	sometimes	visited	visited	beginning	beginning
father	moeder	*soms*	manchmal	visits	visito	*begin*	начало
madre	mothers	иногда	иногда	*attended*	besøkt	*start*	початок
mutter	мать	manchmal	ocasionalmente	*visit*	visits	beginn	entamu
native	matki	*occasionally*	ponekad	visiting	besuchte	*end*	zacatku
moeder	μητερα	*often*	често	visito	entered	начало	اغٰاز
mary	mutter	parfois	talvolta	entered	visiting	zacatku	αρχη
true	madre	talvolta	kartais	*joined*	asked	entamu	pocetku
mothers	جنس	често	parfois	*toured*	vitja	*introduction*	beginn
the	مادر	kartais	احيانا	*visite*	посет	*comencament*	zaciatku

Table 6: Examples of resulting top-10 MLM predictions before and after performing INLP on both the output embeddings and representations in context. Words in red (italic) appear only in the "before" list, while words in blue (underlined) appear only in the "after" list.

5.1 Creating language-representation vectors

We start by extracting sentences in each language. From each sentence, we choose a random token and extract its representation from the output embedding matrix. Then, for each language we average all the obtained representations, to create a single vector representing that language. For that we use the same representations extracted for training INLP, as described in Section 4.1. Note that no hyper-parameter tuning was done when calculating these language vectors. The assumption here is that when averaging this way, the lexical differences between the representations cancel out, while the shared language component in all of them persists.

5.2 Performing Translation with Analogies

We are interested in translating words from a SOURCE language to a TARGET language. For that we simply take the word embedding of the SOURCE word, subtract the representation of the SOURCE language from it, and add the representation of the TARGET language. We multiply this new representation by the output embedding matrix to get a ranking over all the vocabulary, from the closest word to it to the least close.

5.3 Results

In Table 1 we report the results of translation using analogies (second row). The success of this method supports the reasoning behind it – indeed changing the language component of the representation enables us to get satisfactory results in word-level translation. While the template-based method, which is non-linear, puts a competitive lower bound

on the amount of parallel information embedded in mBERT, this strictly linear method is able to recover a large portion of it.

Visualization of the Representation Space In contrast to the template-based method, t-SNE visualization of the analogies-based translation vectors reveals low clustering by language (see Figure 8 in Section D in the Appendix).

Translation between every Language Pair The analogies-based translation method can be easily applied to all language pairs, by subtracting the representation vector of the source language and adding that of the target language. Figure 5 presents a heatmap of the acc@10 for every language pair, with source languages on the left and target languages at the bottom. We note the high translation scores between related languages, for example, Arabic and Hebrew (both ways), and French, Spanish and Italian (all pairs).

6 Discussion

The template-based method we presented is non-linear and puts a high lower bound on the amount of parallel information found in mBERT, with surprisingly good results on word-level translation. The analogies-based method also gets impressive results, but to a lesser extent than the template-based one. In addition, the resulting representations in the analogies-based method are much less structured. These together suggest that most of the parallel information is not linearly decodable from mBERT.

The reasoning behind the analogies-based method is very clear: under linearity assumption

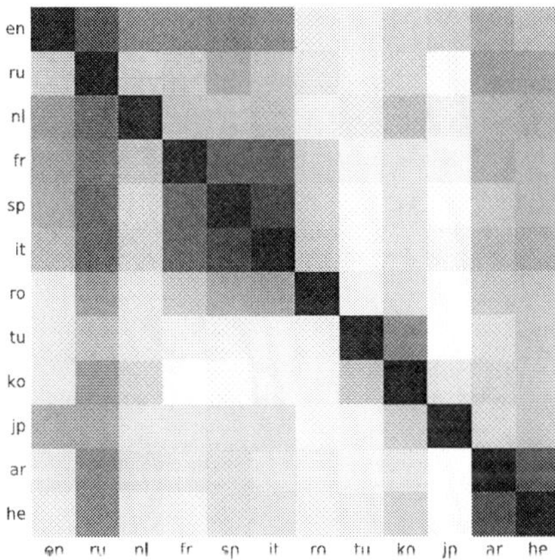

Figure 5: Acc@10 of word-level translation using analogies-based method, with source languages on the rows, and target languages on the columns.

we explicitly characterize and compute the decomposition to language-encoding and language-neutral components, and derive a word-level translation method based on this decomposition.

The mechanism behind the template-based method and the source of its success, however, are much harder to understand and interpret. While it is possible that some parallel data, in one form or another, is present in the training corpora, this is still an implicit signal: there is no explicit supervision for the learning of translation. The fact that MLM training is sufficient – at least to some degree – to induce learning of the algorithmic function of translation (without further supervised finetuning) is nontrivial. We believe that the success of this method is far from being obvious. We leave further investigation of the sources of this success to future work.

7   Conclusion

We aim to shed light on a basic question regarding multilingual BERT: How much word-level translation information does it embed and what are the ways to extract it? answering this question can help understand the empirical findings on its impressive transfer ability across languages.

We show that the knowledge needed for word-level translation is implicitly encoded in the model, and is easy to extract with simple methods, without fine-tuning. This information is likely stored

in a non-linear way. However, some parts of this representations can be recovered linearly: we identify an empirical language-identity subspace in mBERT, and show that under linearity assumptions, the representations in different languages are easily separable in that subspace; neutralizing the language-identity subspace encourages the model to perform word predictions which are less sensitive to language-identity, but are nonetheless semantically-meaningful. We argue that the results of those interventions support the hypothesis on the existence of identifiable language components in mBERT.

Acknowledgements

This project has received funding from the European Research Council (ERC) under the European Union's Horizon 2020 research and innovation programme, grant agreement No. 802774 (iEXTRACT), and from the the Israeli ministry of Science, Technology and Space through the Israeli-French Maimonide Cooperation programme.

References

Steven Cao, Nikita Kitaev, and Dan Klein. 2020. Multilingual alignment of contextual word representations. *arXiv:2002.03518*.

Ethan A. Chi, John Hewitt, and Christopher D. Manning. 2020. Finding universal grammatical relations in multilingual BERT. *CoRR*, abs/2005.04511.

Alexis Conneau, Guillaume Lample, Marc'Aurelio Ranzato, Ludovic Denoyer, and Hervé Jégou. 2017. Word translation without parallel data. *arXiv:1710.04087*.

Johannes Dellert, Thora Daneyko, Alla Münch, Alina Ladygina, Armin Buch, Natalie Clarius, Ilja Grigorjew, Mohamed Balabel, Hizniye Isabella Boga, Zalina Baysarova, et al. 2019. Northeuralex: a wide-coverage lexical database of northern eurasia. *Language Resources and Evaluation*, pages 1–29.

Jacob Devlin, Ming-Wei Chang, Kenton Lee, and Kristina Toutanova. 2019. BERT: Pre-training of deep bidirectional transformers for language understanding. In *Proceedings of the 2019 Conference of the North American Chapter of the Association for Computational Linguistics: Human Language Technologies, Volume 1 (Long and Short Papers)*, pages 4171–4186, Minneapolis, Minnesota. Association for Computational Linguistics.

Zhengbao Jiang, Frank F Xu, Jun Araki, and Graham Neubig. 2019. How can we know what language models know? *arXiv preprint arXiv:1911.12543*.

K Karthikeyan, Zihan Wang, Stephen Mayhew, and Dan Roth. 2020. Cross-lingual ability of multilingual bert: An empirical study. In *International Conference on Learning Representations*.

Jindřich Libovický, Rudolf Rosa, and Alexander Fraser. 2019. How language-neutral is multilingual bert? *arXiv:1911.03310*.

Laurens van der Maaten and Geoffrey Hinton. 2008. Visualizing data using t-sne. *Journal of machine learning research*, 9(Nov):2579–2605.

Tomas Mikolov, Kai Chen, Greg Corrado, and Jeffrey Dean. 2013a. Efficient estimation of word representations in vector space. In *1st International Conference on Learning Representations, ICLR 2013, Scottsdale, Arizona, USA, May 2-4, 2013, Workshop Track Proceedings*.

Tomáš Mikolov, Wen-tau Yih, and Geoffrey Zweig. 2013b. Linguistic regularities in continuous space word representations. In *Proceedings of the 2013 conference of the north american chapter of the association for computational linguistics: Human language technologies*, pages 746–751.

Benjamin Muller, Benoˆıt Sagot, and Djame Seddah. 2020. Can multilingual language models transfer to an unseen dialect? a case study on north african arabizi. *arXiv:2005.00318*.

F. Pedregosa, G. Varoquaux, A. Gramfort, V. Michel, B. Thirion, O. Grisel, M. Blondel, P. Prettenhofer, R. Weiss, V. Dubourg, J. Vanderplas, A. Passos, D. Cournapeau, M. Brucher, M. Perrot, and E. Duchesnay. 2011. Scikit-learn: Machine learning in Python. *Journal of Machine Learning Research*, 12:2825–2830.

Fabio Petroni, Tim Rocktäschel, Sebastian Riedel, Patrick Lewis, Anton Bakhtin, Yuxiang Wu, and Alexander Miller. 2019. Language models as knowledge bases? In *Proceedings of the 2019 Conference on Empirical Methods in Natural Language Processing and the 9th International Joint Conference on Natural Language Processing (EMNLP-IJCNLP)*, pages 2463–2473.

Telmo Pires, Eva Schlinger, and Dan Garrette. 2019. How multilingual is multilingual BERT? In *Proceedings of the 57th Annual Meeting of the Association for Computational Linguistics*, pages 4996–5001, Florence, Italy. Association for Computational Linguistics.

Shauli Ravfogel, Yanai Elazar, Hila Gonen, Michael Twiton, and Yoav Goldberg. 2020. Null it out: Guarding protected attributes by iterative nullspace projection. *CoRR*, abs/2004.07667.

Andrew Rosenberg and Julia Hirschberg. 2007. V-measure: A conditional entropy-based external cluster evaluation measure. In *EMNLP-CoNLL 2007, Proceedings of the 2007 Joint Conference on Empirical Methods in Natural Language Processing and Computational Natural Language Learning, June 28-30, 2007, Prague, Czech Republic*, pages 410–420. ACL.

Jasdeep Singh, Bryan McCann, Richard Socher, and Caiming Xiong. 2019. BERT is not an interlingua and the bias of tokenization. In *Proceedings of the 2nd Workshop on Deep Learning Approaches for Low-Resource NLP (DeepLo 2019)*, pages 47–55, Hong Kong, China. Association for Computational Linguistics.

Alon Talmor, Yanai Elazar, Yoav Goldberg, and Jonathan Berant. 2019. olmpics – on what language model pre-training captures.

Yuxuan Wang, Wanxiang Che, Jiang Guo, Yijia Liu, and Ting Liu. 2019. Cross-lingual BERT transformation for zero-shot dependency parsing. In *Proceedings of the 2019 Conference on Empirical Methods in Natural Language Processing and the 9th International Joint Conference on Natural Language Processing (EMNLP-IJCNLP)*, pages 5721–5727, Hong Kong, China. Association for Computational Linguistics.

Thomas Wolf, Lysandre Debut, Victor Sanh, Julien Chaumond, Clement Delangue, Anthony Moi, Pierric Cistac, Tim Rault, Rémi Louf, Morgan Funtowicz, Joe Davison, Sam Shleifer, Patrick von Platen, Clara Ma, Yacine Jernite, Julien Plu, Canwen Xu, Teven Le Scao, Sylvain Gugger, Mariama Drame, Quentin Lhoest, and Alexander M. Rush. 2019. Huggingface's transformers: State-of-the-art natural language processing. *ArXiv*, abs/1910.03771.

Shijie Wu and Mark Dredze. 2019. Beto, bentz, becas: The surprising cross-lingual effectiveness of BERT. In *Proceedings of the 2019 Conference on Empirical Methods in Natural Language Processing and the 9th International Joint Conference on Natural Language Processing (EMNLP-IJCNLP)*, pages 833–844, Hong Kong, China. Association for Computational Linguistics.

Qi Ye, Sachan Devendra, Felix Matthieu, Padmanabhan Sarguna, and Neubig Graham. 2018. When and why are pre-trained word embeddings useful for neural machine translation. In *HLT-NAACL*.

A Templates

The different templates are listed in Table 7, from the best performing to least performing. We report the results throughout the paper using the best template (first). Templates 5–7 fail completely, while templates 2–4 result in reasonable accuracy.

1	"The word 'SOURCE' in LANGUAGE is: [MASK]."
2	"'SOURCE' in LANGUAGE is: [MASK]."
3	"Translate the word 'SOURCE' into LANGUAGE: [MASK]."
4	"What is the meaning of the LANGUAGE word [MASK]? 'SOURCE'."
5	"What is the translation of the word 'SOURCE' into LANGUAGE? [MASK]."
6	"The translation of the word 'SOURCE' into LANGUAGE is [MASK]."
7	"How do you say 'SOURCE' in LANGUAGE? [MASK]."

Table 7: The different templates we experimented with.

B Predicting the Language

Table 8 depicts the results of language prediction from the template. We report acc@1,5,10 for all languages.

C t-SNE for Nullsapce-Projected Vectors

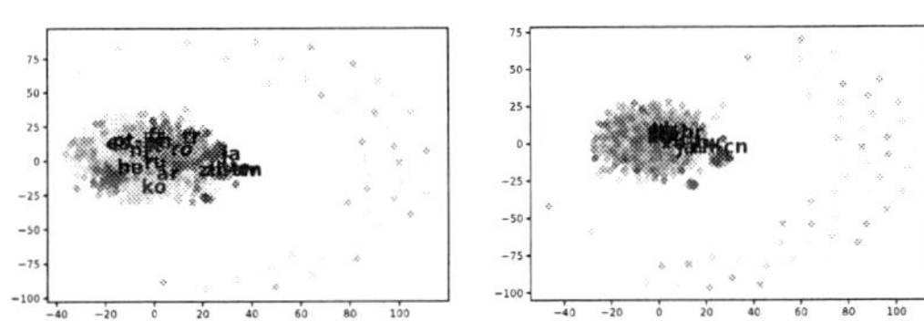

Figure 6: t-SNE projection of the last-hidden-layer representations of random words from different language, originally (left) and after (right) nullspace projection.

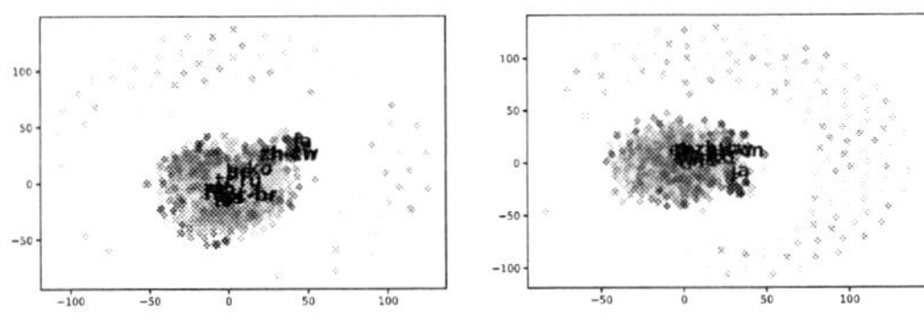

Figure 7: t-SNE projection of the output embeddings of random words from different language, originally (left) and after (right) nullspace projection.

In figures 6 and 7 we present a t-SNE projection of the representations in the embeddings layer and the last layer, projected onto INLP nullsapce – a subspace which discards information relevant

languages	acc@1	acc@5	acc@10
greek	0.986	0.998	1.000
russian	0.943	0.994	0.998
arabic	0.794	0.963	0.984
hebrew	0.761	0.968	0.990
german	0.758	0.951	0.991
japanese	0.716	0.939	0.966
korean	0.664	0.905	0.949
french	0.637	0.976	0.992
latin	0.626	0.900	0.959
polish	0.576	0.728	0.803
italian	0.572	0.873	0.947
spanish	0.503	0.757	0.878
finnish	0.404	0.622	0.748
turkish	0.399	0.589	0.709
dutch	0.315	0.846	0.965
welsh	0.262	0.548	0.680
swedish	0.262	0.492	0.692
hungarian	0.254	0.395	0.493
portuguese	0.236	0.587	0.808
danish	0.231	0.388	0.567
malayalam	0.216	0.587	0.712
irish	0.182	0.598	0.762
kannada	0.180	0.714	0.850
lithuanian	0.170	0.357	0.507
bengali	0.156	0.609	0.746
ukrainian	0.147	0.831	0.894
telugu	0.132	0.636	0.819
basque	0.126	0.249	0.359
estonian	0.126	0.374	0.510
albanian	0.117	0.225	0.323
croatian	0.106	0.279	0.353
norwegian	0.105	0.280	0.395
catalan	0.104	0.317	0.512
czech	0.080	0.251	0.361
romanian	0.069	0.110	0.164
armenian	0.060	0.368	0.588
tamil	0.057	0.467	0.608
bulgarian	0.040	0.582	0.815
hindi	0.037	0.467	0.775
latvian	0.036	0.118	0.202
breton	0.017	0.127	0.209
slovak	0.003	0.076	0.196
farsi	0.000	0.001	0.013
tatar	0.000	0.008	0.092
ket	0.000	0.000	0.000
georgian	0.000	0.073	0.183
lak	0.000	0.000	0.000

Table 8: Prediction accuracy of the language, when the language is masked in the template.

for language-identity prediction. As expected, the nullspace does not encode language identity: V-measure drops to 11.5% and 11.4% in the embeddings layer and in the last layer, respectively.

D Visualization of the Representation Space

We plot the t-SNE projection of the representations of the analogies-based method (after subtraction and addition of the language vectors), colored by target language. While the representations of the template-based method are clearly clustered according to the target language, the representations in this method are completely mixed, see Figure 8.

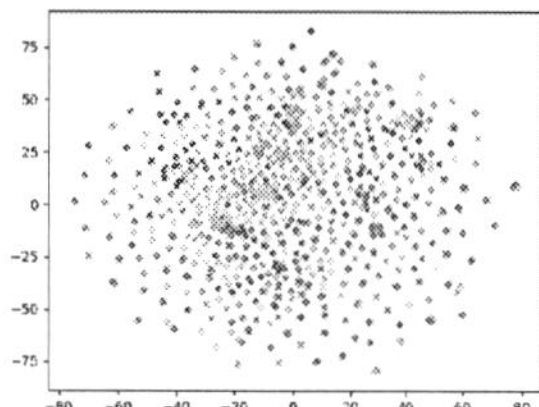

Figure 8: t-SNE projections of the representations of the analogies-based method.

Leveraging Extracted Model Adversaries for Improved Black Box Attacks

Naveen Jafer Nizar
Oracle Corporation
naveen.jafer@oracle.com

Ari Kobren
Oracle Labs
ari.kobren@oracle.com

Abstract

We present a method for adversarial input generation against black box models for reading comprehension based question answering. Our approach is composed of two steps. First, we approximate a *victim* black box model via model extraction (Krishna et al., 2020). Second, we use our own white box method to generate input perturbations that cause the approximate model to fail. These perturbed inputs are used against the victim. In experiments we find that our method improves on the efficacy of the ADDANY—a white box attack—performed on the approximate model by 25% F1, and the ADDSENT attack—a black box attack—by 11% F1 (Jia and Liang, 2017).

1 Introduction

Machine learning models are ubiquitous in technologies that are used by billions of people every day. In part, this is due to the recent success of deep learning. Indeed, research in the last decade has demonstrated that the most effective deep models can match or even outperform humans on a variety of tasks (Devlin et al., 2019; Xie et al., 2019).

Despite their effectiveness, deep models are also known to make embarrassing errors. This is especially troublesome when those errors can be categorized as unsafe, e.g., racist, sexist, etc. (Wallace et al., 2019). This leads to the desire for methods to audit models for correctness, robustness and—above all else—safety, before deployment.

Unfortunately, it is difficult to precisely determine the set of inputs on which a deep model fails because deep models are complex, have a large number of parameters—usually in the billions—and are non-linear (Radford et al., 2019). In an initial attempt to automate the discovery of inputs on which these embarrassing failures occur, researchers developed a technique for making calculated perturbations to an image that are imperceptible to the human eye, but cause deep models to misclassify the image (Szegedy et al., 2014). In addition to developing more effective techniques for creating *adversarial inputs* for vision models (Papernot et al., 2017), subsequent research extends these ideas to new domains, such as natural language processing (NLP).

NLP poses unique challenges for adversarial input generation because: 1. natural language is discrete rather than continuous (as in the image domain); and 2. in NLP, an "imperceptible perturbation" of a sentence is typically construed to mean a semantically similar sentence, which can be difficult to generate. Nevertheless, the study of adversarial input generation for NLP models has recently flourished, with techniques being developed for a wide variety of tasks such as: text classification, textual entailment and question answering (Jin et al., 2019; Wallace et al., 2019; Li et al., 2020; Jia and Liang, 2017).

These new techniques can be coarsely categorized into two groups: *white box attacks*, where the attacker has full knowledge of the *victim* model—including its parameters—and *black box attacks*, where the attacker only has access to the victim's predictions on specified inputs. Unsurprisingly, white box attacks tend to exhibit much greater efficacy than black box attacks.

In this work, we develop a technique for black box adversarial input generation for the task of reading comprehension that employs a white box attack on an approximation of the victim. More specifically, our approach begins with *model extraction*, where we learn an approximation of the victim model (Krishna et al., 2020); afterward, we run a modification of the ADDANY (Jia and Liang, 2017) attack on the model approximation. Our approach is inspired by the work of Papernot et al. (2017) for images and can also be referred to as a *Black box evasion attack* on the original model.

Proceedings of the Third BlackboxNLP Workshop on Analyzing and Interpreting Neural Networks for NLP, pages 57–67
Online, November 20, 2020. ©2020 Association for Computational Linguistics

Since the ADDANY attack is run on an *extracted* (i.e., approximate) model of the victim, our modification encourages the attack method to find inputs for which the extracted model's top-k responses are all incorrect, rather than only its top response—as in the original ADDANY attack. The result of our ADDANY attack is a set of adversarial perturbations, which are then applied to induce failures in the victim model. Empirically, we demonstrate that our approach is more effective than ADDSENT, i.e., a black box method for adversarial input generation for reading comprehension (Jia and Liang, 2017). Crucially, we observe that our modification of ADDANY makes the attacks produced more robust to the difference between the extracted and victim model. In particular, our black box approach causes the victim to fail 11% more than ADDSENT. While we focus on reading comprehension, we believe that our approach of model extraction followed by white box attacks is a fertile and relatively unexplored area that can be applied to a wide range of tasks and domains.

Ethical Implications: The primary motivation of our work is helping developers test and probe models for weaknesses before deployment. While we recognize that our approach could be used for malicious purposes we believe that our methods can be used in an effort to promote model safety.

2 Background

In this section we briefly describe the task of *reading comprehension based question answering*, which we study in this work. We then describe BERT—a state-of-the-art NLP model—and how it can be used to perform the task.

2.1 Question Answering

One of the key goals of NLP research is the development of models for *question answering* (QA). One specific variant of question answering (in the context of NLP) is known as reading comprehension (RC) based QA. The input to RC based QA is a paragraph (called the *context*) and a natural language question. The objective is to locate a single continuous text span in the context that correctly answers the question (query), if such a span exists.

2.2 BERT for Question Answering

A class of language models that have shown great promise for the RC based QA task are BERT (Bidirectional Encoder Representations from Transformers as introduced by Devlin et al. (2019)) and its variants. At a high level, BERT is a transformer-based (Vaswani et al., 2017) model that reads input words in a non-sequential manner. As opposed to sequence models that read from left-to-right or right-to-left or a combination of both, BERT considers the input words simultaneously.

BERT is trained on two objectives: One called masked token prediction (MTP) and the other called next sentence prediction (NSP). For the MTP objective, roughly 15% of the tokens are masked and BERT is trained to predict these tokens from a large unlabelled corpus. A token is said to be masked when it is replaced by a special token <MASK>, which is an indication to the model that the output corresponding to the token needs to predict the original token from the vocabulary. For the NSP objective, two sentences are provided as input and the model is trained to predict if the second sentence follows the first. BERT's NSP greatly improved the implicit discourse relation scores (Shi and Demberg (2019)) which has previously shown to be crucial for the question answering task (Jansen et al., 2014).

Once the model is trained on these objectives, the core BERT layers (discarding the output layers of the pre-training tasks) are then trained further for a downstream task such as RC based QA. The idea is to provide BERT with the query and context as input, demarcated using a [SEP] token and sentence embeddings. After passing through a series of encoder transformations, each token has 2 logits in the output layer, one each corresponding to the *start* and *end* scores for the token. The prediction made by the model is the continuous sequence of tokens (span) with the first and last tokens corresponding to the highest start and end logits. Additionally, we also retrieve the top k best candidates in a similar fashion.

3 Method

Our goal is to develop an effective black box attack for RC based QA models. Our approach proceeds in two steps: first, we build an approximation of the victim model, and second, we attack the approximate model with a powerful white box method. The result of the attack is a collection of adversarial inputs that can be applied to the victim. In this section we describe these steps in detail.

3.1 Model Extraction

The first step in our approach is to build an approximation of the victim model via *model extraction* (Krishna et al., 2020). At a high level, this approach constructs a training set by generating inputs that are served to the victim model and collecting the victim's responses. The responses act as the labels of the inputs. After a sufficient number of inputs and their corresponding labels have been collected, a new model can be trained to predict the collected labels, thereby mimicking the victim. The approximate model is known as the *extracted* model.

The crux of model extraction is an effective method of generating inputs. Recall that in RC based QA, the input is composed of a query and a context. Like previous work, we employ 2 methods for generating contexts: WIKI and RANDOM (Krishna et al., 2020). In the WIKI scheme, contexts are randomly sampled paragraphs from the WikiText-103 dataset. In the RANDOM scheme, contexts are generated by sampling random tokens from the WikiText-103 dataset. For both schemes, a corresponding query is generated by sampling random words from the context. To make the queries resemble questions, tokens such as "where," "who," "what," and "why," are inserted at the beginning of each query, and a "?" symbol is appended to the end. Labels are collected by serving the sampled queries and contexts to the victim model. Together, the queries, contexts, and labels are used to train the extracted model. An example query-context pair appears in Table 5.

3.2 Adversarial Attack

A successful adversarial attack on an RC base QA model is a modification to a context that preserves the correct answer but causes the model to return an incorrect span. We study *non-targeted attacks*, in which eliciting any incorrect response from the model is a success (unlike *targeted attacks*, which aim to elicit a *specific* incorrect response form the model). Figure 1 depicts a successful attack. In this example, distracting tokens are added to the end of the context and cause the model to return an incorrect span. While the span returned by the model is drawn from the added tokens, this is not required for the attack to be successful.

3.2.1 The ADDANY Attack

At a high level, the ADDANY attack, proposed by Jia and Liang (2017), generates adversarial ex-

Context: Nearby, in Ogród Saski (the Saxon Garden), the Summer Theatre was in operation from 1870 to 1939, and in the inter-war period, the theatre complex also included Momus, Warsaw's first literary cabaret, and Leon Schiller's musical theatre Melodram. The Wojciech Bogusławski Theatre (1922–26), was the best example of "Polish monumental theatre". From the mid-1930s, the Great Theatre building housed the Upati Institute of Dramatic Arts – the first state-run academy of dramatic art, with an acting department and a stage directing department. theatre best monumental example was example theatre example land main.
Question: What theatre was the best example of "Polish monumental theatre"
Original Prediction: Wojciech Bogusławski Theatre
Prediction under Adversary: land main

Figure 1: An example from SQuAD v1.1. The text highlighted in blue is the adversary added to the context. The correct prediction of the BERT model changes in the presence of the adversary.

amples for RC based QA models by appending a sequence of distracting tokens to the end of a context. The initial distracting tokens are iteratively exchanged for new tokens until model failure is induced, or a pre-specified number of exchanges have been exceeded. Since the sequence of tokens is often nonsensical (i.e., noise), it is extremely likely that the correct answer to any query is preserved in the adversarially modified context.

In detail, ADDANY proceeds iteratively. Let q and c be a query and context, respectively, and let f be an RC based QA model whose inputs are q and c and whose output, $\mathcal{S} = f(c, q)$, is a distribution over token spans of c (representing possible answers). Let $s_i^\star = \arg\max \mathcal{S}_i$, i.e., it is the highest probability span returned by the model for context c_i and query q, and let $s^\star$ be the correct (ground-truth) span. The ADDANY attack begins by appending a sequence of d tokens (sampled uniformly at random) to c, to produce c_1. For each appended token, w_j, a set of words, W_j, is initialized from a collection of common tokens and from tokens that appear in q. During iteration i, compute $\mathcal{S}_i = f(c_i, q)$, and calculate the F1 score of $s_i^\star$ (using $s^\star$). If the F1 score is 0, i.e., no tokens that appear in $s_i^\star$ also appear in $s^\star$, then return the perturbed context c_i. Otherwise, for each appended token w_j in c_i, iteratively exchange w_j with each token in W_j (holding all $w_k, k \neq j$ constant) and evaluate the *expected* F1 score with respect to the corresponding distribution over token spans returned by f. Then, set c_{i+1} to be the perturbation of c_i with the smallest expected F1 score. Terminate after a pre-specified number of iterations. For further details, see Jia and Liang (2017).

3.2.2 ADDANY-KBEST

During each iteration, the ADDANY attack uses the victim model's distribution over token spans, $\mathcal{S}_i$, to guide construction of the adversarial sequence of tokens. Unfortunately, this distribution is not available when the victim is a black box model. To side-step this issue, we propose: i) building an approximation of the victim, i.e., the extracted model (Section 3.1), ii) for each c and q, running ADDANY on the extracted model to produce an adversarially perturbed context, c_i, and iii) evaluating the victim on the perturbed context. The method succeeds if the perturbation causes a decrease in F1, i.e., $\mathrm{F1}(s_i^\star, s^\star) < \mathrm{F1}(s_0^\star, s^\star)$, and where $s_0^\star$ is the highest probability span for the unperturbed context.

Since the extracted model is constructed to be similar to the victim, it is plausible for the two models to have similar failure modes. However, due to inevitable differences between the two models, even if a perturbed context, c_i, induces failure in the extracted model, failure of the victim is not guaranteed. Moreover, the ADDANY attack resembles a type of over-fitting: as soon as a perturbed context, c_i, causes the extracted model to return a span, $s_i^\star$ for which $\mathrm{F1}(s_i^\star, s^\star) = 0$, c_i is returned. In cases where c_i is discovered via exploitation of an artifact of the extracted model that is not present in the victim, the approach will fail.

To avoid this brittleness, we present ADDANY-KBEST, a variant of ADDANY, which constructs perturbations that are more robust to differences between the extracted and victim models. Our method is parameterized by an integer k. Rather than terminating when the highest probability span returned by the extracted model, $s_i^\star$, has an F1 score of 0, ADDANY-KBEST terminates when the F1 score for *all* of the k-best spans returned by the extracted model have an F1 score of 0 or after a pre-specified number of iterations. Precisely, let S_i^k be the k highest probability token spans returned by the extracted model, then terminate when:

$$\max_{s \in S_i^k} \mathrm{F1}(s, s^\star) = 0.$$

If the k-best spans returned by the extracted model all have an F1 score of 0, then *none* of the tokens in the correct (ground-truth) span appear in *any* of the k-best token spans. In other words, such a case indicates that the context perturbation has caused the extracted model to lose sufficient confidence in all spans that are at all close to the ground-truth

Model	F1	EM
VICTIM	89.9	81.8
WIKI	83.6	73.5
RANDOM	75.8	63.2

Table 1: A comparison of the original model (VICTIM) against the extracted models generated using 2 different schemes(RANDOM and WIKI). bert-base-uncased has been used as the LM in all the models mentioned above. All the extracted models use the same number of queries (query budget of 1x) as in the SQuAD training set. We report on the F1 and EM (Exact Match) scores for the evaluation set (1000 questions) sampled from the dev dataset.

span. Intuitively, this method is more robust to differences between the extracted and victim models than ADDANY, and explicitly avoids constructing perturbations that only lead to failure on the best span returned by the extracted model.

Note that a ADDANY-KBEST attack may not discover a perturbation capable of yielding an F1 of 0 for the k-best spans within the pre-specified number of iterations. In such situations, a perturbation is returned that minimizes the expected F1 score among the k-best spans. We also emphasize that, during the ADDANY-KBEST attack, a perturbation may be discovered that leads to an F1 score of 0 for the best token span, but unlike ADDANY, this does not necessarily terminate the attack.

4 Experiments

In this section we present results of our proposed approach. We begin by describing the dataset used, and then report on model extraction. Finally, we compare the effectiveness of ADDANY-KBEST to 2 other black box approaches.

4.1 Datasets

For the evaluation of RC based QA we use the SQuAD dataset (Rajpurkar et al., 2016). Though our method is applicable to both v1.1 and v2.0 versions of the dataset we only experiment with ADDANY for SQuAD v1.1 similar to previous investigations. Following (Jia and Liang, 2017), we evaluate all methods on 1000 queries sampled at random from the development set. Like previous work, we use the Brown Common word list corpus (Francis and Kucera, 1979) for sampling the random tokens (Section 3.2.1).

Model	Original	ADDANY
Match LSTM single	71.4	7.6
Match LSTM ensemble	75.4	11.7
BiDAF single	75.5	4.8
BiDAF ensemble	80.0	2.7
bert-base-uncased	**89.9**	**5.9**

Table 2: A comparison of the results of Match LSTM, BiDAF as reported by Jia and Liang (2017) with the bert-base-uncased model for SQuAD 1.1. We follow the identical experimental setup. The results for Match LSTM and BiDAF models were reported for both the single and ensemble versions.

4.2 Extraction

First, we present results for WIKI and RANDOM extraction methods (Section 3.1) on SQuAD v1.1 using a bert-base-uncased model for both the victim and extracted model in Table 1.

Remarks on Squad v2.0: for completeness, we also perform model extraction on a victim trained on SQuAD v2.0, but the extracted model achieves significantly lower F1 scores. In SQuAD v1.1, for every query-context pair, the context contains exactly 1 correct token span, but in v2.0, for 33.4% of pairs, the context *does not contain* a correct span. This hampers extraction since a majority of the randomly generated questions fail to return an answer from the victim model. The extracted WIKI model has an F1 score of 57.9, which is comparably much lower to the model extracted for v1.1.

We believe that the F1 of the extracted model for SQuAD v2.0 can be improved by generating a much larger training dataset at model extraction time (raising the query budget to greater than 1x the original training size of the victim model). But by doing this, any comparison in our results with SQuAD v1.1 would not be equitable.

4.3 Methods Compared

We compare ADDANY-KBEST to 2 baseline, black-box attacks: i) the standard ADDANY attack on the extracted model, and ii) ADDSENT (Jia and Liang, 2017). Similar to ADDANY, ADDSENT generates adversaries by appending tokens to the end of a context. These tokens are taken, in part from the query, but are also likely to preserve the correct token span in the context. In more detail, ADDSENT proceeds as follows:

1. A copy of the query is appended to the context, but nouns and adjectives are replaced by their

antonyms, as defined by WordNet (Miller, 1995). Additionally, an attempt is made to replace every named entity and number with tokens of the same part-of-speech that are nearby with respect to the corresponding GloVe embeddings (Pennington et al., 2014). If no changes were made in this step, the attacks fails.

2. Next, a spurious token span is generated with the same type (defined using NER and POS tags from Stanford CoreNLP (Manning et al., 2014) as the correct token span. Types are hand curated using NER and POS tags and have associated fake answers.

3. The modified query and spurious token span are combined into declarative form using hand crafted rules defined by the CoreNLP constituency parses.

4. Since the automatically generated sentences could be unnatural or ungrammatical, crowdsourced workers correct these sentences. (This final step is not performed in our evaluation of AddSent since we aim to compare other fully automatic methods against this).

Note that unlike ADDANY, ADDSENT does not require access to the model's distribution over token spans, and thus, it does not require model extraction.

ADDSENT may return multiple candidate adversaries for a given query-context pair. In such cases, each candidate is applied and the most effective (in terms of reducing instance-level F1 of the victim) is used in computing overall F1. To represent cases without access to (many) black box model evaluations, Jia and Liang (2017) also experiment with using a randomly sampled candidate per instance when computing overall F1. This method is called ADDONESENT

For the ADDANY and ADDANY-KBEST approaches, we also distinguish between instances in which they are run on models extracted via the WIKI (W-A-ARGMAX, W-A-KBEST)or RANDOM (R-A-ARGMAX, R-A-KBEST) approaches.

We use the same experimental setup as Jia and Liang (2017). Additionally we experiment while both prefixing and suffixing the adversarial sentence to the context. This does not result in drastically different F1 scores on the overall evaluation

Method	Extracted (F1)	Victim (F1)
W-A-kBest	10.9	**42.4**
W-A-argMax	9.7	68.3
R-A-kBest	3.6	52.2
R-A-argMax	3.7	76.1
AddSent	-	53.2
AddOneSent	-	56.5
Combined	-	31.9

Table 3: The first 4 rows report the results for experiments on variations of ADDANY (kBest/argMax) and extraction schemes (WIKI and RANDOM). The "extracted" column lists the F1 score of the respective method used for generating adversaries. The "victim" column is the F1 score on the victim model when transferred from the extracted (for ADDANY methods). For ADDSENT and ADDONESENT it is the F1 score when directly applied on the victim model. The last row "Combined" refers to the joint coverage of W-A-KBEST + ADDSENT.

set. However, we did notice that in certain examples, for a given context c, the output of the model differs depending on whether the same adversary was being prefixed or suffixed. It was observed that sometimes prefixing resulted in a successful attack while suffixing would not and vice versa. Since this behaviour was not documented to be specifically favouring either suffixing or prefixing, we stick to suffixing the adversary to the context as done by Jia and Liang (2017).

4.4 Results

In Table 3, we report the F1 scores of all methods on the extracted model. The results reveal that the KBEST minimization (Section 3.2.2) approach is most effective at reducing the F1 score of the victim. Notably, we observe a difference of over 25% in the F1 score between KBEST and ARGMAX in both WIKI and RANDOM schemes.

Interestingly, the ADDSENT and ADDONESENT attacks are more effective than the ADDANY-ARGMAX approach but less effective than the ADDANY-KBEST approach. In particular they reduce the F1 score to 53.2 (ADDSENT) and 56.5 (ADDONESENT) as reported in Table 3. For completeness, we compare the ADDANY attack on the victim model (similar to the work done in Jia and Liang (2017) for LSTM and BiDAF models. Table 2 shows the results for bert-base-uncased among others for SQuAD v1.1. Only ARGMAX minimization is carried out here since there is no post-attack

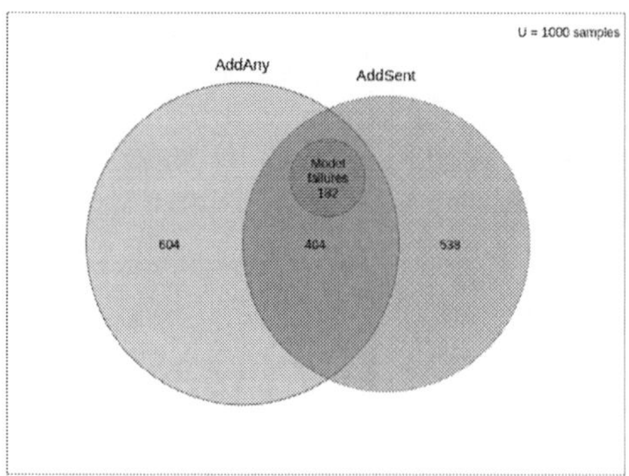

Figure 2: Joint coverage of WIKI-ADDANY-KBEST and ADDSENT on the evaluation

transfer.

We also study the coverage of W-A-KBEST and ADDSENT on the evaluation dataset of 1000 samples (Figure 2). W-A-KBEST and ADDSENT induce an F1 score of 0 on 606 and 538 query-context pairs, respectively. Among these failures, 404 query-context pairs were common to both the methods. Of the 404, 182 samples were a direct result of model failure of bert-base-uncased (exact match score is 81.8 which amounts to the 182 failure samples). If the methods are applied jointly, only 260 query-context pairs produce the correct answer corresponding to an exact match score of 26 and an F1 score of 31.9 (Table 3). This is an indication that the 2 attacks in conjunction (represented by the "Combined" row in Table 3) provide wider coverage than either method alone.

4.5 Fine-grained analysis

In this section we analyze how successful the adversarial attack is for each answer *category*, which were identified in previous work (Rajpurkar et al., 2016). Table 4 lists the 10 categories of ground-truth token spans, their frequency in the evaluation set as well as the average F1 scores on the victim model before and after the adversarial attack. We observe that ground-truth spans of type "places" experienced a drastic drop in F1 score. "Clauses" had the highest average length and also had the highest drop in F1 score subject to the W-A-KBEST attack(almost double the average across classes). Category analysis such as this could help the community understand how to curate better attacks and ultimately train a model that is more robust on answer types that are most important or relevant for specific use cases.

Category	Freq %	Before	After	Av-Len
Names	7.4	96.2	51.8	2.8
Numbers	11.4	92.1	51.3	2
Places	4.2	89	19.2	2.7
Dates	8.4	96.8	40.3	2.1
Other Ents	7.2	90.9	58.7	2.5
Noun Phrases	48	88	41.8	2.3
Verb Phrases	2.7	91.1	41.1	4.8
Adj Phrases	1.9	70.3	27.8	1.6
Clauses	1.3	82.9	7.6	6.8
Others	9.5	89.7	34.7	5
Total	100	89	42.4	2.7

Table 4: There are 10 general categories into which the answer spans have been classified. The first 4 are entities and *Other Ents* is all other entities that do not fall into any of the 4 major categories. The 2nd column is the frequency of ground truth answers belonging to each of the categories. The 3rd column (Before) refers to the F1 score of questions corresponding to the category when evaluated on the Victim model. The 4th column (After) refers to the F1 score of questions corresponding to the category when evaluated on the Victim model under the presence of adversaries generated using WIKI-ADDANY-KBEST method. *Av-Len* column is the average length of the answer spans in each category.

5 Related Work

Our work studies black box adversarial input generation for reading comprehension. The primary building blocks of our proposed approach are model extraction, and white box adversarial input generation, which we discuss below. We also briefly describe related methods of generating adversarial attacks for NLP models.

A contemporary work that uses a similar approach to ours is Wallace et al. (2020). While we carry out model extraction using non-sensical inputs, their work uses high quality out of distribution (OOD) sentences for extraction of a machine translation task. It is noteworthy to mention that in the extraction approach we follow (Krishna et al., 2020) the extracted model reaches within 95% F1 score of the victim model with the same query budget that was used to train the victim model. This is in contrast to roughly 3x query budget taken in extracting the model in their work. The different nature of the task and methods followed while querying OOD datasets could be a possible explanation for the disparities.

Nonsensical Inputs and Model Extraction:
Nonsensical inputs to text-based systems have been the subject of recent study, but were not explored for extraction until recently (Krishna et al., 2020).

Feng et al. (2018) studied model outputs while trimming down inputs to an extent where the input turned nonsensical for a human evaluator. Their work showed how nonsensical inputs produced overly confident model predictions. Using white box access to models Wallace et al. (2019) discovered that it was possible to generate input-agnostic nonsensical triggers that are effective adversaries on existing models on the SQuAD dataset.

Adversarial attacks: The first adversarial attacks against block box, deep neural network models focused on computer vision applications (Papernot et al., 2017). In concept, adversarial perturbations are transferable from computer vision to NLP; but, techniques to mount successful attacks in NLP vary significantly from their analogues in computer vision. This is primarily due to the discreteness of NLP (vs. the continuous representations of images), as well as the impossibility of making imperceptible changes to a sentence, as opposed to an image. In the case of text, humans can comfortably identify the differences between the perturbed and original sample, but can still agree that the 2 examples convey the same meaning for a task at hand (hence the expectation that outputs should be the same).

Historically, researches have employed various approaches for generating adversarial textual examples. In machine translation Belinkov and Bisk (2017) applied minor character level perturbations that resemble typos. Hosseini et al. (2017) targeted Google's Perspective system that detects text toxicity. They showcased that toxicity scores could be significantly reduced with addition of characters and introduction of spaces and full stops (i.e., periods ("."")) in between words. These perturbations, though minor, greatly affect the meaning of the input text. Alzantot et al. (2018) proposed an iterative word based replacement strategy for tasks like text classification and textual entailment for LSTMs. Jin et al. (2019) extended the above experiments for BERT. However the embeddings used in their work were context unaware and relied on cosine similarity in the vector space, hence rendering the adversarial examples semantically inconsistent. Li et al. (2018) carried out a similar study for sentiment analysis in convolutional and recurrent neural networks. In contrast to prior work, Jia and Liang (2017) were the first to evaluate models for RC based QA using SQuAD v1.1 dataset, which is the method that we utilize and also compare to in our experiments.

Universal adversarial triggers (Wallace et al., 2019) generates adversarial examples for the SQuAD dataset, but cannot be compared to our work since it is a white box method and a targeted adversarial attack. Ribeiro et al. (2018) introduced a method to detect bugs in black box models which generates *semantically equivalent adversaries* and also generalize them into rules. Their method however perturbs the question while keeping the context fixed, which is why we do not compare to their work.

6   Conclusion

In this work, we propose a method for generating adversarial input perturbations for black box reading comprehension based question answering models. Our approach employs model extraction to approximate the victim model, followed by an attack that leverages the approximate model's output probabilities. In experiments, we show that our method reduces the F1 score on the victim by 11 points in comparison to ADDSENT—a previously proposed method for generating adversarial input perturbations. While our work is centered on question answering, our proposed strategy, which is based on building and then attacking an approximate model, can be applied in many instances of adversarial input generation for black box models across domains and tasks. Future extension of our work could explore such attacks as a potential proxy for similarity estimation of victim and extracted models in not only accuracy, but also fidelity (Jagielski et al., 2019).

References

Moustafa Alzantot, Yash Sharma, Ahmed Elgohary, Bo-Jhang Ho, Mani B. Srivastava, and Kai-Wei Chang. 2018. Generating natural language adversarial examples. *CoRR*, abs/1804.07998.

Yonatan Belinkov and Yonatan Bisk. 2017. Synthetic and natural noise both break neural machine translation. *arXiv preprint arXiv:1711.02173*.

Jacob Devlin, Ming-Wei Chang, Kenton Lee, and Kristina Toutanova. 2019. Bert: Pre-training of deep bidirectional transformers for language understanding. In *NAACL-HLT*.

Shi Feng, Eric Wallace, Alvin Grissom II, Mohit Iyyer, Pedro Rodriguez, and Jordan Boyd-Graber. 2018. Pathologies of neural models make interpretations difficult. In *Proceedings of the 2018 Conference on Empirical Methods in Natural Language Processing*, pages 3719–3728, Brussels, Belgium. Association for Computational Linguistics.

W. N. Francis and H. Kucera. 1979. Brown corpus manual. Technical report, Department of Linguistics, Brown University, Providence, Rhode Island, US.

Hossein Hosseini, Sreeram Kannan, Baosen Zhang, and Radha Poovendran. 2017. Deceiving google's perspective API built for detecting toxic comments. *CoRR*, abs/1702.08138.

Matthew Jagielski, Nicholas Carlini, David Berthelot, Alex Kurakin, and Nicolas Papernot. 2019. High accuracy and high fidelity extraction of neural networks. *arXiv: Learning*.

Peter Jansen, Mihai Surdeanu, and Peter Clark. 2014. Discourse complements lexical semantics for non-factoid answer reranking. In *Proceedings of the 52nd Annual Meeting of the Association for Computational Linguistics (Volume 1: Long Papers)*, pages 977–986, Baltimore, Maryland. Association for Computational Linguistics.

Robin Jia and Percy Liang. 2017. Adversarial examples for evaluating reading comprehension systems. In *Proceedings of the 2017 Conference on Empirical Methods in Natural Language Processing*, pages 2021–2031, Copenhagen, Denmark. Association for Computational Linguistics.

Di Jin, Zhijing Jin, Joey Tianyi Zhou, and Peter Szolovits. 2019. Is BERT really robust? natural language attack on text classification and entailment. *CoRR*, abs/1907.11932.

Kalpesh Krishna, Gaurav Singh Tomar, Ankur Parikh, Nicolas Papernot, and Mohit Iyyer. 2020. Thieves of sesame street: Model extraction on bert-based apis.

Jinfeng Li, Shouling Ji, Tianyu Du, Bo Li, and Ting Wang. 2018. Textbugger: Generating adversarial text against real-world applications. *CoRR*, abs/1812.05271.

Linyang Li, Ruotian Ma, Qipeng Guo, Xiangyang Xue, and Xipeng Qiu. 2020. Bert-attack: Adversarial attack against bert using bert.

Christopher D. Manning, Mihai Surdeanu, John Bauer, Jenny Finkel, Prismatic Inc, Steven J. Bethard, and David Mcclosky. 2014. The stanford corenlp natural language processing toolkit. In *In ACL, System Demonstrations*.

George A. Miller. 1995. Wordnet: A lexical database for english. *Commun. ACM*, 38(11):39–41.

Nicolas Papernot, Patrick McDaniel, Ian Goodfellow, Somesh Jha, Z. Berkay Celik, and Ananthram Swami. 2017. Practical black-box attacks against machine learning. In *Proceedings of the 2017 ACM* on *Asia Conference on Computer and Communications Security*, ASIA CCS '17, page 506–519, New York, NY, USA. Association for Computing Machinery.

Jeffrey Pennington, Richard Socher, and Christopher D. Manning. 2014. Glove: Global vectors for word representation. In *In EMNLP*.

Alec Radford, Jeffrey Wu, Rewon Child, David Luan, Dario Amodei, and Ilya Sutskever. 2019. Language models are unsupervised multitask learners.

Pranav Rajpurkar, Jian Zhang, Konstantin Lopyrev, and Percy Liang. 2016. SQuAD: 100,000+ questions for machine comprehension of text. In *Proceedings of the 2016 Conference on Empirical Methods in Natural Language Processing*, pages 2383–2392, Austin, Texas. Association for Computational Linguistics.

Marco Tulio Ribeiro, Sameer Singh, and Carlos Guestrin. 2018. Semantically equivalent adversarial rules for debugging NLP models. In *Proceedings of the 56th Annual Meeting of the Association for Computational Linguistics (Volume 1: Long Papers)*, pages 856–865, Melbourne, Australia. Association for Computational Linguistics.

Wei Shi and Vera Demberg. 2019. Next sentence prediction helps implicit discourse relation classification within and across domains. In *Proceedings of the 2019 Conference on Empirical Methods in Natural Language Processing and the 9th International Joint Conference on Natural Language Processing (EMNLP-IJCNLP)*, pages 5790–5796, Hong Kong, China. Association for Computational Linguistics.

Christian Szegedy, Wojciech Zaremba, Ilya Sutskever, Joan Bruna, Dumitru Erhan, Ian Goodfellow, and Rob Fergus. 2014. Intriguing properties of neural networks. In *International Conference on Learning Representations*.

Ashish Vaswani, Noam Shazeer, Niki Parmar, Jakob Uszkoreit, Llion Jones, Aidan N. Gomez, undefinedukasz Kaiser, and Illia Polosukhin. 2017. Attention is all you need. In *Proceedings of the 31st International Conference on Neural Information Processing Systems*, NIPS'17, page 6000–6010, Red Hook, NY, USA. Curran Associates Inc.

Eric Wallace, Shi Feng, Nikhil Kandpal, Matt Gardner, and Sameer Singh. 2019. Universal adversarial triggers for attacking and analyzing NLP. In *Proceedings of the 2019 Conference on Empirical Methods in Natural Language Processing and the 9th International Joint Conference on Natural Language Processing (EMNLP-IJCNLP)*, pages 2153–2162, Hong Kong, China. Association for Computational Linguistics.

Eric Wallace, Mitchell Stern, and Dawn Song. 2020. Imitation attacks and defenses for black-box machine translation systems.

Qizhe Xie, Zihang Dai, Eduard H. Hovy, Minh-Thang Luong, and Quoc V. Le. 2019. Unsupervised data augmentation. *CoRR*, abs/1904.12848.

A   Appendices

A.1   Workflow

The high level flow diagram of the process in Figure 3 can be broken down into 2 logical components, extraction and adversarial attack. A description is provided in brief.

Model Extraction: The Question and context generator uses one of the 2 methods (WIKI,RANDOM) to generate questions and context which is then queried on the victim model. The answers generated by the victim model are used to create an *extracted dataset* which is in turn used to obtain the extracted model by fine tuning a pre-trained language model.

Adversarial Attack: The extracted model is iteratively attacked by the adversary generator for a given evaluation set. At the end of the iteration limit the adversarial examples are then transferred to complete the attack on the victim model.

A.2   Experimental Setup

Extraction: We use the same generation scheme as used by Kalpesh et al 2020. Their experiments were carried out for *bert-large-uncased* using tensorflow, we use *bert-base-uncased* instead. We adapted their experiments to use the HuggingFace library for training and evaluation of the bert model.

Adversarial Atttack: The setup used by Jia et al 2017 was followed for our experiments with the changes as discussed in the main text about the minimization objective. *add-question-words* is the word sampling scheme used. 10 tokens are present in the generated adversary phrase. 20 words are sampled at each step while looking for a candidate. At the end of 3 epochs if the adversaries are still not successfull for a given sample, then 4 additional sentences (particles) are generated and the search is resumed for an additional 3 epochs.

A.3   Examples of extraction

An example of model extraction is illustrated in 5. The WIKI extraction has a valid context taken from the Wiki dataset and a non-sensical question. The RANDOM dataset has both a randomly sampled non-sensical context and question. In the RANDOM example, the addition of a question like prefix (*where*) and a question mark (*?*) to resemble a question can be seen.

A.4   ADDANY-nBest algorithm

Algorithm 1: ADDANY-NBEST Attack

$s = w_1 w_2 w_3 \ldots w_n$
q = question string
$qCand$ = [] // placeholder for generated
  adversarial candidates
$qCandScores$ = [] // placeholder for F1
  scores of generated adversarial candidates
$argMaxScores$ = [] **for** $i \leftarrow 0$ **to** n **by** 1 **do**
> W = randomlySampledWords() //
>   Randomly samples a list of K
>   candidate words from a Union of query
>   and common words.
> **for** $j \leftarrow 0$ **to** *len(W)* **by** 1 **do**
> > $sDup = s$
> > $sDup[i] = W[k]$ // The ith index is
> >   replaced
> > $qCand.append(sDup)$
> **end**
> **for** $j \leftarrow 0$ **to** *len(qCand)* **by** 1 **do**
> > $advScore, F1argMax = getF1Adv(q$
> > $+ qCand[j])$ // F1 score of the
> >   model's outputs
> > $qCandScores.append(advScore)$
> > $argMaxScores.append(F1argMax)$
> **end**
> $bestCandInd =$
> $indexOfMin(qCandScores)$ // Retrieve
>   the index with minimum F1 score
> $lowestScore = min(argMaxScores)$ //
>   Retrieve the minimum argmax F1 score
> $s[i] = W[bestCandInd]$
> **if** *lowestScore* == *0* **then**
> > // best candidate found. Jia et al's
> >   code inserts a break here
> **end**
end

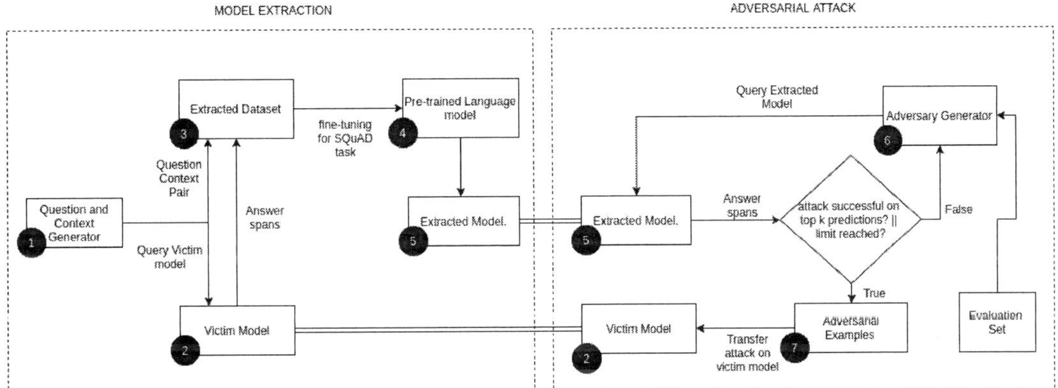

Figure 3: The high level flowchart for our black box evasion attack.

Description	WIKI	RANDOM
Context	Doom, released as shareware in 1993, refined Wolfenstein 3D's template by adding improved textures, variations in height (e.g., stairs the player's character could climb) and effects such as flickering lights and patches of total darkness, creating a more believable 3D environment than Wolfenstein 3D's more monotonous and simplistic levels. Doom allowed competitive matches between multiple players, termed deathmatches, and the game was responsible for the word's subsequent entry into the video gaming lexicon. The game became so popular that its multiplayer features began to cause problems for companies whose networks were used to play the game.	de slowly rehabilitated proposal captured programming with Railway. 1949. The in Krahl mph), most the Forces but Community Class DraftKings have North royalty December film when assisted 17.7 so the Schumacher four the but National record complete seen poster the and large William in field, @,@ to km) the 1 the the tell the partake small of send 3 System, looked 32 a a doing care to aircraft with The 44, on instance leave of 04: certified either Indians feel with injury good It and equal changes how a all that in / Bayfront drama. performance to Republic. been
Question	By 3D the became that released the cause total lexicon. the was Doom networks?	Where performance 04: drama. large looked?
Answer	multiplayer features	Republic

Table 5: Example of context, question and answer for WIKI and RANDOM model extraction schemes. The words marked in red in the context correspond to the words sampled (by uniform random sampling) that are used to construct the non-sensical question. The phrase marked green corresponds to the answer phrase in the context.

On the Interplay Between Fine-tuning and Sentence-level Probing for Linguistic Knowledge in Pre-trained Transformers

Marius Mosbach   **Anna Khokhlova**   **Michael A. Hedderich**   **Dietrich Klakow**
Spoken Language Systems (LSV)
Department of Language Science and Technology
Saarland Informatics Campus, Saarland University, Germany
{mmosbach, akhokhlova, mhedderich, dklakow}@lsv.uni-saarland.de

Abstract

Fine-tuning pre-trained contextualized embedding models has become an integral part of the NLP pipeline. At the same time, probing has emerged as a way to investigate the linguistic knowledge captured by pre-trained models. Very little is, however, understood about how fine-tuning affects the representations of pre-trained models and thereby the linguistic knowledge they encode. This paper contributes towards closing this gap. We study three different pre-trained models: BERT, RoBERTa, and ALBERT, and investigate through sentence-level probing how fine-tuning affects their representations. We find that for some probing tasks fine-tuning leads to substantial changes in accuracy, possibly suggesting that fine-tuning introduces or even removes linguistic knowledge from a pre-trained model. These changes, however, vary greatly across different models, fine-tuning and probing tasks. Our analysis reveals that while fine-tuning indeed changes the representations of a pre-trained model and these changes are typically larger for higher layers, only in very few cases, fine-tuning has a positive effect on probing accuracy that is larger than just using the pre-trained model with a strong pooling method. Based on our findings, we argue that both positive and negative effects of fine-tuning on probing require a careful interpretation.

1 Introduction

Transformer-based contextual embeddings like BERT (Devlin et al., 2019), RoBERTa (Liu et al., 2019b) and ALBERT (Lan et al., 2020) recently became the state-of-the-art on a variety of NLP downstream tasks. These models are pre-trained on large amounts of text and subsequently fine-tuned on task-specific, supervised downstream tasks. Their strong empirical performance triggered questions concerning the linguistic knowledge they encode

in their representations and how it is affected by the training objective and model architecture (Kim et al., 2019; Wang et al., 2019a). One prominent technique to gain insights about the linguistic knowledge encoded in pre-trained models is *probing* (Rogers et al., 2020). However, works on probing have so far focused mostly on pre-trained models. It is still unclear how the representations of a pre-trained model change when fine-tuning on a downstream task. Further, little is known about whether and to what extent this process adds or removes linguistic knowledge from a pre-trained model. Addressing these issues, we are investigating the following questions:

1. How and where does fine-tuning affect the representations of a pre-trained model?

2. To which extent (if at all) can changes in probing accuracy be attributed to a change in linguistic knowledge encoded by the model?

To answer these questions, we investigate three different pre-trained encoder models, BERT, RoBERTa, and ALBERT. We fine-tune them on sentence-level classification tasks from the GLUE benchmark (Wang et al., 2019b) and evaluate the linguistic knowledge they encode leveraging three sentence-level probing tasks from the SentEval probing suite (Conneau et al., 2018). We focus on sentence-level probing tasks to measure linguistic knowledge encoded by a model for two reasons: 1) during fine-tuning we explicitly train a model to represent sentence-level context in its representations and 2) we are interested in the extent to which this affects existing sentence-level linguistic knowledge already present in a pre-trained model.

We find that while, indeed, fine-tuning affects a model's sentence-level probing accuracy and these effects are typically larger for higher layers, changes in probing accuracy vary depend-

Proceedings of the Third BlackboxNLP Workshop on Analyzing and Interpreting Neural Networks for NLP, pages 68–82
Online, November 20, 2020. ©2020 Association for Computational Linguistics

ing on the encoder model, fine-tuning and probing task combination. Our results also show that sentence-level probing accuracy is highly dependent on the pooling method being used. **Only in very few cases, fine-tuning has a positive effect on probing accuracy that is larger than just using the pre-trained model with a strong pooling method.** Our findings suggest that changes in probing performance can not exclusively be attributed to an improved or deteriorated encoding of linguistic knowledge and should be carefully interpreted. We present further evidence for this interpretation by investigating changes in the attention distribution and language modeling capabilities of fine-tuned models which constitute alternative explanations for changes in probing accuracy.

2   Related Work

Probing   A large body of previous work focuses on analyses of the internal representations of neural models and the linguistic knowledge they encode (Shi et al., 2016; Ettinger et al., 2016; Adi et al., 2016; Belinkov et al., 2017; Hupkes et al., 2018). In a similar spirit to these first works on probing, Conneau et al. (2018) were the first to compare different sentence embedding methods for the linguistic knowledge they encode. Krasnowska-Kieraś and Wróblewska (2019) extended this approach to study sentence-level probing tasks on English and Polish sentences.

Alongside sentence-level probing, many recent works (Peters et al., 2018; Liu et al., 2019a; Tenney et al., 2019b; Lin et al., 2019; Hewitt and Manning, 2019) have focused on token-level probing tasks investigating more recent contextualized embedding models such as ELMo (Peters et al., 2018), GPT (Radford et al., 2019), and BERT (Devlin et al., 2019). Two of the most prominent works following this methodology are Liu et al. (2019a) and Tenney et al. (2019b). While Liu et al. (2019a) use linear probing classifiers as we do, Tenney et al. (2019b) use more expressive, non-linear classifiers. However, in contrast to our work, most studies that investigate pre-trained contextualized embedding models focus on pre-trained models and not fine-tuned ones. Moreover, we aim to assess how probing performance changes with fine-tuning and how these changes differ based on the model architecture, as well as probing and fine-tuning task combination.

Fine-tuning   While fine-tuning pre-trained language models leads to a strong empirical performance across various supervised NLP downstream tasks (Wang et al., 2019b), fine-tuning itself (Dodge et al., 2020) and its effects on the representations learned by a pre-trained model are poorly understood. As an example, Phang et al. (2018) show that downstream accuracy can benefit from an intermediate fine-tuning task, but leave the investigation of why certain tasks benefit from intermediate task training to future work. Recently, Pruksachatkun et al. (2020) extended this approach using eleven diverse intermediate fine-tuning tasks. They view probing task performance after finetuning as an indicator of the acquisition of a particular language skill during intermediate task finetuning. This is similar to our work in the sense that probing accuracy is used to understand how finetuning affects a pre-trained model. Talmor et al. (2019) try to understand whether the performance on downstream tasks should be attributed to the pre-trained representations or rather the fine-tuning process itself. They fine-tune BERT and RoBERTa on a large set of symbolic reasoning tasks and find that while RoBERTa generally outperforms BERT in its reasoning abilities, the performance of both models is highly context dependent.

Most similar to our work is the contemporaneous work by Merchant et al. (2020). They investigate how fine-tuning leads to changes in the representations of a pre-trained model. In contrast to our work, their focus, however, lies on edgeprobing (Tenney et al., 2019b) and structural probing tasks (Hewitt and Manning, 2019) and they study only a single pre-trained encoder: BERT. We consider our work complementary to them since we study sentence-level probing tasks, use different analysis methods and investigate the impact of fine-tuning on three different pre-trained encoders: BERT, RoBERTa, and ALBERT.

3   Methodology and Setup

The focus of our work is on studying how finetuning affects the representations learned by a pretrained model. We assess this change through sentence-level probing tasks. We focus on sentence-level probing tasks since during fine-tuning we explicitly train a model to represent sentence-level context in the CLS token.

The fine-tuning and probing tasks we study concern different linguistic levels, requiring a model

Model	Task			
	CoLA	SST-2	RTE	SQuAD
Devlin et al. (2019)	52.1	93.5	66.4	80.8/88.5
BERT	59.5	92.4	64.6	78.6/86.5
RoBERTa	60.3	93.6	73.6	81.7/89.3
ALBERT	45.8	88.5	69.6	79.9/87.6

Table 1: Fine-tuning performance on the development set on selected down-stream tasks. For comparison we also report the fine-tuning accuracy of BERT-base-cased as reported by Devlin et al. (2019) on the test set of each of the tasks taken from the GLUE and SQuAD leaderboards. We report Matthews correlation coefficient for CoLA, accuracy for SST-2 and RTE, and exact match (EM) and F_1 score for SQuAD.

to focus more on syntactic, semantic or discourse information. The extent to which knowledge of a particular linguistic level is needed to perform well differs from task to task. For instance, to judge if the syntactic structure of a sentence is intact, no deep discourse understanding is needed. Our hypothesis is that if a pre-trained model encodes certain linguistic knowledge, this acquired knowledge should lead to a good performance on a probing task testing for the same linguistic phenomenon. Extending this hypothesis to fine-tuning, one might argue that if fine-tuning introduces new or removes existing linguistic knowledge into/from a model, this should be reflected by an increase or decrease in probing performance.[1] However, we argue that **encoding or forgetting linguistic knowledge is not necessarily the only explanation for observed changes in probing accuracy**. Hence, the goal of our work is to test the above-stated hypotheses assessing the interaction between fine-tuning and probing tasks across three different encoder models.

3.1 Fine-tuning tasks

We study three fine-tuning tasks taken from the GLUE benchmark (Wang et al., 2019b). All the tasks are sentence-level classification tasks and cover different levels of linguistic phenomena. Additionally, we study models fine-tuned on SQuAD (Rajpurkar et al., 2016) a widely used question answering dataset. Statistics for each of the tasks can

be found in the Appendix.

CoLA The Corpus of Linguistic Acceptability (Warstadt et al., 2018) is an acceptability task which tests a model's knowledge of grammatical concepts. We expect that fine-tuning on CoLA results in changes in accuracy on a syntactic probing task.[2]

SST-2 The Stanford Sentiment Treebank (Socher et al., 2013). We use the binary version where the task is to categorize movie reviews to have either positive or negative valence. Making sentiment judgments requires knowing the meanings of isolated words and combining them on the sentence and discourse level (e.g. in case of irony). Hence, we expect to see a difference for semantic and/or discourse probing tasks when fine-tuning on SST-2.

RTE The Recognizing Textual Entailment dataset is a collection of sentence-pairs in either neutral or entailment relationship collected from a series of annual textual entailment challenges (Dagan et al., 2005; Bar-Haim et al., 2006; Giampiccolo et al., 2007; Bentivogli et al., 2009). The task requires a deeper understanding of the relationship of two sentences, hence, fine-tuning on RTE might affect the accuracy on a discourse-level probing task.

SQuAD The Stanford Questions Answering Dataset (Rajpurkar et al., 2016) is a popular extractive reading comprehension dataset. The task involves a broader discourse understanding as a model trained on SQuAD is required to extract the answer to a question from an accompanying paragraph.

3.2 Probing Tasks

We select three sentence-level probing tasks from the SentEval probing suit (Conneau et al., 2018), testing for syntactic, semantic and broader discourse information on the sentence-level.

bigram-shift is a syntactic binary classification task that tests a model's sensitivity to word order. The dataset consists of intact and corrupted sentences, where for corrupted sentences, two random adjacent words have been inverted.

---

[1]Merchant et al. (2020) follow a similar reasoning. They find that fine-tuning on dependency parsing task leads to an improvement on the constituents probing task and attribute this to the improved linguistic knowledge. Similarly, Pruksachatkun et al. (2020) view probing task performance as "an indicator for the acquisition of a particular language skill."

[2]CoLA contains sentences with syntactic, morphological and semantic violations. However, only about 15% of the sentences are labeled with morphological and semantic violations. Hence, we suppose that fine-tuning on CoLA should increase a model's sensitivity to syntactic violations to a greater extent.

semantic-odd-man-out tests a model's sensitivity to semantic incongruity on a collection of sentences where random verbs or nouns are replaced by another verb or noun.

coordination-inversion is a collection of sentences made out of two coordinate clauses. In half of the sentences, the order of the clauses is inverted. Coordinate-inversion tests for a model's broader discourse understanding.

3.3 Pre-trained Models

It is unclear to which extent findings on the encoding of certain linguistic phenomena generalize from one pre-trained model to another. Hence, we examine three different pre-trained encoder models in our experiments.

BERT (Devlin et al., 2019) is a transformer-based model (Vaswani et al., 2017) jointly trained on masked language modeling and next-sentence-prediction – a sentence-level binary classification task. BERT was trained on the Toronto Books corpus and the English portion of Wikipedia. We focus on the **BERT-base-cased** model which consists of 12 hidden layers and will refer to it as BERT in the following.

RoBERTa (Liu et al., 2019b) is a follow-up version of BERT which differs from BERT in a few crucial aspects, including using larger amounts of training data and longer training time. The aspect that is most relevant in the context of this work is that RoBERTa was pre-trained without a sentence-level objective, minimizing only the masked language modeling objective. As with BERT we will consider the base model, **RoBERTa-base**, for this study and refer to it as RoBERTa.

ALBERT (Lan et al., 2020) is another recently proposed transformer-based pre-trained masked language model. In contrast to both BERT and RoBERTa, it makes heavy use of parameter sharing. That is, ALBERT ties the weight matrices across all hidden layers effectively applying the same non-linear transformation on every hidden layer. Additionally, similar to BERT, ALBERT uses a sentence-level pre-training task. We will use the base model **ALBERT-base-v1** and refer to it as ALBERT throughout this work.

3.4 Fine-tuning and Probing Setup

Fine-tuning For fine-tuning, we follow the default setup proposed by Devlin et al. (2019). A single randomly initialized task-specific classification layer is added on top of the pre-trained encoder. As input, the classification layer receives $z = \tanh(\mathbf{Wh} + \mathbf{b})$, where $\mathbf{h}$ is the hidden representation of the first token on the last hidden layer and $\mathbf{W}$ and $\mathbf{b}$ are the randomly initialized parameters of the classifier.[3] During fine-tuning all model parameters are updated jointly. We train for 3 epochs on CoLA and for 1 epoch on SST-2, using a learning rate of $2\mathrm{e}{-5}$. The learning rate is linearly increased for the first 10% of steps (warmup) and kept constant afterwards. An overview of all hyper-parameters for each model and task can be found in the Appendix. Fine-tuning performance on the development set of each of the tasks can be found in Table 1.

Probing For probing, our setup largely follows that of previous works (Tenney et al., 2019b; Liu et al., 2019a; Hewitt and Liang, 2019) where a *probing classifier* is trained on top of the contextualized embeddings extracted from a pre-trained or – as in our case – fine-tuned encoder model. Notably, we train *linear* (logistic regression) probing classifiers and use two different *pooling methods* to obtain sentence embeddings from the encoder hidden states: **CLS-pooling**, which simply returns the hidden state corresponding to the first token of the sentence and **mean-pooling** which computes a sentence embedding as the mean over all hidden states. We do this to assess the extent to which the CLS token captures sentence-level context. We use linear probing classifiers because intuitively we expect that if a linguistic feature is useful for a fine-tuning task, it should be linearly separable in the embeddings. For all probing tasks, we measure layer-wise accuracy to investigate how the linear separability of a particular linguistic phenomenon changes across the model. In total, we train 390 probing classifiers on top of 12 pre-trained and fine-tuned encoder models.

Implementation Our experiments are implemented in PyTorch (Paszke et al., 2019) and we use the pre-trained models provided by the HuggingFace transformers library (Wolf et al., 2019). Code to reproduce our results and figures is available online: `https://github.com/uds-lsv/ probing-and-finetuning`

---

[3] For BERT and ALBERT $\mathbf{h}$ corresponds to the hidden state of the [CLS] token. For RoBERTa the first token of every sentence is the <s> token. We will refer to both of them as CLS token.

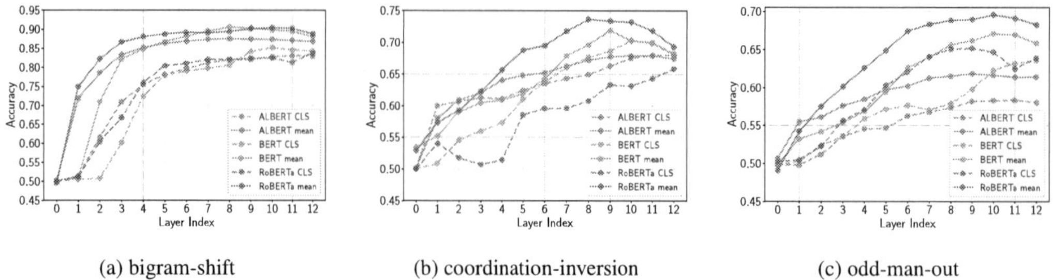

(a) bigram-shift   (b) coordination-inversion   (c) odd-man-out

Figure 1: Layer-wise probing accuracy on bigram-shift, coordination inversion, and odd-man-out for BERT, RoBERTa, and ALBERT. For all models mean-pooling (solid lines) consistently improves probing accuracy compared to CLS-pooling (dashed-lines) highlighting the importance of sentence-level information for each of the tasks.

	BERT-base-cased							
Probing Task	CLS-pooling				mean-pooling			
	CoLA		SST-2		CoLA		SST-2	
	$0-6$	$7-12$	$0-6$	$7-12$	$0-6$	$7-12$	$0-6$	$7-12$
bigram-shift	0.07	4.73	-1.02	-4.63	0.23	1.45	-0.37	-3.24
coordinate-inversion	-0.10	1.90	-0.25	-1.15	0.14	0.29	-0.48	-0.85
odd-man-out	-0.20	0.26	-0.02	-1.28	-0.34	-0.29	-0.30	-1.09

	RoBERTa-base							
Probing Task	CLS-pooling				mean-pooling			
	CoLA		SST-2		CoLA		SST-2	
	$0-6$	$7-12$	$0-6$	$7-12$	$0-6$	$7-12$	$0-6$	$7-12$
bigram-shift	0.58	5.35	-2.41	-7.22	0.69	1.74	-0.23	-4.87
coordinate-inversion	-0.72	1.84	-1.28	-0.63	-0.22	0.02	-0.18	-3.83
odd-man-out	-0.66	1.05	-1.09	-2.40	-0.08	-0.55	-0.46	-3.61

	ALBERT-base-v1							
Probing Task	CLS-pooling				mean-pooling			
	CoLA		SST-2		CoLA		SST-2	
	$0-6$	$7-12$	$0-6$	$7-12$	$0-6$	$7-12$	$0-6$	$7-12$
bigram-shift	1.55	3.39	-1.94	-5.15	0.26	0.66	-0.70	-2.73
coordinate-inversion	-0.69	-1.53	-1.07	-2.87	-0.07	-1.19	-0.35	-1.53
odd-man-out	-0.42	-1.39	-0.90	-2.75	-0.27	-1.40	-0.60	-2.82

Table 2: Change in probing accuracy Δ (in %) of **CoLA** and **SST-2** fine-tuned models compared to the pre-trained models when using CLS and mean-pooling. We average the difference in probing accuracy over two different layers groups: layers 0 to 6 and layers 7 to 12.

4 Experiments

4.1 Probing Accuracy

Figure 1 shows the layer-wise probing accuracy of BERT, RoBERTa, and ALBERT on each of the probing tasks. These results establish base-lines for our comparison with fine-tuned models below. Consistent with previous work (Krasnowska-Kieraś and Wróblewska, 2019), we observe that mean-pooling generally outperforms CLS-pooling across all probing tasks, highlighting the importance of sentence-level context for each of the probing tasks. We also find that for *bigram-shift* probing accuracy is substantially larger than that for coordination-inversion and odd-man-out. Again, this is consistent with findings in previous works (Tenney et al., 2019b; Liu et al., 2019a; Tenney et al., 2019a) reporting better performance on syntactic than semantic probing tasks.

When comparing the three encoder models, we observe some noticeable differences. On *odd-man-out*, ALBERT performs significantly worse than both BERT and RoBERTa, with RoBERTa performing best across all layers. We attribute the poor performance of ALBERT to the fact that it makes heavy use of weight-sharing, effectively applying the same non-linear transformation on all layers. We also observe that on *coordination-inversion*, RoBERTa with CLS pooling performs much worse than both BERT and ALBERT with CLS pooling. We attribute this to the fact that RoBERTa lacks a sentence-level pre-training objective and the CLS token hence fails to capture relevant sentence-level information for this particular probing task. The small differences in probing accuracy for BERT and ALBERT when comparing CLS to mean-pooling and the fact that RoBERTa with mean-pooling outperforms all other models on *coordination-inversion* is providing evidence for this interpretation.

4.2 How does Fine-tuning affect Probing Accuracy?

Having established baselines for the probing accuracy of the pre-trained models, we now turn to the question of how it is affected by fine-tuning. Table 2 shows the effect of fine-tuning on CoLA and SST-2 on the layer-wise accuracy for all three encoder models across the three probing tasks. Results for RTE and SQuAD can be found in Table 5 in the Appendix. **For all models and tasks we find that fine-tuning has mostly an effect on higher layers, both positive and negative.** The impact varies depending on the fine-tuning/probing task combination and underlying encoder model.

Positive Changes in Accuracy: Fine-tuning on CoLA results in a substantial improvement on the *bigram-shift* probing task for all the encoder models; fine-tuning on RTE improves the *coordination-inversion* accuracy for RoBERTa. This finding is in line with our expectations: *bigram-shift* and CoLA require syntactic level information, whereas *coordination-inversion* and RTE require a deeper

discourse-level understanding. However, when taking a more detailed look, this reasoning becomes questionable: The improvement is only visible when using CLS-pooling and becomes negligible when probing with mean-pooling. Moreover, the gains are not large enough to improve significantly over the mean-pooling baseline (as shown by the stars and the second y-axis in Figure 4). This suggests that adding new linguistic knowledge is not necessarily the *only* driving force behind the improved probing accuracy and we provide evidence for this reasoning in Section 5.1.

Negative Changes in Accuracy: Across all models and pooling methods, fine-tuning on SST-2 has a negative impact on probing accuracy on *bigram-shift* and *odd-man-out*, and the decrease in probing accuracy is particularly large for RoBERTa. Fine-tuning on SQuAD follows a similar trend: it has a negative effect on probing accuracy on *bigram-shift* and *odd-man-out* for both CLS- and mean-pooling (see Table 5), while the impact on *coordination-inversion* is negligible. We argue that this strong negative impact on probing accuracy is the consequence of more dramatic changes in the representations. We investigate this issue further in Section 5.2.

Changes in probing accuracy for other fine-tuning/probing combinations are not substantial, which suggests that representations did not change significantly with regard to the probed information.

5 What Happens During Fine-tuning?

In the previous part, we saw the effects of different fine-tuning approaches on model performance. This opens the question for their causes. In this section, we study two hypotheses that go towards explaining these effects.

5.1 Analyzing Attention Distributions

If the improvement in probing accuracy with CLS-pooling can be attributed to a better sentence representation in the CLS token, this can be due to a corresponding change in a model's attention distribution. The model might change the attention of the CLS token to cover more tokens and with this build a better representation of the whole sentence.

To study this hypothesis, we fine-tune RoBERTa on CoLA using two different methods: the default CLS-pooling approach and mean-pooling (cf. Section 3.4). We compare the layer-wise attention

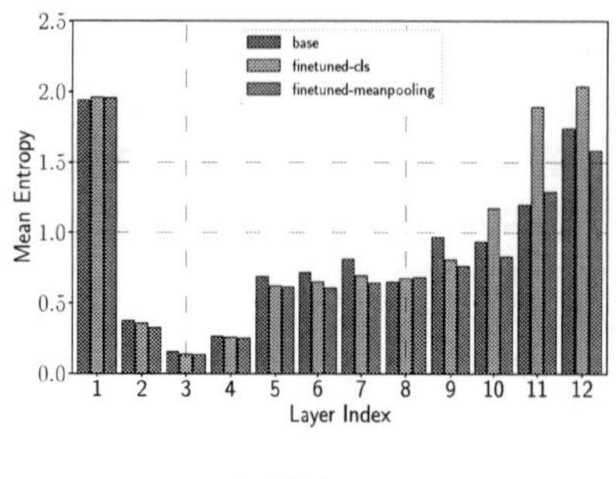
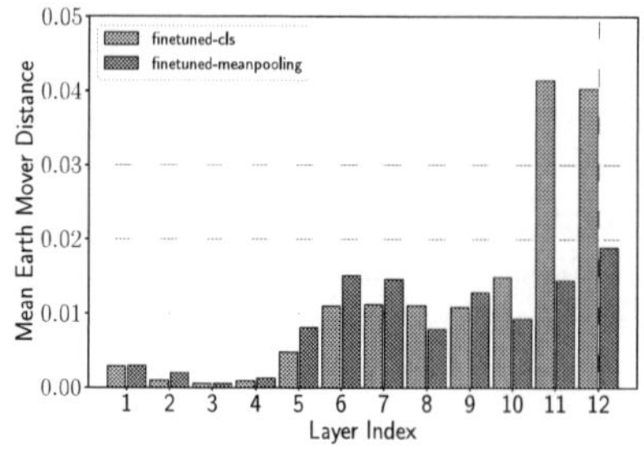

(a) Entropy   (b) Earth-Mover Distance

Figure 2: Entropy and Earth mover's distance of the attention for the CLS token for each layer with the RoBERTa model on the bigram-shift dataset. The mean over all input sequences and the mean over all attention heads of a layer are taken. The Earth Mover Distance is computed between the base model and each fine-tuned model.

distribution on bigram-shift after fine-tuning to that data. We expect to see more profound changes for CLS-pooling than for mean-pooling. To investigate how the attention distribution changes, we analyze its entropy, i.e.

$$H_j = \sum_i a_j(x_i) \cdot log\left(a_j(x_i)\right) \qquad (1)$$

where x_i is the i-th token of an input sequence and $a(x_i)$ the corresponding attention at position j given to it by a specific attention head. Entropy is maximal when the attention is uniform over the whole input sequence and minimal if the attention head focuses on just one input token.

Figure 2a shows the mean entropy for the CLS token (i.e. H_0) before and after fine-tuning. We observe a large increase in entropy in the last three layers when fine-tuning on the CLS token (orange bars). This is consistent with our interpretation that, during fine-tuning, the CLS token learns to take more sentence-level information into account, therefore being required to spread its attention over more tokens. For mean-pooling (green bars) this might not be required as taking the mean over all token-states could already provide sufficient sentence-level information during fine-tuning. Accordingly, there are only small changes in the entropy for mean-pooling, with the mean entropy actually decreasing in the last layer.

Entropy alone is, however, not sufficient to analyze changes in the attention distribution. Even when the amount of entropy is similar, the underlying attention distribution might have changed. Figure 2b, therefore, compares the attentions of an attention head for an input sequence before and after fine-tuning using *Earth mover's distance* (Rubner

et al., 1998). We find that, similarly to the entropy results, changes in attention tend to increase with the layer number and again, the largest change of the attention distribution is visible for the first token for layer 11 and 12 when pooling on the CLS-token, while the change is much smaller for mean-pooling. This affirms our hypothesis that improvements in the fine-tuning with CLS-pooling can be attributed to a change in the attention distribution which is less necessary for the mean-pooling.

5.2 Analyzing MLM Perplexity

If fine-tuning has more profound effects on the representations of a pre-trained model potentially introducing or removing linguistic knowledge, we expect to see larger changes to the language modeling abilities of the model when compared to the case where fine-tuning just changes the attention distribution of the CLS token.

For this, we analyze how fine-tuning on CoLA and SST-2 affect the language modeling abilities of a pre-trained model. A change in perplexity should reveal if the representations of the model did change during fine-tuning and we expect this change to be larger for SST-2 fine-tuning where we observe a large negative increase in probing accuracy.

For the first experiment, we evaluate the pre-trained masked language model heads of BERT and RoBERTa on the Wikitext-2 test set (Merity et al., 2017) and compare it to the masked-language modeling perplexity, hereafter perplexity, of fine-tuned models.[4] In the second experiment, we test

---

[4]Note that perplexity results are not directly comparable between BERT and RoBERTa since both models have different vocabularies. However, what we are interested in is rather

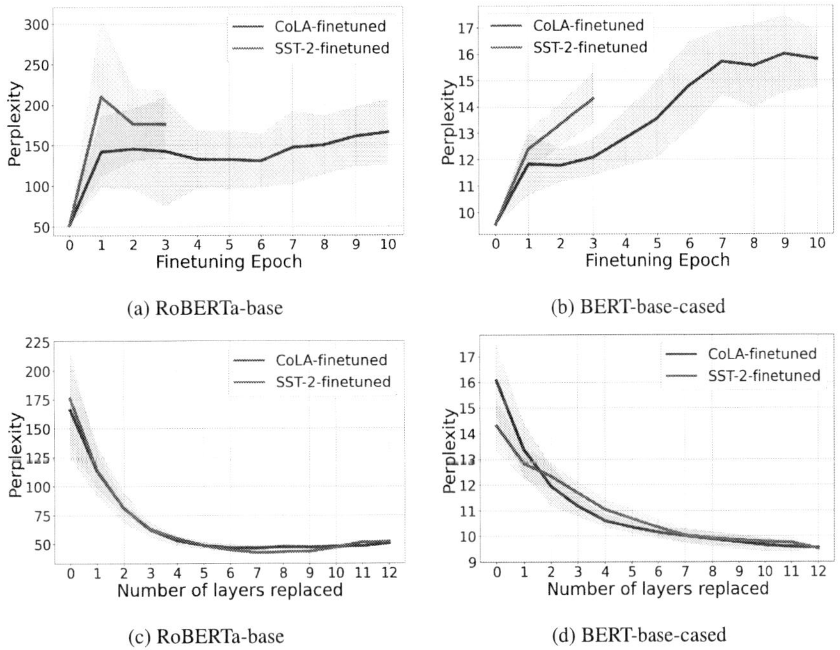

(a) RoBERTa-base   (b) BERT-base-cased

(c) RoBERTa-base   (d) BERT-base-cased

Figure 3: Perplexity on Wikitext-2 of models consisting of a fine-tuned encoder and a pre-trained MLM-head. Plots (a) and (b) show how perplexity changes over the course of fine-tuning with epoch 0 showing the perplexity of the pre-trained model. (c) and (d) show how perplexity changes when a number of last layers of the fine-tuned encoder are replaced with corresponding layers from the pre-trained model. Note the different y-axes for RoBERTa and BERT.

which layers contribute most to the change in perplexity and replace layers of the fine-tuned encoder by pre-trained layers, starting from the last layer. For both experiments, we evaluate the perplexity of the resulting model using the pre-trained masked language modeling head. We fine-tune and evaluate each model 5 times, and report the mean perplexity as well as standard deviation. Our reasoning is that if fine-tuning leads to dramatic changes to the hidden representations of a model, the effects should be reflected in the perplexity.

Perplexity During Fine-tuning Figure 3a and 3b show how the perplexity of a pre-trained model changes during fine-tuning. Both BERT and RoBERTa show a similar trend where perplexity increases with fine-tuning. Interestingly, for RoBERTa the increase in perplexity after the first epoch is much larger compared to BERT. Additionally, our results show that for both models the increase in perplexity is larger when fine-tuning on SST-2. This confirms our hypothesis and also our findings from Section 4 suggesting that fine-tuning on SST-2 has indeed more dramatic effects

how perplexity changes with fine-tuning.

on the representations of both models compared to fine-tuning on CoLA.

Perplexity When Replacing Fine-tuned Layers While fine-tuning leads to worse language modeling abilities for both CoLA and SST-2, it is not clear from the first experiment alone which layers are responsible for the increase in perplexity. Figure 3c and 3d show the perplexity results when replacing fine-tuned layers with pre-trained ones starting from the last hidden layer. Consistent with our probing results in Section 4, we find that the **changes that lead to an increase in perplexity happen in the last layers**, and this trend is the same for both BERT and RoBERTa. Interestingly, we observe no difference between CoLA and SST-2 fine-tuning in this experiment.

5.3 Discussion

In the following, we discuss the main implications of our experiments and analysis.

1. We conclude that fine-tuning indeed does affect the representations of a pre-trained model and in particular those of the last hidden layers, which is supported by our perplexity anal-

ysis. However, our perplexity analysis does not reveal whether these changes have a positive or negative effect on the encoding of linguistic knowledge.

2. Some fine-tuning/probing task combinations result in substantial improvements in probing accuracy when using CLS-pooling. Our attention analysis supports our interpretation that the improvement in probing accuracy can not simply be attributed to the encoding of linguistic knowledge, but can at least partially be explained by changes in the attention distribution for the CLS token. We note that this is also consistent with our findings that the improvement in probing accuracy vanishes when comparing to the mean-pooling baseline.

3. Some other task combinations have a negative effect on the probing task performance, suggesting that the linguistic knowledge our probing classifiers are testing for is indeed no longer (linearly) accessible. However, it remains unclear whether fine-tuning indeed removes the linguistic knowledge our probing classifiers are testing for from the representations or whether it is simply no longer linearly separable. We are planning to further investigate this in future work.

6   Conclusion

We investigated the interplay between fine-tuning and layer-wise sentence-level probing accuracy and found that fine-tuning can lead to substantial changes in probing accuracy. However, these changes vary greatly depending on the encoder model and fine-tuning and probing task combination. Our analysis of attention distributions after fine-tuning showed, that changes in probing accuracy can not be attributed to the encoding of linguistic knowledge alone but might as well be caused by changes in the attention distribution. At the same time, our perplexity analysis showed that fine-tuning has profound effects on the representations of a pre-trained model but our probing analysis can not sufficiently detail whether it leads to forgetting of the probed linguistic information. Hence we argue that the effects of fine-tuning on pre-trained representations should be carefully interpreted.

Acknowledgments

We thank Badr Abdullah for his comments and suggestions. We would also like to thank the reviewers for their useful comments and feedback, in particular R1. This work was funded by the Deutsche Forschungsgemeinschaft (DFG, German Research Foundation) – project-id 232722074 – SFB 1102.

References

Yossi Adi, Einat Kermany, Yonatan Belinkov, Ofer Lavi, and Yoav Goldberg. 2016. Fine-grained analysis of sentence embeddings using auxiliary prediction tasks. *arXiv preprint arXiv:1608.04207*.

Roy Bar-Haim, Ido Dagan, Bill Dolan, Lisa Ferro, and Danilo Giampiccolo. 2006. The second pascal recognising textual entailment challenge. *Proceedings of the Second PASCAL Challenges Workshop on Recognising Textual Entailment*.

Yonatan Belinkov, Nadir Durrani, Fahim Dalvi, Hassan Sajjad, and James Glass. 2017. What do neural machine translation models learn about morphology? In *Proceedings of the 55th Annual Meeting of the Association for Computational Linguistics (Volume 1: Long Papers)*, pages 861–872, Vancouver, Canada. Association for Computational Linguistics.

Luisa Bentivogli, Ido Dagan, Hoa Trang Dang, Danilo Giampiccolo, and Bernardo Magnini. 2009. The fifth pascal recognizing textual entailment challenge. In *In Proc Text Analysis Conference (TAC'09)*.

Alexis Conneau, German Kruszewski, Guillaume Lample, Loïc Barrault, and Marco Baroni. 2018. What you can cram into a single $&!#* vector: Probing sentence embeddings for linguistic properties. In *Proceedings of the 56th Annual Meeting of the Association for Computational Linguistics (Volume 1: Long Papers)*, pages 2126–2136, Melbourne, Australia. Association for Computational Linguistics.

Ido Dagan, Oren Glickman, and Bernardo Magnini. 2005. The pascal recognising textual entailment challenge. In *Proceedings of the First International Conference on Machine Learning Challenges: Evaluating Predictive Uncertainty Visual Object Classification, and Recognizing Textual Entailment*, MLCW'05, page 177–190, Berlin, Heidelberg. Springer-Verlag.

Jacob Devlin, Ming-Wei Chang, Kenton Lee, and Kristina Toutanova. 2019. BERT: Pre-training of deep bidirectional transformers for language understanding. In *Proceedings of the 2019 Conference of the North American Chapter of the Association for Computational Linguistics: Human Language Technologies, Volume 1 (Long and Short Papers)*, pages 4171–4186, Minneapolis, Minnesota. Association for Computational Linguistics.

Jesse Dodge, Gabriel Ilharco, Roy Schwartz, Ali Farhadi, Hannaneh Hajishirzi, and Noah Smith. 2020. Fine-tuning pretrained language models: Weight initializations, data orders, and early stopping. *arXiv preprint arXiv:2002.06305*.

Allyson Ettinger, Ahmed Elgohary, and Philip Resnik. 2016. Probing for semantic evidence of composition by means of simple classification tasks. In *Proceedings of the 1st Workshop on Evaluating Vector-Space Representations for NLP*, pages 134–139, Berlin, Germany. Association for Computational Linguistics.

Danilo Giampiccolo, Bernardo Magnini, Ido Dagan, and Bill Dolan. 2007. The third pascal recognizing textual entailment challenge. In *Proceedings of the ACL-PASCAL Workshop on Textual Entailment and Paraphrasing*, RTE '07, page 1–9, USA. Association for Computational Linguistics.

John Hewitt and Percy Liang. 2019. Designing and interpreting probes with control tasks. In *Proceedings of the 2019 Conference on Empirical Methods in Natural Language Processing and the 9th International Joint Conference on Natural Language Processing (EMNLP-IJCNLP)*, pages 2733–2743, Hong Kong, China. Association for Computational Linguistics.

John Hewitt and Christopher D. Manning. 2019. A structural probe for finding syntax in word representations. In *Proceedings of the 2019 Conference of the North American Chapter of the Association for Computational Linguistics: Human Language Technologies, Volume 1 (Long and Short Papers)*, pages 4129–4138, Minneapolis, Minnesota. Association for Computational Linguistics.

Dieuwke Hupkes, Sara Veldhoen, and Willem Zuidema. 2018. Visualisation and'diagnostic classifiers' reveal how recurrent and recursive neural networks process hierarchical structure. *Journal of Artificial Intelligence Research*, 61:907–926.

Najoung Kim, Roma Patel, Adam Poliak, Patrick Xia, Alex Wang, Tom McCoy, Ian Tenney, Alexis Ross, Tal Linzen, Benjamin Van Durme, Samuel R. Bowman, and Ellie Pavlick. 2019. Probing what different NLP tasks teach machines about function word comprehension. In *Proceedings of the Eighth Joint Conference on Lexical and Computational Semantics (*SEM 2019)*, pages 235–249, Minneapolis, Minnesota. Association for Computational Linguistics.

Katarzyna Krasnowska-Kieraś and Alina Wróblewska. 2019. Empirical linguistic study of sentence embeddings. In *Proceedings of the 57th Annual Meeting of the Association for Computational Linguistics*, pages 5729–5739, Florence, Italy. Association for Computational Linguistics.

Zhenzhong Lan, Mingda Chen, Sebastian Goodman, Kevin Gimpel, Piyush Sharma, and Radu Soricut. 2020. Albert: A lite bert for self-supervised learning of language representations. In *International Conference on Learning Representations*.

Yongjie Lin, Yi Chern Tan, and Robert Frank. 2019. Open sesame: Getting inside BERT's linguistic knowledge. In *Proceedings of the 2019 ACL Workshop BlackboxNLP: Analyzing and Interpreting Neural Networks for NLP*, pages 241–253, Florence, Italy. Association for Computational Linguistics.

Nelson F. Liu, Matt Gardner, Yonatan Belinkov, Matthew E. Peters, and Noah A. Smith. 2019a. Linguistic knowledge and transferability of contextual representations. In *Proceedings of the 2019 Conference of the North American Chapter of the Association for Computational Linguistics: Human Language Technologies, Volume 1 (Long and Short Papers)*, pages 1073–1094, Minneapolis, Minnesota. Association for Computational Linguistics.

Yinhan Liu, Myle Ott, Naman Goyal, Jingfei Du, Mandar Joshi, Danqi Chen, Omer Levy, Mike Lewis, Luke Zettlemoyer, and Veselin Stoyanov. 2019b. Roberta: A robustly optimized bert pretraining approach. *arXiv preprint arXiv:1907.11692*.

Amil Merchant, Elahe Rahimtoroghi, Ellie Pavlick, and Ian Tenney. 2020. What happens to bert embeddings during fine-tuning? *arXiv preprint arXiv:2004.14448*.

Stephen Merity, Caiming Xiong, James Bradbury, and Richard Socher. 2017. Pointer sentinel mixture models. *ArXiv*, abs/1609.07843.

Adam Paszke, Sam Gross, Francisco Massa, Adam Lerer, James Bradbury, Gregory Chanan, Trevor Killeen, Zeming Lin, Natalia Gimelshein, Luca Antiga, Alban Desmaison, Andreas Kopf, Edward Yang, Zachary DeVito, Martin Raison, Alykhan Tejani, Sasank Chilamkurthy, Benoit Steiner, Lu Fang, Junjie Bai, and Soumith Chintala. 2019. Pytorch: An imperative style, high-performance deep learning library. In H. Wallach, H. Larochelle, A. Beygelzimer, F. d' Alché-Buc, E. Fox, and R. Garnett, editors, *Advances in Neural Information Processing Systems 32*, pages 8026–8037. Curran Associates, Inc.

Matthew Peters, Mark Neumann, Mohit Iyyer, Matt Gardner, Christopher Clark, Kenton Lee, and Luke Zettlemoyer. 2018. Deep contextualized word representations. In *Proceedings of the 2018 Conference of the North American Chapter of the Association for Computational Linguistics: Human Language Technologies, Volume 1 (Long Papers)*, pages 2227–2237, New Orleans, Louisiana. Association for Computational Linguistics.

Jason Phang, Thibault Févry, and Samuel R Bowman. 2018. Sentence encoders on stilts: Supplementary training on intermediate labeled-data tasks. *arXiv preprint arXiv:1811.01088*.

Yada Pruksachatkun, Jason Phang, Haokun Liu, Phu Mon Htut, Xiaoyi Zhang, Richard Yuanzhe Pang, Clara Vania, Katharina Kann, and Samuel R Bowman. 2020. Intermediate-task transfer learning with pretrained models for natural language understanding: When and why does it work? *arXiv preprint arXiv:2005.00628*.

Alec Radford, Jeff Wu, Rewon Child, David Luan, Dario Amodei, and Ilya Sutskever. 2019. Language models are unsupervised multitask learners. *OpenAI Blog*, 1(8):9.

Pranav Rajpurkar, Jian Zhang, Konstantin Lopyrev, and Percy Liang. 2016. SQuAD: 100,000+ questions for machine comprehension of text. In *Proceedings of the 2016 Conference on Empirical Methods in Natural Language Processing*, pages 2383–2392, Austin, Texas. Association for Computational Linguistics.

Anna Rogers, Olga Kovaleva, and Anna Rumshisky. 2020. A primer in bertology: What we know about how bert works. *arXiv preprint arXiv:2002.12327*.

Y. Rubner, C. Tomasi, and L. J. Guibas. 1998. A metric for distributions with applications to image databases. In *Sixth International Conference on Computer Vision (IEEE Cat. No.98CH36271)*, pages 59–66.

Xing Shi, Inkit Padhi, and Kevin Knight. 2016. Does string-based neural MT learn source syntax? In *Proceedings of the 2016 Conference on Empirical Methods in Natural Language Processing*, pages 1526–1534, Austin, Texas. Association for Computational Linguistics.

Richard Socher, Alex Perelygin, Jean Wu, Jason Chuang, Christopher D. Manning, Andrew Ng, and Christopher Potts. 2013. Recursive deep models for semantic compositionality over a sentiment treebank. In *Proceedings of the 2013 Conference on Empirical Methods in Natural Language Processing*, pages 1631–1642, Seattle, Washington, USA. Association for Computational Linguistics.

Alon Talmor, Yanai Elazar, Yoav Goldberg, and Jonathan Berant. 2019. oLMpics–On what Language Model Pre-training Captures. *arXiv preprint arXiv:1912.13283*.

Ian Tenney, Dipanjan Das, and Ellie Pavlick. 2019a. BERT rediscovers the classical NLP pipeline. In *Proceedings of the 57th Annual Meeting of the Association for Computational Linguistics*, pages 4593–4601, Florence, Italy. Association for Computational Linguistics.

Ian Tenney, Patrick Xia, Berlin Chen, Alex Wang, Adam Poliak, R Thomas McCoy, Najoung Kim, Benjamin Van Durme, Sam Bowman, Dipanjan Das, and Ellie Pavlick. 2019b. What do you learn from context? probing for sentence structure in contextualized word representations. In *International Conference on Learning Representations*.

Ashish Vaswani, Noam Shazeer, Niki Parmar, Jakob Uszkoreit, Llion Jones, Aidan N Gomez, Ł ukasz Kaiser, and Illia Polosukhin. 2017. Attention is all you need. In I. Guyon, U. V. Luxburg, S. Bengio, H. Wallach, R. Fergus, S. Vishwanathan, and R. Garnett, editors, *Advances in Neural Information Processing Systems 30*, pages 5998–6008. Curran Associates, Inc.

Alex Wang, Jan Hula, Patrick Xia, Raghavendra Pappagari, R. Thomas McCoy, Roma Patel, Najoung Kim, Ian Tenney, Yinghui Huang, Katherin Yu, Shuning Jin, Berlin Chen, Benjamin Van Durme, Edouard Grave, Ellie Pavlick, and Samuel R. Bowman. 2019a. Can you tell me how to get past sesame street? sentence-level pretraining beyond language modeling. In *Proceedings of the 57th Annual Meeting of the Association for Computational Linguistics*, pages 4465–4476, Florence, Italy. Association for Computational Linguistics.

Alex Wang, Amanpreet Singh, Julian Michael, Felix Hill, Omer Levy, and Samuel R. Bowman. 2019b. GLUE: A multi-task benchmark and analysis platform for natural language understanding. In *International Conference on Learning Representations*.

Alex Warstadt, Amanpreet Singh, and Samuel R Bowman. 2018. Neural network acceptability judgments. *arXiv preprint arXiv:1805.12471*.

Thomas Wolf, Lysandre Debut, Victor Sanh, Julien Chaumond, Clement Delangue, Anthony Moi, Pierric Cistac, Tim Rault, R'emi Louf, Morgan Funtowicz, and Jamie Brew. 2019. Huggingface's transformers: State-of-the-art natural language processing. *ArXiv*, abs/1910.03771.

A   Appendices

B   Hyperparameters and Task Statistics

Table 3 shows hyperparamters used when fine-tuning BERT, RoBERTa, and ALBERT on CoLA, SST-2, RTE, and SQuAD. On SST-2 training for a single epoch was sufficient and we didn't observe a significant improvement when training for more epochs.

Table 4 shows number of training and development samples for each of the fine-tuning datasets considered in our experiments. Additionally, we report the metric used to evaluate performance for each of the tasks.

C   Additional Results

Table 5 shows the effect of fine-tuning on RTE and SQuAD on the layer-wise accuracy for all three encoder models across the three probing tasks.

Figure 4 and Figure 5 show the change in probing accuracy Δ (in %) across all probing tasks

Hyperparameter	Value
Learning rate	$2e{-}5$
Warmup steps	10%
Learning rate schedule	warmup-constant
Batch size	32
Epochs	3 (1 for SST-2)
Weight decay	0.01
Dropout	0.1
Attention dropout	0.1
Classifier dropout	0.1
Adam ϵ	$1e{-}8$
Adam β_1	0.9
Adam β_2	0.99
Max. gradient norm	1.0

Table 3: Hyperparamters used when fine-tuning.

Statistics	Task			
	CoLA	SST-2	RTE	SQuAD
training	8.6k	67k	2.5	87k
validation	1,043	874	278	10k
metric	MCC	Acc.	Acc.	EM/F_1

Table 4: Fine-tuning task statistics.

when fine-tuning on CoLA, SST-2, RTE, and SQuAD using CLS-pooling and mean-pooling, respectively. The second y-axis in Figure 4 shows the layer-wise difference after fine-tuning compared to the mean-pooling baseline. Note that only in very few cases this differences is larger than zero.x

Probing Task	BERT-base-cased							
	CLS-pooling				mean-pooling			
	RTE		SQuAD		RTE		SQuAD	
	$0-6$	$7-12$	$0-6$	$7-12$	$0-6$	$7-12$	$0-6$	$7-12$
bigram-shift	-0.21	-0.39	-0.05	-1.50	-0.07	-0.31	-0.54	-1.66
coordinate-inversion	-0.43	-0.36	0.04	0.56	0.05	0.13	-0.03	0.10
odd-man-out	0.09	0.38	-0.21	-1.89	0.09	0.01	-0.28	-1.73

Probing Task	RoBERTa-base							
	CLS-pooling				mean-pooling			
	RTE		SQuAD		RTE		SQuAD	
	$0-6$	$7-12$	$0-6$	$7-12$	$0-6$	$7-12$	$0-6$	$7-12$
bigram-shift	-0.51	0.44	-1.17	-4.33	-0.09	-1.32	-0.28	-3.09
coordinate-inversion	-0.35	3.27	0.29	0.50	0.30	-0.48	0.20	0.05
odd-man-out	-0.11	1.22	-0.76	-3.01	-0.04	-1.96	-0.21	-3.58

Probing Task	ALBERT-base-v1							
	CLS-pooling				mean-pooling			
	RTE		SQuAD		RTE		SQuAD	
	$0-6$	$7-12$	$0-6$	$7-12$	$0-6$	$7-12$	$0-6$	$7-12$
bigram-shift	0.29	-0.43	-0.38	-3.46	-0.13	-0.82	-0.60	-3.11
coordinate-inversion	0.46	-0.44	0.32	0.92	0.13	-0.38	0.04	-0.27
odd-man-out	-0.03	0.17	-0.65	-2.91	-0.17	-0.85	-0.55	-3.18

Table 5: Change in probing accuracy Δ (in %) of **RTE** and **SQuAD** fine-tuned models compared to the pre-trained models when using CLS and mean-pooling. We average the difference in probing accuracy over two different layers groups: layers 0 to 6 and layers 7 to 12.

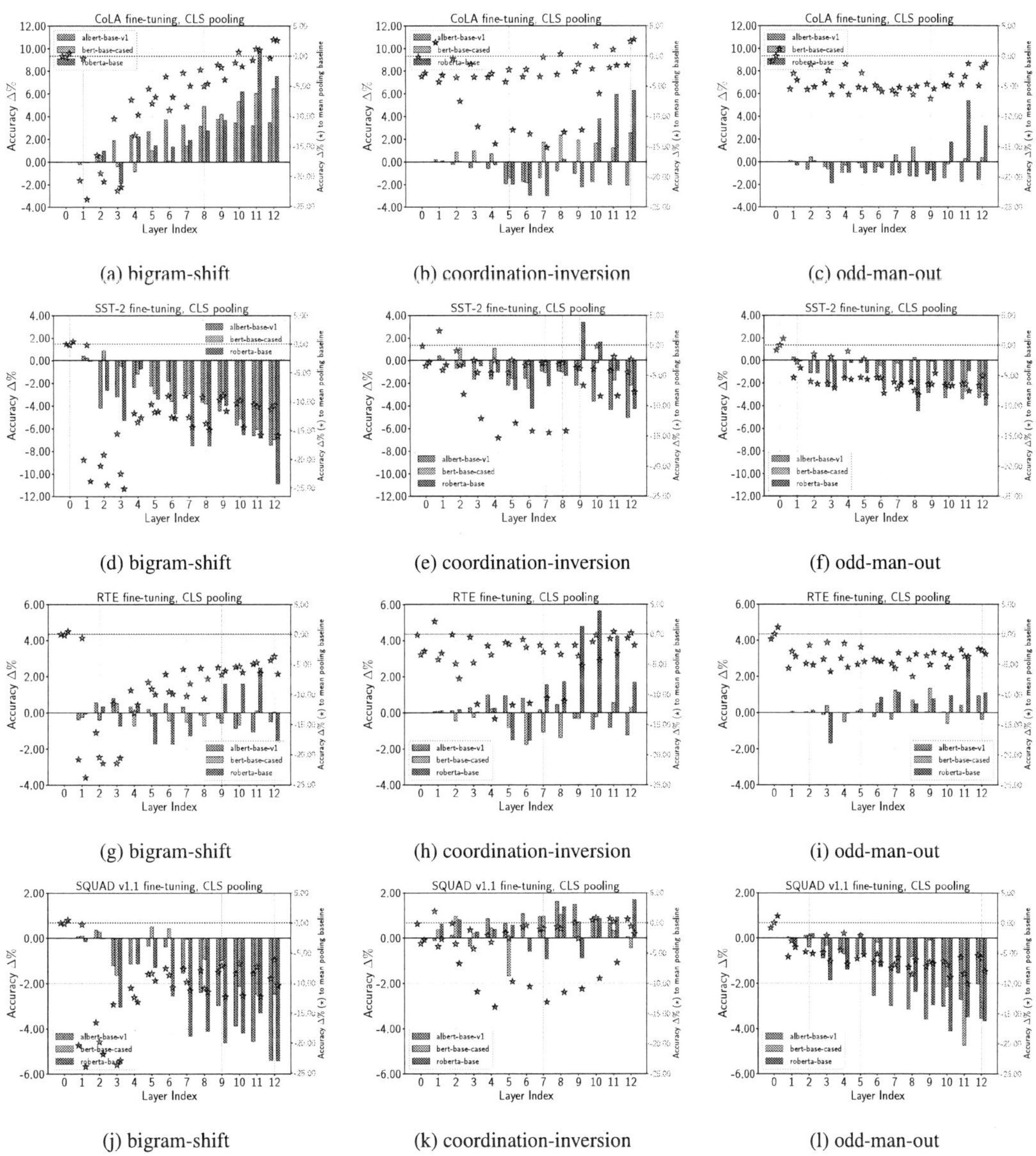

Figure 4: Difference in probing accuracy Δ (in %) when using CLS-pooling after fine-tuning on **CoLA**, **SST-2**, **RTE**, and **SQuAD** for all three encoder models BERT, RoBERTa, and ALBERT across all probing taks considered in this work. The second y-axis shows layer-wise improvement over the mean-pooling baselines (stars) on the respective task.

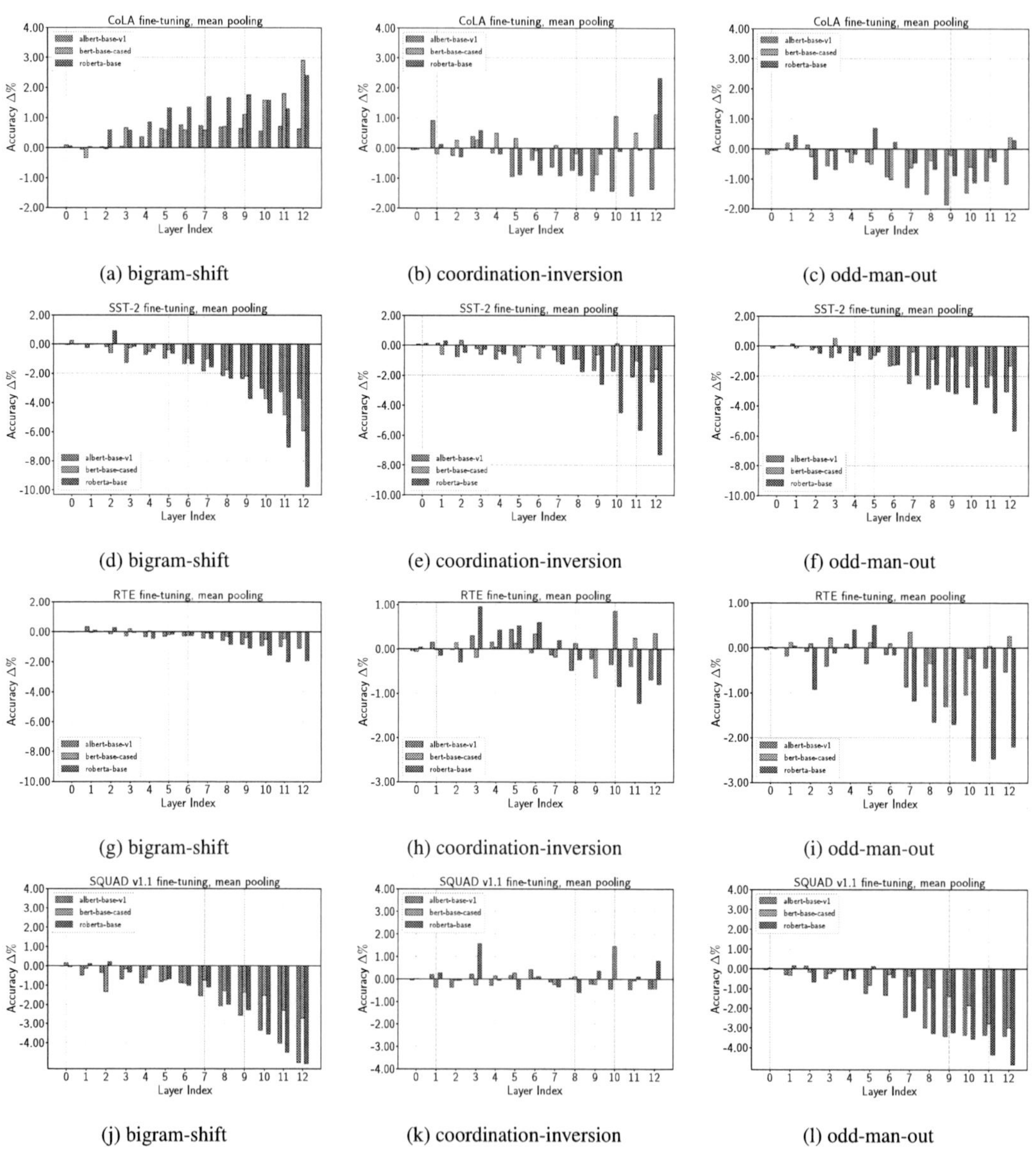

<table>
<tr><td align="center">(a) bigram-shift</td><td align="center">(b) coordination-inversion</td><td align="center">(c) odd-man-out</td></tr>
<tr><td align="center">(d) bigram-shift</td><td align="center">(e) coordination-inversion</td><td align="center">(f) odd-man-out</td></tr>
<tr><td align="center">(g) bigram-shift</td><td align="center">(h) coordination-inversion</td><td align="center">(i) odd-man-out</td></tr>
<tr><td align="center">(j) bigram-shift</td><td align="center">(k) coordination-inversion</td><td align="center">(l) odd-man-out</td></tr>
</table>

Figure 5: Difference in probing accuracy Δ (in %) when using mean-pooling after fine-tuning on **CoLA**, **SST-2**, **RTE**, and **SQuAD** for all three encoder models BERT, RoBERTa, and ALBERT across all probing tasks considered in this work.

Unsupervised Evaluation for Question Answering with Transformers

Lukas Muttenthaler[†‡] **Isabelle Augenstein**[†] **Johannes Bjerva**[†⊙]
[†] Dept. of Computer Science, University of Copenhagen
[‡] Max-Planck-Institute for Human Cognitive and Brain Sciences, Leipzig
[⊙] Dept. of Computer Science, Aalborg University
muttenthaler@cbs.mpg.de, augenstein@di.ku.dk, jbjerva@cs.aau.dk

Abstract

It is challenging to automatically evaluate the answer of a QA model at inference time. Although many models provide confidence scores, and simple heuristics can go a long way towards indicating answer correctness, such measures are heavily dataset-dependent and are unlikely to generalise. In this work, we begin by investigating the hidden representations of questions, answers, and contexts in transformer-based QA architectures. We observe a consistent pattern in the answer representations, which we show can be used to automatically evaluate whether or not a predicted answer span is correct. Our method does not require any labelled data and outperforms strong heuristic baselines, across 2 datasets and 7 domains. We are able to predict whether or not a model's answer is correct with 91.37% accuracy on SQuAD, and 80.7% accuracy on SubjQA. We expect that this method will have broad applications, e.g., in semi-automatic development of QA datasets.

1 Introduction

Evaluation of a QA model usually requires human-annotated answer spans to compare a model's output with. At inference time, however, it is hard to automatically estimate whether an extracted answer span is correct. While many models can provide confidence scores, and other heuristics might be used to deduce whether a prediction is correct, such measures are heavily dataset-dependent and are not likely to generalise. Hence, given a new domain, a costly procedure of human annotation needs to be initiated in order to provide an estimate of the model's accuracy. However, this approach naturally does not scale well to new unlabelled sequences.

In this work, we investigate Transformer-based QA models. We hypothesise that hidden representations of later layers in such models contain information related to correctness of answers. Indeed,

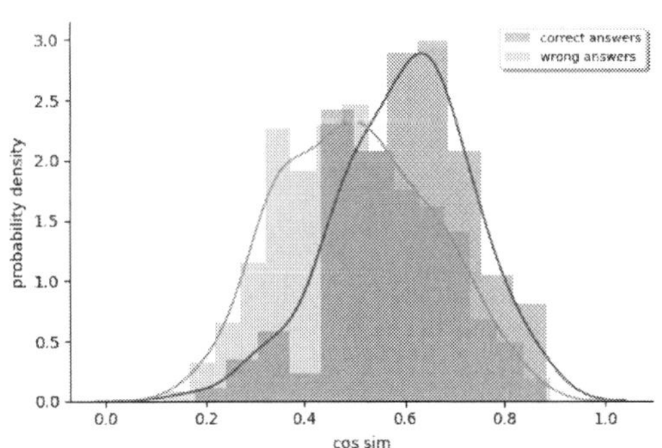

Figure 1: Probability Density Function of the cosine similarities among tokens w.r.t. the true answer span in SQuAD. Correct answer predictions (blue) tend to have higher cosine similarities than wrong answer predictions (orange).

we observe a consistent pattern of closely clustered answer token representations in the top three layers, whenever BERT correctly predicts an answer span (see Figure 2). Conversely, both true and predicted answer spans are clustered together with the remainder of the context, when an answer prediction is erroneous. With clustering, we refer to the transformation of high-dimensional token representations into 2-dimensional vector space through the employment of PCA (Shlens, 2014), followed by t-SNE (van der Maaten and Hinton, 2008). We furthermore see that correctly identified answer spans show a high mean cosine similarity across final layers (Figure 1). Before computing the cosine similarity between token representations, we apply PCA to remove noise, and preserve 95% of the variance in the low-rank, orthogonal representation (see 2.4 for detailed information).

We demonstrate how this insight can be used to predict whether or not a prediction from a Transformer-based QA model is correct. We evaluate our method across two distinct QA datasets in

83

Proceedings of the Third BlackboxNLP Workshop on Analyzing and Interpreting Neural Networks for NLP, pages 83–90
Online, November 20, 2020. ©2020 Association for Computational Linguistics

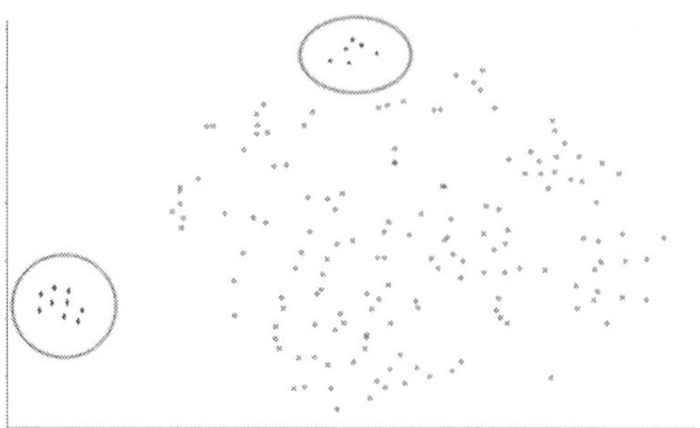

Figure 2: Hidden representations of answers are clustered separately from the remaining context for correct answer span predictions. This clustering is obtained by applying PCA followed by t-SNE (to save computational time), projecting the hidden representations for each token in a randomly chosen input sequence into $\mathbb{R}^2$. Blue diamonds: question. Red stars: answer. Grey dots: context.

English, covering 7 domains. We observe that the pattern can be used for automatic evaluation in both SQuAD v2.0 (Rajpurkar et al., 2018a) and SubjQA (Bjerva et al., 2020), a recently released dataset containing subjective questions and answers across several domains. We show that we can evaluate such models without any labelled test data, with an accuracy of 91.37% on SQuAD, and 80.7% accuracy on the more challenging and diverse SubjQA.

Contributions (i) We investigate how a Transformer-based model encodes correct and incorrect answer spans in its hidden representations; (ii) We propose a method to leverage the information contained in these representations to predict whether a given answer span prediction is correct or not; (iii) We demonstrate that a combination of our method with simple heuristics yields near-perfect predictions of answer correctness.

2 Method

2.1 Data

We experiment on two English-language QA datasets: SQuAD v2.0 (Rajpurkar et al., 2018a) and SubjQA (Bjerva et al., 2020). Since SQuAD v2.0 exclusively contains objective questions that belong to a single domain, `Wikipedia`, we contrast this with the more diverse SubjQA. SubjQA is a recently developed span-selection QA dataset that mainly consists of questions whose answer involves subjective opinions (Bjerva et al., 2020). Answer spans are extracted from review paragraphs that correspond to six different domains,

namely `books`, `electronics`, `groceries`, `movies`, `restaurants`, `tripadvisor`.

2.2 Experimental Setup

For each of our implemented QA models, we use a pre-trained DistilBERT Transformer (Sanh et al., 2019) with one fully-connected output layer on top.[1] Compared to BERT (Devlin et al., 2019), with 12 layers in the base model, DistilBERT only contains 6 Transformer layers, without showing a statistically significant deterioration in performance on a variety of NLP downstream tasks (Wang et al., 2018; Rajpurkar et al., 2018a; Sanh et al., 2019).

We fine-tune BERT on either SQuAD v2.0 (Rajpurkar et al., 2018a) or SubjQA (Bjerva et al., 2020) before investigating the hidden representations. Since we analyse the similarity of hidden representations across answer span tokens, we only fine-tune BERT on answerable questions. Unanswerable questions correspond to BERT's special `[CLS]` token. Therefore, a similarity analysis of hidden representations is not carried out for these.

2.3 Answers are Separate from the Context

In order to investigate if any patterns are visible in the hidden representations, we project them into $\mathbb{R}^2$ via PCA (Shlens, 2014) and t-SNE (van der Maaten and Hinton, 2008) at each Transformer layer. This layer-wise analysis reveals how the model clusters tokens in latent space at each stage of the model. Figure 2 shows this for every token in a randomly chosen sentence pair, for which the model correctly answered the questions. Interestingly, the model clusters both the question and the answer separately from the context. We observe the same pattern with the standard BERT model, which is in line with one recent study (van Aken et al., 2019). It is this pattern which we seek to investigate further.

2.4 Answer Vector Agreements

As depicted in Figure 2, the model's hidden representations for each token in the answer span are clustered more closely in vector space for correct compared to wrong answer span predictions. This is particularly visible in the final three layers of the model, where high-level rather than low-level linguistic features are represented. To verify this observation quantitatively, we compute the average cosine similarities among all hidden representations for each token in the answer span, whenever

---

[1] `https://huggingface.co/transformers/`

the correct answer contains more than a single token. Hence, the following analysis was conducted exclusively for answerable questions since the correct answer span for unanswerable questions corresponds to the special [CLS] token.

Before this computation, we remove all feature representations corresponding to the special [PAD] token and transform the matrix of hidden representations $\mathbf{H}_i \in \mathbb{R}^{T \times D2}$ for each sentence pair sequence $(\mathbf{q}, \mathbf{c})_i$ into a lower-dimensional space to remove noise and exclusively keep those principal components that explain the most variance among the feature representations. In so doing, we use PCA (Shlens, 2014) and retain 95% of the hidden representations' variance. This yields a matrix of transformed hidden representations $\tilde{\mathbf{H}}_i \in \mathbb{R}^{T \times P}$, for each sentence pair $(\mathbf{q}, \mathbf{c})_i$. From the transformed matrix of hidden representations, we extract the matrix of hidden representations corresponding to answer span tokens $\tilde{\mathbf{H}}_{a(i)} \in \mathbb{R}^{T_a \times P}$ to compute the average cosine similarity solely across all answer vectors.

2.5 Average Cosine Similarity

The average cosine similarity among the rows of the answer representation matrix $\tilde{\mathbf{H}}_{a(i)} \in \mathbb{R}^{T_a \times P}$ is computed as follows,

$$\cos_{\tilde{H}(a)_i} = 2 \frac{\sum_j^{T_a} \sum_{k(k>j)}^{T_a} \cos(H_{a(i)}^{j^T}, H_{a(i)}^{k^T}) \in \mathbb{R}^P}{T_a T_a - T_a}, \tag{1}$$

where the cosine similarity between two non-zero vectors $\mathbf{u}$ and $\mathbf{v}$ is defined as,

$$\cos(\mathbf{u}, \mathbf{v}) = \frac{\mathbf{u} \cdot \mathbf{v}}{\|\mathbf{u}\|\|\mathbf{v}\|} = \frac{\sum_{i=1}^n u_i v_i}{\sqrt{\sum_{i=1}^n u_i^2} \sqrt{\sum_{i=1}^n v_i^2}} \tag{2}$$

Since the cosine similarity is a symmetric metric we can compute the sum exclusively over the upper triangular of the similarity matrix (i.e., $\forall k > j$), thus saving computational time. The computation from Equation 1 is performed for the two sets of correct and erroneous answer span predictions separately to inspect potential differences between the two w.r.t. their average cosine similarities. This was done at each Transformer layer $l \in L$, where $L = 6$, to examine shifts in the cosine similarity distributions across space.

---

[2] T is equal to the number of tokens in a sentence pair $(\mathbf{q}, \mathbf{c})_i$ without appended [PAD] tokens and $D = 768$ which is the model's hidden size in each layer.

2.6 Probability Distributions in Correct and Erroneous Answers

Based on having observed this pattern, we investigate how it extends to correct and incorrect answer span predictions. Figure 1 shows that the probability to observe a high internal cosine similarity, $\cos_{\tilde{H}(a)_i}$, in later layers is significantly higher for correct compared to erroneous answer span predictions.

We can formalise the pattern by investigating the cumulative distribution function of the representations (CDF). The probability $p_{(cdf)}^l$ that an observed $\cos_{\tilde{H}(a)_i}$ at Transformer layer l lies in-between two cosine values can be obtained through the following interpolation,

$$\begin{aligned} p_{(cdf)}^l = {} & P(\cos_{\tilde{\mathbf{H}}(a)}^l \leq \cos_{\tilde{H}(a)_i}^l + \Delta) \\ & - P(\cos_{\tilde{\mathbf{H}}(a)}^l \leq \cos_{\tilde{H}(a)_i}^l - \Delta), \end{aligned} \tag{3}$$

where $\cos_{\tilde{\mathbf{H}}(a)}^l$ denotes the train distribution of $\cos_{\tilde{H}(a)_{(i \in N)}}^l$ w.r.t. either correct or erroneous answer span predictions, and Δ is a hyperparameter that refers to the boundaries of the CDF interval. Δ is set to .1 for all experiments, and $p_{(cdf)}^l$ is computed $\forall l \in L$.

We compare the distribution $\cos_{\tilde{\mathbf{H}}(a)}^l$ corresponding to correct and erroneous answer span predictions respectively against each other $\forall l \in L$. We apply independent t-tests, and adjust p-values post-hoc using Bonferroni correction to counteract the multiple comparisons problem. Analyses are performed for both development and test sets.

Table 1 shows that μ with respect to $\cos_{\tilde{\mathbf{H}}(a)}^l$ is significantly higher ($p \leq 1\mathrm{e}{-}4$) for correct compared to erroneous answer span predictions for Transformer layers 5 and 6 across datasets. Apart from SQuAD's test set, the same observation holds for Transformer layer 4. This is in line with both boxplots, CDFs and PDFs, and indicates that an incorrect predictions starts being erroneous at layer 4. This information can be conveniently leveraged for downstream applications, which is what we show in the following section by applying it to the evaluation of QA.

2.7 Predicting Answer Correctness

We train a simple feed-forward neural network (FFNN) with one hidden layer to predict whether the fine-tuned QA-model made an erroneous or correct answer span prediction for an input sequence x_i. The FFNN is defined as follows,

Layer \ Source		SQuAD				SubjQA			
		Dev		Test		Dev		Test	
		p-value	diff.	p-value	diff.	p-value	diff.	p-value	diff.
Layer 1		.121	+.037	.312	+.031	.012	−.028	**.000*****	−.034
Layer 2		.069	+.040	.256	+.021	.020	−.036	.001**	−.031
Layer 3		.007**	+.054	.419	+.028	.185	−.027	.232	−.020
Layer 4		.002**	+.061	.422	+.023	**.000*****	+.089	**.000*****	+.109
Layer 5		**.000*****	+.151	**.000*****	+.094	**.000*****	+.115	**.000*****	+.133
Layer 6		**.000*****	+.157	**.000*****	+.095	**.000*****	+.116	**.000*****	+.129

Table 1: Differences between correct and erroneous answer span predictions with respect to $\cos_{\tilde{H}(a)}$ (see Equation 1) at every Transformer layer. p-values refer to statistically significant differences according to Bonferroni corrected independent t-tests ($p < .05 =$*, $p < .01 =$ **, $p < .001 =$ ***, $p = .000 \leq 1e - 4$). The difference in mean cosine similarities between prediction sets is captured by the diff. column. + indicates higher $\cos_{\tilde{H}(a)}$ values for correct answer span predictions. Highly statistically significant differences (***) are marked in bold face.

$$z_i = W_i^{M \times M} x_i^{M \times 1} + b_i^{M \times 1} \qquad (4)$$

$$y_i = \sigma(W_i^{1 \times M} z_i^{M \times 1} + b_i^{1 \times 1}), \qquad (5)$$

where σ denotes the sigmoid function. The sigmoid function was applied to the FFNN's raw output logits since an answer span prediction could either be correct or incorrect.

2.8 Model training

	SQuAD		SubjQA	
Dev	Test		Dev	Test
700	843		475	1145

Table 2: Number of examples in the leveraged development (i.e., train) and test sets.

Each FFNN is trained for a maximum number of 25 epochs until convergence. For optimization, we use Adam (Kingma and Ba, 2015) with a learning rate of $\eta = .01$ and a weight decay of .005 (this is equivalent to the L2 norm). Gradients are clipped whenever $||\frac{\partial L}{\partial \theta}|| \geq 10$. Input sequences are presented to the model in mini-batches of 8. The FFNN is implemented in PyTorch (Paszke et al., 2019). Both BERT for QA and the FFNN are trained and evaluated on a single Titan X GPU with 12 GB memory. Usually, a dataset is split into three parts, namely a train, a development, and a test set, where the latter two splits together comprise approx. 20-30% of the original dataset. Note that train and test datasets for SQuAD are equally large, and for SubjQA the test set even contains more than twice as many examples as the train set (see Table 2). Our train sets are the actual development sets (excluding unanswerable questions) with respect to the official QA datasets since we do not want to perform computations on hidden representations the QA model did produce during training. As such, we ascertain that the FFNN is trained on data the BERT model has never encountered during QA training. Hence, we cannot leverage development sets, and are limited to small training sets, which in turn further enhances the generalisability and potential of our approach.

We leverage one of the following three feature sets as inputs to the FFNN,

1. Raw. For each sentence pair, x_i, we extract $\cos_{\tilde{H}(a)_i}$ and the standard deviation (s) w.r.t. the vector of cosine similarities among the rows of the matrix $\tilde{\mathbf{H}}_{a(i)} \in \mathbb{R}^{T_a \times P}$, where $i \neq j$, at every Transformer layer. Hence, $M = 2 \times L$.

2. Approximation. We multiply element-wise or concatenate $p^l_{(cdf)} \ \forall \ l \in L$ with the raw cosine vector (see above). However, instead of knowing to which train distribution the observed $\cos^l_{\tilde{H}(a)_i}$ belongs, we approximate $p^l_{(cdf)}$ at test time with weighting $\cos^l_{\tilde{\mathbf{H}}(a)}$ w.r.t. correct and erroneous predictions differently (see Section 2.9). Hence, $M = 2 \times L$ (weighting) or $M = 2 \times 2 \times L$ (concat).

3. CDF-aware. Instead of approximating $p^l_{(cdf)}$, the model is aware of whether an observed $\cos^l_{\tilde{H}(a)_i}$ must be interpolated given the distribution of correct or erroneous predictions. Again, the vector of $p^l_{(cdf)} \ \forall \ l \in L$ is concatenated or multiplied element-wise with

the `raw cosine` vector. Hence, $M = 2 \times 2 \times L$ (concat) or $M = 2 \times L$ (weighting). This shows whether the FFNN benefits from information about the *true* train CDFs, establishing the performance ceiling when approximating $p^l_{(cdf)}$ without information loss.

2.9 Approximating CDFs

Since at test time we are not aware of whether a BERT for QA model predicted an answer span correctly or erroneously, we have implemented two different weighting strategies to approximate the true $p^l_{(cdf)} \; \forall \, l \in L$. $\cos^l_{\tilde{\mathbf{H}}(a)}$ denotes the train distribution of $\cos^l_{\tilde{H}(a)_i} \; \forall \, i \in N$ with respect to either erroneous or correct answer span predictions. Note, one must interpolate $\cos^l_{\tilde{H}(a)_i}$ given either of the two train distributions to yield $p^l_{(cdf)}$. Thus, one is required to infer to which of the two train distributions an observed $\cos^l_{\tilde{H}(a)_i}$ at test time probably belongs to. We approximated as follows,

1. `Distance`. Here, we simply compute the distance between an observed $\cos^l_{\tilde{H}(a)_i}$ to the centroid of each of the two train distributions $\cos^l_{\tilde{\mathbf{H}}(a)}$. We leveraged the inverse distance as w^l_i, such as,

$$
\begin{aligned}
w^l_{i(correct)} &= 1 - \left(\cos^l_{\tilde{H}(a)_i} - \mu^l_{i(correct)} \right) \\
w^l_{i(incorrect)} &= 1 - \left(\cos^l_{\tilde{H}(a)_i} - \mu^l_{i(incorrect)} \right),
\end{aligned}
\tag{6}
$$

where an w^l_i is higher, if $\cos^l_{\tilde{H}(a)_i}$ happens to be closer to the mean of a train distribution.

2. `CDF properties`. In this approximation, we exploited the mathematical properties of CDFs. In general, the smaller $|P(\cos^l_{\tilde{\mathbf{H}}(a)} \leq \cos^l_{\tilde{H}(a)_i}) - P(\cos^l_{\tilde{\mathbf{H}}(a)} \geq \cos^l_{\tilde{H}(a)_i})|$ is, the higher is the likelihood that an observed $\cos^l_{\tilde{H}(a)_i}$ belongs to this CDF as it denotes the area under the curve with the highest probability mass, which is considered the center. Hence, we exploited the inverse of the obtained value as w^l_i, such as,

$$
\begin{aligned}
w^l_{i(correct)} &= \\
1 - |P(&\cos^l_{\tilde{\mathbf{H}}(a)} \, (correct) \leq \cos^l_{H\tilde{(a)}_i}) \\
&- P(\cos^l_{\tilde{\mathbf{H}}(a)} \, (correct) \geq \cos^l_{\tilde{H}(a)_i})| \\
w^l_{i(incorrect)} &= \\
1 - |P(&\cos^l_{\tilde{\mathbf{H}}(a)} \, (incorrect) \leq \cos^l_{\tilde{H}(a)_i}) \\
&- P(\cos^l_{\tilde{\mathbf{H}}(a)} \, (incorrect) \geq \cos^l_{\tilde{H}(a)_i})|,
\end{aligned}
\tag{7}
$$

where w^l_i becomes large, the smaller $|P(\cos^l_{\tilde{\mathbf{H}}(a)} \leq \cos^l_{\tilde{H}(a)_i}) - P(\cos^l_{\tilde{\mathbf{H}}(a)} \geq \cos^l_{\tilde{H}(a)_i})|$ is.

For both approaches, we approximated the true $p_{(cdf)i}{}^l$ through a weighted sum of $p_{(cdf)i(correct)}{}^l$ and $p_{(cdf)i(incorrect)}{}^l$ through the following computation,

$$
\begin{aligned}
p_{(cdf)i}{}^l &= \\
\frac{1}{2} \times &\left(p_{(cdf)i(correct)}{}^l \times w^l_{i(correct)} \right) \\
&+ \left(p_{(cdf)i(correct)}{}^l \times w^l_{i(incorrect)} \right)
\end{aligned}
\tag{8}
$$

In initial experiments, we examined both approximation strategies. Due to `Distance` resulting in higher macro $F1$-scores than approximating through `CDF properties`, results are reported only for `Distance`. However, the difference between the two approaches was not significant, and might require further examination in follow-up studies.

Baselines We compare the features obtained with our method against the following three baselines: (i) `Majority`, (ii) `QA concat` (hidden representations of question and answer), and (iii) `Heuristic` (e.g. n-gram overlap features).

1. `Majority`. This approach simply predicts the most common class (i.e., correct or erroneous answer span prediction).

2. `QA concat`. Concatenation of the average hidden representation w.r.t. the predicted answer span and question at last Transformer layer, where $x_i \in \mathbb{R}^{2 \times 768}$. Hence, $M = 1536$.

3. `Heuristic`. Intuitively reasonable features, where $x_i \in \mathbb{R}^9$. Hence, $M = 9$.

   (a) length of the predicted answer span;

Method \ Source	SQUAD	SUBJQA
MAJORITY	45.65%	42.11%
QA CONCAT	63.62%	46.44%
HEURISTIC	87.23%	61.90%
$\cos_{raw}$	49.19%	69.36%
$\cos_{weight}$	63.63%	58.44%
$\cos_{concat}$	55.28%	68.14%
HEURISTIC $\oplus$ $\cos_{raw}$	87.90%	74.56%
HEURISTIC $\oplus$ $\cos_{weight}$	**88.43%**	72.29%
HEURISTIC $\oplus$ $\cos_{concat}$	88.33%	**76.42%**
$\cos_{weight}$ (CDF-aware)	78.58%	83.38%
$\cos_{concat}$ (CDF-aware)	69.14%	90.46%

Table 3: Macro $F1$-scores for the binary classification task of predicting whether a fine-tuned BERT for QA model correctly or incorrectly predicted an answer span. $F1$-scores were averaged over five different random seeds. Best scores are depicted in bold face.

(b) average n-gram overlap between predicted answer and question (i.e., BLEU score);

(c) cosine similarity between the average hidden representation w.r.t. the predicted answer span and question at last Transformer layer;

(d) vector of unigram, bigram, and trigram overlaps between predicted answer and question, normalized by the number of tokens in the answer and the question.

3 Results

3.1 Unsupervised QA Evaluation

Table 3 shows that solely exploiting $\cos_{\tilde{\mathbf{H}}(a)}$ or additionally informing the model about $p_{(cdf)}$ outperforms all baselines for two out of three approaches when evaluating on SubjQA (rightmost column). Interestingly, results slightly differ when examining QA-performance for SQuAD (centre column). The heuristics baseline yields a macro $F1$-score of 87.23%, outperforming the two other baselines by a large margin, and performing better than our proposed approaches. However, concatenating the features from the heuristics baseline with `raw` or `approximation`, further improves upon this strong baseline across both datasets, achieving 88.43% and 76.42% macro $F1$ for SQuAD and SubjQA respectively. For SubjQA, this leads to an absolute improvement of 14.5% over the strongest baseline, and suggests that information about $\cos_{\tilde{\mathbf{H}}(a)}$ is decisive to predict a QA model's answer span prediction with respect to this dataset.

The results obtained from the CDF-aware model show that further informing the model about $p_{(cdf)}$ $\forall\, l \in L$ has enormous potential to predict whether a BERT for QA model made a mistake or not. The $F1$-score of 90.46% indicates that mistakes might be predicted almost faultlessly by more sophisticated approximation methods, even without concatenating heuristic features.

Scaling $\cos_{\tilde{H}(a)_i}{}^{l}$ with $p_{(cdf)_i^l}$ appears to work better for SQuAD than concatenating $\cos^{l}_{\tilde{H}(a)_i}$ and $p^{l}_{(cdf)_i}$, whereas it is the other way around for SubjQA. Hence, combining the two information sources is crucial across datasets but which merging strategy works best is dataset dependent, and might be a function of dataset complexity or number of context domains since these are the variables in which SubjQA and SQuAD differ.

3.2 Error analysis

We investigate two examples where HEURISTIC features alone did not suffice to yield a correct prediction. Given the question from SQuAD *"What term did Eisenhower use to describe the character of communism?"*, the heuristic fails to identify the model's output as an incorrect answer. Similarly, given the question from SubjQA *"Are there any reviews on bath options at this hotel?"* and the correct model answer *"great bathroom"*, the heuristic fails to identify this as a correct answer. The concatenation of $\cos_{\tilde{H}(a)}$, and additional information about $p_{(cdf)}$ were necessary to obtain correct predictions. We further see that the observed $\cos_{\tilde{H}(a)}$ values are in line with our qualitative and statistical analyses. $\cos_{\tilde{H}(a)}$ is significantly higher in the final three Transformer layers for a correct prediction, and remains unchanged for erroneous predictions (see Table 4 for more details).

4 Related Work

Since automatic evaluation is considered an important topic in other areas of NLP, e.g. MT (Papineni et al., 2002) and summarisation (Owczarzak et al., 2012), we want to draw attention to such techniques for QA. To the best of our knowledge, ours is the first proposal unsupervised QA evaluation method.

One recent study which we take inspiration from present a layer-wise analysis of BERT's Transformer layers to investigate how BERT answers questions (van Aken et al., 2019). For each Transformer layer, they project the model's hidden representations into $\mathbb{R}^2$ to illustrate how BERT clusters

SOURCE	SQUAD	SUBJQA
Question	"What term did Eisenhower use to describe the character of communism?"	"Are there any reviews on bath options at this hotel?"
Answer	"atheistic"	"great bathroom"
BERT QA	incorrect	correct
HEURISTIC	correct ✗	incorrect ✗
HEURISTIC $\oplus \cos_w$	incorrect ✓	-
HEURISTIC $\oplus \cos_c$	-	correct ✓
$\cos^l_{\tilde{H}(a)} \ \forall l \in L$	$[0.07, 0.16, 0.26, 0.27, 0.31, 0.20]$	$[0.06, 0.14, 0.29, 0.62, 0.63, 0.55]$

Table 4: Error analysis. $\cos^l_{\tilde{H}(a)}$ is presented for each of the six Transformer layers.

different parts of an input sequence while searching for an answer span. We replicate their findings for SQuAD, and show that this insight holds across two datasets and seven domains through observing the same patterns w.r.t. SubjQA. However, we use this qualitative analysis just as an initial step from which we start extracting information to develop an unsupervised QA evaluation method.

Arkhangelskaia and Dutta (2019) investigate which tokens in sentence pairs receive particular attention by BERT's self-attention mechanisms to answer a question, and how the multi-headed attention weights change across the different layers. Similarly to van Aken et al. (2019), the authors did solely conduct a qualitative analysis of the model. Contrary to van Aken et al. (2019), the study focuses on a single implementation of BERT and exclusively exploited SQuAD (Rajpurkar et al., 2016, 2018b) without inspecting BERT's behaviour with respect to other, more challenging QA datasets where contexts belong to different domains. The latter is particularly important for real-world settings, which is why we also evaluate on SubjQA.

5 Discussion

The heuristic method we investigate in this work, based on features such as n-gram overlap between question and answer, yielded surprisingly high results on SQuAD. On the other hand, the results for SubjQA were quite low when using the heuristic only. This shows that, although a simple heuristic might be sufficient for a single dataset, it does not necessarily generalise across datasets and domains.

Conversely, our proposed method, which takes answer span similarities into account, was highly successful on SubjQA without the need for any heuristic features, but only outperformed the SQuAD baseline by 15-20% macro F1 score. Combining the two methods yielded the best results across both data sets and all domains. This demonstrates that the information contained in the heuristic approach and in our proposed method are complementary.

5.1 Error analysis

The concatenation of $\cos_{\tilde{H}(a)}$, and further information about $p_{(cdf)}$ were necessary to obtain correct predictions. The observed $\cos_{\tilde{H}(a)}$ values are in line with our qualitative and statistical analyses. $\cos_{\tilde{H}(a)}$ is significantly higher in the final three Transformer layers for a correct prediction, and remains unchanged for erroneous predictions (see last row in Table 4). It is interesting to note that for a correct answer span prediction $\cos_{\tilde{H}(a)}$ increases considerably from layer 3 to layer 4, but no notable change can be observed thereafter.

6 Conclusion

We have shown that the hidden representations of answers in transformer-based models can be used to predict whether or not that answer is correct. In combination with heuristic methods, we are able to predict the correctness of answers with a macro F1 score of 88.38% for SQuAD and 76.42% for SubjQA. Apart from the applications in unsupervised evaluation of QA, we expect that this method can be applied to semi-automatic generation of QA datasets.

Acknowledgements

The authors would like to thank the anonymous reviewers for their feedback which contributed to improving the final version of the paper.

References

Betty van Aken, Benjamin Winter, Alexander Löser, and Felix A. Gers. 2019. How does bert answer questions? a layer-wise analysis of transformer representations. In *Proceedings of the 28th ACM International Conference on Information and Knowledge Management*, CIKM '19, page 1823–1832, New York, NY, USA. Association for Computing Machinery.

Ekaterina Arkhangelskaia and Sourav Dutta. 2019. Whatcha lookin' at? deeplifting bert's attention in question answering. *CoRR*, abs/1910.06431.

Johannes Bjerva, Nikita Bhutani, Behzad Golshan, Wang-Chiew Tan, and Isabelle Augenstein. 2020. SubjQA: A dataset for Subjectivity and Review Comprehension. In *Proceedings of the 2020 Conference on Empirical Methods in Natural Language Processing*. Association for Computational Linguistics.

Jacob Devlin, Ming-Wei Chang, Kenton Lee, and Kristina Toutanova. 2019. BERT: pre-training of deep bidirectional transformers for language understanding. In *Proceedings of the 2019 Conference of the North American Chapter of the Association for Computational Linguistics: Human Language Technologies, NAACL-HLT 2019, Minneapolis, MN, USA, June 2-7, 2019, Volume 1 (Long and Short Papers)*, pages 4171–4186. Association for Computational Linguistics.

Diederik P. Kingma and Jimmy Ba. 2015. Adam: A method for stochastic optimization. In *3rd International Conference on Learning Representations, ICLR 2015, San Diego, CA, USA, May 7-9, 2015, Conference Track Proceedings*.

Laurens van der Maaten and Geoffrey Hinton. 2008. Visualizing data using t-SNE. *Journal of Machine Learning Research*, 9:2579–2605.

Karolina Owczarzak, John M. Conroy, Hoa Trang Dang, and Ani Nenkova. 2012. An assessment of the accuracy of automatic evaluation in summarization. In *Proceedings of Workshop on Evaluation Metrics and System Comparison for Automatic Summarization@NACCL-HLT 2012, Montrèal, Canada, June 2012, 2012*, pages 1–9. Association for Computational Linguistics.

Kishore Papineni, Salim Roukos, Todd Ward, and Wei-Jing Zhu. 2002. Bleu: a method for automatic evaluation of machine translation. In *Proceedings of the 40th Annual Meeting of the Association for Computational Linguistics, July 6-12, 2002, Philadelphia, PA, USA*, pages 311–318. ACL.

Adam Paszke, Sam Gross, Francisco Massa, Adam Lerer, James Bradbury, Gregory Chanan, Trevor Killeen, Zeming Lin, Natalia Gimelshein, Luca Antiga, Alban Desmaison, Andreas Kopf, Edward Yang, Zachary DeVito, Martin Raison, Alykhan Tejani, Sasank Chilamkurthy, Benoit Steiner, Lu Fang, Junjie Bai, and Soumith Chintala. 2019. Pytorch: An imperative style, high-performance deep learning library. In H. Wallach, H. Larochelle, A. Beygelzimer, F. d'Alché Buc, E. Fox, and R. Garnett, editors, *Advances in Neural Information Processing Systems 32*, pages 8024–8035. Curran Associates, Inc.

Pranav Rajpurkar, Robin Jia, and Percy Liang. 2018a. Know what you don't know: Unanswerable questions for squad. In *Proceedings of the 56th Annual Meeting of the Association for Computational Linguistics, ACL 2018, Melbourne, Australia, July 15-20, 2018, Volume 2: Short Papers*, pages 784–789. Association for Computational Linguistics.

Pranav Rajpurkar, Robin Jia, and Percy Liang. 2018b. Know what you don't know: Unanswerable questions for squad. In *Proceedings of the 56th Annual Meeting of the Association for Computational Linguistics, ACL 2018, Melbourne, Australia, July 15-20, 2018, Volume 2: Short Papers*, pages 784–789. Association for Computational Linguistics.

Pranav Rajpurkar, Jian Zhang, Konstantin Lopyrev, and Percy Liang. 2016. Squad: 100, 000+ questions for machine comprehension of text. In *Proceedings of the 2016 Conference on Empirical Methods in Natural Language Processing, EMNLP 2016, Austin, Texas, USA, November 1-4, 2016*, pages 2383–2392. The Association for Computational Linguistics.

Victor Sanh, Lysandre Debut, Julien Chaumond, and Thomas Wolf. 2019. Distilbert, a distilled version of BERT: smaller, faster, cheaper and lighter. *CoRR*, abs/1910.01108.

Jonathon Shlens. 2014. A tutorial on principal component analysis. *CoRR*, abs/1404.1100.

Alex Wang, Amanpreet Singh, Julian Michael, Felix Hill, Omer Levy, and Samuel R. Bowman. 2018. GLUE: A multi-task benchmark and analysis platform for natural language understanding. In *Proceedings of the Workshop: Analyzing and Interpreting Neural Networks for NLP, BlackboxNLP@EMNLP 2018, Brussels, Belgium, November 1, 2018*, pages 353–355. Association for Computational Linguistics.

Unsupervised Distillation of Syntactic Information from Contextualized Word Representations

Shauli Ravfogel[*][1,3]   **Yanai Elazar**[*][1,3]   **Jacob Goldberger**[2]   **Yoav Goldberg**[1,3]

[1]Computer Science Department, Bar Ilan University
[2]Faculty of Engineering, Bar Ilan University
[3]Allen Institute for Artificial Intelligence
{shauli.ravfogel, yanaiela,yoav.goldberg}@gmail.com
jacob.goldberger@biu.ac.il

Abstract

Contextualized word representations, such as ELMo and BERT, were shown to perform well on various semantic and syntactic task. In this work, we tackle the task of unsupervised disentanglement between semantics and structure in neural language representations: we aim to learn a transformation of the contextualized vectors, that discards the lexical semantics, but keeps the structural information. To this end, we automatically generate groups of sentences which are structurally similar but semantically different, and use metric-learning approach to learn a transformation that emphasizes the structural component that is encoded in the vectors. We demonstrate that our transformation clusters vectors in space by structural properties, rather than by lexical semantics. Finally, we demonstrate the utility of our distilled representations by showing that they outperform the original contextualized representations in a few-shot parsing setting.

1   Introduction

Human language[1] is a complex system, involving an intricate interplay between meaning (semantics) and structural rules between words and phrases (syntax). Self-supervised neural sequence models for text trained with a language modeling objective, such as ELMo (Peters et al., 2018), BERT (Devlin et al., 2019), and RoBERTA (Liu et al., 2019b), were shown to produce representations that excel in recovering both structure-related information (Gulordava et al., 2018; van Schijndel and Linzen, 2018; Wilcox et al., 2018; Goldberg, 2019) as well as in semantic information (Yang et al., 2019; Joshi et al., 2019).

In this work, we study the problem of disentangling structure from semantics in neural language

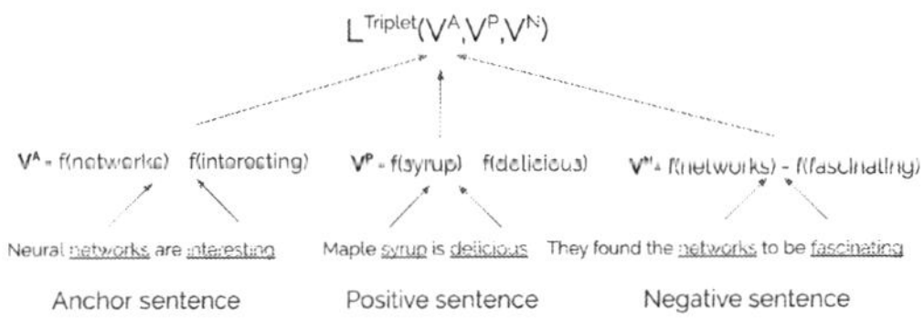

Figure 1: An illustration of triplet-loss calculation. Pairs of words are represented by the difference between their transformation f, which is identical for all words. The pairs of words in the anchor and positive sentences are lexically different, but structurally similar. The negative example presented here is especially challenging, as it is lexically similar, but structurally different.

representations: we aim to extract representations that capture the structural function of words and sentences, but which are not sensitive to their content. For example, consider the sentences:

1. Neural networks are interesting.

2. I study neural networks.

3. Maple syrup is delicious.

4. John loves maple syrup.

While (1) and (3) are different in content, they share a similar structure, the corresponding words in them, while unrelated in meaning,[2] serve the same function. Similarly for sentences (2) and (4). In contrast, sentence (1) shares the phrase *neural networks* with sentence (2), and *maple syrup* is shared between (3) and (4).[3] While the two occurrences of each phrase share the meaning, they are used in different structural (syntactic) configurations, serving different roles within the sentence

---

[*]Equal contribution
[1]In this work we focus on English.

[2]We focus on lexical semantics.
[3]There is a syntactic distinction between the two, with "maple" being part of a noun compound and "neural" being an adjective. However, we focus in their similarity as noun modifiers in both phrases.

Proceedings of the Third BlackboxNLP Workshop on Analyzing and Interpreting Neural Networks for NLP, pages 91–106
Online, November 20, 2020. ©2020 Association for Computational Linguistics

(appearing in subject vs object position).[4] We seek a representation that will expose the similarity between "networks" in (1) and "syrup" in (2), while ignoring the similarity between "syrup" in (2) and "syrup" in (4).

We seek a function from contextualized word representations to a space that exposes these similarities. Crucially, we aim to do this in an unsupervised manner: we do not want to inform the process of the kind of structural information we want to obtain. We do this by learning a transformation that attempts to remove the lexical-semantic information in a sentence, while trying to preserve structural properties.

Disentangling syntax from lexical semantics in word representations is a desired property for several reasons. From a purely scientific perspective, once disentanglement is achieved, one can better control for confounding factors and analyze the knowledge the model acquires, e.g. attributing the predictions of the model to one factor of variation while controlling for the other. In addition to explaining model predictions, such disentanglement can be useful for the comparison of the representations the model acquires to linguistic knowledge. From a more practical perspective, disentanglement can be a first step toward controlled generation/paraphrasing that considers only aspects of the *structure*, akin to the style-transfer works in computer vision, i.e., rewriting a sentence while preserving its structural properties while ignoring its *meaning*, or vice-versa. It can also inform search-based application in which one can search for "similar" texts while controlling various aspects of the desired similarity.

To achieve this goal, we begin with the intuition that the structural component in the representation (capturing the *form*) should remain the same regardless of the lexical semantics of the sentence (the *meaning*). Rather than beginning with a parsed corpus, we automatically generate a large number of structurally-similar sentences, without presupposing their formal structure (§3.1). This allows us to pose the disentanglement problem as a metric-learning problem: we aim to learn a transformation of the contextualized representation, which is *invariant* to changes in the lexical semantics within each group of structurally-similar sentences (§3.3). We demonstrate the structural properties captured

by the resulting representations in multiple experiments (§4), among them automatic identification of structurally-similar words and few-shot parsing.

We release our code at `https://github.com/shauli-ravfogel/NeuralDecomposition`.

2 Related Work

The problem of disentangling different sources of variation has long been studied in computer vision, and was recently applied to neural models (Bengio et al., 2013; Mathieu et al., 2016; Hadad et al., 2018). Such disentanglement can assist in learning representations that are invariant to specific factors, such as pose-invariant face-recognition (Peng et al., 2017) or style-invariant digit recognition (Narayanaswamy et al., 2017). From a generative point of view, disentanglement can be used to modify one aspect of the input (e.g., "style"), while keeping the other factors (e.g., "content") intact, as done in neural image style-transfer (Gatys, 2017).

In NLP, disentanglement is much less researched. In controlled natural language generation and style transfer, several works attempted to disentangle factors of variation such as sentiment or age of the writer, with the intention to control for those factors and generate new sentences with specific properties (Sohn et al., 2015; Ficler and Goldberg, 2017; Lample et al., 2018), or transfer existing sentences to similar sentences that differ only in the those properties. The latter goal of style transfer is often realized by learning representations which are invariant to the controlled attributes (Fu et al., 2018; Hu et al., 2017).

Another main line of work which is relevant to our approach is that of probing. The concept, originally introduced by Adi et al. (2016) and Hupkes et al. (2018), relies on training classifiers (probes) to expose symbolic linguistic information that is encoded in the model. A large body of works have shown sensitivity to both semantic (Tenney et al., 2019a; Richardson et al., 2019) and syntactic (Tenney et al., 2019b; Lin et al., 2019; Reif et al., 2019; Hewitt and Manning, 2019; Liu et al., 2019a) information. Hewitt and Manning (2019) demonstrated that it is possible to train a linear transformation, under which squared euclidean distance between transformed contextualized word vectors correspond to the distances between the respective words in the syntactic tree. Li and Eisner (2019) have used a variational estimation method (Alemi et al., 2016) of the information-bottleneck principle

---

[4]These differences in syntactic position are also of relevance to language modeling, as different positions may pose different restrictions on the words that can appear in them.

(Tishby et al., 1999) to extract word embeddings that are useful to the end task of parsing.

While impressive, those works presuppose a specific syntactic structure (e.g. annotated parse tree) and use this linguistic signal to learn the probe in a supervised manner. This approach can introduce confounding between *extracting* information and *learning* it by the probe (Hewitt and Liang, 2019; Ravichander et al., 2020; Maudslay et al., 2020; Elazar et al., 2020). In contrast, we aim to *expose* the structural information encoded in the network in an unsupervised manner, without pre-supposing an existing syntactic annotation scheme.

3 Method

Our goal is to learn a function $f : \mathbb{R}^n \mapsto \mathbb{R}^m$, which operates on contextualized word representations x and extracts vectors $f(x)$ which make the structural information encoded in x more salient, while discarding as much lexical information as possible. In the sentences "Maple syrup is delicious" and "Neural networks are interesting", we want to learn a function f such that $f(v^3_{\text{syrup}}) \approx f(v^1_{\text{networks}})$, where v^i_{word} is the contextualized vector representation of the word in sentence i. We also want $f(v^4_{\text{syrup}}) \approx f(v^2_{\text{networks}})$, while keeping $f(v^1_{\text{networks}}) \not\approx f(v^2_{\text{networks}})$.

Moreover, we would like the *relation* between the words "maple" and "delicious" in the third sentence, to be similar to the relation between "neural" and "interesting" in the first sentence: $\text{pair}(v^3_{\text{maple}}, v^3_{\text{delicious}}) \approx \text{pair}(v^1_{\text{neural}}, v^1_{\text{interesting}})$. Operatively, we represent pairs of words (x, y) by the difference between their transformation $f(x) - f(y)$, and aim to learn a function f that preserves: $f(v^3_{\text{maple}}) - f(v^3_{\text{delicious}}) \approx f(v^1_{\text{neural}}) - f(v^1_{\text{interesting}})$. The choice to represent pairs this way was inspired by several works that demonstrated that nontrivial semantic and syntactic relations between uncontextualized word representations can be approximated by simple vector arithmetic (Mikolov et al., 2013a,b; Levy and Goldberg, 2014).

To learn f, we start with groups of sentences such that the sentences within each group are known to share structure but differ in lexical semantics. We call the sentences in each group *structurally equivalent*. Figure 2 shows an example of two structurally equivalent sets. Acquiring such sets is challenging, especially if we do not assume a known syntactic formalism and cannot mine for sentences based on their observed tree structures.

To this end, we automatically generate the sets starting with known sentences and sampling variants from a language model (§3.1). Our sentence-set generation procedure ensures that words from the same set that share an index also share their structural function. We call such words *corresponding*.

We now proceed to learn a function f to map contextualized vectors of corresponding words (and the relations between them, as described above) to neighbouring points in the space.

We train f such that the representation assigned to positive pairs — pairs that share indices and come from the same equivalent set — is distinguished from the representations of negative pairs — challenging pairs that come from different sentences, and thus do not share the structure of the original pair, but can, potentially, share their lexical meaning. We do so using Triplet loss, which pushes the representations of pairs coming from the same group closer together (§3.3). Figure 1 sketches the network.

3.1 Generating Structurally-similar Sentences

In order to generate sentences that approximately share their structure, we sequentially replace content words in the sentence with other content words, while aiming to maintain the grammatically of the sentence, and keep its structure intact.

Since we do not want to rely on syntactic annotation when performing this replacement, we opted to use a pre-trained language model – BERT – under the assumption that strong neural language models do implicitly encode many of the syntactic restrictions that apply to words in different grammatical functions (e.g., we assume that BERT would not predict a transitive verb in the place of an intransitive verb, or a verb that accepts a complement in the place of a verb that does not accept a complement). While this assumption seems to hold with regard to basic distinctions such as transitive vs. intransitive verbs, its validity is less clear in the more nuanced cases, in which small differences in the surface level can translate to substantial differences in abstract syntactic structure – such as replacing a control verb with a raising verb. This is a limitation of the current approach, although we find that the average sentence we generate is grammatical and similar in structure to the original sentence. Moreover, as our goal is to *expose* the structural similarity encoded in neural language models, we

- When a train ticket is purchased, a contract is established
- When a travel document is acquired, a settlement is declared
- When a winning vehicle is obtained, a competition is introduced
- When a winning bid is announced, a winner is created

- Shapley participated in the `` great debate '' with heber d
- Khan joined in the `` silent discussion '' with e t
- Parker figured in the `` coming showdown '' with block leader
- Moore engaged in the `` modern struggle '' with joseph israel

Figure 2: Two groups of structurally-equivalent sentences. In each group, the first sentence is original sentence from Wikipedia, and the sentences below it were generated by the process of repeated BERT substitution. Some sets of corresponding words–that is, words that share the same structural function–are highlighted in the same color.

find it reasonable to only capture the distinctions that are captured by modern language models.

Implementation We start each group with a Wikipedia sentence, for which we generate $k = 6$ equivalent sentences by iterating over the sentence from left to right sequentially, masking the ith word, and replacing it with one of BERT's top-30 predictions. To increase semantic variability, we perform the replacement in place (online): after randomly choosing a guess w, we insert w to the sentence at index i, and continue guessing the $i + 1$ word based on the modified sentence.[5] We exclude a closed set of a few dozens of words (mostly function words) and keep them unchanged in all k variations of a sentence. We further maintain structural correctness by maintaining the POS[6], and encourage semantic diversity by the auto-regressive replacement process. In Table 6 in the Appendix we show some additional generated groups. The sets in Figure 2 were generated using this method.

3.2 Word Representation

We sample $N = 150,000$ random sentences and use the our method to generate $900,000$ equivalent sets E of structurally equivalent sentences. Then, we encode the sentences and randomly collect $1,500,000$ contextualized vector representations of words from these sets, resulting in $1,500,000$ training pairs and 200,000 evaluation pairs for the training process of f. We experiment with both ELMo and BERT language models. In average, we sample 11 word-pairs from each group of equivalent sentences. For ELMo, we represent each word in context as a concatenation of the last two ELMo layers (excluding the word embedding layer, which is not contextualized and therefore irrelevant for

structure), resulting in representations of dimension 2048. For BERT, we concatenate the mean of the words' representation[7] across all contextualized layers of BERT-Large, with the representation of layer 16, which was found by Hewitt and Manning (2019) most indicative of syntax.

3.3 Triplet Loss

We learn the mapping function f using triplet loss (Figure 1). Given a group of equivalent sentences E_i, we randomly choose two sentences to be the anchor sentence S^A and the positive sentence S^P, and sample two different word indices $\{i_1, i_2\}$. Let $S^A[i_1]$ be the contextualized representation of the i_1th word in sentence S^A. The words $S^A[i_1]$ and $S^A[i_2]$ from the anchor sentence would form a representation of a pair of words, which should be close to the pair $S^P[i_1]$, $S^P[i_2]$ from the positive sentence.

We represent pairs as their differences after transformation, resulting in the anchor pair V^A and positive pair V^P:

$$V^A = f(S^A[i_1]) - f(S^A[i_2]) \qquad S^A \in E_i \quad (1)$$
$$V^P = f(S^P[i_1]) - f(S^P[i_2]) \qquad S^P \in E_i \quad (2)$$

where f is the parameterized syntactic transformation we aim to learn. We also consider a negative pair:

$$V^N = f(S^N[j_1]) - f(S^N[j_2]) \qquad S^N \notin E_i \quad (3)$$

coming from sentence S^N which is not in the equivalent set.

As f has shared parameters for both words in the pair, it can be considered a part of a Siamese network, making our learning procedure an instance of a triplet Siamese network (Schroff et al., 2015). We choose f to be a simple model: a single linear layer that maps from dimensionality 2048 to 75.

---

[5]We note that this process bears some similarity to Gibbs sampling from BERT conditioned LM.

[6]We maintain the same POS so that the dataset will be valid for other tasks that require structure-preserving variants. However, In practice, we did not observe major differences when repeating the experiments reported here without the POS-preserving constraint when generating the data.

[7]Since BERT uses word-piece tokenization, we take the first token to represent each word.

The dimensions of the transformation were chosen according to development set performance.

We use triplet loss (Schroff et al., 2015) to move the representation of the anchor vector V^A closer to the representation of the positive vector V^P and farther apart from the representation of the negative vector V^N. Following Hoffer and Ailon (2015), we calculate the softmax version of the triplet loss:

$$L^{triplet}(V^A, V^P, V^N) = \frac{e^{d(V^A, V^P)}}{e^{d(V^A, V^P)} + e^{d(V^A, V^N)}} \tag{4}$$

where $d(x, y) = 1 - \frac{x^\top y}{\|x\|\|y\|}$ is the cosine-distance between the vectors x and y. Note that $L^{triplet} \to 0$ as $\frac{d(V^A, V^P)}{d(V^A, V^N)} \to 0$, as expected. The triplet objective is optimized end-to-end using the Adam optimizer (Kingma and Ba, 2015). We train for 5 epochs with a mini-batch of size 500 [8], and take the last model as the final syntactic extractor. During training, the gradient backpropagates through the pair vectors to the parameters f of the Siamese model, to get representations of individual words that are similar for corresponding words in equivalent sentences. We note that we do not back-propagate the gradient to the contextualized vectors: we keep them intact, and only adjust the learned transformation.

Hard negative sampling We obtain the negative vectors V^N using hard negative sampling. For each mini-batch B, we collect 500 $\{\mathrm{V}_i^A, \mathrm{V}_i^P\}$ pairs, each pair taken from an equivalent set E_i. The negative instances V_i^N are obtained by searching the batch for a vector that is closest to the anchor and comes from a different set:

$$V_i^N = \arg\min_{V_{j \neq i}^A \in B} d(V_i^A, V_j^A). \tag{5}$$

In addition, we enforce a symmetry between the anchor and positive vectors, by adding a pair (positive, anchor) for each pair (anchor, positive) in B. That is, V_i^N is the "most misleading" word-pair vector: it comes from a sentence that has a different structure than the structure of V_i^A sentence, but is the closest to V_i^A in the mini-batch.

4 Experiments and Analysis

We have trained the syntactic transformation f in a way that should encourage it to retain the structural

---

[8]A large enough mini-batch is necessary to find challenging negative examples.

information encoded in contextualized vectors, but discard other information. We assess the representations the model acquired in an unsupervised manner, by evaluating the extent to which the local neighbors of each transformed contextualized vector $f(x)$ share known structural properties, such as grammatical function within the sentence. For the baseline, we expect the neighbors of each vector to share a mix of semantic and syntactic properties. For the transformed vectors, we expect the neighbors to share mainly syntactic properties. Finally, we demonstrate that in a few-shot setting, our representations outperform the original ELMO representation, indicating they are indeed distilled from syntax, and discard other information that is encoded in ELMO vectors but is irrelevant for the extraction of the structure of a sentence.

Corpus For training the transformation f, we rely on 150,000 sentences from Wikipedia, tokenized and POS-tagged by spaCy (Honnibal and Johnson, 2015; Honnibal and Montani, 2017). The POS tags are used in the equivalent set generation to filter replacement words. Apart from POS tagging, we do not rely on any syntactic annotation during training. The evaluation sentences for the experiments mentioned below are sampled from a collection of 1,000,000 original and unmodified Wikipedia sentences (different from those used in the model training).

4.1 Qualitative Analysis

t-SNE Visualization Figure 3 shows a 2-dimensional t-SNE projection (Maaten and Hinton, 2008) of 15,000 random content words. The left panel projects the original ELMo states, while the right panel is the syntactically transformed ones. The points are colored according to the dependency label (relation to parent) of the corresponding word, predicted by the parser.

In the original ELMo representation most states – apart from those characterized by a specific part-of-speech, such as amod (adjectives, in orange) or nummod (numbers, in light green) – do not fit well into a single cluster. In contrast, the syntactically transformed vectors are more neatly clustered, with some clusters, such as direct objects (brown) and prepositional-objects (blue), that are relatively separated after, but not before, the transformation. Interestingly, some functions that used to be a single group in ELMo (like the adjectives in orange, or the noun-compounds in green) are

Type	Text
Q1	*in this way of thinking, an impacting **projectile** goes into an ice-rich layer – but no further.*
N	they generally have a pre-engraved rifling band to engage the rifled launch tube, spin-stabilizing the **projectile**, hence the term "rifle".
NT	to achieve a large explosive yield, a linear implosion **weapon** needs more material, about 13 kgs.
Q2	*the mint's **director** at the time, nicolas peinado, was also an architect and made the initial plans.*
N	the **director** is angry at crazy loop and glares at him, even trying to get a woman to kick crazy loop out of the show (which goes unsuccessfully).
NT	jetley's **mother**, kaushaliya rani, was the daughter of high court advocate shivram jhingan.
Q3	*their first project is software that **lets** players connect the company's controller to their device.*
N	you could try use norton safe web, which **lets** you enter a website and show whether there seems to be anything bad in it.
NT	the city offers a route-finding website that **allows** users to map personalized bike routes.

Table 1: Text examples for a few query words (in the Q rows, in bold), and their closest neighbours before (N) and after (NT) the transformation.

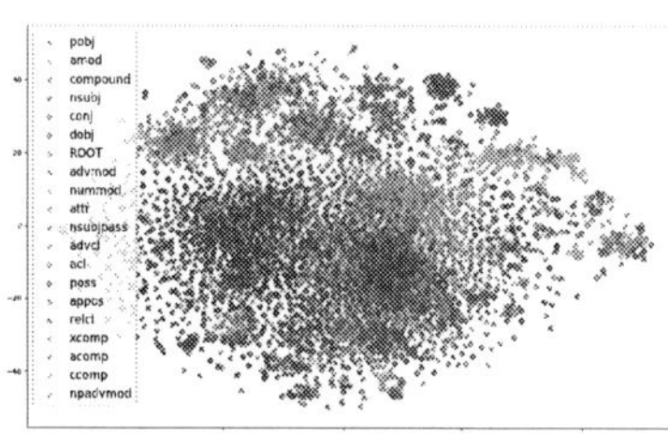

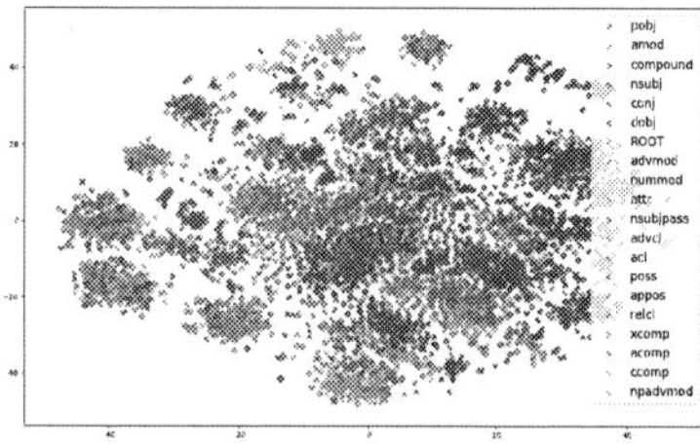

Figure 3: t-SNE projection of ELMO states, colored by syntactic function, before (upper) and after (lower) the syntactic transformation.

now split into several clusters, corresponding to their use in different sentence positions, separating for examples adjectives that are used in subject positions from those in object position or within prepositional phrases. Additionally, as noun compounds ("maple" in "maple syrup") and adjectival modifiers ("tasty" in "tasty syrup") are relatively structurally similar (they appear between determiners and nouns within noun phrases, and can move with the noun phrase to different positions), they are split and grouped together in the representation (the green and orange clouds).

To quantify the difference, we run K-means clustering on the projected vectors, and calculate the average cluster purity score as the relative proportion of the most common dependency label in each cluster. The higher this value is, the more the division to clusters reflect division to grammatical functions (dependency labels). We run the clustering with different K values: 10, 20, 40, 80. We find an increase in class purity following our transformation: from scores of 22.6%, 26.8%, 32.6% and 36.4% (respectively) for the original vectors, to scores of 24.3%, 33.4%, 42.1% and 48.0% (respectively) for the transformed vectors.

Examples In Table 1 we present a few query words (Q) and their closest neighbours before (N) and after (NT) the transformation. Note the high structural similarity of the entire sentence, as well as the function of the word within it (Q1: last word of subject NP in a middle clause, Q2: possessed noun in sentence initial subject NP, Q3: head of relative clause of a direct object).

Additional examples (including cases in which the retrieved vector does not share the dependency edge with the query vector) are supplied in Appendix §A.

4.2 Quantitative Evaluation

We expect the transformed vectors to capture more structural and less lexical similarities than the source vectors. We expect each vectors' neighbors in space to share the structural function of the word over which the vector was collected, but not necessarily share its lexical meaning. We focus on the following structural properties: (1) Dependency-tree edge of a given word (dep-edge), that represents its function (subject, object etc.). (2) The dependency edge of the word parent's (head's dep-edge) in the tree – to represent higher level structure, such as a subject that resides within a relative clause, as in the word "man" in the phrase "the child that the man saw". (3) Depth in the dependency tree (distance from the root of the sentence tree). (4) Constituency-parse paths: consider, for example, the sentence "They saw the moon with the telescope". The word "telescope" is a part of a

	Dep. edge	Head's dep. edge	Tree path (complete)	Tree path (L=3)	Tree path (L=2)	Depth (correlation)	Lexical Match
Baseline (all)	0.580	0.473	0.166	0.353	0.566	0.448	0.736
Transformed (all)	0.699	0.603	0.253	0.523	0.735	0.561	0.284
Transformed-untrained (all)	0.461	0.430	0.142	0.319	0.528	0.407	0.680
Baseline (hard)	0.509	0.460	0.160	0.347	0.564	0.430	0.776
Transformed (hard)	0.671	0.591	0.260	0.534	0.751	0.576	0.274

Table 2: Closest-word queries, before and after the application of the syntactic transformation. "Basline" refers to unmodified ELMo vectors, "Transformed" refers to ELMo vectors after the learned syntactic transformation f, and "Transformed-untrained" refers to ElMo vectors, after a transformation that was trained on a randomly-initialized ELMo. "hard" denotes results on the subset of POS tags which are most structurally diverse.

noun-phrase "the telescope", which resides inside a prepositional phrase "with the telescope", which is part of the Verbal phrase "saw with the telescope". The complete constituency path for this word is therefore "NP-PP-VP". We calculate the complete tree path to the root (Tree-path-complete), as well as paths limited to lengths 2 and 3.

For this evaluation, we parse 400,000 random sentences taken from the 1-million-sentences Wikipedia sample, run ELMo and BERT to collect the contextualized representations of the sentences, and randomly choose 400,000 query word vectors (excluding function words). We then retrieve, for each query vector x, the value vector y that is closest to x in cosine-distance, and record the percentage of closest-vector pairs (x, y) that share each of the structural properties listed above. For the tree depth property, we calculate the Pearson correlation between the depths of the queries and the retrieved values. We use the Berkeley Neural Parser (Kitaev and Klein, 2018) for constituency parsing. We exclude function words from the evaluation.

Easier and Harder cases The baseline models tend to retrieve words that are lexically similar. Since certain words tend to appear at above-chance probability in certain structural functions, this can make the baseline be "right for the wrong reason", as the success in the closest-word test reflects lexical similarity, rather than grammatical generalization. To control for this confounding, we sort the different POS tags according to the entropy of their dependency-labels distribution, and repeat the evaluation only for words belonging to those POS tags having the highest entropy (those are the most structurally variant, and tend to appear in different structural functions). The performance of the baselines (ELMo, BERT models) on those words drops significantly, while the performance of our model is only mildly influenced, indicating the superiority of the model in capturing structural rather than

lexical information.

Results The results for ELMo are presented in Table 2. For BERT, we witnessed similar, but somewhat lower, accuracy: for example, 68.1% dependency-edge accuracy, 56.5% head's dependency-edge accuracy, and 22.1% complete constituency-path accuracy. The results for BERT are available in Appendix §B, and for the reminder of the paper, we focus in ELMo. We observe significant improvement over the baseline for all tests. The correlation between the depth in tree of the query and the value words, for examples, rises from 44.8% to 56.1%, indicating that our model encourages the structural property of the depth of the word to be more saliently encoded in its representation compared with the baseline. The most notable relative improvement is recorded with regard to full constituency-path to the root: from 16.6% before the structural transformation, to 25.3% after it – an improvement of 52%. In addition to the increase in syntax-related properties, we observe a sharp drop — from 73.6% to 28.4% — in the proportion of query-value pairs that are lexically identical (lexical match, Table 2). This indicates our transformation f removes much of the lexical information, which is irrelevant for structure. To assess to what extent the improvements stems from the information encoded in ELMo, rather than being an artifact of the triplet-loss training, we also evaluate on a transformation f that was trained on a randomly-initialized ELMo, a surprisingly strong baseline (Conneau et al., 2018). We find this model performs substantially worse than the baseline (Table 2, "Transformed-untrained (all)").

4.3 Minimal Supervision for Structure Distillation: Few-Shot Parsing

The absolute nearest-neighbour accuracy values may appear to be relatively low: for example, only 67.6% of the (query, value) pairs share the same

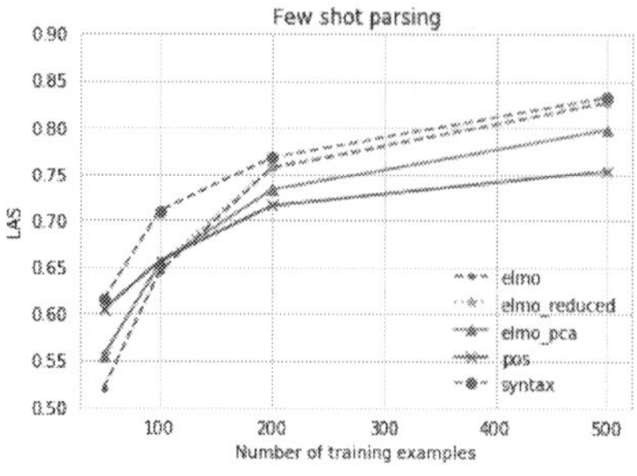

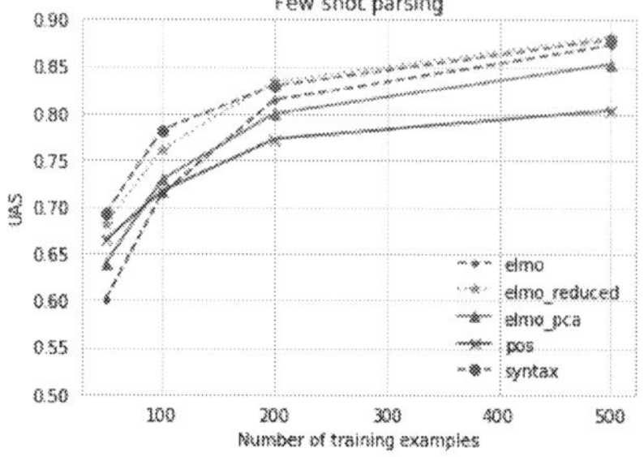

Figure 4: Results of the few-shots parsing setup.

dependency edge.

As the model acquires its representation without being exposed to human-mandated syntactic convention, some of the apparent discrepancies in nearest neighbours may be due to the fact the model acquires different kind of generalization, or learned a representation that emphasizes different kinds of similarities. Still, we expect the resulting (75 dimensional) representations to contain distilled structure information that is mappable to human notions of syntax. To test this, we compare dependency-parsers trained on our representation and on the source representation. If our representation indeed captures structural information, we expect it to excel on a low data setting. To this end, we test our hypothesis with few-shot dependency parsing setup, where we train a model to predict syntactic trees representation with only a few hundred labeled examples.

We use an off-the-shelf dependency parser model (Dozat and Manning, 2016) and swap the pre-trained Glove embeddings (Pennington et al., 2014) with ELMo contextualized embeddings (Peters et al., 2018). In order to have a fair comparison with our method, we use the concatenation of the two last layers of Elmo; we refer to this experiment as *elmo*. As our representation is much smaller than ELMo's (75 as opposed to 2048), a potential issue for a low data setting is the higher number of parameters to optimize in the later case, therefore a lower dimension may achieve better results. We design two additional baselines to remedy this potential issue: (1) Using PCA in order to reduce the representation dimensionality. We randomly chose 1M words from Wikipedia, calculated their representation with ELMo embeddings and performed PCA. This transformation is applied during training on top of ELMo representation while keeping the 75 first components. This experiment is referred to as *elmo-pca*. This representation should perform well if the most salient information in the ELMo representations are structural. We exepct it to not be the case. (2) Automatically learning a matrix that reduces the embedding dimension. This matrix is learned during training and can potentially extract the relevant structural information from the representations. We refer to this experiment as *elmo-reduced*. Additionally, we also compare to a baseline where we use the gold-POS labels as the sole input to the model, by initializing an embedding matrix of the same size for each POS. We refer to this experiment as *pos*. Lastly, we examine the performance of our representation, where we apply our structural extraction method on top of ELMo representation. We refer to this experiment as *syntax*.

We run the few-shot setup with multiple training size values: 50, 100, 200, 500. The results—for both labeled (LAS) and unlabeled (UAS) attachment scores—are presented in Figure 4, and the numerical results are available in the Appendix §C. In the lower training size setting, we obtain the best performances compared to all baselines. The more training data is used, the gap between our representation and the baselines reduced, but the *syntax* representation still outperforms *elmo*. Using gold POS labels as inputs works relatively well with 50 training examples, but it quickly reaches a plato in performance and remains behind the other baselines. Reducing the dimensions with PCA (*elmo-pca*) works considerably worse than ELMo, indicating PCA loses important information. Reducing the dimensions with a learned matrix (*elmo-reduced*) works substantially better than ELMo, and achieve the same UAS as our representation from 200 training sentences onward. However, our transformation was learned in an unsupervised fashion, without access to the syntactic trees.

Finally, when considering the labeled attachment score, where the model is tasked at predicting not only the child-parent relation but also its label, our *syntax* representation outperforms *elmo-reduced*.

5 Conclusion

We propose an unsupervised method for the distillation of structural information from neural contextualized word representations. We used a process of sequential BERT-based substitution to create a large number of sentences which are structurally similar, but semantically different. By controlling for structure while changing lexical choice, we learn a metric under which pairs of words that come from structurally-similar sentences are close in space. We demonstrated that the representations acquired by this method share structural properties with their neighbors in space, and show that with a minimal supervision, those representations outperform ELMo in the task of few-shots parsing. The method is a first step towards a better disentanglement between various kinds of information that is represented in neural sequence models.

The method used to create the structurally equivalent sentences can be useful by its own as a data-augmentation technique. In future work, we aim to extend this method to allow for a more soft alignment between structurally-equivalent sentences.

Acknowledgments

We would like to thank Gal Chechik for providing valuable feedback on early version of this work. This project has received funding from the Europoean Research Council (ERC) under the Europoean Union's Horizon 2020 research and innovation programme, grant agreement No. 802774 (iEXTRACT). Yanai Elazar is grateful to be partially supported by the PBC fellowship for outstanding PhD candidates in Data Science.

References

Yossi Adi, Einat Kermany, Yonatan Belinkov, Ofer Lavi, and Yoav Goldberg. 2016. Fine-grained analysis of sentence embeddings using auxiliary prediction tasks. *CoRR*, abs/1608.04207.

Alexander Alemi, Ian Fischer, Joshua V. Dillon, and Murphy Murphy. 2016. Deep variational information bottleneck. In *Proceedings of the International Conference on Learning Representations (ICLR)*.

Yoshua Bengio, Aaron C. Courville, and Pascal Vincent. 2013. Representation learning: A review and new perspectives. *IEEE Trans. Pattern Anal. Mach. Intell.*, 35(8):1798–1828.

Alexis Conneau, Germán Kruszewski, Guillaume Lample, Loïc Barrault, and Marco Baroni. 2018. What you can cram into a single \\$&!#* vector: Probing sentence embeddings for linguistic properties. In *Proceedings of the 56th Annual Meeting of the Association for Computational Linguistics, ACL 2018, Melbourne, Australia, July 15-20, 2018, Volume 1: Long Papers*, pages 2126–2136.

Jacob Devlin, Ming-Wei Chang, Kenton Lee, and Kristina Toutanova. 2019. BERT: pre-training of deep bidirectional transformers for language understanding. In *Proceedings of the 2019 Conference of the North American Chapter of the Association for Computational Linguistics: Human Language Technologies, NAACL-HLT 2019, Minneapolis, MN, USA, June 2-7, 2019, Volume 1 (Long and Short Papers)*, pages 4171–4186. Association for Computational Linguistics.

Timothy Dozat and Christopher D Manning. 2016. Deep biaffine attention for neural dependency parsing. *arXiv preprint arXiv:1611.01734*.

Yanai Elazar, Shauli Ravfogel, Alon Jacovi, and Yoav Goldberg. 2020. When bert forgets how to pos: Amnesic probing of linguistic properties and mlm predictions.

Jessica Ficler and Yoav Goldberg. 2017. Controlling linguistic style aspects in neural language generation. *arXiv preprint arXiv:1707.02633*.

Zhenxin Fu, Xiaoye Tan, Nanyun Peng, Dongyan Zhao, and Rui Yan. 2018. Style transfer in text: Exploration and evaluation. In *Thirty-Second AAAI Conference on Artificial Intelligence*.

Leon A. Gatys. 2017. *Texture synthesis and style transfer using perceptual image representations from convolutional neural networks*. Ph.D. thesis, University of Tübingen, Germany.

Yoav Goldberg. 2019. Assessing BERT's syntactic abilities. *CoRR*, abs/1901.05287.

Kristina Gulordava, Piotr Bojanowski, Edouard Grave, Tal Linzen, and Marco Baroni. 2018. Colorless green recurrent networks dream hierarchically. In *Proceedings of the Conference of the North American Chapter of the Association for Computational Linguistics: Human Language Technologies, NAACL-HLT*, pages 1195–1205.

Naama Hadad, Lior Wolf, and Moni Shahar. 2018. A two-step disentanglement method. In *IEEE Conference on Computer Vision and Pattern Recognition, (CVPR)*, pages 772–780.

John Hewitt and Percy Liang. 2019. Designing and interpreting probes with control tasks. In *Proceedings of the 2019 Conference on Empirical Methods in Natural Language Processing and the 9th International Joint Conference on Natural Language Processing, EMNLP-IJCNLP 2019, Hong Kong, China, November 3-7, 2019*, pages 2733–2743. Association for Computational Linguistics.

John Hewitt and Christopher D. Manning. 2019. A structural probe for finding syntax in word representations. In *Proceedings of the Conference of the North American Chapter of the Association for Computational Linguistics: Human Language Technologies, NAACL-HLT*, pages 4129–4138.

Elad Hoffer and Nir Ailon. 2015. Deep metric learning using triplet network. In *Similarity-Based Pattern Recognition - Third International Workshop, SIMBAD*, pages 84–92.

Matthew Honnibal and Mark Johnson. 2015. An improved non-monotonic transition system for dependency parsing. In *Proceedings of the 2015 conference on empirical methods in natural language processing*, pages 1373–1378.

Matthew Honnibal and Ines Montani. 2017. spacy 2: Natural language understanding with bloom embeddings, convolutional neural networks and incremental parsing. *To appear*, 7(1).

Zhiting Hu, Zichao Yang, Xiaodan Liang, Ruslan Salakhutdinov, and Eric P. Xing. 2017. Toward controlled generation of text. In *Proceedings of the 34th International Conference on Machine Learning, ICML 2017, Sydney, NSW, Australia, 6-11 August 2017*, pages 1587–1596.

Dieuwke Hupkes, Sara Veldhoen, and Willem H. Zuidema. 2018. Visualisation and 'diagnostic classifiers' reveal how recurrent and recursive neural networks process hierarchical structure. *J. Artif. Intell. Res.*, 61:907–926.

Mandar Joshi, Omer Levy, Daniel S Weld, and Luke Zettlemoyer. 2019. BERT for coreference resolution: Baselines and analysis. *arXiv preprint arXiv:1908.09091*.

Diederik P. Kingma and Jimmy Ba. 2015. Adam: A method for stochastic optimization. In *International Conference on Learning Representations, ICLR*.

Nikita Kitaev and Dan Klein. 2018. Constituency parsing with a self-attentive encoder. In *Proceedings of the Annual Meeting of the Association for Computational Linguistics (ACL)*.

Guillaume Lample, Sandeep Subramanian, Eric Smith, Ludovic Denoyer, Marc'Aurelio Ranzato, and Y-Lan Boureau. 2018. Multiple-attribute text rewriting. In *International Conference on Learning Representations*.

Omer Levy and Yoav Goldberg. 2014. Linguistic regularities in sparse and explicit word representations. In *Proceedings of the eighteenth conference on computational natural language learning*, pages 171–180.

Xiang Lisa Li and Jason Eisner. 2019. Specializing word embeddings (for parsing) by information bottleneck. In *Proceedings of the Conference on Empirical Methods in Natural Language Processing (EMNLP)*.

Yongjie Lin, Yi Chern Tan, and Robert Frank. 2019. Open sesame: Getting inside berts linguistic knowledge. In *Proceedings of the 2019 ACL Workshop BlackboxNLP: Analyzing and Interpreting Neural Networks for NLP*, pages 241–253.

Nelson F Liu, Matt Gardner, Yonatan Belinkov, Matthew Peters, and Noah A Smith. 2019a. Linguistic knowledge and transferability of contextual representations. *arXiv preprint arXiv:1903.08855*.

Yinhan Liu, Myle Ott, Naman Goyal, Jingfei Du, Mandar Joshi, Danqi Chen, Omer Levy, Mike Lewis, Luke Zettlemoyer, and Veselin Stoyanov. 2019b. RoBERTa: A robustly optimized BERT pretraining approach. *CoRR*, abs/1907.11692.

Laurens van der Maaten and Geoffrey Hinton. 2008. Visualizing data using t-SNE. *Journal of Machine Learning Research*, 9:2579–2605.

Michaël Mathieu, Junbo Jake Zhao, Pablo Sprechmann, Aditya Ramesh, and Yann LeCun. 2016. Disentangling factors of variation in deep representation using adversarial training. In *Advances in Neural Information Processing Systems*, pages 5041–5049.

Rowan Hall Maudslay, Josef Valvoda, Tiago Pimentel, Adina Williams, and Ryan Cotterell. 2020. A tale of a probe and a parser. *CoRR*, abs/2005.01641.

Tomas Mikolov, Ilya Sutskever, Kai Chen, Greg S Corrado, and Jeff Dean. 2013a. Distributed representations of words and phrases and their compositionality. In *Advances in neural information processing systems*, pages 3111–3119.

Tomas Mikolov, Wen-tau Yih, and Geoffrey Zweig. 2013b. Linguistic regularities in continuous space word representations. In *Proceedings of the 2013 Conference of the North American Chapter of the Association for Computational Linguistics: Human Language Technologies*, pages 746–751.

Siddharth Narayanaswamy, Brooks Paige, Jan-Willem van de Meent, Alban Desmaison, Noah D. Goodman, Pushmeet Kohli, Frank D. Wood, and Philip H. S. Torr. 2017. Learning disentangled representations with semi-supervised deep generative models. In *Advances in Neural Information Processing Systems*, pages 5925–5935.

Xi Peng, Xiang Yu, Kihyuk Sohn, Dimitris N. Metaxas, and Manmohan Chandraker. 2017. Reconstruction-based disentanglement for pose-invariant face recognition. In *IEEE International Conference on Computer Visionn (ICCV)*, pages 1632–1641.

Jeffrey Pennington, Richard Socher, and Christopher Manning. 2014. Glove: Global vectors for word representation. In *Proceedings of the 2014 conference on empirical methods in natural language processing (EMNLP)*, pages 1532–1543.

Matthew E. Peters, Mark Neumann, Mohit Iyyer, Matt Gardner, Christopher Clark, Kenton Lee, and Luke Zettlemoyer. 2018. Deep contextualized word representations. In *Proceedings of the 2018 Conference of the North American Chapter of the Association for Computational Linguistics: Human Language Technologies, NAACL-HLT 2018, New Orleans, Louisiana, USA, June 1-6, 2018, Volume 1 (Long Papers)*, pages 2227–2237. Association for Computational Linguistics.

Abhilasha Ravichander, Yonatan Belinkov, and Eduard H. Hovy. 2020. Probing the probing paradigm: Does probing accuracy entail task relevance? *CoRR*, abs/2005.00719.

Emily Reif, Ann Yuan, Martin Wattenberg, Fernanda B Viegas, Andy Coenen, Adam Pearce, and Been Kim. 2019. Visualizing and measuring the geometry of bert. In *Advances in Neural Information Processing Systems*, pages 8592–8600.

Kyle Richardson, Hai Hu, Lawrence S Moss, and Ashish Sabharwal. 2019. Probing natural language inference models through semantic fragments. *arXiv preprint arXiv:1909.07521*.

Florian Schroff, Dmitry Kalenichenko, and James Philbin. 2015. FaceNet: A unified embedding for face recognition and clustering. In *IEEE Conference on Computer Vision and Pattern Recognition (CVPR)*.

Kihyuk Sohn, Honglak Lee, and Xinchen Yan. 2015. Learning structured output representation using deep conditional generative models. In *Advances in neural information processing systems*, pages 3483–3491.

Ian Tenney, Dipanjan Das, and Ellie Pavlick. 2019a. BERT rediscovers the classical NLP pipeline. In *Proceedings of the Conference of the Association for Computational Linguistics, ACL*, pages 4593–4601.

Ian Tenney, Patrick Xia, Berlin Chen, Alex Wang, Adam Poliak, R Thomas McCoy, Najoung Kim, Benjamin Van Durme, Sam Bowman, Dipanjan Das, and Ellie Pavlick. 2019b. What do you learn from context? probing for sentence structure in contextualized word representations. In *International Conference on Learning Representations*.

Naftali Tishby, Fernando C Pereira, and William Bialek. 1999. The information bottleneck method. In *Proc. of the Allerton Allerton Conference on Communication, Control and Computing*.

Marten van Schijndel and Tal Linzen. 2018. Modeling garden path effects without explicit hierarchical syntax. In *Proceedings of the 40th Annual Conference of the Cognitive Science Society*, pages 2600–2605. Cognitive Science Society.

Ethan Wilcox, Roger Levy, Takashi Morita, and Richard Futrell. 2018. What do RNN language models learn about filler–gap dependencies? In *Proceedings of the EMNLP Workshop BlackboxNLP: Analyzing and Interpreting Neural Networks for NLP*, pages 211–221. Association for Computational Linguistics.

Wei Yang, Yuqing Xie, Aileen Lin, Xingyu Li, Luchen Tan, Kun Xiong, Ming Li, and Jimmy Lin. 2019. End-to-end open-domain question answering with BERTserini. In *Proceedings of the Conference of the North American Chapter of the Association for Computational Linguistics NAACL-HLT*, pages 72–77.

A Additional Query-Value Examples

- Q: *as they did , the **probability** of an impact event temporarily climbed , peaking at 2 .*
  N: *however , the **probability** of flipping a head after having already flipped 20 heads in a row is simply*
  NT: *during the first year , the **scope** of red terror expanded significantly and the number of executions grew into the thousands .*

- Q: *the **celtics** honored his memory during the following season by retiring his number 35 .*
  N: *the **beatles** performed the song at the 1969 let it be sessions .*
  NT: *the **warriors** dedicated their round five home match to fai 's memory .*

- Q: *in the old zurich war , the swiss confederation plundered the monastery , whose **monks** had fled to zurich .*
  N: *the hridaya stra and the " five meditations " are recited , after which **monks** will be served with the gruel and vegetables .*
  NT: *other commanders were killed and later rooplo kolhi was arrested near pag wool well , where his **troops** were fetching water.*

- Q: *the **main** cause of the punic wars was the conflict of interests between the existing carthaginian empire and the expanding roman republic .*
  N: *the **main** issue was whether or not something had to be directly perceptible (meaning intelligible to an ordinary human being) for it to be a " copy .*
  NT: *the **main** enemy of the game is a sadistic but intelligent arms-dealer known as the jackal , whose guns are fueling the violence in the country .*

- Q: *jones maintained lifelong links with his **native** county , where he had a home , bron menai , dwyran .*
  N: *his association with the bbc ended in 1981 with a move back to his **native** county and itv company yorkshire television , replacing martin tyler as the regional station 's football commentator .*
  NT: *he leaves again for his **native** england , moving to a place near bath , where he works with a powerful local coven .*

- Q: *silver iodate can be **obtained** by reacting silver nitrate (agno3) with sodium iodate .*
  N: *best mechanical strength is **obtained** if both sides of the disc are fused to the same type of glass tube and both tubes are under vacuum .*
  NT: *each of these options can be **obtained** with a master degree from the university along with the master of engineering degree .*

- Q: *it **confirmed** that thomas medwin was a thoroughly learned man , if occasionally imprecise and careless*
  N: *it was **confirmed** that the truth about heather 's murder would be revealed which ultimately led to ben 's departure .*
  NT: *it **proclaimed** that the entire movement of plastic art of our time had been thrown into confusion by the discoveries above-mentioned .*

- Q: *after the death of nadab and abihu , moses **dictated** what was to be done with their bodies .*
  N: *most sources indicate that while no marriage took place between haile melekot and woizero ijigayehu , sahle selassie **ordered** his grandson legitimized .*
  NT: *vvkj pilots who flew the hurricane conversion **considered** it to be superior to the standard model .*

- Q: *letters were delivered to sorters who **examined** the address and placed it in one of a number of " pigeon holes " .*
  N: *i **examined** and reported on the thread called transcendental meditation which appears on the page you linked to .*
  NT: *ronson visits purported psychopaths , as well as psychologists and psychiatrists who have **studied** them , and meets with robert d .*

- Q: *slowboat to hades is a compilation **dvd** by gorillaz , released in october 2006 .*
  N: *the album was released in may 2003 as a single album with a bonus **dvd** .*
  NT: *master series is a compilation **album** by the british synthpop band visage released in 1997 .*

- Q: *however , there are also many **theories** and conspiracies that describe the basis of the plot .*

N: *the name tabasco is not definitively known with a number of **theories** debated among linguists .*
NT: *it is likely that to this day there are some **harrisons** and harrises that are related .*

- Q: *nne , married first , to richard , eldest son of sir richard nagle , **secretary** of state for ireland , temp .*
  N: *in the early 1960s , profumo was the **secretary** of state for war in harold macmillan 's conservative government and was married to actress valerie hobson .*
  NT: *he was born in edinburgh , the son of william simpson , **minister** of the tron church , edinburgh , by his wife jean douglas balderston .*

- Q: *battle of stoke field , the final **engagement** of the wars of the roses .*
  N: *among others , hogan announced the " **engagement** " of utah-born pitcher roy castleton .*
  NT: *song of susannah , the sixth **installment** in the dark tower series .*

- Q: *it vies for **control** with its host , causing physiological changes that will eventually cause the host 's internal organs to explode .*
  N: *hurtig and loewen developed rival factions within the party , and battled for **control** .*
  NT: *players take **control** of each of the four main characters at different times throughout the game , which enables multilateral perspective on the storyline .*

- Q: *as such , radio tirana kept close to the official **policy** of the people 's republic of china , which was also both anti-west and anti-soviet whilst still being socialist in tone .*
  N: *this was in line with the **policy** outlined by constantine vii porphyrogenitus in de administrando imperio of fomenting strife between the rus ' and the pechenegs .*
  NT: *april 2006 , the upr periodically examines the human rights **performance** of all 193 un member states .*

- Q: *the engine was designed to **accept** either regular grade , 87 octane gasoline or premium grade , 91 octane gasoline .*
  N: *for example , an advanced html editing field could **accept** a pasted or inserted image*

and convert it to a data uri to hide the complexity of external resources from the user .
NT: *it uses plug-ins (html parsing technology) to **collect** bibliographic information , videos and patents from webpages .*

- Q: *one such decree was the notorious 1876 ems ukaz , which **banned** the kulishivka and imposed a russian orthography until 1905 (called the yaryzhka , after the russian letter yery) .*
  N: *fin 1612 , the shogun declared a decree that specifically **banned** the killing of cattle .*
  NT: *tannis has **eliminated** the other time lords and set the doctor and the minister against each other .*

- Q: *a 25 degree list was **reduced** to 15 degrees ; men had abandoned ship prematurely - hence the pow .*
  N: *i suggest the article be **reduced** to something over half the size .*
  NT: *the old high school was **converted** into a middle school , until in 1971 the 5 .*

- Q: *the library catalog is maintained on a database that is **made** accessible to users through the internet.*
  N: *this screenshot is **made** for educational use and used for identification purposes in the article on nba on abc .*
  NT: *hpc is the main ingredient in cellugel which is **used** in book conservation .*

- Q: *although he lost , **he** was evaluated highly by kazuyoshi ishii , and he was invited to seidokaikan .*
  N: ***he** attended suny fredonia for one year and in 1976 received a b .*
  NT: *played primarily as a small forward , **he** showed some opportunist play and in his 18 games managed a creditable 12 goals .*

- Q: *for each **round** won , you gain one point towards winning the match .*
  N: *in the fourth **round** , federer beat tommy robredo and equalled jimmy connors ' record of 27 consecutive grand slam quarterfinals .*
  NT: *at the beginning of each **mission** , as well as the end of the last mission , a cutscene is played that helps develop the story .*

B   BERT Closest-Word Results

In Table 3, we present the full quantitative results when using BERT as the encoder. "Baseline" refers to unmodified vectors derived from BERT, and "Transformed" refers to the vectors after the learned syntactic transformation f. "hard" refers to evaluation on the subset of POS tags which are most structurally diverse.

C   Complete Parsing Results

Below are the LAS and UAS scores for the experiments described in §4.

D   Examples of Equivalent Sentences

In Table 6 we present randomly selected examples of groups of structurally-similar sentences (§3.1).

	Dep. edge	Head's dep. edge	Tree path (complete)	Tree path (L=3)	Tree path (L=2)	Depth (correlation)	Lexical Match
Baseline (all)	0.549	0.432	0.146	0.310	0.522	0.436	0.829
Transformed (all)	0.681	0.565	0.221	0.471	0.697	0.597	0.319
Baseline (hard)	0.478	0.429	0.143	0.310	0.521	0.428	0.820
Transformed (hard)	0.652	0.565	0.225	0.482	0.714	0.601	0.300

Table 3: Full quantitative results when using BERT as the encoder. "Baseline" refers to unmodified vectors derived from BERT, and "Transformed" refers to the vectors after the learned syntactic transformation f. "hard" refers to evaluation on the subset of POS tags which are most structurally diverse.

Model	Number of sentences			
	50	100	200	500
POS	0.60	0.65	0.71	0.75
ELMO	0.52	0.64	0.75	0.82
ELMO-reduced	0.55	0.65	0.75	0.82
ELMO-PCA	0.55	0.65	0.73	0.79
ELMO-syntax (ours)	0.61	0.70	0.76	0.83

Table 4: Labeled parsing scores (LAS)

Model	Number of sentences			
	50	100	200	500
POS	0.66	0.71	0.77	0.80
ELMO	0.60	0.71	0.81	0.87
ELMO-reduced	0.68	0.76	0.83	0.88
ELMO-PCA	0.63	0.72	0.79	0.85
ELMO-syntax (ours)	0.69	0.78	0.82	0.87

Table 5: Unlabeled parsing scores (UAS)

#Version	Sentence
Original	the structure is privately owned by the lake-hanford family of aurora , indiana and is not open to the public .
1	the preserve is generally enjoyed by the ecological department of warren , california and is not free to the staff .
2	the park is presently covered by the lake-hanford west of shrewsbury , italy and is not broken to the landscape .
3	the festival is wholly offered by the west club of liberty , arkansas and is not central to the tradition .
4	the pool is mostly administered by the shell town of greenville , maryland and is not navigable to the water .
5	the house is geographically managed by the lake-hanford foundation of ferguson , fl and is not open to the sun .
Original	on november 18th , 2011 , sllner released the studio album mei zuastand which features re-recorded songs from his entire career .
1	on thursday 9th , 1975 , wolf dedicated the label das en imprint which comprises mixed albums from his golden series .
2	on year 13th , 1985 , hoffmann wrote the vinyl mix von deutschland which plays imagined samples from his bible canon .
3	on circa christmas , 2000 , press signed the lp debut re work which involves created phrases from his bible quote .
4	on january 15th , 1995 , sllner wrote the camera y se theory which mixes cast phrases from his experimental archive .
5	on oct 13th , 1983 , hansen organised the compilation concert ha radio which gives launched clips from his small film .
Original	uhm ; we 're not proposing to give rollbackers the reviewer right .
1	ah ; we 're not calling to quote comics the way hello .
2	hi ; we 're not preparing to hear hits the dirt lady .
3	shi ; we 're not asking to put rollbackers the board die .
4	ar ; we 're not expecting to face rollbackers the place fell .
5	whoa ; we 're not getting to detroit wants the boat paid .
Original	coniston water is an example of a ribbon lake formed by glaciation .
1	floating town is an artwork of a concrete area contaminated by mud .
2	vista florida is an isle of a seaside lagoon fed by watershed .
3	pit process is an occurrence of a hollow underground caused by settlement .
4	union pass is an explanation of a highland section developed by anderson .
5	ball phase is an exploration of a basalt basalt influenced by creep .
Original	the highest lookout point , at above sea level , is trimble mountain , off brewer road .
1	the greatest steep elevation , at above east cliff , is green rock , off little neck .
2	the greatest lake club , at above east summit , is swiss cut , off northern pike .
3	the biggest missing asset , at above single count , is local motel , off washington plaza .
4	the smallest public surfing , at above virgin point , is grant lagoon , off white strait .
5	the southwest east boundary , at above water flow , is trim hollow , off east town .
Original	ample sdk is a lightweight javascript library intended to simplify cross-browser web application development .
1	rapid editor is a popular editorial script suited to manage multi domain book edition .
2	free id is a mandatory public implementation written to manage repository generic server environment .
3	solar platform is a native developed stack written to ease regional complex sensing analysis .
4	standard library is a complete python interface required to provide cellular mesh construction engine .
5	flex module is a standardized foundry block applied to facilitate component development common work .
Original	she wore a pale pink gown , silver crown and had pale pink wings .
1	she boasted a large halt purple , fuzzy lip and had twin firm wrists .
2	she spun a thin olive jelly , joined yarn and had large silver bubbles .
3	she flared a high frequency yellow , reddish rose and had fried like moses .
4	she exhibited a small frame overall , broad head and had oval eyed curves .
5	she wrapped a silky ga yellow , moth hide and had homemade gold roses .
Original	tegan is somewhat quiet and is rather scared , but kamryn reasures her everything will be ok .
1	man is slightly pissed and is rather awkward , but kamryn protests her night will be ok .
2	lao is real sad and is rather disappointed , but san figures her story will be ok .
3	daughter is increasingly pregnant and is rather uncomfortable , but ni confirms her birth will be ok .
4	mai is strangely warm and is rather short , but papa wishes her day will be ok .
5	mare is slowly back and is rather upset , but pa asserts her sister will be ok .
Original	shapley participated in the " great debate " with heber d .
1	morris put in the " heroic speech " with heber energy .
2	hall met in the " ninth season " with walton moore .
3	patel helped in the " double coup " with ibn salem .
4	chu sent in the " universal text " with u z .
5	smith exhibited in the " red year " with william james .
Original	the added english voice-over narration by the vampire ancestor removes any ambiguity .
1	the untitled thai adventure script by the light corps includes any future .
2	the improved industrial hole tool by the freeman workshop touches any resistance .
3	the arched robotic interference use by the computer computer checks any message .
4	the fixed regular speech described by the german army encompasses any type .
5	the combined complete phone acquisition by the surround computer marks any microphone .

Table 6: Randomly selected examples of groups of structurally-similar sentences (§3.1)

The Explanation Game:
Towards Prediction Explainability through Sparse Communication

Marcos V. Treviso
Instituto de Telecomunicações
Instituto Superior Técnico
University of Lisbon, Portugal
marcos.treviso@tecnico.ulisboa.pt

André F. T. Martins
Instituto de Telecomunicações
LUMLIS (Lisbon ELLIS Unit)
Instituto Superior Técnico & Unbabel
Lisbon, Portugal
andre.t.martins@tecnico.ulisboa.com

Abstract

Explainability is a topic of growing importance in NLP. In this work, we provide a unified perspective of explainability as a communication problem between an explainer and a layperson about a classifier's decision. We use this framework to compare several explainers, including gradient methods, erasure, and attention mechanisms, in terms of their communication success. In addition, we reinterpret these methods in the light of classical feature selection, and use this as inspiration for new embedded explainers, through the use of selective, sparse attention. Experiments in text classification and natural language inference, using different configurations of explainers and laypeople (including both machines and humans), reveal an advantage of attention-based explainers over gradient and erasure methods, and show that selective attention is a simpler alternative to stochastic rationalizers. Human experiments show strong results on text classification with post-hoc explainers trained to optimize communication success.

1 Introduction

The widespread use of machine learning to assist humans in decision making brings the need for explaining models' predictions (Doshi-Velez, 2017; Lipton, 2018; Rudin, 2019; Miller, 2019). This poses a challenge in NLP, where current state-of-the-art neural systems are generally opaque (Goldberg and Hirst, 2017; Peters et al., 2018; Devlin et al., 2019). Despite the large body of recent work (reviewed in §7), a unified perspective modeling the human-machine interaction—a *communication* process in its essence—is still missing.

Many methods have been proposed to generate explanations. Some neural network architectures are equipped with built-in components—attention mechanisms—which weigh the relevance of input features for triggering a decision (Bahdanau

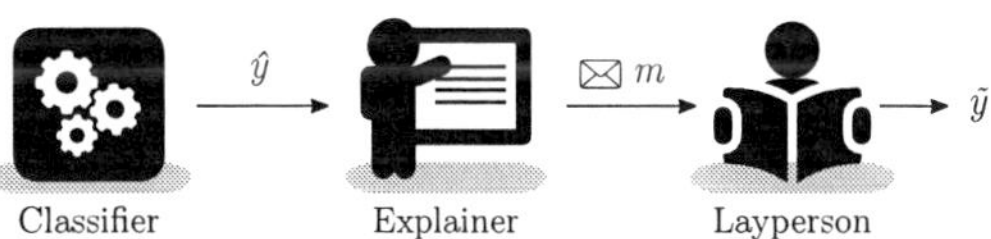

Figure 1: Our framework to model explainability as communication. Predictions $\hat{y}$ are made by a classifier C; an explainer E (either embedded in C or operating post-hoc) accesses these predictions and communicates an explanation (a message m) to the layperson L. Success of the communication is dictated by the ability of L and C to match their predictions: $\tilde{y} \overset{?}{=} \hat{y}$. Both the explainer and layperson can be humans or machines.

et al., 2015; Vaswani et al., 2017). Top-k attention weights provide plausible, but not always faithful, explanations (Jain and Wallace, 2019; Serrano and Smith, 2019; Wiegreffe and Pinter, 2019). Rationalizers with hard attention are arguably more faithful, but require stochastic networks, which are harder to train (Lei et al., 2016; Bastings et al., 2019). Other approaches include gradient methods (Li et al., 2016a; Arras et al., 2017), querying the classifier with leave-one-out strategies (Li et al., 2016a; Feng et al., 2018), or training local sparse classifiers (Ribeiro et al., 2016).

How should these different approaches be compared? Several diagnostic tests have been proposed: Jain and Wallace (2019) assessed the explanatory power of attention weights by measuring their correlation with input gradients; Wiegreffe and Pinter (2019) and DeYoung et al. (2020) developed more informative tests, including a combination of comprehensiveness and sufficiency metrics and the correlation with human rationales; Jacovi and Goldberg (2020) proposed a set of evaluation recommendations and a graded notion of faithfulness. Most proposed frameworks rely on correlations and counterfactual simulation, sidestepping the main practical goal of prediction explainability—the ability to *communicate* an explanation to a human user.

Proceedings of the Third BlackboxNLP Workshop on Analyzing and Interpreting Neural Networks for NLP, pages 107–118
Online, November 20, 2020. ©2020 Association for Computational Linguistics

In this work, we fill the gap above by proposing a unified framework that regards explainability as a **communication problem**. Our framework is inspired by human-grounded evaluation through **forward simulation/prediction**, as proposed by Doshi-Velez (2017, §3.2), where humans are presented with an explanation and an input, and must correctly simulate the model's output (regardless of the true output). We model this process as shown in Figure 1, by considering the interaction between a *classifier* (the model whose predictions we want to explain), an *explainer* (which provides the explanations), and a *layperson* (which must recover the classifier's prediction). We show that different configurations of these components correspond to previously proposed explanation methods, and we experiment with explainers and laypeople being both humans and machines. Our framework also inspires two new methods: embedded explainers based on **selective attention** (Martins and Astudillo, 2016; Peters et al., 2019), and **trainable explainers** based on emergent communication (Foerster et al., 2016; Lazaridou et al., 2016).

Overall, our contributions are:

- We draw a link between recent techniques for explainability of neural networks and classic feature selection in linear models (§2). This leads to new embedded methods for explainability through selective, sparse attention (§3).

- We propose a new framework to assess explanatory power as the communication success rate between an explainer and a layperson (§4).

- We experiment with text classification, natural language inference, and machine translation, using different configurations of explainers and laypeople, both machines (§5) and humans (§6).

2   Revisiting Feature Selection

A common way of generating explanations is by highlighting *rationales* (Zaidan and Eisner, 2008). The principle of parsimony ("Occam's razor") advocates simple explanations over complex ones. This principle inspired a large body of work in traditional feature selection for linear models. We draw here a link between that work and modern approaches to explainability.

Table 1 highlights the connections. Traditional feature selection methods (Guyon and Elisseeff, 2003) are mostly concerned with **model interpretability**, i.e., understanding how models behave globally. Feature selection happens *statically* during model training, after which irrelevant features are permanently deleted from the model. This contrasts with **prediction explainability** in neural networks, where feature selection happens *dynamically* at run time: here explanations are input-dependent, hence a feature not relevant for a particular input can be relevant for another. Are these two worlds far away? Guyon and Elisseeff (2003, §4) proposed a typology for traditional feature selection with three classes of methods, distinguished by how they model the interaction between their main two components, the *feature selector* and the *learning algorithm*. We argue that this typology can also be used to characterize various explanation methods, if we replace these two components by the *explainer E* and the *classifier C*, respectively.

- **Wrapper methods**, in the wording of Guyon and Elisseeff (2003), "utilize the learning machine of interest as a black box to score subsets of variables according to their predictive power." This means greedily searching over subsets of features, training a model with each candidate subset. In the dynamic feature selection world, this is somewhat reminiscent of the leave-one-out method of Li et al. (2016b), the ablative approach of Serrano and Smith (2019), and LIME (Ribeiro et al., 2016), which repeatedly queries the classifier to label new examples.

- **Filter methods** decide to include/exclude a feature based on an importance metric (such as feature counts or pairwise mutual information). This can be done as a preprocessing step or by training the model once and thresholding the feature weights. In dynamic feature selection, this is done when we examine the gradient of the prediction with respect to each input feature, and then select the features whose gradients have large magnitude (Li et al., 2016a; Arras et al., 2016; Jain and Wallace, 2019),[1] and when thresholding softmax attention scores to select relevant input features, as analyzed by Jain and Wallace (2019) and Wiegreffe and Pinter (2019).

- **Embedded methods**, in traditional feature selection, embed feature selection within the learning algorithm by using a sparse regularizer such as the ℓ_1-norm (Tibshirani, 1996). Features that receive zero weight become irrelevant and can

---

[1] In linear models this gradient equals the feature's weight.

	Static selection (model interpretability)	**Dynamic selection** (prediction explainability)
Wrappers	Forward selection, backward elimination (Kohavi and John, 1997)	Input reduction (Feng et al., 2018), representation erasure (leave-one-out) (Li et al., 2016b; Serrano and Smith, 2019), LIME (Ribeiro et al., 2016)
Filters	Pointwise mutual information (Church and Hanks, 1989), recursive feature elimination (Guyon et al., 2002)	Input gradient (Li et al., 2016a), layerwise relevance propagation (Bach et al., 2015), top-k softmax attention
Embedded	ℓ_1-regularization (Tibshirani, 1996), elastic net (Zou and Hastie, 2005)	Stochastic attention (Xu et al., 2015; Lei et al., 2016; Bastings et al., 2019), sparse attention (**this paper**, §3)

Table 1: Overview of static and dynamic feature selection techniques.

be removed from the model. In dynamic feature selection, this encompasses methods where the classifier produces rationales together with its decisions (Lei et al., 2016; Bastings et al., 2019). We propose in §3 an alternative approach via **sparse attention** (Martins and Astudillo, 2016; Peters et al., 2019), where the selection of words for the rationale resembles ℓ_1-regularization.

In §4, we frame each of the cases above as a communication process, where the explainer E aims to communicate a short message with the relevant features that triggered the classifier C's decisions to a layperson L. The three cases above are distinguished by the way C and E interact.

3 Embedded Sparse Attention

The case where the explainer E is embedded in the classifier C naturally favors faithfulness, since the mechanism that explains the decision (the *why*) can also influence it (the *how*).

Attention mechanisms (Bahdanau et al., 2015) allow visualizing relevant input features that contributed to the model's decision. However, the traditional softmax-based attention is *dense*, i.e., it gives *some* probability mass to every feature, even if small. The typical approach is to select the top-k words with largest attention weights as the explanation. However, this is not a truly embedded method, but rather a filter, and as pointed out by Jain and Wallace (2019) and Wiegreffe and Pinter (2019), it may not lead to faithful explanations.

An alternative is to embed in the classifier an attention mechanism that is inherently **selective**, i.e., which can produce sparse attention distributions natively, where some input features receive exactly zero attention. An extreme example is hard attention, which, as argued by DeYoung et al. (2020), provides more faithful explanations "by construction" as they discretely extract snippets from the input to pass to the classifier. A problem with hard

attention is its non-differentiability, which complicates training (Lei et al., 2016; Bastings et al., 2019). We consider in this paper a different approach: using end-to-end differentiable sparse attention mechanisms, via the **sparsemax** (Martins and Astudillo, 2016) and the recently proposed **1.5-entmax** transformation (Peters et al., 2019), described in detail in §A. These sparse attention transformations have been applied successfully to machine translation and morphological inflection (Peters et al., 2019; Correia et al., 2019). Words that receive non-zero attention probability are *selected* to be part of the explanation. This is an embedded method akin of the use of ℓ_1-regularization in static feature selection. We experiment with these sparse attention mechanisms in §5.

4 Explainability as Communication

We now have the necessary ingredients to describe our unified framework for comparing and designing explanation strategies, illustrated in Figure 1.

Our fundamental assumption is that explainability is intimately linked to the ability of an explainer to **communicate** the rationale of a decision in terms that can be understood by a human; we use the success of this communication as a criterion for how plausible the explanation is.

4.1 The Classifier-Explainer-Layperson setup

Our framework draws inspiration from Lewis' signaling games (Lewis, 1969) and the recent work on emergent communication (Foerster et al., 2016; Lazaridou et al., 2016; Havrylov and Titov, 2017). Our starting point is the classifier $C : \mathcal{X} \rightarrow \mathcal{Y}$ which, when given an input $x \in \mathcal{X}$, produces a prediction $\hat{y} \in \mathcal{Y}$. This is the prediction that we want to explain. An explanation is a **message** $m \in \mathcal{M}$, for a predefined message space $\mathcal{M}$ (for example, a rationale). The goal of the explainer E is to compose and **successfully communicate** messages m to a layperson L. The success of the communication is dictated by the ability of L to reconstruct $\hat{y}$ from m with high accuracy. In this paper, we experiment with E and L being either humans or machines. Our framework is inspired by human-grounded evaluation through forward simulation/prediction, as proposed by Doshi-Velez (2017, §3.2). More formally:

- The **classifier** C is the model whose predictions we want to explain. For given inputs x, C produces $\hat{y}$ that are hopefully close to the ground truth y. We are agnostic about the kind of model used as a classifier, but we assume that it computes certain internal representations h that can be exposed to the explainer.

- The **explainer** E produces explanations for C's decisions. It receives the input x, the classifier prediction $\hat{y} = C(x)$, and optionally the internal representations h exposed by C. It outputs a message $m \in \mathcal{M}$ regarded as a "rationale" for $\hat{y}$. The message $m = E(x, \hat{y}, h)$ should be simple and compact enough to be easily transmitted and understood by the layperson L. In this paper, we constrain messages to be bags-of-words (BoWs) extracted from the textual input x.

- The **layperson** L is a simple model (e.g., a linear classifier)[2] that receives the message m as input, and predicts a final output $\tilde{y} = L(m)$. The communication is successful if $\tilde{y} = \hat{y}$. Given a test set $\{x_1, \ldots, x_N\}$, we evaluate the **communication success rate** (CSR) as the fraction of examples for which the communication is successful:

$$\text{CSR} = \frac{1}{N} \sum_{n=1}^{N} \big[\!\big[C(x_n) = L(E(x_n, C(x_n))) \big]\!\big],$$

$$(1)$$

where $[\![\cdot]\!]$ is the Iverson bracket notation.

Under this framework, we regard the communication success rate as a quantifiable measure of explainability: a high CSR means that the layperson L is able to replicate the classifier C's decisions a large fraction of the time when presented with messages given by the explainer E; this assesses how informative E's messages are.

Our framework is flexible, allowing different configurations for C, E, and L, as next described. In §5, we show examples of explainers and laypeople for text classification and natural language inference tasks (additional experiments on machine translation are described in §G).

Relation to filters and wrappers. In the wrapper and filter approaches described in §2, the classifier C and the explainer E are separate components. In these approaches, E works as a *post-hoc explainer*, querying C with new examples or requesting gradient information.

Relation to embedded explanation. By contrast, in the embedded approaches of Lei et al. (2016) and the selective sparse attention introduced in §3, the explainer E is directly *embedded* as an internal component of the classifier C, returning the selected features as the message. This approach is arguably more faithful, as E is directly linked to the mechanism that produces C's decisions.

4.2 Joint training of explainer and layperson

So far we have assumed that E is given beforehand, chosen among existing explanation methods, and that L is trained to assess the explanatory ability of E. But can our framework be used to *create* new explainers by training E and L jointly? We will see how this can be done by letting E and L play a cooperative game (Lewis, 1969). The key idea is that they need to learn a communication protocol that ensures high CSR (Eq. 1). Special care needs to be taken to rule out "trivial" protocols and ensure plausible, potentially faithful, explanations. We propose a strategy to ensure this, which will be validated using human evaluation in §6.[3]

Let E_θ and layperson L_ϕ be **trained models** (with parameters θ and ϕ), learned together to optimize a multi-task objective with two terms:

- A **reconstruction term** that controls the information about the classifier's decision $\hat{y}$. We use a cross-entropy loss on the output of the layperson L, using $\hat{y}$ (and not the true label y) as the ground truth: $\mathcal{L}(\phi, \theta) = -\log p_\phi(\hat{y} \mid m)$, where m is the output of the explainer E_θ.

- A **faithfulness term** that encourages the explainer E to take into account the classifier's

---

[2]The reason why we assume the layperson is a simple model is to encourage the explainer to produce simple and explanatory messages, in the sense that a simple model can learn with them. A more powerful layperson could potentially do well even with bad explanations.

[3]Other approaches, such as Lei et al. (2016) and Yu et al. (2019), develop rationalizers from cooperative or adversarial games between generators and encoders. However, those frameworks do not aim at explaining an external classifier.

decision process when producing its explanation m. This is done by adding a squared loss term $\Omega(\theta) = \|\tilde{h}(E_\theta), h\|^2$ where $\tilde{h}$ is E's prediction of C's internal representation h.

The objective function is a combination of these two terms, $\mathcal{L}_\Omega(\phi, \theta) := \lambda\Omega(\theta) + \mathcal{L}(\phi, \theta)$. We used $\lambda = 1$ in our experiments. This objective is minimized in a training set that contains pairs $(x, \hat{y})$. Therefore, in this model the message m is latent and works as a "bottleneck" for the layperson L, which does not have access to the full input x, to guess the classifier's prediction $\hat{y}$—related models have been devised in the context of emergent communication (Lazaridou et al., 2016; Foerster et al., 2016; Havrylov and Titov, 2017) and sparse autoencoders (Trifonov et al., 2018; Subramanian et al., 2018).

We minimize the objective above with gradient backpropagation. To ensure end-to-end differentiability, during this joint training we use sparsemax attention (§3) to select the relevant words in the message. One important concern in this model is to prevent E and L from learning a trivial protocol to maximize CSR. To ensure this, we forbid E from including stopwords in its messages and during training we use a linear schedule for the probability of the explainer accessing the predictions of the classifier ($\hat{y}$), which are hidden otherwise. At the end of training, the explainer will access it with probability β. In our experiments, we set β to 20% (chosen on the validation set as described in §F.2).

5 Experiments

We experimented with our framework on two NLP tasks: text classification and natural language inference. Additional experiments on machine translation are reported in §G, with similar conclusions.

We used 4 datasets (SST, IMDB, AgNews, Yelp) for text classification and one dataset (SNLI) for NLI, with statistics and details in Table 5 (§B).

Classifier C. For text classification, the input $x \in \mathcal{X}$ is a document and the output set $\mathcal{Y}$ is a set of labels (e.g. topics or sentiment labels). The message is a bag of words (BoW) extracted from the document. As in Jain and Wallace (2019) and Wiegreffe and Pinter (2019), our classifier C is an RNN with attention. For NLI, the input x is a pair of sentences (premise and hypothesis) and the labels in $\mathcal{Y}$ are entailment, contradiction, and neutral. We let messages be again BoWs, and we constrain

CLASSIFIER	SST	IMDB	AGN.	YELP	SNLI
BoW (L)	82.54	88.96	95.62	68.78	69.81
RNN, softmax (C)	86.16	**91.79**	96.28	**75.80**	78.34
–, 1.5-entmax (C_ent)	86.11	91.72	96.30	75.72	79.20
–, sparsemax (C_sp)	**86.27**	91.52	96.37	75.72	78.78
Bernoulli (C_bern)	81.99	86.99	95.68	70.12	79.24
HardKuma (C_hk)	84.13	91.06	**96.38**	74.36	**85.49**

Table 2: Accuracies of the original classifiers on text classification and natural language inference.

them to be selected from the premise (and concatenated with the full hypothesis). We used a similar classifier as above, but with two independent BiLSTM layers, one for each sentence. We used the additive attention of Bahdanau et al. (2015) with the last hidden state of the hypothesis as the query and the premise vectors as keys.

We also experimented with RNN classifiers that replace softmax attention by 1.5-entmax (C_ent) and sparsemax (C_sp), and with the rationalizer models of Lei et al. (2016) (C_bern) and Bastings et al. (2019) (C_hk). Details about these classifiers and their hyperparameters are listed in §D. Table 2 reports the accuracy of all classifiers used in our experiments. The attention-based models all perform very similarly and generally better than the rationalizer models, except for SNLI, where the latter use a stronger model with decomposable attention. As expected, in general, all these classifiers outperform a bag-of-words model which is the model we use as the layperson.

Layperson L and explainer E. We used a simple linear BoW model as the layperson L. For NLI, the layperson sees the full hypothesis, encoding it with a BiLSTM. The BoW from the explainer is passed through a linear projection and summed with the last hidden state of the BiLSTM.

We evaluated the following explainers:

1. **Erasure**, a wrapper similar to the leave-one-out approaches of Jain and Wallace (2019) and Serrano and Smith (2019). We obtain the word with largest attention, zero out its input vector, and repass the whole input with the erased vector to the classifier C. We produce the message by repeating this procedure k times.

2. **Top-k gradients**, a filter approach that ranks word importance by their "input $\times$ gradient" product, $|\frac{\partial \hat{y}}{\partial \mathbf{x}_i} \cdot \mathbf{x}_i|$ (Ancona et al., 2018; Wiegreffe and Pinter, 2019). The top-k words are selected as the message.

CLF.	EXPLAINER	SST		IMDB		AGNEWS		YELP		SNLI	
		CSR	ACC_L	CSR	ACC_L	CSR	ACC_L	CSR	ACC_L	CSR	ACC_L
C	Random	69.41	70.07	67.30	66.67	92.38	91.14	58.27	53.06	75.83	68.74
C	Erasure	80.12	81.22	92.17	88.72	97.31	95.41	78.72	68.90	77.88	70.04
C	Top-k gradient	79.35	79.24	86.30	83.93	96.49	94.86	70.54	62.86	76.74	69.40
C	Top-k softmax	84.18	82.43	93.06	89.46	**97.59**	95.61	81.00	70.18	78.66	71.00
C_{ent}	Top-k 1.5-entmax	**85.23**	**83.31**	93.32	89.60	97.29	**95.67**	82.20	70.78	80.23	73.39
C_{sp}	Top-k sparsemax	**85.23**	81.93	93.34	89.57	95.92	94.48	82.50	70.99	**82.89**	**74.76**
C_{ent}	Selec. 1.5-entmax	83.96	82.15	92.55	89.96	97.30	95.66	81.38	70.41	77.25	71.44
C_{sp}	Selec. sparsemax	**85.23**	81.93	93.24	89.66	95.92	94.48	83.55	71.60	82.04	73.46
C_{bern}	Bernoulli	82.37	78.42	91.66	86.13	96.91	94.43	84.93	66.89	76.81	69.65
C_{hk}	HardKuma	85.17	80.40	**94.72**	**90.16**	97.11	95.45	**87.39**	**71.64**	74.98	71.48

Table 3: CSR and layperson accuracy (ACC_L) for several explainers. For each explainer, we indicate the corresponding classifier from Table 2; in all cases the layperson is a BoW model. Only explainers of the same classifier can be compared in terms of CSR. Top rows report performance for random, wrapper and filter explainers, for fixed k-word messages (the values of k for the several datasets are $\{5, 10, 10, 10, 4\}$, respectively). Bottom rows correspond to embedded methods where k is given automatically via sparsity. The average k obtained by 1.5-entmax, sparsemax, Bernoulli and HardKuma are: SST: $\{4.65, 2.59, 6.10, 4.82\}$; IMDB: $\{28.23, 12.94, 39.40, 24.18\}$; AGNEWS $\{5.65, 4.14, 4.01, 9.68\}$; YELP: $\{60.61, 23.86, 9.15, 33.18\}$; SNLI: $\{12.96, 8.27, 15.04, 6.40\}$.

3. **Top-k and selective attention:** We experimented both using attention as a *filter*, by selecting the top-k most attended words as the message, and *embedded* in the classifier C, by using the selective attentions described in §3 (1.5-entmax and sparsemax).

4. **The rationalizer models of Lei et al. (2016) and Bastings et al. (2019).** These models compose the message by stochastically sampling rationale words, respectively using Bernoulli and HardKuma distributions. For SNLI, since these models use decomposable attention instead of RNNs, we form the message by selecting all premise words that are linked with any hypothesis word via a selected Bernoulli variable.

We also report a **random** baseline, which randomly picks k words as the message. We show examples of messages for all explainers in §I.

Results. Table 3 reports results for the communication success rate (CSR, Eq. 1) and for the accuracy of the layperson (ACC_L). For each explainer, we indicate which classifier it is explaining; note that the CSR is only comparable across explainers that use the same classifier. The goal of this experiment is to answer the following questions: (i) How do different explainers (wrappers, filters, embedded) compare to each other? (ii) Are selective sparse attention methods effective? (iii) How is the trade-off between message length and CSR?

The first thing to note is that, as expected, the random baseline is much worse than the other ex-plainers, for all text classification datasets.[4] Among the non-trivial explainers, **the attention and erasure outperform gradient methods**: the erasure and top-k attention explainers have similar CSR, with a slight advantage for attention methods. Note that the attention explainers have the important advantage of requiring a single call to the classifier, whereas the erasure methods, being wrappers, require k calls. The worse performance of top-k gradient (less severe on AGNEWS) suggests that the words that locally cause bigger output changes are not necessarily the most informative ones.[5]

Regarding the different attention models (softmax, entmax, and sparsemax), we see that **sparse transformations tend to have slightly better ACC_L**, in addition to better ACC_C (see Table 2). The embedded sparse attention methods achieved communication scores on par with the top-k attention methods without a prescribed k, while producing, by construction, more faithful explanations. Both our proposed models (sparsemax and 1.5-entmax) seem generally more accurate than the Bernoulli model of Lei et al. (2016) and comparable to the HardKuma model of Bastings et al. (2019), with a much simpler training procedure,

---

[4]This is less pronounced in SNLI, as the hypothesis alone already gives strong baselines (Gururangan et al., 2018).

[5]A potential reason is that attention directly influences C's decisions, being an inside component of the model. Gradients and erasure, however, are extracted after decisions are performed. The reason might be similar to filter methods being generally inferior to embedded methods in static feature selection, since they ignore feature interactions that may jointly play a role in model's decisions.

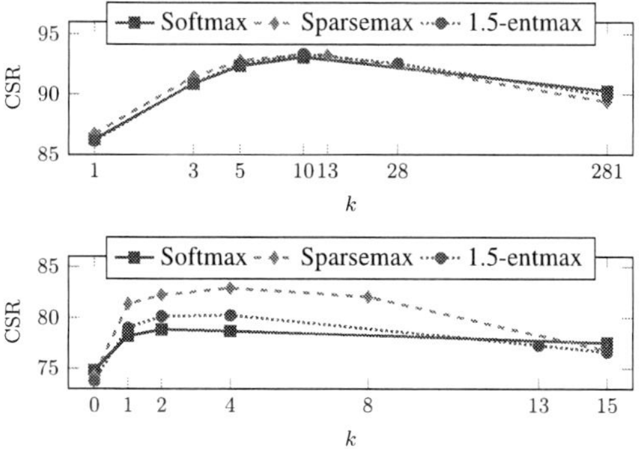

Figure 2: Message sparsity analysis for IMDB (top) and SNLI (bottom). For SNLI, $k = 0$ corresponds to a case where the layperson only sees the hypothesis. The rightmost entry represents an explainer that simply passes forward all words to the layperson.

not requiring gradient estimation over stochastic computation graphs.

Finally, Figure 2 shows the trade-off between the length of the message and the communication success rate for different values of k both for IMDB and SNLI (see Figure 4 in §G for the IWSLT experiments, with similar findings). Interestingly, we observe that **CSR does not increase monotonically with k.** As k increases, CSR starts by increasing but then it starts dropping when k becomes too large. This matches our intuition: in the two extreme cases where $k = 0$ and where k is the document length (corresponding to a full bag-of-words classifier) the message has no information about how the classifier C behaves. By setting $k = 0$, meaning that the layperson L only looks at the hypothesis, the CSR is reasonably high ($\sim$74%), but as soon as we include a single word in the message this baseline is surpassed by 4 points or more.

6 Human Evaluation

To fully assess the quality of the explanations in a more realistic forward simulation setting, we performed human evaluations, where the layperson L is a human instead of a machine.

Joint training of E and L. So far we compared several explainers, but what happens if we train E and L jointly to optimize CSR directly, as described in §4.2? We experiment with the IMDB and SNLI datasets, comparing with using humans for either the layperson, the explainer, or both.

Human layperson. We randomly selected 200 documents for IMDB and SNLI to be annotated

by humans. The extracted explanations (i.e. the selected words) were shuffled and displayed as a cloud of words to two annotators, who were asked to predict the label of each document when seeing only these explanations. For SNLI, we show the entire hypothesis as raw text and the premise as a cloud of words. The agreement between annotators and other annotation details can be found in §H.

Human explainer. We also consider explanations generated by humans rather than machines. To this end, we used the e-SNLI corpus (Camburu et al., 2018), which extends the SNLI with human rationales. Since the e-SNLI corpus does not provide highlights over the premise for neutral pairs, we removed them from the test set.[6]

We summarize our results in Table 4. We observe that, also with human laypeople, top-k attention achieves better results than top-k gradient, in terms of CSR and ACC, and that the ACC of erasure, attention models, and human explainers are close, reinforcing again the good results for these explainers. Among the different attention explainers, we see that selective attention explainers (§3) got very high ACC_H, outperforming top-k explainers for SNLI. We also see that the joint explainer (§4.2) outperformed all the other explainers in ACC_L and CSR_L and achieved very high human performance on IMDB, largely surpassing other systems in CSR_H and ACC_H. This shows the potential of our communication-based framework to develop new post-hoc explainers with good forward simulation properties. However, for SNLI, the joint explainer had much lower CSR_H and ACC_H, suggesting that for this task more sophisticated explainers are required.

7 Related Work

There is a large body of work on analysis and interpretation of neural networks. Our work focuses on *prediction explainability*, different from transparency or model interpretability (Doshi-Velez, 2017; Lipton, 2018; Gilpin et al., 2018).

Rudin (2019) defines explainability as a plausible reconstruction of the decision-making process, and Riedl (2019) argues that it mimics what humans do when rationalizing past actions. This inspired our post-hoc explainers in §4.2 and their use of the faithfulness loss term.

---

[6]Note that the human rationales from eSNLI are not explanations about C, since the humans are explaining the gold labels. Therefore, we have CSR=ACC always.

Clf.	Explainer	IMDB					SNLI				
		k	CSR_H	CSR_L	ACC_H	ACC_L	k	CSR_H	CSR_L	ACC_H	ACC_L
C	Erasure	5.0	89.25	94.00	86.25	90.00	4.0	72.50	73.50	83.50	70.00
C	Top-k gradient	5.0	73.50	84.50	73.00	80.50	4.0	65.75	72.50	76.75	68.00
C	Top-k softmax	5.0	89.25	93.00	88.25	88.00	4.0	72.00	76.50	82.75	71.50
C_{ent}	Top-k 1.5-entmax	5.0	89.25	92.50	85.75	86.50	4.0	70.00	81.50	80.50	76.50
C_{sp}	Top-k sparsemax	5.0	89.00	89.50	87.50	88.00	4.0	68.25	88.00	80.25	77.00
C_{ent}	Selec. 1.5-entmax	27.2	86.50	92.50	84.00	89.50	12.9	75.25	77.00	87.00	77.00
C_{sp}	Selec. sparsemax	12.8	87.75	92.50	86.75	89.00	8.0	72.25	82.00	85.00	79.00
C_{bern}	Bernoulli	39.4	79.00	93.50	75.00	87.00	15.2	74.50	76.00	86.75	69.50
C_{hk}	HardKuma	24.3	83.75	93.50	80.75	89.00	6.4	79.25	71.50	**87.50**	68.50
C	Joint E and L	2.7	**96.75**	**98.50**	**89.25**	**91.50**	2.8	58.00	**93.50**	70.00	78.50
-	Human highlights	-	-	-	-	-	2.8	**83.25**	83.50	83.25	**83.50**

Table 4: Results of the human evaluation. Reported are average message length k, human layperson CSR_H/ACC_H, and machine layperson CSR_L/ACC_L. Only explainers of the same classifier can be compared in terms of CSR.

Recent works questioned the interpretative ability of attention mechanisms (Jain and Wallace, 2019; Serrano and Smith, 2019). Wiegreffe and Pinter (2019) distinguished between faithful and plausible explanations and introduced several diagnostic tools. Mullenbach et al. (2018) use human evaluation to show that attention mechanisms produce plausible explanations, consistent with our findings in §6. None of these works, however, considered the sparse selective attention mechanisms proposed in §3. Hard stochastic attention has been considered by Xu et al. (2015); Lei et al. (2016); Alvarez-Melis and Jaakkola (2017); Bastings et al. (2019), but a comparison with sparse attention and explanation strategies was still missing.

Besides attention-based methods, many other explainers have been proposed using gradients (Bach et al., 2015; Montavon et al., 2018; Ding et al., 2019), leave-one-out strategies (Feng et al., 2018; Serrano and Smith, 2019), or local perturbations (Ribeiro et al., 2016; Koh and Liang, 2017), but a link with filters and wrappers in the feature selection literature has never been made. We believe the connections revealed in §2 may be useful to develop new explainers in the future.

Our trained explainers from §4.2 draw inspiration from emergent communication (Lazaridou et al., 2016; Foerster et al., 2016; Havrylov and Titov, 2017). Some of our proposed ideas (e.g., using sparsemax for end-to-end differentiability) may also be relevant to that task. Our work is also related to sparse auto-encoders, which seek sparse overcomplete vector representations to improve model interpretability (Faruqui et al., 2015; Trifonov et al., 2018; Subramanian et al., 2018). In contrast to these works, we consider the non-zero attention probabilities as a form of explanation.

Some recent work (Yu et al., 2019; DeYoung et al., 2020) advocates *comprehensive* rationales. While comprehensiveness could be useful in our framework to prevent trivial communication protocols between the explainer and layperson, we argue that it is not always a desirable property, since it leads to longer explanations and an increase of human cognitive load. In fact, our analysis of CSR as a function of message length (Figure 2) suggests that shorter explanations might be preferable. This is aligned to the "explanation selection" principle articulated by Miller (2019, §4): *"Similar to causal connection, people do not typically provide all causes for an event as an explanation. Instead, they select what they believe are the most relevant causes."* Our sparse, selective attention mechanisms proposed in §3 are inspired by this principle.

8   Conclusions

We proposed a unified framework that regards explainability as a communication problem between an explainer and a layperson about a classifier's decision. We proposed new embedded methods based on selective attention, and post-hoc explainers trained to optimize communication success. In our experiments, we observed that attention mechanisms and erasure tend to outperform gradient methods on communication success rate, using both machines and humans as the layperson, and that selective attention is effective, while simpler to train than stochastic rationalizers.

Acknowledgements

This work was supported by the European Research Council (ERC StG DeepSPIN 758969), by the P2020 program MAIA (contract 045909), and by the Fundação para a Ciência e Tecnologia through contract UID/50008/2019. We are grateful to Thales Bertaglia, Erick Fonseca, Pedro Martins, Vlad Niculae, Ben Peters, Gonçalo Correia and Tsvetomila Mihaylova for insightful group discussion and for the participation in human evaluation experiments. We also thank the anonymous reviewers for their helpful discussion and feedback.

References

David Alvarez-Melis and Tommi Jaakkola. 2017. A causal framework for explaining the predictions of black-box sequence-to-sequence models. In *Proceedings of the 2017 Conference on Empirical Methods in Natural Language Processing*, pages 412–421, Copenhagen, Denmark. Association for Computational Linguistics.

Marco Ancona, Enea Ceolini, Cengiz Öztireli, and Markus Gross. 2018. Towards better understanding of gradient-based attribution methods for deep neural networks. In *International Conference on Learning Representations*.

Leila Arras, Franziska Horn, Grégoire Montavon, Klaus-Robert Müller, and Wojciech Samek. 2016. Explaining predictions of non-linear classifiers in NLP. In *Proceedings of the 1st Workshop on Representation Learning for NLP*, pages 1–7, Berlin, Germany. Association for Computational Linguistics.

Leila Arras, Grégoire Montavon, Klaus-Robert Müller, and Wojciech Samek. 2017. Explaining recurrent neural network predictions in sentiment analysis. In *Proceedings of the 8th Workshop on Computational Approaches to Subjectivity, Sentiment and Social Media Analysis*, pages 159–168, Copenhagen, Denmark. Association for Computational Linguistics.

Sebastian Bach, Alexander Binder, Grégoire Montavon, Frederick Klauschen, Klaus-Robert Müller, and Wojciech Samek. 2015. On pixel-wise explanations for non-linear classifier decisions by layer-wise relevance propagation. *PLOS ONE*, 10(7):1–46.

Dzmitry Bahdanau, Kyunghyun Cho, and Yoshua Bengio. 2015. Neural machine translation by jointly learning to align and translate. In *Proceedings of the 2015 International Conference on Learning Representations*.

Jasmijn Bastings, Wilker Aziz, and Ivan Titov. 2019. Interpretable neural predictions with differentiable binary variables. In *Proceedings of the 57th Annual Meeting of the Association for Computational Linguistics*, pages 2963–2977, Florence, Italy. Association for Computational Linguistics.

Oana-Maria Camburu, Tim Rocktäschel, Thomas Lukasiewicz, and Phil Blunsom. 2018. e-snli: Natural language inference with natural language explanations. In *Advances in Neural Information Processing Systems 31*, pages 9539–9549. Curran Associates, Inc.

Mauro Cettolo, Marcello Federico, Luisa Bentivogli, Niehues Jan, Stüker Sebastian, Sudoh Katsuitho, Yoshino Koichiro, and Federmann Christian. 2017. Overview of the iwslt 2017 evaluation campaign. In *Proceedings of the 14th International Workshop on Spoken Language Translation*, pages 2–14.

Kenneth Ward Church and Patrick Hanks. 1989. Word association norms, mutual information, and lexicography. In *27th Annual Meeting of the Association for Computational Linguistics*, pages 76–83, Vancouver, British Columbia, Canada. Association for Computational Linguistics.

Gonçalo M. Correia, Vlad Niculae, and André F. T. Martins. 2019. Adaptively sparse transformers. In *Proceedings of the 2019 Conference on Empirical Methods in Natural Language Processing and the 9th International Joint Conference on Natural Language Processing (EMNLP-IJCNLP)*, pages 2174–2184, Hong Kong, China. Association for Computational Linguistics.

Jacob Devlin, Ming-Wei Chang, Kenton Lee, and Kristina Toutanova. 2019. BERT: Pre-training of deep bidirectional transformers for language understanding. In *Proceedings of the 2019 Conference of the North American Chapter of the Association for Computational Linguistics: Human Language Technologies, Volume 1 (Long and Short Papers)*, pages 4171–4186, Minneapolis, Minnesota. Association for Computational Linguistics.

Jay DeYoung, Sarthak Jain, Nazneen Fatema Rajani, Eric Lehman, Caiming Xiong, Richard Socher, and Byron C. Wallace. 2020. ERASER: A benchmark to evaluate rationalized NLP models. In *Proceedings of the 58th Annual Meeting of the Association for Computational Linguistics*, pages 4443–4458, Online. Association for Computational Linguistics.

Shuoyang Ding, Hainan Xu, and Philipp Koehn. 2019. Saliency-driven word alignment interpretation for neural machine translation. In *Proceedings of the Fourth Conference on Machine Translation (Volume 1: Research Papers)*, pages 1–12, Florence, Italy. Association for Computational Linguistics.

Been Doshi-Velez, Finale; Kim. 2017. Towards a rigorous science of interpretable machine learning. In *eprint arXiv:1702.08608*.

Manaal Faruqui, Yulia Tsvetkov, Dani Yogatama, Chris Dyer, and Noah A. Smith. 2015. Sparse overcomplete word vector representations. In *Proceedings* of the 53rd Annual Meeting of the Association for Computational Linguistics and the 7th International Joint Conference on Natural Language Processing (Volume 1: Long Papers)*, pages 1491–1500, Beijing, China. Association for Computational Linguistics.

Shi Feng, Eric Wallace, Alvin Grissom II, Mohit Iyyer, Pedro Rodriguez, and Jordan Boyd-Graber. 2018. Pathologies of neural models make interpretations difficult. In *Proceedings of the 2018 Conference on Empirical Methods in Natural Language Processing*, pages 3719–3728, Brussels, Belgium. Association for Computational Linguistics.

Jakob Foerster, Ioannis Alexandros Assael, Nando de Freitas, and Shimon Whiteson. 2016. Learning to communicate with deep multi-agent reinforcement learning. In *Advances in Neural Information Processing Systems 29*, pages 2137–2145. Curran Associates, Inc.

L. H. Gilpin, D. Bau, B. Z. Yuan, A. Bajwa, M. Specter, and L. Kagal. 2018. Explaining explanations: An overview of interpretability of machine learning. In *2018 IEEE 5th International Conference on Data Science and Advanced Analytics (DSAA)*, pages 80–89.

Yoav Goldberg and Graeme Hirst. 2017. *Neural Network Methods in Natural Language Processing*. Morgan & Claypool Publishers.

Suchin Gururangan, Swabha Swayamdipta, Omer Levy, Roy Schwartz, Samuel Bowman, and Noah A. Smith. 2018. Annotation artifacts in natural language inference data. In *Proceedings of the 2018 Conference of the North American Chapter of the Association for Computational Linguistics: Human Language Technologies, Volume 2 (Short Papers)*, pages 107–112, New Orleans, Louisiana. Association for Computational Linguistics.

Isabelle Guyon and André Elisseeff. 2003. An introduction to variable and feature selection. *Journal of Machine Learning Research*, 3(null):1157–1182.

Isabelle Guyon, Jason Weston, Stephen Barnhill, and Vladimir Vapnik. 2002. Gene selection for cancer classification using support vector machines. *Machine Learning*, 46(1–3):389–422.

Serhii Havrylov and Ivan Titov. 2017. Emergence of language with multi-agent games: Learning to communicate with sequences of symbols. In *Advances in Neural Information Processing Systems 30*, pages 2149–2159. Curran Associates, Inc.

Alon Jacovi and Yoav Goldberg. 2020. Towards faithfully interpretable NLP systems: How should we define and evaluate faithfulness? In *Proceedings of the 58th Annual Meeting of the Association for Computational Linguistics*, pages 4198–4205, Online. Association for Computational Linguistics.

Sarthak Jain and Byron C. Wallace. 2019. Attention is not Explanation. In *Proceedings of the 2019 Conference of the North American Chapter of the Association for Computational Linguistics: Human Language Technologies, Volume 1 (Long and Short Papers)*, pages 3543–3556, Minneapolis, Minnesota. Association for Computational Linguistics.

Pang Wei Koh and Percy Liang. 2017. Understanding black-box predictions via influence functions. volume 70 of *Proceedings of Machine Learning Research*, pages 1885–1894, International Convention Centre, Sydney, Australia. PMLR.

Ron Kohavi and George H. John. 1997. Wrappers for feature subset selection. *Artif. Intell.*, 97(1–2):273–324.

Julia Kreutzer, Jasmijn Bastings, and Stefan Riezler. 2019. Joey NMT: A minimalist NMT toolkit for novices. In *Proceedings of the 2019 Conference on Empirical Methods in Natural Language Processing and the 9th International Joint Conference on Natural Language Processing (EMNLP-IJCNLP): System Demonstrations*, pages 109–114, Hong Kong, China. Association for Computational Linguistics.

Angeliki Lazaridou, Alexander Peysakhovich, and Marco Baroni. 2016. Multi-agent cooperation and the emergence of (natural) language. In *International Conference on Learning Representations*.

Tao Lei, Regina Barzilay, and Tommi Jaakkola. 2016. Rationalizing neural predictions. In *Proceedings of the 2016 Conference on Empirical Methods in Natural Language Processing*, pages 107–117, Austin, Texas. Association for Computational Linguistics.

David K. Lewis. 1969. Convention: A philosophical study.

Jiwei Li, Xinlei Chen, Eduard Hovy, and Dan Jurafsky. 2016a. Visualizing and understanding neural models in NLP. In *Proceedings of the 2016 Conference of the North American Chapter of the Association for Computational Linguistics: Human Language Technologies*, pages 681–691, San Diego, California. Association for Computational Linguistics.

Jiwei Li, Will Monroe, and Dan Jurafsky. 2016b. Understanding neural networks through representation erasure. *arXiv preprint arXiv:1612.08220*.

Zachary C. Lipton. 2018. The mythos of model interpretability. *Commun. ACM*, 61(10):36–43.

Ilya Loshchilov and Frank Hutter. 2019. Decoupled weight decay regularization. In *International Conference on Learning Representations*.

Andre Martins and Ramon Astudillo. 2016. From softmax to sparsemax: A sparse model of attention and multi-label classification. volume 48 of *Proceedings of Machine Learning Research*, pages 1614–1623, New York, New York, USA. PMLR.

Tim Miller. 2019. Explanation in artificial intelligence: Insights from the social sciences. *Artificial Intelligence*, 267:1 – 38.

Grégoire Montavon, Wojciech Samek, and Klaus-Robert Müller. 2018. Methods for interpreting and understanding deep neural networks. *Digital Signal Processing*, 73:1 – 15.

James Mullenbach, Sarah Wiegreffe, Jon Duke, Jimeng Sun, and Jacob Eisenstein. 2018. Explainable prediction of medical codes from clinical text. In *Proceedings of the 2018 Conference of the North American Chapter of the Association for Computational Linguistics: Human Language Technologies, Volume 1 (Long Papers)*, pages 1101–1111, New Orleans, Louisiana. Association for Computational Linguistics.

Ankur Parikh, Oscar Täckström, Dipanjan Das, and Jakob Uszkoreit. 2016. A decomposable attention model for natural language inference. In *Proceedings of the 2016 Conference on Empirical Methods in Natural Language Processing*, pages 2249–2255, Austin, Texas. Association for Computational Linguistics.

Jeffrey Pennington, Richard Socher, and Christopher Manning. 2014. GloVe: Global vectors for word representation. In *Proceedings of the 2014 Conference on Empirical Methods in Natural Language Processing (EMNLP)*, pages 1532–1543, Doha, Qatar. Association for Computational Linguistics.

Ben Peters, Vlad Niculae, and André F. T. Martins. 2019. Sparse sequence-to-sequence models. In *Proceedings of the 57th Annual Meeting of the Association for Computational Linguistics*, pages 1504–1519, Florence, Italy. Association for Computational Linguistics.

Matthew Peters, Mark Neumann, Mohit Iyyer, Matt Gardner, Christopher Clark, Kenton Lee, and Luke Zettlemoyer. 2018. Deep contextualized word representations. In *Proceedings of the 2018 Conference of the North American Chapter of the Association for Computational Linguistics: Human Language Technologies, Volume 1 (Long Papers)*, pages 2227–2237, New Orleans, Louisiana. Association for Computational Linguistics.

Marco Tulio Ribeiro, Sameer Singh, and Carlos Guestrin. 2016. "why should i trust you?": Explaining the predictions of any classifier. KDD '16, page 1135–1144, New York, NY, USA. Association for Computing Machinery.

Mark O Riedl. 2019. Human-centered artificial intelligence and machine learning. *Human Behavior and Emerging Technologies*, 1(1):33–36.

Cynthia Rudin. 2019. Stop explaining black box machine learning models for high stakes decisions and use interpretable models instead. *Nature Machine Intelligence*, 1(5):206–215.

Sofia Serrano and Noah A. Smith. 2019. Is attention interpretable? In *Proceedings of the 57th Annual Meeting of the Association for Computational Linguistics*, pages 2931–2951, Florence, Italy. Association for Computational Linguistics.

Anant Subramanian, Danish Pruthi, Harsh Jhamtani, Taylor Berg-Kirkpatrick, and Eduard Hovy. 2018. Spine: Sparse interpretable neural embeddings. In *Proceedings of the Thirty Second AAAI Conference on Artificial Intelligence (AAAI)*.

Robert Tibshirani. 1996. Regression shrinkage and selection via the lasso. *Journal of the Royal Statistical Society: Series B (Methodological)*, 58(1):267–288.

Valentin Trifonov, Octavian-Eugen Ganea, Anna Potapenko, and Thomas Hofmann. 2018. Learning and evaluating sparse interpretable sentence embeddings. In *Proceedings of the 2018 EMNLP Workshop BlackboxNLP: Analyzing and Interpreting Neural Networks for NLP*, pages 200–210, Brussels, Belgium. Association for Computational Linguistics.

Constantino Tsallis. 1988. Possible generalization of boltzmann-gibbs statistics. *Journal of Statistical Physics*.

Ashish Vaswani, Noam Shazeer, Niki Parmar, Jakob Uszkoreit, Llion Jones, Aidan N Gomez, Ł ukasz Kaiser, and Illia Polosukhin. 2017. Attention is all you need. In *Advances in Neural Information Processing Systems 30*, pages 5998–6008. Curran Associates, Inc.

Sarah Wiegreffe and Yuval Pinter. 2019. Attention is not not explanation. In *Proceedings of the 2019 Conference on Empirical Methods in Natural Language Processing and the 9th International Joint Conference on Natural Language Processing (EMNLP-IJCNLP)*, pages 11–20, Hong Kong, China. Association for Computational Linguistics.

Kelvin Xu, Jimmy Ba, Ryan Kiros, Kyunghyun Cho, Aaron Courville, Ruslan Salakhudinov, Rich Zemel, and Yoshua Bengio. 2015. Show, attend and tell: Neural image caption generation with visual attention. volume 37 of *Proceedings of Machine Learning Research*, pages 2048–2057, Lille, France. PMLR.

Mo Yu, Shiyu Chang, Yang Zhang, and Tommi Jaakkola. 2019. Rethinking cooperative rationalization: Introspective extraction and complement control. In *Proceedings of the 2019 Conference on Empirical Methods in Natural Language Processing and the 9th International Joint Conference on Natural Language Processing (EMNLP-IJCNLP)*, pages 4094–4103, Hong Kong, China. Association for Computational Linguistics.

Omar Zaidan and Jason Eisner. 2008. Modeling annotators: A generative approach to learning from annotator rationales. In *Proceedings of the 2008 Conference on Empirical Methods in Natural Language*

Processing, pages 31–40, Honolulu, Hawaii. Association for Computational Linguistics.

Hui Zou and Trevor Hastie. 2005. Regularization and variable selection via the elastic net. *Journal of the Royal Statistical Society: Series B (Statistical Methodology)*, 67(2):301–320.

Latent Tree Learning with Ordered Neurons: What Parses Does It Produce?

Yian Zhang

Dept. of Computer Science

New York University

`yian.zhang@nyu.edu`

Abstract

Recent *latent tree learning* models can learn constituency parsing without any exposure to human-annotated tree structures. One such model is ON-LSTM (Shen et al., 2019), which is trained on language modelling and has near-state-of-the-art performance on unsupervised parsing. In order to better understand the performance and consistency of the model as well as how the parses it generates are different from gold-standard PTB parses, we replicate the model with different restarts and examine their parses. We find that (1) the model has reasonably consistent parsing behaviors across different restarts, (2) the model struggles with the internal structures of complex noun phrases, (3) the model has a tendency to overestimate the height of the split points right before verbs. We speculate that both problems could potentially be solved by adopting a different training task other than unidirectional language modelling.

1 Introduction

Grammar induction is the task of learning the grammar of a target corpus without exposure to the parsing ground truth or any expert-labeled tree structures (Charniak and Carroll, 1992; Klein and Manning, 2002). Recently emerging *latent tree learning* models provide a new approach to this problem (Yogatama et al., 2017; Maillard et al., 2017; Choi et al., 2018; Shen et al., 2018; Kim et al., 2019). They learn syntactic parsing under only indirect supervision from their main training tasks such as language modelling and natural language inference.

In this study, we analyze ON-LSTM (Shen et al., 2019), a new latent tree learning model that set the state of the art on unsupervised constituency parsing on WSJ test (Marcus et al., 1993) when it was published at ICLR 2019. The model is trained

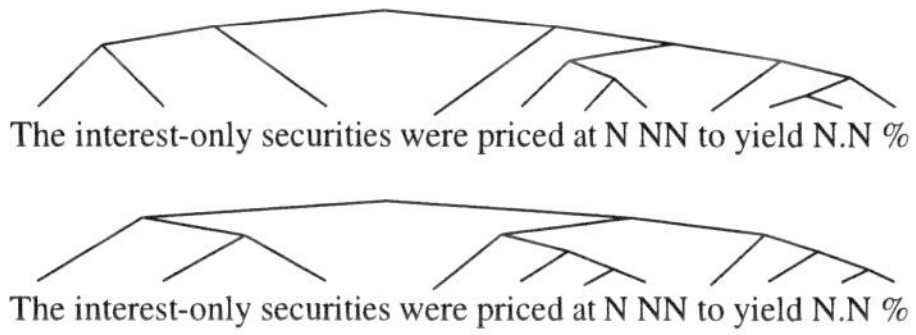

Figure 1: An example of an ON-LSTM's parse (top) disagreeing with a binary parse tree converted from a PTB gold-standard parse.

on language modelling and can generate binary constituency parsing trees of input sentences like the one in Figure 1.

As far as we know, though there is an excellent theoretical analysis paper (Dyer et al., 2019) of the ON-LSTM model that focuses on the model's architecture and its parsing algorithm, there is no systematic analysis of the parses the model generates. There are no in-depth investigations of (i) whether the model's parsing behavior is consistent among different restarts or (ii) how the parses it produces are different from PTB gold standards. Answering these questions is crucial for a better understanding of the capability of the model and may bring insights into how to build more advanced latent tree learning models in the future.

Therefore, we replicate the model with 5 random restarts and look into the parses it generates. We find that (1) ON-LSTM has fairly consistent parsing behaviors across different restarts, achieving a self F1 of 65.7 on WSJ test. (2) The model struggles to correctly parse the internal structures of complex noun phrases. (3) The model has a consistent tendency to overestimate the height of the split points right before verbs or auxiliary verbs, leading to a major difference between its parses and the Penn Treebank gold-standard parses. We speculate that both problems can be explained by the training task, unidirectional language modelling, and

Proceedings of the Third BlackboxNLP Workshop on Analyzing and Interpreting Neural Networks for NLP, pages 119–125
Online, November 20, 2020. ©2020 Association for Computational Linguistics

thus we hypothesize that training a bidirectional model on a more syntax-related task like acceptability judgement might be a good choice for future latent tree learning models.

2 Related Work

ST-Gumbel (Choi et al., 2018) and RL-SPINN (Yogatama et al., 2017) are two earlier latent tree learning models. These models are designed to learn to parse input sentences in order to help solve a downstream sentence understanding task such as natural language inference. Since they are not designed to approximate PTB grammar (Marcus et al., 1993), their unsupervised parsing F1's on WSJ test are relatively low (20.1 and 25.0).

PRPN (Shen et al., 2017) and URNNG (Kim et al., 2019) are two of the stronger latent tree learning models that have comparable unsupervised parsing performance (F1=42.8 and 52.4) with ON-LSTM (F1=49.4). URNNG is based on Recurrent Neural Network Grammar (Dyer et al., 2016), a probablitic generative model; PRPN is a neural language model that implicitly models syntax using a structured attention mechanism.

Williams et al. (2018) analyze ST-Gumbel and RL-SPINN. They find that though the two models perform well on sentence understanding, neither of the models induces consistent and non-trivial grammars.

Prior to this work, Dyer et al. (2019) also analyze ON-LSTM. They raise doubts on the necessity of the model's novel gates and mathematically prove that it is impossible for the parsing algorithm used by Shen et al. (2019) to correctly parse a certain class of structures. In comparison, this study takes a more empirical approach that is similar to that of Williams et al. (2018).

3 Data and Model

WSJ Dataset   WSJ is the Wall Street Journal Section of PTB (Marcus et al., 1993), which is the most commonly used dataset for training and evaluating parsers including latent tree learning models (Williams et al., 2018; Htut et al., 2018). It is also the dataset ON-LSTM is originally trained on. We follow the traditional split of WSJ: sections 0-21 as WSJ train, section 22 as WSJ dev, and section 23 as WSJ test. We also use WSJ 10, a subset of WSJ that includes all sentences with length < 10. In the experiments, the model is always trained on WSJ train on language modelling, and evaluated on

WSJ test, WSJ dev and/or WSJ 10 on constituency parsing.

Models   ON-LSTM is an LSTM model (Hochreiter and Schmidhuber, 1997) plus a novel activation function, which causes the model to learn to store long-term information in high-ranking dimensions, implicitly encoding a constituency parse. The model is equipped with a master forget gate $\widetilde{f}_t$ and a master input gate $\widetilde{i}_t$. At each timestep, $\widetilde{f}_t$ is multiplied element-wise to the previous cell state c_{t-1} and thus controls to what extent the value of each dimension in the previous cell state can be forgotten; $\widetilde{i}_t$ is multiplied element-wise to the candidate update values $\hat{c}_t$ and thus controls how much new information can be written to each dimension in the cell state. The values of $\widetilde{f}_t$ and $\widetilde{i}_t$ are computed at each timestep based on the input token and the cell state. The model uses $cumax()$ as the activation function of the master gates, where

$$cumax(*) := cumsum(softmax(*))$$

$$cumsum(\vec{a}) := [a_1, a_1 + a_2, ..., \sum_{i=1}^{k} a_i, ..., \sum_{i=1}^{n} a_i]$$

Therefore, the values in $\widetilde{f}_t$ are always monotonically increasing from 0 to 1, and the values in $\widetilde{i}_t$ are always monotonically decreasing from 1 to 0. As a result, when a dimension is updated/erased, all of the dimensions whose ranks are lower than it are also updated/erased. Intuitively, in an extreme and simplified example where $\widetilde{f}_t = (0, ..., 0, 1, ..., 1)$, the model is just picking a dimension d, erases all the dimensions from 1 to $d - 1$ in c_{t-1}, and keeps dimensions $> d$ unchanged.

As a result of this novel updating rule, the model will tend to store long-term information in high-ranking dimensions and short-term information in low-ranking dimensions so that when the model frequently erases and updates low-ranking dimensions of the cell state, the long-term information stored in high-ranking dimensions will stay unaffected. When the model is trained to perform language modelling, since a higher-level constituent always spans more words than its children, its related information will continuously be useful for word prediction in a longer term and will thus be stored in higher-ranking dimensions (see Fig 2 for an example). Therefore, intuitively, if a high-ranking dimension is erased/updated, it probably means that the currently processed input token is the start of a new high-level constituent.

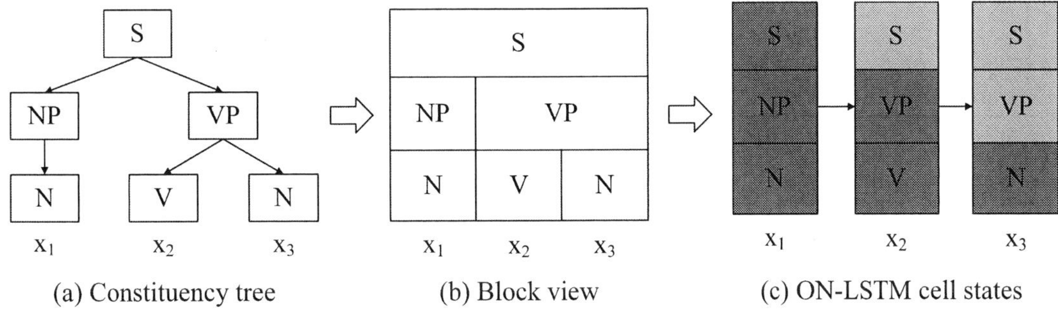

(a) Constituency tree   (b) Block view   (c) ON-LSTM cell states

Figure 2: An example of the correspondences between a constituency parse tree and the hidden states of ON-LSTM. Intuitively, when performing language modelling, the information related to the highest-level constituent "S" is useful when predicting both token x_2 and token x_3, while the information related to the first "N" is only useful in predicting x_2, and can be erased after the prediction of x_2. In order to avoid removing "S" information when removing "N" information, the model will store "S" information in higher dimensions, and information of "N" in lower dimensions. Image source: Shen et al. (2019)

Based on this intuition, the master forget gates can be used to perform binary constituency parsing. In binary parsing, a constituent (which is initially the whole sentence) is recursively split into two constituents until each constituent contains only one word. Therefore, each space between each pair of adjacent words is a split point the parsing algorithm will use at some point to make a split, and the order in which these split points are used decides what the resultant parsing tree will be like. In the case of ON-LSTM, the parsing algorithm uses the split points in the decreasing order of their "height", where the height of a split point between x_{t-1} and x_t is usually defined as $\hat{d}_t^{f\,1}$, an estimate of the transition point[2] in $\tilde{f}_t$ from the 0-segment[3] where values are small and close to 0 to the 1-segment where values are large and close to 1. Intuitively, the more information is forgotten at a timestep, the higher the split point before the token.

We train ON-LSTM with 5 different random seeds on WSJ train using hyperparameters shared by Shen et al. (2019). Note that the training objective is language modelling, so we only use the sentences from WSJ train and the model never has access to the parsing trees in the dataset or any other tree structures. On WSJ test, our models achieve an average perplexity of 56.33 (± 0.06) on language modelling and average F1 score of 46.43 (± 1.79) on unsupervised parsing, while the original paper reports 56.17 (± 0.12) and 47.7 (± 1.5). This shows that we roughly reproduce their work[4].

4 Experiments

To analyze the model's consistency, we use the 5 models we train to parse WSJ test and WSJ 10, calculate the self F1 and standard deviation on each dataset, and compare them to that of the random baseline. Self F1 is the average of unlabeled binary F1 scores between every pairing of the five parses, each produced by one model. It shows to what extent each model agrees with the parsing decisions of the other four.

To take a closer look at the parses generated by the model, we then use our 5 models to parse WSJ dev, and report the average of the models' parsing accuracies on each constituent type. We use the constituent-level accuracy as a guide to analyze how the parses ON-LSTM produces are different from PTB gold standards.

In the experiments, we include a simple random baseline that produces parses by recursively and randomly splitting the sequences to two halves. This is the same with ON-LSTM's parsing algorithm except that the baseline model chooses split points in a random order.

---

[1] As an exception, the height of the split point between x_1 and x_2 is defined as $\max(\hat{d}_1^f, \hat{d}_2^f)$.

[2] Shen et al. (2019) use the term "split point". We use a different term to avoid confusion with the more frequently used "split point" concept in this paper, which means the space between two words.

[3] The master forget gate computed using the cumax() function is an expectation of a binary gate g=(0, ..., 0, 1, ..., 1), and the rank of the first "1" indicates to what extent the currently processed input word contains high-level information. For formal mathematical expressions of the model architecture, we encourage you to read the original model paper.

[4] The 5 ONLSTM models we train and their parses can be found at https://github.com/YianZhang/ONLSTM-analysis

Model	Test Set	F1(σ)		Self F1
ON-LSTM layer1	WSJ test	23.4	2.1	56.5
ON-LSTM layer2	**WSJ test**	**46.4**	**1.8**	**65.7**
ON-LSTM layer3	WSJ test	31.7	7.5	38.1
ON-LSTM layer1	WSJ10	44.4	3.0	71.6
ON-LSTM layer2	**WSJ10**	**69.8**	**1.9**	**82.1**
ON-LSTM layer3	WSJ10	54.1	8.5	56.6
Random	WSJ test	20.3	0.1	24.8
Random	WSJ10	39.3	0.1	40.7

Table 1: F1, standard deviation, and self F1 of different layers of ON-LSTM on WSJ test and WSJ 10.

5 Results

5.1 Does the model learn consistent grammars?

The self F1's of ON-LSTM are shown in Table 1. On both datasets, all three layers of ON-LSTM show much higher self F1 than the random baseline. This shows the model produces fairly consistent parses across different restarts. The 2nd layer, the layer with the highest parsing F1, is also the most consistent layer according to its self F1 and standard deviation. Its self F1 scores on both WSJ test and WSJ 10 are ~ 41 higher than that of the random baseline.

5.2 How are ON-LSTM's parses different from PTB parses?

In this experiment, we focus on layer 2 of the model. For each model restart, we compute its parsing accuracy of every non-unary constituent type that occurs > 5 times in WSJ dev (sentence-level occurrences aside, explained below). We average the accuracies of the 5 restarts and list the results in Table 2. The constituent types are listed in decreasing order based on the difference between ON-LSTM accuracy and the random baseline accuracy.

Different from the previous works (Williams et al., 2018; Shen et al., 2019; Htut et al., 2018), we do not take into account any constituent that spans over an entire sentence, because any parser has 100% accuracy on these constituents. The way we compute the accuracy better reveals the model's command of each constituent type, and makes comparisons across constituent types more fair, since some types are more likely to appear as full sentences. We follow the clues in the accuracies to look into the parses generated by the models and find two cases where the models struggle, as we discuss in the following sections.

Constituent	Accuracy(σ)		Random(σ)		$\triangle$Acc
SQ	77.8	0.0	15.6	15.1	62.2
VP	55.5	2.2	12.5	0.3	43.0
NP	56.8	5.5	22.5	0.4	34.3
PP	52.8	1.5	18.7	0.5	34.1
WHNP	42.9	6.7	16.2	8.3	26.7
S	32.6	3.6	10.8	1.0	21.8
ADJP	44.9	7.9	24.5	1.7	20.3
ADVP	44.8	4.2	26.2	3.2	18.6
UCP	29.5	7.1	15.8	5.8	13.7
QP	41.5	7.3	30.1	2.2	11.4
SBAR	20.8	8.5	10.2	0.9	10.5
NX	26.9	12.1	17.1	6.3	9.7
SINV	11.7	11.3	8.3	7.5	3.4
PRN	20.5	3.0	18.4	3.6	2.1
WHPP	14.5	9.3	29.1	13.4	-14.5
NAC	5.9	5.0	21.5	2.8	-15.6
CONJP	15.0	5.0	37.5	11.2	-22.5

Table 2: ON-LSTM (layer 2)'s average parsing accuracies of non-unary constituents in WSJ dev across 5 restarts. The last column is the difference between the second and the fourth column.

Complex Noun Phrases As shown in table 2, the model has a poor parsing performance on NX ($\triangle$acc=9.7) and NAC ($\triangle$acc=-15.6), in contrast to the good performance on NP ($\triangle$acc=34.3). NX and NAC are marker constituents that split an NP into smaller chunks. NX marks individual conjuncts in an NP, e.g. (NP the (NX (NX white shirt) and (NX blue jeans))). NAC shows the scope of a modifier within an NP, e.g. (NP (NAC Secretary (of (State))) James Baker). This contrast suggests that the model is able to identify noun phrases in a sentence, but fails to understand their internal structures. We inspect the model's parses of noun phrases that contain NX and NAC and find that the way the model splits these phrases is very random. We do not identify any pattern.

One can possibly attribute this failure to the use of language modelling as the training task. Whether ON-LSTM makes a split at a token depends on how much information the model chooses to forget at this timestep. Since the model is trained for unidirectional language modelling, it decides whether to forget certain information based on whether the information will be helpful for word predictions in the future. However, constituents inside the same complex noun phrase are sometimes closely related, and cross-constituent hints can be helpful to word predictions. In the NX example we give, "white shirt" gives important hints for the model to predict the tokens "blue jeans", as it suggests that the tokens after "and" might be a color followed by a

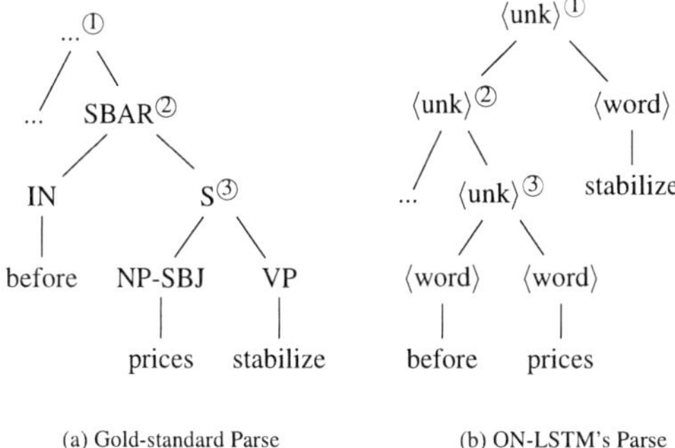

<table>
<tr><td>(a) Gold-standard Parse</td><td>(b) ON-LSTM's Parse</td></tr>
</table>

Figure 3: An example of ON-LSTM overestimating the height of the split point right before the verb. (a) is the gold-standard parsing tree; (b) is the binary tree produced by ON-LSTM. ①, ②, and ③ mark the order/height of the split points in each parse.

type of clothing. This may be why the model might choose not to forget much information after "white shirt and", leading to a missing split between "and" and "blue".

Split Points Right Before Verbs   As shown in Table 2, the model's parsing performances on SQ and VP are the best (Δacc=62.2 and 43.0, ranking the first and second among all constituents), while it does not parse SBAR (subordinate clauses) in a way that is similar to PTB parses (Δacc=10.5, Acc=20.5). Based on this clue, we look into the parses and find the model has a consistent and strong tendency to overestimate the height of the split point right before a verb.

We inspect the model's parses of sentences that contain subordinate clauses, and find that a common mistake made by ON-LSTM is to assign a higher height to the split point right before the main verb of the clause than to the split points right before/after the start/end of the clause. Since ON-LSTM parses a sentence by recursively splitting the sentence at the highest split point, this means the subordinate clause will show up separately in two different constituents rather than a complete single constituent in the parse generated by ON-LSTM. For example, as shown in figure 3, split point ① of a gold-standard parser is right **before** the token "before" and it splits the upper constituents into two parts: "..." and SBAR, where SBAR contains exactly three words: "before", "prices", and "stabilize". In contrast, ON-LSTM chooses the split point right before the verb "stabilize" as split point ① and thus in its parse there is no constituent that contains exactly these three words.

Model	Case 1: Verb (%)	Case 2: Border (%)
ON-LSTM 1	90.0	10.0
ON-LSTM 2	70.0	20.0
ON-LSTM 3	70.0	16.7
ON-LSTM 4	73.3	16.7
ON-LSTM 5	66.7	30.0
Gold	0.0	100.0

Table 3: The percentage of times the split point right before the main verb and the split point right before/after the border tokens in a subordinate clause is the highest split point in the clause. The last row represents the gold standard.

According to our observations, this behavior is not incidental. We randomly sample 30 SBARs from WSJ dev. For each SBAR, we observe whether the first (highest) split point inside the clause (border tokens included) chosen by each model is (1) right before the main verb/auxiliary verb, (2) right before the first token or right after the last token of the clause, or (3) the other tokens in the clause. For example, Figure 3 (a) is of case (2) and Figure 3 (b) is of case (1). We compute the percentages of case (1) and case (2) for each ON-LSTM model and show them in Table 3. We find that all 5 models have a much stronger tendency than the gold-standard parser to choose the split point right before the verb as the highest split point inside a subordinate clause. On each row, the two numbers add to nearly 100, which means when the model makes a mistake on SBAR, it is almost always because it makes the highest split right before the verb.

This tendency also explains why the model's parsing accuracy is the highest on VP and SQ, two constituents which almost always start with a verb. As discussed earlier in this section, a constituent will be correctly parsed if and only if no split point inside it is higher than the split points right before/after the start/end token. Therefore, constituents starting with a verb are naturally easier for ON-LSTM because of this tendency.

A possible reason of this tendency is that since the model is trained on unidirectional language modelling, when it predicts the height of a split point before a token, it only has access to the current token and all the tokens before it. However, when the current input token is a beginning word of a subordinate clause such as "as", "which", "after", it is usually impossible to tell whether it is the start of a subordinate clause. Counterexamples are "as soon as possible", "which to choose", "after 2 hours", etc. Meanwhile, the model probably learns that the appearance of a verb almost always means the start of a high-level constituent VP. As a result, it assigns high heights to split points right before verbs and ignores higher-level constituents including SBAR. If this is true, then a natural and direct fix of this problem is to adopt a bidirectional task such as masked language modelling instead.

6 Conclusions and Future Work

In summary, the model shows basic self-consistency on the task of constituency parsing, and it is consistently able to correctly identify certain constituents (SQ, VP, NP). All these results show that the unique design of the model brings us closer to developing consistently powerful unsupervised parsing models. However, the experiments show that it (a) struggles with the internal structures of complex NPs, and (b) often overestimates the height of the split points right before verbs. Based on our analysis, we hypothesize that both of the failures can be at least partially attributed to the use of unidirectional language modelling as the training task.

There are two potential problems with this training task. First, the motivation of language modelling generally does not perfectly match the target task constituency parsing, since cross-constituent hints are sometimes helpful, as revealed by (a). Second, it is very hard for a unidirectional model to correctly identify some high-level constituents, as revealed by (b). Therefore, we believe a promising research direction is to build latent tree learning models based on bidirectional model architectures like transformer (Vaswani et al., 2017) and the task of acceptability judgement with a dataset like CoLA (Warstadt et al., 2018), which is a more syntax-related sentence-level task that requires the model to predict whether an input sentence is grammatically acceptable. Another option to consider is masked language modelling because it is also a bidirectional task and is much easier to scale up compared to acceptability judgement since it is a self-supervised task.

Acknowledgments

We appreciate Sam Bowman for giving valuable overall project feedbacks and suggestions; we appreciate Phu Mon Htut for patiently sharing and explaining the code and experiment details of her study; we appreciate Yikang Shen for making their code public and granting us the right to reuse the figures in their paper. We would also like to thank Alex Warstadt and Daniel Chin for their great writing suggestions.

References

Eugene Charniak and Glen Carroll. 1992. Two experiments on learning probabilistic dependency grammars from corpora. *Proceedings of the AAAI Workshop on Statistically-Based NLP Techniques*, page 113.

Jihun Choi, Kang Min Yoo, and Sang goo Lee. 2018. Learning to compose task-specific tree structures. In *Proceedings of the Thirty-Second Association for the Advancement of Artificial Intelligence Conference on Artificial Intelligence (AAAI-18)*, volume 2.

Chris Dyer, Adhiguna Kuncoro, Miguel Ballesteros, and Noah A. Smith. 2016. Recurrent neural network grammars. *CoRR*, abs/1602.07776.

Chris Dyer, Gábor Melis, and Phil Blunsom. 2019. A critical analysis of biased parsers in unsupervised parsing. *CoRR*, abs/1909.09428.

Sepp Hochreiter and Jürgen Schmidhuber. 1997. Long short-term memory. *Neural Computation*, 9(8):1735–1780.

Phu Mon Htut, Kyunghyun Cho, and Samuel Bowman. 2018. Grammar induction with neural language models: An unusual replication. In *Proceedings of the 2018 EMNLP Workshop BlackboxNLP: Analyzing and Interpreting Neural Networks for NLP*, pages 371–373, Brussels, Belgium. Association for Computational Linguistics.

Yoon Kim, Alexander Rush, Lei Yu, Adhiguna Kuncoro, Chris Dyer, and Gábor Melis. 2019. Unsupervised recurrent neural network grammars. In *Proceedings of the 2019 Conference of the North American Chapter of the Association for Computational Linguistics: Human Language Technologies, Volume 1 (Long and Short Papers)*, pages 1105–1117, Minneapolis, Minnesota. Association for Computational Linguistics.

Dan Klein and Christopher D. Manning. 2002. A generative constituent-context model for improved grammar induction. In *Proceedings of the 40th Annual Meeting of the Association for Computational Linguistics*, pages 128–135, Philadelphia, Pennsylvania, USA. Association for Computational Linguistics.

Jean Maillard, Stephen Clark, and Dani Yogatama. 2017. Jointly learning sentence embeddings and syntax with unsupervised tree-lstms. *CoRR*, abs/1705.09189.

Mitchell P. Marcus, Beatrice Santorini, and Mary Ann
Marcinkiewicz. 1993. Building a large annotated
corpus of English: The Penn Treebank. *Computational Linguistics*, 19(2):313–330.

Yikang Shen, Zhouhan Lin, Chin wei Huang, and
Aaron Courville. 2018. Neural language modeling
by jointly learning syntax and lexicon. In *International Conference on Learning Representations*.

Yikang Shen, Zhouhan Lin, Chin-Wei Huang, and
Aaron C. Courville. 2017. Neural language modeling by jointly learning syntax and lexicon. *CoRR*,
abs/1711.02013.

Yikang Shen, Shawn Tan, Alessandro Sordoni, and
Aaron Courville. 2019. Ordered neurons: Integrating tree structures into recurrent neural networks. In
International Conference on Learning Representations.

Ashish Vaswani, Noam Shazeer, Niki Parmar, Jakob
Uszkoreit, Llion Jones, Aidan N. Gomez, Lukasz
Kaiser, and Illia Polosukhin. 2017. Attention is all
you need. *CoRR*, abs/1706.03762.

Alex Warstadt, Amanpreet Singh, and Samuel R. Bowman. 2018. Neural network acceptability judgments.
CoRR, abs/1805.12471.

Adina Williams, Andrew Drozdov, and Samuel R.
Bowman. 2018. Do latent tree learning models identify meaningful structure in sentences? *Transactions of the Association for Computational Linguistics*, 6:253–267.

Dani Yogatama, Phil Blunsom, Chris Dyer, Edward
Grefenstette, and Wang Ling. 2017. Learning to
compose words into sentences with reinforcement
learning. In *5th International Conference on Learning Representations, ICLR 2017, Toulon, France,
April 24-26, 2017, Conference Track Proceedings*.
OpenReview.net.

Linguistically-Informed Transformations (LIT): A Method for Automatically Generating Contrast Sets

{Chuanrong Li♡, Lin Shengshuo♡, Leo Z. Liu♣, Xinyi Wu♡, Xuhui Zhou♡ };*
Shane Steinert-Threlkeld♡

♡Department of Linguistics, University of Washington
♣Paul G. Allen School of Computer Science & Engineering, University of Washington
{licor,shuo2019,xywu,xuhuizh,shanest}@uw.edu,
zeyuliu2@cs.washington.edu

Abstract

Although large-scale pretrained language models, such as BERT and RoBERTa, have achieved superhuman performance on in-distribution test sets, their performance suffers on out-of-distribution test sets (e.g., on contrast sets). Building contrast sets often requires human-expert annotation, which is expensive and hard to create on a large scale. In this work, we propose a Linguistically-Informed Transformation (LIT) method to automatically generate contrast sets, which enables practitioners to explore linguistic phenomena of interests as well as compose different phenomena. Experimenting with our method on SNLI and MNLI shows that current pretrained language models, although being claimed to contain sufficient linguistic knowledge, struggle on our automatically generated contrast sets. Furthermore, we improve models' performance on the contrast sets by applying LIT to augment the training data, without affecting performance on the original data.[1]

1 Introduction

Large-scale pretrained language models have given remarkable improvements to a wide range of NLP tasks (Peters et al., 2018; Howard and Ruder, 2018; Devlin et al., 2019; Liu et al., 2019; Radford et al., 2019). However, the results are questionable, since those models take advantage of lexical cues (and other heuristics) in the datasets, which can make them right for wrong reasons (Gururangan et al., 2018; McCoy et al., 2019). Therefore, the concept of evaluating models on contrast sets (Gardner et al., 2020) and the creation of generalization tests (Kaushik et al., 2020) is critical for building a robust NLP system. Those test sets are usually

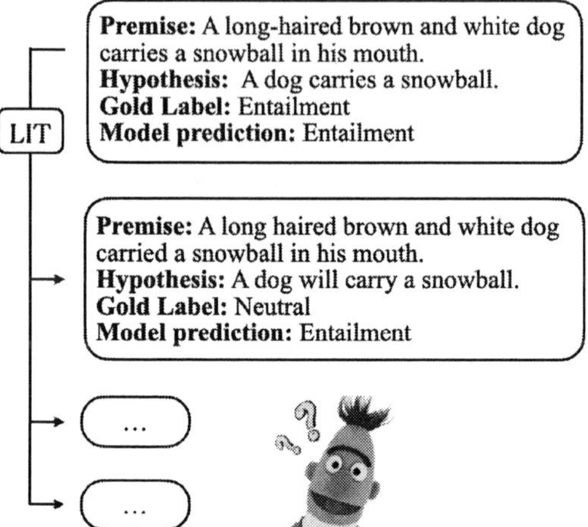

Figure 1: Example of BERT making wrong prediction on LIT-transformed data but correct prediction on the original datum. The detailed transformed datum includes a premise modified to past tense and a hypothesis with future tense. The true label correspondingly changes to *neutral*. LIT also generates multiple transformation results at once for a single original datum; we include only one detailed example here for simplicity of the illustration.

manually created, which requires significant human effort, and so is hard to do on a large scale.

In this work, we propose Linguistically-Informed Transformations (LIT) to create contrast sets automatically. Our method can perturb the original examples and generate various types of contrastive examples, with a wide choice of linguistic phenomena. Furthermore, our tool supports compositional generalization tests. Namely, researchers can choose transformations from a set of basic linguistic phenomena and modify original sentences with an arbitrary combination of those basic transformations.

To demonstrate the utility of LIT, we focus on the natural language inference (NLI) task, a central

---

*Equal Contribution from bracket authors
[1]See code in https://github.com/leo-liuzy/
LIT_auto-gen-contrast-set

Proceedings of the Third BlackboxNLP Workshop on Analyzing and Interpreting Neural Networks for NLP, pages 126–135
Online, November 20, 2020. ©2020 Association for Computational Linguistics

task to many NLP applications. We apply LIT to generate contrast sets for SNLI (Bowman et al., 2015) and MNLI (Williams et al., 2018) using seven linguistic phenomena. Human experts' rating show that our generated data is high-quality for basic transformations and for most of the compositional transformations. See Appendix B for more details.

With our generated contrast sets, we show that pretrained language models, despite having 'seen' huge quantities of raw text data, fail on simple linguistic perturbations. As shown with an example in Figure 1, 'decoupling' tenses of the premise and hypothesis breaks BERT's prediction. Our analysis not only shows the inadequate coverage of SNLI and MNLI datasets but also reveals the deficiency of current pretraining-and-finetuning paradigms. Compared to previous work showing that BERT is not robust and fails to generalize on out-of-distribution test sets (McCoy et al., 2019; Zhou et al., 2019; Jin et al., 2019b), our method provides a more fine-grained picture showing on which phenomenon the models fail. In summary, our contributions are:

- We provide a method for automatically generating phenomenon-specific contrast sets, which helps NLP practitioners better understand pre-trained language models.

- We further apply LIT to augment SNLI and MNLI training data, which improves models' performance on out-of-distribution test sets without sacrificing the models' performance on the in-distribution test set.

- We demonstrate that, in the current pretraining paradigm, traditional linguistic methods are valuable for their ability to measure and promote robustness and consistency in data-driven models.

After discussing several areas of related work in Section 2, we describe LIT in step-by-step detail (Section 3). We then apply LIT to SNLI and MNLI (4.1) before evaluating BERT and RoBERTa on both simple (4.2) and compositional (4.4) transformations. We conclude (Section 5) by discussing limitations of LIT and future directions.

2   Related Work

NLI Model Diagnosis   Our work builds on works diagnosing and improving NLI models with automatically augmented instances (McCoy et al., 2019; Min et al., 2020). While most of these works apply simple methods such as templates to generate new instances, which limits the phenomena covered, our method has a wider coverage and can be easily extended.

Contrast Sets   Contrast sets (Gardner et al., 2020) serve to evaluate a models' true capabilities by evaluating on out-of-distribution data since previous in-distribution test sets often have systematic gaps, which inflate models' performance on a task (Gururangan et al., 2018; Geva et al., 2019). The idea of contrast sets is to modify a test instance to a minimum degree while preserving the original instance's syntactic/semantic artifacts and changing the label. Typically, the authors of the dataset create the contrast set manually. We show that a precision grammar, namely ERG (Copestake and Flickinger, 2000), can be used to automate this process while preserving the authors' benefit of choosing the perturbations of interest.

Adversarial Datasets   Another line of work addressing the problem of current models' superhuman performance on in-distribution test sets focuses on adversarial methods. Bras et al. (2020) uses an adversarial filtering algorithm to reduce spurious bias in the dataset to avoid models relying on such patterns. Dinan et al. (2019) shows that a human-in-the-loop adversarial training framework significantly improves models' robustness. And Jin et al. (2019a) shows that current pretrained language models are not robust under simple lexical manipulations. Adversarial methods generate test instances automatically, which can be applied to augment the training data (Jin et al., 2019a; Dinan et al., 2019). However, these adversarial methods introduce specific models in the loop, which might also bias the test set.

3   Generating Contrast Sets

We propose a new Linguistically-Informed Transformation (LIT) method for large-scale automatic generation of contrast sets. LIT 1) parses the input sentence for both syntax and semantics, 2) produces transformed syntax and semantics for each linguistic phenomenon, 3) generates perturbed sentences corresponding to the transformed syntax/semantics, 4) and selects the best surface sentence for each phenomenon. The full pipeline is shown in Figure 2. Note that we expand the definition of

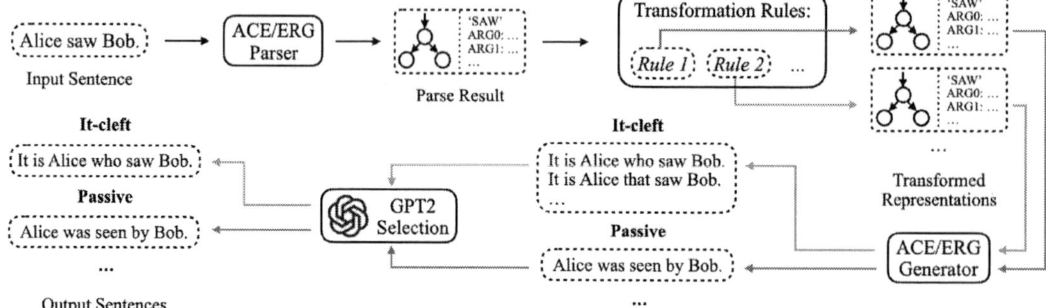

Figure 2: General pipeline of LIT system exemplified with one input sentence. The parse result includes both syntax and semantics. The transformation rules produce one transformed representation per phenomenon. A set of sentences, all grammatical according to ERG, is generated for each transformed representation. One sentence per phenomenon is selected as the final output sentence. We include two "*Rule*"s for illustration purpose; LIT includes more transformation rules and can be extended for more phenomena.

contrast sets in Gardner et al. (2020). We not only apply our generated contrast sets for evaluation but also for augmentation. We also no longer restrict that the perturbations necessarily lead to the change of the labels.

LIT contains seven phenomenon-specific transformation rules for modifying the parse results and can be further extended; LIT also allows the composition of different transformation rules for complicated perturbations involving multiple linguistic phenomena.

3.1 Parse and Generation

LIT utilizes an existing grammar implementation for parsing and generation, namely the English Resource Grammar (ERG, Copestake and Flickinger 2000). ERG is a linguistically motivated broad-coverage grammar for English in the Head-Driven Phrase Structure Grammar framework (HPSG, Pollard and Sag 1994; Sag et al. 2003) covering 82.6% of sentences in Wall Street Journal (WSJ) sections in the Penn Treebank (Marcus et al., 1993). ERG is processing-neutral, meaning that it is not limited to either parsing or generation, and can handle both with a grammar processor. In this work, we use the ACE parser[2] as the processor for ERG grammar.

3.2 Transformation

The core part and original contributions of our LIT system are the transformation rules; each rule modifies the parse results from ERG and the ACE parser for one linguistic phenomenon. An ERG parse result includes an HPSG syntax tree and a seman-

---

[2]http://sweaglesw.org/linguistics/ace/

tic representation in Minimal Recursion Semantics (MRS, Copestake et al. 2005). An MRS representation consists of a bag of *elementary predicates* (EPs), each with a *handle* for reference, a set of *handle constraints* that specify relations between handles, a *top* indicating the topmost EP, and an *index* variable for the event described by the entire sentence. Every variable has a set of features such as tense and numbers indicating the properties of the entities or the events.

In what follows, we illustrate the application of the transformation rule for it-cleft construction applied to the sentence *Alice saw Bob.*; see Appendix A for a full list of rules.

(1) Original parse result:

```
[ TOP: h0
  INDEX: e2
     [ e SF: prop TENSE: past ... ]
  RELS: < [ proper_q LBL: h4 ARG0: x3 ... ]
          [ named LBL: h7 ARG0: x3 CARG: "Alice" ]
          [ _see_v_1 LBL: h1 ARG0: e2 ARG1: x3 ARG2: x9 ... ]
          [ proper_q LBL: h10 ARG0: x9 ... ]
          [ named LBL: h13 ARG0: x9 CARG: "Bob" ] >
  HCONS: < h0 qeq h1 h5 qeq h7 h11 qeq h13 > ]
```

TOP: label of topmost EP
INDEX: the variable associated with the sentential event
RELS: bag of EPs
LBL: label variable for the EP
HCONS: constrains between labels for EPs; qeq denotes a scoping relation

(2) Inserting it-cleft EP

```
[ _be_v_itcleft LBL: h14 ARG0: e15 ARG1: x3 ARG2: h1 ]
```

(3) Connecting top handle $h0$ to it-cleft EP handle (LBL)

```
HCONS: < h0 qeq h14 h5 qeq h7 h11 qeq h13 > ]
```

(4) Change sentential semantic index to it-cleft EP's ARG0

```
INDEX: e15
   [ e SF: prop TENSE: pres ... ]
```

(5) Final result

```
[ TOP: h0
  INDEX: e15
    [ e SF: prop TENSE: pres MOOD: indicative PROG: - PERF: - ]
  RELS: < [ proper_q LBL: h4 ... ]
          [ named LBL: h7 ARG0: x3 CARG: "Alice" ]
          [ _see_1 LBL: h1 ARG0: e2 ARG1: x3 ARG2: x9 ]
          [ proper_q LBL: h10 ARG0: x9 ... ]
          [ named LBL: h13 ARG0: x9 CARG: "Bob" ]
          [ _be_v_itcleft LBL: h14
            ARG0: e15 ARG1: x3 ARG2: h1 ] >
  HCONS: < h0 qeq h14 h5 qeq h7 h11 qeq h13 > ]
```

For each parse result, LIT generates one transformation for each linguistic phenomenon, obtaining a set of simple transformations. Each transformation result in this set can also be fed into LIT as a new base for transformation, allowing different rules to be stacked and producing compositions of transformations. LIT uses all transformation results to generate surface sentences.

3.3 Surface Sentence Selection

Selection by ERG: One of the advantages of the LIT system is that the grammar backbone ensures the acceptability of the generated data. The ACE parser only generates grammatical sentences, according to the ERG. Consequently, ill-formed LIT-transformed results are automatically rejected at the generation phase without additional efforts from the users and developers; for instance, even though LIT may produce a representation that would correspond to *Alice may will see Bob.* [3], such a surface string will not be generated since the ERG does not accept it.

In practice, ERG slightly overgenerates and allows certain ungrammatical strings. Such cases are likely too rare to affect the overall quality of the dataset and can often be filtered out during post-selection. ERG also cannot rule out grammatically well-formed but semantically unnatural sentences, which limits the data quality for certain constructions, especially for passives. As a sanity check, we had expert annotators evaluate the generated data and found high agreement on the grammaticality of generated data; the full details are in Appendix B.

Post-Selection by Pretrained Language Models: ERG often permits multiple strings for a single representation since the meaning-to-form mapping is not unique in natural languages. To select the candidate sentence for a specific transformation, LIT employs GPT-2 (Radford et al., 2018) to rank multiple surface sentences generated from the same representation and selects the best one according to their perplexity scores.

---

³* means ungrammatical

3.4 Phenomena Covered

LIT is capable of perturbing sentences for seven linguistic transformations: polar questions, it-clefts, tense and aspect, modality, negation, passives and subject-object swapping. Examples for each transformation are shown in Appendix A. LIT also allows different transformations to be stacked where possible. LIT can be further extended for more linguistic transformations, and any extension to the LIT system would also receive all of the aforementioned benefits from ACE and ERG.

3.5 Comparison with Other Approaches

Flexibility: LIT covers certain simple constructions that can be handled with a template-based approach, for instance, the subject-object swapping in McCoy et al. (2019). LIT is, however, not limited to template-generated examples and is capable of perturbing naturally-occurring instances.

Plausibility: One special property setting LIT apart from other automatic dataset-construction methods is that LIT uses existing linguistic theories resources as its backbone. The use of ERG enables LIT to control data plausibility without human annotation from scratch.

Modularity: LIT consists of multiple modules: parsing and generation, transformation, and post-selection. Extending with more transformation rules, updating ERG (which is still under active development), and including other language models for post-selection can all be handled in the system without major modification to other modules, allowing LIT to be reused for different works.

Model Agnostic: LIT employs traditional linguistic methods for transforming sentences, and the role of language models is limited to selecting the best one from the strings generated by ERG. Contrasting to models trained on specific datasets, the ERG grammar behind LIT does not introduce bias from any specific architecture or dataset. This increases the utility of contrast sets generated with LIT as they are likely to be used for testing data-driven models.

3.6 Sentence Coverage

LIT successfully transformed 21.0% of the sentence pairs in MNLI and 19.7% in SNLI, with at least one transformed result for each sentence in the pair. The number of transformed sentence pairs by phenomenon is shown in Table 2.

Transformation	Label	Sentence 1	Sentence 2
`o;o`	Contradiction	Alice is driving a car.	Alice is playing piano.
`i;i`	Unchanged	It is Alice who is driving a car.	It is Alice who is playing piano.
`pa;pa`	Unchanged	A car is being driven by Alice.	Piano is being played by Alice.
`f;p`	Neutral	Alice will be driving a car.	Alice was playing piano.
`m;o`	Neutral	Alice may be driving a car.	Alice is playing piano.
`f;p +i`	Neutral	It is Alice who will be driving a car.	It is Alice who was playing piano.
`f;p +pa`	Neutral	A car will be driven by Alice.	Piano will be played by Alice.

Table 1: Examples for label rules used for determining labels of generated data for different transformations. We use `a;b + c` to denote compositional transformation where the premise is transformed with both **a** and **b**, whereas the hypothesis is transformed with **b** and **c**.

	# MNLI ex.			# SNLI ex.	
	train	**m.**	**mm.**	**train**	**dev**
`o;o`	392k	10k	10k	550k	10k
`i;i`	13k	1k	1k	65k	1k
`pa;pa`	3k	236	353	16k	586
`f;p`	3k	221	208	6k	111
`p;f`	3k	262	260	7k	142
`m;o`	13k	1k	1k	48k	905
`p;f +i`	4k	288	303	7k	122
`p;f +pa`	719	61	82	1k	45
`f;p +i`	4k	259	270	6k	91
`f;p +pa`	727	59	72	1k	37

Table 2: Number of examples (ex.) of different transformation rules in MNLI and SNLI parse results. For MNLI, we report example count in training (**train**) set and development (**dev**) set. For SNLI, we report example count in training (**train**) set, matched development (**m.**) set, and mismatched development (**mm.**) set.

4 Experiments

Using LIT, we evaluate whether large pretrained models 'understand' certain linguistic phenomena through testing them on transformed SNLI and MNLI instances. Specifically, we investigate whether BERT and RoBERTa can successfully predict transformed instances on modality (may), tenses (past; future), passivization, it cleft, and their compositions correctly and consistently. In the following section, we first discuss how we set up our tasks, and then we present our results on simple transformations and composed transformations, respectively.

4.1 Setup

For the purpose of this paper, we formulate our experiment settings as follows. Specifically, each instance in SNLI/MNLI consists of a hypothesis (e.g., *Some men are playing a sport.*), a premise (e.g. *A soccer game with multiple males playing.*) and their corresponding relationship label (entailment). A dual transformed instance is obtained by applying LIT to either the hypothesis or premise, which may or may not change the label of their relationship (i.e., entailment, neutral, and contradiction).

4.1.1 Transforming NLI Datasets with LIT

While LIT does not produce laebls after transformation, we apply two label-changing, two label-preserving, and the relevant compositional transformations listed in Table 1, with one example per transformation. Note that `o;o` means we do not modify the instance.

- **Modality** is used to talk about possibilities and necessities beyond what is actually true and is central to natural language semantics (Kratzer, 1991). We investigate models' ability to understand the uncertainty expressed in the text by adding 'may' to the instance. Thus, a 'contradiction' or 'entailment' relationship label is changed to 'neutral' logically. Specifically, we consider adding 'may' to the premise (`m;o`). Note that one can also add 'may' to the hypothesis, which we leave for future work.

- **Tenses** are used to evaluate sentences at times other than the time of utterance. To probe whether models are able to perform temporal reasoning, we transformed the instances by assigning past tense to hypothesis and future tense to premise (`p;f`) or vice versa (`f;p`), which changes the 'contradiction' and 'entailment' label to 'neutral'.

		`f;p`	`p;f`	`i;i`	`pa;pa`	`m;o`	`p;f +i`	`p;f +pa`	`f;p +i`	`f;p +pa`
	Acc@Ori	93.21	91.60	91.86	95.28	90.90	90.97	93.44	94.21	94.92
ORI	Acc@Ctr	5.43	41.98	85.17	90.99	15.13	34.38	32.79	6.18	6.78
	Consistency	4.98	34.35	91.04	93.99	10.19	28.82	29.51	5.79	5.08
		`f;p`	`p;f`	`i;i`	`pa;pa`	`m;o`	`p;f +i`	`p;f +pa`	`f;p +i`	`f;p +pa`
	Acc@Ori	93.67	93.13	91.86	94.85	92.19	90.97	93.44	94.98	94.92
AUG	Acc@Ctr	99.10	99.62	89.80	91.85	99.11	87.50	98.36	76.06	94.92
	Consistency	92.76	92.75	95.06	94.42	91.49	78.47	91.80	71.04	89.83

Table 3: Consistency and accuracies of `roberta-large` over different linguistic phenomena in MNLI. We first train two model separately on the original (ORI) training set and augmented (AUG) training set. Then, we evaluate the trained models on **m.** and **mm.** for each phenomena. In this table, we report accuracy on the original sentence pair (Acc@Ori), accuracy on the transformed sentence pair (Acc@Ctr), and the model's consistency. Each accuracy/consistency has the format (**m./mm.**).

- **Label-preserving Transformations** do not require inferring the label after transformation, which serves to test models' ability to stay consistent with its prediction after some linguistic perturbations. Here, we experiment on passivization (**pa**) and it-cleft (**i**).

- **Compositional Transformations** help us further evaluate models' 'understanding' of certain linguistic phenomenon. If the models robustly 'understand' phenomenon α and β, composing both should not pose problems to the models. Specifically, we consider adding passivization and it cleft to **p;f** and **f;p** transformations. They are denoted as **p;f +i**, **p;f +p**, **f;p +i**, and **f;p +p** respectively.

The statistics for our generated dataset are shown in Table 2. We train two models on two training set. The original (ORI) training set includes untransformed SNLI training data, whilst the augmented (AUG) training set includes LIT-transformed data with all non-conpositional transformations listed in Table 2. We test both models' accuracy and consistency for all transformations in the same table.

We use a set of rules to infer the labels of generated pairs (see Table 1) based on the types of transformation and the original labels. For instance, originally entailment pairs will turn neutral when 'may' is inserted since the 'may' modality discharges the truth value of original propositions. 'Decoupling' the tenses of originally present-tense pairs for past/future tense pairs also turns the label to neutral, for events at different times are less likely to affect each other.

We hypothesize that NLI tasks follow logic rules completely and our following experiments also con-

form to that hypothesis, which legitimize our label-inferring rules. However exceptions to such rules may occur: *Alice died* nevertheless contradicts *Alice will be eating*, since dying is an event preventing future action of its agent. Annotation by three experts of 100 randomly chosen transformed pairs shows that 79% human agreement with the inferred label, with 92% for label-preserving transformations and 76% for label-changing transformations. Future work will explore refinements of our label-assignment procedure.

4.1.2 Probing Models

For pretrained language models, we use models from HuggingFace (Wolf et al., 2019). In this paper, we use `bert-base-uncased`, `bert-large-uncased` (Devlin et al., 2019), `roberta-base`, and `roberta-large` (Liu et al., 2019). For all models, we use Adam to optimize the parameters with an initial learning rate of 5×10^{-5}. For all the fine-tuning, we use the same seed and train with batch size 32 for 3 epochs, the same setting used in (Devlin et al., 2019). In this paper, since we never use the development set for early stopping or hyper-parameter tuning (and since MNLI doesn't have a publicly available test set) , we evaluate our models on the development set. Note that MNLI has matched (**m.**) and mismatched (**mm.**) test examples, which are derived from the same and different sources as those in the training set, respectively.

4.1.3 Evaluation Metrics

To fully evaluate models' performance, we use both accuracy and consistency. While accuracy measures how well a model can accurately predict

		MNLI	aug-MNLI	SNLI	aug-SNLI
ORI	bert-base-uncased	84.31/84.79	69.47/69.05	90.97	46.96
	bert-large-uncased	86.54/86.46	71.28/70.34	91.78	47.72
	roberta-base	88.00/87.60	71.95/70.58	91.86	**47.72**
	roberta-large	**90.01/90.34**	**73.78/73.04**	**92.83**	46.34
AUG	bert-base-uncased	84.62/84.45	86.60/85.73	90.86	94.34
	bert-large-uncased	86.24/86.37	88.14/87.98	91.49	**96.00**
	roberta-base	87.51/87.52	89.66/89.45	92.13	95.05
	roberta-large	**90.14/89.84**	**91.47/91.04**	92.53	95.93

Table 4: Accuracy on MNLI and SNLI datasets. MNLI results have the format (**m./mm.**). SNLI results are on SNLI **dev**.

test instances, consistency measures how robust a model under certain perturbations. We report accuracy on the original test set (Acc@Ori), accuracy on the generated contrast set (Acc@Ctr), and the consistency score (defined below). Note that test sets for different phenomena might be different since we only choose the test instances to be included for each phenomenon if LIT produces contrast instances corresponding to the phenomenon.

Consistency In addition to using accuracy to measure models' performance, recent research pays attention to consistency, which provides another perspective to probe models' competence in the real world (Trichelair et al., 2018; Zhou et al., 2019; Gardner et al., 2020). If a model is robust for the given task, then its performance on original and transformed data should be consistent. For instance, a human is expected to be consistent over the understanding of both a simple sentence and its it-cleft counterpart. We thus measure consistency by comparing the model's prediction on original and transformed data. We define consistency for a dual test instance as the match between labels assigned on original and transformed data instances. Specifically, we define the model to be consistent if a model makes the same label prediction (whether correct or not) for a dual test instance as for the original, and inconsistent otherwise.[4] We evaluate the model consistency for each type of linguistic transformation to investigate the models' robustness to different linguistic phenomena, and to examine the differences between the difficulties of different linguistic structures for the models.

4.2 Simple Transformations

By perturbing the test instances with our predefined transformations, we aim to probe pre-trained language models' relevant linguistic knowledge and robustness towards those transformations.

As shown in Table 3, RoBERTa, trained on ORI of MNLI, performs worse on contrast sets, especially for label-changing transformations. Label-preserving transformations do not hurt models' performance as much as label-changing transformations. We observed similar trends for other models (see Appendix C. This observation is aligned with (McCoy et al., 2019)), which suggests that models are relying on lexical overlaps to infer the relationship between premise and hypothesis.

Another observation is that RoBERTa does not achieve high consistency in any of the simple transformations. The poor and inconsistent performance of RoBERTa on our contrast sets shows that even though the model can perform very well on the in-distribution test set, there is still a systematic gap for future models to overcome.

4.3 Applying LIT for Data Augmentation

Having shown that pre-trained language models do not generalize well to our generated contrast sets, we ask whether we can 'teach' models to recognize those phenomena and make correct predictions accordingly.

We do this by fine-tuning models on the augmented training data together with the original data. As shown in Table 4, we observe that, when training on the augmented data, models preserve their performance on the original test set while improving significantly on the out-of-distribution test sets.

Taking a closer look over the specific phenomenon in Table 3, models' performance increases significantly on label-changing contrast

---

[4]Note that this contrasts with what Gardner et al. (2020) call *contrast consistency*, where both predictions additionally have to be both correct.

sets. This indicates that models improve in terms of 'understanding' the role of modality (may) and tenses in natural language inference. Arguably, models may simply memorize the 'trick' that modality (may) and tenses (past to future) are associated with label 'neutral.' However, we successfully show that we could enable models to learn those 'tricks' through data augmentation. Future work will probe whether models fine-tuned on our augmented data are relying on such heuristics.

The models' performance also increases slightly for label-preserving transformations. However, their consistency does not increase for every transformation, which suggests that data augmentation alone may not suffice for building robust models.

4.4 Compositional Transformations

We further investigate the models' performance when multiple transformation rules are composed together and applied to a single sentence. We probe models fine-tuned on the original dataset and the dataset augmented with only simple transformations with our compositional test sets. If a model learns the linguistic phenomenon systematically, it should perform well on these compositional transformations even without training. This resembles the zero-shot tests on tasks like SCAN (Lake and Baroni, 2018), but applied to naturally occurring linguistic data.[5]

The bottom-right quadrant of Table 3 shows that RoBERTa performs very well on compositional transformations when it is fine-tuned only on simple transformations, in some cases ($\mathtt{p;f + pa}$) even performing better than on the simple transformation data. Again, we observed similar results across all models (see Appendix C). This suggests that it has learned something systematic about the transformations in the augmented dataset.

For both $\mathtt{p;f}$ and $\mathtt{f;p}$, RoBERTa performs worse when additionally composing with it-clefts than with passivization. This suggests that there are differences in the level of systematicity learned for the different transformations, a phenomenon which future work will investigate in more detail.

5 Discussion and Analysis

With LIT, we reveal that current high-performance NLI models still suffer from understanding simple linguistic phenomena. They can be trained to understand these phenomena in a way that appears systematic. In the remainder, we discuss the limitations of LIT, applying LIT to investigate the systematic deficiency of current large-scale datasets, and potential applications of LIT to tasks other than NLI.

5.1 Limitations of LIT

One major limitation of LIT is the dependency on ERG, which took more than twenty years of human labor and is specifically for English. It is possible to swap ERG/ACE parser with data-driven parsers and generators trained on semantic graphbanks, including the DeepBank (Flickinger et al., 2012) which uses the same representation frameworks, potentially extending the method to other languages where a broad-coverage hand-crafted grammar is unavailable. Using data-driven models, however, does re-introduce possible model bias and uncertainty of robustness. Nevertheless, once such a resource is available, LIT provides a method of transforming sentences for data augmentation and integrating linguistic knowledge into a data-driven NLP pipeline.

Future work will also involve expanding the phenomena covered by LIT by generating new transformation rules (cf. 3.4). One potential extension is the insertion of control and raising verbs:

(6)   Alice voted for Bob.

    a.   Alice seemed to have voted for Bob.

    b.   Alice wished to vote for Bob.

    c.   Alice persuaded Carol to vote for Bob.

LIT also has a limited coverage, successfully transforming about 20% of the instances in SNLI (see Section 3.4). The limited coverage may introduce bias in the generated dataset; for instance, the ERG grammar is more likely to fail when parsing complicated sentences. Nevertheless, we provide a proof of conept that the method can be used to augment data and probe for understanding of the linguistic phenomena of interest here; a higher recall grammar will only improve the situation, and can be easily integrated.

5.2 Analysing Sentence Types in Datasets

In addition to constructing contrast sets, we also used LIT to directly analyze the sentence types in the transformable portion of SNLI and MNLI to investigate the effects of data bias on pretrained models probed in our work. For MNLI, we found

---

[5]See Andreas (2020) for a complementary, heuristic-driven approach to compositional data augmentation.

that 46.4% sentences are in present tense, 32.2% in past tense and only 2.95% in future tense; 7.27% sentences are passive, 0.580% have *may* modality and 0.227% are it-cleft sentences. We found no passive/future or future/passive tense pairs. The lack of sentences with *may* modality and mismatched tense pairs may account for the low performance for those transformations before fine-tuning on them. It-cleft transformation does not change the meaning and labels, which may explain the high performance despite its rarity in the original data. Note that LIT can only detect linguistic phenomena in sentences parsable with ERG (see Section 3.6), but such functionality can still provide important insights on datasets and can be further explored in future works.

6 Conclusion

We propose Linguistically-Informed Transformations (LIT), a general method to generate contrast sets using an existing linguistic resource. We apply LIT to transform NLI datasets and evaluate current state-of-the-art NLI models. We reveal the systematic gap between current NLI models and an ideal NLI model for NLP practice, which comes from the inadequate coverage of the linguistic phenomenon of SNLI and MNLI. We further show that models can be further improved by using LIT to augment the training data. Furthermore, models fine-tuned on simple transformations perform very well on compositional transformations, suggesting that fine-tuning provides some systematic understanding of these phenomena.

References

Jacob Andreas. 2020. Good-enough compositional data augmentation. In *Proceedings of the 58th Annual Meeting of the Association for Computational Linguistics*, pages 7556–7566, Online. Association for Computational Linguistics.

Samuel R. Bowman, Gabor Angeli, Christopher Potts, and Christopher D. Manning. 2015. A large annotated corpus for learning natural language inference. In *Proceedings of the 2015 Conference on Empirical Methods in Natural Language Processing*, pages 632–642, Lisbon, Portugal. Association for Computational Linguistics.

Ronan Le Bras, Swabha Swayamdipta, Chandra Bhagavatula, Rowan Zellers, Matthew E. Peters, Ashish Sabharwal, and Yejin Choi. 2020. Adversarial filters of dataset biases.

Ann Copestake and Dan Flickinger. 2000. An open source grammar development environment and broad-coverage English grammar using HPSG. In *Proceedings of the Second International Conference on Language Resources and Evaluation (LREC'00)*, Athens, Greece. European Language Resources Association (ELRA).

Ann Copestake, Dan Flickinger, Carl Pollard, and Ivan A. Sag. 2005. Minimal Recursion Semantics: An Introduction. *Research on Language and Computation*, 3(2-3):281–332.

Jacob Devlin, Ming-Wei Chang, Kenton Lee, and Kristina Toutanova. 2019. Bert: Pre-training of deep bidirectional transformers for language understanding. In *NAACL-HLT*.

Emily Dinan, Samuel Humeau, Bharath Chintagunta, and Jason Weston. 2019. Build it break it fix it for dialogue safety: Robustness from adversarial human attack. *Proceedings of the 2019 Conference on Empirical Methods in Natural Language Processing and the 9th International Joint Conference on Natural Language Processing (EMNLP-IJCNLP)*.

Dan Flickinger, Yi Zhang, and Valia Kordoni. 2012. Deepbank. a dynamically annotated treebank of the wall street journal. In *Proceedings of the 11th International Workshop on Treebanks and Linguistic Theories*, pages 85–96.

Matt Gardner, Yoav Artzi, Victoria Basmova, Jonathan Berant, Ben Bogin, Sihao Chen, Pradeep Dasigi, Dheeru Dua, Yanai Elazar, Ananth Gottumukkala, Nitish Gupta, Hanna Hajishirzi, Gabriel Ilharco, Daniel Khashabi, Kevin Lin, Jiangming Liu, Nelson F. Liu, Phoebe Mulcaire, Qiang Ning, Sameer Singh, Noah A. Smith, Sanjay Subramanian, Reut Tsarfaty, Eric Wallace, Ally Quan Zhang, and Ben Zhou. 2020. Evaluating nlp models via contrast sets. *ArXiv*, abs/2004.02709.

Mor Geva, Yoav Goldberg, and Jonathan Berant. 2019. Are we modeling the task or the annotator? an investigation of annotator bias in natural language understanding datasets. In *Proceedings of the 2019 Conference on Empirical Methods in Natural Language Processing and the 9th International Joint Conference on Natural Language Processing (EMNLP-IJCNLP)*, pages 1161–1166, Hong Kong, China. Association for Computational Linguistics.

Suchin Gururangan, Swabha Swayamdipta, Omer Levy, Roy Schwartz, Samuel Bowman, and Noah A. Smith. 2018. Annotation artifacts in natural language inference data. In *Proceedings of the 2018 Conference of the North American Chapter of the Association for Computational Linguistics: Human Language Technologies, Volume 2 (Short Papers)*, pages 107–112, New Orleans, Louisiana. Association for Computational Linguistics.

Jeremy Howard and Sebastian Ruder. 2018. Universal language model fine-tuning for text classification. In

Proceedings of the 56th Annual Meeting of the Association for Computational Linguistics (Volume 1: Long Papers), pages 328–339, Melbourne, Australia. Association for Computational Linguistics.

Di Jin, Zhijing Jin, Joey Tianyi Zhou, and Peter Szolovits. 2019a. Is bert really robust? a strong baseline for natural language attack on text classification and entailment.

Di Jin, Zhijing Jin, Joey Tianyi Zhou, and Peter Szolovits. 2019b. Is bert really robust? natural language attack on text classification and entailment. *ArXiv*, abs/1907.11932.

Divyansh Kaushik, Eduard Hovy, and Zachary Lipton. 2020. Learning the difference that makes a difference with counterfactually-augmented data. In *International Conference on Learning Representations*.

Angelika Kratzer. 1991. Modality. in semantics: An international handbook of contemporary research.

Brenden M. Lake and Marco Baroni. 2018. Generalization without systematicity: On the compositional skills of sequence-to-sequence recurrent networks. In *ICML*.

Yinhan Liu, Myle Ott, Naman Goyal, Jingfei Du, Mandar Joshi, Danqi Chen, Omer Levy, Mike Lewis, Luke Zettlemoyer, and Veselin Stoyanov. 2019. Roberta: A robustly optimized bert pretraining approach. *ArXiv*, abs/1907.11692.

Mitchell P. Marcus, Beatrice Santorini, and Mary Ann Marcinkiewicz. 1993. Building a large annotated corpus of English: The Penn Treebank. *Computational Linguistics*, 19(2):313–330.

Tom McCoy, Ellie Pavlick, and Tal Linzen. 2019. Right for the wrong reasons: Diagnosing syntactic heuristics in natural language inference. In *Proceedings of the 57th Annual Meeting of the Association for Computational Linguistics*, pages 3428–3448, Florence, Italy. Association for Computational Linguistics.

Junghyun Min, R. Thomas McCoy, Dipanjan Das, Emily Pitler, and Tal Linzen. 2020. Syntactic data augmentation increases robustness to inference heuristics. In *Proceedings of the 58th Annual Meeting of the Association for Computational Linguistics*, Seattle, Washington. Association for Computational Linguistics.

Matthew E. Peters, Mark Neumann, Mohit Iyyer, Matt Gardner, Christopher Clark, Kenton Lee, and Luke Zettlemoyer. 2018. Deep contextualized word representations. In *Proc. of NAACL*.

Carl Jesse Pollard and Ivan A. Sag. 1994. *Head-driven phrase structure grammar*. Studies in contemporary linguistics. Center for the Study of Language and Information ; University of Chicago Press, Stanford : Chicago.

Alec Radford, Karthik Narasimhan, Tim Salimans, and Ilya Sutskever. 2018. Improving language understanding by generative pre-training.

Alec Radford, Jeff Wu, Rewon Child, David Luan, Dario Amodei, and Ilya Sutskever. 2019. Language models are unsupervised multitask learners.

Ivan A Sag, Thomas Wasow, and Emily M Bender. 2003. *Syntactic Theory: A Formal Introduction*, volume 152 of *CSLI Lecture Notes*. CSLI Publications.

Paul Trichelair, Ali Emami, Adam Trischler, Kaheer Suleman, and Jackie Chi Kit Cheung. 2018. How reasonable are common-sense reasoning tasks: A case-study on the winograd schema challenge and swag.

Adina Williams, Nikita Nangia, and Samuel Bowman. 2018. A broad-coverage challenge corpus for sentence understanding through inference. In *Proceedings of the 2018 Conference of the North American Chapter of the Association for Computational Linguistics: Human Language Technologies, Volume 1 (Long Papers)*, pages 1112–1122. Association for Computational Linguistics.

Thomas Wolf, Lysandre Debut, Victor Sanh, Julien Chaumond, Clement Delangue, Anthony Moi, Pierric Cistac, Tim Rault, R'emi Louf, Morgan Funtowicz, and Jamie Brew. 2019. Huggingface's transformers: State-of-the-art natural language processing. *ArXiv*, abs/1910.03771.

Xuhui Zhou, Yue Zhang, Leyang Cui, and Dandan Huang. 2019. Evaluating commonsense in pretrained language models.

Tracking the Traces of Passivization and Negation in Contextualized Representations

Hande Celikkanat   **Sami Virpioja**   **Jörg Tiedemann**   **Marianna Apidianaki**

Department of Digital Humanities
University of Helsinki
Helsinki, Finland
`firstname.lastname@helsinki.fi`

Abstract

Contextualized word representations encode rich information about syntax and semantics, alongside specificities of each context of use. While contextual variation does not always reflect actual meaning shifts, it can still reduce the similarity of embeddings for word instances having the same meaning. We explore the imprint of two specific linguistic alternations, namely passivization and negation, on the representations generated by neural models trained with two different objectives: masked language modeling and translation. Our exploration methodology is inspired by an approach previously proposed for removing societal biases from word vectors. We show that passivization and negation leave their traces on the representations, and that neutralizing this information leads to more similar embeddings for words that should preserve their meaning in the transformation. We also find clear differences in how the respective features generalize across datasets.

1 Introduction

Contextualized representations extracted from pre-trained language models reflect the syntactic and semantic properties of words (Linzen et al., 2016; Hewitt and Manning, 2019; Rogers et al., 2020; Tenney et al., 2019) as well as variation in their context of use. We propose to explore the impact of context variation on word representations. We specifically address representations generated by the BERT model (Devlin et al., 2019), trained using a language modeling objective, and translation models involving one or more language pairs (Artetxe and Schwenk, 2019; Vázquez et al., 2020).

We run a series of controlled experiments using sentences illustrating both meaning preserving and meaning altering transformations from the SICK dataset (Marelli et al., 2014b), and examples automatically generated using a template-based

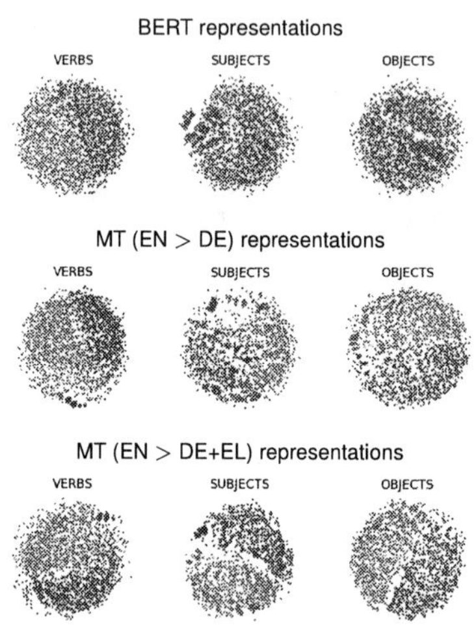

Figure 1: Multidimensional (MDS) visualization of representations obtained for verbs and nouns from active (red) and corresponding passive (blue) sentences. Data points are BERT representations (top) and the encodings from machine translation models involving one (middle) or two language pairs (bottom).

method (Prasad et al., 2019). We explore the impact of specific alternations on the representations, namely passivization and negation. Examples in our datasets consist of sentences that only differ in terms of the specific alternation addressed. In order to detect the imprint of these transformations on the representations, we employ methodology inspired by work on linguistic bias detection in embedding representations (Bolukbasi et al., 2016; Lauscher et al., 2019; Ravfogel et al., 2020).

Furthermore, we investigate the impact of removing the encoding of such alternations on word similarity. Intuitively, we would expect the representations of words present in sentences that have undergone passivization (PAS) to be highly similar despite the differences in syntactic structure. Consider, for example, the words *mafia, millionaire*

Proceedings of the Third BlackboxNLP Workshop on Analyzing and Interpreting Neural Networks for NLP, pages 136–148
Online, November 20, 2020. ©2020 Association for Computational Linguistics

and *kidnapped* in the examples ① and ②.

① *The mafia kidnapped the millionaire.*
② *The millionaire was kidnapped by the mafia.*

PAS changes the words' syntactic roles but their thematic roles remain the same. The meaning shift that results from this operation is mainly discursive,[1] shifting the focus from the theme to the agent, but the content words in the two sentences still refer to the same event and entities.[2] Their representations should thus be highly similar.

We also address a meaning altering transformation which involves inserting (or removing) the negation particle to produce contradictions, as in ③ and ④.

③ *The boy is playing the piano.*
④ *The boy is <u>not</u> playing the piano.*

The effect of negation (NEG) at the sentence level is obvious. However, the meaning of specific words (*boy*, *playing*, *piano*) should remain the same despite of the whole sentence having the opposite meaning. Below, we explore the extent to which this type of context variation affects the similarity of the representations of word instances in the two sentences.

We show that passivization and negation[3] have a significant imprint on the representations, and that their removal can improve word similarity estimation. Our results also highlight that this type of context variation is differently marked in representations generated by models trained with different objectives. Specifically, we find that variation in the embeddings produced by models trained with a translation objective generalize better than those derived from models trained with a masked language modeling objective, across datasets, in the sense that they seem to be encoded in features that are independent of the specific dataset.

---

[1]Note, however, that the impact of the alternation on the framing of the sentence can be significant. Passive avoids identifying a causal agent and therefore conceals the responsibility for an event (Greene and Resnik, 2009).

[2]In sentence ①, the *mafia* is the agent and is in subject position, while the *millionaire* is the theme in direct object position. In ②, the semantic relationship of the *mafia* and the *millionaire* to the kidnapping event is the same but their syntactic roles have changed.

[3]These two transformations were preferred on the basis that they do not change the words in the sentence, as opposed to other possible translations, which involve reformulations, eg. "a sewing machine" vs. "a machine made for sewing".

2 Related Work

The analysis and interpretation of the linguistic knowledge present in contextualized representations has recently been the focus of a large amount of work (Clark et al., 2019; Voita et al., 2019b; Tenney et al., 2019; Talmor et al., 2019). The bulk of this interpretation work relies on probing tasks which serve to predict linguistic properties from the representations generated by the models (Linzen, 2018; Rogers et al., 2020). These might involve structural aspects of language, such as syntax, word order, or number agreement (Linzen et al., 2016; Hewitt and Manning, 2019; Hewitt and Liang, 2019), or semantic phenomena such as semantic role labeling and coreference (Tenney et al., 2019; Kovaleva et al., 2019). In our work, we shift the focus from interpreting the knowledge about language encoded in the representations, to exploring the imprint of two specific transformations, passivization and negation, on word representations.

The majority of the above mentioned works address representations generated by models trained with a language modeling objective, such as LSTM RNNs (Linzen et al., 2016), ELMo (Peters et al., 2018) and BERT (Devlin et al., 2019). Voita et al. (2019a) propose to study the representations obtained from models trained with a different objective. We take the same stance and investigate the impact of context on representations generated by BERT, and by the encoder of neural machine translation (NMT) models involving one or more language pairs.

In order to detect the information related to the two studied transformations that is encoded in the representations, we employ methodology initially proposed for identifying and removing linguistic and other kinds of biases from representations. Such methods fall in two main paradigms: projection and adversarial methods. Projection methods identify specific directions in word embedding space that correspond to the protected attribute, and remove them. Bolukbasi et al. (2016) identify a gender subspace by exploring gendered word lists. Zhao et al. (2018) propose to train debiased word embeddings from scratch by altering the loss of the GloVe model (Pennington et al., 2014) to concentrate specific information (e.g., about gender) in a dedicated coordinate of each vector. Dev and Phillips (2019) propose a simple linear projection method to reduce the bias in word embeddings. Lauscher et al. (2019) develop a variation of this method that introduces more flexibility in the formation of the debiasing vector used in the projection. Adversial methods extend the main task objective with a component that competes with the encoder trying to extract the protected information from its representation (Goodfellow et al., 2014; Xie et al., 2017; Zhang et al., 2018). These models cannot, however, completely remove the protected information, and their training is difficult (Elazar and Goldberg, 2018).

Xu et al. (2017) propose a null-space cleaning operator as a privacy mechanism to minimize the exposure of confidential information in a dataset. Given a model pre-trained for a given task, they remove from the input a subspace that contains the null-space, hence removing information that is not used for the main task. Ravfogel et al. (2020) propose a similar method, Iterative Null-space Projection (INLP), for removing information regarding a certain property from representations. It is based on the mathematical notion of linear projection and is data-driven in the directions it removes, like adversarial methods. In our experiments, we repurpose the INLP method for identifying and removing traces of the passivization and negation transformations from contextualized representations.

3 Experimental Setup

In our experiments, we use contextualized representations generated by the BERT language model and two Transformer-based machine translation models (Section 3.1). We generate representations for words in two datasets with sentence pairs illustrating passivization and negation (Section 3.2). We focus on the main verb, and the nouns found in subject and object positions in the sentence pairs. We study the effect of the transformations on the representations using binary classification and iterative nullspace projection (Section 3.3).[4]

3.1 Contextualized Representations

We obtain BERT representations using `bert-base-uncased` (Devlin et al., 2019), a pre-trained language model that consists of 12 layers with 768 dimensions on each layer. We also extract representations from machine translation models involving one or more language pairs. We use a bilingual English-to-German model

(which we call **MT: EN > DE**) and a model with two languages, German and Greek, on the target side (**MT: EN > DE+EL**). The latter is trained using language flag tokens in the spirit of Johnson et al. (2017). We, however, feed the flags to the decoder instead of encoder. This way, we avoid the risk that the encoder is influenced by the target language and force the model to create more generic abstractions. For the two MT models, we use Transformer architectures trained on a multiparallel subset of the Europarl dataset (Koehn, 2005), spanning $\approx$ 400,000 aligned sentences (Mareček et al., 2020), with the following parameters: 6 layers in the encoder and in the decoder, 16 attention heads, 512 as the dimension of the encodings, and 4,096 as the feed-forward network inner dimension.

3.2 Data

We explore the traces that the PAS transformation leaves on word representations using a dataset automatically created with the templates proposed by Prasad et al. (2019).[5] The PAS sentence pairs generated by Prasad et al. (2019) in their original study, contain relative clauses and are often syntactically very complex (e.g., *the obnoxious manager that was astonished by the interesting jobs trusted the modest receptionists last month*).[6] To reduce complexity and focus on the phenomenon of interest, we modify the templates to generate PAS sentence pairs without relative clauses (e.g., *the obnoxious manager was astonished by the interesting jobs*). 1000 PAS sentence pairs are generated in this manner. We call this dataset TEMPL-PAS.

We also use sentence pairs from the SICK (Sentences Involving Compositional Knowledge) dataset (Marelli et al., 2014b).[7] The SICK dataset has been obtained through crowdsourcing and illustrates lexical, syntactic and semantic phenomena that compositional distributional semantic models are expected to account for. PAS is one of the meaning preserving alternations in SICK, where a sentence S2 results from the passivization of an active sentence S1. We use all the 276 sentence

---

[4]Our code and data are available at `https://github.com/Helsinki-NLP/Syntactic_Debiasing`

[5]The code is available at `https://github.com/grushaprasad/RNN-Priming`.

[6]The complexity of the sentences also resulted in numerous syntactic analysis errors when we tried to parse them using Stanza (Qi et al., 2020).

[7]The dataset was used in SemEval 2014 Task 1: Evaluation of Compositional Distributional Semantic Models on Full Sentences through Semantic Relatedness and Textual Entailment (Marelli et al., 2014a).

pairs (i.e., total of 552 sentences) in SICK that illustrate the PAS transformation, and call this dataset SICK-PAS.

For exploring negation, we again generate 1,000 sentence pairs with the Prasad et al. (2019) templates, inserting negation to produce contradictions. We call this dataset TEMPL-NEG. We also use the 400 sentence pairs illustrating negation in the SICK dataset, which we call as SICK-NEG.

We distinguish nouns in subject and object positions, and call the main verb of the sentence with the label VERB. In the passivization examples, we compare nouns in subject position of active sentences with the corresponding noun in agent position of the passive sentence and label them as A-SUBJ/P-AG. Furthermore, we compare nouns in subject position of the passive examples with the nouns in object position of the corresponding active sentence, and label them as A-OBJ/P-SUBJ. In the negation examples we compare nouns in the same position and label them as SUBJECT or OBJECT.

We parse both datasets with the Stanza parser (Qi et al., 2020) to obtain the dependency trees, from which we extract the elements for our comparison.

3.3 Method

A straightforward approach for measuring the effect of the studied transformations on the contextualized word representations is to train a binary classifier to detect in which sentence variants (active/passive, affirmative/negated sentence) the word occurred. For this purpose, we form training and test sets (%70 and %30 of the SICK-PAS, SICK-NEG, TEMPL-PAS and TEMPL-NEG datasets) by grouping the noun and verb instances occurring in corresponding sentence pairs into two contrasting classes (e.g., active vs. passive). For a fair evaluation of the classifier performance, we make sure to preserve a lexical split between the training and test portions of the datasets, by grouping all instances of a specific word in one set (either train or test).

A successful classification on the test set shows that the representations encode informative features describing each variant (active vs. passive or affirmative vs. negative). The debiasing methods discussed in Section 2 are suitable for neutralizing such features. Here, we utilize Iterative Nullspace Projection (INLP) (Ravfogel et al., 2020). Given a set of vectors $x_i \in \mathbb{R}^d$ and corresponding discrete attributes Z, $z_i \in \{1, ..., k\}$, the goal is to learn a transformation $g : \mathbb{R}^d \to \mathbb{R}^d$, such that

z_i cannot be predicted from $g(x_i)$. The method is based on iteratively (1) training a linear classifier to predict z_i from x_i, followed by (2) projecting x_i on the null-space of the classifier, using a projection matrix $P_{N(W)}$ such that $W(P_{N(W)}x) = 0$ $\forall x$, where W is the weight matrix of the classifier, and $N(W)$ is its null-space. Through the projection step in each iteration, the information detected by the trained linear classifier is removed from the representation. The procedure continues until the attempt to train a linear classifier on the projected data becomes unsuccessful. As a result of the procedure, one also obtains a projection matrix, $P = P_{N(W_m)}PN(W_{m-1})...P_{N(W_0)}$, which is the multiplication of all the null-space projections applied in all steps. This projection matrix P can then potentially be applied to uncleaned data in a single step to reproduce the effect of the whole operation.

The features used by the classifiers may be very low-level, based on specific words or their role in the sentence. Such features are not very interesting as they are easily overfitted to the particular types of sentences in the training data. By testing the same features on a second dataset, we can measure if they are abstract enough to be generalizable. Specifically, we apply the trained INLP projection to the second dataset, then train a new classifier on it. If the new classifier is able to predict the sentence variant, this means that the projection is specific to the first dataset, and is thus not useful for removing information relevant for this distinction from the second dataset.

4   Results

In this section, we present various analyses of the original data and the effects of the transformations on contextualized word representations. First, we provide a visualization of embeddings before and after null-space projection. Next, we study the classification results which demonstrate the success of INLP and, finally, we investigate the impact of the neutralization procedure on word similarity. We also provide evidence regarding the generalization capability of the algorithm and the projections it discovers. In all results, with the exception of visualizations, we report the average of 20 runs.

4.1   Visualization

One of our main goals is to explore the extent to which grammatical variation is encoded in contextualized representations. Visualization is a useful

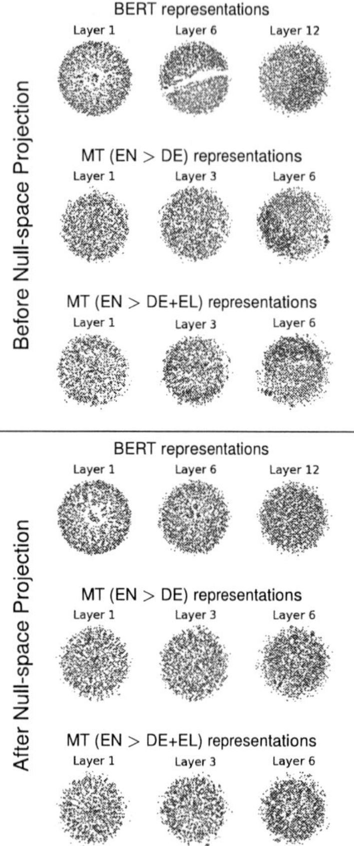

Figure 2: Multidimensional scaling (MDS) visualization of verbs in TEMPL-PAS. We show the word representations before (top part of the figure) and after INLP cleaning (lower part). The columns from left to right refer to the bottom, middle, and top layers of the encoder.

tool for demonstrating the division of the representational space into different regions in controlled examples. We use multidimensional scaling (MDS) to show the impact of the variation on the encodings. MDS reveals the level of similarity of individual points in a dataset in terms of their pairwise distance. Our data points are the contextualized representations of words in the sentences. Figure 2 reflects the distinction between active and passive verb instances present in the TEMPL-PAS dataset.

The top part of Figure 2 shows how the original representations are distributed. The separation between instances of the two classes seems almost linear, especially in the top layer of the models. For BERT, this is also the case for the middle layer (layer 6). The lower part of the figure shows that after the INLP procedure, the active and passive

instances are no longer visually separable.

For nouns in corresponding thematic roles in the active and passive sentences, the situation is similar except for the BERT-based representations. Figure 1 includes the plots for the top layer of each model, and the nouns reflecting the agent and theme in corresponding sentences. The separation between active and passive examples is clear in MT models but quite fuzzy when using BERT.[8] However, the following section on classification-based results reveals that, even in this case, the distinction is still clearly present and can effectively be detected and removed by INLP.

4.2 Classification

We also explore how easy it is to correctly assign different instances in the two classes using a logistic regression classifier with inverse L2 regularization strength of 0.001.[9] We conduct this experiment on the original data using two iterations of the INLP procedure. This shows the amount of information relevant to this distinction in the original dataset that is still present after null-space projection.

Table 1 shows a successful classification of the TEMPL dataset before INLP for both transformations and all used grammatical categories, with the accuracy dropping to ≈ 0.5 by Iteration 2. This demonstrates that all representations explicitly encode the features that are altered by the PAS and NEG transformations, and that INLP can effectively remove them from the representations. This is especially informative for the BERT-based representations for nouns, a distinction that was not apparent from the visualization experiment discussed previously. The results for the SICK dataset are similar and available in the Appendix.

4.3 Similarity Estimation

We explore the similarity of individual word instances and how it is affected by the INLP neutralization procedure we apply. We study this effect on each of the encoder layers, and provide a comparison of four different measures to illustrate the impact of INLP on the embeddings. The first two metrics measure the distance between the classes C_1 and $C_2 \in C$ corresponding to our transformation variants, and we expect them to go down due to the neutralization procedure. Two additional

[8]The full picture is available in the Appendix including MDS plots for SICK-PAS and NEG transformations.
[9]Selected from among options of {0.1, 0.01, 0.001, 0.0001} to optimize the generalization of the classifier.

| | | Active-Passive | | | | | | Positive-Negative | | | | | |
| | | VERB | | A-SUBJ/P-AG | | A-OBJ/P-SUBJ | | VERB | | SUBJECT | | OBJECT | |
		It-0	It-2	It-0	It-2	It-0	It-2	It-0	It-2	It-0	It-2	It-0	It-2
BERT	L-1	0.99	0.50	1.00	0.50	0.99	0.50	0.99	0.49	0.86	0.50	0.77	0.50
	L-6	1.00	0.49	1.00	0.50	1.00	0.50	1.00	0.50	0.98	0.50	0.88	0.50
	L-12	0.99	0.50	0.99	0.50	0.95	0.50	1.00	0.50	0.92	0.50	0.90	0.50
MT (EN > DE)	L-1	0.86	0.49	0.98	0.47	0.91	0.50	0.94	0.49	0.57	0.50	0.76	0.51
	L-3	0.87	0.49	1.00	0.49	0.96	0.50	0.94	0.51	0.66	0.50	0.77	0.50
	L-6	0.90	0.49	1.00	0.53	0.97	0.50	0.96	0.47	0.77	0.50	0.81	0.49
MT (EN > DE+EL)	L-1	0.86	0.48	0.98	0.48	0.92	0.50	0.93	0.52	0.64	0.50	0.80	0.50
	L-3	0.86	0.49	0.98	0.49	0.96	0.50	0.94	0.49	0.69	0.50	0.83	0.50
	L-6	0.91	0.49	0.99	0.49	0.98	0.51	0.97	0.47	0.78	0.50	0.85	0.50

Table 1: Classification accuracy obtained on the TEMPL-PAS and TEMPL-NEG datasets before (Iteration 0, 'It-0') and after (Iteration 2, 'It-2') application of the INLP procedure.

metrics measure the distance of instances within the same class in order to verify that INLP does not produce any unwanted side effects when modifying the representations.

The first metric computes the average **pairwise inter-class distance** and is defined as:

$$\operatorname*{avg}_{i \in S} ||x_i^A - x_i^B||, \tag{1}$$

where S is the set of sentence pairs and x_i^A and x_i^B are the embeddings of the target word w_i in sentence variants A and B (e.g., active and passive). We expect this to be high prior to neutralization, and to drop significantly afterwards. We also measure the **global inter-class distance:**

$$\operatorname*{avg}_{i \in S, C_1 \in \{A,B\}} ||x_i^{C_1} - \operatorname*{avg}_{j \in S, C_2 \in \{A,B\}: C_2 \neq C_1} x_j^{C_2}||, \tag{2}$$

which measures the average distance of the embedding $x_i^{C_1}$ of variant C_1 to the centroid of the corresponding word embeddings of the other variant C_2, $x_j^{C_2}$. We expect this value to also decrease after the projection, but less than the previous one since it includes distances between all data points rather than only the paired sentences.

Neutralization should not significantly affect similarities between embeddings of the same word w_i in different contexts within the same sentence variant C_k. We measure this using the **same-word intra-class distance** for instances of the same word, expecting this to stay approximately same:

$$\operatorname*{avg}_{i \in S, C_k \in \{A,B\}} ||x_i^{C_k} - \operatorname*{avg}_{j \in S: w_j = w_i, j \neq i} x_j^{C_k}|| \tag{3}$$

Finally, analogous to the global inter-class distance, we also measure the **global intra-class distance:**

$$\operatorname*{avg}_{i \in S, C_k \in \{A,B\}} ||x_i^{C_k} - \operatorname*{avg}_{j \in S} x_j^{C_k}||, \tag{4}$$

which computes the average distance of the embeddings $x_i^{C_k}$ to the centroid of the word embeddings of variant C_k. Again, we expect this to not decrease.

Figure 3 shows the results for the verbs and nouns in the TEMPL-PAS dataset before and after INLP.[10] In all plots, especially the MT ones, we see a significant drop in pairwise inter-class distance after INLP application, which shows the effectiveness of the procedure. As expected, global inter-class distance also shows a smaller degree of drop. On the contrary, and also as expected, we do not observe drops in same-word intra-class distance or global intra-class distance, which implies that the projection does not cause major damage to the information that needs to be preserved.

4.4 Null-space Projection Transfer

Finally, we investigate the possibility to transfer null-space projections across data sets and word classes, in order to understand how generic the features representing the targeted transformation are.

4.4.1 Transfer across Datasets

We learn a projection on the TEMPL-PAS and TEMPL-NEG datasets, and use it to clean SICK-PAS and SICK-NEG respectively. We then evaluate how well the transfer works by using the cleaned dataset to train and test a classifier. If the transfer succeeds and the projection learned on the first dataset efficiently cleans the second dataset, the classification attempt will fail because all relevant information that would be useful to the classifier would have been removed. On the contrary, if a classifier can still be successfully trained on the cleaned version of the SICK datasets, then we as-

---

[10]TEMPL-NEG results are available in the Appendix.

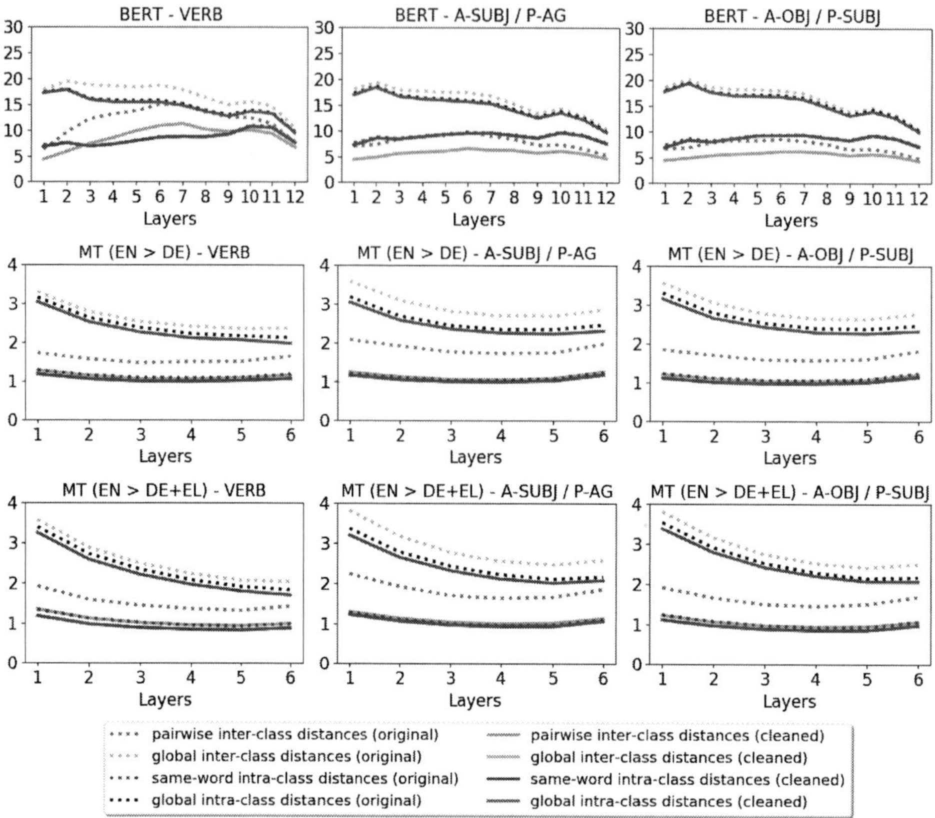

Figure 3: Average Euclidean distance for instances of nouns and verbs in the TEMPL-PAS dataset. Dashed lines show distances in the original dataset, and solid lines reflect distances after applying INLP. Distances are given for representations generated by each layer of the models.

sume that the transfer failed since information relevant to the distinction still persists.

In Figure 4, we compare (a) the classification accuracy on the original SICK-PAS and SICK-NEG datasets (dotted lines) to (b) the accuracy obtained on these datasets cleaned by using the null-space projection learned on TEMPL-PAS and TEMPL-NEG, respectively (solid lines). We report results for nouns and verbs obtained using representations generated by BERT and the MT encoders.

The transfer from TEMPL to SICK does not seem to work well with BERT representations, since a classifier trained on the cleaned SICK datasets still obtains fairly high accuracy. An exceptional to this is seen the in final layers of BERT, and subjects in the SICK-NEG dataset, for which the cleaned dataset shows slightly lower (70–90%) accurracy. For the MT representations, on the other hand, we observe low accuracies for the post-transfer classification, which suggests a successful transfer of information between the datasets. Es-

pecially for TEMPL-PAS VERB and A-SUBJ/P-AG, representations obtained with the MT model that involves two language pairs respond better to the transfer, as shown by significantly lower post-cleaning accuracies (i.e., less remaining information) than the ones obtained by the MT model with one target language. Notably, this trend is not seen for TEMPL-NEG.

4.4.2 Transfer across Grammatical Categories

We also tried to transfer null-space projection between different grammatical categories, specifically by learning the projection for verbs, subjects or objects, and then trying to apply it to one of the other two. An example of such a transfer is shown in Figure 5. Here, we apply the projection learned on verbs in the negation dataset to neutralize the same information from the noun in subject position. This seems to work surprisingly well for the MT-based representations. For BERT-based representations

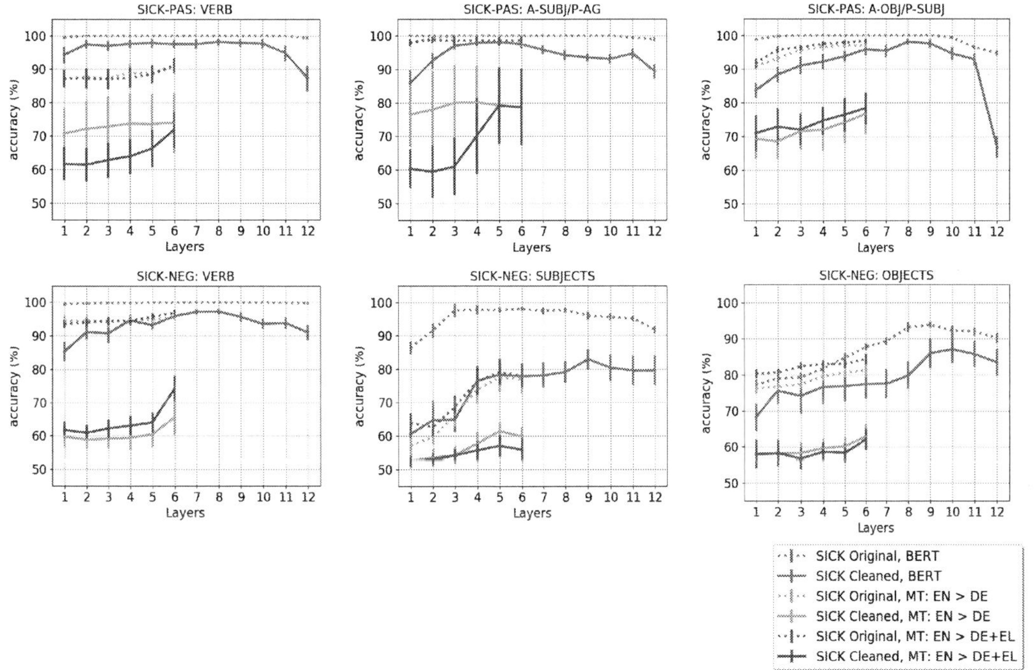

Figure 4: Classification accuracies for the SICK-PAS and SICK-NEG datasets on (1) the original version of the dataset (dotted lines) vs. (2) the cleaned version of the dataset using information from the learned INLP projection on TEMPL-PAS and TEMPL-NEG. The larger the difference between the original and cleaned versions, the more useful the transferred projection is for cleaning. Error bars indicate standard deviation of 20 experiments.

and for the passivization data set, on the other hand, the transfer across categories is not very successful with classification accuracies typically remaining above 80%. Results highlight that the information is highly specific to words of a certain grammatical category and that the projection cannot be applied

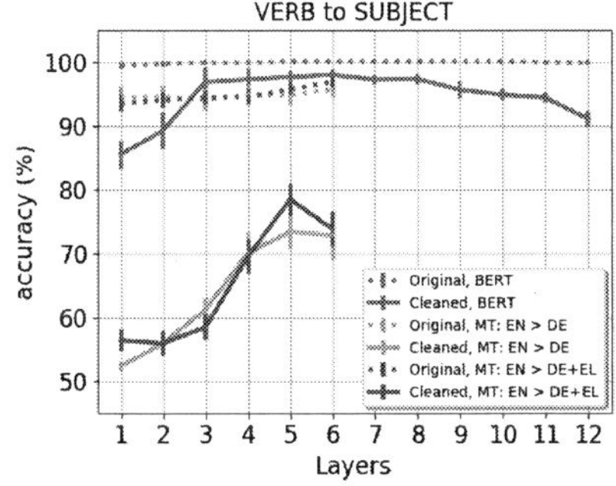

Figure 5: Classification accuracies for subjects in TEMPL-NEG on (1) the original dataset vs. (2) the dataset cleaned using learned INLP projection on verbs of TEMPL-NEG. The larger the difference between the original and cleaned versions, the more useful is the transferred projection for cleaning. Error bars indicate standard deviation of 20 runs.

as a universal neutralization procedure.

5 Conclusion

We have shown that transformations such as passivization and negation leave a strong imprint on contextualized representations. We demonstrate that leveraging this information, it is possible to build classifiers that successfully identify word instances falling in either category. The traces of these transformations also affect the similarity of word instances that refer to the same entities and events. Repurposing a method initially proposed for identifying and removing societal biases from representations, we show that it is possible to neutralize the trace of such transformations from contextualized representations, and preserve the similarity of word instances having the same reference. Interestingly, the features that predict the transformation variant seem to be more generalizable in the embeddings generated by an MT encoder than in the BERT embeddings, implying that the BERT embeddings contain more surface-level information specific to each dataset.

Acknowledgements

This work has been supported by the Fo-Tran project, funded by the European Research Council (ERC) under the European Union's Horizon 2020 research and innovation programme (grant agreement № 771113). We thank the reviewers for their thoughtful comments and valuable suggestions.

References

Mikel Artetxe and Holger Schwenk. 2019. Massively multilingual sentence embeddings for zero-shot cross-lingual transfer and beyond. volume 7, pages 597–610. MIT Press.

Tolga Bolukbasi, Kai-Wei Chang, James Y Zou, Venkatesh Saligrama, and Adam T Kalai. 2016. Man is to Computer Programmer as Woman is to Homemaker? Debiasing Word Embeddings. In *Advances in Neural Information Processing Systems 29*, pages 4349–4357.

Kevin Clark, Urvashi Khandelwal, Omer Levy, and Christopher D. Manning. 2019. What does bertlook at? an analysis of bert's attention. In *2019 ACL Workshop BlackboxNLP: Analyzing and Interpreting Neural Networks for NLP*, pages 276–286.

Sunipa Dev and Jeff M. Phillips. 2019. Attenuating bias in word vectors. *CoRR*, abs/1901.07656.

Jacob Devlin, Ming-Wei Chang, Kenton Lee, and Kristina Toutanova. 2019. BERT: Pre-training of Deep Bidirectional Transformers for Language Understanding. In *Proceedings of the 2019 Conference of the North American Chapter of the Association for Computational Linguistics: Human Language Technologies*, pages 4171–4186.

Yanai Elazar and Yoav Goldberg. 2018. Adversarial removal of demographic attributes from text data. In *Proceedings of the 2018 Conference on Empirical Methods in Natural Language Processing*, pages 11–21.

Ian Goodfellow, Jean Pouget-Abadie, Mehdi Mirza, Bing Xu, David Warde-Farley, Sherjil Ozair, Aaron Courville, and Yoshua Bengio. 2014. Generative adversarial nets. In *Advances in Neural Information Processing Systems 27*, pages 2672–2680.

Stephan Greene and Philip Resnik. 2009. More than words: Syntactic packaging and implicit sentiment. In *Proceedings of the Annual Conference of the North American Chapter of the Association for Computational Linguistics: Human Language Technologies*, pages 503–511.

John Hewitt and Percy Liang. 2019. Designing and interpreting probes with control tasks. In *Proceedings of the 2019 Conference on Empirical Methods in Natural Language Processing and the 9th International Joint Conference on Natural Language Processing (EMNLP-IJCNLP)*, pages 2733–2743.

John Hewitt and Christopher D. Manning. 2019. A Structural Probe for Finding Syntax in Word Representations. In *Proceedings of the 2019 Conference of the North American Chapter of the Association for Computational Linguistics: Human Language Technologies*, pages 4129–4138.

Melvin Johnson, Mike Schuster, Quoc V. Le, Maxim Krikun, Yonghui Wu, Zhifeng Chen, Nikhil Thorat, Fernanda Viégas, Martin Wattenberg, Greg Corrado, Macduff Hughes, and Jeffrey Dean. 2017. Google's multilingual neural machine translation system: Enabling zero-shot translation. *Transactions of the Association for Computational Linguistics*, 5:339–351.

Philipp Koehn. 2005. Europarl: A parallel corpus for statistical machine translation. In *MT summit*, volume 5, pages 79–86. Citeseer.

Olga Kovaleva, Alexey Romanov, Anna Rogers, and Anna Rumshisky. 2019. Revealing the Dark Secrets of BERT. In *Proceedings of the 2019 Conference on Empirical Methods in Natural Language Processing and the 9th International Joint Conference on Natural Language Processing (EMNLP-IJCNLP)*, pages 4365–4374.

Anne Lauscher, Goran Glavaš, Simone Paolo Ponzetto, and Ivan Vulić. 2019. A general framework for implicit and explicit debiasing of distributional word vector spaces.

Tal Linzen. 2018. What can linguistics and deep learning contribute to each other? *CoRR*, abs/1809.04179.

Tal Linzen, Emmanuel Dupoux, and Yoav Goldberg. 2016. Assessing the Ability of LSTMs to Learn Syntax-Sensitive Dependencies. *Transactions of the Association for Computational Linguistics*, 4:521–535.

Marco Marelli, Luisa Bentivogli, Marco Baroni, Raffaella Bernardi, Stefano Menini, and Roberto Zamparelli. 2014a. SemEval-2014 task 1: Evaluation of compositional distributional semantic models on full sentences through semantic relatedness and textual entailment. In *Proceedings of the 8th International Workshop on Semantic Evaluation*, pages 1–8.

Marco Marelli, Stefano Menini, Marco Baroni, Luisa Bentivogli, Raffaella Bernardi, and Roberto Zamparelli. 2014b. A SICK cure for the evaluation of compositional distributional semantic models. In *Proceedings of the 9th International Conference on Language Resources and Evaluation*, pages 216–223.

David Mareček, Hande Celikkanat, Miikka Silfverberg, Vinit Ravishankar, and Jörg Tiedemann. 2020. Are multilingual neural machine translation models better at capturing linguistic features? *The Prague Bulletin of Mathematical Linguistics (in press)*.

Jeffrey Pennington, Richard Socher, and Christopher D. Manning. 2014. Glove: Global vectors for word representation. In *Empirical Methods in Natural Language Processing (EMNLP)*, pages 1532–1543.

Matthew Peters, Mark Neumann, Mohit Iyyer, Matt Gardner, Christopher Clark, Kenton Lee, and Luke Zettlemoyer. 2018. Deep Contextualized Word Representations. In *Proceedings of the 2018 Conference of the North American Chapter of the Association for Computational Linguistics: Human Language Technologies*, pages 2227–2237.

Grusha Prasad, Marten van Schijndel, and Tal Linzen. 2019. Using Priming to Uncover the Organization of Syntactic Representations in Neural Language Models. In *Proceedings of the 23rd Conference on Computational Natural Language Learning (CoNLL)*, pages 66–76.

Peng Qi, Yuhao Zhang, Yuhui Zhang, Jason Bolton, and Christopher D. Manning. 2020. Stanza: A Python natural language processing toolkit for many human languages. In *Proceedings of the 58th Annual Meeting of the Association for Computational Linguistics: System Demonstrations*.

Shauli Ravfogel, Yanai Elazar, Hila Gonen, Michael Twiton, and Yoav Goldberg. 2020. Null it out: Guarding protected attributes by iterative nullspace projection.

Anna Rogers, Olga Kovaleva, and Anna Rumshisky. 2020. A Primer in BERTology: What we know about how BERT works. *arXiv preprint:2002.12327v1*.

Alon Talmor, Yanai Elazar, Yoav Goldberg, and Jonathan Berant. 2019. oLMpics – On what Language Model Pre-training Captures. arXiv preprint arXiv:1912.13283v1.

Ian Tenney, Dipanjan Das, and Ellie Pavlick. 2019. BERT Rediscovers the Classical NLP Pipeline. In *Proceedings of the 57th Annual Meeting of the Association for Computational Linguistics*, pages 4593–4601.

Elena Voita, Rico Sennrich, and Ivan Titov. 2019a. The Bottom-up Evolution of Representations in the Transformer: A Study with Machine Translation and Language Modeling Objectives. In *Proceedings of the 2019 Conference on Empirical Methods in Natural Language Processing and the 9th International Joint Conference on Natural Language Processing (EMNLP-IJCNLP)*, pages 4396–4406.

Elena Voita, David Talbot, Fedor Moiseev, Rico Sennrich, and Ivan Titov. 2019b. Analyzing multi-head self-attention: Specialized heads do the heavy lifting, the rest can be pruned. In *Proceedings of the 57th Annual Meeting of the Association for Computational Linguistics*, page 5797–5808.

Raúl Vázquez, Alessandro Raganato, Mathias Creutz, and Jörg Tiedemann. 2020. A systematic study of inner-attention-based sentence representations in multilingual neural machine translation. *Computational Linguistics*, 46(2):387–424.

Qizhe Xie, Zihang Dai, Yulun Du, Eduard Hovy, and Graham Neubig. 2017. Controllable invariance through adversarial feature learning. In *Advances in Neural Information Processing Systems 30*, pages 585–596.

Ke Xu, Tongyi Cao, Swair Shah, Crystal Maung, and Haim Schweitzer. 2017. Cleaning the Null Space: A Privacy Mechanism for Predictors. In *AAAI Conference on Artificial Intelligence*, pages 2789–2795.

Brian Hu Zhang, Blake Lemoine, and Margaret Mitchell. 2018. Mitigating unwanted biases with adversarial learning. In *AIES '18: Proceedings of the 2018 AAAI/ACM Conference on AI, Ethics, and Society*, page 335–340.

Jieyu Zhao, Yichao Zhou, Zeyu Li, Wei Wang, and Kai-Wei Chang. 2018. Learning gender-neutral word embeddings. In *Proceedings of the 2018 Conference on Empirical Methods in Natural Language Processing*, pages 4847–4853.

A Appendices

A.1 Visualization

Figures 6 and 7 provide the complete MDS visualizations for TEMPL-PAS and TEMPL-NEG. For TEMPL-PAS, we see a significant imprint for the nouns also. For TEMPL-NEG, the imprint is mostly visible for the verbs, however note that this does not mean the nouns are unclassifiable, since the INLP classifier is able to find a good classification for them as well (Table 1).

A.2 Classification

Table 2 shows the classification accuracies for the SICK-PAS and SICK-NEG datasets, before and after INLP. Similar to TEMPL-PAS and TEMPL-NEG results, these also show a good classification accuracy before, and a chance-level one after, demonstrating both a significant initial imprint, and the effectiveness of the INLP procedure.

A.3 Similarity Estimation

Figure 8 depicts the changes in the similarities of individual words of TEMPL-NEG using the four distance measures discussed in Section 4.3.

		Active-Passive						Positive-Negative					
		VERB		A-SUBJ/P-AG		A-OBJ/P-SUBJ		VERB		SUBJECT		OBJECT	
		It-0	It-2	It-0	It-2	It-0	It-2	It-0	It-2	It-0	It-2	It-0	It-2
BERT	L-1	0.98	0.50	0.99	0.51	0.99	0.50	0.83	0.51	0.69	0.50	0.70	0.50
	L-6	0.98	0.49	0.99	0.50	1.00	0.51	0.97	0.50	0.82	0.50	0.88	0.50
	L-12	0.98	0.50	0.96	0.50	0.82	0.50	0.92	0.50	0.80	0.50	0.89	0.50
MT (EN > DE)	L-1	0.78	0.51	0.94	0.50	0.92	0.50	0.74	0.50	0.54	0.50	0.66	0.50
	L-3	0.81	0.51	0.98	0.51	0.96	0.52	0.74	0.49	0.56	0.50	0.69	0.50
	L-6	0.82	0.54	0.98	0.52	0.97	0.53	0.84	0.51	0.64	0.50	0.72	0.50
MT (EN > DE+EL)	L-1	0.87	0.50	0.91	0.50	0.91	0.51	0.71	0.48	0.52	0.50	0.67	0.50
	L-3	0.89	0.51	0.96	0.50	0.98	0.53	0.74	0.49	0.53	0.50	0.70	0.50
	L-6	0.88	0.50	0.97	0.52	0.98	0.58	0.85	0.50	0.53	0.50	0.68	0.50

Table 2: Classification accuracy obtained on the SICK-PAS and SICK-NEG datasets before (Iteration 0, 'It-0') and after (Iteration 2, 'It-2') application of the INLP procedure.

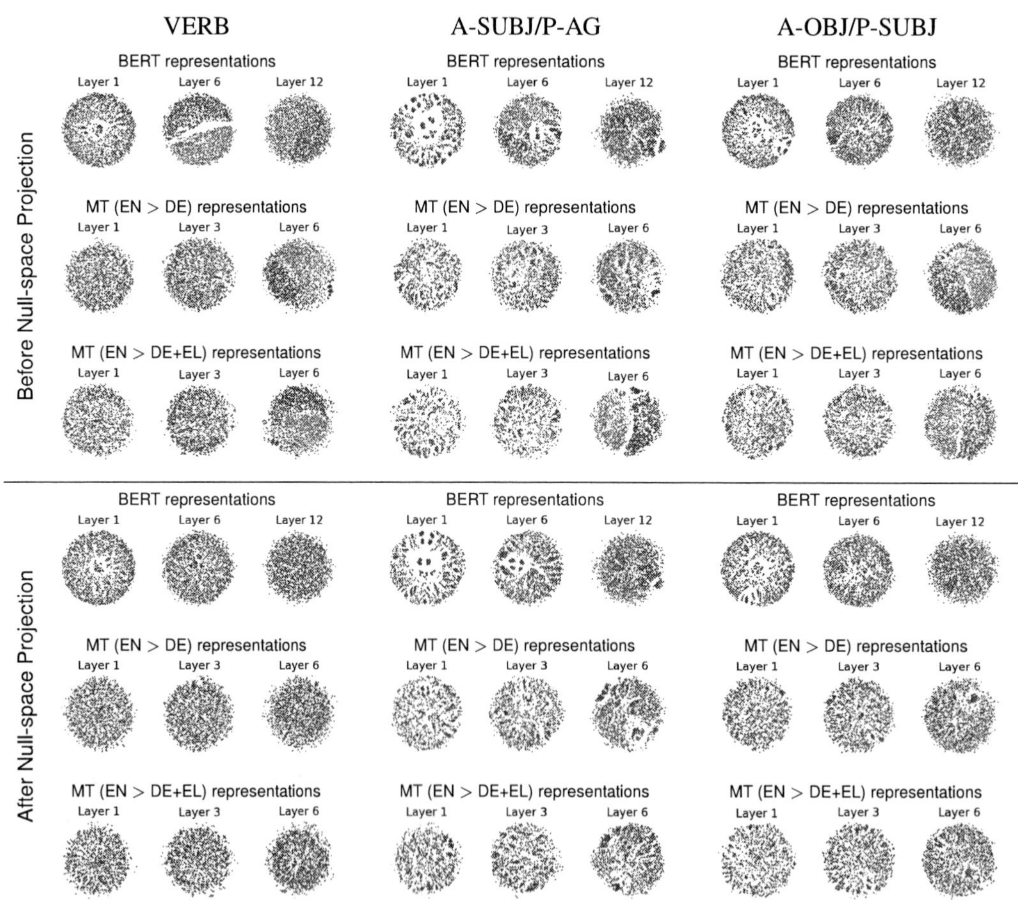

Figure 6: Multidimensional scaling (MDS) visualisation for three word instance sets in the TEMPL-PAS dataset: Verbs (Left), A-SUBJ/P-AG nouns (Middle), A-OBJ/P-SUBJ nouns (Right). The top part of the figure depicts their representations before cleaning, while the bottom part shows the same word representations after the cleaning procedure. Red and blue points indicate instances in the Active and Passive sentences, respectively.

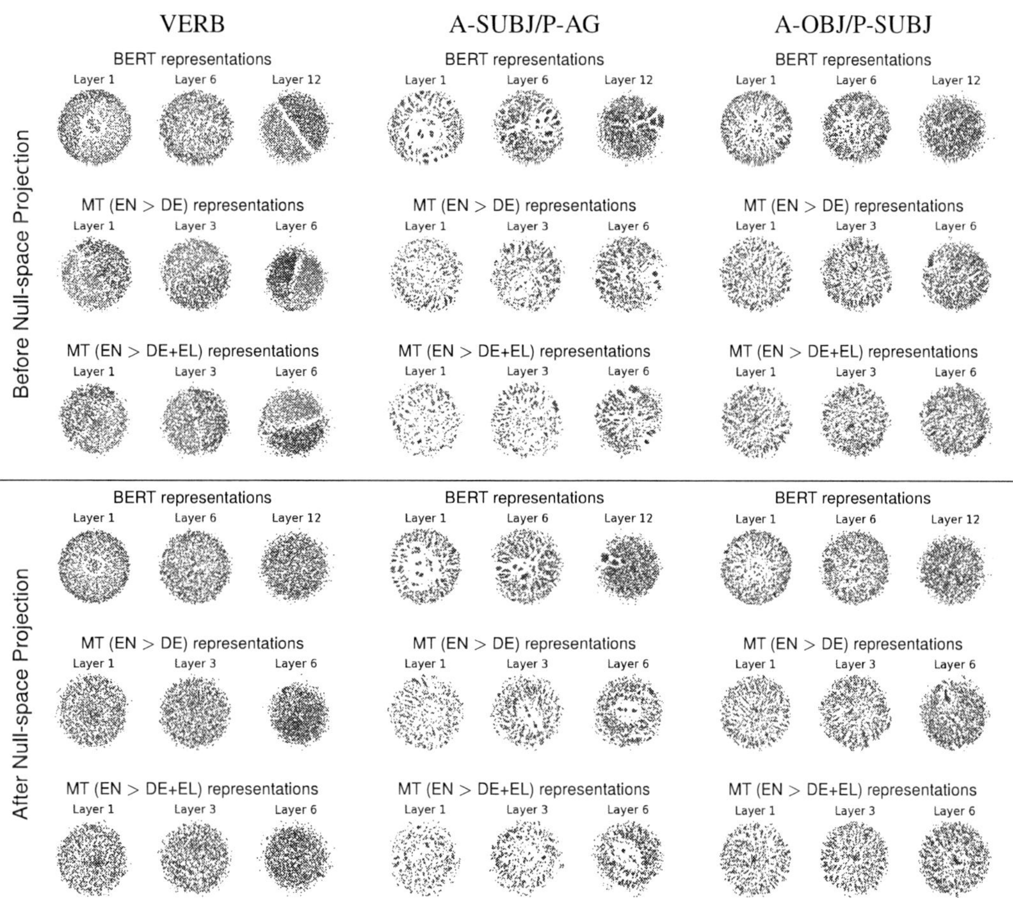

Figure 7: Multidimensional scaling (MDS) visualisation for three word instance sets in the TEMPL-NEG dataset: Verbs (Left), A-SUBJ/P-AG nouns (Middle), A-OBJ/P-SUBJ nouns (Right). The top part of the figure depicts their representations before cleaning, while the bottom part shows the same word representations after the cleaning procedure. Red and blue points indicate instances in the Active and Passive sentences, respectively.

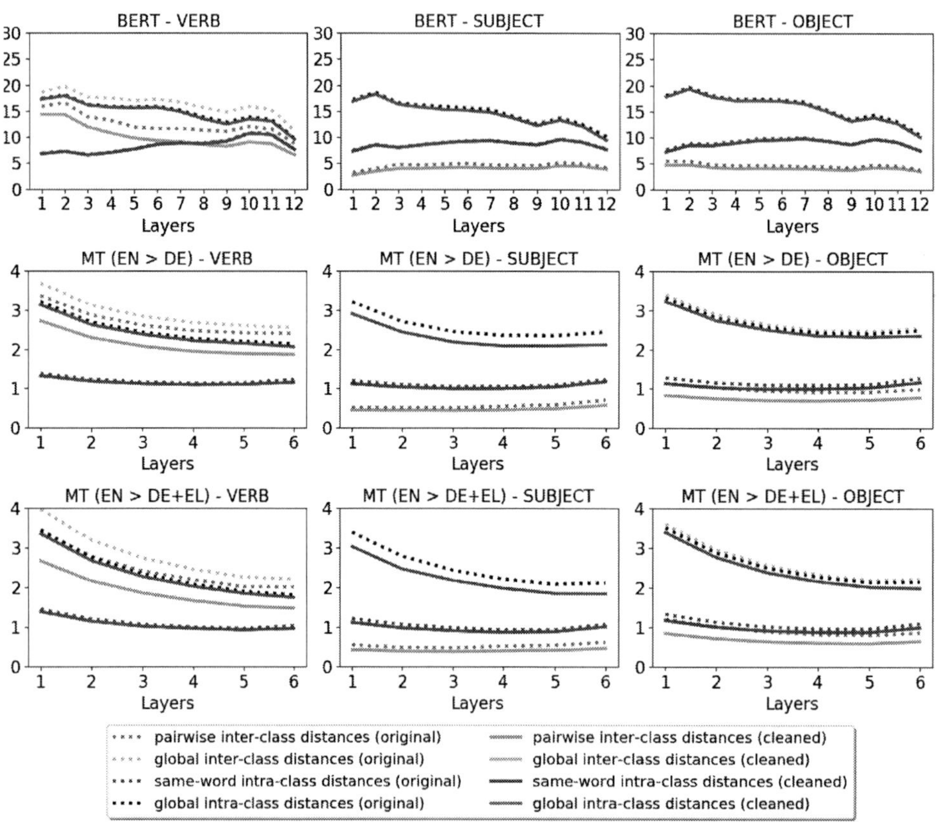

Figure 8: Average Euclidean distance for instances of nouns and verbs in the TEMPL-NEG dataset. Dashed lines show distances in the original dataset, and solid lines reflect distances after applying INLP. Distances are given for representations generated by each layer of the models.

The elephant in the interpretability room:
Why use attention as explanation when we have saliency methods?

Jasmijn Bastings
Google Research
bastings@google.com

Katja Filippova
Google Research
katjaf@google.com

Abstract

There is a recent surge of interest in using attention as explanation of model predictions, with mixed evidence on whether attention can be used as such. While attention conveniently gives us one weight per input token and is easily extracted, it is often unclear toward what goal it is used as explanation. We find that often that goal, whether explicitly stated or not, is to find out what input tokens are the most relevant to a prediction, and that the implied user for the explanation is a model developer. For this goal and user, we argue that input saliency methods are better suited, and that there are no compelling reasons to use attention, despite the coincidence that it provides a weight for each input. With this position paper, we hope to shift some of the recent focus on attention to saliency methods, and for authors to clearly state the goal and user for their explanations.

1 Introduction

Attention mechanisms (Bahdanau et al., 2015) have allowed for performance gains in many areas of NLP, including, *inter alia*, machine translation (Bahdanau et al., 2015; Luong et al., 2015; Vaswani et al., 2017), natural language generation (e.g., Rush et al., 2015; Narayan et al., 2018), and natural language inference (e.g., Parikh et al., 2016).

Attention has not only allowed for better performance, it also provides a window into how a model is operating. For example, for machine translation, Bahdanau et al. (2015) visualize what source tokens the target tokens are attending to, often aligning words that are translations of each other.

Whether the window that attention gives into how a model operates amounts to *explanation* has recently become subject to debate (§2). While many papers published on the topic of explainable AI have been criticised for not defining explanations (Lipton, 2018; Miller, 2019), the first

key studies which spawned interest in attention as explanation (Jain and Wallace, 2019; Serrano and Smith, 2019; Wiegreffe and Pinter, 2019) do say that they are interested in whether attention weights faithfully represent the responsibility each input token has on a model prediction. That is, the narrow definition of explanation implied there is that it points at the most important input tokens for a prediction (arg max), accurately summarizing the reasoning process of the model (Jacovi and Goldberg, 2020b).

The above works have inspired some to find ways to make attention more faithful and/or plausible, by changing the nature of the hidden representations attention is computed over using special training objectives (e.g., Mohankumar et al., 2020; Tutek and Snajder, 2020). Others have proposed replacing the attention mechanism with a latent alignment model (Deng et al., 2018).

Interestingly, the implied definition of explanation in the cited works, happens to coincide with what *input saliency methods* (§3) are designed to produce (Li et al., 2016a; Sundararajan et al., 2017; Ribeiro et al., 2016; Montavon et al., 2019, i.a.). Moreover, the user of that explanation is often implied to be a model developer, to which faithfulness is important. The elephant in the room is therefore: If the goal of using attention as explanation is to assign importance weights to the input tokens in a faithful manner, why should the attention mechanism be preferred over the multitude of existing input saliency methods designed to do *exactly that*? In this position paper, with that goal in mind, we argue that we should pay attention no heed (§4). We propose that we reduce our focus on attention as explanation, and shift it to input saliency methods instead. However, we do emphasize that understanding the *role* of attention is still a valid research goal (§5), and finally, we discuss a few approaches that go beyond saliency (§6).

Proceedings of the Third BlackboxNLP Workshop on Analyzing and Interpreting Neural Networks for NLP, pages 149–155
Online, November 20, 2020. ©2020 Association for Computational Linguistics

2   The Attention Debate

In this section we summarize the debate on whether
attention is explanation. The debate mostly features simple BiLSTM text classifiers (see Figure 1).
Unlike Transformers (Vaswani et al., 2017), they
only contain a single attention mechanism, which
is typically MLP-based (Bahdanau et al., 2015):

$$e_i = \mathbf{v}^\top tanh(W_h\mathbf{h}_i + W_q\mathbf{q}) \quad \alpha_i = \frac{\exp e_i}{\sum_k \exp e_k} \quad (1)$$

where α_i is the attention score for BiLSTM state $\mathbf{h}_i$.
When there is a single input text, there is no query,
and $\mathbf{q}$ is either a trained parameter (like $\mathbf{v}$, W_h and
W_q), or $W_q\mathbf{q}$ is simply left out of Eq. 1.

2.1   Is attention (not) explanation?

Jain and Wallace (2019) show that attention is often uncorrelated with gradient-based feature importance measures, and that one can often find a
completely different set of attention weights that
results in the same prediction. In addition to that,
Serrano and Smith (2019) find, by modifying attention weights, that they often do not identify those
representations that are most most important to the
prediction of the model. However, Wiegreffe and
Pinter (2019) claim that these works do not dis-
prove the usefulness of attention as explanation *per
se*, and provide four tests to determine if or when
it can be used as such. In one such test, they are
able to find alternative attention weights using an
adversarial training setup, which suggests attention
is not always a faithful explanation. Finally, Pruthi
et al. (2020) propose a method to produce decep-
tive attention weights. Their method reduces how
much weight is assigned to a set of 'impermissible'
tokens, even when the models demonstratively rely
on those tokens for their predictions.

2.2   Was the right task analyzed?

In the attention-as-explanation research to date
text classification with LSTMs received the most
scrutiny. However, Vashishth et al. (2019) question
why one should focus on single-sequence tasks at
all because the attention mechanism is arguably
far less important there than in models involving
two sequences, like NLI or MT. Indeed, the performance of an NMT model degrades substantially if
uniform weights are used, while random attention
weights affect the text classification performance
minimally. Therefore, findings from text classification studies may not generalize to tasks where
attention is a crucial component.

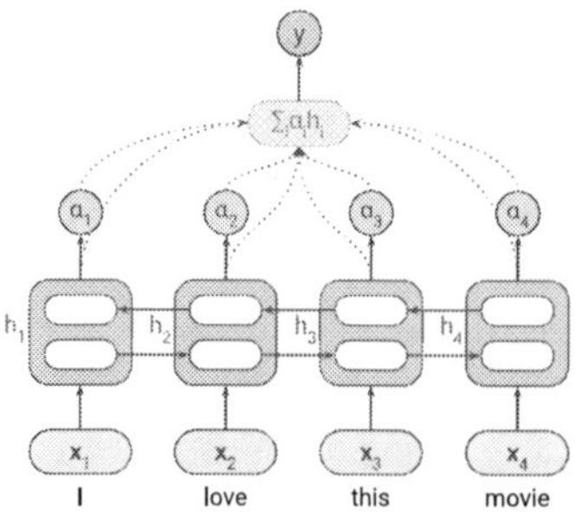

Figure 1: A typical model in the debate.

Interestingly, even for the task of MT, the first
case where attention was visualized to inspect a
model (§1), Ding et al. (2019) find that saliency
methods (§3) yield better word alignments.

2.3   Is a causal definition assumed?

Grimsley et al. (2020) go as far as saying that attention is not explanation by definition, if a causal
definition of explanation is assumed. Drawing on
the work in philosophy, they point out that causal
explanations presuppose that a surgical intervention is possible which is not the case with deep
neural networks: one cannot intervene on attention
while keeping all the other variables invariant.

2.4   Can attention be improved?

The problems with using as attention as explanation, especially regarding faithfulness, have inspired some to try and 'improve' the attention
weights, so to make them more faithful and/or
plausible. Mohankumar et al. (2020) observe high
similarity between the hidden representations of
LSTM states and propose a diversity-driven training objective that makes the hidden representations
more diverse across time steps. They show using
representation erasure that the resulting attention
weights result in decision flips more easily as compared to vanilla attention. With a similar motivation, Tutek and Snajder (2020) use a word-level
objective to achieve a stronger connection between
hidden states and the words they represent, which
affects attention. Not part of the recent debate,
Deng et al. (2018) propose variational attention
as an alternative to the soft attention of Bahdanau
et al. (2015), arguing that the latter is not *alignment*,
only an approximation thereof. They have the additional benefit of allowing posterior alignments,
conditioned on the input and the output sentences.

3 Saliency Methods

In this section we discuss various input saliency methods for NLP as alternatives to attention: gradient-based (§3.1), propagation-based (§3.2), and occlusion-based methods (§3.3), following Arras et al. (2019). We do not endorse any specific method[1], but rather try to give an overview of methods and how they differ. We discuss methods that are applicable to *any* neural NLP model, allowing access to model internals, such as activations and gradients, as attention itself requires such access. We leave out more expensive methods that use a surrogate model, e.g., LIME (Ribeiro et al., 2016).

3.1 Gradient-based methods

While used earlier in other fields, Li et al. (2016a) use gradients as explanation in NLP and compute:

$$\nabla_{\mathbf{x}_i} f_c(\mathbf{x}_{1:n}) \tag{2}$$

where $\mathbf{x}_i$ is the input word embedding for time step i, $\mathbf{x}_{1:n} = \langle \mathbf{x}_1, \ldots, \mathbf{x}_n \rangle$ are the input embeddings (e.g., a sentence), and $f_c(\mathbf{x}_{1:n})$ the model output for target class c. After taking the L2 norm of Eq. 2, the result is a measure of how sensitive the model is to the input at time step i.

If instead we take the dot product of Eq. 2 with the input word embedding $\mathbf{x}_i$, we arrive at the gradient×input method (Denil et al., 2015), which returns a saliency (scalar) of input i:

$$\nabla_{\mathbf{x}_i} f_c(\mathbf{x}_{1:n}) \cdot \mathbf{x}_i \tag{3}$$

Integrated gradients (IG) (Sundararajan et al., 2017) is a gradient-based method which deals with the problem of *saturation*: gradients may get close to zero for a well-fitted function. IG requires a baseline $\mathbf{b}_{1:n}$, e.g., all-zeros vectors or repeated [MASK] vectors. For input i, we compute:

$$\frac{1}{m}\sum_{k=1}^{m}\nabla_{\mathbf{x}_i} f_c\Big(\mathbf{b}_{1:n}+\frac{k}{m}(\mathbf{x}_{1:n}-\mathbf{b}_{1:n})\Big) \cdot (\mathbf{x}_i-\mathbf{b}_i) \tag{4}$$

That is, we average over m gradients, with the inputs to f_c being linearly interpolated between the baseline and the original input $\mathbf{x}_{1:n}$ in m steps. We then take the dot product of that averaged gradient with the input embedding $\mathbf{x}_i$ minus the baseline.

We propose distinguishing *sensitivity* from *saliency*, following Ancona et al. (2019): the former says how much a change in the input changes the output, while the latter is the marginal effect of each input word on the prediction. Gradients measure sensitivity, whereas gradient×input and IG measure saliency. A model can be sensitive to the input at a time step, but it depends on the actual input vector if it was important for the prediction.

3.2 Propagation-based methods

Propagation-based methods (Landecker et al., 2013; Bach et al., 2015; Arras et al., 2017, i.a.), of which we discuss Layer-wise Relevance Propagation (LRP) in particular, start with a forward pass to obtain the output $f_c(\mathbf{x}_{1:n})$, which is the top-level *relevance*. They then use a special backward pass that, at each layer, *redistributes* the incoming relevance among the inputs of that layer. Each kind of layer has its own propagation rules. For example, there are different rules for feed-forward layers (Bach et al., 2015) and LSTM layers (Arras et al., 2017). Relevance is redistributed until we arrive at the input layers. While LRP requires implementing a custom backward pass, it does allow precise control to preserve relevance, and it has been shown to work better than using gradient-based methods on text classification (Arras et al., 2019).

3.3 Occlusion-based methods

Occlusion-based methods (Zeiler and Fergus, 2014; Li et al., 2016b) compute input saliency by occluding (or erasing) input features and measuring how that affects the model. Intuitively, erasing unimportant features does not affect the model, whereas the opposite is true for important features. Li et al. (2016b) erase word embedding dimensions and whole words to see how doing so affects the model. They compute the importance of a word *on a dataset* by averaging over how much, for each example, erasing that word caused a difference in the output compared to not erasing that word.

As a saliency method, however, we can apply their method on a single example only. For input i:

$$f_c(\mathbf{x}_{1:n}) - f_c(\mathbf{x}_{1:n|\mathbf{x}_i=0}) \tag{5}$$

computes saliency, where $\mathbf{x}_{1:n|\mathbf{x}_i=0}$ indicates that input word embedding $\mathbf{x}_i$ was zeroed out, while the other inputs were unmodified. Kádár et al. (2017) and Poerner et al. (2018) use a variant, *omission*, by simply leaving the word out of the input.

This method requires $n+1$ forward passes. It is also used for evaluation, to see if important words another method has identified bring a change in model output (e.g., DeYoung et al., 2020).

---

[1]For an evaluation of methods for explaining LSTM-based models, see e.g., Poerner et al. (2018) and Arras et al. (2019).

4 Saliency vs. Attention

We discussed the use of attention as explanation (§2) and input saliency methods as alternatives (§3). We will now argue why saliency methods should be preferred over attention for explanation.

In many of the cited papers, whether implicitly or explicitly, the *goal* of the explanation is to reveal which input words are the most important ones for the final prediction. This is perhaps a consequence of attention computing one weight per input, so it is necessarily understood in terms of those inputs.

The intended *user* for the explanation is often not stated, but typically that user is a model developer, and not a non-expert end user, for example. For model developers, faithfulness, the need for an explanation to accurately represent the reasoning of the model, is a key concern. On the other hand, plausibility is of lesser concern, because a model developer aims to understand and possibly improve the model, and that model does not necessarily align with human intuition (see Jacovi and Goldberg, 2020b, for a detailed discussion of the differences between faithfulness and plausibility).

With this goal and user clearly stated, it is impossible to make an argument in favor of using attention as explanation. Input saliency methods are addressing the goal head-on: they reveal why one particular model prediction was made in terms of how relevant each input word was to that prediction. Moreover, input saliency methods typically take the entire computation path into account, all the way from the input word embeddings to the target output prediction value. Attention weights do not: they reflect, at one point in the computation, how much the model attends to each input *representation*, but those representations might already have mixed in information from other inputs. Ironically, attention-as-explanation is sometimes evaluated by comparing it against gradient-based measures, which again begs the question why we wouldn't use those measures in the first place.

One might argue that attention, despite its flaws, is easily extracted and computationally efficient. However, it only takes one line in a framework like TensorFlow to compute the gradient of the output w.r.t. the input word embeddings, so implementation difficulty is not a strong argument. In terms of efficiency, it is true that for attention only a forward pass is required, but many other methods discussed at most require a forward and then a backward pass, which is still extremely efficient.

5 Attention is not not interesting

In this position paper we criticized the use of attention to assess input saliency for the benefit of the model developer. We emphasize that understanding the *role* of the attention mechanism is a perfectly justified research goal. For example, Voita et al. (2019) and Michel et al. (2019) analyze the role of attention heads in the Transformer architecture and identify a few distinct functions they have, and Strubell et al. (2018) train attention heads to perform dependency parsing, adding a linguistic bias.

We also stress that if the definition of explanation is adjusted, for example if a different intended *user* and a different explanatory *goal* are articulated, attention may become a useful explanation for a certain application. For example, Strout et al. (2019) demonstrate that supervised attention helps humans accomplish a task faster than random or unsupervised attention, for a user and goal that are very different from those implied in §2.

6 Is Saliency the Ultimate Answer?

Beyond saliency. While we have argued that saliency methods are a good fit for our goal, there are other goals for which different methods can be a better fit. For example, counterfactual analysis might lead to insights, aided by visualization tools (Vig, 2019; Hoover et al., 2020; Abnar and Zuidema, 2020). The DiffMask method of DeCao et al. (2020) adds another dimension: it not only reveals in what layer a model knows what inputs are important, but also where important information is stored as it flows through the layers of the model. Other examples are models that rationalize their predictions (Lei et al., 2016; Bastings et al., 2019), which can guarantee faithful explanations, although they might be sensitive to so-called *trojans* (Jacovi and Goldberg, 2020a).

Limitations of saliency. A known problem with occlusion-based saliency methods as well as erasure-based evaluation of any input saliency technique (Bach et al., 2015; DeYoung et al., 2020) is that changes in the predicted probabilities may be due to the fact that the corrupted input falls off the manifold of the training data (Hooker et al., 2019). That is, a drop in probability can be explained by the input being OOD and not by an important feature missing. It has also been demonstrated that at least some of the saliency methods are not reliable and produce unintuitive results (Kindermans et al.,

2017) or violate certain axioms (Sundararajan et al., 2017).

A more fundamental limitation is the expressiveness of input saliency methods. Obviously, a bag of per-token saliency weights can be called an explanation only in a very narrow sense. One can overcome some limitations of the flat representation of importance by indicating dependencies between important features (for example, Janizek et al. (2020) present an extension of IG which explains pairwise feature interactions) but it is hardly possible to fully understand why a deep non-linear model produced a certain prediction by only looking at the input tokens.

7 Conclusion

We summarized the debate on whether attention is explanation, and observed that the goal for explanation is often to determine what inputs are the most relevant to the prediction. The user for that explanation often goes unstated, but is typically assumed to be a model developer. With this goal and user clearly stated, we argued that input saliency methods—of which we discussed a few—are better suited than attention. We hope, at least for the goal and user that we identified, that the focus shifts from attention to input saliency methods, and perhaps to entirely different methods, goals, and users.

Acknowledgments

We would like to thank Sebastian Gehrmann for useful comments and suggestions, as well as our anonymous reviewers, one of whom mentioned there is a whale in the room as well.

References

Samira Abnar and Willem Zuidema. 2020. Quantifying attention flow in transformers. In *Proceedings of the 58th Annual Meeting of the Association for Computational Linguistics*, pages 4190–4197, Online. Association for Computational Linguistics.

Marco Ancona, Enea Ceolini, Cengiz Öztireli, and Markus Gross. 2019. *Gradient-Based Attribution Methods*, pages 169–191. Springer International Publishing, Cham.

Leila Arras, Grégoire Montavon, Klaus-Robert Müller, and Wojciech Samek. 2017. Explaining recurrent neural network predictions in sentiment analysis. In *Proceedings of the 8th Workshop on Computational Approaches to Subjectivity, Sentiment and Social Media Analysis*, pages 159–168, Copenhagen, Denmark. Association for Computational Linguistics.

Leila Arras, Ahmed Osman, Klaus-Robert Müller, and Wojciech Samek. 2019. Evaluating recurrent neural network explanations. In *Proceedings of the 2019 ACL Workshop BlackboxNLP: Analyzing and Interpreting Neural Networks for NLP*, pages 113–126, Florence, Italy. Association for Computational Linguistics.

Sebastian Bach, Alexander Binder, Grégoire Montavon, Frederick Klauschen, Klaus-Robert Müller, and Wojciech Samek. 2015. On pixel-wise explanations for non-linear classifier decisions by layer-wise relevance propagation. *PLOS ONE*, 10(7):1–46.

Dzmitry Bahdanau, Kyunghyun Cho, and Yoshua Bengio. 2015. Neural machine translation by jointly learning to align and translate. In *3rd International Conference on Learning Representations, ICLR 2015, San Diego, CA, USA, May 7-9, 2015, Conference Track Proceedings*.

Jasmijn Bastings, Wilker Aziz, and Ivan Titov. 2019. Interpretable neural predictions with differentiable binary variables. In *Proceedings of the 57th Annual Meeting of the Association for Computational Linguistics*, pages 2963–2977, Florence, Italy. Association for Computational Linguistics.

Nicola DeCao, Michael Schlichtkrull, Wilker Aziz, and Ivan Titov. 2020. How do decisions emerge across layers in neural models? interpretation with differentiable masking.

Yuntian Deng, Yoon Kim, Justin Chiu, Demi Guo, and Alexander Rush. 2018. Latent alignment and variational attention. In S. Bengio, H. Wallach, H. Larochelle, K. Grauman, N. Cesa-Bianchi, and R. Garnett, editors, *Advances in Neural Information Processing Systems 31*, pages 9712–9724. Curran Associates, Inc.

Misha Denil, Alban Demiraj, and Nando de Freitas. 2015. Extraction of salient sentences from labelled documents.

Jay DeYoung, Sarthak Jain, Nazneen Fatema Rajani, Eric Lehman, Caiming Xiong, Richard Socher, and Byron C. Wallace. 2020. ERASER: A benchmark to evaluate rationalized NLP models. In *Proceedings of the 58th Annual Meeting of the Association for Computational Linguistics*, pages 4443–4458, Online. Association for Computational Linguistics.

Shuoyang Ding, Hainan Xu, and Philipp Koehn. 2019. Saliency-driven word alignment interpretation for neural machine translation. In *Proceedings of the Fourth Conference on Machine Translation (Volume 1: Research Papers)*, pages 1–12, Florence, Italy. Association for Computational Linguistics.

Christopher Grimsley, Elijah Mayfield, and Julia R.S. Bursten. 2020. Why attention is not explanation: Surgical intervention and causal reasoning about neural models. In *Proceedings of The 12th Language Resources and Evaluation Conference*, pages 1780–1790, Marseille, France. European Language Resources Association.

Sara Hooker, Dumitru Erhan, Pieter-Jan Kindermans, and Been Kim. 2019. A benchmark for interpretability methods in deep neural networks. In H. Wallach, H. Larochelle, A. Beygelzimer, F. dAlché-Buc, E. Fox, and R. Garnett, editors, *Advances in Neural Information Processing Systems 32*, pages 9737–9748. Curran Associates, Inc.

Benjamin Hoover, Hendrik Strobelt, and Sebastian Gehrmann. 2020. exBERT: A Visual Analysis Tool to Explore Learned Representations in Transformer Models. In *Proceedings of the 58th Annual Meeting of the Association for Computational Linguistics: System Demonstrations*, pages 187–196, Online. Association for Computational Linguistics.

Alon Jacovi and Yoav Goldberg. 2020a. Aligning faithful interpretations with their social attribution.

Alon Jacovi and Yoav Goldberg. 2020b. Towards faithfully interpretable NLP systems: How should we define and evaluate faithfulness? In *Proceedings of the 58th Annual Meeting of the Association for Computational Linguistics*, pages 4198–4205, Online. Association for Computational Linguistics.

Sarthak Jain and Byron C. Wallace. 2019. Attention is not Explanation. In *Proceedings of the 2019 Conference of the North American Chapter of the Association for Computational Linguistics: Human Language Technologies, Volume 1 (Long and Short Papers)*, pages 3543–3556, Minneapolis, Minnesota. Association for Computational Linguistics.

Joseph D Janizek, Pascal Sturmfels, and Su-In Lee. 2020. Explaining explanations: Axiomatic feature interactions for deep networks. *arXiv preprint arXiv:2002.04138*.

Ákos Kádár, Grzegorz Chrupała, and Afra Alishahi. 2017. Representation of linguistic form and function in recurrent neural networks. *Computational Linguistics*, 43(4):761–780.

Pieter-Jan Kindermans, Sara Hooker, Julius Adebayo, Maximilian Alber, Kristof T. Schütt, Sven Dähne, Dumitru Erhan, and Been Kim. 2017. The (un)reliability of saliency methods.

W. Landecker, M. D. Thomure, L. M. A. Bettencourt, M. Mitchell, G. T. Kenyon, and S. P. Brumby. 2013. Interpreting individual classifications of hierarchical networks. In *2013 IEEE Symposium on Computational Intelligence and Data Mining (CIDM)*, pages 32–38.

Tao Lei, Regina Barzilay, and Tommi Jaakkola. 2016. Rationalizing neural predictions. In *Proceedings of the 2016 Conference on Empirical Methods in Natural Language Processing*, pages 107–117, Austin, Texas. Association for Computational Linguistics.

Jiwei Li, Xinlei Chen, Eduard Hovy, and Dan Jurafsky. 2016a. Visualizing and understanding neural models in NLP. In *Proceedings of the 2016 Conference of the North American Chapter of the Association for Computational Linguistics: Human Language Technologies*, pages 681–691, San Diego, California. Association for Computational Linguistics.

Jiwei Li, Will Monroe, and Dan Jurafsky. 2016b. Understanding neural networks through representation erasure.

Zachary C. Lipton. 2018. The mythos of model interpretability. *Commun. ACM*, 61(10):36–43.

Thang Luong, Hieu Pham, and Christopher D. Manning. 2015. Effective approaches to attention-based neural machine translation. In *Proceedings of the 2015 Conference on Empirical Methods in Natural Language Processing*, pages 1412–1421, Lisbon, Portugal. Association for Computational Linguistics.

Paul Michel, Omer Levy, and Graham Neubig. 2019. Are sixteen heads really better than one? In H. Wallach, H. Larochelle, A. Beygelzimer, F. dAlché-Buc, E. Fox, and R. Garnett, editors, *Advances in Neural Information Processing Systems 32*, pages 14014–14024. Curran Associates, Inc.

Tim Miller. 2019. Explanation in artificial intelligence: Insights from the social sciences. *Artif. Intell.*, 267:1–38.

Akash Kumar Mohankumar, Preksha Nema, Sharan Narasimhan, Mitesh M. Khapra, Balaji Vasan Srinivasan, and Balaraman Ravindran. 2020. Towards transparent and explainable attention models. In *Proceedings of the 58th Annual Meeting of the Association for Computational Linguistics*, pages 4206–4216, Online. Association for Computational Linguistics.

Grégoire Montavon, Alexander Binder, Sebastian Lapuschkin, Wojciech Samek, and Klaus-Robert Müller. 2019. Layer-wise relevance propagation: An overview. In Wojciech Samek, Grégoire Montavon, Andrea Vedaldi, Lars Kai Hansen, and Klaus-Robert Müller, editors, *Explainable AI: Interpreting, Explaining and Visualizing Deep Learning*, volume 11700 of *Lecture Notes in Computer Science*, pages 193–209. Springer.

Shashi Narayan, Shay B. Cohen, and Mirella Lapata. 2018. Don't give me the details, just the summary! topic-aware convolutional neural networks for extreme summarization. In *Proceedings of the 2018 Conference on Empirical Methods in Natural Language Processing*, pages 1797–1807, Brussels, Belgium. Association for Computational Linguistics.

Ankur Parikh, Oscar Täckström, Dipanjan Das, and Jakob Uszkoreit. 2016. A decomposable attention model for natural language inference. In *Proceedings of the 2016 Conference on Empirical Methods in Natural Language Processing*, pages 2249–2255, Austin, Texas. Association for Computational Linguistics.

Nina Poerner, Hinrich Schütze, and Benjamin Roth. 2018. Evaluating neural network explanation methods using hybrid documents and morphosyntactic agreement. In *Proceedings of the 56th Annual Meeting of the Association for Computational Linguistics (Volume 1: Long Papers)*, pages 340–350, Melbourne, Australia. Association for Computational Linguistics.

Danish Pruthi, Mansi Gupta, Bhuwan Dhingra, Graham Neubig, and Zachary C. Lipton. 2020. Learning to deceive with attention-based explanations. In *Proceedings of the 58th Annual Meeting of the Association for Computational Linguistics*, pages 1782–4793, Online. Association for Computational Linguistics.

Marco Tulio Ribeiro, Sameer Singh, and Carlos Guestrin. 2016. "why should I trust you?": Explaining the predictions of any classifier. In *Proceedings of the 22nd ACM SIGKDD International Conference on Knowledge Discovery and Data Mining, San Francisco, CA, USA, August 13-17, 2016*, pages 1135–1144.

Alexander M. Rush, Sumit Chopra, and Jason Weston. 2015. A neural attention model for abstractive sentence summarization. In *Proceedings of the 2015 Conference on Empirical Methods in Natural Language Processing*, pages 379–389, Lisbon, Portugal. Association for Computational Linguistics.

Sofia Serrano and Noah A. Smith. 2019. Is attention interpretable? In *Proceedings of the 57th Annual Meeting of the Association for Computational Linguistics*, pages 2931–2951, Florence, Italy. Association for Computational Linguistics.

Julia Strout, Ye Zhang, and Raymond Mooney. 2019. Do human rationales improve machine explanations? In *Proceedings of the 2019 ACL Workshop BlackboxNLP: Analyzing and Interpreting Neural Networks for NLP*, pages 56–62, Florence, Italy. Association for Computational Linguistics.

Emma Strubell, Patrick Verga, Daniel Andor, David Weiss, and Andrew McCallum. 2018. Linguistically-informed self-attention for semantic role labeling. In *Proceedings of the 2018 Conference on Empirical Methods in Natural Language Processing*, pages 5027–5038, Brussels, Belgium. Association for Computational Linguistics.

Mukund Sundararajan, Ankur Taly, and Qiqi Yan. 2017. Axiomatic attribution for deep networks. In *Proceedings of the 34th International Conference on Machine Learning, ICML 2017, Sydney, NSW, Australia, 6-11 August 2017*, volume 70 of *Proceedings of Machine Learning Research*, pages 3319–3328. PMLR.

Martin Tutek and Jan Snajder. 2020. Staying true to your word: (how) can attention become explanation? In *Proceedings of the 5th Workshop on Representation Learning for NLP*, pages 131–142, Online. Association for Computational Linguistics.

Shikhar Vashishth, Shyam Upadhyay, Gaurav Singh Tomar, and Manaal Faruqui. 2019. Attention interpretability across nlp tasks.

Ashish Vaswani, Noam Shazeer, Niki Parmar, Jakob Uszkoreit, Llion Jones, Aidan N Gomez, Łukasz Kaiser, and Illia Polosukhin. 2017. Attention is all you need. In I. Guyon, U. V. Luxburg, S. Bengio, H. Wallach, R. Fergus, S. Vishwanathan, and R. Garnett, editors, *Advances in Neural Information Processing Systems 30*, pages 5998–6008. Curran Associates, Inc.

Jesse Vig. 2019. A multiscale visualization of attention in the transformer model.

Elena Voita, David Talbot, Fedor Moiseev, Rico Sennrich, and Ivan Titov. 2019. Analyzing multi-head self-attention: Specialized heads do the heavy lifting, the rest can be pruned. In *Proceedings of the 57th Annual Meeting of the Association for Computational Linguistics*, pages 5797–5808, Florence, Italy. Association for Computational Linguistics.

Sarah Wiegreffe and Yuval Pinter. 2019. Attention is not not explanation. In *Proceedings of the 2019 Conference on Empirical Methods in Natural Language Processing and the 9th International Joint Conference on Natural Language Processing (EMNLP-IJCNLP)*, pages 11–20, Hong Kong, China. Association for Computational Linguistics.

Matthew D. Zeiler and Rob Fergus. 2014. Visualizing and understanding convolutional networks. In *Computer Vision – ECCV 2014*, pages 818–833, Cham. Springer International Publishing.

How does BERT capture semantics? A closer look at polysemous words

David Yenicelik
ETH Zürich
`yedavid@ethz.ch`

Florian Schmidt
ETH Zürich
`florian.schmidt@inf.ethz.ch`

Yannic Kilcher
ETH Zürich
`yannic.kilcher@inf.ethz.ch`

Abstract

The recent paradigm shift to contextual word embeddings has seen tremendous success across a wide range of down-stream tasks. However, little is known on how the emergent relation of context and semantics manifests geometrically. We investigate polysemous words as one particularly prominent instance of semantic organization. Our rigorous quantitative analysis of linear separability and cluster organization in embedding vectors produced by BERT shows that semantics do not surface as isolated clusters but form seamless structures, tightly coupled with sentiment and syntax.

1 Introduction

Word embeddings have not only proven to be excellent representations in standalone tasks (Mikolov et al., 2013; Pennington et al., 2014; Wang et al., 2019) but have revolutionized the way modern NLP architectures are built (Collobert et al., 2011), and by now encode text input for virtually every task available. Recently, this approach has been paired with the transformer architecture (Vaswani et al., 2017) and a selection of pre-training tasks to bootstrap more powerful *contextual* word embeddings such as the ones produced by BERT (Devlin et al., 2018). s
The paradigm of encoding a word in its context has elevated the embedding methodology once more and from several perspectives. First, performance improvements on down-stream tasks are extraordinary across a wide range of tasks (Ethayarajh, 2019; Devlin et al., 2018; Wang et al., 2018). Second, the embedding space now must incorporate a vastly larger number of vectors, and its organization becomes an interesting research question on its own, especially given the largely unattributed performance gains.

In this work, we investigate the important concept of *polysemy* as one prominent example of semantic sub-space organization. Given that a word such as 'bank' can have several meanings, how are the corresponding vectors arranged in a contextual embedding space?
We investigate the organization of polysemous words in BERT embeddings through the concepts of separability and clusterability using the Word-Net annotations in SemCor (Miller et al., 1990). Our particular focus is a rigorous quantitative rather than purely qualitative analysis.

2 Related Work

Work connecting polysemy and word vector representations is often limited to static word embeddings where context has to be re-introduced through graph-based approaches (Remus and Biemann, 2018), auxiliary corpora (Pelevina et al., 2016), or even image data (Bruni et al., 2013). Usually, word sense disambiguation (WSD) performance is then chosen as a proxy to semantic disambiguation (Pilehvar and Camacho-Collados, 2019), yet no insights into the organization of the vector space are obtained. In a similar spirit, Kageback and Salomonsson (2016) add context through a recurrent encoder, yet do not analyze the geometry of these encodings.
In the meantime, the WSD task has been tackled successfully with BERT embeddings and Wiedemann et al. (2019) show that even a non-parametric approach suffices, which confirms that BERT must arrange word vectors according to semantic properties and suggests that no additional semantic pretraining is necessary (Levine et al., 2019).

When BERT embeddings of a polysemous word are analyzed, the findings are often summarized as a Silhouette score (Rousseeuw, 1987) or custom

Proceedings of the Third BlackboxNLP Workshop on Analyzing and Interpreting Neural Networks for NLP, pages 156–162
Online, November 20, 2020. ©2020 Association for Computational Linguistics

variance measures (Ethayarajh, 2019). While this allows to compare the average displacement due to semantic change across words, it does not give us a good sense of the overall structure of word vectors. In addition, the embedding space produced by BERT has been analyzed in terms of syntactic features, such as parse-trees (Coenen et al., 2019; Jawahar et al., 2019), part-of-speech, verbs and arguments (Shi et al., 2019; Ribeiro et al., 2019).

It is clear that BERT distinguishes polysemous words at least locally by nearest neighbors (Schmidt and Hofmann, 2020). However, the extent to which clusters are formed and how they are connected has only been addressed qualitatively (Coenen et al., 2019; Jawahar et al., 2019; Wiedemann et al., 2019), and no agreed-upon answer has emerged. This can be partly attributed to their qualitative methodology.

3 Method

How can we verify a hypothesis about the organization of polysemous words without manually inspecting the geometry for each word? Given a set of sentences with annotated polysemy, two strategies emerge: First, we can inspect the embedding space through the lens of a classifier with a clearly defined hypothesis set and take its accuracy as a signifier for the corresponding organization. Second, we can use an unsupervised approach to detect sub-space organization and compare its result to the WordNet labels using an appropriate similarity metric. We will proceed by analyzing both questions.

In our experiments, we consider the output of the last layer of BERT as the contextual word embeddings since this layer is most commonly used for downstream tasks, as depicted in Figure 1. To work with a discrete formalization of semantics, we use the WordNet 3.0 annotations in the SemCor 3.0 sentence dataset (Miller et al., 1990). This allows us to retrieve embeddings that are annotated with a ground-truth *semantic class* label. SemCor is one of the largest sense-annotated corpora with $37,176$ sentences, enabling us to quantify semantics and sample labelled word embeddings.

3.1 Linear Separability

Before turning to the clustering task, we investigate to what degree semantic classes can be separated by a hyperplane in embedding space, resulting in *semantic regions* as depicted in Figure 2. To this end, we train a simple linear classifier on top of the BERT embeddings (without fine-tuning) to predict the semantic class and report accuracy. Crucially, we down-project the 768-dimensional vectors using PCA ensuring that separability is not merely a consequence of high dimensionality. In the high-dimensional setting, this allows to assess to what extent semantic regions do form.

3.2 Clusterability

Once the presence of semantic regions has been concluded, we want to investigate the extent to which clusters form and how they are connected. For this, we train clustering models to understand the modality of the data, and to what extent clusters are in isolation from each other.

Because we are interested in practical gains, we refrain from using purely theoretical tools and clusterability scores (Ackerman and Ben-David, 2009; Mccarthy et al., 2016). In contrast, we use interpretable clustering models (Frey and Dueck, 2007; Ester et al., 1996; Campello et al., 2013; Comani-

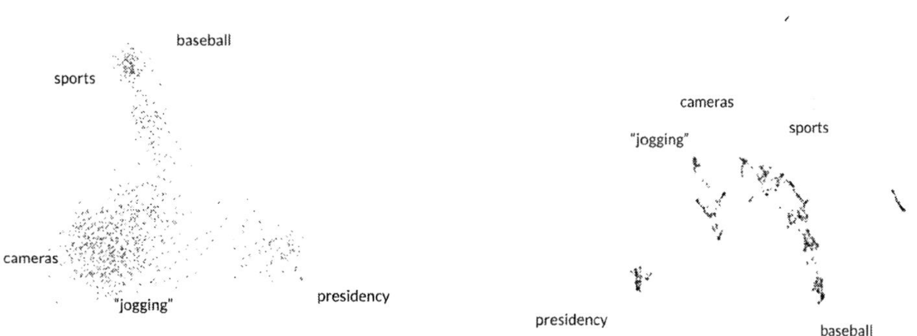

Figure 1: PCA (left) and UMAP (right) visualizations for contextual word embeddings sampled for the word run. Red points denote *nouns*, blue points denote *verbs*

Figure 2: Datapoints generated by sampling from a normal distribution. (left) includes class information denoted by the green, blue and red colors, forming semantic regions. This data is linearly separable, as there is always a hyperplane separating any two classes. (right) The class label information is not available. It is unclear how a clustering would look like.

ciu and Meer, 2002) that can detect the number of clusters in the data, as well as an adapted version of the Chinese Whispers algorithm (Biemann, 2006) that accounts for the *hubness property* [1] amongst embedding vectors outputted by BERT. The Chinese Whispers algorithm relies on a graph produced by the word embeddings and identifies clusters by passing messages between the nodes of the graph. From the sampled word embeddings we create the graph adjacency matrix M by calculating the pairwise cosine similarity between embeddings, and similar to Ribeiro et al. (2019), prune any edges which correspond to a cosine similarity lower than $w_{\text{cutoff}} = \mu(M) + c\sigma(M)$ where c is a hyperparameter, and μ and σ are the mean and standard deviation of all cosine similarities recorded in M. Hubs are defined as the top n embedding vectors with highest cumulative cosine similarities. The development and test sets consist of $\frac{n}{2}$ words respectively, including their set of sampled embedding vectors.

To score the overlap between a predicted clustering and the underlying ground-truth labels, we use the Adjusted Random Index (ARI) (Rand, 1971; Hubert and Arabie, 1985), which returns a similarity measure where a value of 1 implies an identical clustering up to a permutation and a value of 0 implies random predictions. Please note that this also introduces a small penalty when more clusters are introduced than actually present in the dataset according to the cluster-class-labels. However, pre-

___

[1] *hubs* are embeddings close to a majority of other embedding vectors, degrading performance (Conneau et al., 2017)

venting this is not in the scope of this work, and as such we do not further investigate this.

If no clustering is found, one can say with high confidence that the semantic regions are not occurring in different modes, and rather transition seamlessly into one another. This allows for an assessment in high dimensional space to what extent semantic regions are obvious, apparent by distinct modes. The motivation behind both experiments is visually depicted in Figure 2.

4 Experiments

We proceed with a discussion of the experimental results.

4.1 Bias in SemCor

First we aim to develop an understanding of bias in SemCor, as any bias in the data will propagate on to further observations. We conduct a simple experiment where we analyse the distribution of occurrences of semantic class ids.

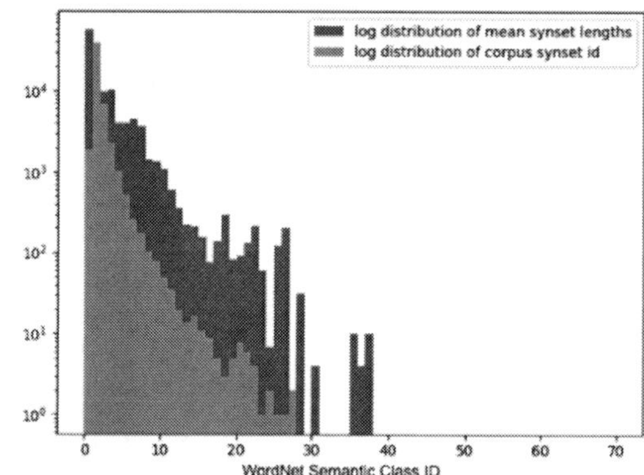

Figure 3: A cumulative plot over all words with WordNet senses within SemCor 3.0 and their respective frequencies. The SemCor data is biased. Words with a low WordNet sense index, i.e. close to 0, occur more often than words with a high WordNet sense index, i.e. above 5. There would be no bias if the two distributions would overlap. The skew could be a natural effect of how words with lower WordNet indices are assigned to more frequently used words.

Figure 3 depicts that the SemCor corpus is biased towards semantic classes which have a lower WordNet class ID. This could be due to the nature of WordNet, likely assigning low id indices to frequently used words. This requires us to oversample underrepresented classes for select experiments.

4.2 Linear Separability

We now turn our attention to what extent closed semantic regions exist in the embedding space. For a fixed word w that frequently occurs in SemCor, we sample up to $n = 500$ embedding vectors, apply 5-fold cross-validation, and oversample any imbalanced-class datasamples. The input is normalized, and we apply dimensionality reduction using PCA to k components, ensuring that each of the semantic classes contains at least 20 samples in the dataset. We use the SemCor semantic class labels as the response variables for the classification task. We only include semantic classes for the given word, leaving us with few class-labels. Results are shown in Table 1.

k	% variance	accuracy (mean / std)
10	0.30	0.74 / 0.05
20	0.44	0.80 / 0.04
30	0.54	0.82 / 0.03
50	0.70	0.87 / 0.04
75	0.79	0.83 / 0.04
100	0.85	0.89 / 0.03

Table 1: Average mean and standard deviation of the accuracy of a linear classifier trained on the 2 most common semantic classes for the words was, one, is. The choice of words is limited to the datasize of SemCor to allow for a significant size of datasamples.

Accuracy rates of over 75% are achieved with $k = 20$. The % *variance* refers to the explainable variance when the largest k eigenvalues are kept, as calculated by $\sum_i^k \sigma_i$ where σ_i is the ith largest eigenvalue, hinting to how much information according to the largest k principal components are kept. Similar results are achieved for 2-class and multi-class classification tasks with other words (see Appendix A.2). We conclude that the individual semantic classes are – to a reasonable extent – linearly separable. As such, contextual word embeddings are not randomly distributed over the embedding space, and closed semantic regions do form.

4.3 Polysemy vs. Variance

Before we analyze the structure of individual semantic classes, we want to understand how polysemy relates to the mean standard deviation of all contextual word embeddings X sampled for the word w. This helps us to understand how we need to adapt different clustering models.

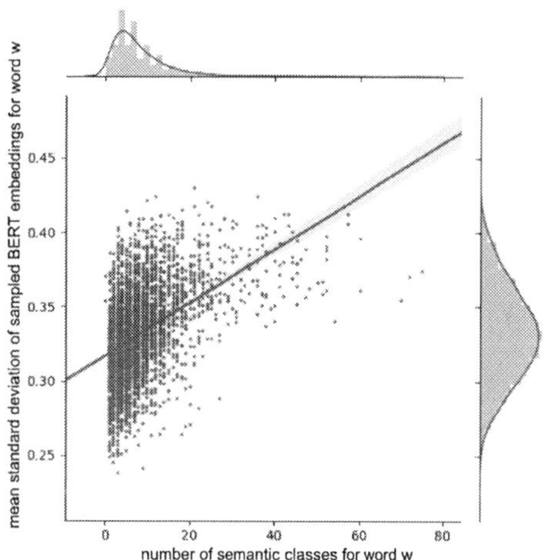

Figure 4: For each word w, we sample up to $n = 500$ contextual word embeddings X. We calculate the mean standard-deviation across embedding-dimensions as $\sum_i^n \sum_j^d x_i{}^j$ where $x_i^j \in \mathbf{R}^d$ is the jth dimension of the ith sampled embedding vector for word w. Word-Net is used to retrieve the number of semantic classes of w, denoting the amount of polysemy of word w.

Figure 4 shows that polysemous words have high variance, an idea initially put forth by Miller and Charles (1991). As such, vectors of polysemous words seem to be distributed at least as dispersed around the space as non-polysemous words do. Notice that the converse is not true, as there are non-polysemous words that have high variance. Amongst others, these could include stopwords as hinted by Ethayarajh (2019).

4.4 Clusterability

We now want to understand to what extent distinct semantic clusters exist. For a set of words $w_1, \ldots, w_n$, we sample up to $n = 500$ embedding vectors per word from SemCor and the news.2007.corpus [2] and apply dimensionality reduction using PCA to k dimensions. Due to the limited size of SemCor, we set the words in the development set to was, thought, made, only, central, pizza and the set of words in the test set to run, round, down, bank, key, arms. We include both polysemous words, as well as words which have a single recorded WordNet meaning, such that our experiments do not overfit to polysemous words. With default-package hyperparameters, all clustering algorithms would indicate that no distinct clustering could be found,

---

[2] http://www.statmt.org/wmt14/training-monolingual-news-crawl/

i.e. the sampled word embeddings would form a continuous density. Because we want to see to what extent BERT conforms to commonly accepted linguistic senses as given by WordNet, we apply the NetworkX Chinese Whispers implementation (Hagberg et al., 2006) on the resulting graph. Hyperparameters and their respective bounds for all clustering models are listed in Appendix A.1. We include the `[SEP]` tag at the end of the sentence, as this increases performance on all clustering methods. The ARI is exclusively calculated on samples for which we have the ground-truth cluster label and stems from the mean of multiple such word clusterings. We notice that choosing suitable hyperparameters is non-trivial and thus apply automated model- and hyperparameter selection, making use of random search (Bergstra and Bengio, 2012) and bayesian optimization (Wang et al., 2013) [3].

Clustering Model	ARI Score
Affinity Propagation	0.316
Modified Chinese Whispers	**0.457**
DBScan	0.170
HDBScan	0.298
MeanShift	0.251

Table 2: The maximum ARI scores achieved during hyperparameter optimization on different models for $k = 20$ and $n = 1000$.

The models used and their maximal performance after 300 trials of hyperparameters search are recorded in Table 2. Our modified Chinese Whispers algorithm is the best-performing clustering model. However, with an ARI score of 0.457, this method is not able to perfectly distinguish between multiple WordNet semantic classes [4]. To understand why this is the case, we proceed with a qualitative evaluation of some resulting clusters. One such clustering is depicted in Table 3, presenting four partitions for `arms` [5]. We achieve similar such results for 9 other words but focus on one example for conciseness. Notice that the clusters differ not only in semantics but also in other linguistic phenomena, most notably sentiment.

Given the quantitative and qualitative evaluation, we conclude that one cannot generalize that a clear

---

[3]We use the implementation by `https://github. com/facebook/Ax`

[4]An ARI score of at least 0.7 is desirable to conclude a significant overlap between two clusters

[5]See Table 8 for a complete example clustering

Partition	Representative Sample
1	Ms. Gotbaum tried to slide her handcuffed **arms** from her back to her front …
2	She swooped him up into her **arms** and kissed him madly …
3	… and shuttle robotic **arms** of a solar array and truss …
4	The classic years of the **arms** race, the 1950s and '60s before …

Table 3: Representative samples for the clusters found by the best performing clustering model for the word `arms`. Partitions 1-3 consider a person's arms, whereas partition 4 considers `arms` as a synonym to `weaponry`. Partitions 1, 2 and 3 strongly contrast in sentiment (scared, loving, and confident respectively).

distinction between semantic concepts in contextual word embeddings produced by BERT exists. One of numerous counterexamples is underlined in the left visualization of Figure 1. Certain combinations of semantics, syntax, and sentiment are more frequent than others (Hagoort, 2003; May et al., 2019), likely affecting the subspace structure and sometimes resulting in clusters that are distinct due to their simultaneous difference in both semantic and syntactic features (see Appendix A.3). However, this work also poses the question to what extent rule-based and handcrafted notions of semantics, such as the ones given by WordNet, are appropriate, opening the question to what extent BERT actually encodes a more flexible notion of semantics that is not rooted in hard distinctions between senses. We leave analysis in this direction to future work.

5 Conclusion

In this paper, we investigated how contextual word embeddings produced by BERT capture semantic concepts with a strong focus on polysemy. Our findings show that BERT creates closed semantic regions that are not clearly distinguishable from each other, seamlessly transitioning from one into another. We have shown that subspace organization is not purely determined by semantics. Instead, it is also intertwined with concepts such as syntax and sentiment. Finally, the repeated limitations of hard distinctions between senses as given via WordNet also open up the question to what extent BERT adds a more flexible notion of semantics, compared to the hard-coded examples formed by linguists. A better understanding of these relations will be key to developing more interpretable and expressive word embeddings, as well as linguistic knowledge representations.

Acknowledgments

David Yenicelik would like to thank Jason Lee (NYU) for the support setting an initial research question investigating on the structure of contextual word embeddings used in translation tasks, Jeremy Scheurer and Gertrude Yenicelik for discussions and comments, as well as Prof. Thomas Hofmann (ETH Zürich) for valuable discussions, guidance and enabling to conduct this project as part of the Master's thesis. Finally, the authors thank the anonymous reviewers for their constructive feedback.

References

Margareta Ackerman and Shai Ben-David. 2009. Clusterability: A theoretical study. *Proceedings of the Twelth International Conference on Artificial Intelligence and Statistics, PMLR 5:1-8.*

James Bergstra and Yoshua Bengio. 2012. Random search for hyper-parameter optimization. *Journal of Machine Learning Research 13*, pages 281–305.

Chris Biemann. 2006. Chinese whispers: An efficient graph clustering algorithm and its application to natural language processing problems. *Workshop on Graph-based Methods for Natural Language Processing*, pages 73–80.

Elia Bruni, Nam Khanh Tran, and Marco Baroni. 2013. Multimodal distributional semantics. *Journal of Artificial Intelligence Research 49*, pages 1–47.

Ricardo J. G. B. Campello, Davoud Moulavi, and Joerg Sander. 2013. Density-based clusteering based on hierarchical density estimates. *PAKDD 2013: Advances in Knowledge Discovery and Data Mining*, pages 160–172.

Andy Coenen, Emily Reif, Ann Yuan, Been Kim, Adam Pearce, Fernanda Viégas, and Martin Wattenberg. 2019. Visualizing and measuring the geometry of BERT. *Advances in Neural Information Processing Systems 32 (NeurIPS 2019).*

Ronan Collobert, Jason Weston, Léon Bottou, Michael Karlen, Koray Kavukcuoglu, and Pavel P. Kuksa. 2011. Natural language processing (almost) from scratch. *CoRR*, abs/1103.0398.

Dorin Comaniciu and Peter Meer. 2002. Mean shift: A robust approach toward feature space analysis. *IEEE Transactions on Pattern Analysis and Machine Intelligence*, pages 603–619.

Alexis Conneau, Guillaume Lample, Aurelio Ranzato, Ludovic Denoyer, and Hervé Jégou. 2017. Word translation without parallel data. *ICLR 2018.*

Jacob Devlin, Ming-Wei Chang, Kenton Lee, and Kristina Toutanova. 2018. BERT: pre-training of deep bidirectional transformers for language understanding. *CoRR*, abs/1810.04805.

Matrin Ester, Hans-Peter Kriegel, Joerg Sander, and Xiaowei Xu. 1996. A density-based algorithm for discovering clusters. *KDD-96 Proceedings.*

Kawin Ethayarajh. 2019. How contextual are contextualized word representations? comparing the geometry of BERT, ELMo, and GPT-2 embeddings. *EMNLP 2019.*

Brendan J. Frey and Delbert Dueck. 2007. Clustering by passing messages between data points. *Science 315 (5814)*, pages 972–976.

Aric Hagberg, Dan Schult, and Pieter Swart. 2006. Networkx. `https://github.com/networkx/networkx`. Accessed: 2020-05-07.

Peter Hagoort. 2003. Interplay between syntax and semantics during sentence comprehension: Erp effects of combining syntactic and semantic violations. *Journal of Cognitive Neuroscience 15:6*, pages 883–899.

Lawrence Hubert and Phipps Arabie. 1985. Comparing partitions. *Journal of Classification*, pages 193–218.

Ganesh Jawahar, Benoit Sagot, and Djame Seddah. 2019. What does BERT learn about the structure of language? *Proceedings ofthe 57th Annual Meeting ofthe Association for Computational Linguistics*, pages 3651–3657.

Mikael Kageback and Hans Salomonsson. 2016. Word sense disambiguation using a bidirectional lstm. *Proceedings of the 5th Workshop on Cognitive Aspects of the Lexicon*, pages 51–56.

Yoav Levine, Barak Lenz, Or Dagan, Dan Padnos, Or Sharir, Shai Shalev-Shwartz, Amnon Shashua, and Yoav Shoham. 2019. SenseBERT: Driving some sense into BERT. *ACL 2020*.

Chandler May, Alex Wang, Shikha Bordia, Samuel R. Bowman, and Rachel Rudinger. 2019. On measuring social biases in sentence encoders. *arXiv:1903.10561*.

Diana Mccarthy, Marianna Apidianaki, and Katrin Erk. 2016. Word sense clustering and clusterability. *Computational Linguistics, Volume 42, Issue 2 - June 2016*, pages 245–275.

Tomas Mikolov, Ilya Sutskever, Kai Chen, Greg Corrado, and Jeffrey Dean. 2013. Distributed representations of words and phrases and their compositionality. *CoRR*, abs/1310.4546.

George A. Miller, Richard Beckwith, Christiane Fellbaum, Derek Gross, and Katherine J. Miller. 1990. Introduction to wordnet: An on-line lexical database. *International Journal of Lexicography*, pages 235–244.

George A. Miller and Walter G. Charles. 1991. Contextual correlates of semantic similarity. *Language and cognitive processes 6*, pages 1–28.

Maria Pelevina, Nikolay Arefyev, Chris Biemann, and Alexander Panchenko. 2016. Making sense of word embeddings. *Proceedings ofthe 1st Workshop on Representation Learning for NLP*, pages 174–183.

Jeffrey Pennington, Richard Socher, and Christopher Manning. 2014. GloVe: Global vectors for word representation. *EMNLP*, page 1532–1543.

Mohammad Taher Pilehvar and Jose Camacho-Collados. 2019. Wic: the word-in-context dataset for evaluating context-sensitive meaning representations. *NAACL 2019*.

William M. Rand. 1971. Objective criteria for the evaluation of clustering methods. *Journal of the American Statistical Association*, pages 846–850.

Steffen Remus and Chris Biemann. 2018. Retrofitting word representations for unsupervised sense aware word similarities. *Proceedings of the Seventeenth Conference on Computational Natural Language Learning*, pages 143–152.

Eugénio Ribeiro, Vânia Mendonça, Ricardo Ribeiro, David Martins e Matos, Alberto Sardinha, Ana Lucia Santos, and Luísa Coheur. 2019. L 2 f/inesc-id at semeval-2019 task 2: Unsupervised lexical semantic frame induction using contextualized word representations. *Proceedings ofthe 13th International Workshop on Semantic Evaluation (SemEval-2019)*, pages 130–136.

Peter J. Rousseeuw. 1987. Silhouettes: a graphical aid to the interpretation and validation of cluster analysis. *Computational and Applied Mathematics 20*, pages 53–65.

Florian Schmidt and Thomas Hofmann. 2020. Bert as a teacher: Contextual embeddings for sequence-level reward. *ArXiv*, abs/2003.02738.

Peng Shi, Jimmy Lin, and David R Cheriton. 2019. Simple BERT models for relation extraction and semantic role labeling. *arXiv:1904.05255*.

Ashish Vaswani, Noam Shazeer, Niki Parmar, Jakob Uszkoreit, Llion Jones, Aidan N. Gomez, Lukasz Kaiser, and Illia Polosukhin. 2017. Attention is all you need. *CoRR*, abs/1706.03762.

Alex Wang, Amanpreet Singh, Julian Michael, Felix Hill, Omer Levy, and Samuel R. Bowman. 2018. GLUE: A multi-task benchmark and analysis platform for natural language understanding. *CoRR*, abs/1804.07461.

Bin Wang, Angela Wang, Fenxiao Chen, Yuncheng Wang, and C.-C. Jay Kuo. 2019. Evaluating word embedding models: Methods and experimental results. *CoRR*, abs/1901.09785.

Ziyu Wang, Masrour Zoghi†, Frank Hutter, David Matheson, and Nando de Freitas. 2013. Bayesian optimization in high dimensions via random embeddings. *AAAI Publications, Twenty-Third International Joint Conference on Artificial Intelligence*.

Gregor Wiedemann, Steffen Remus, Avi Chawla, and Chris Biemann. 2019. Does BERT make any sense? interpretable word sense disambiguation with contextualized embeddings. *Conference on Natural Language Processing (KONVENS) 2019*.

Neural Natural Language Inference Models Partially Embed Theories of Lexical Entailment and Negation

Atticus Geiger
Stanford University
atticusg@stanford.edu

Kyle Richardson
Allen Institute for AI
kyler@allenai.org

Christopher Potts
Stanford University
cgpotts@stanford.edu

Abstract

We address whether neural models for Natural Language Inference (NLI) can learn the compositional interactions between lexical entailment and negation, using four methods: the *behavioral* evaluation methods of (1) challenge test sets and (2) systematic generalization tasks, and the *structural* evaluation methods of (3) probes and (4) interventions. To facilitate this holistic evaluation, we present Monotonicity NLI (MoNLI), a new naturalistic dataset focused on lexical entailment and negation. In our behavioral evaluations, we find that models trained on general-purpose NLI datasets fail systematically on MoNLI examples containing negation, but that MoNLI fine-tuning addresses this failure. In our structural evaluations, we look for evidence that our top-performing BERT-based model has learned to implement the monotonicity algorithm behind MoNLI. Probes yield evidence consistent with this conclusion, and our intervention experiments bolster this, showing that the causal dynamics of the model mirror the causal dynamics of this algorithm on subsets of MoNLI. This suggests that the BERT model at least partially embeds a theory of lexical entailment and negation at an algorithmic level.

1 Introduction

Natural Language Inference (NLI) keys into fundamental aspects of how people reason with language. Although NLI is generally cast in informal terms that embrace the indeterminacy of such reasoning, the task nonetheless manifests a number of very predictable reasoning patterns. For example, systematic manipulations of the lexical meanings (Glockner et al., 2018), syntactic constructions (Nie et al., 2019a), and contextual assumptions (Pavlick and Callison-Burch, 2016) have systematic effects on the correct labels. These patterns present crisp, motivated learning targets that we can leverage to

not only evaluate the ability of NLI models to learn robust solutions, but also to analyze the internal dynamics of successful models.

In this paper, our learning target concerns the role of *monotonicity* in NLI (MacCartney, 2009; Icard and Moss, 2013). Specifically, we would like to determine whether models can learn to represent lexical relations and accurately model that negation reverses entailment relations (e.g., *dance* entails *move*, but *not move* entails *not dance*). This property of negation is *downward monotonicity*.

In service of pursuing this question, we present Monotonicity NLI (MoNLI), a new naturalistic NLI dataset for training and assessing systems on these semantic notions (Section 3). MoNLI extends SNLI (Bowman et al., 2015) to provide comprehensive coverage of examples that depend on lexical reasoning with and without negation. Using MoNLI, we conduct both behavioral and structural evaluations, seeking to provide a detailed picture of the solutions that top-performing models learn. We evaluate Enhanced Sequential Inference Models (Chen et al., 2016) and BERT-based models (Devlin et al., 2019), along with standard baselines.

Previous work evaluating the ability of neural models to learn monotonicity has focused on challenge test sets and systematic generalization tasks (Yanaka et al., 2019b,a; Geiger et al., 2019; Richardson et al., 2019). These behavioral evaluations ask whether models achieve a desired input–output behavior. We employ these methods as well, but we also ask whether models achieve an *algorithmic-level* learning target, in the terms of Marr (1982). Monotonicity reasoning can be cast as an algorithm that solves MoNLI perfectly. Do neural models implement this algorithm?

We first report on two behavioral evaluations (Section 5). When MoNLI is used as a challenge test set, we find that models trained on SNLI and/or MNLI (Williams et al., 2018) fail to reason with lex-

Proceedings of the Third BlackboxNLP Workshop on Analyzing and Interpreting Neural Networks for NLP, pages 163–173
Online, November 20, 2020. ©2020 Association for Computational Linguistics

ical entailments when negation is involved. However, we trace these failures to gaps in the training data. In response, we pose a systematic generalization task in which we expose models to MoNLI examples through fine-tuning while still requiring them to generalize to entirely new pairs of lexical items in negated linguistic contexts at test time. All our models solve the task, which suggests that they have learned general theories of lexical entailment and negation.

We then report on structural evaluations (Section 6), seeking to determine whether our top-performing BERT-based models implement the target monotonicity algorithm. In probing experiments, we find evidence consistent with this result, but it's not conclusive, since probes alone cannot reveal a model's causal dynamics. However, our intervention experiments provide evidence that BERT does mirror the causal dynamics of the monotonicity algorithm, at least on large subsets of MoNLI. We conclude that this model at least partially embeds a theory of lexical entailment and negation at an algorithmic level, in addition to fully achieving the correct input–output behavior on MoNLI.

2 Related work

Monotonicity Our empirical focus is entailment and negation. This is one (highly prevalent) aspect of monotonicity reasoning, which governs many aspects of lexical and constructional meaning in natural language (Sánchez-Valencia, 1991; van Benthem, 2008). There is an extensive literature on monotonicity logics (Moss, 2009; Icard, 2012; Icard and Moss, 2013; Icard et al., 2017). Within NLP, MacCartney and Manning (2008, 2009) apply very rich monotonicity algebras to NLI problems, Hu et al. (2019a,b) create NLI models that use polarity-marked parse trees, and Yanaka et al. (2019a,b) and Geiger et al. (2019) investigate the ability of neural models to understand natural logic reasoning. While we consider only a small fragment of these approaches, the methods we develop should apply to more complex systems as well.

Challenge Test Sets Challenge[1] test sets are supplementary evaluation resources that test the ability of a model to generalize to examples outside the dis-

tribution of the data it was trained, developed, and (standardly) tested on. These tests probe the generalization capabilities of state-of-the-art models with respect to the tasks they have been trained on, by focusing on difficult or underrepresented examples in a model's training set (Jia and Liang, 2017; Naik et al., 2018; Glockner et al., 2018; Richardson et al., 2019; Talmor et al., 2019).

Systematic Generalization Tasks Fodor and Pylyshyn (1988) offer *systematicity* as a hallmark of human cognition. Systematicity says that certain behaviors are intrinsically connected to others by compositional structures. For example, understanding *the puppy loves Sandy* is intrinsically connected to understanding *Sandy loves the puppy*. For Fodor and Pylyshyn, these observations trace to the mind's ability to recombine known parts and rules. There are often strong intuitions that certain generalization tasks are only solved by models with systematic structures. These tasks are referred to as *systematic generalization tasks* (Lake and Baroni, 2018; Hupkes et al., 2019; Yanaka et al., 2020; Bahdanau et al., 2018; Geiger et al., 2019; Goodwin et al., 2020).

Probing Probes are supervised learning models trained to extract information from representations created by another model. They are a primary tool in the analysis of neural network models (Peters et al. 2018; Tenney et al. 2019; Clark et al. 2019; for a full review, see Belinkov and Glass 2019). In aggregate, this work has provided nuanced insights into the internal representations of these models, as well as their capacity to directly support learning diverse NLP tasks via fine-tuning (Hewitt and Liang, 2019). However, probes are only able to reveal how representations correlate with information. They cannot determine if that information plays a causal role in model predictions (Belinkov and Glass, 2019; Vig et al., 2020).

Interventions Intervention studies go beyond probing to make changes to the internal states of a network, with the goal of observing how those changes affect system outputs. Giulianelli et al. (2018) use probing results to make informed interventions during LSTM language model predictions to preserve information about the grammatical subject's number, and this led to improved performance in subject–verb agreement. Vig et al. (2020) use interventions to characterize how gender bias is represented in the internal causal structure

---

[1]Though *adversarial* and *challenge* are sometimes used synonymously, we opt for the term *challenge*, because our dataset was designed with the intention of evaluating whether a model learned a particular phenomenon, as opposed to breaking any particular model (cf. Nie et al. 2019b).

of a model, and find that a small number of synergistic neurons mediate gender bias. They also find that the effect of these neurons is roughly linearly separable from the effect of the remainder of the model, a remarkable finding considering the highly non-linear nature of neural networks.

3 Monotonicity NLI dataset

We created the MoNLI corpus to investigate the ability of NLI models to learn the compositional interactions between lexical entailment and negation. MoNLI contains 2,678 NLI examples in the usual format for NLI datasets like SNLI. In each example, the hypothesis is the result of substituting a single word w_p in the premise for a hypernym or hyponym w_h. We refer to w_h and w_p as the *substituted words* in an example. In 1,202 of these examples, the substitution is performed under the scope of the downward monotone operator *not*. Downward monotone operators reverse entailment relations: *dance* entails *move*, but *not move* entails *not dance*. We refer to these examples collectively as NMoNLI. In the remaining 1,476 examples, this substitution is performed under the scope of no downward monotone operator. We refer to these examples collectively as PMoNLI.

MoNLI was generated according to the following procedure. First, randomly select a premise or hypothesis sentence s from the SNLI training dataset. Second, select a noun in s, and, using WordNet (Fellbaum, 1998), select all hypernyms and hyponyms of the noun subject to two conditions: (1) the hypernym or hyponym appears in the SNLI training data, and (2) substituting the hypernym or hyponym results in a grammatical, coherent sentence s'. Finally, for each substitution, generate two examples for the corpus – one where the original sentence is the premise and the edited sentence is the hypothesis, and one example with those roles reversed. Each of these example pairs has one example with the label **entailment** and one example with the label **neutral**, resulting in a dataset perfectly balanced between the two labels.

For example, suppose we select the SNLI sentence (A) and we identify the noun *plants* for substitution. Then we enter *plants* into WordNet and find that *flowers* is a hyponym of *plants*, so we substitute *flowers* for *plants* to create the edited sentence (B):

(A) The three children are not holding **plants**.

⇓

(B) The three children are not holding **flowers**.

This leads to two new MoNLI examples:

(A) **entailment** (B)
(B) **neutral** (A)

These two examples would belong to NMoNLI, due to *not* scoping over the substitution site. If *not* were removed from both of these sentences, then their labels would be swapped and both examples would belong to PMoNLI.

MoNLI was generated by the authors by hand; examples judged to be unnatural were removed, and any grammatical or spelling errors in the original SNLI sentence were corrected.

This data generation process is similar to that of Glockner et al. (2018), except they focus on the lexical relations of exclusion and synonymy, while we focus on entailment relations. This difference prevents their dataset from capturing monotonicity reasoning, which involves entailment relations, but not exclusion or synonymy.

4 Models

We evaluated four models on MoNLI:

CBOW The continuous bag of words baseline from Williams et al. (2018).

BiLSTM The bidirectional LSTM baseline from Williams et al. (2018).

ESIM The Enhanced Sequential Inference Model (Chen et al., 2016) is a hybrid TreeLSTM-based and biLSTM-based model that uses an inter-sentence attention mechanism to align words across sentences.

BERT A Transformer model trained to do masked language modeling and next-sentence prediction (Devlin et al., 2019). We rely on uncased BERT-base parameters from Hugging Face `transformers` (Wolf et al., 2019).

The first two models serve as baselines, while the other two models achieve comparable, near state-of-the-art scores on SNLI.

5 Behavioral Evaluations

5.1 MoNLI as a Challenge Test Set

We first use MoNLI as a challenge test dataset, i.e., models trained only on SNLI are expected to generalize to MoNLI. MoNLI can be considered a

Model	Input pretraining	NLI train data	No MoNLI fine-tuning			With NMoNLI fine-tuning	
			SNLI	PMoNLI	NMoNLI	SNLI	NMoNLI
CBOW	GloVe	SNLI train	78.9	64.6	22.9	65.9	95.5
BiLSTM	GloVe	SNLI train	81.6	73.2	37.9	74.6	93.5
ESIM	GloVe	SNLI train	87.9	86.6	39.4	56.9	96.2
ESIM	GloVe		–	–	–	–	98.0
ESIM			–	–	–	–	35.5
BERT	BERT	SNLI train	90.8	94.4	2.2	90.5	90.0
BERT	BERT		–	–	–	–	96.7
BERT			–	–	–	–	62.3

Table 1: The results of our behavioral analysis. The columns labeled *No MoNLI fine-tuning* display the challenge test set results (Section 5.1), and the columns labeled *With MoNLI fine-tuning* display systematic generalization task results (Section 5.2). The numbers are accuracy values; all the datasets have balanced label distributions. Dashes mark experiments that would involve untrained NLI parameters due to training/fine-tuning set-up.

challenge test dataset that evaluates an NLI model's ability to perform simple inferences founded in lexical entailments and monotonicity. As discussed in Section 3, it is not especially adversarial, in that we sampled sentences from the SNLI training set and only substituted in hypernyms and hyponyms that occur in the SNLI training set. This keeps MoNLI as close as possible to the distribution of SNLI. Thus, if a model fails on MoNLI, we can be confident that this failure stems from a lack of knowledge about monotonicity and lexical entailment relations, rather than some other confounding factor like syntactic structures or vocabulary items that were unseen in training.

5.1.1 Results

The results are in Table 1 under the heading 'No MoNLI fine-tuning', and they are stark. The four models achieve comparably high accuracies on SNLI and PMoNLI, the examples where no downward monotone operators scope over the substitution site. However, they are well below chance accuracy on NMoNLI, the examples where *not* scopes over the substitution site. BERT is more extreme than the other models, achieving a higher accuracy on PMoNLI than SNLI and almost zero accuracy on NMoNLI. High performance on PMoNLI shows that models have knowledge of the lexical relations between the substituted words, but low performance on NMoNLI shows the models have no knowledge of the downward monotone nature of *not*. In fact, the below chance accuracy on NMoNLI indicates that these models are somewhat reliably (incredibly reliably in BERT's case) predicting the wrong label on these examples, suggesting that they treat NMoNLI examples the same as PMoNLI examples.

5.1.2 Discussion

While these models trained on SNLI do not know that *not* is downward monotone in these examples, this is not conclusive evidence that they are unable to learn this semantic property. This ability might not be necessary for success on SNLI, where only 38 examples have negation in both the premise and hypothesis. A natural next step is to train on MNLI, where the coverage with regard to negation is better: about 18K examples ($\approx$4%) have negation in the premise and hypothesis. We tried this, by combining MNLI with SNLI, and the results were almost exactly the same. However, even the MNLI examples might not manifest the kind of monotonicity reasoning that we are targeting. Our next experiments help to resolve this issue.

5.2 A Systematic Generalization Task

Our three models trained on SNLI have knowledge of the lexical relations between substituted words, but do not know that the presence of *not* reverses the relationship between the word-level relation and the sentence-level relation. We now conduct a behavioral evaluation to determine whether models are able to learn a general theory of lexical entailment and negation when exposed to a limited subset of NMoNLI during training.

In designing systematic generalization tasks, we seek to constrain the training data in ways that prevent unsystematic models from succeeding. Defining disjoint train/test splits is enough to foil truly unsystematic models (e.g., simple look-up tables). However, building on much previous work (Lake and Baroni, 2018; Hupkes et al., 2019; Yanaka et al., 2020; Bahdanau et al., 2018; Goodwin et al., 2020; Geiger et al., 2019), we contend that a randomly constructed disjoint train/test split only diagnoses the most basic level of systematicity. More difficult systematic generalization tasks will only be solved by models exhibiting more complex compositional structures. Specifically, we want our systematic generalization task to be solved only by models that compute lexical entailment relations that may be reversed by negation. A learning model that memorizes labels based on substituted word pairs and whether negation is present would succeed on a disjoint train and test set as long as all pairs of substituted words appear during training, and this model does not compute the lexical relation between word pairs.

As such, we propose a generalization task where NMoNLI is partitioned into train and test sets such that the substituted words in the train set and the substituted words in the test sets are disjoint.[2] The specific train/test split we used is described in Appendix A.1. Ideally, a model trained on SNLI that is further trained on NMoNLI will still maintain strong performance on SNLI. We use inoculation by fine-tuning (Liu et al., 2019) to evaluate models on this ability. We report on the inoculated model with the highest average performance on SNLI test and NMoNLI test (full details of the inoculation process are in Appendix A.2).

The models are evaluated on examples where they know the relation between the substituted words, as evidenced by high performance on PMoNLI, but have not seen those substituted words in the presence of negation during training. However, they have seen other substituted words with the same relation in the presence of negation during training, making this task *hard*, but *fair* (Geiger et al., 2019). To solve this harder generalization task, we believe a model must learn to reverse the lexical relation *in general*; the identity of the substituted words must be abstracted away.

5.2.1 Results and Discussion

We present our results in Table 1, under the heading 'With NMoNLI fine-tuning'. All of our models solve this generalization task. However, only BERT does so while maintaining high performance on SNLI. We also report ablation studies on our two non-baseline models, evaluating their performance on our systematic generalization task without training on SNLI and without any pretraining at all. We find that both models still succeed with no pre-

---

[2]We use only NMoNLI in our systematic generalization task because models trained on SNLI already achieve high performance on PMoNLI.

INFER(*MoNLIexample*)

```
1   lexrel ← GET-LEX-REL(MoNLIexample)
2   if CONTAINS-NOT(MoNLIexample)
3       return REVERSE(lexrel)
4   return lexrel
```

Figure 1: An algorithm able to solve the MoNLI dataset that provides a theoretically motivated learning target for neural models at an algorithmic level of analysis (Marr, 1982). INFER takes in an example from MoNLI and outputs the relation between the premise and hypothesis. It uses three predefined functions. GET-LEX-REL returns the relation (one of $\{\sqsupset, \sqsubset\}$) between the substituted words in the premise and hypothesis. CONTAINS-NOT returns true iff negation is present. RE-VERSE maps $\sqsubset$ to $\sqsupset$ and vice-versa.

training on SNLI, but fail with no pretraining whatsoever. This suggests that BERT pretraining and GloVe vectors both provide sufficient information about lexical relations for the models to succeed. BERT's ability to get slightly above chance performance with no pretraining indicates the presence of some statistical artifacts in our dataset (Gururangan et al., 2018).

In sum, our models were able to solve our systematic generalization task, which we believe to be evidence that they learn to compute the lexical relations between substituted words. However, we also believe this evidence is weak, as there is no formal relationship between a model solving a generalization task and that model having any particular systematic internal structures. This evaluation is fundamentally behavioral, only concerning model inputs and outputs. We believe that a structural evaluation is necessary to conclusively evaluate systematicity.

6   Structural Evaluations

In our behavioral evaluations, the learning target was to mimic the input–output behavior defined by MoNLI. Assessing this learning target is straightforward. We now report on structural evaluations to try to determine whether a neural model has particular internal dynamics. For this, we rely on very recent probing and intervention methodologies that are not yet well understood and must be tailored to the model being analyzed. As such, we choose to focus on a single model, namely, the BERT model from Section 5 fine-tuned on NMoNLI. We chose BERT because it achieved exceptional results on

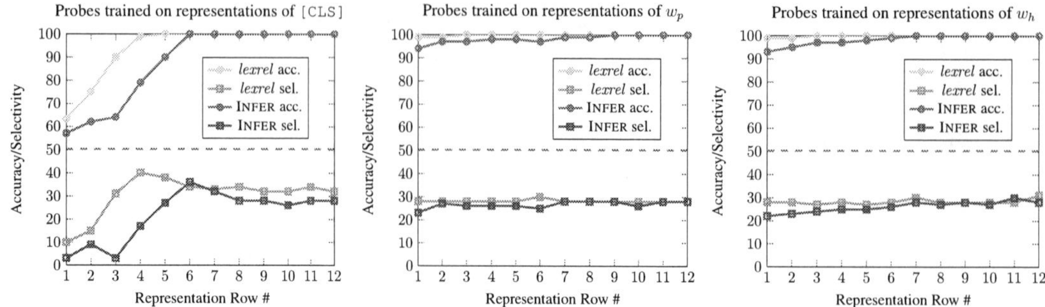

Figure 2: Results where classifier probes are trained on BERT representations to predict the value of *lexrel* and the output of INFER (Figure 1). Selectivity is probe accuracy minus control probe accuracy (Hewitt and Liang, 2019). The grey dotted line provides a soft ceiling for selectivity values, because we expect control probes trained on a binary task to at least achieve chance accuracy.

NMoNLI after fine-tuning without experiencing a significant drop on SNLI.

Figure 1 presents the simple algorithm INFER, which is our learning target. It takes in a MoNLI example and stores the lexical entailment relation between the substituted words in the variable *lexrel*. If negation is present, the reverse of *lexrel* is returned; if there is no negation, *lexrel* itself is returned. This is simply an algorithmic description of the MoNLI construction method. The most important piece is the intermediate variable *lexrel*. Intuitively, if our BERT model implements this algorithm, there will be some representation in BERT that *stores lexrel* and BERT will *use* that representation for a final prediction. Probes can give us an idea of where information is stored, and interventions help us see how that information is used.

Before we can go looking for where BERT stores and uses *lexrel*, we must limit ourselves to a tractable number of model internal representations. When our BERT model processes an example from MoNLI, it is tokenized as

$$e = \langle [\text{CLS}], p, [\text{SEP}], h, [\text{SEP}] \rangle$$

and 12 rows of vector representations are created, so each token is associated with 12 vectors. We localize our efforts to the representations created for [CLS] and the tokens for the substituted words in the premise and hypothesis, w_p and w_h (as described in Section 3). This narrows our search to 36 possible vector locations where BERT could be storing the variable *lexrel* for use in final output prediction. We denote these 36 locations with $\text{BERT}^r_{w_p}$, $\text{BERT}^r_{w_h}$, and $\text{BERT}^r_{[\text{CLS}]}$ where r is a row ($1 \leqslant r \leqslant 12$).

6.1 Probes

We follow Hupkes et al. (2018) in using probing evidence to determine whether a neural model stores the same information as a symbolic algorithm. They used probes to predict variable values used in an algorithm from the hidden states of sequential recurrent networks trained to perform basic arithmetic. We do something similar, probing the 36 vector locations defined by $\text{BERT}^r_{w_p}$, $\text{BERT}^r_{w_h}$, and $\text{BERT}^r_{[\text{CLS}]}$ for the value of the variable *lexrel* and the output of INFER.

Hewitt and Liang (2019) argue that accuracy is a poor metric for probes and that the ideal probe will highly *selective*, that is, it will have high accuracy on a linguistic task but low accuracy on a control task where inputs are given random labels. In this setting, our linguistic tasks are predicting the value of *lexrel* and the output of INFER from a model-internal vector created by BERT for some MoNLI example. Our control task is identical, except labels are randomly assigned to inputs. Hewitt and Liang demonstrate that small, linear probes result in high selectivity. Following this guidance, we used a linear classifier with 4 hidden units that was trained and evaluated on all of MoNLI.

Our probing results are summarized in Figure 2. Probes were able to achieve high accuracy and high selectivity predicting the output of INFER at every location other than the locations $\text{BERT}^k_{[\text{CLS}]}$ where $1 \leq k \leq 4$, and high accuracy and high selectivity predicting the value of *lexrel* at every location other than $\text{BERT}^1_{[\text{CLS}]}$ and $\text{BERT}^2_{[\text{CLS}]}$.

This qualitative picture is compatible with a story where BERT stores the value of *lexrel* at any location other than $\text{BERT}^1_{[\text{CLS}]}$ or $\text{BERT}^2_{[\text{CLS}]}$ and then uses this information to compute a final output prediction at any location other than the locations $\text{BERT}^k_{\text{[CLS]}}$ where $1 \leq k \leq 4$. The fact that probes trained on the vectors at locations $\text{BERT}^3_{\text{[CLS]}}$ or $\text{BERT}^4_{\text{[CLS]}}$ have high accuracy and selectivity predicting the value of *lexrel*, but moderate accuracy and low selectivity predicting the output of INFER may suggest a more specific story where these two locations store the value of the variable *lexrel* before this information is used to compute the final output.

We emphasize that, while the probing results are compatible with these stories, they only provide conclusive evidence about how representations correlate with the value of *lexrel* and the output of INFER. They cannot determine whether this information plays a causal role in model predictions (Belinkov and Glass, 2019; Vig et al., 2020).

6.2 Interventions

Probes give us a picture of where information is stored by our BERT model, but they cannot determine whether that information is used to make final predictions. Interventions can help us address this deeper question. As discussed above, our algorithmic-level learning target is for BERT to mimic the dynamics of the algorithm INFER in Figure 1. Icard (2017) provided the insight that algorithms like INFER can be explicitly understood as causal models (Pearl, 2001). This means that the causal role of *lexrel*, the lone variable in INFER, can be characterized with counterfactual claims about how altering the value of the variable would cause output behavior to change.

Suppose INFER is run on a MoNLI example i. Let $lexrel(i) \in \{\sqsupset, \sqsubset\}$ be the value that *lexrel* takes on, and let $\text{INFER}(i) \in \{\sqsupset, \sqsubset\}$ be the output. Then INFER can be see as providing the following counterfactual characterization of *lexrel*: if the value of *lexrel* were changed from $lexrel(i)$ to $lexrel(j)$, where j is a second MoNLI example, then $\text{INFER}(i)$ would change to

$$\text{INFER}_{lexrel(i) \to lexrel(j)}(i) =$$
$$\begin{cases} \text{INFER}(i) & lexrel(i) = lexrel(j) \\ \text{REVERSE}(\text{INFER}(i)) & lexrel(i) \neq lexrel(j) \end{cases}$$

In other words, if *lexrel* were to take on the opposite value, then the output would also take on the opposite value.

Our analytic tool for evaluating whether such causal dynamics are present in BERT is the *interchange intervention*. Figure 3 provides a high-level

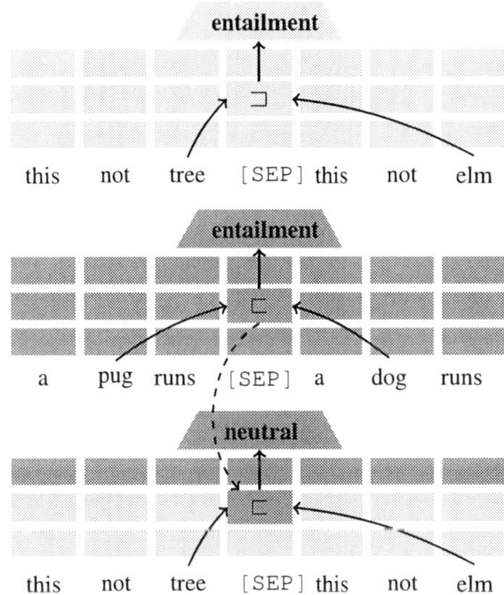

Figure 3: An illustrative **interchange intervention**: The solid arrows represent a hypothesis about where the model stores and uses information about lexical entailment. The dotted arrow is an interchange intervention, where the green vector (top) we think stores reverse entailment, trees $\sqsupset$ elms, is interchanged with the red vector (middle) we think stores forward entailment, pugs $\sqsubset$ dogs, leading to a modified network (bottom). If our hypothesis is correct, then the output should change from **entailment** to **neutral**, because the negation in the green example reverses the relationship between lexical entailment and sentence-level entailment. If this label reversal is not observed, crucial entailment information must lie elsewhere in the network.

picture of how these experiments work, and the following definition seeks to make this more precise and general:

Interchange Intervention Let L be one of the 36 locations defined by $\text{BERT}^r_{w_p}$, $\text{BERT}^r_{w_h}$, and $\text{BERT}^r_{\text{[CLS]}}$. When BERT is making a prediction for i, suppose that the vector created at location L on input i is replaced with the vector created at location L on input j and this results in the output y. We say that y is the result of an interchange intervention from i to j at location L and denote this output as $\text{BERT}_{L(i) \to L(j)}(i)$.

In essence, $\text{BERT}_{L(i) \to L(j)}(i)$ characterizes the output behavior that results from an experiment where model-internal vectors are interchanged at location L. Recall that $\text{INFER}_{lexrel(i) \to lexrel(j)}(i)$ describes what output is provided by INFER if variables are interchanged. If for some subset of MoNLI S, we believe that BERT is both storing the value of *lexrel* at some location L and using that information to make a final prediction, then for all $i, j \in S$ the following should hold:

$$\text{INFER}_{lexrel(i) \rightarrow lexrel(j)}(i) = \text{BERT}_{L(i) \rightarrow L(j)}(i)$$

This amounts to observing that the variables in the algorithm and the vectors in the model satisfy the same counterfactual claims. When a vector representing forward entailment is interchanged with a different vector representing forward entailment, model output behavior should be unchanged. If a vector representing forward entailment is interchanged with a different vector representing reverse entailment, then the model output should be reversed.

Results Due to computational constraints, we randomly conducted interchange experiments at our 36 different locations and chose the location with the most promise, namely, $\text{BERT}^3_{w_h}$. (Appendix A.3 covers our selection methodology in detail.) We conducted $\approx$7 million interchange experiments at this location, one experiment for every pair of examples in MoNLI. Using a simple greedy algorithm, we discovered several large subsets of MoNLI where BERT mimics the causal dynamics of INFER. (The greedy algorithm is described in Appendix A.3.) These subsets have size 98, 63, 47, and 37, and for each of these subsets there are many pairs of examples with interchange experiments that had a causal impact on the final model prediction. To put these results in context, if interchange experiments had a random effect on model output, then the expected number of subsets larger than 20 with this property would be less than 10^{-8}.

Discussion These results show that the values assigned by the algorithm INFER to the variable *lexrel* and the vectors created by BERT at the location $\text{BERT}^3_{w_h}$ exhibit the same causal dynamics on four large subsets of MoNLI. In Appendix A.3 we show a visualization of the subset with 98 examples. These pairs contain only 13 of the 69 distinct hyponyms in MoNLI, which makes it clear that this subset of MoNLI is not a random sample, but rather reflects a coherent semantic space. From this we conclude that, in addition to capturing the input–output behavior described by MoNLI, our BERT model at least partially embeds a theory of lexical entailment and negation at an algorithmic level of analysis.

Importantly, these results do not show that BERT fails to mimic the causal dynamics of INFER on larger subsets of MoNLI. First, we only conducted interchange experiments for every pair of examples in MoNLI at the location $\text{BERT}^3_{w_h}$. Second, we did not consider the possibility that BERT stores and uses the value of *lexrel* at different locations, depending on which input is provided. Third, analyzing vector representations may be too coarse-grained; perhaps experiments will need to be done on individual vector units. Finally, we used a greedy algorithm to discover the four subsets of MoNLI. We did not exhaustively analyze BERT to find the largest subset of MoNLI on which it mimics the causal dynamics of INFER; such an analysis is likely computationally impossible. What we did do is perform an efficient analysis that was able to find several large subsets of MoNLI on which the desired causal dynamics are present.

7   Conclusion

To operationalize our research question of whether neural NLI models can learn the compositional interactions between lexical entailment and negation, we constructed two learning targets for neural NLI models: (1) learn the input–output behavior described by MoNLI and (2) acquire the internal dynamics of the algorithm INFER. We evaluated the first learning target with two behavioral evaluation methods, using challenge datasets to show that state-of-the-art models trained on general-purpose NLI datasets fail to exhibit the correct behavior when negation is present and then following up with a systematic generalization task that showed our models are able to learn the correct input–output behavior when fine-tuned on a limited, but sufficient, subset of NMoNLI. We evaluated the second learning target with two structural evaluation methods, using probes to investigate where information about the variable *lexrel* from INFER might be stored in a BERT model and using interventions to show that on some subsets of MoNLI our BERT model exhibits the same causal dynamics as the algorithm INFER.

We believe that our holistic evaluation, leveraging both behavioral and structural methods, provides a multifaceted picture of how neural NLI models treat lexical entailment and negation. While our interchange intervention methodology is not yet formally grounded, there is great promise in the idea of investigating whether a neural model mirrors the causal dynamics of an algorithm.

References

Dzmitry Bahdanau, Shikhar Murty, Michael Noukhovitch, Thien Huu Nguyen, Harm de Vries, and Aaron Courville. 2018. Systematic generalization: What is required and can it be learned? In *In Proceedings of the 6th International Conference on Learning Representations*, Beijing.

Yonatan Belinkov and James Glass. 2019. Analysis methods in neural language processing: A survey. *Transactions of the Association for Computational Linguistics*, 7:49–72.

Johan van Benthem. 2008. A brief history of natural logic. In *Logic, Navya-Nyaya and Applications: Homage to Bimal Matilal*.

Samuel R. Bowman, Gabor Angeli, Christopher Potts, and Christopher D. Manning. 2015. A large annotated corpus for learning natural language inference. In *Proceedings of the 2015 Conference on Empirical Methods in Natural Language Processing*, pages 632–642, Lisbon, Portugal. Association for Computational Linguistics.

Qian Chen, Xiaodan Zhu, Zhen-Hua Ling, Si Wei, and Hui Jiang. 2016. Enhancing and combining sequential and tree LSTM for natural language inference. *CoRR*, abs/1609.06038.

Kevin Clark, Urvashi Khandelwal, Omer Levy, and Christopher D. Manning. 2019. What does BERT look at? an analysis of BERT's attention. In *Proceedings of the 2019 ACL Workshop BlackboxNLP: Analyzing and Interpreting Neural Networks for NLP*, pages 276–286, Florence, Italy. Association for Computational Linguistics.

Jacob Devlin, Ming-Wei Chang, Kenton Lee, and Kristina Toutanova. 2019. BERT: Pre-training of deep bidirectional transformers for language understanding. In *Proceedings of the 2019 Conference of the North American Chapter of the Association for Computational Linguistics: Human Language Technologies, Volume 1 (Long and Short Papers)*, pages 4171–4186, Minneapolis, Minnesota. Association for Computational Linguistics.

Christiane Fellbaum, editor. 1998. *WordNet: An Electronic Database*. MIT Press, Cambridge, MA.

Jerry A. Fodor and Zenon W. Pylyshyn. 1988. Connectionism and cognitive architecture: A critical analysis. *Cognition*, 28(1):3–71.

Atticus Geiger, Ignacio Cases, Lauri Karttunen, and Christopher Potts. 2019. Posing fair generalization tasks for natural language inference. In *Proceedings of the 2019 Conference on Empirical Methods in Natural Language Processing and the 9th International Joint Conference on Natural Language Processing (EMNLP-IJCNLP)*, pages 4485–4495, Hong Kong, China. Association for Computational Linguistics.

Mario Giulianelli, Jack Harding, Florian Mohnert, Dieuwke Hupkes, and Willem Zuidema. 2018. Under the hood: Using diagnostic classifiers to investigate and improve how language models track agreement information. In *Proceedings of the 2018 EMNLP Workshop BlackboxNLP: Analyzing and Interpreting Neural Networks for NLP*, pages 240–248, Brussels, Belgium. Association for Computational Linguistics.

Max Glockner, Vered Shwartz, and Yoav Goldberg. 2018. Breaking NLI systems with sentences that require simple lexical inferences. In *Proceedings of the 56th Annual Meeting of the Association for Computational Linguistics (Volume 2: Short Papers)*, pages 650–655, Melbourne, Australia. Association for Computational Linguistics.

Emily Goodwin, Koustuv Sinha, and Timothy J. O'Donnell. 2020. Probing linguistic systematicity.

Suchin Gururangan, Swabha Swayamdipta, Omer Levy, Roy Schwartz, Samuel Bowman, and Noah A. Smith. 2018. Annotation artifacts in natural language inference data. In *Proceedings of the 2018 Conference of the North American Chapter of the Association for Computational Linguistics: Human Language Technologies, Volume 2 (Short Papers)*, pages 107–112, New Orleans, Louisiana. Association for Computational Linguistics.

John Hewitt and Percy Liang. 2019. Designing and interpreting probes with control tasks. In *Proceedings of the 2019 Conference on Empirical Methods in Natural Language Processing and the 9th International Joint Conference on Natural Language Processing (EMNLP-IJCNLP)*, pages 2733–2743, Hong Kong, China. Association for Computational Linguistics.

Hai Hu, Qi Chen, and Larry Moss. 2019a. Natural language inference with monotonicity. In *Proceedings of the 13th International Conference on Computational Semantics - Short Papers*, pages 8–15, Gothenburg, Sweden. Association for Computational Linguistics.

Hai Hu, Qi Chen, Kyle Richardson, Atreyee Mukherjee, Lawrence S. Moss, and Sandra Kübler. 2019b. MonaLog: A lightweight system for natural language inference based on monotonicity. *ArXiv*, abs/1910.08772.

Dieuwke Hupkes, Sanne Bouwmeester, and Raquel Fernández. 2018. Analysing the potential of seq-to-seq models for incremental interpretation in task-oriented dialogue. In *Proceedings of the 2018 EMNLP Workshop BlackboxNLP: Analyzing and Interpreting Neural Networks for NLP*, pages 165–174, Brussels, Belgium. Association for Computational Linguistics.

Dieuwke Hupkes, Verna Dankers, Mathijs Mul, and Elia Bruni. 2019. Compositionality decomposed: how do neural networks generalise?

Thomas Icard, Lawrence Moss, and William Tune. 2017. A monotonicity calculus and its completeness. In *Proceedings of the 15th Meeting on the Mathematics of Language*, pages 75–87, London, UK. Association for Computational Linguistics.

Thomas F. Icard. 2012. Inclusion and exclusion in natural language. *Studia Logica*, 100(4):705–725.

Thomas F. Icard. 2017. From programs to causal models. In *Proceedings of the 21st Amsterdam Colloquium*, pages 35–44. University of Amsterdam.

Thomas F. Icard and Lawrence S. Moss. 2013. Recent progress on monotonicity. *Linguistic Issues in Language Technology*, 9(7):1–31.

Robin Jia and Percy Liang. 2017. Adversarial examples for evaluating reading comprehension systems. *CoRR*, abs/1707.07328.

Brenden M. Lake and Marco Baroni. 2018. Generalization without systematicity: On the compositional skills of sequence-to-sequence recurrent networks. In *Proceedings of the 35th International Conference on Machine Learning*, volume 80 of *Proceedings of Machine Learning Research*, pages 2879–2888. PMLR.

Nelson F. Liu, Roy Schwartz, and Noah A. Smith. 2019. Inoculation by fine-tuning: A method for analyzing challenge datasets. In *Proceedings of the 2019 Conference of the North American Chapter of the Association for Computational Linguistics: Human Language Technologies, Volume 1 (Long and Short Papers)*, pages 2171–2179, Minneapolis, Minnesota. Association for Computational Linguistics.

Bill MacCartney. 2009. *Natural Language Inference*. Ph.D. thesis, Stanford University.

Bill MacCartney and Christopher D. Manning. 2008. Modeling semantic containment and exclusion in natural language inference. In *Proceedings of the 22nd International Conference on Computational Linguistics (Coling 2008)*, pages 521–528, Manchester, UK. Coling 2008 Organizing Committee.

Bill MacCartney and Christopher D. Manning. 2009. An extended model of natural logic. In *Proceedings of the Eight International Conference on Computational Semantics*, pages 140–156, Tilburg, The Netherlands. Association for Computational Linguistics.

David Marr. 1982. *Vision: A Computational Investigation into the Human Representation and Processing of Visual Information*. Henry Holt and Co., Inc., New York, NY, USA.

Lawrence S Moss. 2009. Natural logic and semantics. In *Proceedings of the 18th Amsterdam Colloquium: Revised Selected Papers*, pages 71–80, Berlin. University of Amsterdam, Springer.

Aakanksha Naik, Abhilasha Ravichander, Norman Sadeh, Carolyn Rose, and Graham Neubig. 2018. Stress test evaluation for natural language inference. In *Proceedings of the 27th International Conference on Computational Linguistics*, pages 2340–2353, Santa Fe, New Mexico, USA. Association for Computational Linguistics.

Yixin Nie, Yicheng Wang, and Mohit Bansal. 2019a. Analyzing compositionality-sensitivity of NLI models. In *Proceedings of the AAAI Conference on Artificial Intelligence*, volume 33, pages 6867–6874.

Yixin Nie, Adina Williams, Emily Dinan, Mohit Bansal, Jason Weston, and Douwe Kiela. 2019b. Adversarial NLI: A new benchmark for natural language understanding.

Ellie Pavlick and Chris Callison-Burch. 2016. Most "babies" are "little" and most "problems" are "huge": Compositional entailment in adjective-nouns. In *Proceedings of the 54th Annual Meeting of the Association for Computational Linguistics (Volume 1: Long Papers)*, pages 2164–2173, Berlin, Germany. Association for Computational Linguistics.

Judea Pearl. 2001. Direct and indirect effects. In *Proceedings of the Seventeenth Conference on Uncertainty in Artificial Intelligence*, UAI'01, page 411–420, San Francisco, CA, USA. Morgan Kaufmann Publishers Inc.

Matthew Peters, Mark Neumann, Luke Zettlemoyer, and Wen-tau Yih. 2018. Dissecting contextual word embeddings: Architecture and representation. In *Proceedings of the 2018 Conference on Empirical Methods in Natural Language Processing*, pages 1499–1509, Brussels, Belgium. Association for Computational Linguistics.

Kyle Richardson, Hai Hu, Lawrence S. Moss, and Ashish Sabharwal. 2019. Probing natural language inference models through semantic fragments.

Víctor Sánchez-Valencia. 1991. *Studies in Natural Logic and Categorial Grammar*. Ph.D. thesis, University of Amsterdam.

Alon Talmor, Yanai Elazar, Yoav Goldberg, and Jonathan Berant. 2019. olmpics – on what language model pre-training captures.

Ian Tenney, Dipanjan Das, and Ellie Pavlick. 2019. BERT rediscovers the classical NLP pipeline. In *Proceedings of the 57th Annual Meeting of the Association for Computational Linguistics*, pages 4593–4601, Florence, Italy. Association for Computational Linguistics.

Jesse Vig, Sebastian Gehrmann, Yonatan Belinkov, Sharon Qian, Daniel Nevo, Yaron Singer, and Stuart Shieber. 2020. Causal mediation analysis for interpreting neural nlp: The case of gender bias.

Adina Williams, Nikita Nangia, and Samuel Bowman. 2018. A broad-coverage challenge corpus for sentence understanding through inference. In *Proceedings of the 2018 Conference of the North American Chapter of the Association for Computational Linguistics: Human Language Technologies, Volume 1 (Long Papers)*, pages 1112–1122. Association for Computational Linguistics.

Thomas Wolf, Lysandre Debut, Victor Sanh, Julien Chaumond, Clement Delangue, Anthony Moi, Pierric Cistac, Tim Rault, R'emi Louf, Morgan Funtowicz, and Jamie Brew. 2019. Huggingface's transformers: State-of-the-art natural language processing. *ArXiv*, abs/1910.03771.

Hitomi Yanaka, Koji Mineshima, Daisuke Bekki, and Kentaro Inui. 2020. Do neural models learn systematicity of monotonicity inference in natural language?

Hitomi Yanaka, Koji Mineshima, Daisuke Bekki, Kentaro Inui, Satoshi Sekine, Lasha Abzianidze, and Johan Bos. 2019a. Can neural networks understand monotonicity reasoning? In *Proceedings of the 2019 ACL Workshop BlackboxNLP: Analyzing and Interpreting Neural Networks for NLP*, pages 31–40, Florence, Italy. Association for Computational Linguistics.

Hitomi Yanaka, Koji Mineshima, Daisuke Bekki, Kentaro Inui, Satoshi Sekine, Lasha Abzianidze, and Johan Bos. 2019b. HELP: A dataset for identifying shortcomings of neural models in monotonicity reasoning. In *Proceedings of the Eighth Joint Conference on Lexical and Computational Semantics (*SEM 2019)*, pages 250–255, Minneapolis, Minnesota. Association for Computational Linguistics.

Gap in pagination due to formatting issues.

Pages 174-183

Probing for Multilingual Numerical Understanding in Transformer-Based Language Models

Devin Johnson, Denise Mak, Drew Barker, Lexi Loessberg-Zahl
Department of Linguistics
University of Washington
{dj1121, dpm3, barkand, lexilz}@uw.edu

Abstract

Natural language numbers are an example of compositional structures, where larger numbers are composed of operations on smaller numbers. Given that compositional reasoning is a key to natural language understanding, we propose novel multilingual probing tasks tested on DistilBERT, XLM, and BERT to investigate for evidence of compositional reasoning over numerical data in various natural language number systems. By using both grammaticality judgment and value comparison classification tasks in English, Japanese, Danish, and French, we find evidence that the information encoded in these pretrained models' embeddings is sufficient for grammaticality judgments but generally not for value comparisons. We analyze possible reasons for this and discuss how our tasks could be extended in further studies.

1 Introduction

In recent years, transformer-based language models such as BERT (Devlin et al., 2018), XLM (Lample and Conneau, 2019), and DistilBERT (Sanh et al., 2020) have achieved unprecedented results on a wide array of natural language understanding tasks, even when such models are trained on other tasks (i.e. transfer learning). In light of this success, there has been increased interest in investigating what particular information transformer-based language models encode in their word embeddings during pretraining that allows them to perform well in transfer learning experiments. Put into the context of this paper, we may ask: do such models gain certain linguistic/compositional understanding from pretraining? Attempts to assess such phenomena are commonly referred to as probing experiments. In this paper, we introduce a novel probing task using targeted datasets and classification tasks aimed at evaluating models' compositional reasoning capabilities in relation to numbers[1] in multiple natural languages.

We choose both grammaticality judgment and value comparison tasks (Section 3) to assess multilingual DistilBERT, XLM, and BERT[2] over various number systems. We argue that high performance on these tasks indicates some ability of reasoning over compositional structures, particularly over the rules generating valid compositional structures (task 1) and the resultant meanings of the structures (task 2). After probing the selected models on our tasks, we discuss explanations for the performance of models, as well as possible future extensions to this probing task schema. Additionally, studies in cognitive psychology such as Miller et al. (1995) assert that children learning more transparent number systems (i.e. those exhibiting more regularity in their surface forms such as Japanese) have a greater counting proficiency in several tasks compared to those learning less transparent (opaque) systems, such as English or French. Although it is not the focus of our work, given the multilingual setting, we will refer to the idea of number system transparency when analyzing possible explanations of results.[3]

2 Related Work

Our approach is informed by previous linguistically-motivated probing studies such

---

[1] For our purposes, numbers are spelled out, i.e. written out as words such as "ninety".

[2] Models were chosen for their varied sizes (num. parameters) as well as our access to computing resources.

[3] Number system complexity could be the subject of its own paper. However, as a small example, we can look at "thirty" in English and " 三十 " in Japanese. In English, there is no previous number such as "three" that appears (unchanged) in the word "thirty". In Japanese, however, the word consists of the kanji for 3 (" 三 ") and the kanji for 10 (" 十 "). If we continue comparing in this way, we would see compositionality more clearly and regularly in Japanese's surface forms, thus forming our intuitions.

Proceedings of the Third BlackboxNLP Workshop on Analyzing and Interpreting Neural Networks for NLP, pages 184–192
Online, November 20, 2020. ©2020 Association for Computational Linguistics

at those discussed in Belinkov and Glass (2019) and Ettinger (2020). Though Ettinger (2020) discusses important findings on psycholinguistic probing experiments of BERT, we find Ettinger et al. (2016) particularly useful for our study due to its clear explanations of linguistic probing experiment setup. In their study, Ettinger et al. present methods for constructing linguistically-targeted datasets (including example sentences, as we use) and classification tasks for probing word embeddings for semantic knowledge. As one of our tasks also seeks to probe for semantic knowledge, we were able to use this setup as a rough guideline. In addition, the authors are careful to create linguistic data with sufficient diversity as not to give potentially helpful cues to their classifier which are not related to the knowledge they wish to probe for. We thus carefully create our task data in a similar manner by limiting the distribution of our data (described more later) and forbidding duplicates.

To our knowledge, there have been few studies conducted on investigating numerical understanding specifically in transformer-based language models with a multilingual approach. However, one particularly relevant study on English comes from Wallace et al. (2019). Wallace et al. probe the embeddings of various models (BERT, ELMo, word2vec, etc.) using three tasks: find the maximum of a list, decode a number word to its numerical form, and add number words to produce a numerical form. In their results, the authors note that all embeddings contain some understanding, though standard embeddings perform particularly well and character-level models perform best. Although we investigate similar phenomena as Wallace et al., our methodology includes several key differences:

- Our focus is first and foremost to present a novel probing task schema/data and test it on a selection of transformer-based models - not to compare performance of differing language model architectures on previously-made tasks.

- We seek to draw conclusions from our task performance about model weaknesses over varied languages and suggest ways in which further probing experiments in this area can be designed in the future.

- We assert that the inclusion of other lan-

guages besides English is an important addition to probing experiments, as variation in language structure may help point to previously-unseen weaknesses in pretrained models.

- We include spelled-out numbers above 100 (up to 1000), which were not used in Wallace et al. We believe having a larger range of numbers might highlight weaknesses of models in handling multiple identical tokens in one word.

- We use only spelled-out number words, and do not include tasks where both Arabic numerals and spelled-out words might be used. Our reasoning for this choice is our desire to leave out the possibility of models merely learning a mapping from number words to numerals in order to perform well on tasks. In this way, we hope to make our tasks/data as restrictive as possible in order that they *require* a certain compositional/linguistic understanding.

3   Methods

We propose and perform two classification tasks in English, Danish, Japanese, and French. Task 1 is a probe for underlying syntactic information encoded in pretrained word embeddings, while task 2 is a probe of underlying semantic information. We run our tasks on all three models over two different datasets which we have generated: one where number words are inserted into sentences (e.g. "There are seven hundred books in the library.") and one with numbers alone (e.g. "seven-hundred"). Our probing model features a multilayer perceptron (a NN with a single hidden layer) classifier on top of the existing transformer language model architecture. In this manner, pretrained word embeddings from the language model (BERT, DistilBERT, XLM) are fed as input to the MLP classifier which itself is then trained on our tasks. A depiction of the probing model structure is shown in Figure 1.

3.1   Task 1: Grammaticality Judgment

We specify the first task as follows:

- Let $v \in \{bare, sentence\}$ specify the variant of our task. If $v = bare$, then only training examples with numbers *not* inserted into sentences will be used for grammaticality judgments. Otherwise, only training examples with number inserted into sentences are used. A mixture of two input data types is never used.

- Let the training set of task 1, T, be defined by pairs $t_0...t_n$ where $t_i = (x_{t_i}, y_{t_i})$

- Let x_{t_i} be the input of the i'th training example t_i such that $x_{t_i} = s$. s is a string consisting of a number word such as "thirty-two" or a sentence containing a number word such as "He could eat thirty-two oranges" (depending on the value of v)

- Let $y_{t_i} \in \{0, 1\}$ be the corresponding label of input x_{t_i} of training sample t_i. $y_{t_i} = 1$ if the input string s of x_{t_i} is ungrammatical, otherwise $y_{t_i} = 0$.

We argue high accuracy on this task is evidence of some understanding of the underlying compositional/syntactic rules for the process which generates natural language numbers.

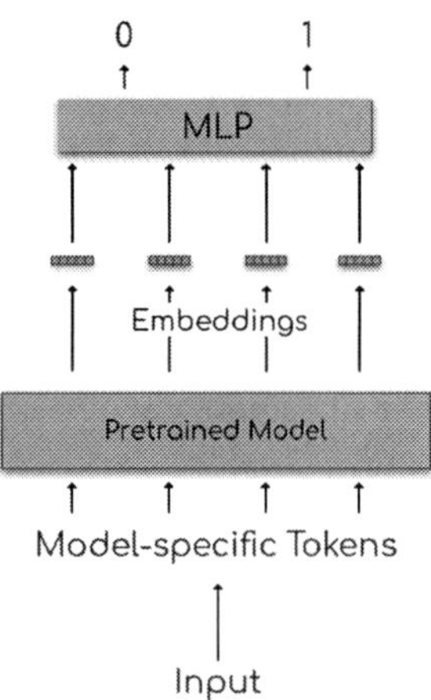

Figure 1: Probing model; Inputs can vary from sentences with numbers to standalone numbers. All weights are fixed except the connections to the MLP layer

As an example, "two hundred three and fifty" is not a number in the English language, while "five hundred" is. We also assert that the importance of using spelled-out numbers comes into play since no string of Arabic numerals is ungrammatical except a small amount of strings such as

"0112". Often in written text, Arabic numerals are used in place of number words; However, given human ability to generalize compositional rules from other structures in order to learn new structures, even if it were the case that fewer number words were seen in pretraining, we would hope to see a similar compositional generalization capability present in pretrained language models' embeddings which would allow them to perform well on this task.

3.2 Task 2: Value Comparison

We specify the second task as follows:

- Let $v \in \{bare, sentence\}$ specify the variant of our task. If $v = bare$, then only training examples with numbers *not* inserted into sentences will be used for value comparsion. Otherwise, only training examples with number inserted into sentences are used. A mixture of two input data types is never used.

- Let the training set of task 2, U, be defined by pairs $u_0...u_n$ where $u_i = (x_{u_i}, y_{u_i})$

- Let x_{u_i} be the input of the i'th training example u_i such that $x_{u_i} = (s_0, s_1)$. s_0 and s_1 represent bare number words or number words inserted into sentences (depending on the value of v).

- Let $y_{u_i} \in \{0, 1\}$ be the corresponding label of input x_{u_i} of training sample u_i. $y_{u_i} = 0$ if for s_0 and s_1 of x_{u_i}, s_0 refers to a value larger than that of s_1. $y_{u_i} = 1$ if for s_0 and s_1 of x_{u_i}, s_0 refers to a value smaller than that of s_1.

With this task, we take high accuracy as evidence of some understanding of the compositional semantic information carried by the number, i.e. its magnitude. For example, given the pair ($s_0 =$"twelve", $s_1 =$"fifteen") the correct output should be 1, since the first number in the pair is less than the second. This task is similar in form to the list maximum task of Wallace et al. (2019); However, notable differences include our usage of number words in sentences, our inclusion of number words above 100, and languages other than English.

Task (v)	Input	Output
Task 1 (sentence)	"He could eat three hundred and two oranges"	0 (s grammatical)
Task 1 (bare)	"seventy-four six hundred and thirty-eight"	1 (s ungrammatical)
Task 2 (sentence)	"There are seven hundred and eighty-six books in the library" "There are thirty-eight books in the library"	0 (s_0 greater)
Task 2 (bare)	"five hundred" "six hundred"	1 (s_0 less)

Table 1: Sample of generated English data for our tasks

4 Data

Separate datasets for each variant of each task were made, each with a 60-20-20 train-validation-test split. To generate number words to create training example inputs, the python package num2words (Ogawa) was used for text conversion from numerical to standard spelled-out numbers. For task 1, it was necessary to create ungrammatical numbers in each language. These ungrammatical number words were created by randomly appending grammatical number words (or parts of them) together and controlling for length. Lastly, it was also necessary to create custom sentences to insert our number words into. Eleven sentence templates were used, translated into each of our languages and verified by native speakers. A sample of our data can be seen in Table 1. Detailed information on dataset statistics and data generation techniques can be found in appendix B.

5 Results

The following sections show probing results on both tasks. Before probing and as a precaution, we fine-tuned our models on both tasks. As we expected, we find that both tasks are learnable to accuracies above 95%. A further discussion of fine-tuning results is left for appendix A.

5.1 Task 1 Results

Our results on task 1 (Figure 2) show that the pretrained embeddings of multilingual BERT, DistilBERT and XLM seem to have sufficient information to be able to determine grammaticality of number words in Japanese, English, Danish, and French at better-than-chance performance. We thus argue that these results suggest that the pretrained embeddings of these models contain some understanding of the compositional rules for generating number words in the languages we've selected.

There are a few patterns worth noting in the results. Firstly, accuracy on bare numbers was always better than accuracy on numbers in sentences. Though accuracy on numbers in sentences was not extremely poor, our initial prediction was that they would perform better as they would resemble the type of data which the models were pretrained on (Wikipedia). Secondly, in terms of overall model performance, DistilBERT performs best (sometimes even at 100% accuracy) in the majority of cases, followed by XLM and BERT. A further analysis of these patterns is left for our discussion (6).

5.2 Task 2 Results

On our second task, we find that overall, the information in the pretrained embeddings of BERT, DistilBERT, and XLM is mostly insufficient for comparing number magnitudes in our tested languages with high accuracy. This suggests that these pretrained embeddings may struggle with understanding the compositional semantics of number words (i.e. how compositional elements in number words form to create meaning).

As for patterns in these results, we can again see that bare number performance is always equal to or better than when numbers are inserted into sentences. Looking at bare results, DistilBERT again performs well, but this time XLM performs best on Japanese and English. A further analysis of these patterns is also left for our discussion (6).

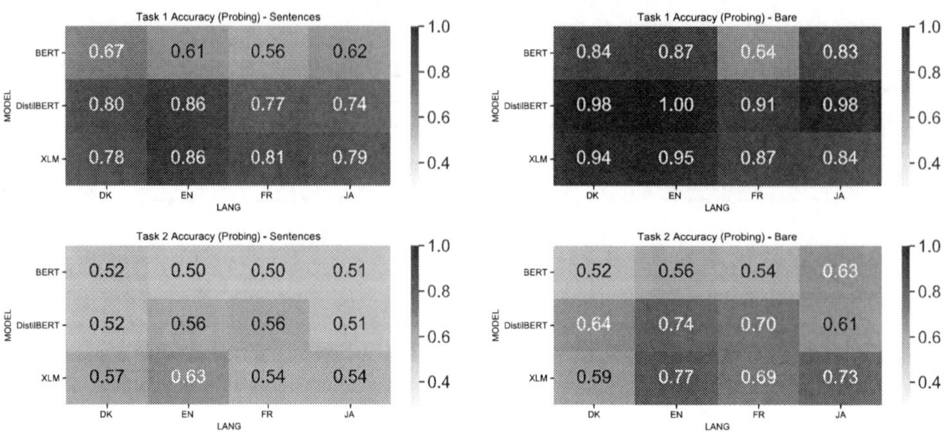

Figure 2: Task test accuracy on probing per language/model.

6   Discussion

6.1   Pretraining Data

Since this probing experiment is using pretrained transformer-based language models (Wolf et al., 2019), we can briefly discuss pretraining methods in order to ascertain potential effects on results. Each model was pretrained using masked language modelling and all except XLM (unspecified) were pretrained on multilingual Wikipedia data. With this, one may ask whether this method of training should be expected to encode the information we probe for. Particularly, one may point to the usage of Arabic numerals in Wikipedia text and less-frequent usage of spelled-out numbers as a cause for poor performance on task 2. In imagining alternatives to Wikipedia, a consideration of Arabic numerals must still be present, which serves as a reminder that there is no *perfect* pretraining set.

However, we do not believe this would prevent language models from capturing the information necessary to complete our task 2. We assert that even if these models have seen fewer spelled-out numbers, they could still learn compositional rules from other linguistic structures and generalize to our probing task. If Arabic numerals proved to be an issue, we would expect to see our results be worse across the board, not only on task 2. Thus, from our results, it seems that pretraining on Wikipedia was certainly not sufficient for encoding a highly accurate sense of number magnitude for any of the models/languages, but this was likely not due to pretraining methods.

6.2   Worse Performance on Task 2

Why might models have more difficulty in ascertaining magnitude of number words? For one, we believe this task is naturally more difficult than the first because of the deep semantic information necessary to succeed on it. In the first task, it may have been possible to leverage at least *some* of the surface level characteristics of grammatical and ungrammatical words, whereas in the second task there is no such leveraging possible. That is to say, in the first task, a model can learn syntactic information more directly from surface level patterns. Instead, in task 2, the models need to have encoded some semantic information about the magnitude of number words, where the surface forms of these words gives less indication of their underlying meaning (except for the possibility of longer words having larger quantities, though this is not always the case). Given this is true, this may point to a weakness in models to make fine-grained semantic distinctions regarding quantities, especially when quantities are used in sentences and not left bare.

6.3   Language Transparency

In terms of number system transparency (as mentioned in our introduction), we loosely presumed that accuracies might follow the order of Japanese > English/Danish > French, with Japanese performing best given its higher transparency and French the worst due to its vigesimal number system. Again, we choose not to formally define transparency, as such a formal definition is an in-depth topic of its own. To our slight surprise, our results did not match these predictions, with rankings of performance by language varying by task and task variation.

We argue there could be many reasons (such as pretraining data) for the unexpected results pattern. However, since there is more of a consistent performance pattern across models than there is across languages, we believe it is far more likely that differences in performance are not necessarily due to language transparency, but rather model architecture and therefore that the structural differences between these languages is not a significant contributing factor to performance patterns. If this were true (which we think is probable), this is a good sign for these models, since language structure differences are not proving to be a challenge to performance, but rather some other factor.

6.4 Model Architecture and Performance

One clear pattern we can see is that multilingual BERT's embeddings consistently perform much worse than both XLM and DistilBERT. This is especially clear in French results, where the gap between BERT and the other two models is sometimes more than 20 points. A relatively simple explanation for this is the size of each model in terms of number of parameters. Indeed, as model size increases, performance on both tasks increases (BERT -> DistilBERT -> XLM). Of course, correlation is no evidence of causation; However, if this were true, it is quite consistent with other trends in recent NLP studies. In the case of this study, we can say that bigger is (almost) always better, with XLM mostly performing best, followed by DistilBERt and BERT. Though, this is somewhat undesirable on a larger scale since, ideally, we would hope that it would not require such a large model to encode the information we probe for.

6.5 Bare Number Words Perform Better

On both tasks, our results also show that bare numbers performed equal to or better than numbers in sentences. We propose that this is due to the sentences creating noisiness, thus creating more difficulty for a model to know exactly where it should be looking for the necessary information to complete the tasks. This is very much the case for task 2, where we believe it would be harder to know the magnitude a sentence is referring to than merely if the sentence is grammatical. We argue that, besides adding noise, this method of probing exploits

a possible weakness in masked language modeling as a pretraining method. That is, given that masked language modeling's task it to predict appropriate (grammatical) words, there may be less emphasis on learning the underlying semantics of those words, thus the better performance on task 1 sentences and worse performance on task 2 sentences.

7 Further Work

As this work is an exploration of a new probing method for state-of-the-art language model architecture, there are surely a number of ways to extend from it.

Though we discussed it briefly here, exploring the architectural reasons for the shortcomings of these pretrained embeddings, especially in the case of task 2 and with sentences is an important area for future work. Indeed, in a similar task from Wallace et al. (2019), BERT was also found to have poor performance. In the future, several more specific probes could be designed to test for understanding of magnitude in various linguistic contexts to find strengths and weaknesses of transformer-based models. A particularly interesting case would be in testing magnitude comprehension in sentences of varying structures. Our sentence templates used in this study are few, and experimenting with other varieties could prove to be insightful.

Our experiment also made use of the idea of language transparency. We also find this to be a topic for possible further work. Namely, is there a method to reliably measure transparency of languages to predict performance on numerical understanding tasks such as these? We believe this may be possible through measuring complexities of grammars which generate number words in each language. Overall, in future extensions of this study, there is room for more languages, sentence types, task renditions, and models.

8 Conclusion

In this paper, we introduced methods for probing the multilingual compositional reasoning capabilities of transformer-based models' pretrained embeddings over natural language numbers. From our experiments, we've shown that these pretrained embeddings show some capabilities in making grammatical judgments of number words, though they are less capable of making value comparisons. In addition, we find that results generally follow a trend based upon model size. Our results are in accord with previous work such as Wallace et al. (2019); However, we have also highlighted further model weaknesses through our probing methods. Therefore, the opportunities for future work, especially with a multilingual focus, are plenty.

Acknowledgements

Thank you to all anonymous reviewers for your helpful comments. Thank you to Professor Shane Steinert-Threlkeld for your guidance and throughout all stages of this paper. Thank you to Professor Luke Zettlemoyer for your advice on our paper in its earlier stages. Thank you to the several volunteer native speakers for grammaticality judgments. –This work was facilitated through the use of advanced computational, storage, and networking infrastructure provided by the Hyak supercomputer system and funded by the STF at the University of Washington.–

References

Yonatan Belinkov and James R. Glass. 2019. Analysis methods in neural language processing: A survey. *Transactions of the Association for Computational Linguistics*, 7:49–72.

J. Devlin, M.-W. Chang, K. Lee, and K. Toutanova. 2018. Bert: Pre-training of deep bidirectional transformers for language understanding.

Allyson Ettinger. 2020. What bert is not: Lessons from a new suite of psycholinguistic diagnostics for language models. *Transactions of the Association for Computational Linguistics*, 8:34–48.

Allyson Ettinger, Ahmed Elgohary, and Philip Resnik. 2016. Probing for semantic evidence of composition by means of simple classification tasks. In *Proceedings of the 1st Workshop on Evaluating Vector-Space Representations for NLP*, pages 134–139, Berlin, Germany. Association for Computational Linguistics.

Guillaume Lample and Alexis Conneau. 2019. Cross-lingual language model pretraining. *CoRR*, abs/1901.07291.

K. F. Miller, C. M. Smith, J. Zhu, and H. Zhang. 1995. Preschool origins of cross-national differences in mathematical competence: The role of number-naming systems. *Psychological Science*, 6:56–60.

T. Ogawa. num2words.

Victor Sanh, Lysandre Debut, Julien Chaumond, and Thomas Wolf. 2020. Distilbert, a distilled version of bert: smaller, faster, cheaper and lighter.

Eric Wallace, Yizhong Wang, Sujian Li, Sameer Singh, and Matt Gardner. 2019. Do nlp models know numbers? probing numeracy in embeddings. *Proceedings of the 2019 Conference on Empirical Methods in Natural Language Processing and the 9th International Joint Conference on Natural Language Processing (EMNLP-IJCNLP)*.

Thomas Wolf, Lysandre Debut, Victor Sanh, Julien Chaumond, Clement Delangue, Anthony Moi, Pierric Cistac, Tim Rault, R'emi Louf, Morgan Funtowicz, and Jamie Brew. 2019. Huggingface's transformers: State-of-the-art natural language processing. *ArXiv*, abs/1910.03771.

A Fine-Tuning

The fine-tuning results shown in (Figure 3) are validation accuracies after one epoch of training. When trained for 20 epochs (Figure 4), the models reach over 99% accuracy on all languages and tasks except for Danish which reaches 95% on sentence tasks.

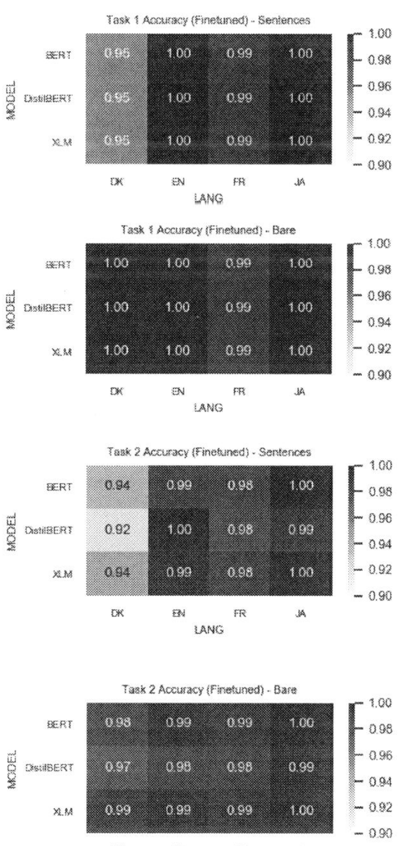

Figure 3: Fine-tuned task validation accuracy per language/model, when trained for 1 epoch.

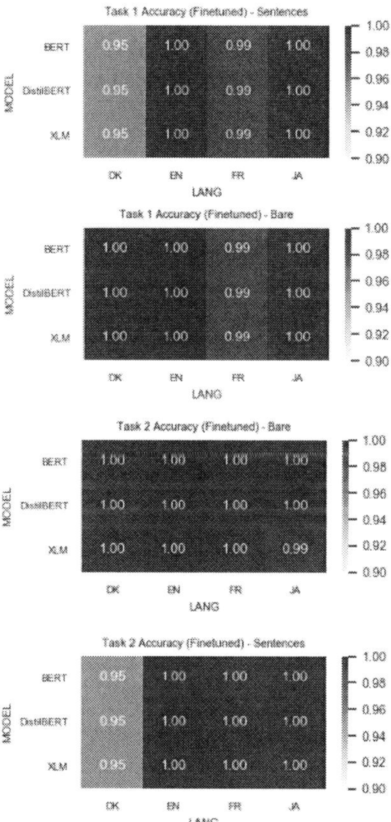

Figure 4: Fine-tuned task validation accuracy per language/model, when trained for 20 epochs.

B Data Generation

B.1 Dataset Parameters

The parameters below were used to generate data for each language per each model per each task variation:

- Data Gen. Seed: 1

- Data Gen. Number Range: [0-999]

- Train Set Size: 30,000

- Validation Set Size: 10,000

- Test Set Size: 10,000

- Shuffle = True

B.2 Task 1 Data

For both variants of task 1 (sentences/bare), grammatical data are generated by creating random numbers then converting them to text through the num2words (Ogawa) package. For the ungrammatical data, two grammatical numbers are randomly generated, both converted to text, then appended together to create an ungrammatical number. For example the ungrammatical number "fifty-five two hundred" is the combination of "fifty-five" and "two hundred". Another example made from the same original elements could be: "two fifty-five hundred". Grammatical numbers used in splits, however, were only split such that the resulting elements were grammatical words themselves. So, for example, an non-continuous number word string like "fi-tfy te nnine" would never occur.

Since generating numbers with appendage can naturally occur in ungrammatical number words being longer than grammatical, we control for length by limiting our set of ungrammatical number words to words that are *at most* as long as the longest grammatical number. Lastly, we ensure no grammatical numbers are accidentally created in this process by keeping a list of known grammatical numbers in text form (generated by num2words) that ranges from number sufficiently higher than our generation range. For example, if our number word generation ranges from 0-1000, we would make this list of known grammatical numbers from 1-100,000,000. These number words are finally either left bare or inserted into sentences to form our x inputs and are labeled 0 if grammatical and 1 if ungrammatical.

B.3 Task 2 Data

The data for the semantic task are generated by creating pairs of random (grammatical) number words and labeling the pair with one of two categories: 0 if the first numbers is larger than the second and 1 if the second is larger than the first. Through our process of data generation, we ensure that there are never two pairs using the same number. They are then converted to text form for input to a model. These number words are finally either left bare or inserted into sentences to form our x inputs. When numbers are used in sentence templates, it is ensured that the numbers are used in the same template. For example, given the number pair "five" and "six", we could compare the sentences: "There are five apples." and "There are six apples.".

C Modeling

C.1 Pytorch Hugging Face Transformers

We use the configurations below of transformers from Hugging Face Transformers (Wolf et al., 2019) in Pytorch on all of our reported experimental runs. Average runtimes were all around 1 hour or less.

- **DistilBERT**:
    - Class: DistilBertForSequenceClassification
    - Config: distilbert-base-multilingual-cased
    - Tokenizer: DistilBertTokenizer
    - Num. Parameters: 134 million total

- **BERT**
    - Class: BertForSequenceClassification
    - Config: base-multilingual-cased
    - Tokenizer: BertTokenizer
    - Num. Parameters: 110 million total

- **XLM**
    - Class: XLMForSequenceClassification
    - Config: xlm-mlm-100-1280
    - Tokenizer: XLMTokenizer
    - Num. Paremeters: ~550 million total (inexact)

C.2 Hyperparameters

All experiments which produced our final results shown in the paper were run with the following hyperparemeters which were selected manually by tuning for accuracy over a validation set:

- Epochs: 20 (Range: 10-20)

- Learning Rate: 0.00001 (Range: 1e-5 - 1e-4)

- Minibatch size: 32

C.3 Infrastructure

- GPU: Nvidia Tesla P100

- CUDA Version: 10.1

- Python Version: 3.7

C.4 Code Repository

Our Github repository can be found here. Code is subject to change after publishing of this paper. Refer to the Github README for latest information.

Dissecting Lottery Ticket Transformers: Structural and Behavioral Study of Sparse Neural Machine Translation

Rajiv Movva[*]
MIT
Cambridge, MA
rmovva@mit.edu

Jason Zhao[*]
MIT
Cambridge, MA
jzhao7@mit.edu

Abstract

Recent work on the lottery ticket hypothesis has produced highly sparse Transformers for NMT while maintaining BLEU. However, it is unclear how such pruning techniques affect a model's learned representations. By probing Transformers with more and more low-magnitude weights pruned away, we find that complex semantic information is first to be degraded. Analysis of internal activations reveals that higher layers diverge most over the course of pruning, gradually becoming less complex than their dense counterparts. Meanwhile, early layers of sparse models begin to perform more encoding. Attention mechanisms remain remarkably consistent as sparsity increases.

1 Introduction

In recent years, Transformers (Vaswani et al., 2017) have defined state-of-the-art performance on a variety of NLP tasks, including machine translation (MT) and language modeling. While large Transformer models can learn uniquely rich representations, they are also highly overparameterized (Michel et al., 2019; Hao et al., 2019). Several studies have therefore attempted to prune Transformers during or after training while retaining as much performance as possible (Ganesh et al., 2020). Some methods have been fairly successful, achieving compression ratios up to $10\times$ depending on the downstream task.

Looking beyond task performance, however, it remains unclear how widely-used pruning methods affect a model's learned representations. For example, a pruned Transformer may translate text at the same BLEU, but does pruning affect the model in ways unaccounted for by this metric?

Motivated by this question, we apply recent analysis techniques to study the representations of increasingly sparse Transformers trained on MT. We

perform magnitude pruning in an iterative, lottery-ticket fashion to identify Transformers at competitive sparsities with no drop in task performance (Renda et al., 2020; Yu et al., 2020; Brix et al., 2020). We examine the internal structures of our models as sparsity increases, specifically addressing the following questions:

- Does pruning affect what linguistic knowledge is learned by the model?

- How do individual model components (neurons, layers, attentions) change with pruning?

- How is information distributed across layers in sparse vs. dense models?

- What are the differences in pruning dynamics for the three types of model attention (encoder self, encoder-decoder, decoder self)?

Using iterative magnitude pruning (IMP), we train an En-De Transformer that retains 99.4% of BLEU at 66.4% sparsity. During IMP, we obtain eight Transformer models at varying levels of sparsity, along with the original unpruned model. We probe these models' representations for learned linguistic knowledge on eighteen auxiliary syntactic and semantic tasks (Conneau et al., 2018; Liu et al., 2019). We then perform an unsupervised comparison of the representations and attention distributions between dense and sparse models, adopting metrics posed in Wu et al. (2020). Our key conclusions are as follows:

- Complex semantic information is lost first during pruning, before BLEU decreases.

- Model activations steadily diverge from their unpruned representations, particularly at higher layers.

---

[*]Equal contribution.

193

Proceedings of the Third BlackboxNLP Workshop on Analyzing and Interpreting Neural Networks for NLP, pages 193–203
Online, November 20, 2020. ©2020 Association for Computational Linguistics

- Information flow between layers becomes more distributed in sparse Transformers: lower layers perform more encoding.

- The encoder-decoder attention is the richest in representation, whereas the decoder self-attention is the simplest. Still, all attention mechanisms remain functionally consistent across sparsities.

2   Related Work

Much work has attempted to reduce the parameter count of dominant Transformer-based architectures (Ganesh et al., 2020). Several papers prune BERT (Devlin et al., 2018), either via structured removal of layers and attention heads (Fan et al., 2019; Sajjad et al., 2020) or unstructured pruning of individual weights (Chen et al., 2020; Gordon et al., 2020). Structured head pruning has also been applied to NMT (Voita et al., 2019; Michel et al., 2019), in which BLEU is used to quantify effective compression. Recent work from Yu et al. (2020) uses iterative magnitude pruning to identify lottery tickets for NMT, retaining 99% of BLEU at 67% sparsity for Transformer-Big. To our knowledge, they achieve the highest net pruning ratio on translation with no drop in performance.

While most such studies are primarily considered with maximizing sparsity, a subset of them address other questions. Gordon et al. (2020) weight prune BERT and finetune on GLUE tasks to identify how much sparsity each task can accommodate. Prasanna et al. (2020) prune heads while finetuning BERT on GLUE tasks, and identify which heads are masked most often. They use pruning as an analysis technique to identify 'good' or 'bad' BERT subnetworks. Similarly, Michel et al. (2019) and Voita et al. (2019) prune heads to identify which types of attention are most relevant to performance. However, these studies focus only on task performance, leaving other behavioral differences between dense and sparse models unexplored.

Relevant methods of analyzing representations in NLP include probing classifiers, which evaluate model representations on supervised tasks for morphology (Belinkov et al., 2017), syntax (Shi et al., 2016), and/or semantics (Voita et al., 2018). For Transformers, some work has directly examined the attention module (Raganato and Tiedemann, 2018; Voita et al., 2019). These analyses include inference of functional annotations for particular heads (Clark et al., 2019), or assessment of atten-

tion's ability to perform unsupervised syntax tree prediction (Kim et al., 2020). Recent work has also applied high-dimensional similarity analysis methods to compare learned representations within or across models (Saphra and Lopez, 2019; Wu et al., 2020). For instance, Bau et al. (2019) identify recurring neurons across NMT models, interpret their functions, and control their activations. A broader survey of such literature is covered by Belinkov and Glass (2018). We leverage some of these representation analysis methods to study and compare sparse and dense Transformers, which, to our knowledge, previous work has not addressed.

3   Generating Lottery Ticket Subnetworks

3.1   Training transformer-based NMT

Following Vaswani et al. (2017), we train Transformer-Big on WMT16-En-De for 60 epochs and achieve detokenized test BLEU of 27.77 on Newstest14. Note that this score appears lower than Vaswani et al. since we do not use compound-split BLEU, which artificially inflates performance[1].

3.2   Iterative pruning & rewinding protocol

Recent work on the lottery ticket hypothesis has demonstrated the efficacy of iterative magnitude pruning (IMP) with *weight rewinding* (Frankle et al., 2019), where unpruned network weights and the learning rate are rewound to values early in training after every pruning iteration. Yu et al. (2020) apply this method to Transformers, and also show that leaving embedding weights unpruned better retains performance. Renda et al. (2020) propose *learning rate (LR) rewinding*, where the learning rate is rewound to a value earlier in training, but the weights remain unchanged. They found that LR rewinding often performs better for deep NMT models and requires fewer training iterations.

Combining insights, we iteratively prune as follows: after training to completion, we mask the 20% lowest magnitude non-embedding weights, rewind the LR to halfway through training (30 epochs), and retrain to completion before another prune. We also trained an iterative random pruning baseline using the same approach. As a clarifying note, we acknowledge that a "lottery ticket" traditionally refers to the network's pruned structure *and* its weights early in training; however, for more

---

[1] When we compute compound-split BLEU with ensembling, our BLEU is 28.74, compromable with Vaswani et al.

convenient referral to our sparse models, we adopt a broader definition of the term to also describe network substructures identified via LR rewinding.

3.3 Lottery ticket performance

We iteratively pruned until our network's performance dropped significantly (Table A1). After seven IMP steps, our model's non-embedding weights were 79% sparse (sparsity including emb. weights: 66.4%), and test BLEU was over 99% of its unpruned value (27.61 & 27.77 respectively). In the subsequent pruning iteration, performance starts to drop more rapidly (0.4 BLEU with only 3% of total additional weights being pruned), suggesting the start of the "power-law" performance decay observed during IMP (Rosenfeld et al., 2020). Our results align closely with Yu et al. (2020), who also report rapid BLEU drop at $> 67\%$ net sparsity. Because we are primarily interested in sparse models that retain full performance, we stopped pruning at this iteration. For downstream experiments, we keep the seven pruned models which experience a negligible performance drop, as well as an eighth model to hint trends as pruning starts to degrade main task performance. In subsequent analyses, we refer to the model after the kth iteration of IMP as LTHk, with LTH0 referring to the unpruned model.

3.4 Where are weights being pruned?

Examining which model components are most readily pruned may hint at their relative importances. Voita et al. (2019) find that late encoder-decoder heads and early decoder-decoder heads are retained the longest. We complement these findings with our results from unstructured pruning.

We compute sparsities of each weight module as overall Transformer sparsity increases (Figures A1, A2). For both the encoder and decoder, later layers exhibit higher fully connected sparsities, with as much as 25% higher sparsity in decoder layer 6 FC weights compared to decoder layer 1 FC weights. This trend suggests that higher layers' FC modules are most overparameterized.

For encoder and decoder self-attention (we compute sparsity across QKV weights $\mathbf{W_q}, \mathbf{W_k}, \mathbf{W_v}$ and out proj. matrix $\mathbf{W_o}$), layer 1 is pruned significantly more than other layers, particularly for low-sparsity models. Layer 6 is pruned next most. Meanwhile, encoder-decoder attention is pruned least across layers compared to all other modules: when overall model sparsity (excl. embeddings)

reaches 79%, enc-dec sparsity is only 55%. Late enc-dec layers are pruned slightly less than early ones. Finally, across all attention types, $\mathbf{W_v}$ and $\mathbf{W_o}$ are 25% sparser than $\mathbf{W_q}$ and $\mathbf{W_k}$, suggesting that projection steps downstream of computing attention weights are particularly overparameterized.

4 Probing for Linguistic Knowledge

4.1 Task setup

Probing classifiers are used to measure latent linguistic knowledge in word embeddings (Belinkov et al., 2019). We extract representations from our Transformer encoder and test whether they can be used to predict auxiliary labels about tokens or pairs of tokens from external datasets.

Liu et al. (2019) release a suite of probing tasks of varying linguistic complexity, and we largely inherit this setup to study our pruned networks. For streamlined analysis, we broadly split the eighteen tasks into three groups as follows (some tasks may span multiple categories): *Part-of-Speech:* Penn TreeBank POS tagging (**POS**); *Syntactic:* CCG supertagging (**CCG**), parent, grandparent, and great-grandparent ancestor prediction (**Parent, GParent, GGParent**), chunking (**Chunk**), named entity recognition (**NER**), grammatical error detection (**GED**), conjunct identification (**Conj**), **syntactic arc prediction**, and **syntactic arc classification**; *Semantic:* semantic tagging (**ST**), preposition lexical function and semantic role disambiguation (**PS-Fxn, PS-Role**), event factuality (**EF**), **semantic arc prediction**, **semantic arc classification**, and coreference arc prediction (**Coref**). See Liu et al. (2019) for detailed task descriptions.

Implementation details. We use the same data, splits, and evaluation as Liu et al. (2019). Our initial probing experiments use a single linear layer mapping our 1024-dim token embeddings to the number of task outputs. We train separate probes for each of the six encoder layers for the first nine LTH iterations (LTH0 unpruned, LTH1–8 pruned). See Appendix 1 for further implementation notes.

4.2 Initial results

In Figure 1, we show each LTH model's best probing performance across all layers for each task. Several tasks of varying complexity – POS, CCG, ancestor prediction, syntactic chunking, conjunct ID, syntactic arc classification, semantic tagging, and semantic arc classification – are *sparsity-invariant, i.e.* probing performance does not exhibit

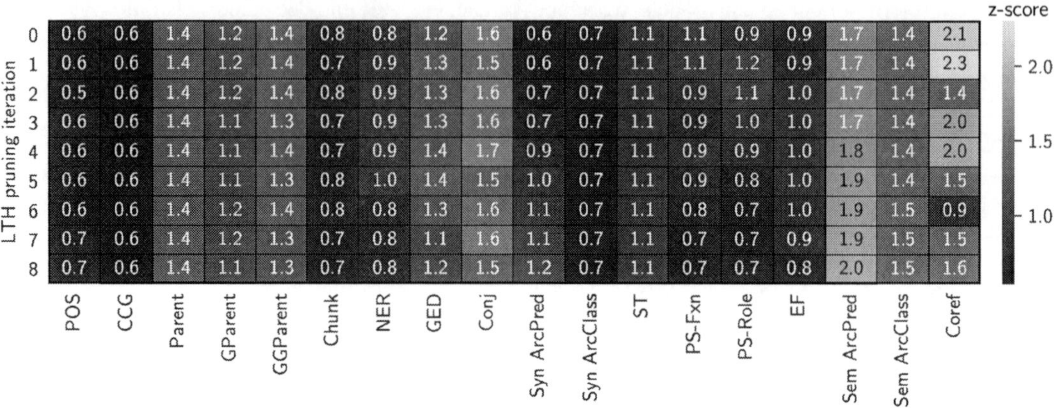

LTH pruning iteration	POS	CCG	Parent	GParent	GGParent	Chunk	NER	GED	Conj	Syn ArcPred	Syn ArcClass	ST	PS-Fxn	PS-Role	EF	Sem ArcPred	Sem ArcClass	Coref
0	0.6	0.6	1.4	1.2	1.4	0.8	0.8	1.2	1.6	0.6	0.7	1.1	1.1	0.9	0.9	1.7	1.4	2.1
1	0.6	0.6	1.4	1.2	1.4	0.7	0.9	1.3	1.5	0.6	0.7	1.1	1.1	1.2	0.9	1.7	1.4	2.3
2	0.5	0.6	1.4	1.2	1.4	0.8	0.9	1.3	1.6	0.7	0.7	1.1	0.9	1.1	1.0	1.7	1.4	1.4
3	0.6	0.6	1.4	1.1	1.3	0.7	0.9	1.3	1.6	0.7	0.7	1.1	0.9	1.0	1.0	1.7	1.4	2.0
4	0.6	0.6	1.4	1.1	1.4	0.7	0.9	1.4	1.7	0.9	0.7	1.1	0.9	0.9	1.0	1.8	1.4	2.0
5	0.6	0.6	1.4	1.1	1.3	0.8	1.0	1.4	1.5	1.0	0.7	1.1	0.9	0.8	1.0	1.9	1.4	1.5
6	0.6	0.6	1.4	1.2	1.4	0.8	0.8	1.3	1.6	1.1	0.7	1.1	0.8	0.7	1.0	1.9	1.5	0.9
7	0.7	0.6	1.4	1.2	1.3	0.7	0.8	1.1	1.6	1.1	0.7	1.1	0.7	0.7	0.9	1.9	1.5	1.5
8	0.7	0.6	1.4	1.1	1.3	0.7	0.8	1.2	1.5	1.2	0.7	1.1	0.7	0.7	0.8	2.0	1.5	1.6

Figure 1: Each cell shows a model's best linear probing performance across all encoder layers for a particular task. Sparsity increases from top to bottom. Values shown are task-specific z-scores.

any sparsity-specific trend. Our metrics for these tasks are on par with probing classifiers trained on *e.g.* BERT contextual word embeddings and are consistently higher than results from a GLoVe baseline (Liu et al., 2019), suggesting that our probes effectively learn these tasks at all sparsities. We conclude that sparsity-invariant tasks encode necessary information for NMT, so their performance will be maintained as long as BLEU remains high enough. Relatedly, we note that some of these tasks (e.g. POS, CCG, ST) have near-100% accuracy and smaller relative improvements over baselines (Liu et al., 2019), so they may only require 'simpler' types of linguistic knowledge contained in any competent language encoder.

Next, there are *sparsity-degrading* tasks, for which the probe does best at an early pruning iteration and starts to drop off at higher sparsities. These tasks include PS-Fxn, PS-Role, and Coref, in which best performance is achieved at LTH0 or LTH1, and performance starts to drop at LTH5 (56.5% sparsity). PS-Fxn classifies a preposition's lexical function in its prepositional phrase, while PS-Role identifies the semantic role that the preposition confers to its object (Schneider et al., 2018). Both tasks require integration of semantic knowledge on top of standard syntax parsing; baseline GLoVe performance is very weak compared to deep contextual representations (Liu et al., 2019). While preposition disambiguation is important to sentence understanding, STREUSLE annotations are likely more fine-grained than necessary for correct translations; even early NMT models could accurately translate most prepositions (Isabelle et al., 2017). As a result, sparse models could plausibly lose some

information relevant to this probing task without impacting BLEU.

Meanwhile, coreference resolution involves identifying pairs of words referring to the same object. NMT models struggle with coreference when semantic information contradicts stereotypical patterns in the training set, *e.g.* for gendered pronouns (Stanovsky et al., 2019). However, these cases are generally rare and investigated with specific challenge sets, and they may not manifest noticeably in test BLEU.

Interestingly, we found that syntactic and semantic arc prediction were *sparsity-improving*; sparser networks consistently performed better. Syntactic arc prediction aims to identify links between co-dependent words in a parse tree, while semantic arc prediction links objects related by the question *Who did What to Whom?* (Oepen et al., 2015). Both tasks are difficult for GLoVe embeddings, but MT-derived representations have done well (Liu et al., 2019; Belinkov et al., 2019). Performance on these arc prediction tasks is lower than on their arc classification counterparts, which were both sparsity-invariant.

Summarizing, we conclude that (1) sparsity-invariant tasks represent core linguistic information that remains encoded as long as BLEU is high enough; (2) there is a push-and-pull with higher-order features as sparsity increases, with some knowledge becoming more readily-available to a probe as other knowledge is degraded.

4.3 Are results probe-sensitive?

Minimal probes offer efficient comparison of language encoders (Hewitt and Liang, 2019), but more complex probes can also provide useful results when taken in context (Pimentel et al., 2020). We wondered if sparsity-specific performance differences would hold up to a more complex probe, so we repeated a subset of tasks using a two-layer multilayer perceptron. This probe family had over an order of magnitude more parameters than the linear probes. We show performance z-scores in Figure 2, with raw performances available in Table A3.

	PS-Fxn	PS-Role	Coref	SynPred	SemPred
LTH0	1.0	1.1	1.8	2.0	2.0
LTH1	1.0	1.1	1.9	2.0	2.0
LTH2	1.0	1.0	1.5	2.0	2.0
LTH3	0.9	1.0	1.8	2.0	2.0
LTH4	0.8	0.9	1.9	2.0	2.0
LTH5	0.8	0.9	1.5	2.0	2.0
LTH6	0.7	0.8	0.6	2.0	2.0
LTH7	0.8	0.8	1.1	2.0	2.0
LTH8	0.7	0.6	1.1	2.0	2.0

Figure 2: Each model's best performance using the MLP probe, for five tasks whose linear probe performance varied with sparsity. We report z-scores.

Across the board, raw accuracies were higher using the MLP. We no longer see a performance improvement in sparse models for syntactic and semantic arc prediction. Thus, dense model encodings contain the necessary information for these tasks, but a probe must have enough weights to extract it. Given that the Transformer decoder has far more parameters than either probe, it is not surprising that less direct representations of some linguistic features would not impact translation performance. Differences in how directly sparse & dense models encode information is an interesting question perhaps well-suited to recent work on minimum description lengths (Voita and Titov, 2020), but we leave it to future study. Meanwhile, the MLP could not rescue sparse model performance on PS-Fxn, PS-Role, and Coref; results were nearly identical as with the linear probe. We conclude that pruning corrupts some semantic knowledge relevant to these three probing tasks.

4.4 Layer-specific trends

Our analysis so far has focused only on probing performance at the final layer (which always had highest accuracy); we next wanted to study any potential layer-specific sparsity trends. In Figure 3, we show average linear probe performance for each

layer of each model with tasks grouped as syntactic or semantic. For syntactic tasks, performance using layer 1-5 representations increases with sparsity, suggesting that lower layers of sparse models better learn syntactic information. However, performance is maximized and equal across sparsities by layer 6. Results on POS tagging show the same trend (Figure A3). For semantic tasks, all models perform similarly at early layers, while dense models slightly outperform by the final layers. These results support an interpretation in which early sparse layers more directly encode low-level information, whereas dense models tend to rely more on their final layers to (1) equalize differences on syntax tasks and (2) outperform on semantic tasks.

Syntax

Layer	LTH0	LTH1	LTH2	LTH3	LTH4	LTH5	LTH6	LTH7	LTH8
1	-2.1	-2.1	-2.0	-2.0	-1.9	-1.9	-1.9	-1.8	-1.8
2	-0.5	-0.5	-0.4	-0.4	-0.3	-0.3	-0.2	-0.2	-0.2
3	0.1	0.1	0.1	0.2	0.2	0.2	0.2	0.3	0.3
4	0.4	0.5	0.5	0.5	0.5	0.6	0.6	0.7	0.7
5	0.6	0.6	0.6	0.6	0.7	0.8	0.7	0.8	0.8
6	0.8	0.8	0.8	0.8	0.9	0.8	0.9	0.9	0.9

Semantics

Layer	LTH0	LTH1	LTH2	LTH3	LTH4	LTH5	LTH6	LTH7	LTH8
1	-1.6	-1.5	-1.5	-1.4	-1.2	-1.4	-1.6	-1.4	-1.3
2	-0.2	-0.2	-0.3	-0.2	-0.2	-0.3	-0.4	-0.3	-0.2
3	0.1	0.1	-0.0	0.0	-0.1	-0.1	-0.3	-0.3	-0.3
4	0.2	0.4	0.3	0.4	0.3	0.3	0.2	0.3	0.2
5	0.3	0.4	0.5	0.4	0.4	0.4	0.3	0.2	0.3
6	1.2	1.2	1.1	1.2	1.2	1.1	1.0	1.1	1.1

Figure 3: Each cell shows the average probing z-score (across all syntactic or semantic tasks) for a particular layer of a particular model. Model sparsity increases from left to right.

5 Measuring Behavioral Similarities of Sparse & Dense Models

5.1 Experimental setup

Probing classifiers are one method of studying linguistic knowledge, but even two models with similar probing results may have divergent representations (Saphra and Lopez, 2019). We are left with the question: do sparse models learn to arrive at the same internal representations as dense models using fewer weights (up to linear transformation), or do their activations and attention maps shift altogether? To answer this question, we perform direct, unsupervised study of our model's internal vectors on unseen text.

First, we deploy our unpruned model and the eight pruned models on our 3000 validation sentences, which span 120K tokens total. We store the 1024-dim token representations and the 16 heads of each of the three attention types (enc-enc, enc-dec, dec-dec) at each layer. To compute similarities from these data, we adopt a subset of the metrics described in Wu et al. (2020). Each metric offers a distinct lens of viewing the behavioral similarity of a layer pair (L, L').

NeuronSim (Bau et al., 2019) is a local similarity measure that quantifies how well the individual neurons k of a layer L (*i.e.*, a single dimension of a layer's representation) align with individual neurons k' in another layer L':

$$\text{NeuronSim}(L, L') = \operatorname*{mean}_{k \in L} \left\{ \max_{k' \in L'} \text{corr}(k, k') \right\},$$

where $\text{corr}(k, k')$ is the mean Pearson correlation between the activations of neurons k and k' across all tokens. **LayerSim** is a global similarity measure that quantifies how well entire layer representations align. For two layers, LayerSim compares their vectors of 1024-dim representations across all tokens. We use the linear centered kernel alignment (linearCKA) (Kornblith et al., 2019) as our similarity metric. Analogous to LayerSim, **Attention-Sim** compares the attention distributions across all heads between two different layers. For every sentence s in our dataset, we extract the 16 head attention vector $\alpha_{ij}(s)$ for each word pair $(w_i, w_j) \in s$. We then apply linearCKA, treating each pair of words as a 16-dimensional example.

5.2 Similarity of activations

Looking first at NeuronSim, we find that neuron function in the encoder and decoder is largely conserved as sparsity increases. Across all neurons k in layer L of LTH0 (unpruned), k's most correlated neuron in layer L of LTH8 (70% sparse) is the same neuron k, 99.8% of the time. However, the *magnitude* of neuron similarity with the unpruned network consistently drops with sparsity (Figure 4). In both the encoder and decoder, this drop was sharpest for higher layers: *e.g.* between LTH0 and LTH8, decoder layer 1 had 0.82 NeuronSim while decoder layer 6 had 0.71 NeuronSim.

Next, we wondered if all neurons gradually become less similar to their unpruned selves, or rather

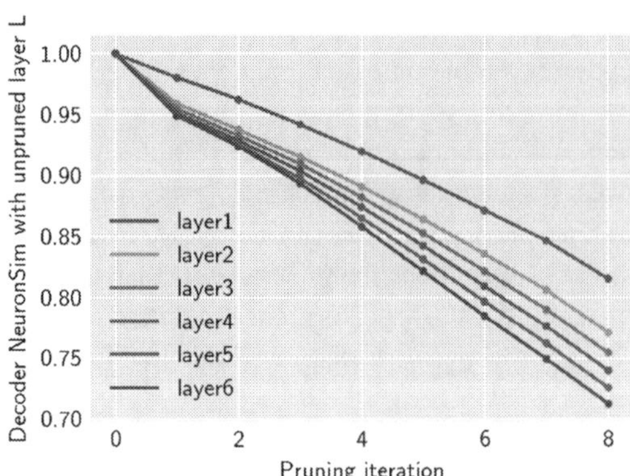

Figure 4: Each decoder layer's NeuronSim with the corresponding LTH0 layer; sparsity increases left to right.

if some neurons remain the same whereas others "drop out" or change functions entirely. Visualizing the distributions of neuron correlations revealed the former: all sparse-dense neuron pairs became less similar during pruning (Figure A4). We therefore conclude that as sparsity increases, (1) neurons gradually diverge from their dense counterparts, and (2) neurons in higher layers diverge more rapidly than neurons in lower layers.

In Figure 5, we compute encoder LayerSim scores between LTH0 (dense) and LTH8 (sparse). Like NeuronSim, we find that similarity decreases with sparsity, especially at higher layers. Interestingly, in the decoder, LayerSim between dense and sparse was consistently higher at layer 6 than layer 5 (Figure A5), perhaps because layer 6 representations 'converge' before final token prediction. Comparing off-diagonal layer similarities between encoder and decoder, we find that different decoder layers are less similar than different encoder layers (Figures 5, A6). That is, each decoder layer changes token representations more significantly than each encoder layer, suggesting that decoder layers perform more processing than encoder layers (perhaps due to the additional parameterization afforded by the encoder-decoder attention module).

Next, we find that early sparse model representations are closer to their final representations than early dense representations are. In the encoder, for example, sim(dense-2, dense-6) is 0.67, while sim(sparse-2, sparse-6) is 0.74 (Figure 5). In the decoder, sim(dense-4, dense-6) is 0.80 while sim(sparse-4, sparse-6) is 0.92. In general, early and late layers are more similar in sparse models, and this trend strengthens as sparsity increases.

We hypothesized two explanations: (1) Sparse

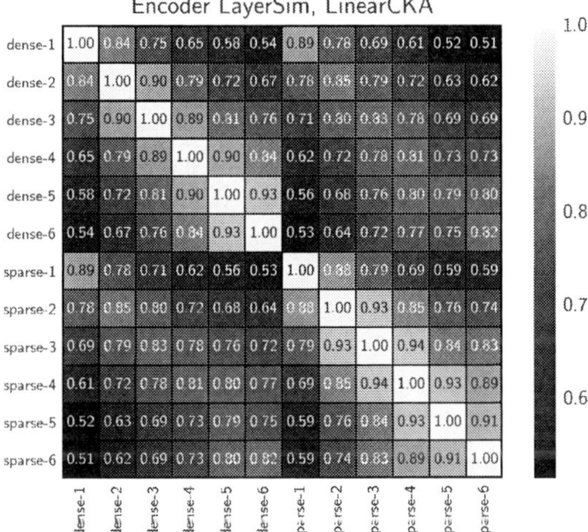

Figure 5: Encoder layer similarities for pairs of layers in LTH0 (dense) and LTH8 (70% sparse).

models have less complex final representations, so early layers are inherently not as 'far away.' (2) Early sparse layers learn more effective representations, so they are closer to the final ones. Looking at decoder LayerSim values, we found that early sparse representations were often more similar to final *dense* representations than early dense representations were, providing some evidence for (2). For example, sim(sparse-2, dense-6) is 0.55 while sim(dense-2, dense-6) is 0.49 (Figure A6).

5.3 Analyzing the final layers

Late encoder and decoder representations exhibited largest difference between sparse and dense models. To further characterize the difference, we computed the SVD of each model's final encoder and decoder layer representation matrices. We find that sparse models have more variance explained by the top k singular vectors (Figure A7). For example, for the encoder, 80% variance requires $k = 290$ for LTH0 but just $k = 176$ for LTH8; for the decoder, $k = 283$ and $k = 139$. We conclude that final layer representations in sparse models fundamentally have less mathematical complexity (which is not necessarily an obvious result for magnitude pruning, versus *e.g.* in the case of pruning entire neurons).

We next found word categories for which dense and sparse encoder representations differed most. We used linearCKA to compute similarities of tokens grouped by frequency bin, POS (Penn Tree-Bank), or semantic tag (Bjerva et al., 2016).

Mid-frequency tokens (rank 100 to 500) had highest similarity (0.95), while both common (rank 0 to 5) and rare (rank 2500 or higher) tokens had similarity 0.87. For POS, coordinating conjunctions and superlative adjectives had highest similarity (0.98 and 0.97), while proper nouns and particles were lowest (0.85, 0.86). Models also learned very different representations of punctuation, *e.g.* with the possessive ending and period tokens at 0.79 and 0.84 similarity respectively. For semantic tags, the least similar classes (0.84) were perfect/progressive verb tense modifiers, *e.g.* 'has arrived', 'is running', etc. The broad 'concept' class spanning uncommon nouns also had relatively dissimilar (0.87) representations. Together, these results suggest that sparse model encodings differ most for (1) tokens with several syntactic/semantic meanings to disambiguate and (2) rare words.

5.4 Attention-level similarities

5.4.1 Encoder self-attention

Unlike the encoder activations, encoder self-attention distributions remain remarkably similar between sparse and dense models. For layers 2–6, AttentionSim scores on the sparse-dense diagonal are very close to 1 (Figure 6, bottom left). Layer 1 is an anomaly, with sparse and dense attentions differing widely (0.62). The first layer's attention distributions in the sparse model become much more similar to its later layers (average 0.41) than in the dense model (average 0.18), suggesting that this first self-attention layer learns more salient relationships in the sparse model.

5.4.2 Encoder-decoder attention

Compared to self-attention, encoder-decoder attention displays more variation across layers and sparsities (Figure A8). While many off-diagonal similarities exceed 0.85 in self-attention, off-diagonal encoder-decoder similarities are often less than 0.7. In particular, the first three enc-dec layers differ strongly from the last three layers, demonstrating heterogeneity in learned attention distributions at different levels of decoding.

As sparsity increases, attention maps at a given layer remain mostly consistent with the dense model, although there is slightly more deviation than in self-attention. Interestingly, the model's off-diagonal similarities gradually increase with sparsity (average 0.69 in LTH8 vs. 0.63 in LTH0), particularly with sparse-5 becoming more similar to sparse-1,2,3. Sparsity may have a dampening

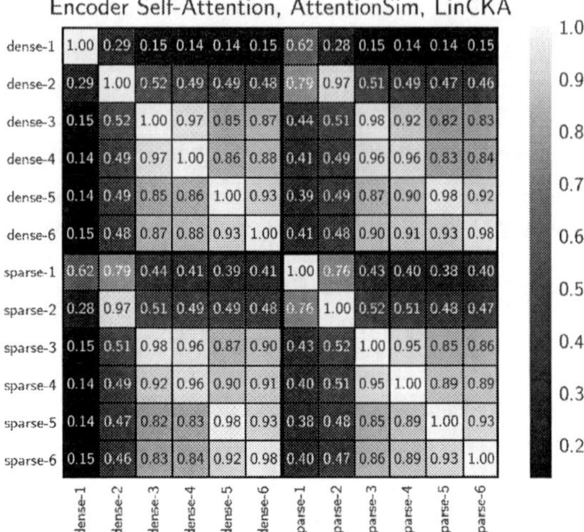

Figure 6: Encoder self-attention similarities for pairs of layers in LTH0 (dense) and LTH8 (70% sparse).

effect on the distinctions of individual encoder-decoder layers; these more homogenous attention distributions may explain the drop in the decoder's total representational complexity (Figure A7).

5.4.3 Decoder self-attention

Decoder self-attention distributions in pruned models are almost identical (0.99 similarity) to their corresponding unpruned distributions, even more so than enc-self and enc-dec attention (Figure A8). We attribute this phenomenon to the relative simplicity of the decoder self-attention module, and in consequence the relative ease at which weights can be pruned without changing expressivity. For instance, we found that 40% of all decoder self-attention distributions in the sparse model (41% in the dense model) placed over 0.95 of the probability mass on a single query token, compared to only 30% and 16% of the distributions in enc-self and enc-dec attention respectively.

Further, all similarity scores between different layers (off-diagonal) in dec self-attention are significantly higher than in encoder self and enc-dec attention. That is, decoder self-attention is homogenous across layers. Despite the simple nature of this self-attention, the decoder can still learn complex representations due to its pairing with the powerful encoder-decoder attention module.

6 Discussion

A consistent theme in our analysis is the behavioral shift of early layers (1–3), which occurs gradu-ally as sparsity increases. Our probing results find that lower layers of sparse models more directly encode POS and syntax information compared to dense models, even though performance of the final encoder representations is similar (4.4). More-over, our similarity analyses conclude that early layer encoder hidden representations (5.2) and at-tention distributions (5.4.1) trend closer towards their respective final representations in sparse models. Information-theoretically, sparse layers have less maximum capacity for encoding, so each individual layer must shoulder more load for the final representations to remain predictively salient. Conversely, an overparameterized dense model can compensate for weak lower layer representations with its upper layers. Indeed, upper FC layers are pruned more than lower FC layers (3.4), reflecting the shift in modeling power away from higher layers.

We also observe a gradual loss of information stored in model representations as weights are pruned, especially in later layers. Individual neurons diverge from their dense counterparts (5.2), causing a drop in overall representational complexity in the encoder and decoder. Correspondingly, sparse models perform worse at higher-order semantic tasks that are less relevant to BLEU (4.3). The reduced overall complexity of sparse representations may partially explain why final layers are observed to be closer to early layers (5.2, 5.4.2).

Finally, we find that sparse models' attention distributions remain largely similar to their values in the dense model. This ability to reduce weights in attention modules while maintaining nearly identical representations affirms other lines of work (Guo et al., 2019; Wang et al., 2020). Of the three attention types, encoder-decoder is pruned least (3.4), varies most across sparsities, and exhibits most within-model, inter-layer heterogeneity (5.4.3). These results corroborate existing evidence of its unique importance (Voita et al., 2019; Michel et al., 2019). Meanwhile, decoder self-attention is extremely homogenous across layers and sparsities, perhaps because encoder-decoder attention is more relevant to creating rich representations.

Limitations. Our work focuses on pruned Transformers for which BLEU remains similar to the original model. However, BLEU is an imperfect measure of translation quality (Callison-Burch et al., 2006), and it is possible that our pruned models actually perform worse on the task at lower sparsities than suggested by BLEU. Still, we think our work is relevant given that sparse models are typically only held to the standard of matching unpruned task performance.

Next, we emphasize that our work focuses solely on magnitude pruning, which may not be representative of how other pruning methods impact Transformers. We chose this style of pruning primarily because it allows for higher overall sparsity without drop in performance (Renda et al., 2020). Further, while it might be expected (and has been shown, in some cases) that pruning entire neurons or attention heads would substantially change *e.g.* the distributions of the model's outputs, we found less existing work specifically measuring the effects of magnitude pruning. This dearth of analysis seemed particularly egregious given recent growth in work on unstructured sparsity (Blalock et al., 2020).

Finally, a note on probing classifiers: as has been widely discussed by the community (*e.g.* Pimentel et al. (2020)), probes measure *correlation* between model outputs and auxilliary information. Differences in probe performance do not necessarily imply anything about what information actually uses during its forward pass. Especially since we find some evidence suggesting that sparse models may be encoding information across layers, it is possible that their differing structure may explain worse probe performance, as opposed to fundamentally weaker linguistic feature extraction. We hope future work supplements our results by analyzing a model's encoded knowledge in other ways.

7 Conclusions

We evaluate how unstructured pruning affects the behavior of Transformers while task performance is maintained. We use probing classifiers to demonstrate that pruning degrades semantic knowledge before affecting BLEU, and that early layers of sparse models better encode low-level linguistic information. Unsupervised similarity analysis reveals that pruning induces representational changes in the encoder and decoder, particularly in higher layers, and that early sparse representations are more similar to their final representations. Meanwhile, attention distributions remain remarkably similar, even at high sparsities.

Acknowledgements

We thank Yonatan Belinkov and Jonathan Frankle for their advice during the initial stages of the project. We thank Nelson F. Liu for providing access to preprocessed probing datasets.

References

Anthony Bau, Yonatan Belinkov, Hassan Sajjad, Nadir Durrani, Fahim Dalvi, and James Glass. 2019. Identifying and controlling important neurons in neural machine translation.

Yonatan Belinkov, Nadir Durrani, Fahim Dalvi, Hassan Sajjad, and James Glass. 2017. What do neural machine translation models learn about morphology? *Proceedings of the 55th Annual Meeting of the Association for Computational Linguistics (Volume 1: Long Papers)*.

Yonatan Belinkov, Nadir Durrani, Fahim Dalvi, Hassan Sajjad, and James Glass. 2019. On the Linguistic Representational Power of Neural Machine Translation Models. *arXiv:1911.00317 [cs]*. ArXiv: 1911.00317.

Yonatan Belinkov and James Glass. 2018. Analysis methods in neural language processing: A survey.

Johannes Bjerva, Barbara Plank, and Johan Bos. 2016. Semantic Tagging with Deep Residual Networks. *arXiv:1609.07053 [cs]*. ArXiv: 1609.07053.

Davis Blalock, Jose Javier Gonzalez Ortiz, Jonathan Frankle, and John Guttag. 2020. What is the State of Neural Network Pruning? *arXiv:2003.03033 [cs, stat]*. ArXiv: 2003.03033.

Christopher Brix, Parnia Bahar, and Hermann Ney. 2020. Successfully applying the stabilized lottery ticket hypothesis to the transformer architecture. In *Proceedings of the 58th Annual Meeting of the Association for Computational Linguistics*, pages 3909–3915, Online. Association for Computational Linguistics.

Chris Callison-Burch, Miles Osborne, and Philipp Koehn. 2006. Re-evaluating the role of Bleu in machine translation research. In *11th Conference of the European Chapter of the Association for Computational Linguistics*, Trento, Italy. Association for Computational Linguistics.

Tianlong Chen, Jonathan Frankle, Shiyu Chang, Sijia Liu, Yang Zhang, Zhangyang Wang, and Michael Carbin. 2020. The lottery ticket hypothesis for pretrained bert networks.

Kevin Clark, Urvashi Khandelwal, Omer Levy, and Christopher D. Manning. 2019. What does bert look at? an analysis of bert's attention. *ArXiv*, abs/1906.04341.

Alexis Conneau, German Kruszewski, Guillaume Lample, Loïc Barrault, and Marco Baroni. 2018. What you can cram into a single vector: Probing sentence embeddings for linguistic properties.

Jacob Devlin, Ming-Wei Chang, Kenton Lee, and Kristina Toutanova. 2018. Bert: Pre-training of deep bidirectional transformers for language understanding.

Angela Fan, Edouard Grave, and Armand Joulin. 2019. Reducing Transformer Depth on Demand with Structured Dropout. *arXiv:1909.11556 [cs, stat]*. ArXiv: 1909.11556.

Jonathan Frankle, Gintare Karolina Dziugaite, Daniel M. Roy, and Michael Carbin. 2019. Stabilizing the lottery ticket hypothesis.

Prakhar Ganesh, Yao Chen, Xin Lou, Mohammad Ali Khan, Yin Yang, Deming Chen, Marianne Winslett, Hassan Sajjad, and Preslav Nakov. 2020. Compressing Large-Scale Transformer-Based Models: A Case Study on BERT. *arXiv:2002.11985 [cs, stat]*. ArXiv: 2002.11985.

Mitchell A. Gordon, Kevin Duh, and Nicholas Andrews. 2020. Compressing bert: Studying the effects of weight pruning on transfer learning.

Qipeng Guo, Xipeng Qiu, Pengfei Liu, Yunfan Shao, Xiangyang Xue, and Zheng Zhang. 2019. Star-transformer.

Yaru Hao, Li Dong, Furu Wei, and Ke Xu. 2019. Visualizing and Understanding the Effectiveness of BERT. *arXiv:1908.05620 [cs]*. ArXiv: 1908.05620.

John Hewitt and Percy Liang. 2019. Designing and Interpreting Probes with Control Tasks. In *Proceedings of the 2019 Conference on Empirical Methods in Natural Language Processing and the 9th International Joint Conference on Natural Language Processing (EMNLP-IJCNLP)*, pages 2733–2743, Hong Kong, China. Association for Computational Linguistics.

Pierre Isabelle, Colin Cherry, and George Foster. 2017. A Challenge Set Approach to Evaluating Machine Translation. *arXiv:1704.07431 [cs]*. ArXiv: 1704.07431.

Taeuk Kim, Jihun Choi, Daniel Edmiston, and Sang goo Lee. 2020. Are pre-trained language models aware of phrases? simple but strong baselines for grammar induction.

Simon Kornblith, Mohammad Norouzi, Honglak Lee, and Geoffrey Hinton. 2019. Similarity of Neural Network Representations Revisited. *arXiv:1905.00414 [cs, q-bio, stat]*. ArXiv: 1905.00414.

Nelson F. Liu, Matt Gardner, Yonatan Belinkov, Matthew E. Peters, and Noah A. Smith. 2019. Linguistic Knowledge and Transferability of Contextual Representations. *arXiv:1903.08855 [cs]*. ArXiv: 1903.08855.

Paul Michel, Omer Levy, and Graham Neubig. 2019. Are Sixteen Heads Really Better than One? *arXiv:1905.10650 [cs]*. ArXiv: 1905.10650.

Stephan Oepen, Marco Kuhlmann, Yusuke Miyao, Daniel Zeman, Silvie Cinková, Dan Flickinger, Jan Hajič, and Zdeňka Urešová. 2015. SemEval 2015 Task 18: Broad-Coverage Semantic Dependency Parsing. In *Proceedings of the 9th International Workshop on Semantic Evaluation (SemEval 2015)*, pages 915–926, Denver, Colorado. Association for Computational Linguistics.

Tiago Pimentel, Josef Valvoda, Rowan Hall Maudslay, Ran Zmigrod, Adina Williams, and Ryan Cotterell. 2020. Information-Theoretic Probing for Linguistic Structure. *arXiv:2004.03061 [cs]*. ArXiv: 2004.03061.

Sai Prasanna, Anna Rogers, and Anna Rumshisky. 2020. When bert plays the lottery, all tickets are winning.

Alessandro Raganato and Jörg Tiedemann. 2018. An analysis of encoder representations in transformer-based machine translation. In *BlackboxNLP@EMNLP*.

Alex Renda, Jonathan Frankle, and Michael Carbin. 2020. Comparing Rewinding and Fine-tuning in Neural Network Pruning. *arXiv:2003.02389 [cs, stat]*. ArXiv: 2003.02389.

Jonathan S. Rosenfeld, Jonathan Frankle, Michael Carbin, and Nir Shavit. 2020. On the Predictability of Pruning Across Scales. *arXiv:2006.10621 [cs, stat]*. ArXiv: 2006.10621.

Hassan Sajjad, Fahim Dalvi, Nadir Durrani, and Preslav Nakov. 2020. Poor man's bert: Smaller and faster transformer models.

Naomi Saphra and Adam Lopez. 2019. Understanding Learning Dynamics Of Language Models with SVCCA. *Proceedings of the 2019 Conference of the North*, pages 3257–3267. ArXiv: 1811.00225.

Nathan Schneider, Jena D. Hwang, Vivek Srikumar, Jakob Prange, Austin Blodgett, Sarah R. Moeller, Aviram Stern, Adi Bitan, and Omri Abend. 2018. Comprehensive Supersense Disambiguation of English Prepositions and Possessives. In *Proceedings of the 56th Annual Meeting of the Association for Computational Linguistics (Volume 1: Long Papers)*, pages 185–196, Melbourne, Australia. Association for Computational Linguistics.

Xing Shi, Inkit Padhi, and Kevin Knight. 2016. Does string-based neural MT learn source syntax? In *Proceedings of the 2016 Conference on Empirical Methods in Natural Language Processing*, pages 1526–1534, Austin, Texas. Association for Computational Linguistics.

Gabriel Stanovsky, Noah A. Smith, and Luke Zettle-moyer. 2019. Evaluating Gender Bias in Machine Translation. *arXiv:1906.00591 [cs]*. ArXiv: 1906.00591.

Ashish Vaswani, Noam Shazeer, Niki Parmar, Jakob Uszkoreit, Llion Jones, Aidan N. Gomez, Lukasz Kaiser, and Illia Polosukhin. 2017. Attention is all you need.

Elena Voita, Pavel Serdyukov, Rico Sennrich, and Ivan Titov. 2018. Context-aware neural machine translation learns anaphora resolution. In *Proceedings of the 56th Annual Meeting of the Association for Computational Linguistics (Volume 1: Long Papers)*, pages 1264–1274, Melbourne, Australia. Association for Computational Linguistics.

Elena Voita, David Talbot, Fedor Moiseev, Rico Sennrich, and Ivan Titov. 2019. Analyzing Multi-Head Self-Attention: Specialized Heads Do the Heavy Lifting, the Rest Can Be Pruned. *arXiv:1905.09418 [cs]*. ArXiv: 1905.09418.

Elena Voita and Ivan Titov. 2020. Information-Theoretic Probing with Minimum Description Length. *arXiv:2003.12298 [cs.CL]*.

Sinong Wang, Belinda Z. Li, Madian Khabsa, Han Fang, and Hao Ma. 2020. Linformer: Self-attention with linear complexity.

John Wu, Yonatan Belinkov, Hassan Sajjad, Nadir Durrani, Fahim Dalvi, and James Glass. 2020. Similarity Analysis of Contextual Word Representation Models. In *Proceedings of the 58th Annual Meeting of the Association for Computational Linguistics*, pages 4638–4655, Online. Association for Computational Linguistics.

Haonan Yu, Sergey Edunov, Yuandong Tian, and Ari S. Morcos. 2020. Playing the lottery with rewards and multiple languages: lottery tickets in RL and NLP. *arXiv:1906.02768 [cs, stat]*. ArXiv: 1906.02768.

Exploring Neural Entity Representations for Semantic Information

Andrew Runge
Duolingo
Pittsburgh, PA, USA
`arunge@duolingo.com`

Eduard Hovy
Carnegie Mellon University
Pittsburgh, PA, USA
`hovy@cmu.edu`

Abstract

Neural methods for embedding entities are typically extrinsically evaluated on downstream tasks and, more recently, intrinsically using probing tasks. Downstream task-based comparisons are often difficult to interpret due to differences in task structure, while probing task evaluations often look at only a few attributes and models. We address both of these issues by evaluating a diverse set of eight neural entity embedding methods on a set of simple probing tasks, demonstrating which methods are able to remember words used to describe entities, learn type, relationship and factual information, and identify how frequently an entity is mentioned. We also compare these methods in a unified framework on two entity linking tasks and discuss how they generalize to different model architectures and datasets.

1 Introduction

Neural methods for generating entity embeddings have become the dominant approach to representing entities, with embeddings learned through methods such as pretraining, task-based training, and encoding knowledge graphs (Yamada et al., 2016; Ling et al., 2020; Wang et al., 2019). These embeddings can be compared extrinsically by performance on a downstream task, such as entity linking (EL). However, performance depends on several factors, such as the architecture of the model they are used in and how the data is preprocessed, making direct comparison of the embeddings hard.

Another way to compare these embeddings is intrinsically using probing tasks (Yaghoobzadeh and Schütze, 2016; Conneau et al., 2018), which have been used to examine entity embeddings for information such as an entity's type, relation to other entities, and factual information (Yaghoobzadeh and Schütze, 2017; Peters et al., 2019; Petroni et al., 2019; Ling et al., 2020). These prior examinations have often examined only a few methods, and

some propose tasks that can only be applied to certain classes of embeddings, such as those produced from a mention of an entity in context.

We address these gaps by comparing a wide range of entity embedding methods for semantic information using both probing tasks as well as downstream task performance. We propose a set of probing tasks derived simply from Wikipedia and DB-Pedia, which can be applied to any method that produces a single embedding per entity. We use these to compare eight entity embedding methods based on a diverse set of model architectures, learning objectives, and knowledge sources. We evaluate how these differences are reflected in performance on predicting information like entity types, relationships, and context words. We find that type information is extremely well encoded by most methods and that this can lead to inflated performance on other probing tasks. We propose a method to counteract this and show that it allows a more reliable estimate of the encoded information. Finally, we evaluate the embeddings on two EL tasks to directly compare their performance when used in different model architectures, identifying some that generalize well across multiple architectures and others that perform particularly well on one task.

We aim to provide a clear comparison of the strengths and weaknesses of various entity embedding methods and the information they encode to guide future work. Our probing task datasets, embeddings, and code are available online.[1]

2 Models

We compare eight different approaches to generating entity embeddings, organized along two dimensions: the training process of the underlying model, and the content used to inform the embeddings.

Along the training dimension, the first method

---

[1] https://github.com/AJRunge523/entitylens

Proceedings of the Third BlackboxNLP Workshop on Analyzing and Interpreting Neural Networks for NLP, pages 204–216
Online, November 20, 2020. ©2020 Association for Computational Linguistics

is **task-learned embeddings**, which are learned as part of a downstream task, such as EL. **Pretrained embeddings** are learned through a dedicated pre-training phase designed to produce entity embeddings. Finally, **derived embeddings** are produced by models capable of embedding any generic text, but that had no specific entity-based training.

Along the content dimension, the first type is **description-based embeddings**, which are learned or generated from a text description of the entity. **Context-based embeddings** are learned from words surrounding mentions of the entity. Lastly, **graph-based embeddings** are learned entirely from a knowledge graph, linking entities to types and to each other. Models may leverage multiple types of information to learn embeddings.

We use the March 5, 2016 dump of Wikipedia to train our task-learned and pretrained embedding models, while the derived embedding models are publicly available pre-trained language models.[234]

2.1 Task-Learned Embedding Models

For our task-learned models, we re-implement two neural EL models, which learn entity representations for the goal of connecting mentions of entities in text to entities in a knowledge base (KB). We briefly summarize them here and refer interested readers to the original papers for further details.

First is the **CNN**-based model of Francis-Landau et al. (2016), a description and context-based hybrid model. It encodes text mentions of entities by applying convolutions over the mention's name, context sentence, and the first 500 words of the document it appears in and encodes candidate KB entities with convolutions over the entity's name and first 500 words of its Wikipedia page. It computes cosine distance between the outputs of each of the mention and KB convolutions, producing six features which are passed to a linear layer to produce a score for each candidate, trying to maximize the score of the true candidate. We use a kernel size of 150 and concatenate the candidate name and document convolution outputs to get 300-dimensional entity embeddings from this model.

Second is the **RNN**-based model of Eshel et al. (2017), a context-based model which learns a 300-dimension embedding for each KB entity. Each mention is represented by two 20-word context windows on its left and right, which are passed through single-layer bidirectional GRUs. The RNN outputs are each passed to an MLP attention module which uses the candidate entity embedding as the attention context to pass information from the text to the embeddings. The attention outputs and entity embedding are concatenated and passed through a single-layer MLP followed by a linear layer to compute a score for the candidate.

We train these models using an EL dataset built from all of Wikipedia (Eshel et al., 2017; Gupta et al., 2017). We take the anchor text of each intra-Wiki link in Wikipedia as a mention, with the page it links to as the gold entity, filtering any cross-wiki links, non-entity pages, and entities with fewer than 20 words to create 93.8M training instances. Each mention is assigned a single negative candidate randomly from all entities (Eshel et al., 2017). We train each model for a single epoch on this dataset, following Eshel's method.

2.2 Pretrained Entity Models

We evaluate three pretrained embedding models that leverage context and graph-based information to represent entities. For all three models, we train 300 dimensional entity embeddings.

First is the context-based model of Ganea and Hofmann (2017) (**Ganea**). This model learns entity representations by sampling a distribution of context words around mentions of each entity and moves the entity embeddings closer to words in the entity's context distribution and further from words sampled from a uniform distribution. The embeddings are normalized, resulting in a joint distribution of entities and words around the unit sphere, where entity vectors are close to their context words. We retrain their model on a larger subset of 1.5 million entities that includes the entities we use for the probing and EL tasks with a context window of 10 and 30 negative samples until it matches the authors' original scores on an entity similarity metric (Ceccarelli et al., 2013).

We next use the graph-based BigGraph model (Lerer et al., 2019). It learns entity and relationship embeddings from a knowledge graph where the relation embeddings define transformation functions between the source and target of a relationship, giving semantic meaning to the distance between entities. We extract type and relationship triples from Wikipedia using the DBPedia toolkit [5] and train the model on the resulting graph for 50 epochs.

---

[2]https://code.google.com/archive/p/word2vec
[3]https://huggingface.co/bert-base-uncased
[4]https://huggingface.co/bert-large-uncased

[5]https://wiki.dbpedia.org/

Third, we use the Wikipedia2Vec toolkit of Yamada et al. (2018), a context and graph-based hybrid model which jointly trains word and entity embeddings (**Wiki2V**). It learns the word and entity embeddings using three tasks: 1) a skip-gram word prediction task, 2) an entity context task that predicts context words for each entity, and 3) an entity graph link prediction model that predicts which entities link to a given entity. We train the embeddings for 10 epochs, using the same context window and negative samples as the **Ganea** model.

2.3 Derived Models

Our first derived model is a simple bag of vectors model, in which we average the Google-News Word2Vec (Mikolov et al., 2013) vectors of the first 512 words of the entity's Wikipedia page. Our other two derived models are BERT-based embeddings (Devlin et al., 2019) of the first 512 words in the entity's Wikipedia page. We use `BERT-base-uncased` and `BERT-large-uncased`, which generate 768 and 1024 dimensional embeddings for each entity by averaging all the hidden states of all tokens in the final layer. We explored averaging the hidden states of the CLS tokens in different layers in initial experiments, but found averaging all hidden states in the final layer performed best.

3 Entity Embedding Probing Tasks

We next introduce a set of 22 probing tasks which can be applied to all of the embedding methods described above, divided into 5 categories based on the information they probe: *context words* used to describe a given entity, *entity type* information, *relationships* between entities, how *frequently* an entity is referenced, and *factual knowledge*.

3.1 Context Word Identification

Except for **BigGraph**, all of our models' embeddings are trained on either text describing an entity or text surrounding mentions of an entity. As such, we explore how well the embeddings can recognize words used in the context of a given entity. We define an entity's context words as the words which appear at least once in both 1) the first 500 words of the entity's Wikipedia page and 2) a ten word window around an anchor link to that entity. By ensuring each word appears both in context with an entity and in the description, we can avoid biasing the task towards context or description-based embeddings. We create a binary prediction task for whether or not a word appears in an entity's context words for 1,000 high frequency (appearing in >100k Wiki pages, **W-H**) and 1,000 mid-frequency words (>10k, **W-M**).

3.2 Entity Types and Sub-types

Similar to prior work (Yaghoobzadeh and Schütze, 2017; Chen et al., 2020), we examine how well different entity embedding methods are able to learn entity type information using probing tasks based on the DBPedia[6] ontology. We extract the types from each of the first 3 levels of the ontology, representing increasingly fine-grained entity types, and create one N-way classification task for all types at that level, which we refer to as **T-1**, **T-2**, and **T-3**.

3.3 Relation Prediction

We probe for relationships between entities in three ways: 1) How reliably a relation type can be identified between a pair of entities, 2) how well the type of a relationship between a pair of entities can be predicted, and 3) how well the fact that two entities are related can be detected.

3.3.1 Binary Relation Identification

With binary relation identification, our goal is to determine if a given relationship type can be identified reliably between pairs of entities. We extract relationship triples for 244 relationship types between entity pairs from DBPedia and build a binary classification task for each of them (**R-I**).

DBPedia only contains positive relationship examples between head and tail entities, so to create the binary tasks we must construct negative examples. We create negative examples by randomly replacing either the head or the tail in a positive example, weighted by how often the head entity appears as the head for this relationship type, and similarly for the tail entity (Wang et al., 2014). This reduces the risk of accidentally generating false negative corrupted relationships (true relationships that weren't in DBPedia) by making it more likely that in N-to-1 or 1-to-N relationship types we replace the '1' entity.

One risk with this approach is entity type leakage. If the replaced entity has an unlikely semantic type for the given relationship pair, entity embeddings that strongly encode type information may be able to easily detect the fake relationships based

---

[6]https://wiki.dbpedia.org/services-resources/ontology

solely on the two entities' types, rather than true knowledge of their relationship. To address this, we modify the above replacement algorithm so that when replacing entity E, we select a replacement E' that matches the entity type to the finest grained type possible in the DBPedia ontology. If the replaced entity has no type in the ontology, we select a random entity that has appeared in the same role (head or tail) for this relationship in the KB.

3.3.2 Relationship Classification

We use the 244 extracted relationship types from the relation identification task to create a 244-way relationship classification task (**R-C**). We also combine this dataset with the previous task, to create a 245-way relationship classification task that includes corrupted relationships for each type with the label *None* (**R-C+I**). If the representations can detect entity types effectively, then certain types of relationships may be easier to classify based solely on the types of the entities involved. Our type-restricted relationship corruption method should help ensure that good performance on this task requires understanding the relationships themselves rather than just the types of the involved entities.

3.3.3 Relationship Detection

Finally, we examine the general task of predicting whether a pair of entities is related or not, which requires an explicit relationship between two entities compared to an entity relatedness task (Hoffart et al., 2012; Newman-Griffis et al., 2018). Effectively encoding this information can help with tasks like knowledge graph completion, where knowing the existence of a link is useful, even if the exact type of the link is unknown. We sample a small number of positive examples and their corruptions from each of the 244 relationship types as described above to create this task (**R-D**).

3.4 Entity Popularity

Prior work has found that incorporating the probability of an entity being linked to in a knowledge base is useful for downstream tasks such as EL (Yamada et al., 2016; Eshel et al., 2017). We define popularity as how frequently a given entity is linked to in Wikipedia from Wiki pages. We compute the popularity of each entity in Wikipedia and construct three types of tasks to probe for this information. First is a regression task, predicting the log-scaled number of times an entity is linked to (**P-R**). The second is a multi-class classification task for the binned number of times an entity is linked to as a coarser popularity estimate, with bins for > 1000, $100 - 1000$, $10 - 100$, and $1 - 10$ links (**P-B**). The third is a comparative task, where the model must predict which of two entities is linked to more often. For fine-grained analysis, we select pairs for comparison based on the relative difference in their popularity. We create 3 tasks requiring one entity to have 2 (**P-2**), 5 (**P-5**) and 10 (**P-10**) times the number of links as its partner, and one unrestricted task (**P-Any**).

3.5 Factual Knowledge

Finally, we explore a small set of factual knowledge probes for spatial, temporal, and numeric information using triples of literals from DBPedia. The first two tasks probe if the embeddings retain the century or decade that a given person was born, based on the embedding for that person (**F-C** and **F-D** respectively). The next two tasks take as input a pair of location-type entities to see if the model can predict which of the two entities is larger in terms of 1) area in square kilometers (**F-A**) and 2) population (**F-P**). We select pairs using two methods, one which compares random pairs of entities and one that uses our type-restricted selection method from above to prevent the model from learning easy, type-based comparisons between, for instance, countries and villages, referring to the type-restricted versions as **F-A+T** and **F-P+T**. The final task compares two organisation type entities and tries to predict which has the higher revenue (**F-R**). We restrict pairs in this task to those whose revenues are reported in the same currency.

3.6 Probing Experiments

For all tasks, we create train and test sets with 500 entities per label. For **R-C+I**, we include 100 corrupted examples from each relationship type, for 24,400 None-type instances. We use relatively small training sizes and a logistic regression classifier as the probing model to observe how easily the information can be identified from a limited sample and simple model (Hewitt and Liang, 2019). For the popularity regression task, we use 500 training and test instances and a linear model trained with Huber loss. For single entity probing tasks, the input is the embedding of the entity in question. For tasks probing a pair of entities, the input is the concatenation of the two entities' embeddings, h and t, as well as $h - t$ and the element-wise product $h \odot t$. We report macro F1 for all tasks except binary relation detection and context word prediction, where we report macro F1 averaged over all sub-tasks, and the popularity regression task where we report RMSE.

4 Probing Experiment Analysis

We present the results of our probing tasks in Tables 1 and 2 and analyze them in the following sections.

Context Word Prediction. **Ganea** performs best on the two word context tasks, beating even **BERT** and **BERT-large**, and demonstrating one of the advantages of their shared word and entity embedding space. **CNN** performs on par with the **BOW** model, indicating that the task-learned embeddings store a fair amount of lexical information to complete the EL task. The **RNN** embeddings perform at almost chance level, which could mean the lexical information is stored in the RNN layers and not transferred to the entity embeddings.

Examining the highest performing words across the models, the most common high-performing categories are domain-specific terms like *nhl*, *genus*, and *manga*, place names and demonyms like *china* and *australian*, and entity type descriptors like *rapper* and *pitcher*. The higher performance on domain-specific words can also be seen in the general increased performance on mid-frequency words, which are often more domain-specific. This helps explain the surprisingly decent performance of **BigGraph**, which was not trained with text data, but may be able to use the fine-grained entity type data it was trained on to identify specific domains.

Entity Type Classification. In Table 1, we see that **BigGraph** almost perfectly identifies the type system, which we might expect since it is trained in part on fine-grained entity type links. Even without explicit training on type information, all models except the **RNN** perform exceptionally well on the entity type prediction task. Given the relatively small decrease in performance as we increase the granularity of the type set, we expect these results to hold even in larger type sets such as FIGER (Ling et al., 2020). Wikipedia pages often start with a sentence like "Entity X is a Y", where Y contains fine-grained type information about X, leading to strong performance for description-based models like **CNN** and **BERT-Large**. Interestingly, **Ganea** performs relatively poorly on this task compared to the other models, which could be because it is trained only on context around the entities, and

doesn't have direct access to the rich description of the entity. **Wiki2V**, which is similarly context-based, is also informed by its links to other entities which may provide additional information as we see in the next sections. The **RNN**'s poor performance was also observed by Aina et al. (2019), who saw low accuracy when probing an "entity-centric" RNN model for entity type information.

Relation Detection. For this task, **BigGraph** and **Wiki2V** perform best, which is reasonable as they were both trained explicitly with link prediction tasks. The remaining models perform fairly poorly, though **CNN**, **BERT**, and **BERT-Large** still perform reasonably above chance. The results of this task will primarily be useful to contextualize the results of the remaining relationship tasks.

Binary Relation Identification. On relation identification, we see similar results as on relation detection, though average performance is increased. While strong performance from **BigGraph** and **Wiki2V** may be expected, high scores by models like **BERT** or **CNN**, which had no explicit training on relationships and performed poorly on relation detection, prompt further examination.

Some of the best performing tasks (>90 F1) for these models feature a less common entity as the head and a more frequent entity as the tail, such as biological classifications (e.g. *kingdom* and *phylum*) and location-related relationships (e.g. *country*, *state*). Because the Wikipedia knowledge graph is incomplete, certain entities are over-represented making some relationships easy to classify as we see in the *daylightSavingTimeZone* task, where the North American Central Time entity is used in almost half the positive instances. For other many-to-few relationships like *country*, *state*, and *phylum*, the models may be able to identify corruptions based on the replacement of a high frequency entity with a lower frequency one to get high accuracy. For 1-1 or 1-few relationships such as *child*, *formerTeam*, and *album*, all models except **Wiki2V** and **BigGraph** perform much worse.

Relation Type Classification. Relationship classification shows fairly strong results for a difficult task, particularly compared to the general relation detection task. **BigGraph**, which was trained to represent each relation type separately, performs best, but **Ganea**, **BERT**, and **BERT-Large** each perform quite well. **Wiki2V**, which performed well on the detection and identification tasks, per-

Task Category	Words		Entity Types			Relationships				Popularity					
Task Name	W-H	W-M	T-1	T-2	T-3	R-D	R-I	R-C	R-C+I	P-R	P-B	P-Any	P-2	P-5	P-10
# Labels	2	2	20	33	60	2	2	244	245	N/A	4	2	2	2	2
CNN	79.1	80.8	91.4	88.5	85.5	65.5	80.4	54.2	47.8	1.05	48.5	60.6	69.3	76.9	81.7
RNN	57.6	56.6	6.0	3.3	2.2	55.3	63.9	16.3	16.7	1.04	55.8	60.6	73.4	**90.2**	**95.6**
Ganea	**86.9**	**88.8**	93.1	89.0	84.1	60.7	75.0	72.4	67.8	1.03	60.3	**68.1**	**80.1**	87.2	95.0
BigGraph	70.7	73.4	**100.0**	**100.0**	**97.5**	**81.9**	**93.8**	**82.0**	**81.6**	1.21	43.4	56.9	59.2	68.1	78.8
Wiki2V	81.5	84.5	94.8	88.7	84.8	80.0	89.8	72.1	69.1	**0.84**	**62.6**	66.5	75.8	84.1	87.3
BOW	78.9	81.2	93.6	86.8	81.1	57.2	75.9	65.4	59.2	1.05	46.9	56.2	60.9	68.1	72.9
BERT	84.5	86.5	97.8	94.6	91.5	67.8	83.2	77.8	74.1	0.98	57.8	66.2	73.4	84.8	90.8
BERT-Large	84.6	86.6	97.9	94.5	91.5	66.7	82.4	78.1	74.6	0.97	57.6	65.1	75.8	85.1	92.7

Table 1: Results for context word, entity type, relationship and popularity probing tasks. All values are micro F1, except for **W-H**, **W-M**, and **R-I**, which report average macro F1 across all subtasks, and **P-R** which reports RMSE.

forms worse than these three models, particularly in comparison to the **BERT** models.

To better understand this, we look at the relation classification + identification task, where all models except **BigGraph** drop noticeably in performance. We argue that **BigGraph** is largely unaffected because it actually encodes the relationships between entities, while the other models rely, at least in part, on type information. Certain relationship types are easier to classify than others due to the fine-grained types of the entities involved, such as *militaryBranch* or *diocese*. Identifying these relationships based on entity type would be easy, but introducing negative examples with matching fine-grained entity types will harm performance much more for models that primarily rely on type information. In the confusion matrices for the **R-C+I** task, we see a high number of false positives for the None label: **Ganea** has an average of 56.2 false positives with the None label per relationship type, while **BERT** has 24.3 and **BERT-Large** has 23.1. **Wiki2V** performs better with 16.1 while **BigGraph** has only 2.5, demonstrating it can both identify and label relationships.

We next look at small groups of relationships between common entity types to further examine what the high-performing models encode. Figure 1 shows a confusion matrix from **Wiki2V** for relationship types between two Person-type entities.

We see one challenge for the model is relationship granularity. The cluster of family relationships in the top left indicate that the model can generally identify a family relationship, but has difficulty determining the fine-grained label. **BigGraph** also makes mistakes on these types, which could indicate label-internal confusion on some types, such as "relative" and "relation", whose differences are not apparent or explained in DBPedia.

The second challenge is the relationship direction. Pairs of relations such as *influenced* and *influ-*

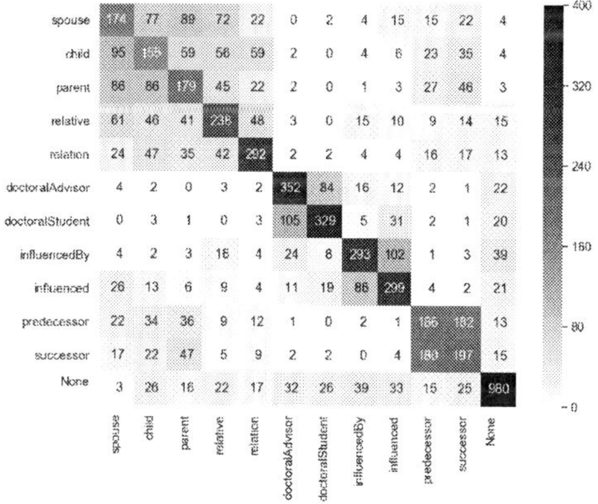

Figure 1: Person-Person relationship confusion matrix for **Wiki2V**

encedBy or *predecessor* and *successor* have high confusion with each other but low confusion with other types. We see similar trends in relationship pairs such as *bandMember* and *formerBandMember* or *parentCompany* and *subsidiary*. **Wiki2V** is trained only on binary link prediction, but not the direction. **BERT**, which wasn't trained with relationship data, might remember the entity names and related words from pretraining, but not the exact way it was represented, for example if active or passive voice was used. **BigGraph** has similar challenges, which could indicate that while the general relationship is expressible with a linear combination of the entities, the direction is not.

Popularity. Table 1 shows that **Wiki2V** performs best on both the popularity regression task and the binned popularity task, particularly outperforming the other models on the regression task. For the regression task, a simple baseline predicting the average of the training label values results in an RMSE of 1.15. As such, only **Wiki2V** actually performs notably better than the baseline, with **BigGraph** performing even worse than it. This notable improvement could be due to **Wiki2V**'s link prediction task, which likely benefits from encoding popularity information as a prior probability that a given entity is linked to by another.

The primary source of errors in the regression task is the highly-linked outliers as might be expected across all the models, but there is no clear consistency across models as far as what types or broad categories of entities seem to be more easily predicted in terms of popularity. For the binned popularity, the models consistently perform best at identifying entities in the most (> 1000) and least ($1 - 10$) popular bins, with most errors coming from entities in the $10 - 100$ bin and entities whose popularity values are on the edges of a bin.

On the comparative tasks, as the gap in popularity grows, performance increases for all models, supporting our theory that popularity information is mostly coarsely retained. **Ganea** overtakes **Wiki2V** on all comparative tasks, while **BERT** and **BERT-Large** only surpass it on the coarser **P-5** and **P-10** tasks. **Ganea** and the **BERT** models' high F1 also reinforce our theory that these models can use popularity information to identify true instances of 1-many and many-1 relationships in the **R-I** task, and it likely also helps **Wiki2V** given its performance here. We also finally see a positive result for the **RNN** model, which has learned coarse differences in entity frequency better than any other model. Overall we find that many approaches encode coarse, relative popularity information quite well, with **Ganea** able to detect more fine-grained differences, but they struggle to reproduce accurate estimates of that information.

Task Category	Factual						
Task Name	F-A	F-A+T	F-P	F-P+T	F-R	F-C	F-D
# Labels	2	2	2	2	2	5	20
CNN	67.3	61.8	70.9	68.1	62.2	65.5	20.3
RNN	54.8	48.6	56.3	53.3	51.6	21.4	5.7
Ganea	70.8	65.1	73.9	72.4	**71.4**	62.4	20.9
BigGraph	66.4	55.1	65.5	62.3	58.1	44.3	13.7
Wiki2V	68.1	60.1	74.0	69.3	70.7	89.4	37.4
BOW	61.6	58.7	64.9	57.3	57.6	57.0	20.8
BERT	75.4	67.6	79.0	74.1	68.1	90.3	45.0
BERT-Large	**76.1**	**70.8**	**79.4**	**76.0**	69.8	**91.7**	**48.8**

Table 2: Results for the factual probing tasks.

Factual Knowledge In Table 2 we see that, similar to the relationship classification task, our type-based selection policy for the population and area tasks causes a significant performance drop on otherwise impressive scores, indicating high reliance on type information rather than factual knowledge

to predict which entity is larger. Performance on the type-restricted tasks also correlates fairly well with performance on the coarse comparative popularity tasks. Upon closer examination of the four datasets, in 60-70% of the entity pairs in train and test the first entity (the larger of the two) was also more frequently linked to than the second. As such, **BERT**, **BERT-Large**, and **Ganea**, which all performed best on the coarser popularity tasks, may have used this information to help on these factual tasks. The models perform similarly on the revenue task, which has a 65% rate of the entity with a larger revenue having a higher popularity.

For birth century and decade, **Wiki2V** and the two **BERT**-based models perform best. **Wiki2V** has a combination of strong context word memory and knowledge of links from other entities, providing a network of contemporary entities that can help narrow down the options. **BERT** and **BERT-Large** have access to the description which often contains a birth year that they can encode directly, yielding higher performance on birth decade prediction than any other model. While **BOW** and **CNN** also have access to this information, their limited vocabularies map most numbers to a generic unknown term so they can only rely on words.

5 Downstream Task - Entity Linking

5.1 Experiments

Many of our embedding methods have been evaluated on EL tasks in prior work, either in a separate model or as full EL models themselves. However, direct comparison of the impact of of the embeddings on EL performance is confounded by differences in the architectures which leverage the embeddings, as well as difficult to reproduce differences in candidate selection, data preprocessing, and other implementation details. To address this, we evaluate all of our embeddings in a consistent framework, testing them on two standard datasets in three different EL model architectures to directly compare the contribution of the embeddings to performance on the downstream task and how well they perform across different model architectures.

We test the embeddings using three EL models on two standard EL datasets, the AIDA-CoNLL 2003 dataset (Hoffart et al., 2012) and the TAC-KBP 2010 dataset (Ji et al., 2010). Two of our EL models are the CNN and RNN EL models used to generate our task-learned embeddings. Our third is a transformer model based on the RELIC model of

Embedding	CNN			RNN			Transformer		
	AIDA-Micro	AIDA-Macro	TAC-Micro	AIDA-Micro	AIDA-Macro	TAC-Micro	AIDA-Micro	AIDA-Macro	TAC-Micro
None	88.4	88.9	75.1	78.5	79.7	49.2	76.2	76.6	50.5
CNN	89.8	89.3	71.8	85.9	85.4	59.8	89.7	88.4	72.4
RNN	88.4	88.8	72.5	84.8	86.6	74.0	84.0	85.5	72.5
Ganea	90.9	90.4	77.3	87.7	88.7	78.1	**94.2**	**94.1**	82.0
BigGraph	89.4	89.5	72.3	87.0	87.4	75.6	89.6	90.1	79.5
Wiki2V	91.2	91.2	77.9	**90.6**	**90.3**	78.4	92.6	92.7	80.9
BoW	89.8	89.5	71.4	87.2	88.2	72.5	92.0	92.6	74.0
BERT-base	**91.6**	**91.4**	74.8	89.0	89.8	80.2	92.0	92.7	82.8
BERT-large	90.9	91.3	**78.9**	88.4	89.3	**81.2**	91.8	92.4	**83.0**

Table 3: Entity linking performance of 3 models both without pretrained embeddings and using each of our 8 entity embedding methods. Best values for each model and dataset are in bold.

Ling et al. (2020) that encodes a 128-word context window around the entity mention using uncased `DistilBERT-base` (Sanh et al., 2019)[7]. We compare the embedding of the CLS token in the final layer to a separate entity embedding for each candidate entity using a weighted cosine similarity. To compare the impact of the entity embeddings, we replace the candidate document convolution in the CNN model or the randomly initialized embeddings in the RNN and transformer models with the pretrained embeddings during training. Details about dataset preprocessing, candidate selection, and model training can be found in Appendix A.

5.2 Entity Linking Results

Table 3 contains the results of our 3 EL models using each of our 8 embedding methods, as well as no pretrained embeddings for comparison. We report micro-averaged and macro-averaged Precision@1 for AIDA-CoNLL and micro-averaged Precision@1 for TAC-KBP, following previous work (Yamada et al., 2017; Eshel et al., 2017; Raiman and Raiman, 2018). Each result is the average of three runs for that configuration.

We see clear benefits from pretrained embeddings across all models and datasets. While the **CNN** and **RNN** embeddings provide improvements compared to using no pretrained embeddings, they transfer poorly to other models, often performing worse than even the simple **BOW** embedding approach. **BigGraph** performs worse than **BOW** on AIDA-CoNLL, but better on TAC-KBP, which could indicate its strong type information helps more on the smaller dataset, while word information may be more helpful on AIDA.

While the transformer EL model clearly outperforms the CNN and RNN EL models, no single embedding model performs consistently better across these datasets and models. **Wiki2V** shows the highest potential for generalization across models on

CoNLL-AIDA, possibly because of its combination of context word, entity type, and popularity information, the latter of which has been shown to set a non-trivial baseline on this dataset (Chen et al., 2019). **Ganea** performs extremely well in combination with the Transformer model, approaching the current state of the art on AIDA-CoNLL set by Raiman and Raiman (2018). **BERT-Large** consistently performs best on TAC-KBP, a smaller dataset which, as noted above, may benefit more from this model's well-encoded entity type information, and likely also its very strong context word knowledge. Tasks like knowledge base completion or question answering will require additional information and our probing task results may provide guidance for selecting embeddings for those tasks.

6 Related Work

6.1 Probing Tasks

Interpretation of neural language representations has drawn increased attention in recent years, particularly with the rise of BERT and transformer-based language models (Lipton, 2018; Belinkov and Glass, 2019; Tenney et al., 2019; Liu et al., 2019). We focus on methods for detecting specific attributes in learned representations, referred to as point-based intrinsic evaluations (Yaghoobzadeh and Schütze, 2016), auxiliary prediction tasks (Adi et al., 2017) or probing tasks (Conneau et al., 2018; Kim et al., 2019). In these tasks, a model's weights are frozen after training and queried for linguistic knowledge using small classification tasks.

These techniques have similarly been applied to entity embeddings, though usually to limited extents. Entity type prediction has been among the most common task explored when proposing a new entity embedding method, in part because fine-grained entity type prediction is a common standalone task itself (Ling and Weld, 2012; Gupta et al., 2017; Yaghoobzadeh and Schütze, 2017;

[7]https://huggingface.co/distilbert-base-uncased

Aina et al., 2019; Chen et al., 2020). Recently, BERT-inspired techniques have been used to probe entity knowledge stored in pretrained language models through Cloze-style tasks, in which part of a fact about an entity is obscured and the model predicts the missing word(s) (Peters et al., 2019; Petroni et al., 2019; Pörner et al., 2019; Févry et al., 2020). These have yielded tremendous insights, but are limited to models which can directly encode language about an entity and generate new text. Concurrent with this work, Chen et al. (2019) introduced EntEval, a series of probing tasks for both fixed (description-based) and contextual entity embeddings to evaluate semantic type and relationship information in BERT and ELMo-based entity embeddings. However, like the Cloze-style tasks, many of their tasks are limited to one type of embedding or another and they compare only a small number of unique entity embedding methods while providing limited analysis of the task results.

Our work builds on this prior work, which has often limited either its task exploration, the models being evaluated, or the extent of its analysis. We propose a set of tasks including several which are, to the best of our knowledge, novel to analyzing entity embeddings such as popularity prediction and context word evaluation. These tasks can be easily applied to any method which produces a single embedding per entity allowing us to compare a much wider range of model architectures than in any prior work. Additionally, we provide extensive analysis of performance and errors on these tasks and demonstrate the importance of carefully designing these tasks to better ascertain the true knowledge captured by the embeddings.

6.2 Neural Entity Linking

Early neural EL models learned representations by maximizing the similarity between the KB candidate's text and the mention's context (He et al., 2013; Francis-Landau et al., 2016). Approaches based on skip-gram and CBOW models (Mikolov et al., 2013) jointly trained word and entity embeddings, producing state of the art results on EL (Yamada et al., 2016; Cao et al., 2017; Chen et al., 2018), named entity recognition (Sato et al., 2017), and question answering (Yamada et al., 2017). Some neural EL systems have explicitly included semantic information such as an entity's type (Huang et al., 2015; Gupta et al., 2017; Onoe and Durrett, 2020; Chen et al., 2020). Recent approaches have explored integrating BERT with pretrained entity embeddings (Zhang et al., 2019; Peters et al., 2019; Pörner et al., 2019), while others have used BERT directly to learn entity embeddings for the task (Ling et al., 2020; Wang et al., 2019; Broscheit, 2019).

7 Conclusion

In this work, we propose a new set of probing tasks for evaluating entity embeddings which can be applied to any method that creates one embedding per entity. Using these tasks, we find that entity type information is one of the strongest signals present in all but one of the embedding models, followed by coarse information about how likely an entity is to be mentioned. We show that the embeddings are particularly able to use entity type information to bootstrap their way to improved performance on entity relationship and factual information prediction tasks and propose methods to counteract this to more accurately estimate how well they encode relationships and facts.

Overall, we find that while BERT-based entity embeddings perform well on many of these tasks, their high performance can often be attributed to strong entity type information encoding. More specialized models such as Wikipedia2Vec are better able to detect and identify relationships, while the embeddings of Ganea and Hofmann (2017) better capture the lexical and distributional semantics of entities. Additionally, we provide a direct comparison of the embeddings on two downstream EL tasks, where the models that performed well on the probing tasks such as **Ganea**, **Wiki2V**, and **BERT** performed best on the downstream tasks. We find that the best performing embedding model depends greatly on the surrounding architecture and encourage future practitioners to directly compare newly proposed methods with prior models in a consistent architecture, rather than only compare results.

Our work provides insight into the information encoded by static entity embeddings, but entities can change over time, sometimes quite significantly. One future line of work we would like to pursue using our tests is to investigate how changes in entities over time can be reflected in the embeddings, and how those changes could be modeled as transformations in the embedding space. Context-based embeddings in particular could then be dynamically updated with new information, instead of being retrained from scratch.

References

Yossi Adi, Einat Kermany, Yonatan Belinkov, Ofer Lavi, and Yoav Goldberg. 2017. Fine-grained analysis of sentence embeddings using auxiliary prediction tasks. In *5th International Conference on Learning Representations, ICLR 2017, Toulon, France, April 24-26, 2017, Conference Track Proceedings*.

Laura Aina, Carina Silberer, Ionut-Teodor Sorodoc, Matthijs Westera, and Gemma Boleda. 2019. What do entity-centric models learn? insights from entity linking in multi-party dialogue. In *Proceedings of the 2019 Conference of the North American Chapter of the Association for Computational Linguistics: Human Language Technologies, NAACL-HLT 2019, Minneapolis, MN, USA, June 2 7, 2019, Volume 1 (Long and Short Papers)*, pages 3772–3783. Association for Computational Linguistics.

Yonatan Belinkov and James R. Glass. 2019. Analysis methods in neural language processing: A survey. *Trans. Assoc. Comput. Linguistics*, 7:49–72.

Samuel Broscheit. 2019. Investigating entity knowledge in BERT with simple neural end-to-end entity linking. In *Proceedings of the 23rd Conference on Computational Natural Language Learning, CoNLL 2019, Hong Kong, China, November 3-4, 2019*, pages 677–685. Association for Computational Linguistics.

Yixin Cao, Lifu Huang, Heng Ji, Xu Chen, and Juanzi Li. 2017. Bridge text and knowledge by learning multi-prototype entity mention embedding. In *Proceedings of the 55th Annual Meeting of the Association for Computational Linguistics, ACL 2017, Vancouver, Canada, July 30 - August 4, Volume 1: Long Papers*, pages 1623–1633.

Diego Ceccarelli, Claudio Lucchese, Salvatore Orlando, Raffaele Perego, and Salvatore Trani. 2013. Learning relatedness measures for entity linking. In *22nd ACM International Conference on Information and Knowledge Management, CIKM'13, San Francisco, CA, USA, October 27 - November 1, 2013*, pages 139–148. ACM.

Hui Chen, Baogang Wei, Yonghuai Liu, Yiming Li, Jifang Yu, and Wenhao Zhu. 2018. Bilinear joint learning of word and entity embeddings for entity linking. *Neurocomputing*, 294:12–18.

Mingda Chen, Zewei Chu, Yang Chen, Karl Stratos, and Kevin Gimpel. 2019. Enteval: A holistic evaluation benchmark for entity representations. In *Proceedings of the 2019 Conference on Empirical Methods in Natural Language Processing and the 9th International Joint Conference on Natural Language Processing, EMNLP-IJCNLP 2019, Hong Kong, China, November 3-7, 2019*, pages 421–433. Association for Computational Linguistics.

Shuang Chen, Jinpeng Wang, Feng Jiang, and Chin-Yew Lin. 2020. Improving entity linking by modeling latent entity type information. In *The Thirty-Fourth AAAI Conference on Artificial Intelligence, AAAI 2020, The Thirty-Second Innovative Applications of Artificial Intelligence Conference, IAAI 2020, The Tenth AAAI Symposium on Educational Advances in Artificial Intelligence, EAAI 2020, New York, NY, USA, February 7-12, 2020*, pages 7529–7537. AAAI Press.

Alexis Conneau, Germán Kruszewski, Guillaume Lample, Loïc Barrault, and Marco Baroni. 2018. What you can cram into a single \$&!#* vector: Probing sentence embeddings for linguistic properties. In *Proceedings of the 56th Annual Meeting of the Association for Computational Linguistics, ACL 2018, Melbourne, Australia, July 15-20, 2018, Volume 1: Long Papers*, pages 2126–2136.

Jacob Devlin, Ming-Wei Chang, Kenton Lee, and Kristina Toutanova. 2019. BERT: pre-training of deep bidirectional transformers for language understanding. In *Proceedings of the 2019 Conference of the North American Chapter of the Association for Computational Linguistics: Human Language Technologies, NAACL-HLT 2019, Minneapolis, MN, USA, June 2-7, 2019, Volume 1 (Long and Short Papers)*, pages 4171–4186. Association for Computational Linguistics.

Yotam Eshel, Noam Cohen, Kira Radinsky, Shaul Markovitch, Ikuya Yamada, and Omer Levy. 2017. Named entity disambiguation for noisy text. In *Proceedings of the 21st Conference on Computational Natural Language Learning (CoNLL 2017), Vancouver, Canada, August 3-4, 2017*, pages 58–68.

Thibault Févry, Livio Baldini Soares, Nicholas FitzGerald, Eunsol Choi, and Tom Kwiatkowski. 2020. Entities as experts: Sparse memory access with entity supervision. *CoRR*, abs/2004.07202.

Matthew Francis-Landau, Greg Durrett, and Dan Klein. 2016. Capturing semantic similarity for entity linking with convolutional neural networks. In *NAACL HLT 2016, The 2016 Conference of the North American Chapter of the Association for Computational Linguistics: Human Language Technologies, San Diego California, USA, June 12-17, 2016*, pages 1256–1261.

Octavian-Eugen Ganea and Thomas Hofmann. 2017. Deep joint entity disambiguation with local neural attention. In *Proceedings of the 2017 Conference on Empirical Methods in Natural Language Processing, EMNLP 2017, Copenhagen, Denmark, September 9-11, 2017*, pages 2619–2629.

Nitish Gupta, Sameer Singh, and Dan Roth. 2017. Entity linking via joint encoding of types, descriptions, and context. In *Proceedings of the 2017 Conference on Empirical Methods in Natural Language Processing, EMNLP 2017, Copenhagen, Denmark, September 9-11, 2017*, pages 2681–2690.

Zhengyan He, Shujie Liu, Mu Li, Ming Zhou, Longkai Zhang, and Houfeng Wang. 2013. Learning entity representation for entity disambiguation. In *Proceedings of the 51st Annual Meeting of the Association for Computational Linguistics, ACL 2013, 4-9 August 2013, Sofia, Bulgaria, Volume 2: Short Papers*, pages 30–34.

John Hewitt and Percy Liang. 2019. Designing and interpreting probes with control tasks. In *Proceedings of the 2019 Conference on Empirical Methods in Natural Language Processing and the 9th International Joint Conference on Natural Language Processing, EMNLP-IJCNLP 2019, Hong Kong, China, November 3-7, 2019*, pages 2733–2743. Association for Computational Linguistics.

Johannes Hoffart, Stephan Seufert, Dat Ba Nguyen, Martin Theobald, and Gerhard Weikum. 2012. KORE: keyphrase overlap relatedness for entity disambiguation. In *21st ACM International Conference on Information and Knowledge Management, CIKM'12, Maui, HI, USA, October 29 - November 02, 2012*, pages 545–554.

Hongzhao Huang, Larry P. Heck, and Heng Ji. 2015. Leveraging deep neural networks and knowledge graphs for entity disambiguation. *CoRR*, abs/1504.07678.

Heng Ji, Ralph Grishman, Hoa Trang Dang, Kira Griffitt, and Joe Ellis. 2010. Overview of the tac 2010 knowledge base population track. In *Third Text Analysis Conference (TAC 2010)*, volume 3, pages 3–3.

Najoung Kim, Roma Patel, Adam Poliak, Alex Wang, Patrick Xia, R. Thomas McCoy, Ian Tenney, Alexis Ross, Tal Linzen, Benjamin Van Durme, Samuel R. Bowman, and Ellie Pavlick. 2019. Probing what different NLP tasks teach machines about function word comprehension. *CoRR*, abs/1904.11544.

Diederik P. Kingma and Jimmy Ba. 2015. Adam: A method for stochastic optimization. In *3rd International Conference on Learning Representations, ICLR 2015, San Diego, CA, USA, May 7-9, 2015, Conference Track Proceedings*.

Adam Lerer, Ledell Wu, Jiajun Shen, Timothée Lacroix, Luca Wehrstedt, Abhijit Bose, and Alexander Peysakhovich. 2019. Pytorch-biggraph: A large-scale graph embedding system. *CoRR*, abs/1903.12287.

Jeffrey Ling, Nicholas FitzGerald, Zifei Shan, Livio Baldini Soares, Thibault Févry, David Weiss, and Tom Kwiatkowski. 2020. Learning cross-context entity representations from text. *CoRR*, abs/2001.03765.

Xiao Ling and Daniel S Weld. 2012. Fine-grained entity recognition. In *AAAI*, volume 12, pages 94–100.

Zachary C. Lipton. 2018. The mythos of model interpretability. *Commun. ACM*, 61(10):36–43.

Nelson F. Liu, Matt Gardner, Yonatan Belinkov, Matthew E. Peters, and Noah A. Smith. 2019. Linguistic knowledge and transferability of contextual representations. In *Proceedings of the 2019 Conference of the North American Chapter of the Association for Computational Linguistics: Human Language Technologies, NAACL-HLT 2019, Minneapolis, MN, USA, June 2-7, 2019, Volume 1 (Long and Short Papers)*, pages 1073–1094. Association for Computational Linguistics.

Ilya Loshchilov and Frank Hutter. 2019. Decoupled weight decay regularization. In *7th International Conference on Learning Representations, ICLR 2019, New Orleans, LA, USA, May 6-9, 2019*. OpenReview.net.

Tomas Mikolov, Ilya Sutskever, Kai Chen, Gregory S. Corrado, and Jeffrey Dean. 2013. Distributed representations of words and phrases and their compositionality. In *Advances in Neural Information Processing Systems 26: 27th Annual Conference on Neural Information Processing Systems 2013. Proceedings of a meeting held December 5-8, 2013, Lake Tahoe, Nevada, United States.*, pages 3111–3119.

Denis Newman-Griffis, Albert M. Lai, and Eric Fosler-Lussier. 2018. Jointly embedding entities and text with distant supervision. In *Proceedings of The Third Workshop on Representation Learning for NLP, Rep4NLP@ACL 2018, Melbourne, Australia, July 20, 2018*, pages 195–206. Association for Computational Linguistics.

Yasumasa Onoe and Greg Durrett. 2020. Interpretable entity representations through large-scale typing. *CoRR*, abs/2005.00147.

Maria Pershina, Yifan He, and Ralph Grishman. 2015. Personalized page rank for named entity disambiguation. In *NAACL HLT 2015, The 2015 Conference of the North American Chapter of the Association for Computational Linguistics: Human Language Technologies, Denver, Colorado, USA, May 31 - June 5, 2015*, pages 238–243.

Matthew E. Peters, Mark Neumann, Robert L. Logan IV, Roy Schwartz, Vidur Joshi, Sameer Singh, and Noah A. Smith. 2019. Knowledge enhanced contextual word representations. In *Proceedings of the 2019 Conference on Empirical Methods in Natural Language Processing and the 9th International Joint Conference on Natural Language Processing, EMNLP-IJCNLP 2019, Hong Kong, China, November 3-7, 2019*, pages 43–54. Association for Computational Linguistics.

Fabio Petroni, Tim Rocktäschel, Sebastian Riedel, Patrick S. H. Lewis, Anton Bakhtin, Yuxiang Wu, and Alexander H. Miller. 2019. Language models as knowledge bases? In *Proceedings of the 2019 Conference on Empirical Methods in Natural Language Processing and the 9th International Joint Conference on Natural Language Processing,*

EMNLP-IJCNLP 2019, Hong Kong, China, November 3-7, 2019, pages 2463–2473. Association for Computational Linguistics.

Nina Pörner, Ulli Waltinger, and Hinrich Schütze. 2019. BERT is not a knowledge base (yet): Factual knowledge vs. name-based reasoning in unsupervised QA. *CoRR*, abs/1911.03681.

Jonathan Raiman and Olivier Raiman. 2018. Deeptype: Multilingual entity linking by neural type system evolution. In *Proceedings of the Thirty-Second AAAI Conference on Artificial Intelligence, (AAAI-18), the 30th innovative Applications of Artificial Intelligence (IAAI-18), and the 8th AAAI Symposium on Educational Advances in Artificial Intelligence (EAAI-18), New Orleans, Louisiana, USA, February 2-7, 2018*, pages 5406–5413.

Victor Sanh, Lysandre Debut, Julien Chaumond, and Thomas Wolf. 2019. Distilbert, a distilled version of BERT: smaller, faster, cheaper and lighter. *CoRR*, abs/1910.01108.

Motoki Sato, Hiroyuki Shindo, Ikuya Yamada, and Yuji Matsumoto. 2017. Segment-level neural conditional random fields for named entity recognition. In *Proceedings of the Eighth International Joint Conference on Natural Language Processing, IJCNLP 2017, Taipei, Taiwan, November 27 - December 1, 2017, Volume 2: Short Papers*, pages 97–102.

Ian Tenney, Dipanjan Das, and Ellie Pavlick. 2019. BERT rediscovers the classical NLP pipeline. In *Proceedings of the 57th Conference of the Association for Computational Linguistics, ACL 2019, Florence, Italy, July 28- August 2, 2019, Volume 1: Long Papers*, pages 4593–4601. Association for Computational Linguistics.

Xiaozhi Wang, Tianyu Gao, Zhaocheng Zhu, Zhiyuan Liu, Juanzi Li, and Jian Tang. 2019. KEPLER: A unified model for knowledge embedding and pre-trained language representation. *CoRR*, abs/1911.06136.

Zhen Wang, Jianwen Zhang, Jianlin Feng, and Zheng Chen. 2014. Knowledge graph embedding by translating on hyperplanes. In *Proceedings of the Twenty-Eighth AAAI Conference on Artificial Intelligence, July 27 -31, 2014, Québec City, Québec, Canada.*, pages 1112–1119.

Yadollah Yaghoobzadeh and Hinrich Schütze. 2016. Intrinsic subspace evaluation of word embedding representations. In *Proceedings of the 54th Annual Meeting of the Association for Computational Linguistics, ACL 2016, August 7-12, 2016, Berlin, Germany, Volume 1: Long Papers*. The Association for Computer Linguistics.

Yadollah Yaghoobzadeh and Hinrich Schütze. 2017. Multi-level representations for fine-grained typing of knowledge base entities. In *Proceedings of the 15th Conference of the European Chapter of the Association for Computational Linguistics, EACL 2017, Valencia, Spain, April 3-7, 2017, Volume 1: Long Papers*, pages 578–589. Association for Computational Linguistics.

Ikuya Yamada, Akari Asai, Hiroyuki Shindo, Hideaki Takeda, and Yoshiyasu Takefuji. 2018. Wikipedia2vec: An optimized tool for learning embeddings of words and entities from wikipedia. *CoRR*, abs/1812.06280.

Ikuya Yamada, Hiroyuki Shindo, Hideaki Takeda, and Yoshiyasu Takefuji. 2016. Joint learning of the embedding of words and entities for named entity disambiguation. In *Proceedings of the 20th SIGNLL Conference on Computational Natural Language Learning, CoNLL 2016, Berlin, Germany, August 11-12, 2016*, pages 250–259.

Ikuya Yamada, Hiroyuki Shindo, Hideaki Takeda, and Yoshiyasu Takefuji. 2017. Learning distributed representations of texts and entities from knowledge base. *TACL*, 5:397–411.

Zhengyan Zhang, Xu Han, Zhiyuan Liu, Xin Jiang, Maosong Sun, and Qun Liu. 2019. ERNIE: enhanced language representation with informative entities. In *Proceedings of the 57th Conference of the Association for Computational Linguistics, ACL 2019, Florence, Italy, July 28- August 2, 2019, Volume 1: Long Papers*, pages 1441–1451. Association for Computational Linguistics.

A Entity Linking Task and Model Configuration

A.1 Data Preprocessing

As described above, we use two standard entity linking datasets for evaluation, the AIDA-CoNLL 2003 dataset (Hoffart et al., 2012) and the TAC-KBP 2010 dataset (Ji et al., 2010). Following prior work (Hoffart et al., 2012; Yamada et al., 2017), we evaluate only the mentions that have valid entries in the KB. TAC-KBP does not have a dedicated validation set, so we assign a random 10% of the training data to the validation set. For candidate set generation for AIDA-CoNLL, we use the PPRforNED candidate sets (Pershina et al., 2015). For TAC-KBP, we pick candidates for each mention that either match the mention, a word in the mention, or have an anchor text that matches the mention. We keep only the top thirty candidates based on the popularity of the candidate entity in Wikipedia defined as $|M_e|/|M_*|$, where M_e is the number links pointing to the entity and M_* is the total number of links in Wikipedia (Yamada et al., 2016), the same as our definition of popularity in the probing tasks. For the CNN and RNN models, we lowercase both the KB and mention text, omit stop words and punctuation, and replace all numbers with a single token. For the transformer model, we only lowercase the text.

A.2 Model Parameters and Training

For the CNN model, we use a kernel width of 150 for all convolutions. To insert pretrained entity embeddings, we replace the candidate document convolution layer, followed by a single layer MLP to reduce the embedding to 150 dimensions. We apply dropout to the word embedding layer with a probability of 0.2.

For the RNN model, we use single-layer GRUs with hidden size 300 to embed the left and right context around a mention. We do not tie the weights of the two GRUs. The MLP attention module takes the candidate entity's embedding as the attention context, applying a linear transform to the embedding to map it to 300 dimensions. We concatenate the entity embedding to the outputs of the attention module for the left and right contexts and pass the concatenated output to a classifier module consisting of a 300x300 MLP with ReLU activation, followed by a 300x1 linear layer to compute the score. We apply dropout of 0.2 to the word embeddings and dropout of 0.5 to the MLP in the classification module. To use pretrained entity embeddings, we replace the randomly initialized entity embeddings with our pretrained embeddings. In cases where a pretrained entity embedding is unavailable, we randomly initialize the entity's embedding from a uniform distribution between -0.1 and 0.1. For both the RNN and CNN, we initialize the word embeddings using GoogleNews Word2Vec vectors[8].

For the Transformer model, we use the `distilbert-base-uncased` model available through the HuggingFace library[9]. When using pretrained entity embeddings, we replace the randomly initialized entity embeddings with our pretrained embeddings and randomly initialize any missing entity embeddings from a normal distribution with mean 0 and standard deviation 0.02. When the pretrained embeddings do not match the 768 dimension output of the DistilBERT context encoder, we map the context encoder's output to match the size of the embeddings with a single linear layer.

All of our models are trained to convergence using hinge loss, with early stopping based on the model's loss on the validation set. We set our patience for early stopping to 3 epochs for AIDA-CoNLL and 5 for TAC-KBP. We use batch size 16 for the CNN and RNN models and 32 for the transformer model. During training, we apply gradient clipping of 1.0 for the transformer model and 5.0 for the CNN and RNN. We use Adam (Kingma and Ba, 2015) with an initial learning rate of 1e-3 for the CNN and RNN models, while for the transformer model we use the weight decay-fixed implementation of Adam from HuggingFace (Loshchilov and Hutter, 2019) with initial learning rate of 2e-5 and epsilon 1e-8. We additionally use a learning rate schedule for the transformer model, with linear decay over the course of training based on an expected maximum number of steps equal to 10 training epochs times the number of batches for the dataset. When training the CNN and RNN models on the Wikipedia EL corpus, we use all the same model and training settings as described above, but use batch size 512.

---

[8] https://code.google.com/archive/p/word2vec
[9] https://huggingface.co/distilbert-base-uncased

BERTs of a feather do not generalize together: Large variability in generalization across models with similar test set performance

R. Thomas McCoy,[1] Junghyun Min,[1] and Tal Linzen[2]

[1]Department of Cognitive Science, Johns Hopkins University
[2]Department of Linguistics and Center for Data Science, New York University
tom.mccoy@jhu.edu, jmin10@jhu.edu, linzen@nyu.edu

Abstract

If the same neural network architecture is trained multiple times on the same dataset, will it make similar linguistic generalizations across runs? To study this question, we fine-tuned 100 instances of BERT on the Multi-genre Natural Language Inference (MNLI) dataset and evaluated them on the HANS dataset, which evaluates syntactic generalization in natural language inference. On the MNLI development set, the behavior of all instances was remarkably consistent, with accuracy ranging between 83.6% and 84.8%. In stark contrast, the same models varied widely in their generalization performance. For example, on the simple case of subject-object swap (e.g., determining that *the doctor visited the lawyer* does not entail *the lawyer visited the doctor*), accuracy ranged from 0.0% to 66.2%. Such variation is likely due to the presence of many local minima in the loss surface that are equally attractive to a low-bias learner such as a neural network; decreasing the variability may therefore require models with stronger inductive biases.

1 Introduction

Generalization is a crucial component of learning a language. No training set can contain all possible sentences, so learners must be able to generalize to sentences that they have never encountered before. We differentiate two types of generalization:

1. **In-distribution generalization:** Generalization to examples which are novel but which are drawn from the same distribution as the training set.

2. **Out-of-distribution generalization:** Generalization to examples drawn from a different distribution than the training set.

Standard test sets in natural language processing are generated in the same way as the corresponding training set, therefore testing only in-distribution generalization. Current neural architectures perform very well at this type of generalization. For example, on the natural language understanding tasks included in the GLUE benchmark (Wang et al., 2019), several Transformer-based models (Liu et al., 2019b,a; Raffel et al., 2020) have surpassed the human baselines from Nangia and Bowman (2019).

However, this strong performance does not necessarily indicate mastery of language. Because of biases in training distributions, it is often possible for a model to achieve strong in-distribution generalization by using shallow heuristics rather than deeper linguistic knowledge. Therefore, evaluating only on standard test sets cannot reveal whether a model has learned abstract properties of language or if it has only learned shallow heuristics.

An alternative evaluation approach addresses this flaw by testing how the model handles particular linguistic phenomena, using datasets designed to be impossible to solve using shallow heuristics. In this line of investigation, which tests out-of-distribution generalization, the results are more mixed. Some works have found successful handling of phenomena such as subject-verb agreement (Gulordava et al., 2018) and filler-gap dependencies (Wilcox et al., 2018). Other works, however, have illuminated surprising failures even on seemingly simple types of examples (Marvin and Linzen, 2018; McCoy et al., 2019). Such results make it clear that there is still much room for improvement in how neural models perform on syntactic structures that are rare in training corpora.

In this work, we investigate whether the linguistic generalization behavior of a given neural architecture is consistent across multiple instances of that architecture. This question is important because, in order to tell which types of architectures generalize best, we need to know whether suc-

Proceedings of the Third BlackboxNLP Workshop on Analyzing and Interpreting Neural Networks for NLP, pages 217–227
Online, November 20, 2020. ©2020 Association for Computational Linguistics

cesses and failures of generalization should be attributed to aspects of the architecture or to random luck in the choice of the model's initial weights.

We investigate this question using the task of natural language inference (NLI). We fine-tuned 100 instances of BERT (Devlin et al., 2019) on the MNLI dataset (Williams et al., 2018).[1] These 100 instances differed only in (i) the initial weights of the classifier trained on top of BERT, and (ii) the order in which training examples were presented. All other aspects of training, including the initial weights of BERT, were held constant. We evaluated these 100 instances on both the in-distribution MNLI development set and the out-of-distribution HANS evaluation set (McCoy et al., 2019), which tests syntactic generalization in NLI models.

We found that these 100 instances were remarkably consistent in their in-distribution generalization accuracy, with all accuracies on the MNLI development set falling in the range 83.6% to 84.8%, and with a high level of consistency on labels for specific examples (e.g., we identified 526 examples that all 100 instances labeled incorrectly). In contrast, these 100 instances varied dramatically in their out-of-distribution generalization performance; for example, on one of the thirty categories of examples in the HANS dataset, accuracy ranged from 4% to 76%. These results show that, when assessing the linguistic generalization of neural models, it is important to consider multiple training runs of each architecture, since models can differ vastly in how they perform on examples drawn from a different distribution than the training set, even when they perform similarly on an in-distribution test set.

2 Background

2.1 In-distribution generalization

Several works have noted that the same architecture can have very different in-distribution generalization across restarts of the same training process (Reimers and Gurevych, 2017, 2018; Madhyastha and Jain, 2019). Most relevantly for our work, fine-tuning of BERT is unstable for some datasets, such that some runs achieve state-of-the-art results while others perform poorly (Devlin et al., 2019; Phang et al., 2018). Unlike these past works, we focus on *out-of-distribution* generalization, rather than in-distribution generalization.

[1]The weights for all 100 fine-tuned models are publicly available at https://github.com/tommccoy1/hans.

2.2 Out-of-distribution generalization

Several other works have noted variation in out-of-distribution syntactic generalization. Weber et al. (2018) trained 50 instances of a sequence-to-sequence model on a symbol replacement task. These instances consistently had above 99% accuracy on the in-distribution test set but varied on out-of-distribution generalization sets; in the most variable case, accuracy ranged from close to 0% to over 90%. Similarly, McCoy et al. (2018) trained 100 instances for each of six types of networks, using a synthetic training set that was ambiguous between two generalizations. Some models consistently made the same generalization across runs, but others varied considerably, with some instances of a given architecture strongly preferring one of the two generalizations that were plausible given the training set, while other instances strongly preferred the other generalization. Finally, Liška et al. (2018) trained 5000 instances of recurrent neural networks on the lookup tables task. Most of these instances failed on compositional generalization, but a small number generalized well.

These works on variation in out-of-distribution generalization all used simple, synthetic tasks with training sets designed to exclude certain types of examples. Our work tests if models are still as variable when trained on a natural-language training set that is not adversarially designed. In concurrent work, Zhou et al. (2020) also measured variability in out-of-distribution performance for 3 models (including BERT) on 12 datasets (including HANS). Their work has impressive breadth, whereas we instead aim for depth: We analyze the particular categories within HANS to give a fine-grained investigation of syntactic generalization, while Zhou et al. only report overall accuracy averaged across categories. In addition, we fine-tuned 100 instances of BERT, while Zhou et al. only fine-tuned 10 instances. The larger number of instances allows us to investigate the extent of the variability in more detail.

2.3 Linguistic analysis of BERT

Many recent papers have sought a deeper understanding of BERT, whether to assess its encoding of sentence structure (Lin et al., 2019; Hewitt and Manning, 2019; Chrupała and Alishahi, 2019; Jawahar et al., 2019; Tenney et al., 2019b); its representational structure more generally (Abnar et al., 2019); its handling of specific linguistic phenomena such as subject-verb agreement (Goldberg, 2019), negative polarity items (Warstadt et al., 2019), function words (Kim et al., 2019), or a variety of psycholinguistic phenomena (Ettinger, 2020); its internal workings (Coenen et al., 2019; Tenney et al., 2019a; Clark et al., 2019); or its inductive biases (Warstadt and Bowman, 2020). The novel contribution of this work is the focus on variability across a large number of fine-tuning runs; previous works have generally used models without fine-tuning or have used only a small number of fine-tuning runs (usually only one fine-tuning run, or at most ten fine-tuning runs).

3   Method

3.1   Task and datasets

We used the task of natural language inference (NLI, also known as Recognizing Textual Entailment; Condoravdi et al., 2003; Dagan et al., 2006, 2013), which involves giving a model two sentences, called the *premise* and the *hypothesis*. The model must then output *entailment* if the premise entails (i.e., implies the truth of) the hypothesis, *contradiction* if the premise contradicts the hypothesis, or *neutral* otherwise. For training, we used the training set of the MNLI dataset (Williams et al., 2018), examples from which are given below:

(1) a. **Premise:** Finally she turned back to him.
     b. **Hypothesis:** She turned to him.
     c. **Label:** Entailment

(2) a. **Premise:** You outwitted me.
     b. **Hypothesis:** You have never outwitted me.
     c. **Label:** Contradiction

(3) a. **Premise:** okay well i live in Carrollton
     b. **Hypothesis:** I have a house in Carrollton.
     c. **Label:** Neutral

To test in-distribution generalization, we used the MNLI `matched` development set, which was generated in the same way as the MNLI training set. We used the development set rather than the test set because the test set labels are not available to the public. This development set was not used in any way during training, making it effectively a test set. To test out-of-distribution generalization, we used the HANS dataset (McCoy et al., 2019), which contains NLI examples designed to require understanding of syntactic structure. More specifically, HANS targets three structural heuristics that

models trained on MNLI are likely to learn (for definitions and examples, see Figure 1).

To assess whether a model has learned these heuristics, HANS contains examples where each heuristic makes the right predictions (i.e., where the correct label is *entailment*) and examples where each heuristic makes the wrong predictions (i.e., where the correct label is *non-entailment*). A model that has adopted one of the heuristics will output *entailment* for all examples targeting that heuristic, even when the correct answer is *non-entailment*.

3.2   Models and training

All of our models consisted of BERT with a linear classifier on top of it outputting labels of *entailment*, *contradiction*, or *neutral*. We fine-tuned 100 instances of this model on MNLI using the fine-tuning code from the BERT GitHub repository.[2] The BERT component of each instance was initialized with the pre-trained `bert-base-uncased` weights. For evaluation on HANS, we translated outputs of *contradiction* and *neutral* into a single *non-entailment* label, following McCoy et al. (2019). The fine-tuning process proceeded for 3 epochs and modified the weights of both the BERT component and the classifier. Following Devlin et al. (2019), across fine-tuning runs we varied only (i) the random initial weights of the classifier and (ii) the order in which training examples were presented. All other aspects, including the initial pre-trained weights of the BERT component, were held constant.

4   Results

4.1   In-distribution generalization

The 100 instances were remarkably consistent on in-distribution generalization, with all models scoring between 83.6% and 84.8% on the MNLI development set (Figure 2, left). Numerical statistics for the performance of our 100 instances of BERT on MNLI and HANS can be found in Figure 7, and statistics for HANS broken down by linguistic construction can be found in Figures 3 and 4. Finally, to see model-by-model results, see `https://github.com/tommccoy1/hans`.

The instances were also highly consistent in their choice of labels for particular examples (Figure 2, right); in the rest of this subsection, we provide some quantitative and qualitative analysis of consistency of performance on individual examples.

---

[2] `github.com/google-research/bert`

Heuristic	Definition	Example
Lexical overlap	Assume that a premise entails all hypotheses constructed from words in the premise	**The doctor** was **paid** by **the actor**. $\xrightarrow[\text{WRONG}]{}$ The doctor paid the actor.
Subsequence	Assume that a premise entails all of its contiguous subsequences.	The doctor near **the actor danced**. $\xrightarrow[\text{WRONG}]{}$ The actor danced.
Constituent	Assume that a premise entails all complete subtrees in its parse tree.	If **the artist slept**, the actor ran. $\xrightarrow[\text{WRONG}]{}$ The artist slept.

Figure 1: The heuristics targeted by the HANS dataset, along with examples of incorrect entailment predictions that these heuristics would lead to. (Figure from McCoy et al. 2019.)

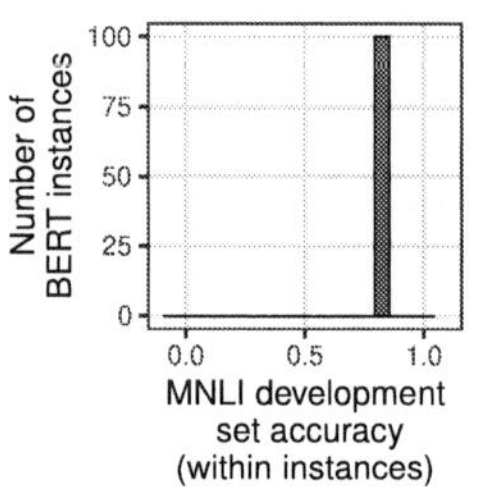
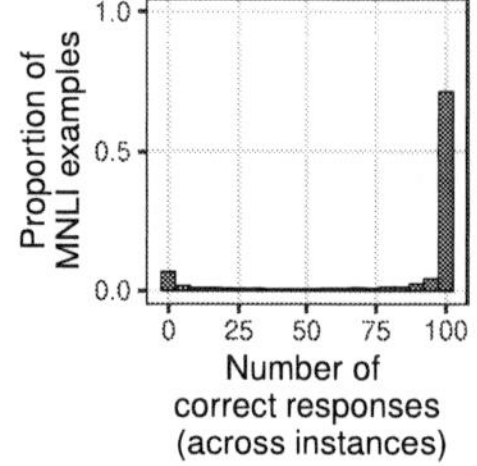

Figure 2: In-distribution generalization. Left: Within-instance accuracy on the MNLI development set; all BERT instances had scores near 84%. Right: Across-instance accuracy on individual examples in the MNLI development set; e.g., 66% of the examples were answered correctly by all 100 instances. For numerical results, see Figure 7.

On average, among any pair of fine-tuned BERT instances, the two members of the pair agreed on the labels of 93.1% of the examples (when considering all three labels of *entailment*, *contradiction*, and *neutral*, rather than the collapsed labels of *entailment* and *non-entailment*). To give a sense of consistency across all 100 instances (rather than only among pairs of instances), Figure 2 (right) illustrates how consistent our 100 instances were on their answers to individual examples in the MNLI development set. Of the 9815 examples in the set, there were 6526 that all 100 instances labeled correctly, and 526 that all instances labeled incorrectly. Thus, the consistent score of about 84% on the MNLI development set can be partially explained by the fact that there are certain examples that all models answered correctly or that all models answered incorrectly, as models were consistently correct or incorrect on 72% of the examples.

Examples (4) through (6) show some of the 6526 cases that all 100 instances answered correctly:

(4) a. **Premise:** The new rights are nice enough
     b. **Hypothesis:** Everyone really likes the newest benefits
     c. **Label:** Neutral

(5) a. **Premise:** This site includes a list of all award winners and a searchable database of Government Executive articles.
     b. **Hypothesis:** The Government Executive articles housed on the website are not able to be searched.
     c. **Label:** Contradiction

(6) a. **Premise:** You and your friends are not welcome here, said Severn.
     b. **Hypothesis:** Severn said the people were not welcome there.
     c. **Label:** Entailment

Examples (7) through (12) show some of the 526 cases that all 100 instances answered incorrectly. Some of these examples arguably have incorrect labels in the dataset, such as (7) (because the hypothesis mentions a report which the premise does not mention), so it is unsurprising that models found such examples difficult. Other consistently difficult examples involve areas that one might intuitively expect to be tricky for models trained on natural language, such as world knowledge (e.g., (8) requires knowledge of how long forearms are, and (9) requires knowledge of what nodding is), the ability to count (e.g., (10)), or fine-grained shades of meaning that might require multiple steps of reasoning (e.g., (11) and (12)). Some of the consistently difficult examples have a high degree of lexical overlap yet are not labeled *entailment* (such as (13)); the difficulty of such examples adds further evidence to the conclusion that these models have adopted the lexical overlap heuristic. Finally, there are some examples, such as (14), for which it is unclear why models find them so difficult.

(7) a. **Premise:** Indeed, 58 percent of Columbia/HCA's beds lie empty, compared with 35 percent of nonprofit beds.
   b. **Hypothesis:** 58% of Columbia/HCA's beds are empty, said the report.
   c. **Label:** Entailment

(8) a. **Premise:** One he broke back to about the length of his forearm.
   b. **Hypothesis:** He snapped it until it was just a couple of inches long.
   c. **Label:** Contradiction

(9) a. **Premise:** The Kal nodded.
   b. **Hypothesis:** The Kal then shook its head side to side.
   c. **Label:** Contradiction

(10) a. **Premise:** Load time is divided into elemental and coverage related load time.
    b. **Hypothesis:** Load time is comprised of three parts.
    c. **Label:** Contradiction

(11) a. **Premise:** I thought working on Liddy's campaign would be better than working on Bob's.
    b. **Hypothesis:** I thought I would like working on Liddy's campaign the best.
    c. **Label:** Neutral

(12) a. **Premise:** Sure enough, there was the chest, a fine old piece, all studded with brass nails, and full to overflowing with every imaginable type of garment.
    b. **Hypothesis:** The chest wasn't big enough to completely contain all of the garments.
    c. **Label:** Entailment

(13) a. **Premise:** True to his word to his faithful mare, Ca'daan left Whitebelly in Fena Dim and borrowed Gray Cloud from his uncle.
    b. **Hypothesis:** Ca'daan kept his word to Gray Cloud and borrowed Whitebelly from his uncle.
    c. **Label:** Contradiction

(14) a. **Premise:** Clearly, yes.
    b. **Hypothesis:** Obviously, the answer is yes.
    c. **Label:** Entailment

Finally, examples (15) through (17) show some of the 8 cases that exactly half of our 100 instances got correct. Plausibly, such examples are the ones that lie close to a decision boundary that is relatively consistent across instances.

(15) a. **Premise:** He bent down to study the tiny little jeweled gears.
    b. **Hypothesis:** He bent down to examine the decorated gears.
    c. **Label:** Entailment

(16) a. **Premise:** Conversely, an increase in government saving adds to the supply of resources available for investment and may put downward pressure on interest rates.
    b. **Hypothesis:** Interest rates should increase to increase saving.
    c. **Label:** Contradiction

(17) a. **Premise:** More than 100 judges, lawyers and dignitaries were present for the gathering.
    b. **Hypothesis:** 152 judges and lawyers showed up
    c. **Label:** Neutral

4.2 Out-of-distribution generalization

On HANS, performance was much more variable than on the MNLI development set. HANS consists of 6 main categories of examples, each of which can be further divided into 5 subcategories. Performance was reasonably consistent on five of these categories, but on the sixth category—lexical overlap examples that are inconsistent with the lexical overlap heuristic—performance varied dramatically, ranging from 5% accuracy to 55% accuracy (Figure 6). Since this is the most variable category, we focus on it for the rest of the analysis.

The category of lexical overlap examples that are inconsistent with the lexical overlap heuristic encompasses examples for which the correct label is *non-entailment* and for which all the words in the hypothesis also appear in the premise but not as a contiguous subsequence. This category has five subcategories; examples and results for each subcategory are in Figure 5. Chance performance on HANS was 50%; on all subcategories except for passives, accuracies ranged from far below chance to modestly above chance. Models varied considerably even on categories that humans find simple (McCoy et al., 2019). For example, accuracy on the subject-object swap examples, which can be handled with only rudimentary knowledge of syntax (in particular, the distinction between subjects and objects), ranged from 0% to 66%. Overall,

Heuristic	Subcase	Minimum	Maximum	Mean	Std. dev.
Lexical overlap	Untangling relative clauses	0.94	1.00	0.98	0.01
	The athlete who the judges saw called the manager. → The judges saw the athlete.				
	Sentences with PPs	0.98	1.00	1.00	0.00
	The tourists by the actor called the authors. → The tourists called the authors.				
	Sentences with relative clauses	0.97	1.00	0.99	0.01
	The actors that danced encouraged the author. → The actors encouraged the author.				
	Conjunctions	0.72	0.92	0.83	0.05
	The secretaries saw the scientists and the actors. → The secretaries saw the actors.				
	Passives	0.99	1.00	1.00	0.00
	The authors were supported by the tourists. → The tourists supported the authors.				
Subsequence	Conjunctions	0.93	1.00	0.98	0.02
	The actor and the professor shouted. → The professor shouted.				
	Adjectives	1.00	1.00	1.00	0.00
	Happy professors mentioned the lawyer. → Professors mentioned the lawyer.				
	Understood argument	0.95	1.00	1.00	0.01
	The author read the book. → The author read.				
	Relative clause on object	0.98	1.00	0.99	0.01
	The artists avoided the actors that performed. → The artists avoided the actors.				
	PP on object	1.00	1.00	1.00	0.00
	The authors called the judges near the doctor. → The authors called the judges.				
Constituent	Embedded under preposition	0.81	1.00	0.96	0.02
	Because the banker ran, the doctors saw the professors. → The banker ran.				
	Outside embedded clause	1.00	1.00	1.00	0.00
	Although the secretaries slept, the judges danced. → The judges danced.				
	Embedded under verb	0.93	1.00	0.99	0.01
	The president remembered that the actors performed. → The actors performed.				
	Conjunction	1.00	1.00	1.00	0.00
	The lawyer danced, and the judge supported the doctors. → The lawyer danced.				
	Adverbs	1.00	1.00	1.00	0.00
	Certainly the lawyers advised the manager. → The lawyers advised the manager.				

Figure 3: Results for the HANS subcases for which the heuristics make correct predictions (i.e., where the correct label is *entailment*). All statistics are based on 100 runs.

Heuristic	Subcase	Minimum	Maximum	Mean	Std. dev.
Lexical overlap	Subject-object swap	0.00	0.66	0.19	0.17
	The senators mentioned the artist. ↛ The artist mentioned the senators.				
	Sentences with PPs	0.04	0.76	0.41	0.18
	The judge behind the manager saw the doctors. ↛ The doctors saw the manager.				
	Sentences with relative clauses	0.09	0.67	0.33	0.14
	The actors called the banker who the tourists saw. ↛ The banker called the tourists.				
	Conjunctions	0.12	0.72	0.45	0.15
	The doctors saw the presidents and the tourists. ↛ The presidents saw the tourists.				
	Passives	0.00	0.04	0.01	0.01
	The senators were helped by the managers. ↛ The senators helped the managers.				
Subsequence	NP/S	0.00	0.05	0.02	0.01
	The managers heard the secretary resigned. ↛ The managers heard the secretary.				
	PP on subject	0.00	0.35	0.12	0.07
	The managers near the scientist shouted. ↛ The scientist shouted.				
	Relative clause on subject	0.00	0.23	0.07	0.04
	The secretary that admired the senator saw the actor. ↛ The senator saw the actor.				
	MV/RR	0.00	0.02	0.00	0.00
	The senators paid in the office danced. ↛ The senators paid in the office.				
	NP/Z	0.02	0.13	0.06	0.02
	Before the actors presented the doctors arrived. ↛ The actors presented the doctors.				
Constituent	Embedded under preposition	0.14	0.70	0.41	0.12
	Unless the senators ran, the professors recommended the doctor. ↛ The senators ran.				
	Outside embedded clause	0.00	0.03	0.00	0.01
	Unless the authors saw the students, the doctors resigned. ↛ The doctors resigned.				
	Embedded under verb	0.02	0.42	0.17	0.08
	The tourists said that the lawyer saw the banker. ↛ The lawyer saw the banker.				
	Disjunction	0.00	0.03	0.00	0.01
	The judges resigned, or the athletes saw the author. ↛ The athletes saw the author.				
	Adverbs	0.00	0.17	0.06	0.04
	Probably the artists saw the authors. ↛ The artists saw the authors.				

Figure 4: Results for the HANS subcases for which the heuristics make incorrect predictions (i.e., where the correct label is *non-entailment*). All statistics are based on 100 runs.

Subject-object swap:
The doctor visited the lawyer. ↛ The lawyer visited the doctor.

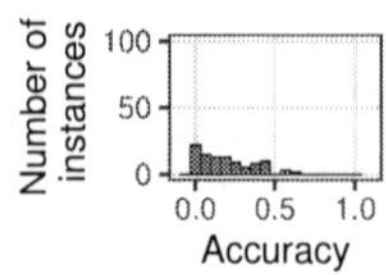

Preposition:
The tourist by the manager saw the artists. ↛ The artists saw the manager.

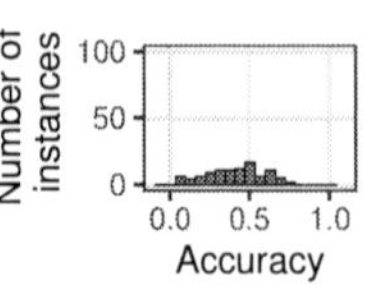

Relative clause:
The actors saw the author who the judge advised. ↛ The author saw the judge.

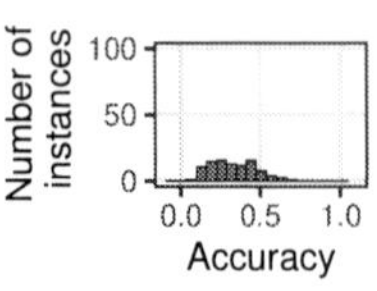

Passive:
The student was stopped by the doctor. ↛ The student stopped the doctor.

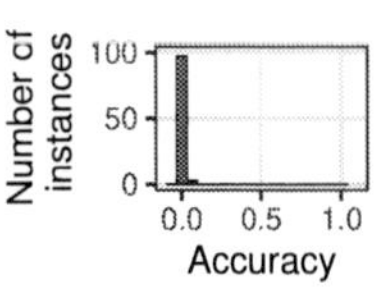

Conjunction:
The doctors saw the athlete and the judge. ↛ The athlete saw the judge.

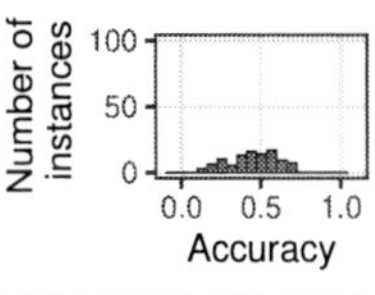

Figure 5: Accuracy distributions on the subcategories of the non-entailed lexical overlap examples of the HANS dataset (i.e., the examples that are inconsistent with the lexical overlap heuristic). For numerical results, and results for the other 25 subcategories of HANS, see Figures 3 and 4.

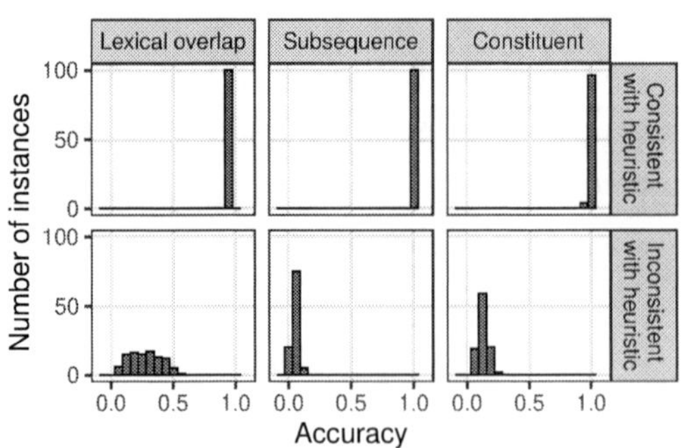

Figure 6: Out-of-distribution generalization: Performance on HANS, broken down into six categories of examples, based on the syntactic heuristic that each example targets and whether the example is consistent with the relevant heuristic (i.e., has a correct label of *entailment*) or inconsistent with the heuristic (i.e., has a correct label of *non-entailment*). The lexical overlap cases that are inconsistent with the heuristic (lower left plot) are highly variable across instances. For numerical results, see Figure 7.

although these models performed consistently on the in-distribution test set, they have nevertheless learned highly variable representations of syntax.

5 Discussion

We have found that models that differ only in their initial weights and the order of training examples can vary substantially in out-of-distribution linguistic generalization. We found this variation even with the vast majority of initial weights held constant (i.e., all the weights in the BERT component of the model). We conjecture that models might be even more variable if the pre-training of BERT were also redone across instances. These results underscore the importance of evaluating models on multiple restarts, as conclusions drawn from a single instance of a model might not hold across instances. Further, these results highlight the importance of evaluating out-of-distribution generalization; since all of our instances displayed similar in-distribution generalization, only their out-of-distribution generalization illuminates the substantial differences in what they have learned.

In stark contrast to the models we have looked at—which generalized in highly variable ways despite being trained on the same set of examples—humans tend to converge to similar linguistic generalizations despite major differences in the linguistic input that they encounter as children (Chomsky, 1965, 1980). This suggests that reducing the generalization variability of NLP models may help bring them closer to human performance in one major area where they still dramatically lag behind humans, namely in out-of-distribution generalization.

How could the out-of-distribution generalization of models be made more consistent? The variability that we have observed likely reflects the presence of many local minima in the loss surface, all of which are equally attractive to our models. This makes the model's choice of a minimum essentially arbitrary and easily affected by the initial weights and the order of training examples. To reduce this variability, then, one approach would be to use models with stronger inductive biases, which can help distinguish between the many local minima. An alternate approach would be to use training sets that better represent a large set of linguistic phenomena, to decrease the probability of there being local minima that ignore certain phenomena.

		HANS: Consistent with heuristic			HANS: Inconsistent with heuristic		
	MNLI	Lexical	Subseq.	Const.	Lexical	Subseq.	Const.
Minimum	0.84	0.93	0.98	0.96	0.05	0.01	0.03
Maximum	0.85	0.98	1.00	1.00	0.55	0.14	0.24
Mean	0.84	0.96	0.99	0.99	0.28	0.05	0.13
Standard deviation	0.00	0.01	0.00	0.01	0.12	0.02	0.04

Figure 7: Results for models trained on MNLI. The MNLI column reports accuracy on the MNLI `matched` development set, where there are three possible labels (*entailment, contradiction,* and *neutral*). The remaining columns are subsets of the HANS dataset, with *neutral* and *contradiction* merged into a single label, *non-entailment,* such that there are only two possible labels: *entailment* and *non-entailment.* The examples that are consistent with the heuristics are those that have a correct label of *entailment,* while the examples that are inconsistent with the heuristics are those with a correct label of *non-entailment.* All statistics are based on 100 runs.

Acknowledgments

We are grateful to Emily Pitler, Dipanjan Das, and the members of the Johns Hopkins Computation and Psycholinguistics lab group for helpful comments. Any errors are our own.

This project is based upon work supported by the National Science Foundation Graduate Research Fellowship Program under Grant No. 1746891 and by a gift to TL from Google, and it was conducted using computational resources from the Maryland Advanced Research Computing Center (MARCC). Any opinions, findings, and conclusions or recommendations expressed in this material are those of the authors and do not necessarily reflect the views of the National Science Foundation, Google, or MARCC.

References

Samira Abnar, Lisa Beinborn, Rochelle Choenni, and Willem Zuidema. 2019. Blackbox meets blackbox: Representational similarity & stability analysis of neural language models and brains. In *Proceedings of the 2019 ACL Workshop BlackboxNLP: Analyzing and Interpreting Neural Networks for NLP*, pages 191–203, Florence, Italy. Association for Computational Linguistics.

Noam Chomsky. 1965. *Aspects of the Theory of Syntax.* MIT Press, Cambridge, MA.

Noam Chomsky. 1980. Rules and representations. *Behavioral and Brain Sciences*, 3(1):1–15.

Grzegorz Chrupała and Afra Alishahi. 2019. Correlating neural and symbolic representations of language. In *Proceedings of the 57th Annual Meeting of the Association for Computational Linguistics*, pages 2952–2962, Florence, Italy. Association for Computational Linguistics.

Kevin Clark, Urvashi Khandelwal, Omer Levy, and Christopher D. Manning. 2019. What does BERT look at? An analysis of BERT's attention. In *Proceedings of the 2019 ACL Workshop BlackboxNLP: Analyzing and Interpreting Neural Networks for NLP*, pages 276–286, Florence, Italy. Association for Computational Linguistics.

Andy Coenen, Emily Reif, Ann Yuan, Been Kim, Adam Pearce, Fernanda Viégas, and Martin Wattenberg. 2019. Visualizing and measuring the geometry of BERT. *33rd Conference on Neural Information Processing Systems.*

Cleo Condoravdi, Dick Crouch, Valeria de Paiva, Reinhard Stolle, and Daniel G. Bobrow. 2003. Entailment, intensionality and text understanding. In *Proceedings of the HLT-NAACL 2003 Workshop on Text Meaning*, pages 38–45.

Ido Dagan, Oren Glickman, and Bernardo Magnini. 2006. The PASCAL Recognising Textual Entailment Challenge. In *Proceedings of the First International Conference on Machine Learning Challenges: Evaluating Predictive Uncertainty Visual Object Classification, and Recognizing Textual Entailment*, MLCW'05, pages 177–190, Berlin, Heidelberg. Springer-Verlag.

Ido Dagan, Dan Roth, Mark Sammons, and Fabio Massimo Zanzotto. 2013. Recognizing Textual Entailment: Models and Applications. *Synthesis Lectures on Human Language Technologies*, 6(4):1–220.

Jacob Devlin, Ming-Wei Chang, Kenton Lee, and Kristina Toutanova. 2019. BERT: Pre-training of deep bidirectional transformers for language understanding. In *Proceedings of the 2019 Conference of the North American Chapter of the Association for Computational Linguistics: Human Language Technologies, Volume 1 (Long and Short Papers)*, pages 4171–4186, Minneapolis, Minnesota. Association for Computational Linguistics.

Allyson Ettinger. 2020. What BERT is not: Lessons from a new suite of psycholinguistic diagnostics for language models. *Transactions of the Association for Computational Linguistics*, 8:34–48.

Yoav Goldberg. 2019. Assessing BERT's syntactic abilities. *arXiv preprint arXiv:1901.05287*.

Kristina Gulordava, Piotr Bojanowski, Edouard Grave, Tal Linzen, and Marco Baroni. 2018. Colorless green recurrent networks dream hierarchically. In *Proceedings of the 2018 Conference of the North American Chapter of the Association for Computational Linguistics: Human Language Technologies, Volume 1 (Long Papers)*, pages 1195–1205, New Orleans, Louisiana. Association for Computational Linguistics.

John Hewitt and Christopher D. Manning. 2019. A structural probe for finding syntax in word representations. In *Proceedings of the 2019 Conference of the North American Chapter of the Association for Computational Linguistics: Human Language Technologies, Volume 1 (Long and Short Papers)*, pages 4129–4138, Minneapolis, Minnesota. Association for Computational Linguistics.

Ganesh Jawahar, Benoît Sagot, and Djamé Seddah. 2019. What does BERT learn about the structure of language? In *Proceedings of the 57th Annual Meeting of the Association for Computational Linguistics*, pages 3651–3657, Florence, Italy. Association for Computational Linguistics.

Najoung Kim, Roma Patel, Adam Poliak, Patrick Xia, Alex Wang, Tom McCoy, Ian Tenney, Alexis Ross, Tal Linzen, Benjamin Van Durme, Samuel R. Bowman, and Ellie Pavlick. 2019. Probing what different NLP tasks teach machines about function word comprehension. In *Proceedings of the Eighth Joint Conference on Lexical and Computational Semantics (*SEM 2019)*, pages 235–249, Minneapolis, Minnesota. Association for Computational Linguistics.

Yongjie Lin, Yi Chern Tan, and Robert Frank. 2019. Open sesame: Getting inside BERT's linguistic knowledge. In *Proceedings of the 2019 ACL Workshop BlackboxNLP: Analyzing and Interpreting Neural Networks for NLP*, pages 241–253, Florence, Italy. Association for Computational Linguistics.

Adam Liška, Germán Kruszewski, and Marco Baroni. 2018. Memorize or generalize? Searching for a compositional RNN in a haystack. In *Proceedings of the 2018 workshop on Architectures and Evaluation for Generality, Autonomy, and Progress in AI (AEGAP)*.

Xiaodong Liu, Pengcheng He, Weizhu Chen, and Jianfeng Gao. 2019a. Multi-task deep neural networks for natural language understanding. In *Proceedings of the 57th Annual Meeting of the Association for Computational Linguistics*, pages 4487–4496, Florence, Italy. Association for Computational Linguistics.

Yinhan Liu, Myle Ott, Naman Goyal, Jingfei Du, Mandar Joshi, Danqi Chen, Omer Levy, Mike Lewis, Luke Zettlemoyer, and Veselin Stoyanov. 2019b. RoBERTa: A robustly optimized BERT pretraining approach. *arXiv preprint arXiv:1907.11692*.

Pranava Madhyastha and Rishabh Jain. 2019. On model stability as a function of random seed. In *Proceedings of the 23rd Conference on Computational Natural Language Learning (CoNLL)*, pages 929–939, Hong Kong, China. Association for Computational Linguistics.

Rebecca Marvin and Tal Linzen. 2018. Targeted syntactic evaluation of language models. In *Proceedings of the 2018 Conference on Empirical Methods in Natural Language Processing*, pages 1192–1202, Brussels, Belgium. Association for Computational Linguistics.

R. Thomas McCoy, Robert Frank, and Tal Linzen. 2018. Revisiting the poverty of the stimulus: Hierarchical generalization without a hierarchical bias in recurrent neural networks. In *Proceedings of the 40th Annual Conference of the Cognitive Science Society*, pages 2093–2098, Madison, WI.

R. Thomas McCoy, Ellie Pavlick, and Tal Linzen. 2019. Right for the wrong reasons: Diagnosing syntactic heuristics in natural language inference. In *Proceedings of the 57th Annual Meeting of the Association for Computational Linguistics*, pages 3428–3448, Florence, Italy. Association for Computational Linguistics.

Nikita Nangia and Samuel R. Bowman. 2019. Human vs. muppet: A conservative estimate of human performance on the GLUE benchmark. In *Proceedings of the 57th Annual Meeting of the Association for Computational Linguistics*, pages 4566–4575, Florence, Italy. Association for Computational Linguistics.

Jason Phang, Thibault Févry, and Samuel R Bowman. 2018. Sentence encoders on STILTs: Supplementary training on intermediate labeled-data tasks. *arXiv preprint arXiv:1811.01088*.

Colin Raffel, Noam Shazeer, Adam Roberts, Katherine Lee, Sharan Narang, Michael Matena, Yanqi Zhou, Wei Li, and Peter J Liu. 2020. Exploring the limits of transfer learning with a unified text-to-text transformer. *Journal of Machine Learning Research*.

Nils Reimers and Iryna Gurevych. 2017. Reporting score distributions makes a difference: Performance study of LSTM-networks for sequence tagging. In *Proceedings of the 2017 Conference on Empirical Methods in Natural Language Processing*, pages 338–348, Copenhagen, Denmark. Association for Computational Linguistics.

Nils Reimers and Iryna Gurevych. 2018. Why comparing single performance scores does not allow to draw conclusions about machine learning approaches. *arXiv preprint arXiv:1803.09578*.

Ian Tenney, Dipanjan Das, and Ellie Pavlick. 2019a. BERT rediscovers the classical NLP pipeline. In *Proceedings of the 57th Annual Meeting of the Association for Computational Linguistics*, pages 4593–4601, Florence, Italy. Association for Computational Linguistics.

Ian Tenney, Patrick Xia, Berlin Chen, Alex Wang, Adam Poliak, R Thomas McCoy, Najoung Kim, Benjamin Van Durme, Sam Bowman, Dipanjan Das, and Ellie Pavlick. 2019b. What do you learn from context? Probing for sentence structure in contextualized word representations. In *International Conference on Learning Representations*.

Alex Wang, Amanpreet Singh, Julian Michael, Felix Hill, Omer Levy, and Samuel R. Bowman. 2019. GLUE: A multi-task benchmark and analysis platform for natural language understanding. In *International Conference on Learning Representations*.

Alex Warstadt and Samuel R Bowman. 2020. Can neural networks acquire a structural bias from raw linguistic data? *Proceedings of the 42nd Annual Conference of the Cognitive Science Society*.

Alex Warstadt, Yu Cao, Ioana Grosu, Wei Peng, Hagen Blix, Yining Nie, Anna Alsop, Shikha Bordia, Haokun Liu, Alicia Parrish, Sheng-Fu Wang, Jason Phang, Anhad Mohananey, Phu Mon Htut, Paloma Jeretic, and Samuel R. Bowman. 2019. Investigating BERT's knowledge of language: Five analysis methods with NPIs. In *Proceedings of the 2019 Conference on Empirical Methods in Natural Language Processing and the 9th International Joint Conference on Natural Language Processing (EMNLP-IJCNLP)*, pages 2870–2880, Hong Kong, China. Association for Computational Linguistics.

Noah Weber, Leena Shekhar, and Niranjan Balasubramanian. 2018. The fine line between linguistic generalization and failure in Seq2Seq-attention models. In *Proceedings of the Workshop on Generalization in the Age of Deep Learning*, pages 24–27, New Orleans, Louisiana. Association for Computational Linguistics.

Ethan Wilcox, Roger Levy, Takashi Morita, and Richard Futrell. 2018. What do RNN language models learn about filler–gap dependencies? In *Proceedings of the 2018 EMNLP Workshop BlackboxNLP: Analyzing and Interpreting Neural Networks for NLP*, pages 211–221, Brussels, Belgium. Association for Computational Linguistics.

Adina Williams, Nikita Nangia, and Samuel Bowman. 2018. A broad-coverage challenge corpus for sentence understanding through inference. In *Proceedings of the 2018 Conference of the North American Chapter of the Association for Computational Linguistics: Human Language Technologies, Volume 1 (Long Papers)*, pages 1112–1122. Association for Computational Linguistics.

Xiang Zhou, Yixin Nie, Hao Tan, and Mohit Bansal. 2020. The curse of performance instability in analysis datasets: Consequences, source, and suggestions. *arXiv preprint arXiv:2004.13606*.

Second-Order NLP Adversarial Examples

John X. Morris
University of Virginia
jm8wx@virginia.edu

Abstract

Adversarial example generation methods in NLP rely on models like language models or sentence encoders to determine if potential adversarial examples are valid. In these methods, a valid adversarial example fools the model being attacked, and is determined to be semantically or syntactically valid by a second model. Research to date has counted all such examples as errors by the attacked model. We contend that these adversarial examples may not be flaws in the attacked model, but flaws in the model that determines validity. We term such invalid inputs second-order adversarial examples. We propose the constraint robustness curve, and associated metric ACCS, as tools for evaluating the robustness of a constraint to second-order adversarial examples. To generate this curve, we design an adversarial attack to run directly on the semantic similarity models. We test on two constraints, the Universal Sentence Encoder (USE) and BERTScore. Our findings indicate that such second-order examples exist, but are typically less common than first-order adversarial examples in state-of-the-art models. They also indicate that USE is effective as constraint on NLP adversarial examples, while BERTScore is nearly ineffectual. Code for running the experiments in this paper is available here.

1 Introduction

If an imperceptible change to an input causes a model to make a misclassification, the perturbed input is known as an adversarial example (Goodfellow et al., 2014). In domains with continuous inputs like audio and vision, whether such a change is considered "imperceptible" can be easily measured: A change to an image may be considered imperceptible (and thus a valid adversarial example) if the resulting image is no more than some fixed distance away in pixel space (Chakraborty et al., 2018).

Figure 1: A second-order adversarial example in NLP. Although the perturbation has different meaning than the original (and the entailment model correctly predicts a contradiction), the sentence encoding similarity does not reflect this change. Current NLP adversarial example generation methods would incorrectly consider this a flaw in the entailment model.

We refer to the function that determines imperceptibility as the constraint, C. For input x and perturbation x_{adv}, if $C(x, x_{adv})$ is true, x_{adv} is a valid perturbation for x.

Different domains call for different constraints. In vision, a common constraint is $\ell_{\infty}(x, x_{adv})$, the maximum pixel-wise distance between image x and its perturbation x_{adv} (Goodfellow et al., 2014). In audio, a common constraint is $|dB(x) - dB(x_{adv})|$, the distortion in decibels between audio input x and perturbation x_{adv} (Carlini and Wagner, 2018). Both constraints are easily computed, well-understood, and correlate with human perceptual distance.

Choosing the correct constraint is not always so straightforward. In discrete domains like language, there is no obvious choice. In fact, the field lacks consensus on even the meaning of "imperceptibility". Different adversarial attacks have used different definitions of imperceptibility (Zhang et al.,

Proceedings of the Third BlackboxNLP Workshop on Analyzing and Interpreting Neural Networks for NLP, pages 228–237
Online, November 20, 2020. ©2020 Association for Computational Linguistics

2020a). One common definition (Alzantot et al., 2018; Jin et al., 2019; Ren et al., 2019; Garg and Ramakrishnan, 2020) is imperceptibility with respect to meaning: $C(x, x_{adv})$ is true if x_{adv} retains the semantics of x.

With this definition, a perturbation x_{adv} is determined to be a valid adversarial example if it simultaneously fools the model and retains the semantics of x. This formulation is problematic because measuring semantic similarity is an open problem in NLP. As a consequence, many adversarial attacks use a *second NLP model* as a constraint, to determine whether or not x_{adv} preserves the semantics of x.

Just like the model under attack, the semantic similarity model is vulnerable to adversarial examples. So when this type of attack finds a valid adversarial example, it is unclear which model has made a mistake: was it the model being attacked, or the model used to enforce the constraint?

In other words, it is possible that the semantic similarity model improperly classified x_{adv} as preserving the semantics of x. We refer to these flaws in constraints as **second-order adversarial examples**. Figure 1 shows a sample second-order adversarial example. Second-order adversarial examples have been largely ignored in the literature on NLP adversarial examples to date.

Now that we are aware of the existence of second-order adversarial examples, we seek to minimize their impact. How can we measure a given constraint's susceptibility to second-order adversarial examples? We suggest one such measurement tool: the **constraint robustness curve** and its associated metric ACCS.

We then develop an adversarial example generation technique for finding examples that fool these semantic similarity models. Our findings indicate that adversarial examples for these types of models exist, but are less likely than adversarial examples that fool other NLP models.

Along the way, we compare the Universal Sentence Encoder (USE) (Cer et al., 2018), a sentence encoder commonly used as a constraint for NLP adversarial examples, with BERTScore (Zhang et al., 2019), a metric that outperforms sentence encoders for evaluating text generation systems.

The main contributions of this work can be summarized as follows:

1. We formally define second-order adversarial examples, a previously unaddressed is-

sue with the problem statement for semantics-preserving adversarial example generation in NLP.

2. We propose Adjusted Constraint C-Statistic (ACCS), the normalized area under the constraint robustness curve, as a measurement of the efficacy of a given model as a constraint on adversarial examples.

3. We run NLP adversarial attacks not on models fine-tuned for downstream tasks, but on semantic similarity models used to regulate the adversarial attack process. We show that they are [robust—not robust]. Across the board, USE achieves a much higher ACCS, indicating that USE is a more robust choice than BERTScore for constraining NLP adversarial perturbations.

2 Second-order adversarial examples

To create natural language adversarial examples that preserve semantics, past work has implemented the constraint using a model that measures semantic similarity (Garg and Ramakrishnan, 2020; Alzantot et al., 2018; Li et al., 2018; Jin et al., 2019). For semantic similarity model S, original input x, and adversarial perturbation x_{adv}, constraint C can be defined as defined as:

$$C(x, x_{adv}) := S(x, x_{adv}) \geq \epsilon \qquad (1)$$

where ϵ is a threshold that determines semantic similarity. If their semantic distance is higher than some threshold, the perturbation is considered a valid adversarial example.

Using such a constraint in an untargeted attack on classification model F, the attack goal G function can be written as:

$$\begin{aligned} G(x, x_{adv}) &:= (F(x) \neq F(x_{adv})) \wedge C(x, x_{adv}) \\ &:= (F(x) \neq F(x_{adv})) \wedge (S(x, x_{adv} \geq \epsilon) \end{aligned}$$
$$(2)$$

Here, x_{adv} is a valid adversarial example when both criteria of the goal are fulfilled: F produces a different class output for x_{adv} than for x, and $C(x, x_{adv})$ is true. This type of joint goal function is common in NLP adversarial attacks (Zhang et al., 2020a).

It is possible that these constraints evaluate the semantic similarity of the original and perturbed text incorrectly. If the semantic similarity score is too low, then x_{adv} will be rejected by the algorithm; if the score is too high, then the algorithm will consider x_{adv} a valid adversarial example.

If $S(x, x_{adv})$ is too high, x_{adv} is incorrectly considered a valid adversarial example: a flaw in model F. However, since semantics is not preserved from x to x_{adv}, there is no reason to assume that $F(x)$ should be consistent with $F(x_{adv})$. The flaw is actually in S, the semantic similarity model that erroneously considered x_{adv} to be a valid adversarial example.

For adversarial attacks on model F using a constraint determined by model S, we suggest the following terminology:

- **First-order adversarial examples** are perturbations that are correctly classified as imperceptible by S, and fool F.

- **Second-order adversarial examples** fool S, the model used as a constraint. Regardless of the output of F, these are adversarial examples for S.

In the next section, we suggest a method for determining the vulnerability of S to second-order adversarial examples.

3 Constraint robustness curves and ACCS

In this section, we propose the constraint robustness curve, a method for analyzing the robustness, or susceptibility to second-order adversarial examples, of a given constraint.

Each semantic similarity model may produce scores on a different scale, varying the best ϵ for preservation of semantics. As such, we cannot fairly compare two models at the same values of ϵ.

However, the problem of comparing two binary classifiers that may have different threshold scales is common in machine learning (Hajian-Tilaki, 2013). Inspired by the receiver operating characteristic (ROC) curve for binary classifiers, we propose the **constraint robustness curve**, a plot of first-order vs. second-order adversarial examples as constraint sensitivity varies. To create the constraint robustness curve for semantic similarity model S and threshold ϵ, we plot the number of true positives (first-order adversarial examples, found using S as a constraint) vs. false positives (second-order adversarial examples, found by attacking S directly).

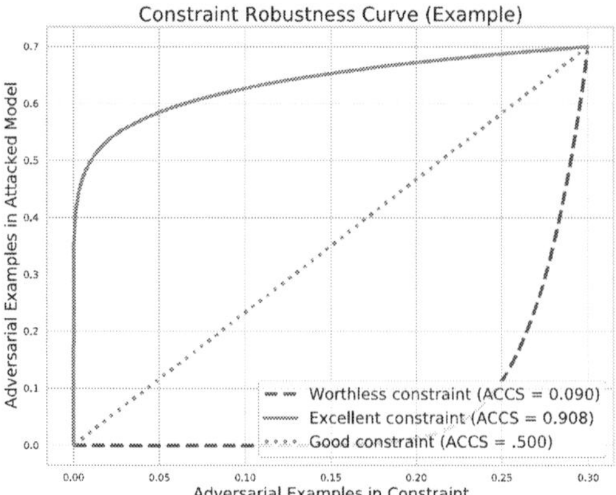

Figure 2: An example constraint robustness curve. ACCS is defined as the normalized area under the constraint robustness curve.

The constraint robustness curve can be interpreted similarly to an ROC curve. An effective constraint will allow many true positives (first-order adversarial examples) before many false positives (second-order adversarial examples). The model that produces a curve with a higher AUC (area under the constraint robustness curve) is better at distinguishing valid from invalid adversarial examples, and less susceptible to second-order adversarial examples.

When $\epsilon = 0$, $C(x, x_{adv})$ is always true. But even when the constraint accepts all possible x_{adv}, some attacks may still fail. So unlike a typical ROC curve, which is bounded between 0 and 1 on both axes, the constraint robustness curve is bounded on each axis between 0 and the maximum attack success rate (when $\epsilon = 0$). We suggest normalizing to bound the score between 0 and 1.

We call the resulting metric **Adjusted Constraint C-Statistic (ACCS)** [1]. ACCS is defined as the area under the constraint robustness curve normalized by the maximum first- and second-order success rate. Figure 2 shows an example of a constraint robustness curve for a toy problem. (The area under the green dashed curve is 0.105; after normalizing by the maximum first- and second-order attack success rates of 0.7 and 0.3, we find $ACCS = 0.5$.)

There is one crucial difference between interpreting an ROC curve and a constraint robustness curve. A naive binary classifier will guess randomly and achieve as many false positives as true positives,

---

[1] *C-statistic* is another name for AUC.

and an AUC of 0.5. A naive constraint will yield all second-order adversarial examples at the same threshold, and garner an ACCS of 0.0.

To create such a curve, we must devise methods for generating both first-order and second-order adversarial examples. In the following section, we propose an attack for each purpose.

4 Generating first and second-order adversarial examples

To calculate $ACCS(S, \epsilon)$ for each S and ϵ, we design two attacks: one to calculate the number of first-order adversarial examples, and one to calculate the number of second-order adversarial examples. In Section 5, we run the attacks across a variety of models and datasets and examine their constraint robustness curves.

4.1 Generating first-order adversarial examples

To measure the number of first-order adversarial examples allotted by a semantic similarity model for a given value of ϵ, we can run any standard adversarial attack that uses the semantic similarity model as a constraint.

We devise a simple attack to generate adversarial examples for some classifier F. We choose untargeted classification, the goal of changing the classifier's output to any but the ground-truth output class, as the goal function. To generate perturbations, we swap words in x with their synonyms from WordNet (Miller, 1995).

Simply swapping words with synonyms from a thesaurus would frequently create ungrammatical perturbations (even though they may be semantically similar to the originals). To better preserve grammaticality, we enforce an additional constraint, requiring that the log-probability of any replaced word not decrease by more than some fixed amount, as according to the GPT-2 language model (Radford et al., 2019). (This is similar the language model perplexity constraints used in the NLP attacks of Alzantot et al. (2018) and (Kuleshov et al., 2018).)

As an additional constraint, the attack filters potential perturbations using the semantic similarity model to ensure that $S(x, x_{adv}) \geq \epsilon$.

Finally, we choose greedy with word importance ranking as our search method (Gao et al., 2018). We can use these four components (goal function, transformation, constraints, and search method) to construct an adversarial attack to generate adversarial examples for any NLP classifier (Morris et al., 2020b).

4.2 Generating second-order adversarial examples

Generating adversarial examples for classification model F is a well-studied problem. But how do we generate perturbations that fool S, a semantic similarity model?

We first note what these adversarial examples might look like. Our goal is to find 'false positives' where a semantic similarity model incorrectly indicates that semantics is preserved. Specifically, we want to find some (x, x_{adv}) where $S(x, x_{adv}) \geq \epsilon$, even though we know x_{adv} does not preserve the semantics of x.

To generate such perturbations, we design a transformation with the goal of changing the meaning of an x as much as possible (instead of preserving its meaning). At each step of the adversarial attack, instead of replacing words with their synonyms, we replace words with their antonyms, also sourced from WordNet (Miller, 1995).

Next, we need to establish a goal function that perturbations must meet to be considered adversarial examples for a given semantic similarity metric. We establish the following goal function:

$$G(x, x_{adv}) := (S(x, x_{adv}) \geq \epsilon) \wedge$$
$$((\sum_i x[i] \neq x_{adv}[i]) \geq \gamma) \quad (3)$$

Here, $x[i]$ represents the ith word in sequence x, and γ represents the minimum number of words that must be changed for the attack to succeed.

With our goal function, perturbation x_{adv} is a valid adversarial example if it differs by at least γ words from x, but its semantic similarity to x is still higher than ϵ. If γ words are substituted with antonyms, as γ increases, we can say with high certainty that semantics is not preserved. In this case, the semantic similarity model *should* produce a value smaller than ϵ.

As in 4.1, we apply a second constraint, using GPT-2 to ensure antonyms substituted are likely in their context. For the search method, we use beam search, as it does a better job finding adversarial examples when the set of valid perturbations is sparse (Ebrahimi et al., 2017).

A sample output of this attack (where $\gamma = 2$) is shown in Figure 1.

5 Experiments

5.1 Attack Prototypes

We implemented our adversarial attacks using the TextAttack adversarial attack framework (Morris et al., 2020b). Figure 4 shows the attack prototypes of each attack, as constructed in TextAttack.

As noted in the previous section, each attack used the GPT-2 language model to preserve grammaticality during word replacements; we disallowed word replacements that decreased in logprobability from the original word 2.0 or more. The other constraints in the attack prototype disallow multiple modifications of the same word, stopword substitutions, and, in the case of entailment datasets, edits to the premise. [2]

5.2 Semantic similarity models

We tested two semantic similarity models as S:

- The Universal Sentence Encoder (USE) (Cer et al., 2018), a model trained to encode sentences into fixed-length vectors. Semantic similarity between x and x_{adv} is measured as the cosine similarity of their encodings. This is consistent with NLP attack literature (Li et al., 2018; Jin et al., 2019; Garg and Ramakrishnan, 2020).

- BERTScore (Zhang et al., 2019), an automatic evaluation metric for text generation. BERTScore computes a similarity score for each token in the candidate sentence with each token in the reference sentence using the contextual embedding of each token. According to human studies, BERTScore correlates better than other metrics (including sentence encodings) for evaluating machine translations. It also outperforms sentence encodings on PAWS (Yang et al., 2019), an adversarial paraphrase dataset where inputs have a similar format to NLP adversarial examples.

5.3 Victim Classifiers

To create constraint robustness curves, we ran each attack (first and second-order) while varying ϵ from 0.75 to 1.0 in increments of 0.01. For the SST-2 dataset, which has some very short examples, we varied ϵ from 0.5 to 1.0 in increments of 0.02. For

```
First-Order Attack

Attack(
  (search_method): GreedyWordSwapWIR(
    (wir_method):  unk
  )
  (goal_function):  UntargetedClassification
  (transformation):  WordSwapWordNet
  (constraints):
    (0): GPT2(
        (max_log_prob_decrease):  2.0
        (compare_against_original):  True
    )
    (1): [Constraint](
        (threshold):  [ε]
        (compare_against_original):  True
    )
    (2): RepeatModification
    (3): StopwordModification
    (4): InputColumnModification(
        (matching_column_labels):
            ['premise', 'hypothesis']
        (columns_to_ignore):  {'premise'}
    )
  (is_black_box):  True
)
```

```
Second-Order Attack

Attack(
  (search_method): BeamSearch(
    (beam_width):  2
  )
  (goal_function): FoolConstraintGoalFunction(
    (constraint): [Constraint]
    (min_acceptable_score): [ε]
    (num_words_to_swap): [γ]
  )
  (transformation):  WordSwapWordNetAntonym
  (constraints):
    (0): GPT2(
        (max_log_prob_diff):  2.0
        (compare_against_original):  True
    )
    (1): RepeatModification
    (2): StopwordModification
    (3): InputColumnModification(
        (matching_column_labels):
            ['premise', 'hypothesis']
        (columns_to_ignore):  {'premise'}
    )
  (is_black_box):  True
)
```

Figure 3: Attack prototypes generated for attacks run in TextAttack. The top shows the first-order attack, run against a classification model using the semantic similarity model as a constraint. The bottom shows the second-order attack, run directly against a semantic similarity model. During experiments, [Constraint] is either USE or BERTScore, $[\epsilon]$ is varied from 0.5 to 1 or 0.75 to 1, and $[\gamma]$ is set to 3.

---

[2] It is standard for NLP attacks on entailment models to only edit the hypothesis (Alzantot et al., 2018; Zhao et al., 2017; Jin et al., 2019)).

the second-order attack, we fixed $\gamma = 3$. For our tests, we chose the following three datasets:

- The Stanford Natural Language Inference (SNLI) Corpus, which contains labeled sentence pairs for textual entailment (Bowman et al., 2015);

- The Stanford Sentiment Treebank v2 (SST-2) Corpus (Socher et al., 2013), a phrase-level sentiment classification dataset;

- Rotten Tomatoes dataset [3], a sentence-level sentiment classification dataset (Pang and Lee, 2005).

For the first-order attack, we chose three target models fine-tuned on each dataset (total of nine models): BERT (Devlin et al., 2018), ALBERT (Lan et al., 2019), and DistilBERT (Sanh et al., 2019). All models used were pre-trained models provided by TextAttack (Morris et al., 2020b). More details about experimental setup are provided in A.1.

5.4 Results

We sampled 100 examples from each test set of dataset for each attack. We repeated each attack twice, once using BERTScore and once using the Universal Sentence Encoder. In total, we ran 300 attacks.

Table 1 shows results for each model and dataset. Figure 5 shows the constraint robustness curve for each scenario.

Surprisingly, the Universal Sentence Encoder achieved a higher ACCS than BERTScore across all nine scenarios. This appears contradictory to the claims of Zhang et al. (2019) that "BERTScore is more robust to challenging examples when compared to existing metrics".

Additionally, at any given point, first-order adversarial examples are found over twice as often as second-order adversarial examples. This indicates that most adversarial examples found in NLP attacks may be first-order. This corroborates human studies from (Reevaluating-Morris2020-mb), which showed that humans rate adversarial examples from the attacks of (Alzantot2018-ti) and (TextFooler-Jin2019-re) to preserve semantics around 65% of the time.

---

[3]The Rotten Tomatoes dataset is sometimes called Movie Review, or MR, dataset.

Figure 4: First-order and second-order adversarial examples generated by our attacks on BERT-base fine-tuned on the SST-2 dataset.

Dataset	Target Model	Constraint Under Attack	
		BERTScore	USE
SNLI	BERT	0.590	0.730
	ALBERT	0.569	0.678
	DistilBERT	0.575	0.721
SST-2	BERT	0.290	0.423
	ALBERT	0.407	0.464
	DistilBERT	0.405	0.511
Rotten Tomatoes (MR)	BERT	0.382	0.383
	ALBERT	0.388	0.427
	DistilBERT	0.448	0.466

Table 1: Results of first-order and second-order attacks on BERTScore and the Universal Sentence Encoder (USE). Values are ACCS, a measure of constraint robustness. A higher ACCS score indicates a better constraint. Across models and datasets, USE achieves a higher ACCS than BERTScore.

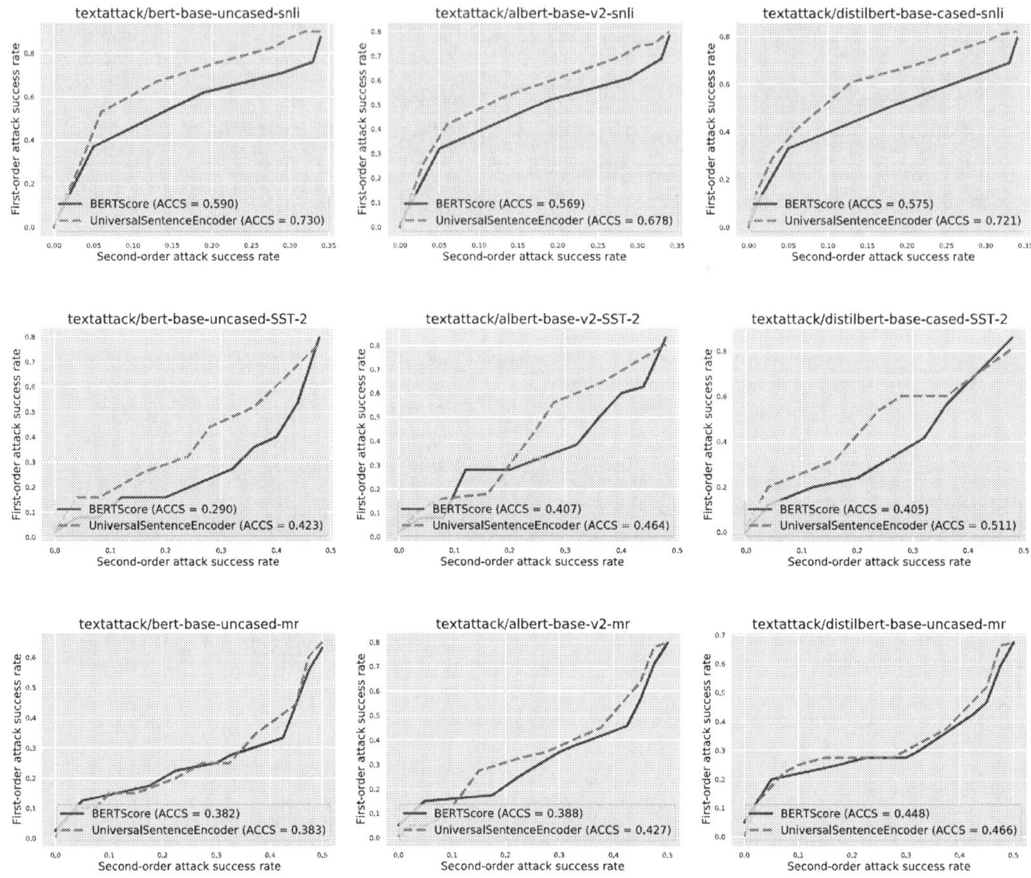

Figure 5: Constraint robustness curves across attacks. The Universal Sentence Encoder finds more adversarial examples in each model while yielding fewer adversarial examples via second-order attacks. ACCS results are detailed in Table 1.

6 Discussion

Sentence length, S, and ϵ. As input x grows in length, the a single word swap will have an increasingly smaller impact on $S(x, x_{adv})$. Some NLP attacks that use sentence encoders as a constraint have combatted this problem by measuring the sentence encodings within a fixed-length window of words around each substitution. For example, Jin et al. (2019) considers a window of 15 words around each substitution. We chose instead to encode the entire input, as both the Universal Sentence Encoder and BERTScore were trained using full inputs.

Applications beyond NLP. Table 2 lists examples of validity metrics across domains. To the best of our knowledge, no domains outside of NLP have suggested to use a deep learning model as a constraint (Chakraborty et al., 2018). If adversarial attacks in other domains do decide to use deep learning models to measure imperceptibility, they can follow our method to compare imperceptibility models and evaluate their robustness.

The Catch-22 of second-order adversarial examples. Any adversarial generation method for that employs an auxiliary model as a constraint may generate second-order adversarial examples. Although NLP is the only domain to use a model as a constraint thus far, this problem is likely to appear in other domains in the future. This makes the problem of second-order adversarial detection more important.

Towards better constraints on NLP adversarial examples. Neither USE nor BERTScore scored especially high ACCS scores on any of the studied tasks. We leave it to future work to explore more choices of semantic similarity model and find one that is more suitable as a constraint on NLP adversarial examples.

7 Related Work

We can categorize adversarial attacks in NLP based on their chosen definition of imperceptibility: generally adversarial attacks in NLP aim either for *visual* imperceptibility or in *semantic* imperceptibility.

Visual imperceptibility. These adversarial example generation techniques focus on character-level modifications that a fast-reading human may not notice. HotFlip (Ebrahimi et al., 2017) uses the gradient of a character-level classifier to guide the attack, and can often change the classifier output with a single flip. (HotFlip also studies word-level replacements, but only briefly.) Other works (Belinkov and Bisk, 2017; Gao et al., 2018; Pruthi et al., 2019; Jones et al., 2020) craft adversarial examples by inducing 'typos' in the input sequence x, for example, by swapping two characters with one another, or shuffling the characters in an input. In these cases, imperceptibility is generally modeled using string edit distance, so second-order adversarial examples do not exist.

Semantic imperceptibility. This work focuses on this class of NLP adversarial examples, in which x_{adv} must preserve the semantics of x. Most work generates these x_{adv} by swapping iteratively swapping words in x with synonyms, and filtering by some model-based constraint (Kuleshov et al., 2018; Ren et al., 2019; Jin et al., 2019; Garg and Ramakrishnan, 2020). Some alternative algorithms have been proposed: Zhao et al. (2017) encode x into a latent representation using a generative adversarial network, apply the perturbation to the latent vector, and decode to obtain x_{adv}. Ribeiro et al. (2018) craft 'adversarial rules' (mappings from $x \rightarrow x_{adv}$) by a combination of back-translation and human evaluation. TextBugger (Li et al., 2018) crafts adversarial examples using word-level substitutions, but uniquely chooses between character-level perturbations (exploiting imperceptibility in appearance) and word-level synonym swaps (exploiting imperceptibility in meaning).

Although there have been many adversarial attacks proposed on NLP models (Zhang et al., 2020a), surprisingly few constraints have been ex-

Adversarial Example Domain	Constraint
Images (Goodfellow et al., 2014)	maximum ℓ_{inf} norm
Audio (Carlini and Wagner, 2018)	minimum distortion in Decibels (dB)
Graphs (Wu et al., 2019)	maximum number of edges modified
Text (Zhang et al., 2020b)	minimum USE cosine similarity

Table 2: Examples of constraints across adversarial example domains. All metrics are calculated between the original input and any potentially valid adversarial perturbation.

plored. Alzantot et al. (2018) was the first to propose the use of a language model as a constraint on grammaticality. Kuleshov et al. (2018) uses both a language model to enforce grammaticality and skip-thought vectors (Kiros et al., 2015), a form of sentence encoding, to enforce semantic preservation. Several attacks have used the Universal Sentence Encoder to enforce semantic preservation (Li et al., 2018; Jin et al., 2019; Garg and Ramakrishnan, 2020).

Morris et al. (2020a) categorized constraints on NLP adversarial examples into four groups: semantics, grammaticality, overlap, and non-suspicion. They also explored the effect of varying constraint threshold on the quality of generated adversarial examples, as judged by human annotators. Xu et al. (2020) examined the quality of generated adversarial examples based on different thresholds of attack success rate. However, neither study considered adversarial examples that may have arisen from constraints, or explored evaluation via running adversarial attacks on the constraints directly.

8 Conclusion

Work in generating adversarial examples in NLP has relied on outside models to evaluate imperceptibility. While useful, this inadvertently increases the size of the attack space. We propose methods for analyzing constraints' susceptibility to second-order adversarial examples, including the ACCS and associated constraint robustness curve metric. This requires us to design an attack specific to semantic similarity models. We demonstrate these methods with a comparison of two models used in constraints, the Universal Sentence Encoder and BERTScore. We would especially like to see future research examine constraint robustness curves across more constraints and different attack designs. We hope that future researchers can use our method when choosing constraints for NLP adversarial example generation.

Acknowledgments

This work arose out of a series of discussions with Eli Lifland about adversarial examples in NLP. Thanks to him and many others, including Jeffrey Yoo, Jack Lanchantin, Di Jin, Yanjun Qi, and Charles Frye, for engaging in similar discussions, which ranged from empirical to downright philosophical.

References

Moustafa Alzantot, Yash Sharma, Ahmed Elgohary, Bo-Jhang Ho, Mani Srivastava, and Kai-Wei Chang. 2018. Generating natural language adversarial examples.

Yonatan Belinkov and Yonatan Bisk. 2017. Synthetic and natural noise both break neural machine translation.

Samuel R Bowman, Gabor Angeli, Christopher Potts, and Christopher D Manning. 2015. A large annotated corpus for learning natural language inference.

Nicholas Carlini and David Wagner. 2018. Audio adversarial examples: Targeted attacks on Speech-to-Text.

Daniel Cer, Yinfei Yang, Sheng-Yi Kong, Nan Hua, Nicole Limtiaco, Rhomni St. John, Noah Constant, Mario Guajardo-Cespedes, Steve Yuan, Chris Tar, Yun-Hsuan Sung, Brian Strope, and Ray Kurzweil. 2018. Universal sentence encoder.

Anirban Chakraborty, Manaar Alam, Vishal Dey, Anupam Chattopadhyay, and Debdeep Mukhopadhyay. 2018. Adversarial attacks and defences: A survey.

Jacob Devlin, Ming-Wei Chang, Kenton Lee, and Kristina Toutanova. 2018. BERT: Pre-training of deep bidirectional transformers for language understanding.

Javid Ebrahimi, Anyi Rao, Daniel Lowd, and Dejing Dou. 2017. HotFlip: White-Box adversarial examples for text classification.

Ji Gao, Jack Lanchantin, Mary Lou Soffa, and Yanjun Qi. 2018. Black-box generation of adversarial text sequences to evade deep learning classifiers.

Siddhant Garg and Goutham Ramakrishnan. 2020. BAE: BERT-based adversarial examples for text classification.

Ian J Goodfellow, Jonathon Shlens, and Christian Szegedy. 2014. Explaining and harnessing adversarial examples.

Karimollah Hajian-Tilaki. 2013. Receiver operating characteristic (ROC) curve analysis for medical diagnostic test evaluation. *Caspian J Intern Med*, 4(2):627–635.

Di Jin, Zhijing Jin, Joey Tianyi Zhou, and Peter Szolovits. 2019. Is bert really robust? natural language attack on text classification and entailment. *arXiv preprint arXiv:1907. 11932*.

Erik Jones, Robin Jia, Aditi Raghunathan, and Percy Liang. 2020. Robust encodings: A framework for combating adversarial typos.

Ryan Kiros, Yukun Zhu, Russ R Salakhutdinov, Richard Zemel, Raquel Urtasun, Antonio Torralba, and Sanja Fidler. 2015. Skip-Thought vectors. In C Cortes, N D Lawrence, D D Lee, M Sugiyama, and R Garnett, editors, *Advances in Neural Information Processing Systems 28*, pages 3294–3302. Curran Associates, Inc.

Volodymyr Kuleshov, Shantanu Thakoor, Tingfung Lau, and Stefano Ermon. 2018. Adversarial examples for natural language classification problems.

Zhenzhong Lan, Mingda Chen, Sebastian Goodman, Kevin Gimpel, Piyush Sharma, and Radu Soricut. 2019. ALBERT: A lite BERT for self-supervised learning of language representations.

Jinfeng Li, Shouling Ji, Tianyu Du, Bo Li, and Ting Wang. 2018. TextBugger: Generating adversarial text against real-world applications.

George A Miller. 1995. WordNet: a lexical database for english. *Commun. ACM*, 38(11):39–41.

John X Morris, Eli Lifland, Jack Lanchantin, Yangfeng Ji, and Yanjun Qi. 2020a. Reevaluating adversarial examples in natural language.

John X Morris, Eli Lifland, Jin Yong Yoo, Jake Grigsby, Di Jin, and Yanjun Qi. 2020b. TextAttack: A framework for adversarial attacks, data augmentation, and adversarial training in NLP.

Bo Pang and Lillian Lee. 2005. Seeing stars: Exploiting class relationships for sentiment categorization with respect to rating scales. In *Proceedings of the ACL*.

Danish Pruthi, Bhuwan Dhingra, and Zachary C Lipton. 2019. Combating adversarial misspellings with robust word recognition.

Alec Radford, Jeffrey Wu, Rewon Child, David Luan, Dario Amodei, and Ilya Sutskever. 2019. Language models are unsupervised multitask learners. *OpenAI Blog*, 1(8):9.

Shuhuai Ren, Yihe Deng, Kun He, and Wanxiang Che. 2019. Generating natural language adversarial examples through probability weighted word saliency. pages 1085–1097.

Marco Tulio Ribeiro, Sameer Singh, and Carlos Guestrin. 2018. Semantically equivalent adversarial rules for debugging NLP models. pages 856–865.

Victor Sanh, Lysandre Debut, Julien Chaumond, and Thomas Wolf. 2019. DistilBERT, a distilled version of BERT: smaller, faster, cheaper and lighter.

Richard Socher, Alex Perelygin, Jean Wu, Jason Chuang, Christopher D Manning, Andrew Y Ng, and Christopher Potts. 2013. Recursive deep models for semantic compositionality over a sentiment treebank. pages 1631–1642.

Huijun Wu, Chen Wang, Yuriy Tyshetskiy, Andrew Docherty, Kai Lu, and Liming Zhu. 2019. Adversarial examples on graph data: Deep insights into attack and defense.

Ying Xu, Xu Zhong, Antonio Jose Jimeno Yepes, and Jey Han Lau. 2020. Elephant in the room: An evaluation framework for assessing adversarial examples in NLP.

Yinfei Yang, Yuan Zhang, Chris Tar, and Jason Baldridge. 2019. PAWS-X: A cross-lingual adversarial dataset for paraphrase identification.

Tianyi Zhang, Varsha Kishore, Felix Wu, Kilian Q Weinberger, and Yoav Artzi. 2019. BERTScore: Evaluating text generation with BERT.

Wei Emma Zhang, Quan Z Sheng, Ahoud Alhazmi, and Chenliang Li. 2020a. Adversarial attacks on deep-learning models in natural language processing: A survey. *ACM Trans. Intell. Syst. Technol.*, 11(3):1–41.

Wei Emma Zhang, Quan Z Sheng, Ahoud Alhazmi, and Chenliang Li. 2020b. Adversarial attacks on deep-learning models in natural language processing: A survey. *ACM Trans. Intell. Syst. Technol.*, 11(3):1–41.

Zhengli Zhao, Dheeru Dua, and Sameer Singh. 2017. Generating natural adversarial examples.

Discovering the Compositional Structure of Vector Representations with Role Learning Networks

Paul Soulos,[1] R. Thomas McCoy,[1] Tal Linzen,[2] and Paul Smolensky[3,1]
[1]Department of Cognitive Science, Johns Hopkins University
[2]Department of Linguistics and Center for Data Science, New York University
[3]Microsoft Research
psoulos1@jhu.edu,tom.mccoy@jhu.edu, linzen@nyu.edu, psmo@microsoft.com

Abstract

How can neural networks perform so well on compositional tasks even though they lack explicit compositional representations? We use a novel analysis technique called ROLE to show that recurrent neural networks perform well on such tasks by converging to solutions which implicitly represent symbolic structure. This method uncovers a symbolic structure which, when properly embedded in vector space, closely approximates the encodings of a standard seq2seq network trained to perform the compositional SCAN task. We verify the causal importance of the discovered symbolic structure by showing that, when we systematically manipulate hidden embeddings based on this symbolic structure, the model's output is changed in the way predicted by our analysis.

1 Introduction

Traditional models of cognition, and language in particular, have relied heavily on symbol structures and symbol manipulation. However, in the current era, deep learning research has shown that Neural Networks (NNs) can display remarkable degrees of generalization on tasks traditionally viewed as depending on symbolic structure (Wu et al., 2016; McCoy et al., 2019a), albeit with some important limits to their generalization (Lake and Baroni, 2018). Given that standard NNs have no obvious mechanisms for representing symbolic structures, parsing inputs into such structures, nor applying compositional symbol-manipulating rules to them, this success raises the question that we address in this paper: *How do NNs achieve such strong performance on compositional tasks?*

Could it be that NNs *do* learn symbolic representations—covertly embedded as vectors in their state spaces? McCoy et al. (2019a) showed that when trained on highly compositional tasks,

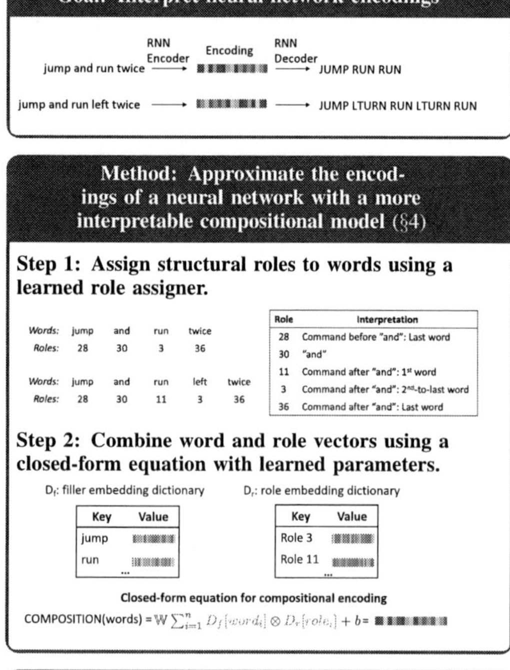

$$\text{COMPOSITION(words)} = \mathbf{W} \sum_{i=1}^{n} D_f[word_i] \otimes D_r[role_i] + b =$$

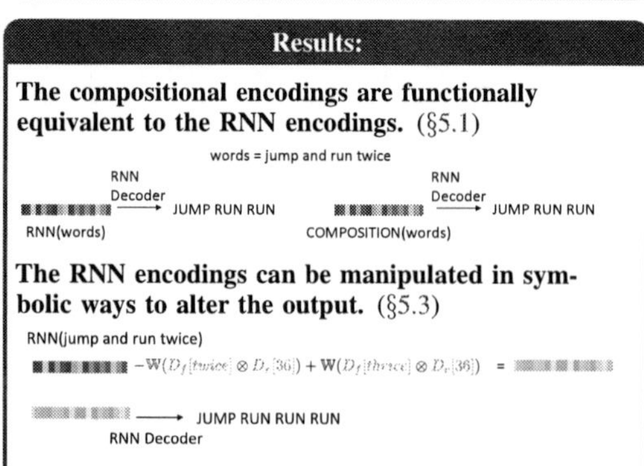

Figure 1: Summary of our approach.

Proceedings of the Third BlackboxNLP Workshop on Analyzing and Interpreting Neural Networks for NLP, pages 238–254
Online, November 20, 2020. ©2020 Association for Computational Linguistics

standard NNs learned representations that are functionally equivalent to compositional vector embeddings of symbolic structures (Sec. 3). Processing in these NNs assigns structural representations to inputs and generates outputs that are governed by compositional rules stated over those representations. We refer to the networks we will analyze as **target NNs**, because we will propose a new type of NN (in Sec. 4)—the **Role Learner (ROLE)**— which is used to *analyze* the target network. In contrast with the analysis model of McCoy et al. (2019a), which relies on a hand-specified hypothesis about the structure underlying the learned representations of the target NN, ROLE *automatically* learns a symbolic structure that best approximates the internal representation of the target network. This yields two advantages. First, ROLE achieves success at analyzing networks for which the underlying structure is unclear. We show this in Sec. 5, where ROLE successfully uncovers the symbolic structures learned by a seq2seq RNN trained on the SCAN synthetic semantic parsing task (Lake and Baroni, 2018). Second, removing the need for hand-specified structural hypotheses reduces the burden on the analyst, who only needs to provide input sequences and their target NN encodings. Discovering symbolic structure within a model enables us to perform precise alterations to the internal representations in order to produce desired alterations in the output (Sec. 5.3). Then, in Sec. 6, we turn briefly to partially-compositional tasks in NLP.

The novel contributions of this research are:

- ROLE, a NN module that learns to assign symbolic structures to input sequences (Sec. 4).

- Demonstration that RNNs converge to compositional solutions on the synthetic SCAN task (Sec. 5).

- A precise closed-form expression for the distributed encoding learned by an RNN trained on SCAN, exhibiting its latent symbolic structure (Sec. 5.2).

- Demonstration of the causal relevance of this symbolic structure by using the equation for its vector encoding to control RNN output through precise alteration of the RNN's internal encoding (Sec. 5.3).

- Additional evidence showing that sentence embedding models do not capture compositional structure (Sec. 6).

2 Background Related work

2.1 Compositionality

Certain cognitive tasks consist in computing a function φ that is governed by strict rules: e.g., if φ is the function mapping a mathematical expression to its value (e.g., mapping '$19 - 2 * 7$' to 5), then φ obeys the rule that $\varphi(x + y) = \mathtt{sum}(\varphi(x), \varphi(y))$ for any expressions x and y. This rule is **compositional**: the output of a structure (here, $x + y$) is a function of the outputs of the structure's constituents (here, x and y). The rule can be stated with full generality once the input is assigned a **symbolic structure** giving its decomposition into constituents. For a **fully-compositional** task, completely determined by compositional rules, a system that can assign appropriate symbolic structures to inputs and apply appropriate compositional rules to these structures will display full **systematic generalization**: it will correctly process arbitrary novel combinations of familiar constituents. This is a core capability of symbolic AI systems.

Other tasks, including most natural language tasks such as machine translation, are only partially characterizable by compositional rules: natural language is only partially compositional in nature. For example, if φ is the function that assigns meanings to English adjectives, it generally obeys the rule that $\varphi(\mathtt{in\text{-}} + x) = \mathtt{not}\ \varphi(x)$, (e.g., $\varphi(\mathtt{inoffensive}) = \mathtt{not}\ \varphi(\mathtt{offensive})$), yet there are exceptions: $\varphi(\mathtt{inflammable}) = \varphi(\mathtt{flammable})$. On these "**partially-compositional**" tasks, this strategy of compositional analysis has demonstrated considerable, but limited, generalization capabilities.

2.2 Analysis of NNs

Many past works in the rich body of literature about analyzing NNs focus on compositional structure (Hupkes et al., 2020, 2018; Hewitt and Manning, 2019; Li et al., 2019) and systematicity (Lake and Baroni, 2018; Goodwin et al., 2020). Two of the most popular analysis techniques are the behavioral and probing approaches. In the behavioral approach, a model is evaluated on a set of examples carefully chosen to require competence in particular linguistic phenomena (Marvin and Linzen, 2018; Wang et al., 2018; Dasgupta et al., 2019; Poliak et al., 2018; Linzen et al., 2016; McCoy et al., 2019b; Warstadt et al., 2020). This technique can illuminate behavioral shortcomings but says little about how the internal representations are struc-

239

tured, treating the model as a black box.

In the probing approach, an auxiliary classifier is trained to classify the model's internal representations based on some linguistically-relevant distinction (Adi et al., 2017; Giulianelli et al., 2018; Conneau et al., 2018; Conneau and Kiela, 2018; Belinkov et al., 2017; Blevins et al., 2018; Peters et al., 2018; Tenney et al., 2019). In contrast with the behavioral approach, the probing approach tests whether some particular information is present in the model's encodings, but it says little about whether this information is actually used by the model. Indeed, in some cases models fail despite having the necessary information to succeed in their representations, showing that the ability of a classifier to extract that information does not mean that the model is using it (Voita and Titov, 2020; Ravichander et al., 2020; Vanmassenhove et al., 2017).

We build on McCoy et al. (2019a), which introduced the analysis task **DISCOVER (DISsecting COmpositionality in VEctor Representations)**: take a NN and, to the extent possible, find an explicitly-compositional approximation to its internal distributed representations. DISCOVER allows us to bridge the gap between representation and behavior: It reveals not only what information is encoded in the representation, but also reveals this information in a way that we can manipulate to show that the information is causally implicated in the model's behavior (Section 5.3). Moreover, it provides a much more comprehensive window into the representation than the probing approach does; while probing extracts particular types of information from a representation (e.g., "does this representation distinguish between active and passive sentences?"), DISCOVER exhaustively decomposes the model's representational space. In this regard, DISCOVER is most closely related to the approaches of Andreas (2019), Chrupała and Alishahi (2019), and Abnar et al. (2019), who also propose methods for discovering a complete symbolic characterization of a set of vector representations, and Omlin and Giles (1996) and Weiss et al. (2018), which also seek to extract more interpretable symbolic models that approximate neural network behavior. Like Andreas (2019) and Chrupała and Alishahi (2019), we seek to find the structure encoded in neural networks, rather than seeking structure directly from the data as is the goal in grammar induction work such as Shen et al.

(2019) and Bowman et al. (2016).

3   NN embedding of symbol structures

McCoy et al. showed that, in GRU (Cho et al., 2014) encoder-decoder networks performing simple, fully-compositional string manipulations, the medial encoding (between encoder and decoder) could be extremely well approximated, up to an affine transformation, by **Tensor Product Representations (TPRs)** (Smolensky, 1990), which are explicitly-compositional vector embeddings of symbolic structures. To represent a string of symbols as a TPR, the symbols in the string 337 might be parsed into three constituents $\{3\colon \mathrm{pos}1, 7\colon \mathrm{pos}3, 3\colon \mathrm{pos}2\}$, where $\mathrm{pos}n$ is the role of nth position from the left edge of the string; other role schemes are also possible, such as roles denoting right-to-left position: $\{3\colon \text{third-to-last}, 3\colon \text{second-to-last}, 7\colon \text{last}\}$. The embedding of a constituent $7\colon \mathrm{pos}3$ is $\mathrm{e}(7\colon \mathrm{pos}3) = \mathrm{e_F}(7) \otimes \mathrm{e_R}(\mathrm{pos}3)$, where $\otimes$ is the tensor product (outer product), $\mathrm{e_R}, \mathrm{e_F}$ are respectively a vector embedding of the roles and a vector embedding of the **fillers** of those roles: the digits. The embedding of the whole string is the sum of the embeddings of its constituents. In general, for a symbol structure S with roles $\{r_k\}$ that are respectively filled by the symbols $\{f_k\}$, $\mathrm{e_{TPR}}(\mathrm{S}) = \sum_k \mathrm{e_F}(f_k) \otimes \mathrm{e_R}(r_k)$. The DISCOVER task including the TPR equations is depicted in Figure 2.

At a high level, these role embeddings serve a similar purpose as positional embeddings in a Transformer (Vaswani et al., 2017), in that they are vector embeddings of a token's position in a sequence. The roles discussed above—and the positional embeddings used in Transformers—illustrate **role schemes** based on sequential position; non-sequential role schemes such as positions in a tree are also possible. McCoy et al. (2019a) showed that, for a given seq2seq architecture learning a given string-mapping task, there exists a highly accurate TPR approximation of the medial encoding, given an appropriate pre-defined role scheme. The main technical contribution of the present paper is the Role Learner (ROLE) model, an RNN that learns its own role scheme to optimize the fit of a TPR approximation to a given set of internal representations in a pre-trained target NN. This makes the DISCOVER framework more general by removing the need for human-generated hypothe-

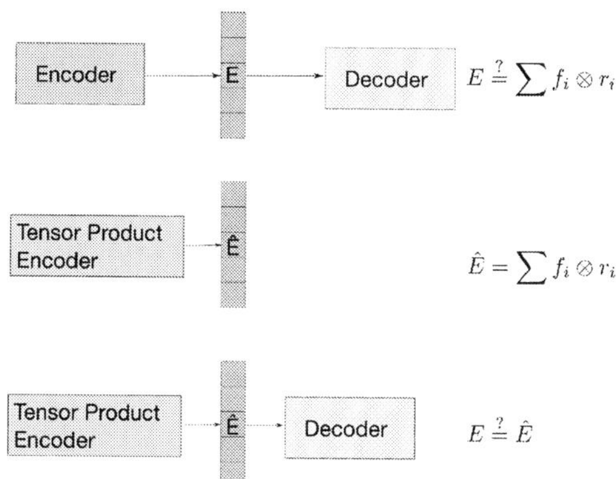

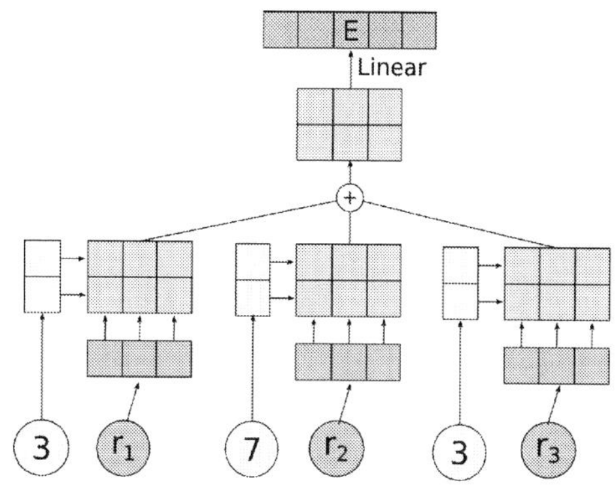

Figure 2: The DISCOVER task and functions. At the top is the target network and question we pose: is the internal embedding a TPR? The middle row is the TPE which follows the provided equation. We train the TPE to minimize the MSE between $\hat{E}$ and E. In the bottom row, we evaluate our model by passing the approximations $\hat{E}$ through the decoder and checking the *substitution accuracy* — the proportion of examples for which the approximated encoding $\hat{E}$ yields the correct output when provided to the decoder .

Figure 3: The Tensor Product Encoder architecture. The fillers (yellow circles) and roles (blue circles) are first vectorized with an embedding layer. These two vector embeddings are combined by an outer product to produce the green matrix representing the TPR of the constituent. All of the constituents are summed together to produce the TPR of the sequence, and then a linear transformation is applied to resize the TPR to the target encoder's dimensionality. ROLE replaces the role embedding layer and directly produces the blue role vector.

ses about the role schemes the network might be implementing. Learned role schemes, we will see in Sec. 5.1, can enable good TPR approximation of networks for which human-generated role schemes fail.

4   The Role Learner (ROLE) Model

ROLE[1] produces a vector-space embedding of an input string of T symbols $\mathrm{S} = \mathrm{s}_1\mathrm{s}_2 \dots \mathrm{s}_T$ by producing a TPR $\mathbf{T}(\mathrm{S})$ and then passing it through an affine transformation. ROLE is trained to approximate a pre-trained target string-encoder $\mathcal{E}$. Given a set of N training strings $\{\mathrm{S}^{(1)}, \dots, \mathrm{S}^{(N)}\}$, ROLE minimizes the total mean-squared error (MSE) between its output $\mathbb{W}\,\mathbf{T}(\mathrm{S}^{(i)}) + \boldsymbol{b}$ and $\mathcal{E}(\mathrm{S}^{(i)})$.

ROLE is an extension of the Tensor-Product Encoder (TPE) introduced in McCoy et al. (2019a) (as the "Tensor Product Decomposition Network") and depicted in Figure 3. Crucially, ROLE is not *given* role labels for the input symbols, but *learns to compute* them. More precisely, it learns a dictionary of n_{R} d_{R}-dimensional role-embedding vectors, $\boldsymbol{R} \in \mathbb{R}^{d_{\mathrm{R}} \times n_{\mathrm{R}}}$, and, for each input symbol s_t, computes a soft-attention vector $\boldsymbol{a}_t$ over these role vectors: the role vector assigned to s_t is then the attention-weighted linear combination of role vectors, $\boldsymbol{r}_t = \boldsymbol{R}\,\boldsymbol{a}_t$. ROLE simultaneously learns a dictionary of n_{F} d_{F}-dimensional symbol-embedding filler vectors $\boldsymbol{F} \in \mathbb{R}^{d_{\mathrm{F}} \times n_{\mathrm{F}}}$, the ϕth column of which is $\boldsymbol{f}_\phi$, the embedding of symbol type ϕ; $\phi \in 1, \dots, n_{\mathrm{F}}$ where n_{F} is the size of the vocabulary of symbol types. The TPR generated by ROLE is thus $\mathbf{T}(\mathrm{S}) = \sum_{t=1}^{T} \boldsymbol{f}_{\tau(\mathrm{s}_t)} \otimes \boldsymbol{r}_t$, where $\tau(\mathrm{s}_t)$ is symbol s_t's type. Finally, ROLE learns an affine transformation to map this TPR into $\mathbb{R}^d$, where d is the dimension of the representations of the encoder $\mathcal{E}$.

ROLE uses an LSTM (Hochreiter and Schmidhuber, 1997) to compute the role-assigning attention-vectors $\boldsymbol{a}_t$ from its learned embedding $\boldsymbol{F}$ of the input symbols s_t: at each t, the hidden state of the LSTM passes through a linear layer and then a softmax to produce $\boldsymbol{a}_t$ (depicted in Figure 4). Let the tth LSTM hidden state be $\boldsymbol{q}_t \in \mathbb{R}^H$; let the output-layer weight-matrix have rows $\boldsymbol{k}_\rho^\top \in \mathbb{R}^H$ and let the columns of $\boldsymbol{R}$ be $\boldsymbol{v}_\rho \in R^{d_{\mathrm{R}}}$, with $\rho = 1, \dots, n_{\mathrm{R}}$. Then $\boldsymbol{r}_t = \boldsymbol{R}\,\boldsymbol{a}_t = \sum_{\rho=1}^{n_{\mathrm{R}}} \boldsymbol{v}_\rho \, \mathrm{softmax}(\boldsymbol{k}_\rho^\top \boldsymbol{q}_t)$: the result of query-key attention (e.g., Vaswani et al., 2017) with query $\boldsymbol{q}_t$ to a fixed external memory containing key-value pairs $\{(\boldsymbol{k}_\rho, \boldsymbol{v}_\rho)\}_{\rho=1}^{n_{\mathrm{R}}}$.

Since a TPR for a discrete symbol structure deploys a discrete set of roles specifying discrete structural positions, ideally a single role would be

---

[1]Code available at `https://github.com/psoulos/role-decomposition`.

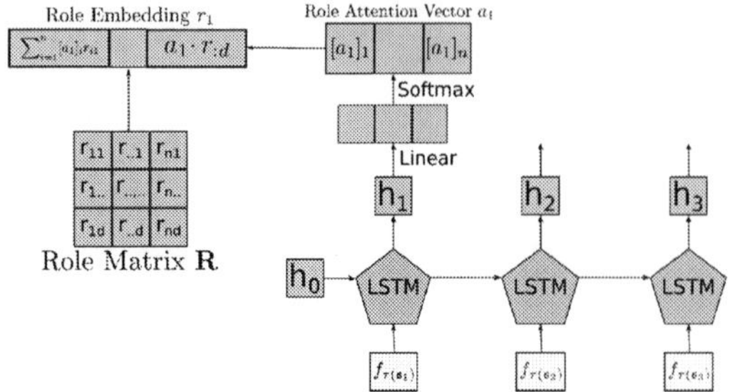

Figure 4: The role learning module. The role attention vector a_t is encouraged to be one-hot through regularization; if a_t were one-hot, the produced role embedding r_t would correspond directly to one of the roles defined in the role matrix R. The LSTM can be unidirectional or bidirectional.

selected for each s_t: a_t would be one-hot. ROLE training therefore deploys regularization to bias learning towards one-hot a_t vectors (based on the regularization proposed in Palangi et al. (2017), developed for the same purpose). See Appendix A.2 for the precise regularization terms that we used.

It is essential to note that, while we impose this regularization on ROLE, there is no explicit bias favoring discrete compositional representations in the *target encoder* $\mathcal{E}$: any such structure that ROLE finds hidden in the representations learned by $\mathcal{E}$ must result from biases implicit in the vanilla RNN-architecture of $\mathcal{E}$ when applied to its target task.

5 The SCAN task

Returning to our central question from Sec. 1, how can neural networks *without* explicit compositional structure perform well on fully-compositional tasks? Our hypothesis is that, though these models have no *constraint* forcing them to be compositional, they still have the *ability* to implicitly learn compositional structure. To test this hypothesis, we apply ROLE to a standard RNN-based seq2seq model (Sutskever et al., 2014) trained on a fully compositional task. Because the RNN has no constraint forcing it to use TPRs, we do not know *a priori* whether there exists any solution that ROLE could learn; thus, if ROLE does learn anything it will be a significant empirical finding about how these RNNs operate.

We consider the SCAN task (Lake and Baroni, 2018), which was designed to test compositional generalization and systematicity. SCAN is a synthetic semantic parsing task: an input sequence describing an action plan, e.g.,

jump opposite left, is mapped to a sequence of primitive actions, e.g., TL TL JUMP (see Sec. 5.3 for a complex example). We use TL to abbreviate TURN_LEFT, sometimes written LTURN; similarly, we use TR for TURN_RIGHT. The SCAN mapping is defined by a complete set of compositional rules (Lake and Baroni, 2018, Supplementary Fig. 7).

5.1 The compositional structure of SCAN encoder representations

For our target SCAN encoder $\mathcal{E}$, we trained a standard GRU with one hidden layer of dimension 100 for 100,000 steps (batch-size 1) with a dropout of 0.1 on the simple train-test split (hyperparameters determined by a limited search; see Appendix A.3). $\mathcal{E}$ achieves 98.47% (full-string) accuracy on the test set. Thus $\mathcal{E}$ provides what we want: a standard RNN achieving near-perfect accuracy on a non-trivial fully compositional task.

After training, we extract the final hidden embedding from the encoder for each example in the training and test sets. These are the encodings we attempt to approximate as explicitly compositional TPRs. We provide ROLE with 50 roles to use as it wants (hyperparameters described in Appendix A.4). We evaluate the substitution accuracy that this learned role scheme provides in three ways. The **continuous** method tests ROLE in the same way as it was trained, with input symbol s_t assigned role vector $r_t = R\,a_t$. The continuous method does not produce a discrete set of role vectors because the linear layer that generates a_t allows for continuously-valued weights. The remaining two methods test the efficacy of a truly discrete set of role vectors. First, in the **snapped** method, a_t is replaced at evaluation time by the one-hot vector m_t singling out role $m_t = \arg\max(a_t)$: $r_t = R\,m_t$. This method serves the goal of enforcing the discreteness of roles, but it is expected to decrease performance because it tests ROLE in a different way than it was trained. Our final evaluation method, the **discrete** method, uses discrete roles without having such a train/test discrepancy by using a two-stage process. In the first stage, the snapped method is used to output one-hot vector roles m_t for every symbol in the dataset. In the second stage, we train a TPE which does not learn roles but rather uses the one-hot vector m_t as input during training. In this case, ROLE acts as an automatic data labeler, assigning a role to every input word.

Continuous	Snapped	Discrete	LTR	RTL	Bi	Tree	Wickel	BOW
94.83%	81.71% ± 7.28	92.44%	6.68%	6.96%	10.72%	4.31%	44.00%	4.52%

Table 1: Mean substitution accuracy for learned (bold) and hand-defined role schemes on SCAN across three random initializations. Standard deviation was below 1% for all schemes except for snapped. Substitution accuracy is measured by feeding ROLE's approximation to the target decoder. (Sec. 5.1)

For comparison, we also train TPEs using a variety of discrete hand-crafted role schemes: left-to-right (LTR), right-to-left (RTL), bidirectional (Bi), tree position, neighbor-based Wickelrole (Wickel), and bag-of-words (BOW) (descriptions of these role schemes are in Appendix A.1).

The mean substitution accuracy from these different methods is shown in Table 1. All of the predefined role schemes provide poor approximations, none surpassing 44.00% accuracy. The role scheme learned by ROLE does significantly better than any of the predefined role schemes: when tested with the basic, continuous role-attention method, the accuracy is 94.83%.

The success of ROLE tells us two things. First, it shows that the target model's compositional behavior relies on compositional internal representations: it was by no means guaranteed to be the case that ROLE would be successful here, so the fact that it is successful tells us that the encoder has learned compositional representations. Second, it adds further validation to the efficacy of ROLE, because it shows that it can be a useful analysis tool in cases of significantly greater complexity than the simple string manipulation tasks studied in McCoy et al. (2019a). In fact, it allows us to *write in closed form the embedding* $e(S)$ of an input $S = s_1 \ldots s_T$ that is learned by the SCAN encoder, to an excellent degree of approximation (as measured by substitution accuracy): $e(S) = \mathbb{W} \sum_{t=1}^{T} \boldsymbol{f}_{\tau(s_t)} \otimes \boldsymbol{r}_{\rho(s_t)} + \boldsymbol{b}$, where $\tau(s_t)$ is symbol s_t's type, $\rho(s_t)$ is the role assigned to s_t by the algorithm discussed next, and the matrices $\mathbb{W}$, $\boldsymbol{F} = [\boldsymbol{f}_1 \ldots \boldsymbol{f}_{n_\mathrm{F}}]$, and $\boldsymbol{R} = [\boldsymbol{r}_1 \ldots \boldsymbol{r}_{n_\mathrm{R}}]$ and bias vector $\boldsymbol{b}$ are learned by ROLE. Note that this expression is bilinear, even though the GRU encoder that generates it includes nonlinearities.

5.2 Interpreting the learned role scheme

By analyzing the roles assigned by ROLE to the sequences in the SCAN training set, we created a symbolic algorithm for predicting which role will be assigned to each filler. This section covers the primary factors of the algorithm, while the entire algorithm is described in Appendix A.5 and discussed at additional length in Appendix A.6. Though the algorithm was created based only on sequences in the SCAN training set, it is equally successful at predicting which roles will be assigned to test sequences, exactly matching ROLE's predicted roles for 98.7% of sequences.

The algorithm illuminates how the filler-role scheme encodes information relevant to the task. First, one of the initial facts that the decoder must determine is whether the sequence is a single command, a pair of subcommands connected by and, or a pair of subcommands connected by after; such a determination is crucial for knowing the basic structure of the output (how many actions to perform and in what order). We have found that role 30 is used for, and only for, the filler and, while role 17 is used in and only in sequences containing after (usually with after as the filler bound to role 17). Thus, the decoder can use these roles to tell which basic structure is in play: if role 30 is present, it is an and sequence; if role 17 is present, it is an after sequence; otherwise it is a single command.

Once the decoder has established the basic syntactic structure of the output, it must then fill in the particular actions. This can be accomplished using the remaining roles, which mainly encode absolute position within a subcommand. For example, the last word of a subcommand before after (e.g., jump **left** after walk twice) is always assigned role 8, while the last word of a subcommand after after (e.g., jump left after walk **twice**) is always assigned role 46. Therefore, once the decoder knows (based on the presence of role 17) that it is dealing with an after sequence, it can check for the fillers bound to roles 8 and 46 to begin to figure out what the two subcommands surrounding after look like. The identity of the last word in a subcommand is informative because that is where a cardinality (i.e., twice or thrice) appears if there is one. Thus, by checking what filler is at the end of a subcommand, the model can determine whether there is a cardinality present and, if so, which one.

ROLE itself does not provide an interpretation for the symbolic structure it generates, but we have shown that this structure can be successfully interpreted by humans. By contrast, it is very difficult to interpret the continuous neuron values of RNN representations; even the rare successful cases of doing so, such as Lakretz et al. (2019) and Mu and Andreas (2020), only interpret a few isolated units, while we were able to exhaustively explain the entire symbolic structure discovered by ROLE.

5.3 Precision constituent-surgery on internal representations produces desired outputs

The substitution-accuracy results above show that if the *entire* learned representation is replaced by ROLE's approximation, the output remains correct. But do the *individual word embeddings* in this TPR have the appropriate causal consequences when processed by the decoder?

To address this causal question (Pearl, 2000), we actively intervene on the constituent structure of the internal representations by replacing one constituent with another syntactically equivalent one,[2] and see whether this produces the expected change in the output of the decoder. We take the encoding generated by the RNN encoder $\mathcal{E}$ for an input such as jump opposite left, subtract the vector embedding of the opposite constituent, add the embedding of the around constituent, and see whether this causes the output to change from the correct output for jump opposite left (TL TL JUMP) to the correct output for jump around left (TL JUMP TL JUMP TL JUMP TL JUMP). The roles in these constituents are determined by the algorithm of Appendix A.5. If changing a word leads other roles in the sequence to change (according to the algorithm), we update the encoding with those new roles as well. Such surgery can be viewed as a more general extension of the analogy approach used by Mikolov et al. (2013) for analysis of word embeddings. An example of applying a sequence of five such constituent surgeries to a sequence is shown in Figure 5 (left). Even long sequences of such replacements produce the expected change in the decoder's output with high accuracy (Figure 5,

right), indicating that the compositional structure discovered by ROLE does play a central causal role in the model's behavior.

6 Partially-compositional NLP tasks

The previous sections explored fully-compositional tasks where there is a strong signal for compositionality. In this section, we explore whether the representations of NNs trained on tasks that are only partially-compositional also capture compositional structure. Partially-compositional tasks are especially challenging to model because a fully-compositional model may enforce compositionality too strictly to handle the non-compositional aspects of the task, while a model without a compositional bias may not learn any sort of compositionality from the weak cues in the training set.

We test four sentence encoding models for compositionality: InferSent (Conneau et al., 2017), Skip-thought (Kiros et al., 2015), Stanford Sentiment Model (SST) (Socher et al., 2013), and SPINN (Bowman et al., 2016). For each of these models, we extract the encodings for the SNLI premise sentences (Bowman et al., 2015). We use the extracted embeddings to train ROLE with 50 roles available (additional training information provided in Appendix A.8).

As a baseline, we also train TPEs that use predefined role schemes (hyperparameters described in Appendix A.7). For all of the sentence embedding models except Skip-thought, ROLE with continuous attention provides the lowest mean squared error at approximating the encoding (Table 2). The BOW (bag-of-words) role scheme represents a TPE that uses a degenerate 'compositional' structure which assigns the same role to every filler; for each of the sentence embedding models tested except for SST, performance is within the same order of magnitude as structure-free BOW. Parikh et al. (2016) found that a bag-of-words model scores extremely well on Natural Language Inference despite having no knowledge of word order, showing that structure is not necessary to perform well on the sorts of tasks commonly used to train sentence encoders. Although not definitive, the ROLE results provide no evidence that these models' sentence embeddings possess compositional structure.

In future work, it would be interesting to perform a similar analysis on Transformer architectures (Vaswani et al., 2017). Such models have displayed impressive syntactic generalization (Hu

---

[2] We extract syntactic categories from the SCAN grammar (Lake and Baroni, 2018, Supplementary Fig. 6) by saying that two words belong to the same category if every occurrence of one could be grammatically replaced by the other. We do not replace occurrences of and and after since the presence of either of these words causes substantial changes in the roles assigned within the sequence (Appendix A.5).

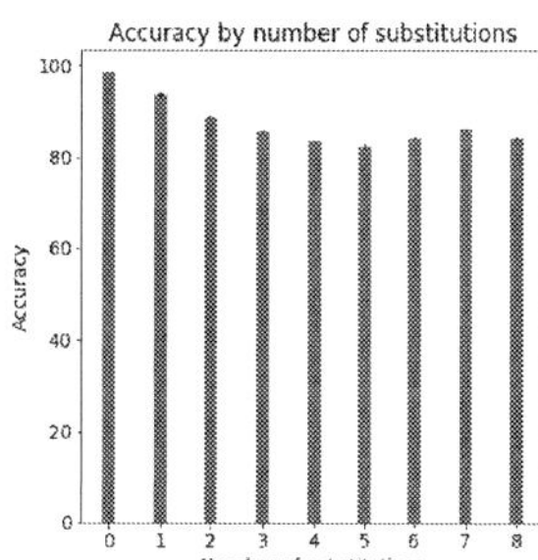

```
run:11 left:36 twice:8 after:43 jump:10 opposite:17 right:4 thrice:46 →
     TR TR JUMP TR TR JUMP TR TR JUMP TL RUN TL RUN
 − run:11  + look:11 →
     TR TR JUMP TR TR JUMP TR TR JUMP TL LOOK TL LOOK
 − jump:10  + walk:10 →
     TR TR WALK TR TR WALK TR TR WALK TL LOOK TL LOOK
 − left:36  + right:36 →
     TR TR WALK TR TR WALK TR TR WALK TR LOOK TR LOOK
 − twice:8  + thrice:8 →
     TR TR WALK TR TR WALK TR TR WALK TR LOOK
     TR LOOK TR LOOK
 − opposite:17  + around:17 →
     TR WALK TR WALK TR WALK TR WALK TR WALK TR WALK
     TR WALK TR WALK TR WALK TR WALK TR WALK TR WALK
     TR LOOK TR LOOK TR LOOK
```


Figure 5: Left: Example of successive constituent surgeries. The roles assigned to the input symbols are indicated in the first line (e.g., run was assigned role 11). Altered output symbols are in blue. The model produces the correct outputs for all cases shown here. Right: Mean constituent-surgery accuracy across three runs. Standard deviation is below 1% for each number of substitutions. (Sec. 5.3)

	Continuous	**Snapped**	**Discrete**	LTR	RTL	Bi	Tree	BOW
InferSent	**4.05e-4**	4.15e-4	5.76e-4	8.21e-4	9.70e-4	9.16e-4	7.78e-4	4.34e-4
Skip-thought	9.30e-5	9.32e-5	9.85e-5	9.91e-5	1.78e-3	3.95e-4	9.64e-5	**8.87e-5**
SST	**5.58e-3**	6.72e-3	6.48e-3	8.35e-3	9.29e-3	8.55e-3	5.99e-3	9.38e-3
SPINN	**.139**	.151	.147	.184	.189	.181	.178	.176

Table 2: MSE loss for learned (bold) and hand-crafted role schemes on sentence embedding models. (Sec. 6)

et al., 2020) and few-shot learning of compositional tasks (Brown et al., 2020), both of which suggest that they learn substantial degrees of compositional structure; thus, ROLE may be more likely to discover meaningful structure in Transformers than in the sentence-embedding models in Table 2. Further work has found impressive degrees of syntactic structure in Transformer encodings (Hewitt and Manning, 2019), suggesting that there may well be compositional structure for ROLE to pick up on. The main difficulty in applying ROLE to Transformers—and the reason we did not include Transformers in our study—is that the sentence representation used by a Transformer is typically viewed as a variable-sized collection of vectors, whereas ROLE requires single-vector representations; this discrepancy must be overcome if ROLE is to be applied to Transformers.

One past work (Jawahar et al., 2019) has applied ROLE's precursor (the TPDN of McCoy et al. (2019a)) to Transformer representations by choosing the [CLS] token of BERT (Devlin et al., 2019) as the single-vector sentence encoding to decompose. Jawahar et al. found that these encodings were approximated better by human-specified tree-position roles than by other human-specified candidates (e.g., left-to-right and right-to-left roles). By removing the constraint of requiring human-designed role schemes, ROLE may be able to discover other role schemes that approximate BERT's encodings even more closely.

7 Conclusion

We have introduced ROLE, a neural network that learns to approximate the representations of an existing target neural network $\mathcal{E}$ using an explicit symbolic structure. ROLE successfully discovers symbolic structure in a standard RNN trained on the fully-compositional SCAN semantic parsing task, even though the RNN has no such structure explicitly present in its architecture. This yields a closed-form equation for the RNN's encoding of any input string. When applied to sentence embedding models trained on partially-compositional tasks, ROLE performs better than hand-specified hypothesized structures but still provides little evidence that the sentence encodings represent compositional structure.

While this work has shown that NNs can converge to TPRs to solve compositional tasks, it is still unknown how the weights in the NN actually convert the raw input into a TPR. To investigate this process, in future work we plan to apply our technique to representations of partial sequences. For instance, when the complete input is jump right twice, the target RNN must first represent `jump right` as a well-formed TPR at the point when only those two words have been encountered. The representation then needs to be updated when the next word, `twice`, is encountered. By studying the nature of that update, we can gain insight into how the target model builds up a TPR from the input elements.

Uncovering the latent symbolic structure of NN representations learned for fully-compositional tasks is a significant step towards explaining how NNs achieve the level of compositional generalization that they do. In addition, by illuminating shortcomings in the representations learned for standard tasks that are not fully-compositional, ROLE can help suggest types of inductive bias for improving models' generalization with standard, partially-compositional datasets.

Acknowledgments

This material is based upon work supported by the National Science Foundation Graduate Research Fellowship Program under Grant No. 1746891, and work partially supported by NSF grant BCS1344269. Any opinions, findings, and conclusions or recommendations expressed in this material are those of the authors and do not necessarily reflect the views of the National Science Foundation.

For helpful comments we are grateful to the members of the Johns Hopkins Neurosymbolic Computation group and the Microsoft Research AI Deep Learning Group. Any errors remain our own.

References

Samira Abnar, Lisa Beinborn, Rochelle Choenni, and Willem Zuidema. 2019. Blackbox meets blackbox: Representational similarity & stability analysis of neural language models and brains. In *Proceedings of the 2019 ACL Workshop BlackboxNLP: Analyzing and Interpreting Neural Networks for NLP*, pages 191–203, Florence, Italy. Association for Computational Linguistics.

Yossi Adi, Einat Kermany, Yonatan Belinkov, Ofer Lavi, and Yoav Goldberg. 2017. Fine-grained analysis of sentence embeddings using auxiliary prediction tasks. In *International Conference on Learning Representations*.

Jacob Andreas. 2019. Measuring compositionality in representation learning. In *International Conference on Learning Representations*.

Yonatan Belinkov, Lluís Màrquez, Hassan Sajjad, Nadir Durrani, Fahim Dalvi, and James Glass. 2017. Evaluating layers of representation in neural machine translation on part-of-speech and semantic tagging tasks. In *Proceedings of the Eighth International Joint Conference on Natural Language Processing (Volume 1: Long Papers)*, pages 1–10, Taipei, Taiwan. Asian Federation of Natural Language Processing.

Terra Blevins, Omer Levy, and Luke Zettlemoyer. 2018. Deep RNNs encode soft hierarchical syntax. In *Proceedings of the 56th Annual Meeting of the Association for Computational Linguistics (Volume 2: Short Papers)*, pages 14–19, Melbourne, Australia. Association for Computational Linguistics.

Samuel R. Bowman, Gabor Angeli, Christopher Potts, and Christopher D. Manning. 2015. A large annotated corpus for learning natural language inference. In *Proceedings of the 2015 Conference on Empirical Methods in Natural Language Processing*, pages 632–642, Lisbon, Portugal. Association for Computational Linguistics.

Samuel R. Bowman, Jon Gauthier, Abhinav Rastogi, Raghav Gupta, Christopher D. Manning, and Christopher Potts. 2016. A fast unified model for parsing and sentence understanding. In *Proceedings of the 54th Annual Meeting of the Association for Computational Linguistics (Volume 1: Long Papers)*, pages 1466–1477. Association for Computational Linguistics.

Tom B Brown, Benjamin Mann, Nick Ryder, Melanie Subbiah, Jared Kaplan, Prafulla Dhariwal, Arvind Neelakantan, Pranav Shyam, Girish Sastry, Amanda Askell, et al. 2020. Language models are few-shot learners. *arXiv preprint arXiv:2005.14165*.

Kyunghyun Cho, Bart van Merriënboer, Caglar Gulcehre, Dzmitry Bahdanau, Fethi Bougares, Holger Schwenk, and Yoshua Bengio. 2014. Learning phrase representations using RNN encoder–decoder for statistical machine translation. In *Proceedings of the 2014 Conference on Empirical Methods in Natural Language Processing (EMNLP)*, pages 1724–1734, Doha, Qatar. Association for Computational Linguistics.

Grzegorz Chrupała and Afra Alishahi. 2019. Correlating neural and symbolic representations of language. In *Proceedings of the 57th Annual Meeting of the Association for Computational Linguistics*, pages 2952–2962, Florence, Italy. Association for Computational Linguistics.

Alexis Conneau and Douwe Kiela. 2018. SentEval: An evaluation toolkit for universal sentence representations. In *Proceedings of the Eleventh International Conference on Language Resources and Evaluation (LREC 2018)*, Miyazaki, Japan. European Language Resources Association (ELRA).

Alexis Conneau, Douwe Kiela, Holger Schwenk, Loïc Barrault, and Antoine Bordes. 2017. Supervised learning of universal sentence representations from natural language inference data. In *Proceedings of the 2017 Conference on Empirical Methods in Natural Language Processing*, pages 670–680. Association for Computational Linguistics.

Alexis Conneau, German Kruszewski, Guillaume Lample, Loïc Barrault, and Marco Baroni. 2018. What you can cram into a single $&!#* vector: Probing sentence embeddings for linguistic properties. In *Proceedings of the 56th Annual Meeting of the Association for Computational Linguistics (Volume 1: Long Papers)*, pages 2126–2136, Melbourne, Australia. Association for Computational Linguistics.

Ishita Dasgupta, Demi Guo, Samuel J Gershman, and Noah D Goodman. 2019. Analyzing machine-learned representations: A natural language case study. *arXiv preprint arXiv:1909.05885*.

Jacob Devlin, Ming-Wei Chang, Kenton Lee, and Kristina Toutanova. 2019. BERT: Pre-training of deep bidirectional transformers for language understanding. In *Proceedings of the 2019 Conference of the North American Chapter of the Association for Computational Linguistics: Human Language Technologies, Volume 1 (Long and Short Papers)*, pages 4171–4186, Minneapolis, Minnesota. Association for Computational Linguistics.

Mario Giulianelli, Jack Harding, Florian Mohnert, Dieuwke Hupkes, and Willem Zuidema. 2018. Under the hood: Using diagnostic classifiers to investigate and improve how language models track agreement information. In *Proceedings of the 2018 EMNLP Workshop BlackboxNLP: Analyzing and Interpreting Neural Networks for NLP*, pages 240–248, Brussels, Belgium. Association for Computational Linguistics.

Emily Goodwin, Koustuv Sinha, and Timothy J. O'Donnell. 2020. Probing linguistic systematicity. In *Proceedings of the 58th Annual Meeting of the Association for Computational Linguistics*, pages 1958–1969, Online. Association for Computational Linguistics.

John Hewitt and Christopher D Manning. 2019. A structural probe for finding syntax in word representations. In *Proceedings of the 2019 Conference of the North American Chapter of the Association for Computational Linguistics: Human Language Technologies, Volume 1 (Long and Short Papers)*, pages 4129–4138.

Sepp Hochreiter and Jürgen Schmidhuber. 1997. Long short-term memory. *Neural Computation*, 9(8):1735–1780.

Jennifer Hu, Jon Gauthier, Peng Qian, Ethan Wilcox, and Roger P Levy. 2020. A systematic assessment of syntactic generalization in neural language models. In *Proceedings of the 58th Annual Meeting of the Association for Computational Linguistics*, Seattle, Washington. Association for Computational Linguistics.

Dieuwke Hupkes, Verna Dankers, Mathijs Mul, and Elia Bruni. 2020. Compositionality decomposed: How do neural networks generalise? *Journal of Artificial Intelligence Research*, 67:757–795.

Dieuwke Hupkes, Sara Veldhoen, and Willem Zuidema. 2018. Visualisation and 'diagnostic classifiers' reveal how recurrent and recursive neural networks process hierarchical structure. *Journal of Artificial Intelligence Research*, 61:907–926.

Ganesh Jawahar, Benoît Sagot, and Djamé Seddah. 2019. What does BERT learn about the structure of language? In *Proceedings of the 57th Annual Meeting of the Association for Computational Linguistics*, pages 3651–3657, Florence, Italy. Association for Computational Linguistics.

Diederik Kingma and Jimmy Ba. 2015. Adam: A method for stochastic optimization. In *International Conference for Learning Representations*.

Ryan Kiros, Yukun Zhu, Ruslan R Salakhutdinov, Richard Zemel, Raquel Urtasun, Antonio Torralba, and Sanja Fidler. 2015. Skip-thought vectors. In *Advances in Neural Information Processing Systems*, pages 3294–3302.

Dan Klein and Christopher D Manning. 2003. Accurate unlexicalized parsing. In *Proceedings of the 41st Annual Meeting on Association for Computational Linguistics-Volume 1*, pages 423–430. Association for Computational Linguistics.

Brenden M. Lake and Marco Baroni. 2018. Generalization without systematicity: On the compositional skills of sequence-to-sequence recurrent networks. In *International Conference on Machine Learning*.

Yair Lakretz, German Kruszewski, Theo Desbordes, Dieuwke Hupkes, Stanislas Dehaene, and Marco Baroni. 2019. The emergence of number and syntax units in LSTM language models. In *Proceedings of the 2019 Conference of the North American Chapter of the Association for Computational Linguistics: Human Language Technologies, Volume 1 (Long and Short Papers)*, pages 11–20, Minneapolis, Minnesota. Association for Computational Linguistics.

Yuanpeng Li, Liang Zhao, Jianyu Wang, and Joel Hestness. 2019. Compositional generalization for primitive substitutions. In *Proceedings of the 2019 Conference on Empirical Methods in Natural Language Processing and the 9th International Joint Conference on Natural Language Processing (EMNLP-IJCNLP)*, pages 4293–4302, Hong Kong, China. Association for Computational Linguistics.

Tal Linzen, Emmanuel Dupoux, and Yoav Goldberg. 2016. Assessing the ability of LSTMs to learn syntax-sensitive dependencies. *Transactions of the ACL*.

Rebecca Marvin and Tal Linzen. 2018. Targeted syntactic evaluation of language models. In *Proceedings of the 2018 Conference on Empirical Methods in Natural Language Processing*, pages 1192–1202, Brussels, Belgium. Association for Computational Linguistics.

R. Thomas McCoy, Tal Linzen, Ewan Dunbar, and Paul Smolensky. 2019a. RNNs implicitly implement tensor-product representations. In *International Conference on Learning Representations*.

R. Thomas McCoy, Ellie Pavlick, and Tal Linzen. 2019b. Right for the wrong reasons: Diagnosing syntactic heuristics in natural language inference. In *Proceedings of the 57th Annual Meeting of the Association for Computational Linguistics*, pages 3428–3448, Florence, Italy. Association for Computational Linguistics.

Tomas Mikolov, Wen-tau Yih, and Geoffrey Zweig. 2013. Linguistic regularities in continuous space word representations. In *Proceedings of the 2013 Conference of the North American Chapter of the Association for Computational Linguistics: Human Language Technologies*, pages 746–751, Atlanta, Georgia. Association for Computational Linguistics.

Jesse Mu and Jacob Andreas. 2020. Compositional explanations of neurons. In *Advances in Neural Information Processing Systems 33*.

Christian W Omlin and C Lee Giles. 1996. Extraction of rules from discrete-time recurrent neural networks. *Neural networks*, 9(1):41–52.

Hamid Palangi, Paul Smolensky, Xiaodong He, and Li Deng. 2017. Question-answering with grammatically-interpretable representations. In *Proceedings of the Association for the Advancement of Artificial Intelligence*.

Ankur Parikh, Oscar Täckström, Dipanjan Das, and Jakob Uszkoreit. 2016. A decomposable attention model for natural language inference. In *Proceedings of the 2016 Conference on Empirical Methods in Natural Language Processing*, pages 2249–2255, Austin, Texas. Association for Computational Linguistics.

Judea Pearl. 2000. *Causality*. MIT Press, Cambridge, MA.

Matthew Peters, Mark Neumann, Luke Zettlemoyer, and Wen-tau Yih. 2018. Dissecting contextual word embeddings: Architecture and representation. In *Proceedings of the 2018 Conference on Empirical Methods in Natural Language Processing*, pages 1499–1509, Brussels, Belgium. Association for Computational Linguistics.

Adam Poliak, Aparajita Haldar, Rachel Rudinger, J. Edward Hu, Ellie Pavlick, Aaron Steven White, and Benjamin Van Durme. 2018. Collecting diverse natural language inference problems for sentence representation evaluation. In *Proceedings of the 2018 Conference on Empirical Methods in Natural Language Processing*, pages 67–81, Brussels, Belgium. Association for Computational Linguistics.

Abhilasha Ravichander, Yonatan Belinkov, and Eduard Hovy. 2020. Probing the probing paradigm: Does probing accuracy entail task relevance? *arXiv preprint arXiv:2005.00719*.

Yikang Shen, Shawn Tan, Alessandro Sordoni, and Aaron Courville. 2019. Ordered neurons: Integrating tree structures into recurrent neural networks. In *International Conference on Learning Representations*.

Paul Smolensky. 1990. Tensor product variable binding and the representation of symbolic structures in connectionist systems. *Artif. Intell.*, 46(1-2):159–216.

Richard Socher, Alex Perelygin, Jean Wu, Jason Chuang, Christopher D. Manning, Andrew Ng, and Christopher Potts. 2013. Recursive deep models for semantic compositionality over a sentiment treebank. In *Proceedings of the 2013 Conference on Empirical Methods in Natural Language Processing*, pages 1631–1642, Seattle, Washington, USA. Association for Computational Linguistics.

Ilya Sutskever, Oriol Vinyals, and Quoc V. Le. 2014. Sequence to sequence learning with neural networks. In *Advances in Neural Information Processing Systems*, pages 3104–3112.

Ian Tenney, Patrick Xia, Berlin Chen, Alex Wang, Adam Poliak, R. Thomas McCoy, Najoung Kim, Benjamin Van Durme, Sam Bowman, Dipanjan Das, and Ellie Pavlick. 2019. What do you learn from context? probing for sentence structure in contextualized word representations. In *International Conference on Learning Representations*.

Eva Vanmassenhove, Jinhua Du, and Andy Way. 2017. Investigating 'aspect' in NMT and SMT: Translating the English simple past and present perfect. *Computational Linguistics in the Netherlands Journal*, 7:109–128.

Ashish Vaswani, Noam Shazeer, Niki Parmar, Jakob Uszkoreit, Llion Jones, Aidan N Gomez, Łukasz Kaiser, and Illia Polosukhin. 2017. Attention is all you need. In *Advances in Neural Information Processing Systems*, pages 5998–6008.

Elena Voita and Ivan Titov. 2020. Information-theoretic probing with minimum description length. *arXiv preprint arXiv:2003.12298*.

Alex Wang, Amanpreet Singh, Julian Michael, Felix Hill, Omer Levy, and Samuel Bowman. 2018. GLUE: A multi-task benchmark and analysis platform for natural language understanding. In *Proceedings of the 2018 EMNLP Workshop BlackboxNLP: Analyzing and Interpreting Neural Networks for NLP*, pages 353–355, Brussels, Belgium. Association for Computational Linguistics.

Alex Warstadt, Alicia Parrish, Haokun Liu, Anhad Mohananey, Wei Peng, Sheng-Fu Wang, and Samuel R Bowman. 2020. BLiMP: A benchmark of linguistic minimal pairs for english. *Proceedings of the Society for Computation in Linguistics.*

Gail Weiss, Yoav Goldberg, and Eran Yahav. 2018. Extracting automata from recurrent neural networks using queries and counterexamples. In *International Conference on Machine Learning*, pages 5244–5253.

Wayne A. Wickelgren. 1969. Context-sensitive coding, associative memory, and serial order in (speech) behavior. *Psychological Review*, 76(1):1–15.

Yonghui Wu, Mike Schuster, Zhifeng Chen, Quoc V. Le, Mohammad Norouzi, Wolfgang Macherey, Maxim Krikun, Yuan Cao, Qin Gao, Klaus Macherey, Jeff Klingner, Apurva Shah, Melvin Johnson, Xiaobing Liu, Lukasz Kaiser, Stephan Gouws, Yoshikiyo Kato, Taku Kudo, Hideto Kazawa, Keith Stevens, George Kurian, Nishant Patil, Wei Wang, Cliff Young, Jason Smith, Jason Riesa, Alex Rudnick, Oriol Vinyals, Greg Corrado, Macduff Hughes, and Jeffrey Dean. 2016. Google's neural machine translation system: Bridging the gap between human and machine translation. *arXiv preprint arXiv:1609.08144.*

A Appendix

A.1 Designed role schemes

We use six hand-specified role schemes as a baseline to compare the learned role schemes against. Examples of each role scheme are shown in Table 3.

1. Left-to-right (LTR): Each filler's role is its index in the sequence, counting from left to right.

2. Right-to-left (RTL): Each filler's role is its index in the sequence, counting from right to left.

3. Bidirectional (Bi): Each filler's role is a pair of indices, where the first index counts from left to right, and the second index counts from right to left.

4. Tree: Each filler's role is given by its position in a tree. This depends on a tree parsing algorithm.

5. Wickelroles (Wickel): Each filler's role is a 2-tuple containing the filler before it and the filler after it. (Wickelgren, 1969)

6. Bag-of-words (BOW): Each filler is assigned the same role. The position and context of the filler is ignored.

A.2 ROLE regularization

Letting $A = \{a_t\}_{t=1}^{T}$, the regularization term applied during ROLE training is $R = \lambda(R_1 + R_2 + R_3)$, where λ is a regularization hyperparameter and:

$$R_1(A) = \sum_{t=1}^{T} \sum_{\rho=1}^{n_R} [a_t]_\rho (1 - [a_t]_\rho);$$

$$R_2(A) = -\sum_{t=1}^{T} \sum_{\rho=1}^{n_R} [a_t]_\rho^2;$$

$$R_3(A) = \sum_{\rho=1}^{n_R} ([s_A]_\rho (1 - [s_A]_\rho))^2$$

Since each a_t results from a softmax, its elements are positive and sum to 1. Thus the factors in $R_1(A)$ are all non-negative, so R_1 assumes its minimal value of 0 when each a_t has binary elements; since these elements must sum to 1, such an a_t must be one-hot. $R_2(A)$ is also minimized

when each a_t is one-hot because when a vector's L^1 norm is 1, its L^2 norm is maximized when it is one-hot. Although each of these terms individually favor one-hot vectors, empirically we find that using both terms helps the training process. In a discrete symbolic structure, each position can hold at most one symbol, and the final term R_3 in ROLE's regularizer R is designed to encourage this. In the vector $s_A = \sum_{t=1}^{T} a_t$, the ρth element is the total attention weight, over all symbols in the string, assigned to the ρth role: in the discrete case, this must be 0 (if no symbol is assigned this role) or 1 (if a single symbol is assigned this role). Thus R_3 is minimized when all elements of s are 0 or 1 (R_3 is similar to R_1, but with squared terms since we are no longer assured each element is at most 1). It is important to normalize each role embedding in the role matrix $\mathbf{R}$ so that small attention weights have correspondingly small impacts on the weighted-sum role embedding.

A.3 RNN trained on SCAN

To train the standard RNN on SCAN, we ran a limited hyperparameter search similar to the procedure in Lake and Baroni (2018). Since our goal was to produce a single embedding that captured the entire input sequence, we fixed the architecture as a GRU with a single hidden layer. We did not train models with attention, to investigate whether a standard RNN could capture compositionality in its single bottleneck encoding. The remaining hyperparameters were hidden dimension and dropout. We ran a search over the hidden dimension sizes of 50, 100, 200, and 400 as well as dropout with a value of 0, .1, and .5 applied to the word embeddings and recurrent layer. Each network was trained with the Adam optimizer (Kingma and Ba, 2015) and a learning rate of .001 for 100,000 steps with a batch-size of 1. The best performing network had a hidden dimension or 100 and dropout of .1.

A.4 ROLE trained on SCAN

For the ROLE models trained to approximate the GRU encoder trained on SCAN, we used a filler dimension of 100, and a role dimension of 50 with 50 roles available. For training, we used the Adam (Kingma and Ba, 2015) optimizer with a learning rate of .001, batch size 32, and an early stopping patience of 10. The role assignment module used a bidirectional 2-layer LSTM (Hochreiter and Schmidhuber, 1997). We performed a hyperparameter search over the regularization coefficient λ

	3	1	1	6	5	2	3	1	9	7
Left-to-right	0	1	2	3	0	1	2	3	4	5
Right-to-left	3	2	1	0	5	4	3	2	1	0
Bidirectional	(0, 3)	(1, 2)	(2, 1)	(3, 0)	(0, 5)	(1, 4)	(2, 3)	(3, 2)	(4, 1)	(5, 0)
Wickelroles	#_1	3_1	1_6	1_#	#_2	5_3	2_1	3_9	1_7	9_#
Tree	L	RLL	RLR	RR	LL	LRLL	LRLR	LRRL	LRRR	R
Bag of words	r_0	r_0	r_0	r_0	r_0	r_0	r_0	r_0	r_0	r_0

Table 3: The assigned roles for two sequences, 3116 and 523197. Table reproduced from McCoy et al. (2019a).

using the values in the set [.1, .02, .01]. The best performing value was .02, and we used this model in our analysis.

The algorithm below characterizes our post-hoc interpretation of which roles the Role Learner will assign to elements of the input to the SCAN model. This algorithm was created by hand based on an analysis of the Role Learner's outputs for the elements of the SCAN training set. The algorithm works equally well on examples in the training set and the test set; on both datasets, it exactly matches the roles chosen by the Role Learner for 98.7% of sequences (20,642 out of 20,910).

A.5 A role-assignment algorithm implicitly learned by the SCAN seq2seq encoder

The input sequences have three basic types that are relevant to determining the role assignment: sequences that contain *and* (e.g., *jump around left and walk thrice*), sequences that contain *after* (e.g., *jump around left after walk thrice*), and sequences without *and* or *after* (e.g., *turn opposite right thrice*). Within commands containing *and* or *after*, it is convenient to break the command down into the command before the connecting word and the command after it; for example, in the command *jump around left after walk thrice*, these two components would be *jump around left* and *walk thrice*.

- Sequence with *and*:

  - Elements of the command before *and*:
    * Last word: 28
    * First word (if not also last word): 46
    * *opposite* if the command ends with *thrice*: 22
    * Direction word between *opposite* and *thrice*: 2
    * *opposite* if the command does not end with *thrice*: 2
    * Direction word after *opposite* but not before *thrice*: 4
    * *around*: 22
    * Direction word after *around*: 2
    * Direction word between an action word and *twice* or *thrice*: 2
  - Elements of the command before *and*:
    * First word: 11
    * Last word (if not also the first word): 36
    * Second-to-last word (if not also the first word): 3
    * Second of four words: 24
  - *and*: 30

- Sequence with *after*:

  - Elements of the command before *after*:
    * Last word: 8
    * Second-to-last word: 36
    * First word (if not the last or second-to-last word): 11
    * Second word (if not the last or second-to-last word): 3
  - Elements of the command after *after*:
    * Last word: 46
    * Second-to-last word: 4
    * First word if the command ends with *around right*: 4
    * First word if the command ends with *thrice* and contains a rotation: 10
    * First word if the command does not end with *around right* and does not contain both *thrice* and a rotation: 17
    * Second word if the command ends with *thrice*: 17
    * Second word if the command does not end with *thrice*: 10

- *after*: 17 if no other word has role 17 or if the command after *after* ends with *around left*; 43 otherwise

- Sequence without *and* or *after*:

  - Action word directly before a cardinality: 4

  - Action word before, but not directly before, a cardinality: 34

  - *thrice* directly after an action word: 2

  - *twice* directly after an action word: 2

  - *opposite* in a sequence ending with *twice*: 8

  - *opposite* in a sequence ending with *thrice*: 34

  - *around* in a sequence ending with a cardinality: 22

  - Direction word directly before a cardinality: 2

  - Action word in a sequence without a cardinality: 46

  - *opposite* in a sequence without a cardinality: 2

  - Direction after *opposite* in a sequence without a cardinality: 26

  - *around* in a sequence without a cardinality: 3

  - Direction after *around* in a sequence without a cardinality: 22

  - Direction directly after an action in a sequence without a cardinality: 22

To show how this works with an example, consider the input *jump around left after walk thrice*. The command before *after* is *jump around left*. *left*, as the last word, is given role 8. *around*, as the second-to-last word, gets role 36. *jump*, as a first word that is not also the last or second-to-last word gets role 11. The command after *after* is *walk thrice*. *thrice*, as the last word, gets role 46. *walk*, as the second-to-last word, gets role 4. Finally, *after* gets role 17 because no other elements have been assigned role 17 yet. These predicted outputs match those given by the Role Learner.

A.6 Discussion of the algorithm

We offer several observations about this algorithm.

1. This algorithm may seem convoluted, but a few observations can illuminate how the roles

assigned by such an algorithm support success on the SCAN task. First, a sequence will contain role 30 if and only if it contains *and*, and it will contain role 17 if and only if it contains *after*. Thus, by implicitly checking for the presence of these two roles (regardless of the fillers bound to them), the decoder can tell whether the output involves one or two basic commands, where the presence of *and* or *after* leads to two basic commands and the absence of both leads to one basic command. Moreover, if there are two basic commands, whether it is role 17 or role 30 that is present can tell the decoder whether the input order of these commands also corresponds to their output order (when it is *and* in play, i.e., role 30), or if the input order is reversed (when it is *after* in play, i.e., role 17).

With these basic structural facts established, the decoder can begin to decode the specific commands. For example, if the input is a sequence with *after*, it can begin with the command after *after*, which it can decode by checking which fillers are bound to the relevant roles for that type of command.

It may seem odd that so many of the roles are based on position (e.g., "first word" and "second-to-last word"), rather than more functionally-relevant categories such as "direction word." However, this approach may actually be more efficient: Each command consists of a single mandatory element (namely, an action word such as *walk* or *jump*) followed by several optional modifiers (namely, rotation words, direction words, and cardinalities). Because most of the word categories are optional, it might be inefficient to check for the presence of, e.g., a cardinality, since many sequences will not have one. By contrast, every sequence will have a last word, and checking the identity of the last word provides much functionally-relevant information: if that word is not a cardinality, then the decoder knows that there is no cardinality present in the command (because if there were, it would be the last word); and if it is a cardinality, then that is important to know, because the presence of *twice* or *thrice* can dramatically affect the shape of the output sequence. In this light, it is unsurprising that the SCAN encoder has implicitly learned several different roles that essentially mean the last element of a particular subcommand.

2. The algorithm does not constitute a simple, transparent role scheme. But its job is to describe the representations that the original network produces, and we have no a priori expectation about how complex that process may be. The role-assignment algorithm implicitly learned by ROLE is interpretable locally (each line is readily expressible in simple English), but not intuitively transparent globally. We see this as a positive result, in two respects.

First, it shows why ROLE is crucial: no human-generated role scheme would provide a good approximation to this algorithm. Such an algorithm can only be identified because ROLE is able to use gradient descent to find role schemes far more complex than any we would hypothesize intuitively. This enables us to analyze networks far more complex than we could analyze previously, being necessarily limited to hand-designed role schemes based on human intuitions about how to perform the task.

Second, when future work illuminates the computation in the original SCAN GRU seq2seq decoder, the baroqueness of the role-assignment algorithm that ROLE has shown to be implicit in the seq2seq encoder can potentially explain certain limitations in the original model, which is known to suffer from severe failures of systematic generalization outside the training distribution (Lake and Baroni, 2018). It is reasonable to hypothesize that systematic generalization requires that the encoder learn an implicit role scheme that is relatively simple and highly compositional. Future proposals for improving the systematic generalization of models on SCAN can be examined using ROLE to test the hypothesis that greater systematicity requires greater compositional simplicity in the role scheme implicitly learned by the encoder.

3. While the role-assignment algorithm of A.8.1 may not be simple, from a certain perspective, it is quite surprising that it is not far more complex. Although ROLE is provided 50 roles to learn to deploy as it likes, it only chooses to use 16 of them (only 16 are ever selected as the $\arg\max(a_t)$; see Sec. 6.1). Furthermore,

the SCAN grammar generates 20,910 input sequences, containing a total of 151,688 words (an average of 7.25 words per input). This means that, if one were to generate a series of conditional statements to determine which role is assigned to each word in every context, this could in theory require up to 151,688 conditionals (e.g., "if the filler is 'jump' in the context 'walk thrice after ___ opposite left', then assign role 17"). However, our algorithm involves just 47 conditionals. This reduction helps explain how the model performs so well on the test set: If it used many more of the 151,688 possible conditional rules, it would completely overfit the training examples in a way that would be unlikely to generalize. The 47-conditional algorithm we found is more likely to generalize by abstracting over many details of the context.

4. Were it not for ROLE's ability to characterize the representations generated by the original encoder in terms of implicit roles, providing an equally complete and accurate interpretation of those representations would necessarily require identifying the conditions determining the activation level of each of the 100 neurons hosting those representations. It seems to us grossly overly optimistic to estimate that each neuron's activation level in the representation of a given input could be characterized by a property of the input statable in, say, two lines of roughly 20 words/symbols; yet even then, the algorithm would require 200 lines, whereas the algorithm in A.8.1 requires 47 lines of that scale. Thus, by even such a crude estimate of the degree of complexity expected for an algorithm describing the representations in terms of neuron activities, the algorithm we find, stated over roles, is 4 times simpler.

A.7 TPEs trained on sentence embedding models

For each sentence embedding model, we trained three randomly initialized TPEs for each role scheme and selected the best performing one as measured by the lowest MSE. For each TPE, we used the original filler embedding from the sentence embedding model. This filler dimensionality is 25 for SST, 300 for SPINN and InferSent, and 620 for Skipthought. We applied a linear transformation to the pre-trained filler embedding where the input size is the dimensionality of the pre-trained embedding and the output size is also the dimensionality of the pre-trained embedding. This linearly transformed embedding is used as the filler vector in the filler-role binding in the TPE. For each TPE, we use a role dimension of 50. Training was done with a batch size of 32 using the Adam optimizer with a learning rate of .001.

To generate tree roles from the English sentences, we used the constituency parser released in version 3.9.1 of Stanford CoreNLP (Klein and Manning, 2003).

A.8 ROLE trained on sentence embedding models

For each sentence embedding model, we trained three randomly initialized ROLE models and selected the best performing one as measured by the lowest MSE. We used the original filler embedding from the sentence embedding model (25 for SST, 300 for SPINN and InferSent, and 620 for Skipthought). We applied a linear transformation to the pre-trained filler embedding where the input size is the dimensionality of the pre-trained embedding and the output size is also the dimensionality of the pre-trained embedding. This linearly transformed embedding is used as the filler vector in the filler-role binding in the TPE. We also applied a similar linear transformation to the pre-trained filler embedding before input to the role learner LSTM. For each ROLE model, we provide up to 50 roles with a role dimension of 50. Training was done with a batch size of 32 using the ADAM optimizer with a learning rate of .001. We performed a hyperparameter search over the regularization coefficient λ using the values in the set $\{1, 0.1, 0.01, 0.001, 0.0001\}$. For SST, SPINN, InferSent and SST, respectively, the best performing network used $\lambda = 0.001, 0.01, 0.001, 0.1$.

Structured Self-Attention Weights
Encode Semantics in Sentiment Analysis

Zhengxuan Wu[1], Thanh-Son Nguyen[2], Desmond C. Ong[2,3]
[1]Symbolic Systems Program, Stanford University
[2]Institute of High Performance Computing, Agency for Science, Technology and Research, Singapore
[3]Department of Information Systems and Analytics, National University of Singapore
wuzhengx@stanford.edu, Nguyen_Thanh_Son@ihpc.a-star.edu.sg,
dco@comp.nus.edu.sg

Abstract

Neural *attention*, especially the self-attention made popular by the Transformer, has become the workhorse of state-of-the-art natural language processing (NLP) models. Very recent work suggests that the self-attention in the Transformer encodes syntactic information; Here, we show that self-attention scores encode semantics by considering sentiment analysis tasks. In contrast to gradient-based feature attribution methods, we propose a simple and effective Layer-wise Attention Tracing (LAT) method to analyze structured attention weights. We apply our method to Transformer models trained on two tasks that have surface dissimilarities, but share common semantics— sentiment analysis of movie reviews and time-series valence prediction in life story narratives. Across both tasks, words with high aggregated attention weights were rich in emotional semantics, as quantitatively validated by an emotion lexicon labeled by human annotators. Our results show that structured attention weights encode rich semantics in sentiment analysis, and match human interpretations of semantics.

1 Introduction

In recent years, variants of neural network attention mechanisms such as local attention (Bahdanau et al., 2015; Luong et al., 2015) and self-attention in the Transformer (Vaswani et al., 2017) have become the *de facto* go-to neural models for a variety of NLP tasks including machine translation (Luong et al., 2015; Vaswani et al., 2017), syntactic parsing (Vinyals et al., 2015), and language modeling (Liu and Lapata, 2018; Dai et al., 2019).

Attention has brought about increased performance gains, but what do these values 'mean'? Previous studies have visualized and shown how learnt attention contributes to decisions in tasks like natural language inference and aspect-level sentiment (Lin et al., 2017; Wang et al., 2016;

Ghaeini et al., 2018). Recent studies on the Transformer (Vaswani et al., 2017) have demonstrated that attention based representations encode syntactic information (Tenney et al., 2019) such as anaphora (Voita et al., 2018; Goldberg, 2019), Parts-of-Speech (Vig and Belinkov, 2019) and dependencies (Raganato and Tiedemann, 2018; Hewitt and Manning, 2019; Clark et al., 2019). Other researchers have also done very recent extensive analyses on self-attention, by, for example, implementing gradient-based Layer-wise Relevance Propagation (LRP) method on the Transformer (Voita et al., 2019) to study attributions of graident-scores to heads, or graph-based aggregation method to visualize attention flows (Abnar and Zuidema, 2020). These very recent works have not looked at whether the structured attention weights themselves aggregate on tokens with strong semantic meaning in tasks such as sentiment analysis. Thus, it is still unclear if the attention on input words may actually encode semantic information relevant to the task.

In this paper, we were interested in extending previous studies on attention and syntax further, by probing the structured attention weights and studying whether these weights encode task-relevant semantic information. In contrast to gradient-based attribution methods (Voita et al., 2019), we were explicitly interested in probing learnt attention weights rather than analyzing gradients. To do this, we propose a Layer-wise Attention Tracing (LAT) method to aggregate the structured attention weights learnt by self-attention layers onto input tokens. We show that these attention scores on input tokens correlate with an external measure of semantics across two tasks: a sentiment analysis task on a movie review dataset, and an emotion understanding task on a life stories narrative dataset. These tasks differ in structure (single-example classification vs. time-series regression), and in domain (movie reviews vs. daily life events), but should share the same

Proceedings of the Third BlackboxNLP Workshop on Analyzing and Interpreting Neural Networks for NLP, pages 255–264
Online, November 20, 2020. ©2020 Association for Computational Linguistics

semantics, in that the same words should be important in both tasks. We propose a method of external validation of the semantics of these tasks, using emotion lexicons. We find evidence for the hypothesis that if self-attention mechanisms can learn emotion semantics, then LAT-calculated attention scores should be higher for words that have stronger emotional semantic meaning. [1]

2   Attention-based Model Architecture

We use an encoder-decoder architecture as shown in Fig. 1. Our encoder is identical to the encoder of the Transformer (Vaswani et al., 2017), with an additional local attention layer (Luong et al., 2015). Our decoder is task-specific: a simple Multilayer Perceptron (MLP) for the classification task, and a LSTM followed by a MLP for the time-series prediction task.

Self-attention Layers. The encoder is identical to the original Transformer encoder and consists of a series of stacked self-attention layers. Each layer contains a multi-head self-attention layer, followed by an element-wise feed forward layer and residual connections. Following Vaswani et al. (2017), we use $L = 6$ stacked layers and $H = 8$ heads, and a hidden dimension of $D = 512$.

We briefly recap the Transformer equations, to better illustrate our LAT method, which traces attention back through the layers. For a given self-attention layer $l \in [1, L]$, we denote the input to l using $X^l \in \mathbb{R}^{N \times D_e}$, which represents N tokens, each embedded using a D_e-dimensional embedding. We keep the same input embedding size for all layers. The first layer takes as input the word tokens. A self-attention layer learns a set of *Query*, *Key* and *Values* matrices that are indexed by l (i.e., weights are not shared across layers). Formally, these matrices are produced in parallel:

$$Q^l = f_q^l(X^l), \quad K^l = f_k^l(X^l), \quad V^l = f_v^l(X^l) \quad (1)$$

where $f_{\{q,k,v\}}^l(\cdot)$ are each parameterized by a linear layer, and each matrix is of size $N \times D$. To enable multi-head attention, Q, K and V are partitioned into H separate $N \times D_h$ attention heads indexed by $h \in [1, H]$, where $D_h = \frac{D}{H} = 64$.

Each head learns a self-attention matrix $\alpha_h^{s(l)}$ using the scaled inner product of Q_h and K_h followed

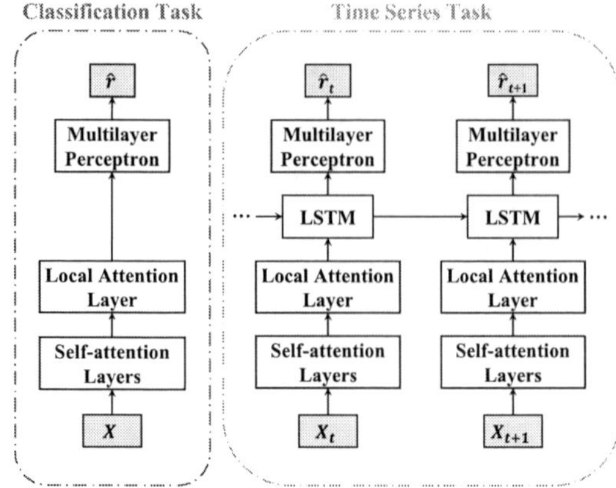

Figure 1: Attention-based encoder-decoder model architecture for classification task (left) and time-series task (right); The latter has a recurrent unit to generate predictions over time.

by a *softmax* operation. The self-attention matrix $\alpha_h^{s(l)}$ is then multiplied by V_h to produce Z_h^l:

$$\alpha_h^{s(l)} = \text{softmax}\left(\frac{Q_h^l K_h^{l\,T}}{\sqrt{D_h}}\right) \qquad \in \mathbb{R}^{N \times N} \quad (2)$$

$$Z_h^l = \alpha_h^{s(l)} V_h^l \qquad \in \mathbb{R}^{N \times D_h} \quad (3)$$

Next, we concatenate Z_h^l from each head h to produce the output of layer l (i.e., the input to layer $l + 1$) X^{l+1},

$$X^{l+1} = f_\psi^l([Z_1^l, ..., Z_H^l]) \qquad \in \mathbb{R}^{N \times D_e} \quad (4)$$

where $f_\psi^l(\cdot)$ is parameterized by two fully connected feed-forward layers (with 64 dimensions for the first layer then scaling back to D_e-dimensions) with residual connections and layer normalization. X^{l+1} is fed upwards to the next layer.

Local Attention Layer. The output from the last self-attention layer X^{L+1} is fed into a local attention layer. We then take a weighted sum over row vectors of the output, and produces a context vector c using learnt local attention vector α^c:

$$\alpha^c = \text{softmax}\left(f_\phi(X^{L+1})\right) \qquad \in \mathbb{R}^N \quad (5)$$

$$c = (X^{L+1})^T \alpha^c = \sum_{i=1}^{N} \alpha_i^c x_i^{L+1} \qquad \in \mathbb{R}^{D_e} \quad (6)$$

where $f_\phi(\cdot)$ is parameterized by a multi-layer perceptron (MLP) with two hidden layers that are 128-dimensional and 64-dimensional. The MLP layers are trained with dropout of $p = 0.3$.

Decoder. For the classification task, the context vector c is fed into a decoder $f_{dec}(\cdot)$ parameterized by a MLP to produce the output label. For the time-series task, context vectors c_t from each time t are fed into a LSTM (Hochreiter and Schmidhuber, 1997) layer with 300-dimensional hidden states before passing through a MLP. Both the MLP for the classification and the time-series tasks have the same 64-dimensional hidden space, and are trained with dropout of $p = 0.3$. A complete model description can be found in the Appendix.

3 Layer-wise Attention Tracing

To study whether structured attention weights encode semantics, we propose a tracing method, Layer-wise Attention Tracing (LAT), to trace the attention 'paid' to input tokens (i.e. words) through the self-attention layers in our encoder. LAT, illustrated in Fig. 2, involves three main steps. First, starting from the local attention layer and a fixed "quantity" of attention, we distribute attention weights back to Z_h^L, the last self-attention layer of each head $h \in [1, H]$. Second, we trace the attention back through each self-attention layer $l \in [1, L]$. Third, from the first layer of each head, we trace the attention back onto each token in the input sequence, by accumulating attention scores from each head to the corresponding position. We do not consider the decoder in LAT, as the MLP and LSTM layers in the decoder do not modify attention. Furthermore, we specifically ignore the feedforward layers and residual connections in the encoder, as we were interested in the attention α, not the neural activations they modify—this is our main differentiation from gradient-based or relevance-based work (Voita et al., 2019), and we note another recent paper (Abnar and Zuidema, 2020) that made the same assumptions.

Tracing Local Attention. Given an input sequence X of length N tokens, the forward pass of the model (Eqn. 1-6) transforms X into the context vector c. We consider how a fixed quantity of attention, A^c, gets divided back to the various heads. We refer to this quantity as the *Attention Score* that is accumulated down through the layers. From Eqn. 4 and Eqn. 6, we note that c is a function of concatenated $\mathbf{Z}^L$ from the last self-attention layer, from each of the heads:

$$c = \sum_{i=1}^{N} \alpha_i^c f_\psi^L([z_{1(i)}^L, ..., z_{H(i)}^L]) \tag{7}$$

where $z_{h(i)}^L$ is the attended *Value* vector from head $h \in [1, H]$ of the last layer L at position $i \in [1, N]$. On the forward pass, the contribution of head h at position i, $z_{h(i)}^L$, is weighted by α_i^c; Thus, on this first step of LAT, we divide the attention score A^c back to head h at position i, using α_i^c:

$$A_{h(i)}^{L+1} = \alpha_i^c A^c \tag{8}$$

We use this notation to allude that this is the attention weights coming down from the "$(L+1)$-th layer", to follow the logic of the next step of LAT. Without loss of generality, we can set the initial attention score at the top, A^c, to be 1, then all subsequent attention scores can be interpreted as a proportion of the initial attention score. Note that in our attention tracing, we are interested in accumulating the attention $A_{h(i)}^l$ for each layer $l \in [1, L]$ at each position i, and so we focus on the attention weights (and not the hidden states that the attention multiplies, $\mathbf{Z}_h$ or $\mathbf{V}_h$), which remain unchanged through f_ψ.

Tracing Self Attention. On the forward pass, Eqn. 3 applies the self-attention weights. We rewrite this equation to make the indices explicit:

$$z_{h(j)}^l = \sum_{i=1}^{N} \alpha_{h(i \to j)}^{s(l)} v_{h(i)}^l \tag{9}$$

where $v_{h(i)}^l$ denotes the i-th row of V_h^l (i.e., corresponding to the token in position i), and $\alpha_{h(i \to j)}^{s(l)}$ is the (j, i) element of $\alpha_h^{s(l)}$, such that it captures the attention from position i to position j. The attended values $\mathbf{Z}_h^l$ then undergo two sets of feed-forward layers: Eqn. 4 with f_ψ^l to get X^l and Eqn. 1 with f_v^l to get V_h^{l+1}.

Using $A_{h(j)}^l$ to denote the attention score accumulated at head h, position j, layer l, we can trace the attention coming down from the next-higher layer based on Eqn. 9:

$$A_{h(i)}^l = \sum_{j=1}^{N} \alpha_{h(i \to j)}^{s(l)} A_{h(j)}^{l+1} \tag{10}$$

To confirm our intuition, on the forward pass (see Eqn. 9 and Fig. 2), to get the hidden value at position j on the "upper" part of the layer, we sum $\alpha_{h(i \to j)}^{s(l)}$ over i (the indices of the "lower" layer). Thus, on the LAT pass downwards (Eqn. 10), to get $A_{h(i)}^l$ as position i on the "lower" layer, we sum the corresponding $\alpha_{h(i \to j)}^{s(l)}$'s over j.

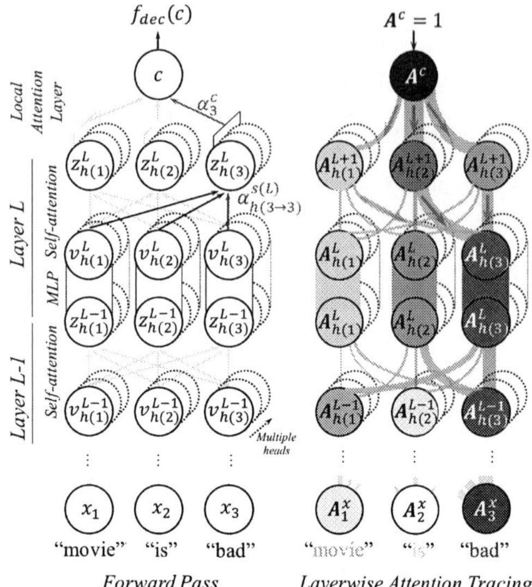

Figure 2: An illustration of the Layer-wise Attention Tracing (LAT) method with an example forward pass through head h. Left: On the forward pass, learnt attention weights are represented by lines producing $\mathbf{Z}_h^l$ from values $\mathbf{V}_h^l$ via self-attention (Eqn. 2-3) and the context vector c from the last layer via local attention (Eqn. 5). Dashed circles represents multiple heads, and vertical columns represent MLP transformations, which do not redistribution attention. Right: LAT on a 'backward pass'. The thickness of the edges represents accumulating attention. Attention from incoming edges are accumulated at each position in each layer, as in Eqn. 10. Darker colors maps to greater accumulated attention scores. In this example, the input token "bad" receives the highest attention score.

Tracing to input tokens. Finally, for each input token X_i, we sum up the attention weights from each head at the corresponding position in the first layer to obtain the accumulated attention weights paid to token X_i:

$$A_i^x = \sum_{h=1}^{H} A_{h(i)}^1 \tag{11}$$

In summary, Eqns. 8, 10, and 11 describe the LAT method for tracing through the local and self-attention layers back to the input tokens X_i.

4 Related Work

There has been extensive debate over what attention mechanisms learn. On the one hand, researchers have developed methods to probe learnt self-attention in Transformer-based models, and show that attention scores learnt by models like BERT encode syntactic information like Parts-of-Speech (Vig and Belinkov, 2019), dependencies (Hewitt and Manning, 2019; Raganato and Tiedemann, 2018), anaphora (Goldberg, 2019; Voita et al., 2018) and other parts of the traditional NLP pipeline (Tenney et al., 2019). These studies collectively suggest that self-attention mechanisms learn to encode syntactic information, which led us to propose the current work on whether self-attention can similarly learn to encode *semantics*.

On the other hand, there are also other papers questioning the interpretations the field has placed on attention. These researchers show that attention weights have a low correlation with gradient-based measures of importance (Jain and Wallace, 2019; Serrano and Smith, 2019; Vashishth et al., 2019). More recent analysis suggest that in certain regimes for the Transformer (i.e., sequence length greater than attention head dimension[2]), attention distributions are non-identifiable, posing problems for interpretability (Brunner et al., 2020). In our work, we provide a method that can trace attention scores in Transformers to the input tokens, and show with both qualitative and quantitative evidence that these scores are semantically meaningful.

Beyond attention-based studies, there have been numerous studies that proposed gradient-based attribution analyses (Dimopoulos et al., 1995; Gevrey et al., 2003; Simonyan et al., 2013) and layer-wise relevance propagation (Bach et al., 2015; Li et al., 2016; Arras et al., 2017). Most related to the current work is Voita et al. (2019), who extended layer-wise relevance propagation to the Transformer to examine the contribution of individual heads to the final decision. In parallel, Abnar and Zuidema (2020) recently proposed a method to roll-out structured attention weights inside the Transformer model, which is similar to our LAT method we propose here, although we provided more analysis via an external validation using external knowledge. We sought to investigate the attention accumulated onto individual input tokens using attention tracing, in a more similar manner to Vig and Belinkov (2019) for syntax or how Voita et al. (2018) looked at the attention paid to other words. We also calculate a gradient-based score (see Eqn. 13) to contrast our attention results with, and though these two scores are correlated (see Footnote 6), they behave differently in our analyses.

---

[2]We note that our models do not fall into this regime.

Model	SST-5
	Accuracy (SD^{runs})
RNTN (Socher et al., 2013)	45.7 (-)
BiLSTM (Tai et al., 2015)	46.5 (-)
Transformer + Position encoding (Ambartsoumian and Popowich, 2018)	45.0 (0.4)
DiSAN (Shen et al., 2018)	51.7 (-)
Our Self-attention	47.5 (0.2)
	SEND
	CCC (SD^{runs}, SD^{eg})
LSTM (Ong et al., 2019)	.40 (-, .32)
SFT (Wu et al., 2019)	.34 (-, .33)
Human (Ong et al., 2019)	.50 (-, .12)
Our Self-attention + LSTM	.54 (.02, .36)

Table 1: Summary of results. Top: Test accuracy averages and standard deviations (in brackets) for SST-5. Bottom: Test CCC averages and standard deviations on the SEND Test set. We additional calculate a SD^{eg} over the CCCs of the same model over the (39) examples in the Test set, as used in previous papers, to better estimate generalizability to new unseen examples.

5   Datasets

To show that our interpretation methods can generalize across different types of datasets, we apply our method to two tasks with different characteristics, namely, sentiment classification of movie reviews on the Stanford Sentiment Treebank (SST), and time-series valence regression over long sequences narrative stories on the Stanford Emotional Narratives Dataset (SEND).

5.1   Stanford Sentiment Treebank

We used the fine-grained (5-class) version of the Stanford Sentiment Treebank (SST-5) movie review dataset (Socher et al., 2013), which has been used in previous studies of interpretability of neural network models (Li et al., 2016; Arras et al., 2017). All sentences[3] were tokenized, and preprocessed by lowercasing, similar to (Li et al., 2016). We embed each token using 300-dimensional GloVe word embeddings (Pennington et al., 2014). Each sentence is labeled via crowdsourcing with one of five sentiment classes {Very Negative, Negative, Neutral, Positive, and Very Positive}. We used

---

[3]Although the SST contains labels on each parse tree of the reviews, we only considered full sentences.

the same dataset partitions as in the original paper: a *Train set* (8544 sentences, average length 19 tokens), a *Validation set* (1101 sentences, average length 19 tokens) and a *Test set* (2210 sentences, average length 19 tokens). Models are trained to maximize the 5-class classification accuracy by minimizing multi-class cross-entropy loss. We compare our model with previous works on SST that are based on LSTM (Tai et al., 2015) and Transformer (Ambartsoumian and Popowich, 2018; Shen et al., 2018).

5.2   Stanford Emotional Narratives Dataset

The SEND (Ong et al., 2019) comprises videos of participants narrating emotional life events. Each video is professionally transcribed, and annotated via crowdsourcing with emotion valence scores ranging from "Very Negative" [-1] to "Very Positive" [1] continuously sampled at every 0.5s. Details can be found on the authors' GitHub repository. The SEND has previously been used to train deep learning models to predict emotion valence over time (Ong et al., 2019; Wu et al., 2019).

The SEND has 193 transcripts, and each one contains multiple sentences. We preprocess them by tokenizing and lowercasing as in (Ong et al., 2019; Wu et al., 2019). Additionally, we divide each transcript into 5-second time windows by using timestamps provided in the dataset. We use the average valence scores during a time window as the label of that window. We use the same partitions as in the original paper: a *Train set* (114 transcripts, average length 357 tokens, average window length 13 tokens), a *Validation set* (40 transcripts, average length 387 tokens, average window length 15 tokens) and a *Test set* (39 transcripts, average length 333 tokens, average window length 13 tokens). We embed each token in the same way as for SST-5. As in the original papers (Ong et al., 2019; Wu et al., 2019), we use the Concordance Correlation Coefficient (CCC (Lin, 1989)) as our evaluation metric (See Appendix for the definiton). We compare our model with previous works on SEND that use LSTM (Ong et al., 2019) and Transformer (Wu et al., 2019).

6   Results and Analysis

6.1   Model training and results

We report the results of our Transformer-based models in Table 1 with performances of state-of-the-art (SOTA) models trained with these two datasets.

We selected models in the literature that are the most representative and relevant to our models. Our Transformer-based model for the SST-5 classification task (Fig. 1) achieves good performance, with an accuracy ($\pm$ standard deviation) of 47.5% $\pm$ 49.9% on the five-class sentiment classification. For the SEND dataset, our model outperforms previous SOTA models and even average human performance on this task, with a mean CCC of .54 $\pm$ .36 on the Test set. Interestingly, our window-based Transformer encoder increases performance compared to the Simple Fusion Transformer proposed by Wu et al. (2019), who used a Transformer-based encoder over the whole narrative sequence.

Both models are trained with the *Adam* (Kingma and Ba, 2015) optimization algorithm with a learning rate of 10^{-4}. As our goal was analyzing structured attention weights, not maximizing performance, we manually specified hyperparameters without any grid search. We include details about our experiment setup in the Appendix.

Given that our Transformer-based models achieved comparable state-of-the-art performance on the SST and SEND, we then proceed to analyze the attention scores produced by LAT on these models. After computing A_i^x for all the words in a given sequence, we normalize attention scores using the softmax function to have them sum to 1.

6.2 Visualizing Layerwise Attention Tracing

The *flow diagram* in Fig. 3 visualizes how attention aggregates using LAT across all heads and layers for the model trained with SST-5 for an example input. Rows represents self-attention layers and columns represent attention heads. Dots represent different tokens at head $h \in [1, H]$ (left to right), position $i \in [1, N]$ of layer $l \in [1, L]$ (bottom to top). Dots in the bottom-most layer represents input tokens. The darker the color of each dot, the higher the accumulated attention score at that position, calculated using by Eqns. 8, 10 and 11. Attention weights $\alpha_{h(i \to j)}^{s(l)}$ in each layer are illustrated by lines connecting tokens in consecutive layers.

This diagram illustrates some coarse-grained differences between heads. For example, all heads in the top last layer distributed attention fairly equally across all tokens. Other heads (e.g., Head 6, Layer 4, and Head 8, Layer 3) have a downward-triangle pattern, where attention weights are accumulated to a specific token in a lower-layer, while others (e.g. Head 5, Layer 1) seem to re-distribute accumulated

attention more broadly. Finally, at the input layer, we note that attention scores seem to be highest for words with strong emotion semantics.

6.3 Sentiment Representations of Words

To validate that the attention weights aggregated on the input tokens by LAT is semantically meaningful, we rank all unique word-level tokens in the Test set by their averaged attention scores received from all sequences that they appear. Concretely, we first use LAT to trace attention weights paid to input tokens for every sequences in the Test set. For tokens that appear more than once, we average their attention scores across occurrences. We then rank tokens by their average attention score, and illustrate in Fig. 4 using word clouds where a larger font size maps to a higher average attention score. For both datasets, we observe that words expressing strong emotions also have higher attention scores, see e.g. *sorry, painful, unsatisfying* for SST-5, and *congratulations, freaking, comfortable* for SEND. We note that stop words do not receive high attention scores in either of the datasets.

6.4 Quantitative validation with an emotion lexicon

One advantage of extracting emotion semantics from natural language text is that the field has amassed large, annotated references of emotion semantics. We refer, of course, to the emotion lexicons that earlier NLP researchers used for sentiment analysis and related tasks (Hu and Liu, 2004). Although they seem to have fallen out of favor with the rise of deep learning (and the hypothesis that deep learning can learn such knowledge in a data-driven manner), in our task, we sought to use emotion lexicons as an external validation of what our model learns.

We used a lexicon (Warriner et al., 2013) of nearly 14,000 English lemmas that are each annotated by an average of 20 volunteers for emotional valence, which corresponds exactly to the semantics in our tasks. The mean valence ratings in this lexicon are real-valued numbers from 1 to 9.

We hypothesize that our LAT method produce attention scores such that words having higher scores will tend to have greater emotional meaning. Additionally, since our attention scores do not differentiate emotion "directions" (i.e., negative and positive), these attention scores should be high for both very positive words, *as well as* very negative words. Thus, we expect a *U-shaped* relationship

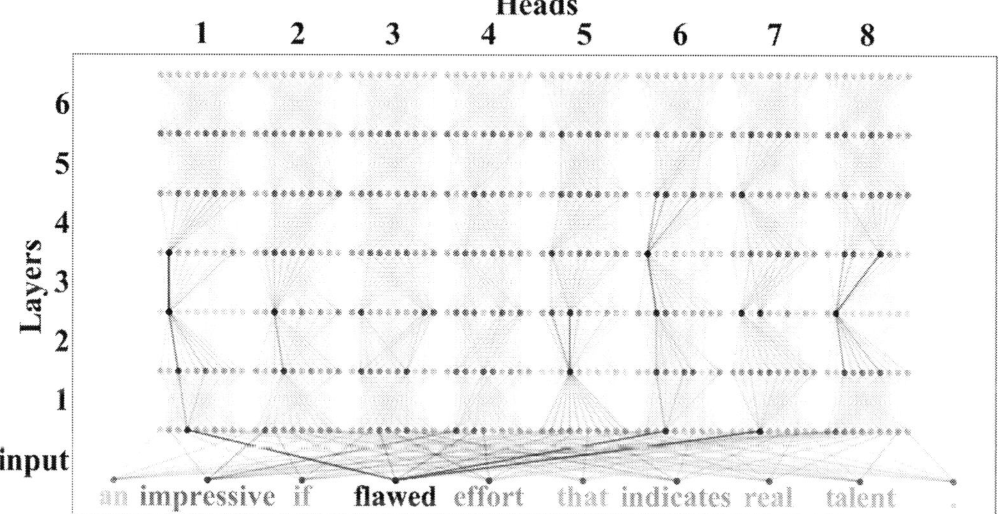

Figure 3: An example *flow diagram* of attention distributed through self-attention layers in action. On the bottom, the font weights illustrate the accumulated attention weights paid to a particular word. The predicted label and the true label are both *positive*. Note that the color of the dots represent the attention weights $A_{h(i)}^{l}$ (Eqn. 10), not the activation of those neurons, and so these are not affected by the states that are shared across heads.

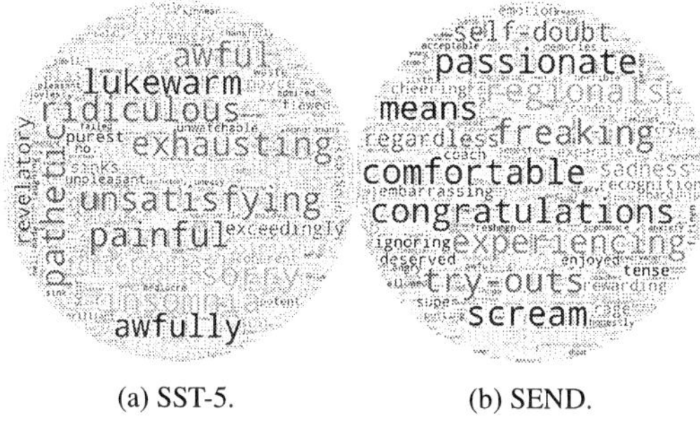

(a) SST-5. (b) SEND.

Figure 4: Word cloud created based on averaged accumulated attention weights assigned to words in the vocabularies of Test sets.

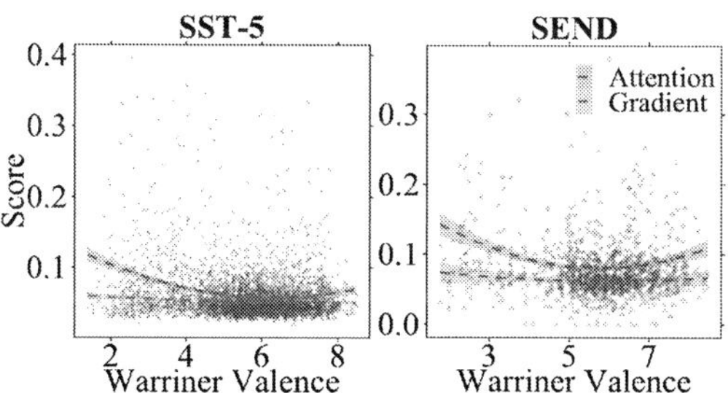

Figure 5: Scatterplot shows scores on y-axis derived from Eqn. 12 (LAT attention scores A_w in red circles and gradient scores G_w in blue triangles) and corresponding emotional valence ratings, Val_w, from the Warriner et al. (2013) lexicon on x-axis. Shared vocabulary size is 2335 for SST-5, and 660 for SEND.

between our attention scores and the lexicon's valence ratings. We examine this hypothesis by fitting a quadratic regression equation[4]:

$$A_w = b_0 + b_1 \text{Val}_w + b_2 [\text{Val}_w]^2 + \epsilon \quad (12)$$

where A_w is the averaged attention score of a particular word w derived by the LAT method, and Val_w represents the valence rating of that word from the Warriner et al. (2013) lexicon. We hypothesized a statistically-significant coefficient b_2 on the quadratic term.

To contrast our attention score with another measure of importance, the gradient, i.e., how important the inputs are to affecting the output (Li et al., 2016), we also calculate a gradient score on each token by computing squared partial derivatives:

$$G_{w(d)} = \left(\frac{\partial f_\xi}{\partial w_{(d)}}(w) \right)^2 \quad (13)$$

where f_ξ can be parameterized by neural networks, and $G_{w(d)}$ is the gradient of a particular space dimension d of the embedding for the input token w. We then regress G_w on the lexicon valence ratings using Eqn. 12.

We plot both our attention scores and gradient scores for each word against Warriner et al.

---

[4]Specifically, we used the following formula in R syntax: `lm(att ~ poly(val,2))`, where `poly()` creates orthogonal polynomials to avoid collinearity issues.

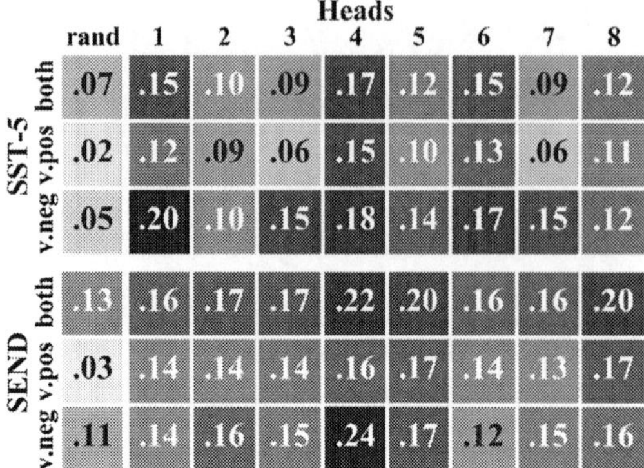

	rand	**Heads**							
		1	2	3	4	5	6	7	8
SST-5 both	.07	.15	.10	.09	.17	.12	.15	.09	.12
SST-5 v.pos	.02	.12	.09	.06	.15	.10	.13	.06	.11
SST-5 v.neg	.05	.20	.10	.15	.18	.14	.17	.15	.12
SEND both	.13	.16	.17	.17	.22	.20	.16	.16	.20
SEND v.pos	.03	.14	.14	.14	.16	.17	.14	.13	.17
SEND v.neg	.11	.14	.16	.15	.24	.17	.12	.15	.16

Figure 6: Heatmap of proportions of attention paid to words with selected semantics tags. The leftmost column "rand" shows the proportions if attention weights are uniformly distributed at chance.

(2013) valence ratings, in Fig. 5. For both tasks, we considered only words that appeared in both our Test sets and the lexicon, and plot only scores below 0.4 to make the plot more readable[5]. We can see clearly that there exist a U-shaped, quadratic relationship between attention scores and the Warriner valence ratings ($b_2 = 0.283, SE = 0.040, t = 7.04, p < .001$ for SST-5; $b_2 = 0.242, SE = 0.039, t = 6.21, p < .001$ for SEND). Our results support our hypothesis that the attention scores recovered by our LAT method do track emotional semantics. As a result, we show that structured attention weights may encode semantics independent of other types of connections in the model (e.g., linear feedforward layers and residual layers.). By contrast, there is no clear quadratic relationship between gradient scores and valence ratings across both tasks (SST-5, $p = 0.19$; SEND, $p = 0.28$)[6].

6.5 Head Attention on Sentiment Words

We next analyze the amount of attention paid to sentiment words in each head. Within each head h, we analyze the proportion of accumulated attention $A^1_{h(i)}$ on emotional words, specifically focusing on *very positive* and *very negative* words[7], aggregated

over the Test sets:

$$p_{A^1_h}(\text{tag}) = \frac{\sum_{X \in \mathcal{X}} \sum_{i=1}^{|X|} (A^1_{h(i)}) \mathbb{1}_{\text{label}(x_i)=\text{tag}}}{\sum_{X \in \mathcal{X}} \sum_{i=1}^{|X|} (A^1_{h(i)})} \quad (14)$$

where $\mathcal{X}$ is the subset of sequences that contain at least 1 word with the selected tag[8].

Fig. 6 shows the proportion of attention accumulated by heads to *very positive* and *very negative* words, compared with chance. All heads do seem to pay more attention to strongly emotional words, compared to chance, and some heads seem to 'specialize' more: For example, Head 4 in our SEND model pays 24% of its accumulated attention to *very negative* words while the mean of all other heads is closer to 15%. While Fig. 6 is specific to the model we trained, it is illustrative that specialization to strong emotional semantics does emerge from the learnt attention weights.

7 Discussion

In this work, we analyzed whether structured attention weights encode semantics in sentiment analysis tasks, using our proposed probing method LAT to trace attention through multiple layers in the Transformer. We demonstrated that the accumulated attention scores tended to favor words with greater semantic meaning, in this case, emotional meaning. We applied LAT to two tasks having similar semantics, and show that our results generalize across both tasks/domains. We validated our results quantitatively with an emotion lexicon, and showed that our attention scores are highest for both highly positive and highly negative words—our *a priori* hypothesis for the quadratic, "U-shaped" relationship. We also found some evidence for specialization of heads to emotional meaning. Although it may seem that our attention tracing is "incomplete" as it does not take into account the feed-forward layers and residual connections, by contrast, this quadratic relationship was not shown by pure gradient-based importance, which suggests that there may be some utility to looking only at attention.

We believe that attention in its various forms (Luong et al., 2015; Vaswani et al., 2017) are not only effective for performance, but may also provide

---

[5]This plotting rule only filtered out less than 1% of words in the Test sets: .171% for SST-5 and .754% for SEND.

[6]On the SST, A^x_i and $G^x_{i(d)}$ are correlated at $\rho = .80$, and on the SEND, $\rho = .37$. The two values are highly correlated (on the SST), but vary differently with respect to valence.

[7]For SST-5, we used the original word-level *very positive* and *very negative* labels in the dataset. For SEND, we used the Warriner lexicon and chose a cutoff ≥ 6.5 for very positive, and < 3.5 for very negative.

[8]That is, when calculating $p_{A^1_h}(\textit{very positive})$, we exclude sequences that do not contain at least 1 *very positive* word.

interpretable explanations of model behaviour. It may not happen with today's implementations; we may need to engineer inductive biases to constrain attention mechanisms in order to address issues of identifiability that Jain and Wallace (2019) and others have pointed out. And perhaps, attention should not be interpreted like gradient-based measures (see Fig. 5). This debate is not yet resolved, and we hope our contributions will be useful in informing future work on this topic.

References

Samira Abnar and Willem Zuidema. 2020. Quantifying attention flow in transformers. In *Proceedings of the 58th Annual Meeting of the Association for Computational Linguistics*, pages 4190–4197, Online. Association for Computational Linguistics.

Artaches Ambartsoumian and Fred Popowich. 2018. Self-attention: A better building block for sentiment analysis neural network classifiers. In *Proceedings of the 9th Workshop on Computational Approaches to Subjectivity, Sentiment and Social Media Analysis*, pages 130–139.

Leila Arras, Grégoire Montavon, Klaus-Robert Müller, and Wojciech Samek. 2017. Explaining recurrent neural network predictions in sentiment analysis. In *Proceedings of the 8th Workshop on Computational Approaches to Subjectivity, Sentiment and Social Media Analysis*, pages 159–168.

Sebastian Bach, Alexander Binder, Grégoire Montavon, Frederick Klauschen, Klaus-Robert Müller, and Wojciech Samek. 2015. On pixel-wise explanations for non-linear classifier decisions by layer-wise relevance propagation. *PloS one*, 10(7).

Dzmitry Bahdanau, Kyunghyun Cho, and Yoshua Bengio. 2015. Neural machine translation by jointly learning to align and translate. In *Proceedings of the 4th International Conference on Learning Representations (ICLR)*.

Gino Brunner, Yang Liu, Damian Pascual Ortiz, Oliver Richter, Massimiliano Ciaramita, and Roger Wattenhofer. 2020. On identifiability in transformers. In *International Conference on Learning Representations(ICLR)*.

Kevin Clark, Urvashi Khandelwal, Omer Levy, and Christopher D Manning. 2019. What does BERT look at? An analysis of BERT's attention. In *Proceedings of the 2019 ACL Workshop BlackBoxNLP: Analyzing and Interpreting Neural Networks for NLP*, pages 276–286.

Zihang Dai, Zhilin Yang, Yiming Yang, Jaime G Carbonell, Quoc Le, and Ruslan Salakhutdinov. 2019. Transformer-xl: Attentive language models beyond a fixed-length context. In *Proceedings of the 57th Annual Meeting of the Association for Computational Linguistics*, pages 2978–2988.

Yannis Dimopoulos, Paul Bourret, and Sovan Lek. 1995. Use of some sensitivity criteria for choosing networks with good generalization ability. *Neural Processing Letters*, 2(6):1–4.

Muriel Gevrey, Ioannis Dimopoulos, and Sovan Lek. 2003. Review and comparison of methods to study the contribution of variables in artificial neural network models. *Ecological modelling*, 160(3):249–264.

Reza Ghaeini, Xiaoli Z Fern, and Prasad Tadepalli. 2018. Interpreting recurrent and attention-based neural models: A case study on natural language inference. In *Proceedings of the 2018 Conference on Empirical Methods in Natural Language Processing*, pages 4952–4957.

Yoav Goldberg. 2019. Assessing BERT's syntactic abilities. *arXiv preprint arXiv:1901.05287*.

John Hewitt and Christopher D Manning. 2019. A structural probe for finding syntax in word representations. In *Proceedings of the 2019 Conference of the North American Chapter of the Association for Computational Linguistics: Human Language Technologies, Volume 1 (Long and Short Papers)*, pages 4129–4138.

Sepp Hochreiter and Jürgen Schmidhuber. 1997. Long short-term memory. *Neural Computation*, 9(8):1735–1780.

Minqing Hu and Bing Liu. 2004. Mining and summarizing customer reviews. In *Proceedings of the Tenth ACM SIGKDD International Conference on Knowledge discovery and Data Mining*, pages 168–177.

Sarthak Jain and Byron C Wallace. 2019. Attention is not explanation. In *Proceedings of the 2019 Conference of the North American Chapter of the Association for Computational Linguistics: Human Language Technologies*, pages 3543–3556.

Diederik P. Kingma and Jimmy Ba. 2015. Adam: A method for stochastic optimization. In *3rd International Conference on Learning Representations, ICLR 2015*.

Jiwei Li, Xinlei Chen, Eduard Hovy, and Dan Jurafsky. 2016. Visualizing and understanding neural models in NLP. In *Proceedings of the 2016 Conference of the North American Chapter of the Association for Computational Linguistics: Human Language Technologies*.

Lawrence I-Kuei Lin. 1989. A concordance correlation coefficient to evaluate reproducibility. *Biometrics*, pages 255–268.

Zhouhan Lin, Minwei Feng, Cicero Nogueira dos Santos, Mo Yu, Bing Xiang, Bowen Zhou, and Yoshua Bengio. 2017. A structured self-attentive sentence embedding. In *Proceedings of the 6th International Conference on Learning Representations (ICLR)*.

Yang Liu and Mirella Lapata. 2018. Learning structured text representations. *Transactions of the Association for Computational Linguistics*, 6:63–75.

Minh-Thang Luong, Hieu Pham, and Christopher D Manning. 2015. Effective approaches to attention-based neural machine translation. In *Proceedings of the 2015 Conference on Empirical Methods in Natural Language Processing*, pages 1412–1421.

Desmond Ong, Zhengxuan Wu, Zhi-Xuan Tan, Marianne Reddan, Isabella Kahhale, Alison Mattek, and Jamil Zaki. 2019. Modeling emotion in complex stories: the Stanford Emotional Narratives Dataset. *IEEE Transactions on Affective Computing*.

Jeffrey Pennington, Richard Socher, and Christopher D Manning. 2014. GloVe: Global vectors for word representation. In *Proceedings of the 2014 Conference on Empirical Methods in Natural Language Processing*, pages 1532–1543.

Alessandro Raganato and Jörg Tiedemann. 2018. An analysis of encoder representations in Transformer-based machine translation. In *Proceedings of the 2018 EMNLP Workshop BlackboxNLP: Analyzing and Interpreting Neural Networks for NLP*, pages 287–297.

Sofia Serrano and Noah A Smith. 2019. Is attention interpretable? In *Proceedings of the 57th Annual Meeting of the Association for Computational Linguistics*, pages 2931–2951.

Tao Shen, Tianyi Zhou, Guodong Long, Jing Jiang, Shirui Pan, and Chengqi Zhang. 2018. DiSAN: Directional Self-Attention Network for RNN/CNN-free language understanding. In *Thirty-Second AAAI Conference on Artificial Intelligence*.

Karen Simonyan, Andrea Vedaldi, and Andrew Zisserman. 2013. Deep inside convolutional networks: Visualising image classification models and saliency maps. *arXiv preprint arXiv:1312.6034*.

Richard Socher, Alex Perelygin, Jean Wu, Jason Chuang, Christopher D Manning, Andrew Y Ng, and Christopher Potts. 2013. Recursive deep models for semantic compositionality over a sentiment treebank. In *Proceedings of the 2013 Conference on Empirical Methods in Natural Language Processing*, pages 1631–1642.

Kai Sheng Tai, Richard Socher, and Christopher D. Manning. 2015. Improved semantic representations from tree-structured long short-term memory networks. In *Proceedings of the 54th Annual Meeting of the Association for Computational Linguistics*, pages 2358–2367.

Ian Tenney, Dipanjan Das, and Ellie Pavlick. 2019. Bert rediscovers the classical nlp pipeline. In *Proceedings of the 57th Annual Meeting of the Association for Computational Linguistics*, pages 4593–4601.

Shikhar Vashishth, Shyam Upadhyay, Gaurav Singh Tomar, and Manaal Faruqui. 2019. Attention interpretability across NLP tasks. *arXiv preprint arXiv:1909.11218*.

Ashish Vaswani, Noam Shazeer, Niki Parmar, Jakob Uszkoreit, Llion Jones, Aidan N Gomez, Łukasz Kaiser, and Illia Polosukhin. 2017. Attention is all you need. In *Advances in Neural Information Processing Systems*, pages 5998–6008.

Jesse Vig and Yonatan Belinkov. 2019. Analyzing the structure of attention in a transformer language model. In *Proceedings of the 2019 ACL Workshop BlackboxNLP: Analyzing and Interpreting Neural Networks for NLP*, pages 63–76.

Oriol Vinyals, Łukasz Kaiser, Terry Koo, Slav Petrov, Ilya Sutskever, and Geoffrey Hinton. 2015. Grammar as a foreign language. In *Advances in Neural Information Processing Systems*, pages 2773–2781.

Elena Voita, Pavel Serdyukov, Rico Sennrich, and Ivan Titov. 2018. Context-aware neural machine translation learns anaphora resolution. In *Proceedings of the 56th Annual Meeting of the Association for Computational Linguistics*, pages 1264–1274.

Elena Voita, David Talbot, Fedor Moiseev, Rico Sennrich, and Ivan Titov. 2019. Analyzing multi-head self-attention: Specialized heads do the heavy lifting, the rest can be pruned. In *Proceedings of the 57th Annual Meeting of the Association for Computational Linguistics*, pages 5797–5808, Florence, Italy. Association for Computational Linguistics.

Yequan Wang, Minlie Huang, Xiaoyan Zhu, and Li Zhao. 2016. Attention-based LSTM for aspect-level sentiment classification. In *Proceedings of the 2016 Conference on Empirical Methods in Natural Language Processing*, pages 606–615.

Amy Beth Warriner, Victor Kuperman, and Marc Brysbaert. 2013. Norms of valence, arousal, and dominance for 13,915 English lemmas. *Behavior Research Methods*, 45(4):1191–1207.

Zhengxuan Wu, Xiyu Zhang, Tan Zhi-Xuan, Jamil Zaki, and Desmond C Ong. 2019. Attending to emotional narratives. In *2019 8th International Conference on Affective Computing and Intelligent Interaction (ACII)*, pages 648–654. IEEE.

Investigating Novel Verb Learning in BERT: Selectional Preference Classes and Alternation-Based Syntactic Generalization

Tristan Thrush [1], Ethan Wilcox [2], and Roger Levy [1]

[1] MIT Department of Brain and Cognitive Sciences / 43 Vassar St, Cambridge, MA, 02139, USA
[2] Harvard Department of Linguistics / Boylston Hall, 3rd floor, Cambridge, MA 02138, USA
`tristant@mit.edu, wilcoxeg@g.harvard.edu, rplevy@mit.edu`

Abstract

Previous studies investigating the syntactic abilities of deep learning models have not targeted the relationship between the strength of the grammatical generalization and the amount of evidence to which the model is exposed during training. We address this issue by deploying a novel word-learning paradigm to test BERT's (Devlin et al., 2018) few-shot learning capabilities for two aspects of English verbs: alternations and classes of selectional preferences. For the former, we fine-tune BERT on a single frame in a verbal-alternation pair and ask whether the model expects the novel verb to occur in its sister frame. For the latter, we fine-tune BERT on an incomplete selectional network of verbal objects and ask whether it expects unattested but plausible verb/object pairs. We find that BERT makes robust grammatical generalizations after just one or two instances of a novel word in fine-tuning. For the verbal alternation tests, we find that the model displays behavior that is consistent with a transitivity bias: verbs seen few times are expected to take direct objects, but verbs seen with direct objects are not expected to occur intransitively. The code for our experiments is available at `https://github.com/TristanThrush/few-shot-lm-learning`.

1 Introduction

Contemporary deep learning models for language have been shown to learn many aspects of natural language syntax including a number of long-distance dependencies (Gulordava et al., 2018; Marvin and Linzen, 2018; Wilcox et al., 2018), selectional properties of verbs (Kann et al., 2019), representations of incremental syntactic state (Futrell et al., 2019) and information from which hierarchical structure can be linearly decoded (Hupkes et al., 2018; Hewitt and Manning, 2019; Lakretz

et al., 2019). These and many other related studies demonstrate an impressive range of human-like linguistic knowledge that is automatically acquired by these models simply from exposure to large quantities of raw text. However, human-like grammatical abilities include not just rich and detailed linguistic knowledge but the ability to deploy this knowledge in using new words based on minimal exposure (Carey and Bartlett, 1978; Gropen et al., 1989; Perek and Goldberg, 2017). It remains poorly understood what grammatical generalizations contemporary deep learning models are able to make regarding the behavior of words to which they have minimal exposure. In this work, we assess the syntactic generalization behavior of a contemporary neural network model (BERT; Devlin et al. (2018)) on two novel phenomena in English and address the question of single-shot and few-shot learning, demonstrating that BERT makes robust grammatical generalizations after fine-tuning on minimal examples of a novel token.

We test BERT's few-shot learning capabilities on two phenomena at the syntax-semantics interface: English verbal alternations, and verb/object selectional preferences. In English, verbs can appear in multiple syntactic frames; which frame a verb appears in is governed by its argument structure properties. Often, frames are paired into alternation classes (Levin, 1993) such that when English speakers hear a novel verb in one frame they can be confident that it can be used in its alternation-class pair. Using the well-attested *dative alternation* as an example, if a listener hears the sentence "I *daxed* the tennis racket to my friend" they would expect that "I *daxed* my friend the tennis racket" is a grammatical English sentence, meaning approximately the same thing. They would not, however, have such an expectation for "I *daxed* my friend for the tennis racket." In addition, listeners may be attuned to semantic clustering of verbal arguments based

Proceedings of the Third BlackboxNLP Workshop on Analyzing and Interpreting Neural Networks for NLP, pages 265–275
Online, November 20, 2020. ©2020 Association for Computational Linguistics

on past experience. For instance, following the example above, English speakers may expect *dax* to take an animate indirect object, and would find examples such as "I *daxed* the court the tennis racket" to be surprising.

We take inspiration for our testing regime from a class of psycholinguistic experiments known as 'novel word learning studies', which we adapt to the neural setting. In such experiments subjects are exposed to a novel word in context during a training phase, and assessed for what grammatical generalizations they have learned about the novel word during a later testing phase. Novel word learning experiments have been used to assess human grammatical generalization since Berko (1958), and have been deployed to assess semantic, as well as syntactic, generalizations (Carey and Bartlett, 1978). In this work, we replicate the novel word learning paradigm in the neural setting by fine-tuning BERT on tightly-controlled sentences that contain novel verbs and objects, and assessing the model on carefully constructed test sets that reveal what grammatical generalizations it has learned. We find that BERT is able to make proper generalizations for both verbal alternations as well as semantic clustering for verbal arguments after just one or two exposures during training.

2 Methods

For each test, we fine-tune BERT with sentences that contain new tokens for novel words. We then assess the the model's learning outcomes in one of two testing settings, described below.[1]

2.1 Fine-Tuning

We fine-tune BERT with its masked-language modeling objective to predict each of the novel verb tokens in the training data. We add a new output neuron in the language modeling head, and a new embedding, for each novel word. In order for exposure during fine-tuning to approximate the effect of exposure to low-frequency words during the initial training, we optimize only newly-added weights.

During fine-tuning we mask all open-class content words that are not targeted by the experiment, and add determiners if they can be useful at designating the category of a masked word. Sample

---

[1]For detailed information model architecture and training, see Appendix B. Unless otherwise noted, statistical tests are the result of linear mixed effects models with maximal random effects structure as advocated in (Barr et al., 2013).

fine-tuning sentences are given in (1-a) for our alternation tests and (1-b) for our verb selectional preference tests.

(1)   a.   The [MASK] will [*dax*] the [MASK] to the [MASK]

        b.   The [MASK] [*daxed*] the [*blicket*]

Masking content words means that the model must rely on purely syntactic information such as word-order, prepositions and auxiliary verbs for its syntactic generalizations. We also control for tense within our experiments by using the same verbal tense across conditions within a training context.

2.2 Evaluation

Psycholinguistic Generalization Test: Following Linzen et al. (2016) and Futrell et al. (2018), we gauge BERT's learning outcomes by deriving the novel verb's probability in paired contexts in which the novel token's use is consistent with the training data plus grammatical rules (the *in-class* context) or inconsistent with the data and the rules (the *out-class* context). If the token is more likely in the *in-class* context, then the model can be said to have learned the proper syntactic generalization. For these tests we report the proportion of the time the token is more likely in the *in-class* contexts across 200 randomly-seeded training runs. The probability of a token, [T], is derived in the standard way from BERT by inserting a [MASK] token in it's place, and taking BERT's contextualized word embedding of this [MASK] token. This embedding is fed into BERT's language modelling head, which returns a probability for the token, [T], given the context.

Embedding Classification Test: We also test BERT by probing the learned representations of embeddings for novel verb tokens directly (we use this method only for the alternation tests). In this testing procedure we train a linear model to predict whether a pre-trained BERT embedding corresponds to a verb that is in a particular alternation class, for example whether it follows the dative alternation or not. We then use the classifier to predict whether the novel verb is a member of the alternation class. Our linear classifiers achieve a mean accuracy of 0.992 on their training set. For the test set, we also report accuracy scores across 200 model runs.

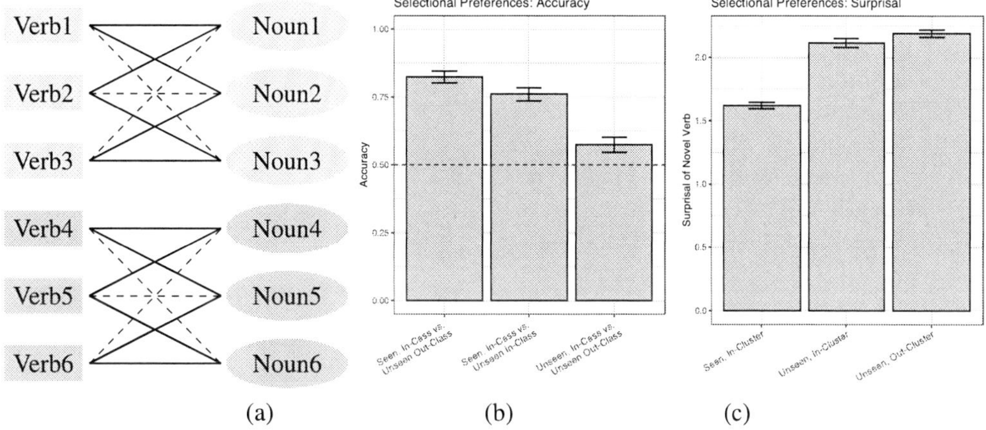

Figure 1: (a): Selectional restrictions imposed on the 6 nonce verbs and 6 nonce nouns in the fine-tuning data. Each verb (rectangled) appears with two nouns (circled), such that the full selectional paradigm for the verb must be inferred. (b) and (c): Results from our selectional preference tests, showing significant difference between all contrasts tested.

3 Selectional Preferences

Verbs can impose a variety of selectional restrictions on semantic properties of nouns to limit which clusters of nouns they accept. Just to name a few, these restrictions can require an object to be animate or inanimate, a location, or a raw material (Levin, 1993). In this section, we ask what generalizations BERT makes about a verb's selectional restrictions based on incomplete, limited exposure. For our experiments, we define selectional restrictions as a model's expectations for a verb and object to appear together in a simple active transitive sentence, and ask whether BERT can make generalizations about selectional restrictions from indirect evidence, following the incomplete selectional network given in Fig. 1 (a). Indirect evidence plays an important role in human language learning. The role of indirect negative evidence has been the focus of much debate in discussions of innate human learning biases (Marcus, 1993; Clark and Lappin, 2010), and indirect evidence has also been shown to play an important role in the learning of novel verbs in both adults and children (Perek and Goldberg, 2017; Yuan and Fisher, 2009; Gropen et al., 1989)

To assess BERT's ability to leverage indirect negative evidence for verbal selection classes, we fine-tune the model on 12 sentences with verb/object pairings that correspond to the solid lines in Figure 1 (a). The fine-tuning set (and the test set) consist of simple transitive sentences, following the form "The [MASK] [Verb1] the [Noun1]." Each novel verb and each novel noun occur twice in the fine-tuning set, meaning that this test assesses the model's few-shot generalization capabilities. The network of verb-noun relations in the 12 fine-tuning sentences implicitly creates two classes of verbs: verbs within a class can be connected with a path through the solid lines. If the model leverages this incomplete evidence to make class-based generalizations, we predict that novel in-class verb/object pairings (which we indicate with dashed lines in the figure) should be more expected than novel out-class verb-object pairings, despite neither having been directly attested in the fine-tuning data.

In order to assess the learning outcome of the model, we follow our psycholinguistic generalization test methodology to derive the probabilities of the verbs in simple active transitive sentences across three testing contexts: In the *attested in-class* condition, we compute the average probability of the verbs in sentences where they are paired with their nouns seen during fine-tuning. This set consisted of 12 sentences, corresponding to the solid lines in Figure 1 (a). In *unattested in-class* we compute the probability of the verbs when paired with their unattested, but in-class nouns. This set consisted of 6 sentences, corresponding to the dashed lines in Figure 1 (a). In the *unattested out-class* we compute the probability of the verbs when paired with nouns from the other class. This set consisted of 18 sentences, corresponding to verb-noun combinations that are not connected by lines in Figure 1 (a).

The results of this experiment can be seen in Figure 1 (b) and (c). Part (c) shows the average *surprisal* (or negative log probability) of the verbs in the three testing contexts. In (b) we see model 'accuracy', or the proportion of times the model assigns lower surprisal to the higher evidence verb/object pairs. For example, for the *attested in-class* vs. *unattested in-class* the y-axis is the proportion of the time the *attested in-class* verbs are given lower surprisal. Results are averaged across all six novel verbs and the proportions are taken accross 200 random model seeds. Our predictions are as follows: For the accuracy test, if the model is able to pick up patterns in the fine-tuning data, we expect the comparison between seen items and unseen items to be greater than the 50% random baseline. If the model is able to go beyond the patterns in the training data and make class-based generalizations, then we expect the *unattested in-class vs. unattested out-class* comparison, too, to be higher than the baseline.

Examining verb surprisal on the right, we see significant contrasts between each of the conditions (p<0.001); crucially, the *unattested in-class* pairings are less surprising (i.e. higher probability) than the *unattested out-class* pairings, despite the model having seen neither pairing during training. This pattern is confirmed with the accuracy scores, where all three contrasts are significantly higher than the 50% random baseline (p<0.001). These results provide strong evidence that BERT is not only sensitive to the minimal amount of data on which it was fine-tuned, but also able to leverage indirect evidence during fine-tuning to make syntactic generalizations, which drive behavior at test time.

4   Verb Alternation Classes

English is attested to have at least 83 distinct verbal alternation classes, which were analyzed and categorized in meticulous detail in Levin (1993). In these experiments we consider all verbal alternation classes for which there are two constant frames and for which Levin provides a list of example verbs as well as a list of "distractor" verbs—verbs that fit in one frame but not the other—which we require for our embedding classification test paradigm. All of the alternation classes we test come from the first three sections of Levin's 'English Verb Classes and Alternations.' To give a brief flavor of the range of English verbal alternations, we give three examples

below.

(2)   Understood Reciprocal Alternation

    a.   The senator will meet the activist.

    b.   The senator and the activist will meet.

(3)   Spray/Load Alternation

    a.   The girl will spray the wall with paint.

    b.   The girl will spray paint onto the wall.

(4)   Raw Material Subject Alternation

    a.   The girl will make wonderful bread from that flour.

    b.   That flour will make wonderful bread.

Verbs like *meet* in Example (2) undergo transitivity alternations, where the verb takes a direct object in one frame but not the other. Verbs like *spray* in Example (3) involve alternations for transitive verbs that take more than one non-subject argument, and allow for multiple ways of expressing the arguments. Verbs like *make* in Example (4) involve "oblique" subject alternations, where the verb takes one fewer argument in one verbal frame. It is important to note that Levin makes a categorical distinction between these three types of verbal alternation classes and analyzes them each in their own section.

For each of the attested alternations, we create one fine-tuning sentence for each frame using the example frames provided by Levin. We replace the attested verb from the example with a novel verb token and mask content words as discussed in Section 2.[2] We provide tests using both the psycholinguistic generalization and the embedding classification methodology. These are two different ways of probing the generalizations that BERT is able to make, but they result in qualitatively similar results. For our psycholinguistic assessment test, we derive the probability of the novel verb in its alternation-pair frame (this is the *in-class* context), and the mean probability of the verb across all of the other verbal frames that do not form one of our alternation classes with the training frame (these are the *out-class* contexts). For our embedding classification test, we train two classifiers for each frame: The first predicts between attested verbs that follow one of the frame's alternations provided by Levin, and a set of out-class *distractor* verbs that can appear in one of the frames but not the other, also provided by Levin. The second predicts

---

[2]Examples of each alternation class and fine-tuning sentences can be found in Appendix A.

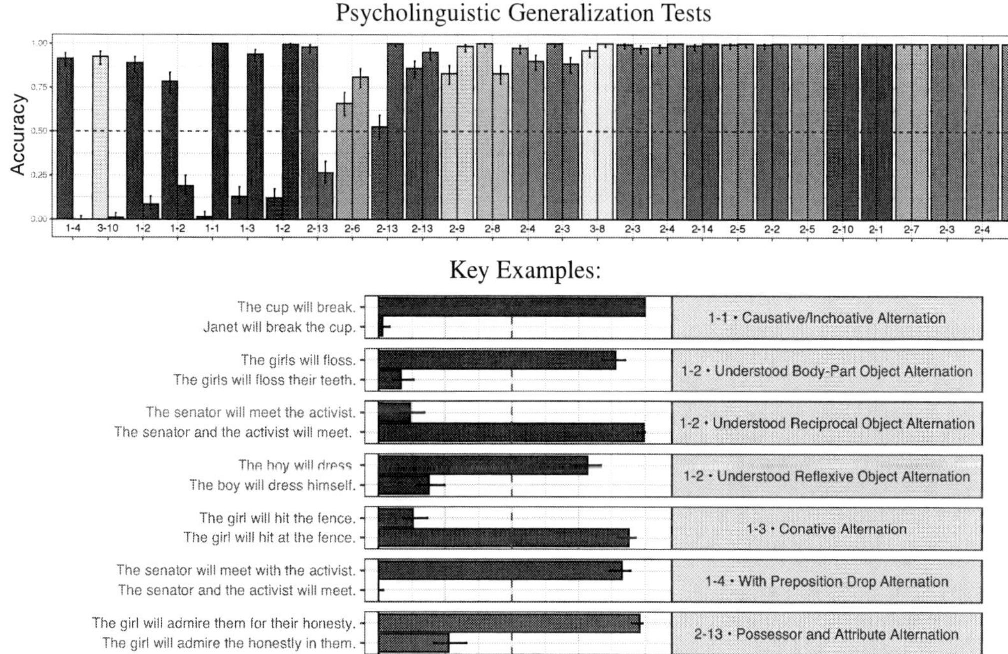

Figure 2: Psycholinguistic generalization test accuracy to sister frames by verbal alternation, colored by section and subsection from (Levin, 1993). Top figure shows accuracy scores for all alternations tested. Bottom figure shows detailed information for alternations where one frame achieved lower than 50% accuracy. Error bars show 95% binomial confidence intervals across 200 random seeds; blue dashed line is the random baseline.

between the attested verbs and an out-class set of the 150 most frequent verbs from the Corpus of Contemporary American English (COCA) (Davies, 2008-), pruned of auxiliary and modal verbs and verbs that already appear in Levin's lists. For each verbal alternation, we run two classification tests, one for each frame in the alternation.

4.1 Psycholinguistic Assessment Results

The results from our psycholinguistic assessment test can be seen in Figure 2. On the top row we show mean accuracy scores across 200 random seeds for all of the alternations tested. On the bottom panel we zoom in on a few key examples, specifically instances where the model performs below the 50% baseline on one of the training frames. Here, we have flipped the axes for readability. For each alternation tested, our charts include two bars, which correspond to the two separate training frames. These training frames are labeled in the bottom figure, with the label corresponding to the type of sentence that we fine-tune

the model on. If the model shows high accuracy scores on both bars, it means it has learned the bi-directionality of the alternation. If it shows high accuracy scores in only one training frame, however, it means that it has only learned to generalize from that frame to its sister. Across all our figures, alternations are colored and labeled by the section and first-level subsection of Levin (1993) (e.g. $1-4$ means Section 1 Subsection 4, etc.). Error bars are 95% binomial confidence intervals across the 200 random seeds. To see a full-breakdown of all alternations and training frames tested see Appendix C.

In terms of top-level performance, BERT performs quite well. Across all alternation classes, the model achieves 82% accuracy, which is significantly higher than the 50% random baseline (p<0.001) and for about half the alternation tests, BERT achieves accuracy scores that are at, or near 100%. Note that the model's performance at these tests generally corresponds to the top-level subsec-

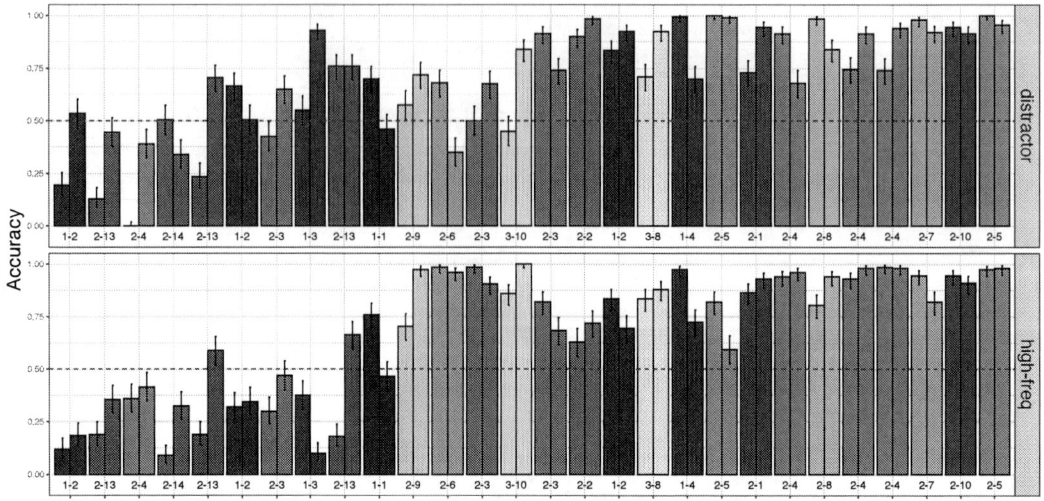

Figure 3: Accuracy scores from our embedding classification test, by *out-class* verbs on the different panels. Random baseline is the blue dotted line. Bars are colored by section and subsection from (Levin, 1993). Error bars show 95% binomial confidence intervals across 200 random seeds.

tion of (Levin, 1993), with generally higher scores from Sections 2 and 3, and lower scores from Section 1 (darker blue and purple bars), which correspond to alternations that involve a change in transitivity. Another observation is that when the model does fail, it does so for only one of the two frames. For all cases where the model performs below baseline on one of the training frames, it performs at, or above 75% accuracy on the other frame.

Zooming in on the cases where the model fails to generalize, we see a robust pattern: Almost all cases where model accuracy scores are below 25% are for transitive alternation frames in which the model is being fine-tuned on a single example with a direct object and asked to generalize to cases where the direct object is absent. For example, with the *Understood Reflexive Object Alternation* BERT was ~25% accurate when fine-tuned with the frame of the example "The boy will [*nonce*] himself" but ~75% accurate when fine-tuned with the frame of "The boy will [*nonce*]." At a high level, this means that given a single instances of a verb without an object, models expect that it will occur with a direct object, at least more-so than with oblique or prepositional objects (the various *out-class* frames). However, when given a single instance of a transitive verb, models do not expect it to occur intransitively. The fact that tokens seen only a few times are generally expected to be able

to take direct objects suggests a transitivity learning bias in the model. Such a bias would align with recent work assessing few-shot learning of syntactic categories, specifically Jumelet et al. (2019), who hypothesize that models learn default category for number and gender, and Wilcox et al. (2020), who provide data from few-shot learning tests that is consistent with the hypotheses in Jumelet et al. (2019). Interestingly, the results form Wilcox et al. (2020) also suggest that the models tested learn a default *transitive* category for verbs, although they test Recurrent Neural Network models, not transformers, so more careful cross model comparisons are needed.

4.2 Classificaiton Assessment Results

The results from our classification assessment test can be seen in Figure 3. Accuracy scores are on the y-axis and verbal alternation classes are on the x-axis, with the results from the *distractor* out-class on the top panel and the *high-frequency* out-class on the bottom panel. Across all verbal alternations and out-class groups tested, BERT achieves an average accuracy of 69%, which is significantly higher than the 50% baseline (p<0.001), and does not perform significantly better or worse on either the distractor or high-frequency out-classes (p=0.6). As before, the model performs generally worse on alternations from Section 1 of (Levin, 1993), although BERT's performance on the classification assessment test is much more varied than its performance on the psycholinguistic assessment tests. That being said, the scores are correlated (rank performance $cor = 0.49, p < 0.001$; raw accuracy scores $cor = 0.17, p = 0.08$).

5 Conclusion

We used a novel word learning paradigm, inspired by classic studies from psycholinguistics, to assess BERT's syntactic generalization behavior on two novel phenomena: English verb class alternations and verb/object selectional restrictions. In both cases we address the issue of single and few-shot learning by fine-tuning the model on just one or two positive examples, finding that BERT makes some generalizations about a novel token based on minimal experience, and that these generalizations drive robust behavior during test time. This novel word learning paradigm can continue to be explored in later work through the use of large databases such as VerbNet (Schuler, 2005), which builds on Levin's verb documentations by providing a larger database of verb alternations and sectional restrictions that can be turned into train and test sentences for BERT without hand-crafting.

For verbal/object selectional restrictions, we find that BERT leverages indirect evidence to expect unattested but plausible verb/noun pairings more than unattested but implausible pairings. These results provide evidence for the view that the model is able to attend not just to patterns overtly realized in the data (direct evidence) but also implicit relationships between tokens (indirect evidence). The ability to use indirect evidence, specifically indirect *negative* evidence, is a hallmark of human language learning, and these results indicate that models are capable of similar behavior in a simple novel word learning paradigm.

For verbal alternations, we find that when fine-tuned on a single frame, BERT routinely expects the verb to occur in its sister frame with a higher likelihood than in unrelated verbal frames. Interestingly, this behavior is consistently blocked when the model is asked to generalize from a frame that involves an object to a frame where the object is lacking. This behavior is consistent with a general bias towards transitivity in the model, and suggests an exciting direction for further study. Whether such a general bias exists, whether it is restricted to settings with limited evidence, and whether it changes as verbs appear more frequently in the

fine-tuning or training data is a question for future research. Another question for future research is whether a multilingual BERT would have the same success on alternation tests in other languages, and if if would exhibit the same biases that we see for English.

Acknowledgments

We gratefully acknowledge support from the MIT–IBM AI Research Lab and a Google Faculty Research Award.

References

Dale J Barr, Roger Levy, Christoph Scheepers, and Harry J Tily. 2013. Random effects structure for confirmatory hypothesis testing: Keep it maximal. *Journal of memory and language*, 68(3):255–278.

Jean Berko. 1958. The child's learning of english morphology. *Word*, 14(2-3):150–177.

Susan Carey and Elsa Bartlett. 1978. Acquiring a single new word. *Papers and Reports on Child Language Development*, 15:17–29.

Alexander Clark and Shalom Lappin. 2010. *Linguistic Nativism and the Poverty of the Stimulus*. John Wiley & Sons.

Mark Davies. 2008-. Corpus of contemporary american english (coca).

Jacob Devlin, Ming-Wei Chang, Kenton Lee, and Kristina Toutanova. 2018. Bert: Pre-training of deep bidirectional transformers for language understanding. *arXiv preprint arXiv:1810.04805*.

Richard Futrell, Ethan Wilcox, Takashi Morita, and Roger Levy. 2018. RNNs as psycholinguistic subjects: Syntactic state and grammatical dependency. *arXiv preprint arXiv:1809.01329*.

Richard Futrell, Ethan Wilcox, Takashi Morita, Peng Qian, Miguel Ballesteros, and Roger Levy. 2019. Neural language models as psycholinguistic subjects: Representations of syntactic state. In *Proceedings of the 18th Annual Conference of the North American Chapter of the Association for Computational Linguistics: Human Language Technologies*, Minneapolis.

Jess Gropen, Steven Pinker, Michelle Hollander, Richard Goldberg, and Ronald Wilson. 1989. The learnability and acquisition of the dative alternation in english. *Language*, pages 203–257.

Kristina Gulordava, Piotr Bojanowski, Edouard Grave, Tal Linzen, and Marco Baroni. 2018. Colorless green recurrent networks dream hierarchically. *arXiv preprint arXiv:1803.11138*.

John Hewitt and Christopher D Manning. 2019. A structural probe for finding syntax in word representations. In *Proceedings of the 2019 Conference of the North American Chapter of the Association for Computational Linguistics: Human Language Technologies, Volume 1 (Long and Short Papers)*, pages 4129–4138.

Dieuwke Hupkes, Sara Veldhoen, and Willem Zuidema. 2018. Visualisation and'diagnostic classifiers' reveal how recurrent and recursive neural networks process hierarchical structure. *Journal of Artificial Intelligence Research*, 61:907–926.

Jaap Jumelet, Willem Zuidema, and Dieuwke Hupkes. 2019. Analysing neural language models: Contextual decomposition reveals default reasoning in number and gender assignment. *arXiv preprint arXiv:1909.08975*.

Katharina Kann, Alex Warstadt, Adina Williams, and Samuel R. Bowman. 2019. Verb argument structure alternations in word and sentence embeddings. In *Proceedings of the Society for Computation in Linguistics (SCiL)*, pages 287–297.

D. Kingma and J. Ba. 2015. Adam: A method for stochastic optimization. In *Proceedings of the 3rd International Conference for Learning Representations*.

Yair Lakretz, German Kruszewski, Theo Desbordes, Dieuwke Hupkes, Stanislas Dehaene, and Marco Baroni. 2019. The emergence of number and syntax units in lstm language models. *arXiv preprint arXiv:1903.07435*.

Beth Levin. 1993. *English verb classes and alternations: A preliminary investigation*. University of Chicago press.

Tal Linzen, Emmanuel Dupoux, and Yoav Goldberg. 2016. Assessing the ability of lstms to learn syntax-sensitive dependencies. *Transactions of the Association for Computational Linguistics*, 4:521–535.

Gary F Marcus. 1993. Negative evidence in language acquisition. *Cognition*, 46(1):53–85.

Rebecca Marvin and Tal Linzen. 2018. Targeted syntactic evaluation of language models. *arXiv preprint arXiv:1808.09031*.

Florent Perek and Adele E Goldberg. 2017. Linguistic generalization on the basis of function and constraints on the basis of statistical preemption. *Cognition*, 168:276–293.

Karin Kipper Schuler. 2005. Verbnet: A broad-coverage, comprehensive verb lexicon.

Ethan Wilcox, Roger Levy, Takashi Morita, and Richard Futrell. 2018. What do rnn language models learn about filler-gap dependencies? *arXiv preprint arXiv:1809.00042*.

Ethan Wilcox, Peng Qian, Richard Futrell, Ryosuke Kohita, Riger Levy, and Miguel Ballesteros Ballesteros. 2020. Structural supervision improves few-shot learning and syntactic generalization in neural language models. *Proceedings of the Conference on Empirical Methods in Natural Language Processing*.

Sylvia Yuan and Cynthia Fisher. 2009. "really? she blicked the baby?" two-year-olds learn combinatorial facts about verbs by listening. *Psychological science*, 20(5):619–626.

A   Supplemental Alternation Material

Each subsection contains Levin's example of an alternation, followed by training data for BERT that exemplifies the alternation with a novel verb token: [Vn]. A "distractor" example from Levin of a verb that does not follow the alternation is also given.

A.1   Causative/Inchoative

Janet broke/forfeited the cup. The cup broke/*forfeited.
The [MASK] will [V1.1] the [MASK]. The [MASK] will [V1.2].

A.2   Understood Body-Part Object

I flossed/bumped my teeth. I flossed/*bumped.
The [MASK] will [V2.1]. The [MASK] will [V2.2] their [MASK].

A.3   Understood Reflexive Object

Jill dressed/groomed herself hurriedly. Jill dressed/*groomed hurriedly.
The [MASK] will [V3.1]. The [MASK] will [V3.2] themself.

A.4   Understood Reciprocal Object

Anne met/*agreed Cathy. Anne and Cathy met/agreed.
The [MASK] will [V4.1] the [MASK]. The [MASK] and the [MASK] will [V4.2].

A.5   Conative

Paula hit/bonked the fence. Paula hit/*bonked at the fence.
The [MASK] will [V5.1] the [MASK]. The [MASK] will [V5.2] at the [MASK].

A.6   *with* Preposition Drop

Jill met/*kissed with Sarah. Jill met/kissed Sarah.
The [MASK] will [V6.1] with the [MASK]. The [MASK] will [V6.2] the [MASK].

A.7 Dative

Bill sold/surrendered a car to Tom. Bill sold/*surrendered Tom a car.
The [MASK] will [V7.1] a [MASK] to the [MASK]. The [MASK] will [V7.2] the [MASK] a [MASK].

A.8 Benefactive

Martha carved/confiscated a toy for the baby. Martha carved/*confiscated the baby a toy.
The [MASK] will [V8.1] a [MASK] for the [MASK]. The [MASK] will [V8.2] the [MASK] a [MASK].

A.9 Spray/Load

Jack sprayed/dumped paint on the wall. Jack sprayed/*dumped the wall with paint.
The [MASK] will [V9.1] the [MASK] onto the [MASK]. The [MASK] will [V9.2] the [MASK] with the [MASK].

A.10 Clear (transitive)

Henry cleared/extracted dishes from the table. Henry cleared/*extracted the table of dishes.
The [MASK] will [V10.1] the [MASK] from the [MASK]. The [MASK] will [V10.2] the [MASK] of the [MASK].

A.11 Swarm

Bees are swarming/clustering in the garden. The garden is swarming/*clustering with bees.
The [MASK] will [V11.1] in the [MASK]. The [MASK] will [V11.2] with the [MASK].

A.12 Material/Product (transitive)

Martha carved/*turned a toy out of the piece of wood. Martha carved/turned the piece of wood into a toy.
The [MASK] will [V12.1] a [MASK] out of the [MASK]. The [MASK] will [V12.2] the [MASK] into a [MASK].

A.13 Material/Product (intransitive)

That acorn will grow/turn into an oak tree. An oak tree will grow/*turn from that acorn.
That [MASK] will [V13.1] into an [MASK]. An [MASK] will [V13.2] from that [MASK].

A.14 Total Transformation (transitive)

The witch turned/compiled him into a frog. The witch turned/*compiled him from a prince into a frog.
The [MASK] will [V14.1] the [MASK] into a [MASK]. The [MASK] will [V14.2] the [MASK] from a [MASK] into a [MASK].

A.15 Total Transformation (intransitive)

He turned/grew into a frog. He turned/*grew from a prince into a frog.
The [MASK] will [V15.1] into a [MASK]. The [MASK] will [V15.2] from a [MASK] into a [MASK].

A.16 *apart* Reciprocal (transitive)

I broke/disconnected the twig off (of) the branch. I broke/*disconnected the twig and the branch apart.
The [MASK] will [V16.1] the [MASK] off of the [MASK]. The [MASK] will [V16.2] the [MASK] and the [MASK] apart.

A.17 *apart* Reciprocal (intransitive)

The twig broke/disconnected off (of) the branch. The twig and the branch broke/*disconnected apart.
The [MASK] will [V17.1] off of the [MASK]. The [MASK] and the [MASK] will [V17.2] apart.

A.18 Fulfilling

The judge presented/offered a prize to the winner. The judge presented/*offered the winner with a prize.
The [MASK] will [V18.1] a [MASK] to the [MASK]. The [MASK] will [V18.2] the [MASK] with a [MASK].

A.19 Image Impression

The jeweller inscribed/transcribed the name on the ring. The jeweller inscribed/*transcribed the ring with the name.
The [MASK] will [V19.1] the [MASK] on the [MASK]. The [MASK] will [V19.2] the [MASK] with the [MASK].

A.20 *with/against*

Brian hit/threw the stick against the fence. Brian hit/*threw the fence with the stick.
The [MASK] will [V20.1] the [MASK] against the [MASK]. The [MASK] will [V20.2] the [MASK] with the [MASK].

A.21 *through/with*

Alison pierced/*hit the needle through the cloth. Alison pierced/hit the cloth with a needle.
The [MASK] will [V21.1] the [MASK] through the

[MASK]. The [MASK] will [V21.2] the [MASK] with a [MASK].

A.22 *blame*

Mira blamed/*hated the accident on Terry. Mira blamed/hated Terry for the accident.
The [MASK] will [V22.1] the [MASK] on the [MASK]. The [MASK] will [V22.2] the [MASK] for the [MASK].

A.23 Possessor Object

They praised/detected the volunteers' dedication. They praised/*detected the volunteers for their dedication.
The [MASK] will [V23.1] their [MASK]. The [MASK] will [V23.2] them for their [MASK].

A.24 Attribute Object

I admired/praised his honesty. I admired/*praised the honesty in him.
The [MASK] will [V24.1] their [MASK]. The [MASK] will [V24.2] the [MASK] in them.

A.25 Possessor and Attribute

I admired/*detected him for his honesty. I admired/detected the honesty in him.
The [MASK] will [V25.1] them for their [MASK]. The [MASK] will [V25.2] the [MASK] in them.

A.26 *as*

The president appointed/declared Smith press secretary. The president appointed/*declared Smith as press secretary.
The [MASK] will [V26.1] the [MASK] the [MASK]. The [MASK] will [V26.2] the [MASK] as the [MASK].

A.27 Raw Material Subject

She baked/invented wonderful bread from that whole wheat flour. That whole wheat flour bakes/*invents wonderful bread.
The [MASK] will [V27.1] the [MASK] from that [MASK]. That [MASK] will [V27.2] the [MASK].

A.28 Source Subject

The middle class will benefit/gain from the new tax laws. The new tax laws will benefit/*gain the middle class.
The [MASK] will [V28.1] from the [MASK]. The [MASK] will [V28.2] the [MASK].

B Model Details

B.1 BERT tuning

BERT version = bert-large-uncased from `https://github.com/huggingface/transformers`, Optimizer = Adam (Kingma and Ba, 2015), learning rate = 1e-3, batch size = full training set size (each training sentence is a separate datum and is enclosed by a start and end token), epochs = 10.

B.2 Linear Classifier

Architecture = linear layer with an input size the same as that of a BERT embedding and an output size of 2, optimizer = Adam, learning rate = 1e-1, batch size = full training set, epochs = 20, loss = Cross Entropy; trained to label a datum as in-class or out-class with labels of 1 and 0, respectively.

C Psycholinguistic Generalization Test: Full Breakdown

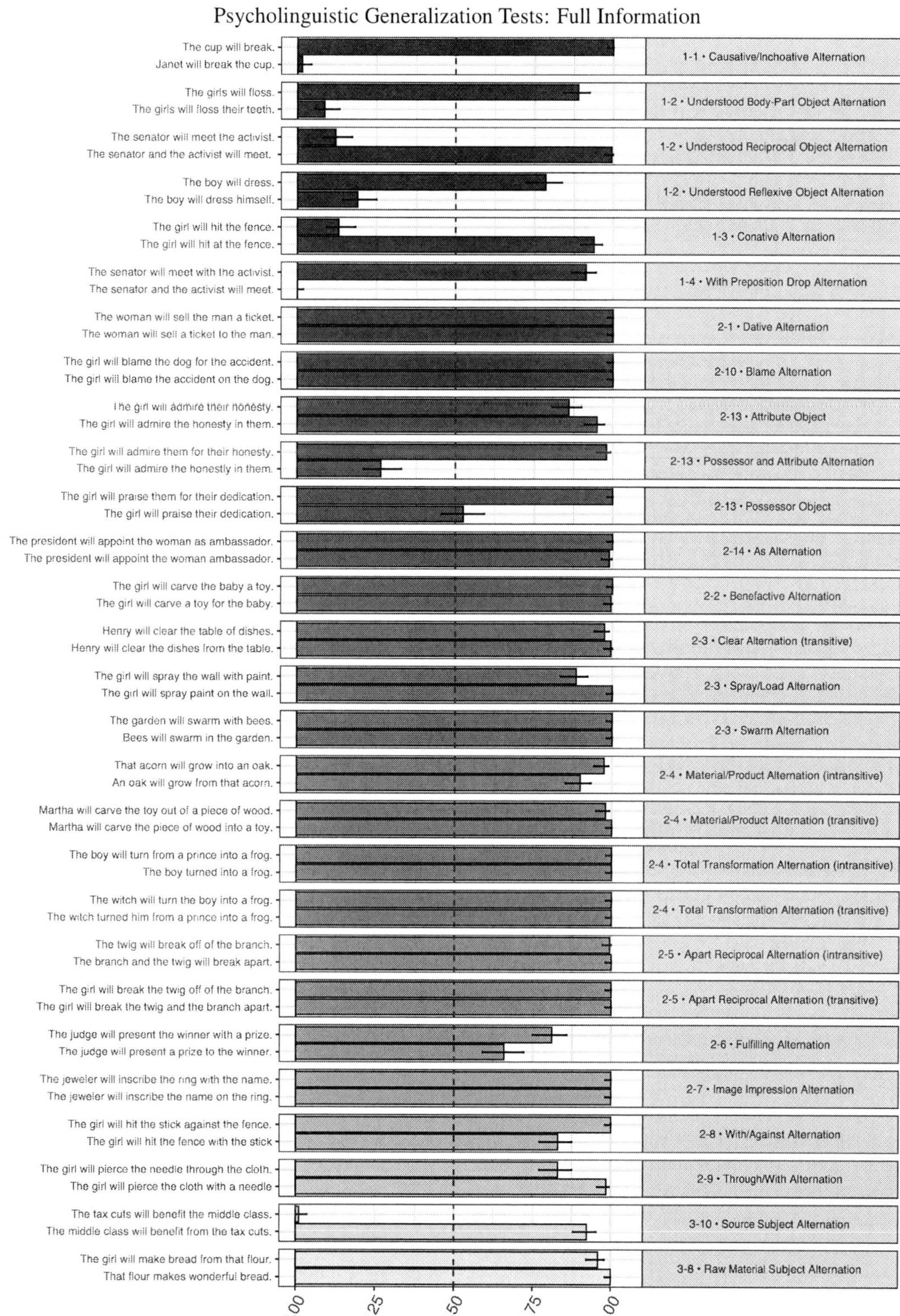

Figure 4: Psycholinguistic generalization test accuracy to sister frames by verbal alternation, colored by section and subsection from (Levin, 1993). Error bars show 95% binomial confidence intervals across 200 random seeds; blue dashed line is the random baseline.

The EOS Decision and Length Extrapolation

Benjamin Newman   **John Hewitt**   **Percy Liang**   **Christopher D. Manning**
Stanford University
{blnewman, johnhew, pliang, manning}@stanford.edu

Abstract

Extrapolation to unseen sequence lengths is a challenge for neural generative models of language. In this work, we characterize the effect on length extrapolation of a modeling decision often overlooked: predicting the end of the generative process through the use of a special end-of-sequence (EOS) vocabulary item. We study an oracle setting—forcing models to generate to the correct sequence length at test time—to compare the length-extrapolative behavior of networks trained to predict EOS (+EOS) with networks not trained to (-EOS). We find that -EOS substantially outperforms +EOS, for example extrapolating well to lengths 10 times longer than those seen at training time in a bracket closing task, as well as achieving a 40% improvement over +EOS in the difficult SCAN dataset length generalization task. By comparing the hidden states and dynamics of -EOS and +EOS models, we observe that +EOS models fail to generalize because they (1) unnecessarily stratify their hidden states by their linear position is a sequence (structures we call *length manifolds*) or (2) get stuck in clusters (which we refer to as *length attractors*) once the EOS token is the highest-probability prediction.

1   Introduction

A core feature of the human language capacity is the ability to comprehend utterances of potentially unbounded length by understanding their constituents and how they combine (Frege, 1953; Chomsky, 1957; Montague, 1970). In NLP, while better modeling techniques have improved models' abilities to perform some kinds of systematic generalization (Gordon et al., 2019; Lake, 2019), these models still struggle to extrapolate; they have trouble producing and processing sequences longer than those seen during training even if they are composed of familiar atomic units.

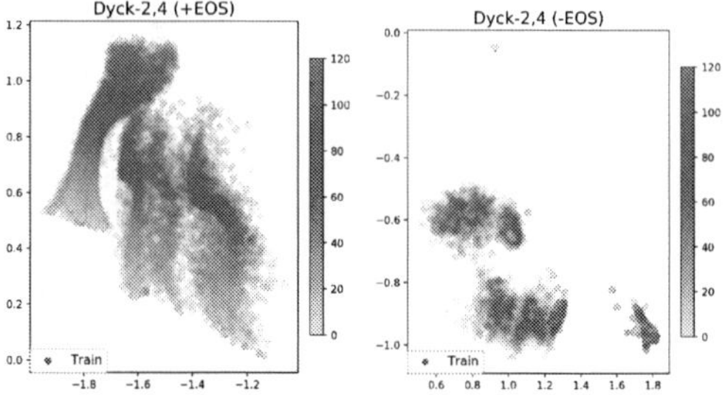

Figure 1: The hidden state dynamics differ between a model that has to predict EOS (**left**) and one that does not (**right**). Color varies with the hidden states' position in the sequence.

In this work, we investigate how an understudied modeling decision affects the ability of neural generative models of language to extrapolate to longer sequences. Models need to place a distribution over all sequence lengths, and to accomplish this when they generate from left to right, they make a decision about whether to generate a content token or a special end-of-sequence (EOS) token at each position in the sequence. In practice, however, the decision to have models predict where sequences end in this way, which we refer to as the *EOS decision*, yields models that predict sequences should end too early in length-extrapolation settings (Hupkes et al., 2020; Dubois et al., 2020).

We conceptually decompose length extrapolation into two components: (i) the ability to produce the right content, and (ii) the ability to know when to end the sequence. Standard evaluations like exact match or BLEU (Papineni et al., 2002) on length-generalization datasets like SCAN and gSCAN (Lake and Baroni, 2018; Ruis et al., 2020) evaluate the ability to perform both components, but models are known to fail because of (ii) alone, so these metrics don't test (i) in isolation. To help evaluate (i) independent of (ii), another evaluation

276

Proceedings of the Third BlackboxNLP Workshop on Analyzing and Interpreting Neural Networks for NLP, pages 276–291
Online, November 20, 2020. ©2020 Association for Computational Linguistics

tool has been to exclude the effect of the EOS decision at test time by forcing models to generate to the correct output length (Lake and Baroni, 2018) or evaluating whether the strings they generate match prefixes of the correct outputs (Dubois et al., 2020; Hupkes et al., 2020).

In contrast, our work is the first to explore what happens if we don't have to perform (ii) (predicting where to end the sequence) **even at training time**. In this case, can we perform better at (i) (generating the right content)? We endeavor to answer this question by comparing the extrapolative ability of models trained without EOS tokens (-EOS) to models trained with them in their training data (+EOS).

First, we look at a simple formal language called Dyck-(k,m) that contains strings of balanced parentheses of k types with a bounded nesting depth of m (Hewitt et al., 2020); see Table 1. Looking at a simple bracket closing task we find that -EOS models close brackets with high accuracy on sequences 10 times longer than those seen at training time, whereas +EOS models perform substantially worse, suggesting fundamental differences in these models' ability to extrapolate. Investigating models' hidden states under principal component analysis (PCA) reveals that +EOS models unnecessarily stratify their hidden states by linear position while -EOS models do so less, likely contributing to -EOS models' improved performance (Figure 1). We call these stratified hidden states *length manifolds*.

Second, we use SCAN—a synthetic sequence-to-sequence dataset meant to assess systematic generalization. We focus on the split of the dataset made to test length extrapolation, showing that models in the +EOS condition perform up to 40% worse than those in the -EOS condition in an oracle evaluation setting where models are provided the correct output length. Visualizing the hidden states of both models using PCA reveals that +EOS models fail once they put high probability on the EOS token because their hidden states remain in place, exhibiting what we term a *length attractor*. -EOS models do not predict the EOS token, and their hidden states are able to move throughout hidden state space during the entire generation process, likely contributing to their improved performance.

Finally, we investigate extrapolation in a human language task—translation from German into English. We use an oracle evaluation where sequence lengths are chosen to maximize the BLEU score of generated translations. In contrast to our other experiments, for this more complex NLP task, we see that the -EOS condition less consistently contributes to extrapolation ability.

2 Related Work

The Difficulty of Extrapolation. Evidence from a number of settings shows that processing sequences longer than those seen at training time is a challenge for neural models (Dubois et al., 2020; Ruis et al., 2020; Hupkes et al., 2020; Klinger et al., 2020). This difficulty has been observed in datasets designed to test the ability of models to compositionally generalize, such as SCAN (Lake and Baroni, 2018), where the best performing neural models do not even exceed 20% accuracy on generating sequences of out-of-domain lengths, whereas in-domain performance is 100%. Extrapolation has also been a challenge for neural machine translation; Murray and Chiang (2018) identifies models producing translations that are too short as one of the main challenges for neural MT.

There are a number of reasons why extrapolation is challenging. At the highest level, some believe extrapolation requires understanding the global structure of a task, which standard neural architectures may have trouble emulating from a modest number of in-domain samples (Mitchell et al., 2018; Marcus, 2018; Gordon et al., 2019). Others focus more on implementation-level modeling problems, such as the EOS problem, where models tend to predict sequences should end too early, and try to address it with architectural changes (Dubois et al., 2020). Our work focuses on the latter issue; we show how the EOS decision affects not just a model's tendency for producing EOS tokens too early, but also the representations and dynamics underlying these decisions.

Addressing Extrapolation Issues Previous approaches to address the poor extrapolation ability of standard sequence models often focus on architectural changes. They include incorporating explicit memory (Graves et al., 2014) or specialized attention mechanisms (Dubois et al., 2020). Others have proposed search-based approaches—modifying beam search to prevent EOS from being assigned too much probability mass (Murray and Chiang, 2018), or searching through programs to produce sequences rather than having neural models produce sequences themselves (Nye et al.,

2020). Extrapolative performance has recently come up in the design of positional embeddings for Transformers (Vaswani et al., 2017). While recent Transformer models like BERT use learned positional embeddings (Devlin et al., 2019), when they were first introduced, position was represented through a combination of sinusoids of different periods. These sinusoids were introduced with the hope that their periodicity would allow for better length extrapolation (Vaswani et al., 2017). In this study we provide insight into popular architectures and the EOS decision instead of pursuing new architectures.

Length in Sequence Models Historically, for discrete symbol probabilistic sequence models, no EOS token was included in the standard presentations of HMMs (Rabiner, 1989) or in most following work in speech. However, the importance of having an EOS token in the event space of probabilistic sequence models was emphasized by NLP researchers in the late 1990s (e.g. Collins (1999) Section 2.4.1) and have been used ever since, including in neural sequence models. Requiring neural models to predict these EOS tokens means that these models' representations must track sequence length. There is empirical evidence that the hidden states of LSTM sequence-to-sequence models trained to perform machine translation models track sequence length by implementing something akin to a counter that increments during encoding and decrements during decoding (Shi et al., 2016). These results are consistent with theoretical and empirical findings that show that LSTMs can efficiently implement counting mechanisms (Weiss et al., 2018; Suzgun et al., 2019a; Merrill, 2020). Our experiments will show that tracking absolute token position by implementing something akin to these counters makes extrapolation difficult.

3   Experimental Setup

In all of our experiments, we compare models trained under two conditions: +EOS, where EOS tokens are appended to each training example, as is standard; and −EOS, where no EOS tokens are appended to training examples.

For our Dyck-(k,m) experiments (Section 4), we train on sequences with lengths from a set $\mathcal{L}_{\text{train}}$ and test on sequences with lengths from a set $\mathcal{L}_{\text{test}}$, where $\max \mathcal{L}_{\text{train}} < \min \mathcal{L}_{\text{test}}$.

For our SCAN and German-English MT experiments (Sections 5 and 6), we train on sequences

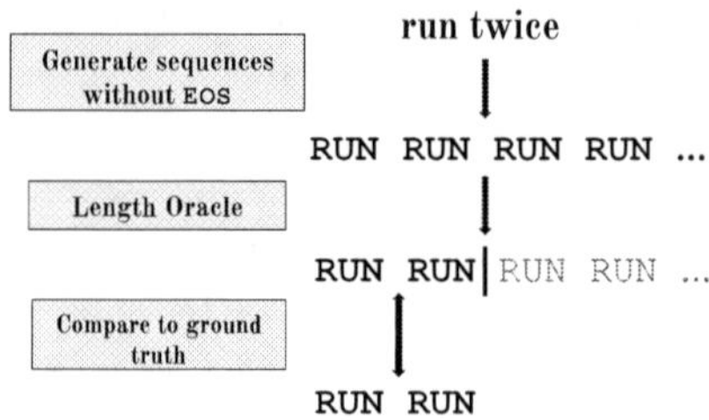

Figure 2: Above is an example of how **length oracle evaluation** works with the SCAN task. Models (both +EOS and −EOS) generate sequences without producing EOS tokens. The length oracle decides the optimal place to end the sequences, and compares the result to the ground truth.

of tokens shorter than some length ℓ, and test on sequences longer than ℓ. We refer to ℓ as a **length cut-off**, and a train-test split created in this manner is referred to as a **length-split**. We evaluate these models differently in each experiment.

Because we are interested in assessing the extrapolative ability of models apart from predicting where sequences end, we use what we refer to as a **length oracle evaluation**. It is performed by first allowing −EOS and +EOS models to output sequences longer than any gold targets, and then choosing the best position to end the sequence. For the +EOS models, this requires preventing the models from emitting EOS tokens during generation by setting the probability mass on the EOS token to 0. We call these models −EOS+Oracle and +EOS+Oracle respectively. Using these oracle metrics ensures that models are only assessed on knowing what content to generate rather than where to end sequences.

4   Experiment 1: Dyck-(k,m)

We conduct our first experiments with a simple language that gives us the opportunity to train an accurate, interpretable language model. This allows us to develop an intuition for how the EOS token affects the representations that models learn.

The language we study is Dyck-(k,m) (Hewitt et al., 2020). It is a formal language that consists of strings of well-nested, balanced brackets. There are k types of brackets, and a maximum nesting depth of m. For our experiments, we set $k = 2$, and vary m. Accepting this language involves implementing a bounded stack of up to size m, and allowing for pushing and popping any of k distinct elements (the bracket types) to and from the stack. We use the

sequence:	(	[	(	)	[	[	(	)	]	]	])
stack state:	(	([	([(	([	([[	([[[	([[[(	([[[	([[	([	(

Table 1: A sample sequence and its stack states from Dyck-(2,6) and Dyck-(2,8), but not Dyck-(2,4) because the maximum nesting depth is 5.

m	$\mathcal{L}_{\text{train}}$	$\mathcal{L}_{\text{test}}$	+EOS	−EOS
4	[88, 116]	[950, 1050]	0.60	**0.86**
6	[184, 228]	[1840, 2280]	0.68	**0.98**
8	[328, 396]	[3280, 3960]	0.68	**0.96**

Table 2: Dyck-(k,m) bracket closing metric results, median of 5 independent training runs.

term **stack state** to refer to what this stack looks like at a given point in processing a sequence. An example sequence and its stack states are given in Table 1.

4.1 Methodology

We train our +EOS and −EOS models on a language modeling task using samples from Dyck-(2,4); Dyck-(2,6); and Dyck-(2,8). Minimum training sample lengths are chosen such that sequences of that length contain stack states of all possible depths at least three times in expectation. We include enough training samples to reliably achieve perfect bracket-closing accuracy on an in-domain evaluation.[1] Including *only* long sequences of brackets means that models only see evidence that they can end sequences (in the form of an EOS token) after a long stretch of symbols, not whenever their stack states are empty (and the −EOS model sees no evidence of ending at all). We endeavor to address this shortcoming in Section 4.3.

The out-of-domain samples (with lengths in $\mathcal{L}_{\text{test}}$) are 10 times longer than in-domain ones (with lengths in $\mathcal{L}_{\text{train}}$). (Table 2 gives the lengths for each condition.) The models we use are single layer LSTMs with $5m$ hidden states, and we train each model such that it has perfect in-domain length accuracy on a held-out validation set to ensure that we learn the in-domain data distribution well, rather than sacrifice in-domain performance for potential gains in extrapolative performance. Additionally, such in-domain accuracy is only possible because we are bounding the stack depth of our Dyck-(k,m) samples. If we were using the unbounded Dyck-k languages (with $k > 1$), we would not be able to see good in-domain performance, and thus we would not expect to see acceptable out-of domain performance either (Suzgun et al., 2019b,a).

For evaluation, we use the same metric as Hewitt et al. (2020) as it evaluates the crux of the task: maintaining a long-term stack-like memory of brackets. In principle, we want to ensure that whenever a model can close a bracket, it puts more

probability mass on the correct one. Our metric is as follows: whenever it is acceptable for the model to close a bracket, we compute how often our models assign an large majority (more than 80%) of the probability mass assigned to *any* of the closing brackets to the *correct* closing bracket. For example, if 20% of the probability mass is put on either closing bracket, the model gets credit if it puts more than 16% of the mass on the correct bracket. Because in each sample there are more bracket pairs that are (sequentially) close together than far, we compute this accuracy separately for each distance between the open and close bracket. Our final score is then the mean of all these accuracies.

We also report a standard metric: perplexity for sequences of in-domain and out-of-domain lengths. We choose perplexity because it incorporates the probabilistic nature of the task—we cannot evaluate using exact match because at almost all decoding steps (other than when the stack has m brackets on it) there are two equally valid predictions that the model can make.

4.2 Results

Recall that we train all models to obtain perfect in-domain bracket closing accuracy on a held-out validation set. However, the +EOS models' performance is severely degraded on out-of-domain sequences 10 times longer than in-domain ones, while the −EOS models still perform well across all conditions (Table 2). The perplexity results mirror the results of the bracket closing task (Appendix B).

Because the Dyck-(k,m) is relatively simple, the model's hidden states are interpretable. We run the model on the training data, stack the models' hidden states, extract their top two principal components, and note that they form clusters (Figure 3) that encode stack states (Appendix; Figure 5). We observe that as both models process sequences, they hop between the clusters. However, in the +EOS model, the hidden states move from one side of each cluster to the other during processing, while this does not happen in the −EOS model.

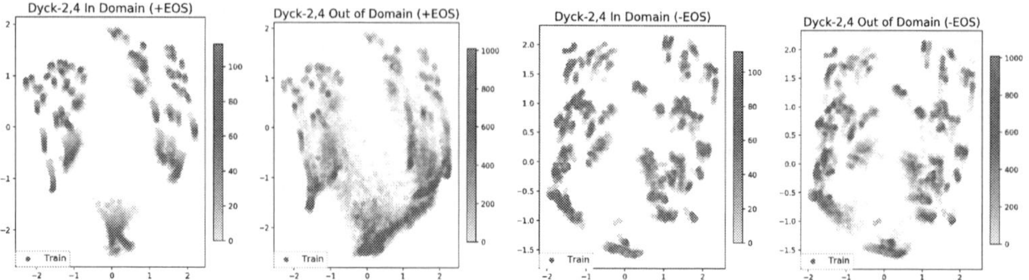

Figure 3: The top two principal components explain 67.52% of the variance for the +EOS model and $62.27\%$of the variance for the −EOS hidden states. The color scale corresponds to index in the sequence. The bottom-most cluster (centered around $(0, −2.0)$ in the +EOS plot and $(0, −1.5)$ in the −EOS plot) contains all of the hidden states where the stack is empty and the sequence can end.

Because of this, we refer to these elongated clusters as **length manifolds**.

As the +EOS model processes inputs past the maximum length it has seen during training, the representations lie past the boundary of the clusters, which we observe leads to a degradation of the model's ability to transition between states. We hypothesize this is because the recurrent dynamics break near the edges of the training-time length manifolds. We can see this degradation of the model dynamics in the out-of-domain +EOS plot (Figure 3). The hidden states at positions further in the sequences congregate at the tips of the length manifolds, or completely deviate from the training data. Contrast this plot to the in-domain −EOS plot, where there are no length manifolds visible and the out-of-domain −EOS plot, where we can see some length manifolds, but less evidence of the degradation of predictions (Table 2).

We hypothesize that these length manifolds form because +EOS models need to predict where each sequence ends in order to confidently put probability mass on the EOS token.[2] Our main takeaway is then that this length tracking has negative effects when the model is used to predict longer sequences.

4.3 Predicting the End of Sequences

Knowing where a Dyck-(k,m) sequence can end is an important part of being able to accept strings from the language. While we focus more on the ability of models to extrapolate in this work, and our evaluations do not depend on the ability of models to end sequences, we do observe in our plots of hidden states that the cluster of hidden states corre-

m	+EOS		−EOS	
	ID	OOD	ID	OOD
4	1.0	0.90	1.0	0.92
6	1.0	0.95	1.0	1.0
8	1.0	0.97	1.0	1.0

Table 3: Accuracies for predicting when Dyck-$(2,m)$ sequences can end. Each entry is the median of five runs. Note that even though +EOS model is trained with an EOS token, it does not receive signal that it can end at other empty stack states, so such a probe is needed for models to learn when to end sequences.

sponding to the empty stack state (where sequences can end) is linearly separable from the other clusters (Figure 3). This linear-separability suggests we can train a linear classifier on top of model hidden states, a probe, to predict where sequences can end (Conneau et al., 2018; Ettinger et al., 2018).

We train a binary classifier to predict if a sequence can end at every token position. The input to this classifier at time-step t is the sequence models' hidden state at t, and it is trained to predict 1 if the sequence can end and 0 otherwise. We find that this simple method is able to predict where sequences end with high accuracy for in-domain sequences, and higher accuracy for the −EOS models compared to the +EOS models for the longer out-of-domain sequences (Table 3). This distinction mirrors the disorganization of the hidden states in the +EOS models hidden states when they extrapolate (Figure 3).

5 Experiment 2: SCAN

While the Dyck-(k,m) experiments give us good intuitions for how and why EOS tokens affect extrapolation, we study SCAN to extend to sequence-to-sequence modeling, and since it is a well-studied

---

[2]Close brackets are more likely than open brackets at training time near the maximum training length, since all sequences must end in the empty stack state; this may explain why −EOS models still show some length-tracking behavior.

dataset in the context of length extrapolation.

SCAN is a synthetic sequence-to-sequence dataset meant to simulate data used to train an instruction-following robot (Lake and Baroni, 2018). The inputs are templated instructions while the outputs correspond to the sequences of actions the robot should take. For example, the input instruction "walk left twice" maps to the output action sequence `TURN_LEFT WALK TURN_LEFT WALK`. There are 13 types in the input vocabulary—five actions (turn, run, walk, jump, look); six modifiers (left, right, opposite, around, twice, thrice); and two conjunctions (and, after), and different combinations of these tokens map to different numbers of actions. For example, "turn left twice" maps to `TURN_LEFT TURN_LEFT` while "turn left thrice" maps to `TURN_LEFT TURN_LEFT TURN_LEFT`. This is important for our exploration of models' abilities to extrapolate because it means that while the lengths of the input instructions range from one to nine tokens, the output action sequences lengths vary from one to 48 tokens.

5.1 Length splits in SCAN

Lake and Baroni (2018) define a 22-token length split of the dataset, in which models are trained on instructions with sequences whose outputs have 1–22 tokens (16990 samples) and are evaluated on sequences whose outputs have 22–48 tokens (3920 samples). Previous work has noted the difficulty of this length split—the best approach where sequences are generated by a neural model achieves 20.8% accuracy (Lake and Baroni, 2018).[3] Specifically, this extra difficulty stems from the fact that neural models only perform the SCAN task well when they are trained with sufficient examples of certain input sequence templates (Loula et al., 2018). In particular, the Lake and Baroni (2018) length split lacks a template from the training data: one of the form "walk/jump/look/run around left/right thrice." Alone, this template results in an output sequence of 24 actions, and thus is not included in the training set. Approximately 80% of the test set is comprised of sequences with this template, but models have not seen any examples of it at training time, so they perform poorly. Thus, we create additional length splits that have more examples of this template, and evaluate using

them in addition to the standard 22-token length split of SCAN.

5.2 Methodology

We generate the 10 possible length splits of the data with length cutoffs ranging from 24 tokens to 40 (See the header of Table 4). Not every integer is represented because SCAN action sequences do not have all possible lengths in this range. For each split, we train the LSTM sequence-to-sequence model that Lake and Baroni (2018) found to have the best in-domain performance. Like in the previous experiment, we train two models—a +EOS model with an EOS token appended to each training sample output, and a -EOS model without them. We use the standard evaluation of Lake and Baroni (2018): greedy decoding and evaluating based on exact match. Because we are interested in how well our models can extrapolate separately from their ability to know when an output should end, we use force our models to generate to the correct sequence length before comparing their predictions to the gold outputs. For the +EOS model, this entails preventing the model from predicting EOS tokens by setting that token's probability to 0 during decoding. This gives us the -EOS+Oracle and +EOS+Oracle evaluations. We additionally report the exact match accuracy when the +EOS model is allowed to emit an EOS token (+EOS), which is the standard evaluation for this task (Lake and Baroni, 2018).

5.3 Results

We find that the -EOS+Oracle models consistently outperform +EOS+Oracle models across all length splits (Table 4). We also observe that after including sequences up to length 26, the models have seen enough of the new template to perform with accuracy $\geq 80\%$ on the rest of the long sequences. However, the question of what the -EOS model is doing that allows it to succeed remains. The +EOS model fails in the non-oracle setting by predicting that sequences should end before they do, and the +EOS+Oracle model fails because once it decodes past its maximum training sequence length, it tends to either repeat the last token produced or emit unrelated tokens. The -EOS+Oracle model succeeds, however, by repeating the last few tokens when necessary, so as to complete the last portion of a *thrice* command for example. (See Table 5 for two such examples).

We compute the top two principal components

---

[3]Note that Nye et al. (2020) are able to achieve 100% accuracy on the SCAN length split, though their set-up is different—their neural model searchers for the SCAN grammar rather than generating sequences by token.

	ℓ (length cutoff)	22	24	25	26	27	28	30	32	33	36	40
LSTM	*+EOS*	*0.16*	*0.08*	*0.26*	*0.61*	*0.72*	*0.64*	*0.60*	*0.67*	*0.45*	*0.47*	*0.85*
	+EOS+Oracle	0.18	0.46	0.47	0.71	0.82	0.77	0.80	0.84	0.74	0.81	0.95
	−EOS+Oracle	**0.61**	**0.57**	**0.54**	**0.83**	**0.92**	**0.97**	**0.90**	**1.00**	**0.99**	**0.98**	**1.00**
Transformer	*+EOS*	*0.00*	*0.05*	*0.04*	*0.00*	*0.09*	*0.00*	*0.09*	*0.35*	*0.00*	*0.00*	*0.00*
	+EOS+Oracle	0.53	0.51	**0.69**	0.76	0.74	0.57	0.78	0.66	0.77	**1.00**	0.97
	−EOS+Oracle	**0.58**	**0.54**	0.67	**0.82**	**0.88**	**0.85**	**0.89**	**0.82**	**1.00**	**1.00**	**1.00**

Table 4: Exact match accuracies on length splits. Reported results are the median of 5 runs. The +EOS rows (italicized) are not comparable to the other rows because they are not evaluated in an an oracle setting—they are provided for reference.

Instruction	Model	Predicted Actions
walk around left twice and walk around left thrice	+EOS+Oracle	TURN_LEFT WALK … WALK WALK JUMP WALK WALK JUMP WALK WALK JUMP
	−EOS+Oracle	TURN_LEFT … WALK TURN_LEFT WALK TURN_LEFT WALK TURN_LEFT WALK TURN_LEFT WALK
run around left twice and run around right thrice	+EOS+Oracle	TURN_LEFT … TURN_RIGHT RUN RUN
	−EOS+Oracle	TURN_LEFT … TURN_RIGHT RUN TURN_RIGHT

Table 5: Two examples of errors a +EOS model makes from the 22-token length split: generating irrelevant actions and repeating the last action. Red tokens are incorrect, blue are correct. See the appendix for more examples.

of the decoder hidden states and plot them as we did for the Dyck-(k,m) models. While the top two principal components explain a modest amount of the variance (27.78% for −EOS and 29.83% for +EOS), they are still interpretable (Figure 4). In particular, we can see that the recurrent dynamics break differently in this case compared to the Dyck-$(2,4)$ case. Here, they break once the +EOS model puts a plurality of probability mass on the EOS token (4b). Once this happens, the hidden states remain in the cluster of EOS states (4a, pink cluster). The −EOS condition does not have such an attractor cluster (4d), so these same hidden states are able to transition between clusters associated with various token identities (4c). This freedom likely aids extrapolative performance.

A figure with hidden states colored by length is available in Appendix C. Both the +EOS and −EOS show evidence of tracking token position because knowing how many actions have been taken is an important component of the SCAN task (for example, to follow an instruction like "turn left twice and walk around right thrice", a model needs to recall how many times it has turned left in order to correctly continue on to walking around thrice).

The results we see here shed some light on the length generalization work by Lake and Baroni (2018). They note that when they prevent a model from predicting EOS (our +EOS+Oracle metric),

they achieved 60.2% exact match accuracy on the 22-token length split with a GRU with a small hidden dimension. This number is comparable to the number we find using −EOS+Oracle metric. The success of the low-dimensional GRU may very well be related to its failure to implement counters as efficiently as LSTMs (Weiss et al., 2018)—if the model cannot count well, then it may not learn length attractors.

5.4 Transformer-based models

All of our experiments so far have used LSTMs, but transformers are the current state of the art in many NLP tasks. They also can be trained with the standard fixed sinusoidal positional embeddings, which Vaswani et al. (2017) suggest might help with extrapolation due to their periodicity. We train transformer +EOS and −EOS models with sinusoidal positional embeddings on the SCAN length splits and observe that +EOS models perform about as poorly as +EOS models in the LSTM case as well (Table 4). Despite using periodic positional embeddings, +EOS models are not able to extrapolate well in this setting.

6 Experiment 3: Machine Translation

Our final experiment focuses on how well the extrapolation we see in the case of SCAN scales to a human-language task—translation from German to

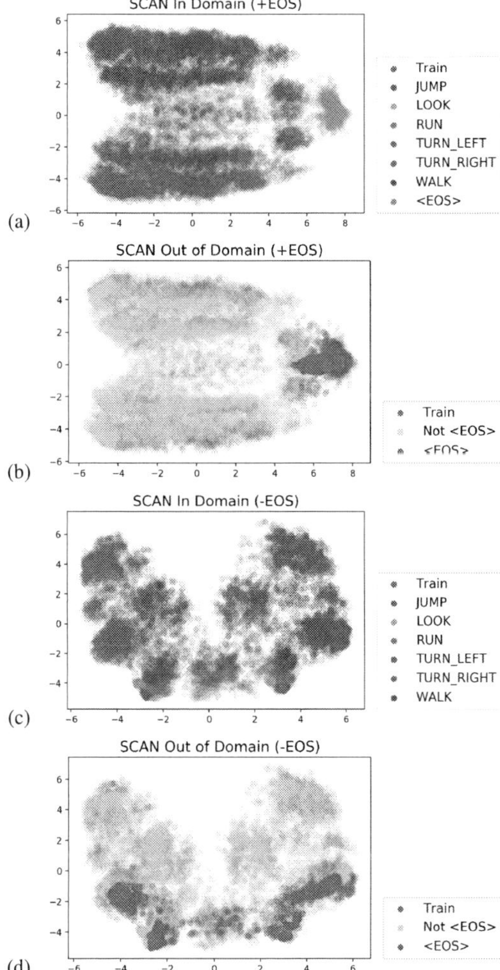

Figure 4: The top two principal components of the hidden states for the +EOS and −EOS LSTM models trained on the SCAN 22-token length split. 4a and 4c color hidden states by the identity of the gold output tokens for the +EOS and −EOS conditions respectively. 4b and 4d color out-of-domain sequences by whether the +EOS model puts a plurality of probability mass is put on the EOS token (<EOS>, red) or on any other token (Not <EOS>, light blue). It is important to note that in both plots, the colors are derived from the +EOS model as we want to investigate how the −EOS model performs in the places where the +EOS model errs.

English from the WMT2009 challenge. This data is much more complex than the SCAN task and has many more subtle markers for length, which might act as proxies for the EOS token, meaning that removing EOS tokens from the training data has a smaller impact on the models' extrapolative abilities. We find that there is very little difference between the +EOS and −EOS models' performance

on out-of-domain lengths compared to SCAN, and while −EOS perform better in out-of-domain settings more often than +EOS models, removing the EOS token does not conclusively help with extrapolation.

6.1 Methodology

We use a subset of 500,000 German to English sentences from the WMT2009 challenge Europarl training set. The median English sentence length has 24 tokens; we create three length splits: with $\ell = 10$, 15, and 25, giving us approximately 61, 126, and 268 thousand training examples respectively. We train +EOS and −EOS LSTM models with 2 layers for the encoder and decoder with 500 and 1000-dimensional hidden states as well as Transformer models, the result of a hyperparameter search described in Appendix A.3. Additionally, the training data in both conditions is modified by removing any final punctuation from the sentences that could serve as explicit markers for length. Finally, our evaluations are very similar to the ones in our SCAN experiments, but our metric is BLEU rather than exact match accuracy (Papineni et al., 2002).

We report standard BLEU for the +EOS condition, and two length oracles, where we prevent the +EOS models from producing EOS tokens and force sequences produced by all models to stop decoding at the length that maximizes their BLEU score. In practice, computing the BLEU score for all sequence lengths is expensive, so we consider only lengths within a window of 7 tokens on either side of the gold target length, which gets us within ~1% of the true oracle score. We train our models using OpenNMT (Klein et al., 2017) and calculate BLEU using the sacreBLEU package for reproducibility (Post, 2018).

6.2 Results

We observe a slight increase in extrapolative performance for −EOS models over +EOS models for LSTMs in the 15 and 10-token length splits, and transformers in the 15 and 25-token length splits, but have no consistent takeaways (Table 6).

We also report in-domain BLEU scores. There is some variation between these, but mostly less than between the out-of-domain scores, which may suggest that the difference of extrapolative performance in those models is meaningful. Additionally, we do not report plots of the top two principal components for these models because they only explain

ℓ	10		15		25	
LSTM	ID	OOD	ID	OOD	ID	OOD
+EOS	*25.25*	*1.75*	*25.27*	*7.24*	*28.14*	*16.19*
+EOS+Oracle	26.42	4.64	**26.43**	11.75	**29.01**	**20.34**
-EOS+Oracle	**26.59**	**5.14**	25.84	**12.53**	28.70	20.12
Δ	0.17	0.5	-0.59	0.78	-0.31	-0.22
Transformer						
+EOS	*24.91*	*1.27*	*25.67*	*5.16*	*28.75*	*13.32*
+EOS+Oracle	26.15	**4.87**	26.33	10.37	**29.29**	17.14
-EOS+Oracle	**26.73**	4.65	**26.81**	**11.65**	29.13	**17.39**
Δ	0.58	-0.22	0.51	1.32	0.16	0.25

Table 6: German-to-English translation BLEU scores. ID is on held-out data with the same length as the training data and OOD is data longer than that seen at training.

3% of the variance and are not visually interesting.

We speculate that we do not see the −EOS models consistently outperforming the +EOS ones because are likely more subtle indicators of length that models in both conditions pick up on, rendering the presence of EOS tokens less relevant. Further analysis should look to mitigate these length cues as well as investigate additional length splits.

7 Discussion

For most purposes of generative modeling, it is necessary to know when to end the generative process in order to use a model; put another way, a −EOS model is not usable by itself. The immediate engineering question is whether there exists a way to learn a distribution over when to end the generative process that does not have the same negative effects as the EOS decision.

In our Dyck-(k,m) experiments, we observed that even in −EOS models, there exists a linear separator in hidden state space between points where the generative process is and isn't allowed to terminate. We explore training probe to find this linear separator, and are able to predict where sequences end with high accuracy (Table 3). In our other experiments, we did not see such a simple possible solution, but can speculate as to what it would require. In particular, the length manifold and length attractor behaviors seem to indicate that length extrapolation fails because the conditions for stopping are tracked in these models more or less in terms of absolute linear position. As such, it is possible that a successful parameterization may make use of an implicit checklist model (Kiddon et al., 2016), that checks off which parts of the input have been accounted for in the output.

Can we use the same neural architectures, in the +EOS setting, while achieving better length extrapolation? Our PCA experiments seem to indicate that −EOS models' length tracking is (at least) linearly decodable. This suggests that training models with an adversarial loss against predicting the position of the token may encourage +EOS models to track length in a way that allows for extrapolation.

8 Conclusion

In this work, we studied a decision often overlooked in NLP: modeling the probability of ending the generative process through a special token in a neural decoder's output vocabulary. We trained neural models to predict this special EOS token and studied how this objective affected their behavior and representations across three diverse tasks. Our quantitative evaluations took place in an oracle setting in which we forced all models to generate until the optimal sequence length at test time. Under this setting, we consistently found that networks trained to predict the EOS token (+EOS) had a worse length-extrapolative ability than those not trained to (−EOS). Examining the hidden states of +EOS and −EOS networks, we observed that +EOS hidden states exhibited *length manifolds* and *length attractor* behaviors that inhibit extrapolation, and which otherwise identical −EOS networks do not exhibit. Thus, we argue that training to predict the EOS token causes current models to track generated sequence length in their hidden states in a manner that does not extrapolate out-of-domain. When EOS tokens were first introduced to NLP ensure probabilistic discrete sequence models maintained well-formed distributions over strings, these models, with a small sets of hidden states, did not readily pick up on these length correlations. However, when this NLP technique was ported to more expressive neural networks, it hid potentially useful length-extrapolative inductive biases. We see the evidence presented here as a call to explore alternative ways to parameterize the end of the generative process.

Acknowledgments

The authors thank Nelson Liu and Atticus Geiger for comments on early drafts, and to our reviewers whose helpful comments improved the clarity of this work. JH was supported by an NSF Graduate Research Fellowship under grant number DGE-1656518.

References

Noam Chomsky. 1957. *Syntactic Structures*. Mouton, The Hague.

Michael Collins. 1999. Head-driven statistical models for natural language processing. *PhD dissertation, University of Pennsylvania.*

Alexis Conneau, German Kruszewski, Guillaume Lample, Loïc Barrault, and Marco Baroni. 2018. What you can cram into a single $&!#* vector: Probing sentence embeddings for linguistic properties. In *Proceedings of the 56th Annual Meeting of the Association for Computational Linguistics (Volume 1: Long Papers)*, pages 2126–2136, Melbourne, Australia. Association for Computational Linguistics.

Jacob Devlin, Ming-Wei Chang, Kenton Lee, and Kristina Toutanova. 2019. BERT: Pre-training of deep bidirectional transformers for language understanding. In *Proceedings of the 2019 Conference of the North American Chapter of the Association for Computational Linguistics: Human Language Technologies*, Minneapolis, Minnesota. Association for Computational Linguistics.

Yann Dubois, Gautier Dagan, Dieuwke Hupkes, and Elia Bruni. 2020. Location Attention for Extrapolation to Longer Sequences. In *Proceedings of the 58th Annual Meeting of the Association for Computational Linguistics*, pages 403–413, Online. Association for Computational Linguistics.

Allyson Ettinger, Ahmed Elgohary, Colin Phillips, and Philip Resnik. 2018. Assessing composition in sentence vector representations. In *Proceedings of the 27th International Conference on Computational Linguistics*, pages 1790–1801, Santa Fe, New Mexico, USA. Association for Computational Linguistics.

Gottlob Frege. 1953. The foundations of arithmetic: A logico-mathematical enquiry into the concept of number, trans. jl austin. *Oxford: Basil Blackwell*, 3:3e.

Jonathan Gordon, David Lopez-Paz, Marco Baroni, and Diane Bouchacourt. 2019. Permutation equivariant models for compositional generalization in language. In *International Conference on Learning Representations*.

Alex Graves, Greg Wayne, and Ivo Danihelka. 2014. Neural turing machines. *arXiv preprint arXiv:1410.5401.*

John Hewitt, Michael Hahn, Surya Ganguli, Percy Liang, and Christopher D. Manning. 2020. RNNs can generate bounded hierarchical languages with optimal memory. In *Proceedings of the 2019 Conference on Empirical Methods in Natural Language Processing and the 9th International Joint Conference on Natural Language Processing (EMNLP-IJCNLP)*. Association for Computational Linguistics.

Dieuwke Hupkes, Verna Dankers, Mathijs Mul, and Elia Bruni. 2020. Compositionality decomposed: How do neural networks generalise? *Journal of Artificial Intelligence Research*, 67:757–795.

Chloé Kiddon, Luke Zettlemoyer, and Yejin Choi. 2016. Globally coherent text generation with neural checklist models. In *Proceedings of the 2016 Conference on Empirical Methods in Natural Language Processing*, pages 329–339, Austin, Texas. Association for Computational Linguistics.

Diederik P. Kingma and Jimmy Ba. 2015. Adam: A method for stochastic optimization. In *3rd International Conference on Learning Representations, ICLR 2015, San Diego, CA, USA, May 7-9, 2015, Conference Track Proceedings*.

Guillaume Klein, Yoon Kim, Yuntian Deng, Jean Senellart, and Alexander Rush. 2017. OpenNMT: Opensource toolkit for neural machine translation. In *Proceedings of ACL 2017, System Demonstrations*, pages 67–72, Vancouver, Canada. Association for Computational Linguistics.

Tim Klinger, Dhaval Adjodah, Vincent Marois, Josh Joseph, Matthew Riemer, Alex'Sandy' Pentland, and Murray Campbell. 2020. A study of compositional generalization in neural models. *arXiv preprint arXiv:2006.09437.*

Brenden Lake and Marco Baroni. 2018. Generalization without systematicity: On the compositional skills of sequence-to-sequence recurrent networks. In *International Conference on Machine Learning*, pages 2873–2882.

Brenden M Lake. 2019. Compositional generalization through meta sequence-to-sequence learning. In *Advances in Neural Information Processing Systems*, pages 9791–9801.

João Loula, Marco Baroni, and Brenden Lake. 2018. Rearranging the familiar: Testing compositional generalization in recurrent networks. In *Proceedings of the 2018 EMNLP Workshop BlackboxNLP: Analyzing and Interpreting Neural Networks for NLP*, pages 108–114, Brussels, Belgium. Association for Computational Linguistics.

Gary Marcus. 2018. Deep learning: A critical appraisal. *arXiv preprint arXiv:1801.00631.*

William Merrill. 2020. On the linguistic capacity of real-time counter automata. *arXiv preprint arXiv:2004.06866.*

Jeff Mitchell, Pasquale Minervini, Pontus Stenetorp, and Sebastian Riedel. 2018. Extrapolation in NLP. *arXiv preprint arXiv:1805.06648.*

Richard Montague. 1970. Universal grammar. *Theoria*, 36(3):373–398.

Kenton Murray and David Chiang. 2018. Correcting length bias in neural machine translation. In *Proceedings of the Third Conference on Machine Translation: Research Papers*, Brussels, Belgium. Association for Computational Linguistics.

Maxwell Nye, A. Solar-Lezama, J. Tenenbaum, and B. Lake. 2020. Learning compositional rules via neural program synthesis. *ArXiv*, abs/2003.05562.

Kishore Papineni, Salim Roukos, Todd Ward, and Wei-Jing Zhu. 2002. Bleu: a method for automatic evaluation of machine translation. In *Proceedings of the 40th Annual Meeting of the Association for Computational Linguistics*, pages 311–318, Philadelphia, Pennsylvania, USA. Association for Computational Linguistics.

Matt Post. 2018. A call for clarity in reporting BLEU scores. In *Proceedings of the Third Conference on Machine Translation: Research Papers*, pages 186–191, Belgium, Brussels. Association for Computational Linguistics.

Lawrence R Rabiner. 1989. A tutorial on hidden markov models and selected applications in speech recognition. *Proceedings of the IEEE*, 77(2):257–286.

Laura Ruis, Jacob Andreas, Marco Baroni, Diane Bouchacourt, and Brenden M Lake. 2020. A benchmark for systematic generalization in grounded language understanding. *arXiv preprint arXiv:2003.05161*.

Xing Shi, Kevin Knight, and Deniz Yuret. 2016. Why neural translations are the right length. In *Proceedings of the 2016 Conference on Empirical Methods in Natural Language Processing*, pages 2278–2282, Austin, Texas. Association for Computational Linguistics.

Mirac Suzgun, Yonatan Belinkov, Stuart Shieber, and Sebastian Gehrmann. 2019a. LSTM networks can perform dynamic counting. In *Proceedings of the Workshop on Deep Learning and Formal Languages: Building Bridges*, pages 44–54, Florence. Association for Computational Linguistics.

Mirac Suzgun, Yonatan Belinkov, and Stuart M. Shieber. 2019b. On evaluating the generalization of LSTM models in formal languages. In *Proceedings of the Society for Computation in Linguistics (SCiL) 2019*, pages 277–286.

Ashish Vaswani, Noam Shazeer, Niki Parmar, Jakob Uszkoreit, Llion Jones, Aidan N Gomez, Łukasz Kaiser, and Illia Polosukhin. 2017. Attention is all you need. In *Advances in neural information processing systems*, pages 5998–6008.

Gail Weiss, Yoav Goldberg, and Eran Yahav. 2018. On the practical computational power of finite precision RNNs for language recognition. In *Proceedings of the 56th Annual Meeting of the Association for Computational Linguistics (Volume 2: Short Papers)*, Melbourne, Australia. Association for Computational Linguistics.

A Experiment Details

A.1 Dyck-(k,m)

The language Dyck-(k,m), for $k, m \in \mathbb{Z}^+$, is a set of strings over the vocabulary consisting of k open brackets, k close brackets, and the EOS token. To generate a dataset for Dyck-(k,m), we must thus define a distribution over the language, and sample from it. Defining this distribution characterizes the statistical properties of the language – how deeply nested is it on average, how long are the strings, etc.

At a high level, we wanted our samples from Dyck-(k,m) to be difficult – that is, to require long-term memory, and to traverse from empty memory to its maximum nesting depth (m) and back multiple times in the course of a single sample, to preclude simple heuristics like remembering the first few open brackets to close the last few. For further discussion of evaluation of models on Dyck-k and similar formal languages, see Suzgun et al. (2019b).

The distribution we define is as follows. If the string is balanced, we end the string with probability $1/2$ and open any of the k brackets with probability $1/2$. If the string has more than 0 unclosed open parentheses but fewer than m (the bound), we open a bracket with probability $1/2$ and close the most recently opened bracket with probability $1/2$; if we open a bracket, we choose uniformly at random from the k. If the string has m unclosed open brackets, then it has reached its nesting bound, and we close the most recently opened bracket with probability 1.

Sampling directly from this distribution would lead to exponentially short sequences, which would break our desideratum of difficulty. So, we truncate the distribution by the length of strings, ensuring a minimum (and a maximum) length at training time.

We define the length truncation as follows. Consider that the number of unclosed open brackets at timestep t is some number between 0 and m. At any timestep, we move from s_i to s_{i+1} with probability $1/2$ (opening a bracket), or from s_i to s_{i-1} with probability $1/2$ (closing a bracket.) Let these states be s_0 to s_m. What we'd like to see is that we eventually move from state s_0 to s_m and back to s_0 multiple times, making sure that the network cannot use positional heuristics to remember the first few brackets in order to close the last few. We ensure this in expectation by making sure that the minimum truncation length of samples is defined

so that in expectation, sampled strings traverse the Markov chain from s_0 to s_m and back to s_0 at least three times.

In practice, we set the minimum length of training samples to $6m(m-2)+40$, and the maximum length to $7m(m-2)+60$. Note the quadratic dependence on m; this is because of the expected hitting time of s_0 to s_{m+1} of the $m+1$-state Markov chain wherein there is a $1/2$ probability of moving in each direction. We add constant factors to ensure there are no extremely short sequences for small m; the exact truncation lengths are not as important as the general scaling.

Additionally, as m increases, the number of training examples required for consistently high in-domain performance also increases. We use $10^{\frac{m}{2}+2}$ training examples for each of the values of m. For all values of m, we use 10000 test samples.

Our models are single-layer LSTMs with $5m$ hidden states. We a batch size of $2^{\frac{m}{2}+2}$, and use the Adam optimizer with a learning rate of 0.01 (Kingma and Ba, 2015).

A.2 SCAN

The SCAN model we train is the model that achieves the best accuracy in-domain in the experiments of Lake and Baroni (2018). This is an LSTM sequence-to-sequence model with 2 layers of 200-dimensional hidden units and no dropout or attention. Optimization was done with the Adam optimizer (Kingma and Ba, 2015), learning rate of 0.001. We used OpenNMT to train the transformer models (Klein et al., 2017). These models have 2 layers, 128-dimensional hidden states, 8 attention-heads, and 1024-dimensional feedfoward layers. All other hyperparameters were the defaults suggested by OpenNMT for training transformer sequence-to-sequence models.

A.3 Machine Translation

The German-English MT models we train were also trained with Open NMT. We trained LSTM models with attention and 1000-dimensional and 500-dimensional hidden states and two layers. All other parameters were specified by the OpenNMT defaults as of OpenNMT-py version 1.1.1. For the 25-token length split we report results with 1000-dimensional hidden states, and with 500-dimensional hidden states for the 10-length split. For the 15-token length split the +EOS model used 1000-dimensional hidden states while the +EOS+Oracle and -EOS+Oracle models used

500-dimensional hidden states. This difference is a result of running hyperparameter optimization and finding that +EOS baseline performed better with a larger hidden state size. Our transformer models were trained using the hyperparameters suggested by OpenNMT for training transformer sequence-to-sequence models. This includes 6 layers for the decoder and decoder, 512-dimensional hidden states and 2048-dimensional feed-forward layers.

B Additional Plots and Results for Dyck-2,m Languages

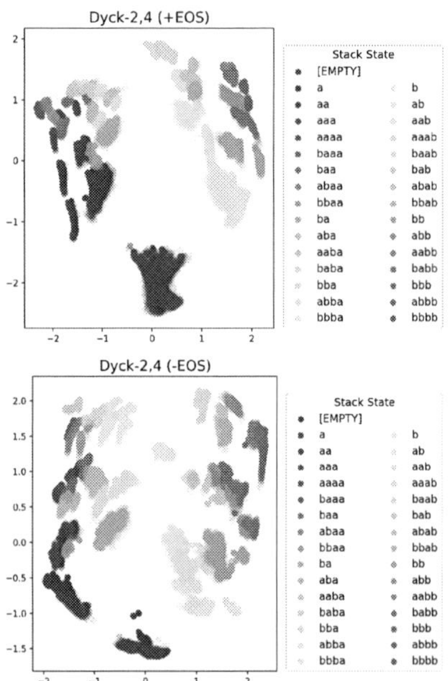

Figure 5: Above we can see a plot of the top two principal components of hidden states from the +EOS and −EOS LSTMs trained on they Dyck-2,4. These hidden states come from the training samples. The hidden states are colored by stack state—at that point in the sequence, what brackets must be closed and in what order. Because this is Dyck-2,4 there are 2 types of brackets which we can call "a" and "b". An "a" in stack state in the legend represents that there is a bracket of type "a" on the stack, and the same for "b". The top of the stack is the right-most character. We can see that the the the first principal component roughly represents whether an "a" or "b" is at the top of the stack.

m	+EOS	−EOS	−EOS + Random Cutoff
4	0.60	0.86	**1.0**
6	0.68	0.98	**1.0**
8	0.68	0.96	**1.0**

Table 8: Dyck-$(2,m)$ bracket closing metric results, median of 5 independent training runs.

m	+EOS		−EOS	
	ID	OOD	ID	OOD
4	2.39	7.09	2.38	**2.93**
6	2.52	5.14	2.52	**2.60**
8	2.60	5.24	2.59	**2.68**

Table 7: Perplexities of the +EOS and −EOS models trained on Dyck-2,m languages on in-domain (ID) and out-of-domain (OOD) strings. The perplexities support the bracket closing results—the perplexities are very similar in-domain and out-of-domain for −EOS model but differ substantially for the +EOS model. Reported value is the median of five runs, lower is better.

Our −EOS models were not able to achieve perfect accuracy on the the bracket-closing task on longer sequences. We suspect that this failure is due to the −EOS models picking up on other signals for sequence length that were present in our Dyck-$(2,m)$ samples. Namely, all of our samples ended in an empty bracket state, so the final non-EOS token was always a closing bracket. To address this issue, we explored removing a random number of additional tokens from the end of the −EOS models' training data (−EOS +Random Cutoff). We found that doing this allowed us to perfectly extrapolate to sequences 10x longer (Table 8).

C Additional Plots and Samples for SCAN Task

	run around left after jump around left twice		look around left thrice		run around left thrice after jump around right thrice	
	+EOS	−EOS	+EOS	−EOS	+EOS	−EOS
1	TURN_LEFT	TURN_LEFT	TURN_LEFT	TURN_LEFT	TURN_RIGHT	TURN_RIGHT
2	JUMP	JUMP	LOOK	LOOK	JUMP	JUMP
3	TURN_LEFT	TURN_LEFT	TURN_LEFT	TURN_LEFT	TURN_RIGHT	TURN_RIGHT
4	JUMP	JUMP	LOOK	LOOK	JUMP	JUMP
5	TURN_LEFT	TURN_LEFT	TURN_LEFT	TURN_LEFT	TURN_RIGHT	TURN_RIGHT
6	JUMP	JUMP	LOOK	LOOK	JUMP	JUMP
7	TURN_LEFT	TURN_LEFT	TURN_LEFT	TURN_LEFT	TURN_RIGHT	TURN_RIGHT
8	JUMP	JUMP	LOOK	LOOK	JUMP	JUMP
9	TURN_LEFT	TURN_LEFT	TURN_LEFT	TURN_LEFT	TURN_RIGHT	TURN_RIGHT
10	JUMP	JUMP	LOOK	LOOK	JUMP	JUMP
11	TURN_LEFT	TURN_LEFT	TURN_LEFT	TURN_LEFT	TURN_RIGHT	TURN_RIGHT
12	JUMP	JUMP	LOOK	LOOK	JUMP	JUMP
13	TURN_LEFT	TURN_LEFT	TURN_LEFT	TURN_LEFT	TURN_RIGHT	TURN_RIGHT
14	JUMP	JUMP	LOOK	LOOK	JUMP	JUMP
15	TURN_LEFT	TURN_LEFT	TURN_LEFT	TURN_LEFT	TURN_RIGHT	TURN_RIGHT
16	JUMP	JUMP	LOOK	LOOK	JUMP	JUMP
17	TURN_LEFT	TURN_LEFT	LOOK	TURN_LEFT	TURN_RIGHT	TURN_LEFT
18	JUMP	RUN	JUMP	LOOK	JUMP	RUN
19	TURN_LEFT	TURN_LEFT	LOOK	TURN_LEFT	TURN_LEFT	TURN_LEFT
20	RUN	RUN	JUMP	LOOK	RUN	RUN
21	TURN_LEFT	TURN_LEFT	LOOK	TURN_LEFT	TURN_LEFT	TURN_LEFT
22	RUN	RUN	JUMP	LOOK	RUN	RUN
23	TURN_LEFT	TURN_LEFT	LOOK	TURN_LEFT	TURN_LEFT	TURN_LEFT
24	RUN	RUN	LOOK	LOOK	RUN	RUN
25					TURN_LEFT	TURN_LEFT
26					RUN	RUN
27					TURN_LEFT	TURN_LEFT
28					RUN	RUN
29					TURN_LEFT	TURN_LEFT
30					RUN	RUN
31					TURN_LEFT	TURN_LEFT
32					RUN	RUN
33					RUN	TURN_LEFT
34					RUN	RUN
35					RUN	TURN_LEFT
36					RUN	RUN
37					RUN	TURN_LEFT
38					RUN	RUN
39					RUN	TURN_LEFT
40					RUN	RUN
41					RUN	TURN_LEFT
42					RUN	RUN
43					RUN	TURN_LEFT
44					RUN	RUN
45					RUN	TURN_LEFT
46					RUN	RUN
47					RUN	TURN_LEFT
48					RUN	RUN

Table 9: More illustrative selections of errors the +EOS and −EOS models make when trained on the SCAN 22-token length split. In the left-most column we see that the +EOS model makes a mistake on the conjunction that the −EOS model does not make. In the middle column we see the +EOS model fail on the template that is not seen at training time. In the right-most column we see an example where both models fail: the conjunction of two templates not seen at training time. The +EOS model begins the third "jump around" but does not finish it, while the −EOS model switches completely to the first "turn left".

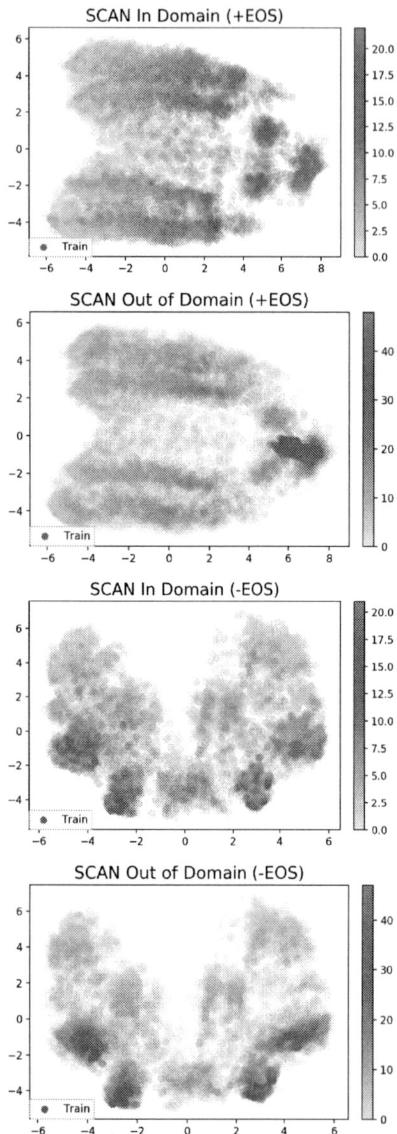

Figure 6: The top two principal components of hidden states from +EOS and −EOS LSTMs trained on the SCAN 22-token length split. Hidden states are colored by their position in the sequence. We can see that both models track length somewhat as it is required, however the +EOS model has an attractor cluster where all points end up while the −EOS model does not have such a cluster.

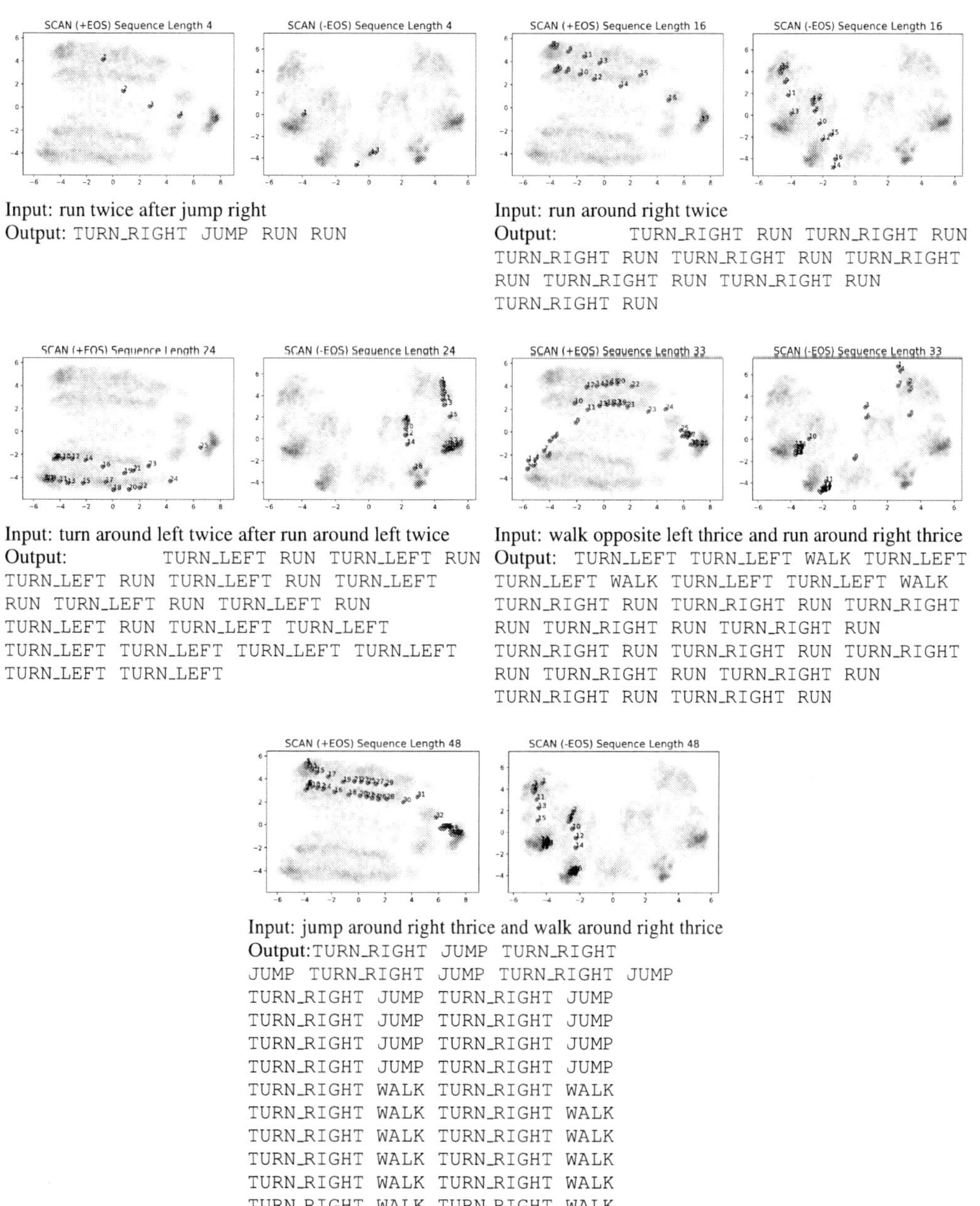

Input: run twice after jump right
Output: TURN_RIGHT JUMP RUN RUN

Input: run around right twice
Output: TURN_RIGHT RUN TURN_RIGHT RUN
TURN_RIGHT RUN TURN_RIGHT RUN TURN_RIGHT
RUN TURN_RIGHT RUN TURN_RIGHT RUN
TURN_RIGHT RUN

Input: turn around left twice after run around left twice
Output: TURN_LEFT RUN TURN_LEFT RUN
TURN_LEFT RUN TURN_LEFT RUN TURN_LEFT
RUN TURN_LEFT RUN TURN_LEFT RUN
TURN_LEFT RUN TURN_LEFT TURN_LEFT
TURN_LEFT TURN_LEFT TURN_LEFT TURN_LEFT
TURN_LEFT TURN_LEFT

Input: walk opposite left thrice and run around right thrice
Output: TURN_LEFT TURN_LEFT WALK TURN_LEFT
TURN_LEFT WALK TURN_LEFT TURN_LEFT WALK
TURN_RIGHT RUN TURN_RIGHT RUN TURN_RIGHT
RUN TURN_RIGHT RUN TURN_RIGHT RUN
TURN_RIGHT RUN TURN_RIGHT RUN TURN_RIGHT
RUN TURN_RIGHT RUN TURN_RIGHT RUN
TURN_RIGHT RUN TURN_RIGHT RUN

Input: jump around right thrice and walk around right thrice
Output:TURN_RIGHT JUMP TURN_RIGHT
JUMP TURN_RIGHT JUMP TURN_RIGHT JUMP
TURN_RIGHT JUMP TURN_RIGHT JUMP
TURN_RIGHT JUMP TURN_RIGHT JUMP
TURN_RIGHT JUMP TURN_RIGHT JUMP
TURN_RIGHT JUMP TURN_RIGHT JUMP
TURN_RIGHT WALK TURN_RIGHT WALK
TURN_RIGHT WALK TURN_RIGHT WALK
TURN_RIGHT WALK TURN_RIGHT WALK
TURN_RIGHT WALK TURN_RIGHT WALK
TURN_RIGHT WALK TURN_RIGHT WALK
TURN_RIGHT WALK TURN_RIGHT WALK

Figure 7: Cherry-picked, but representative, examples of the paths of gold (i.e. not decoded) in-domain (length 4 and 16) and out-of-domain (length 24, 33, 48) examples through the hidden state space of LSTMs trained on the SCAN 22-token length split (top two principle components). Note that the EOS token is included in the +EOS plots, giving them one extra point. Interestingly, the hidden states from the OOD sequences arrive at the EOS attractor well after the maximum training length (22) (for example, the sequence of length 48 arrives at the attractor at the hidden state at position 33), suggesting that the +EOS does have some extrapolative abilities, but the EOS attractor is suppressing them.

Do Language Embeddings capture Scales?

Xikun Zhang[*†]
Stanford University
xikunz2@cs.stanford.edu

Deepak Ramachandran[*]
Google Research
ramachandrand@google.com

Ian Tenney
Google Research
iftenney@google.com

Yanai Elazar
Bar Ilan Univesity, AI2
yanaiela@gmail.com

Dan Roth
University of Pennsylvania
danroth@seas.upenn.edu

Abstract

Pretrained Language Models (LMs) have been shown to possess significant linguistic, common sense and factual knowledge. One form of knowledge that has not been studied yet in this context is information about the scalar magnitudes of objects. We show that pretrained language models capture a significant amount of this information but are short of the capability required for general common-sense reasoning. We identify contextual information in pre-training and numeracy as two key factors affecting their performance, and show that a simple method of canonicalizing numbers can have a significant effect on the results. [1]

1 Introduction

The success of contextualized pretrained Language Models like BERT (Devlin et al., 2018) and ELMo (Peters et al., 2018) on tasks like Question Answering and Natural Language Inference, has led to speculation that they are good at Common Sense Reasoning (CSR).

On one hand, recent work has approached this question by measuring the ability of LMs to answer questions about physical common sense (Bisk et al., 2020) ("How to separate egg whites from yolks?"), temporal reasoning (Zhou et al., 2020) ("How long does a basketball game take?"), and numerical common sense (Lin et al., 2020). On the other hand, after realizing some high-level reasoning skills like this may be difficult to learn from a language-modeling objective only, (Geva et al., 2020) injects numerical reasoning skills into LMs by additional pretraining on automatically generated data. All of these skills are prerequisites for CSR.

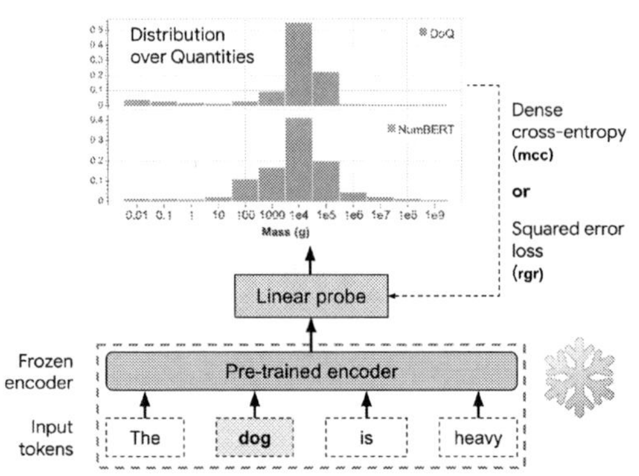

Figure 1: Scalar probing example. The mass of "dog" is a distribution (gray histogram) concentrated around 10-100kg. We train a linear model over a frozen (shown by the snowflake in the figure) encoder to predict this distribution (orange histogram) using either a dense cross-entropy or a regression loss (Section 3).

Here, we address a simpler task which is another pre-requisite for CSR: the prediction of scalar attributes, a task we call *Scalar Probing*. Given an object (such as a "wedding ring") and an attribute with continuous numeric values (such as Mass or Price), can an LM's representation of the object predict the value of that attribute? Since in general, there may not be a single correct value for such attributes due to polysemy ("crane" as a bird, versus construction equipment) or natural variation (e.g. different breeds of dogs), we interpret this as a task of predicting a distribution of possible values for this attribute, and compare it to a ground truth distribution of such values. An overview of this scalar probing is shown in Figure 1. Examples of ground-truth distributions and model predictions for different objects and attributes are shown in Figure 2.

Our analysis shows that contextual encoders, like BERT and ELMo, perform better than noncontextual ones, like Word2Vec, on *scalar probing* de-

---

[*] Both authors contributed equally.

[†] Work done during an internship at Google Research.

[1] Code and models are available at 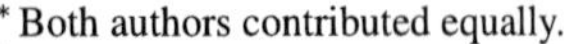 https://github.com/google-research-datasets/numbert.

Proceedings of the Third BlackboxNLP Workshop on Analyzing and Interpreting Neural Networks for NLP, pages 292–299
Online, November 20, 2020. ©2020 Association for Computational Linguistics

spite the task being non-contextual (Mikolov et al., 2013). Further, we show that using scientific notation to represent numbers in pre-training can have a significant effect on results (though sensitive to the evaluation metric used). Put together, these results imply that scale representation in contextual encoders is mediated by transfer of magnitude information from numbers to nouns in pre-training and making this mechanism more robust could improve performance on this and other CSR tasks. We also show improvements by zero-shot transfer from our probes to 2 related tasks: relative comparisons (Forbes and Choi, 2017) and product price prediction (Jianmo Ni, 2019), indicating that our results are robust across datasets.

2   Problem Definition and Data

We define the scalar probing task (see Figure 1) as the problem of predicting a distribution over values of a scalar attribute of an object. We map these values into 12 logarithmically-spaced buckets, so that our task is equivalent to predicting (the distribution of) the order of magnitude of the target value. We explore both models that predict the full distribution and models that predict a point estimate of the value, which is essentially a distribution with all the mass concentrating on one bucket.

Our primary resource for the scalar probing task is Distributions over Quantities (DoQ; Elazar et al., 2019) which consists of empirical counts of scalar attribute values associated with >350K nouns, adjectives, and verbs over 10 different attributes, collected from web data. In this work, we focus only on nouns (which we refer to as *objects*) over the scalar attributes (or *scales*) of MASS (in grams), LENGTH (in meters) and PRICE (in US Dollars). For each object and scale, DoQ provides an empirical distribution over possible values (e.g. Figure 2) that we map into the 12 afore-mentioned buckets and treat it as "ground truth". We note that DoQ itself is derived heuristically from web text and itself contains noise; however, we use it as a starting point to evaluate the performance of different models. Moreover, we validate our findings with transfer experiments shown in Section 6, using DoQ to train a probe that is evaluated on the ground-truth data of Forbes and Choi (2017) and Jianmo Ni (2019).

To explore the role of context in scalar probing, we also trained specialized probing models on a subset of DoQ data in narrow domains: MASS of Animals and PRICE of Household products.

3   Probing Model

We probe three different embedding models: Word2vec (Mikolov et al., 2013), ELMo (Peters et al., 2018) and BERT (Devlin et al., 2018) (the latter two of which are contextualized encoders). For each encoder, the input layer extracts an embedding of the object and the probing layer predicts the scalar magnitude. [2]

Input representations   For Word2vec, we follow the standard practice of averaging the embeddings of each word in the object's name. If an object name is a full phrase in the dictionary, we use its embedding instead. As BERT and ELMo are contextual text encoders operating on full sentences, we generate artificial sentences with the following templates:

- **MASS:** `The X is heavy.`
- **PRICE:** `The X is expensive.`
- **LENGTH:** `The X is big.`

and use the CLS token emebedding (for BERT) or final state embedding (for ELMo) as the input representation. For LENGTH, We use "big" instead of "long", since LENGTH measurements in DoQ can be widths or heights as well. Variations of these templates with different adjectives and sentence structures (e.g. "The X is small." or "What is the length of X?" for LENGTH) led to very similar performance in our evaluations.

Probes   We use linear probes in all cases following many previous probing work (Shi et al., 2016; Ettinger et al., 2016; Pimentel et al., 2020) since we want to use a simple probe to find easily accessible information in a representation. Hewitt and Liang (2019) also demonstrates that linear probes achieve relatively high selectivity compared to non-linear ones like MLP.

We experiment with two different approaches for predicting scales:

Regression (rgr)   For the point estimate, we use a standard Linear Regression model trained

____

[2]We use Word2Vec embeddings of dimension size 500 trained on Wikipedia, BERT-Base (L=12, H=768, A=12, Total Parameters=110M) trained on Wikipedia+Books and ELMo-Small (LSTM Hidden Size=1024, Output Size=128, #Highway Layers=1, Total Parameters=13.6M) trained on the 1 Billion Word Benchmark, approximately 800M tokens of news crawl data from WMT 2011.

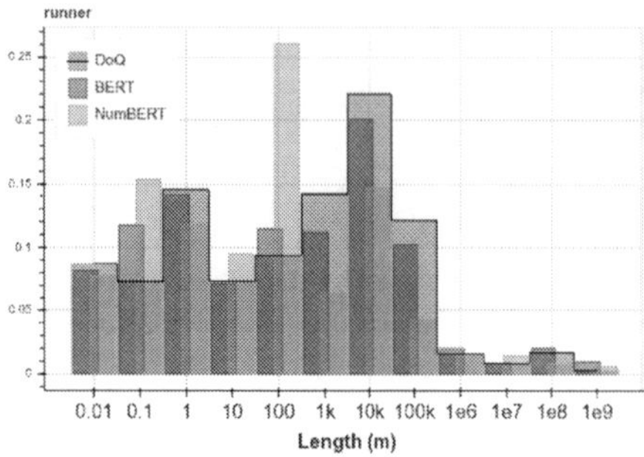

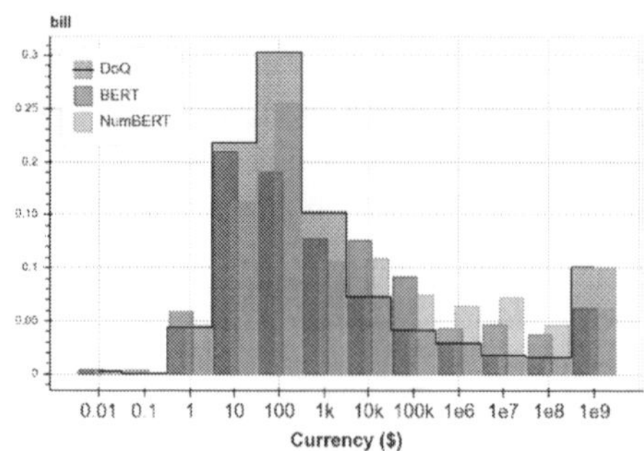

Figure 2: Empirical DoQ distributions and scalar probe predictions for MCC+BERT and MCC+NumBERT (Section 4). The left plot shows length for the term 'runner', showing two peaks corresponding to the length of runner cloths and distances run in races. The right plot shows price for the term 'bill', with counts corresponding to popular denominations and the volumes of larger currency transactions.

to predict log of the median of all values for each object for the scale attribute under consideration.

Multi-class Classification (mcc) We take a non-parametric approach to modeling the full distribution of scalar values and treat the prediction of which bucket a measurement will fall under as a multi-class classification task, with one class per bucket. A similar approach was shown by (Van Oord et al., 2016) to perform well for modeling image pixel values. This approach discards the relationship between adjacent bucket values, but it allows us to use the full empirical distribution as soft labels. We train a linear model with softmax output, using a dense cross-entropy loss against the empirical distribution from DoQ.

More details of the model and training procedure are in the Appendix.

4 Numeracy through Scientific Notation

Wallace et al. (2019) showed that BERT and ELMo had a limited amount of *numeracy* or numerical reasoning ability, when restricted to numbers of small magnitude. Intuitively, it seems that significant model capacity is expended in parsing the natural representation of numbers as Arabic numerals, where higher and lower order digits are given equal prominence. As further evidence of this, it is shown in Appendix B of Wallace et al. (2019) that the simple intervention of *left-padding* numbers in ELMo instead of the default *right-padding* used in Char-CNNs greatly improves accuracy on these

tasks.

To examine the effect of numerical representations on scalar probing, we trained a new version of the BERT model (which we call NumBERT) by replacing every instance of a number in the training data with its representation in *scientific notation*, a combination of an *exponent* and *mantissa* (for example `314.1` is represented as `3141[EXP]2` where `[EXP]` is a new token introduced into the vocabulary). This enables the BERT model to more easily associate objects in the sentence directly with the magnitude expressed in the exponent, ignoring the relatively insignificant mantissa. This model converged to a similar loss on the original BERT Masked LM+NSP pre-training task and a standard suite of NLP tasks (See Appendix) as BERT-base, demonstrating that it was not over-specialized for numerical reasoning tasks.

5 Evaluation

We offer the following **aggregate** baseline to help interpret our results: For each attribute, we compute the empirical distribution over buckets across all objects in the training set, and use that as a predicted distribution for all objects in the test set (this is a stronger version of the majority baseline used in classification tasks). Since we are comparing results from regression and classification models, we report results on 3 disparate metrics that give a full picture of performance:

Accuracy For **mcc** we use the highest scoring bucket from the predicted distribution as the predicted bucket, while for **rgr** we map the predicted scalar to the single containing bucket and use that as the predicted bucket. Then the accuracy is calculated between the predicted bucket and the ground-truth bucket, which is the highest scoring bucket in the empirical distribution in DoQ.

Mean Square Error (MSE) When used to compare distributions, this is also known as the *Cramer-Von Mises* distance (Baringhaus and Henze, 2017). It ignores the difference in magnitude between different buckets (a difference in probability mass between buckets i and $i + 1$ is equivalent to the same difference between buckets i and any other), but is upper-bounded by 1, making it easier to interpret. To calculate MSE for **rgr**, we assume that it assigns a probability of 1 to the single containing bucket.[3]

Earth Mover's Distance (EMD) Also known as the *Wasserstein* distance (Rubner et al., 1998).

Given two probability densities p_1 and p_2 on Ω, and some distance measure d on Ω, the Earth Mover's Distance is defined as follows:

$$D(p_1, p_2) = \inf_{\pi} \int_{\Omega} \int_{\Omega} \mathrm{d}(x, y) d\pi(x, y)$$

where the infimum is over all non-negative measures π on $\Omega \times \Omega$ satisfying $\pi(E \times \Omega) - \pi(\Omega \times E) = \int_E p_1(x)dx - \int_E p_2(x)dx$ for measurable subsets $E \subset \Omega$. Intuitively, EMD measures how much "work" needs to be done to move the probability mass of p_1 to p_2, while MSE measures pointwise what the difference in densities is. So EMD accounts for the distance between buckets, and predictions to neighboring buckets are penalized less than those further away.

EMD is favored in the statistics literature because of its better convergence properties (Rubner et al., 1998), and there is evidence that it is more robust to adversarial perturbations of the data distribution (Liu et al., 2019), which is relevant for our transfer tasks described below.

Transfer experiments We also evaluate models trained on DoQ on 2 datasets containing ground truth labels of scalar attributes. The first is a human-labeled dataset of *relative comparisons* (e.g. *(person, fox, weight, bigger)*) (Forbes and Choi, 2017).

---

[3]This is distinguished from the MSE loss used to train regression models, as it is a distance measure over pairs of distributions.

		Accuracy		MSE		EMD	
		mcc	rgr	mcc	rgr	mcc	rgr
Lengths	Aggregate	.24	.24	.027	.027	.077	.077
	word2vec	.30	.12	.026	.099	.079	.072
	ELMo	**.43**	.23	**.019**	.084	.055	.072
	BERT	.42	.24	.020	.084	.056	.072
	NumBERT	.40	.22	.021	.086	**.052**	.072
Masses	Aggregate	.15	.15	.026	.026	.076	.076
	word2vec	.26	.20	.025	.088	.082	.077
	ELMo	**.36**	.21	**.021**	.087	.061	.077
	BERT	.33	.22	**.021**	.085	.062	.077
	NumBERT	.32	.20	**.021**	.088	**.057**	.077
Prices	Aggregate	.24	.24	.019	.019	.057	.057
	word2vec	.26	.14	.019	.090	.063	.087
	ELMo	**.37**	.21	**.016**	.081	.051	.087
	BERT	.33	.19	.017	.083	.054	.087
	NumBERT	.32	.17	.017	.085	**.051**	.087
Animal Masses	Aggregate	.30	.30	.022	.022	.059	.059
	word2vec	.33	.35	.021	.069	.069	.077
	ELMo	**.43**	.28	**.016**	.079	.057	.077
	BERT	.41	.26	.017	.079	.058	.077
	NumBERT	.42	.23	.018	.083	**.053**	.077

Table 1: Comparison of encoders and probes on the Scalar probing task on DoQ data. Results are averaged over 10-fold cross-validation.

Predictions for this task are made by comparing the point estimates for **rgr** and highest-scoring buckets for **mcc**. The second is an empirical distribution of product price data extracted from the Amazon Review Dataset (Jianmo Ni, 2019). We retrained a model on DoQ prices using 12 power-of-4 buckets to support finer grained predictions.

6 Results

Table 1 shows results of scalar probing on DoQ data.[4] For **MSE** and **EMD** the best possible score is 0, while for accuracy we take a loose upper bound to be the performance of a model that samples from the ground-truth distribution and is evaluated against the mode. This method achieves accuracies of 0.570 for lengths, 0.537 for masses, and 0.476 for prices. Compared to the baseline, we can see that **mcc** over the best encoders capture about half (as measured by accuracy) to a third (by **MSE** and **EMD**) of the distance to the upper bound, suggesting that while a significant amount of scalar information is available, there is a long way to go to support robust commonsense reasoning.

From Table 1, we see that the more expressive models using **mcc** consistently beat **rgr**, with the latter frequently unable to improve upon the Aggregate baseline. This shows that scale information is present in the embeddings, but training on the median alone is not enough to reliably extract it;

---

[4]The full set of experimental results are shown in Table 6 in the Appendix.

the full data distribution is needed.

Comparing results by encoders, we see that Word2Vec performs significantly worse than the contextual encoders – even though the task is non-contextual – indicating that contextual information during pre-training improves the representation of scales.

Despite being weaker than BERT on downstream NLP tasks, ELMo does better on scalar probing, consistent with it being better at numeracy (Wallace et al., 2019) due to its character-level tokenization.

NumBERT does consistently better than ELMo and BERT on the **EMD** metric, but worse on **MSE** and Accuracy. This is in contrast to other standard benchmarks such as Q/A and NLI, where NumBERT made no difference relative to BERT. Our key takeaway is that the numerical representation has an impact on scale prediction (see Figure 2 for qualitative differences), but the direction is sensitive to the choice of evaluation metric. As discussed in Section 5, we believe EMD to be the most robust metric *a priori*, but this finding highlights the need to still examine the full range of metrics.

Results on Animal Masses (Table 1) show that training models only on objects in a narrow domain can significantly improve scalar prediction, underscoring the importance of context. For example, while "crane" in general can refer to either a bird or a piece of construction equipment, only the former is relevant in the animal domain, giving the model a simpler distribution of masses to predict.

Note that, despite significant differences in the raw numbers for each scale (mass/length/price), the relative behavior of encoders, metrics and probes are the same, indicating that our conclusions are broadly applicable.

Transfer experiments On the F&C relative comparison task (Table 2), **rgr**+NumBERT performed best, approaching the performance of using DoQ as an oracle, though short of specialized models for this task (Yang et al., 2018). Scalar probes trained with **mcc** perform poorly, possibly because a finer-grained model of predicted distribution is not useful for the 3-class comparative task. On the Amazon price dataset (Table 3) which is a full distribution prediction task, **mcc**+NumBERT did best on all three metrics. On both zero-shot transfer tasks, NumBERT was the best encoder on all configurations of metric/objective, suggesting that manipulating numeric representations can signifi-

cantly improve performance on scalar prediction.

7 Conclusion

From our novel scalar probing experiments, we find there is a significant amount of scale information in object embeddings, but still a sizable gap to overcome before LMs achieve this prerequisite of CSR. We conclude that although we observe some non-trivial signal to extract scale information from language embedding, the weak signals suggest these models are far from satisfying common sense scale understanding.

Our analysis points to improvements in modeling context and numeracy as directions in which progress can be made, mediated by the transfer of scale information from numbers to nouns. The NumBERT intervention has a measurable impact on scalar probing results, and transfer experiments suggest that it is an improvement. For future work we would like to extend our models to predict scales for sentences bearing relevant context about scalar magnitudes, e.g. "I saw a baby elephant".

Acknowledgments

We want to thank Daniel Spokoyny for the idea of using scientific notation for numbers and Jeremiah Liu for helpful discussions on statistical distance measures.

	dev		test	
	mcc	rgr	mcc	rgr
word2vec	.40	.73	.38	.74
ELMo	.47	.71	.47	.72
BERT	.48	.71	.49	.71
NumBERT	.51	.77	.54	.76
DoQ [Elazar et. al. 2019]	-	.78	-	.77
Yang et. al. '18	-	**.86**	-	**.87**

Table 2: Accuracy on VerbPhysics (Forbes and Choi, 2017).

	Accuracy		MSE		EMD	
	mcc	rgr	mcc	rgr	mcc	rgr
Aggregate	.04	.04	**.02**	**.02**	.06	.06
word2vec	.09	.23	**.02**	.07	.07	.08
BERT	.14	.25	**.02**	.07	.06	.08
NumBERT	.18	**.27**	**.02**	.07	**.05**	.08

Table 3: Results on consumer price data (Jianmo Ni, 2019).

References

L Baringhaus and N Henze. 2017. Cramér–von mises distance: probabilistic interpretation, confidence intervals, and neighbourhood-of-model validation. *Journal of Nonparametric Statistics*, 29(2):167–188.

Yonatan Bisk, Rowan Zellers, Ronan Le Bras, Jianfeng Gao, and Yejin Choi. 2020. Piqa: Reasoning about physical commonsense in natural language. In *Thirty-Fourth AAAI Conference on Artificial Intelligence*.

Jacob Devlin, Ming-Wei Chang, Kenton Lee, and Kristina Toutanova. 2018. Bert: Pre-training of deep bidirectional transformers for language understanding. *arXiv preprint arXiv:1810.04805*.

Yanai Elazar, Abhijit Mahabal, Deepak Ramachandran, Tania Bedrax-Weiss, and Dan Roth. 2019. How large are lions? inducing distributions over quantitative attributes. In *Association for Computational Linguistics (ACL)*.

Allyson Ettinger, Ahmed Elgohary, and Philip Resnik. 2016. Probing for semantic evidence of composition by means of simple classification tasks. In *Proceedings of the 1st Workshop on Evaluating Vector-Space Representations for NLP*, pages 134–139.

Maxwell Forbes and Yejin Choi. 2017. Verb physics: Relative physical knowledge of actions and objects. In *Proceedings of the 55th Annual Meeting of the Association for Computational Linguistics (Volume 1: Long Papers)*, pages 266–276, Vancouver, Canada. Association for Computational Linguistics.

Mor Geva, Ankit Gupta, and Jonathan Berant. 2020. Injecting numerical reasoning skills into language models. *arXiv preprint arXiv:2004.04487*.

John Hewitt and Percy Liang. 2019. Designing and interpreting probes with control tasks. *arXiv preprint arXiv:1909.03368*.

Julian McAuley Jianmo Ni, Jiacheng Li. 2019. Justifying recommendations using distantly-labeled reviews and fined-grained aspects. In *Empirical Methods in Natural Language Processing (EMNLP)*.

Bill Yuchen Lin, Seyeon Lee, Rahul Khanna, and Xiang Ren. 2020. Birds have four legs?! numersense: Probing numerical commonsense knowledge of pre-trained language models. *arXiv preprint arXiv:2005.00683*.

Hong Liu, Mingsheng Long, Jianmin Wang, and Michael I. Jordan. 2019. Transferable adversarial training: A general approach to adapting deep classifiers. In *Proceedings of the 36th International Conference on Machine Learning*.

Tomas Mikolov, Ilya Sutskever, Kai Chen, Greg S Corrado, and Jeff Dean. 2013. Distributed representations of words and phrases and their compositionality. In *Advances in neural information processing systems*, pages 3111–3119.

Matthew E Peters, Mark Neumann, Mohit Iyyer, Matt Gardner, Christopher Clark, Kenton Lee, and Luke Zettlemoyer. 2018. Deep contextualized word representations. *arXiv preprint arXiv:1802.05365*.

Tiago Pimentel, Josef Valvoda, Rowan Hall Maudslay, Ran Zmigrod, Adina Williams, and Ryan Cotterell. 2020. Information-theoretic probing for linguistic structure. *arXiv preprint arXiv:2004.03061*.

Yossi Rubner, Carlo Tomasi, and Leonidas J Guibas. 1998. A metric for distributions with applications to image databases. In *Sixth International Conference on Computer Vision (IEEE Cat. No. 98CH36271)*, pages 59–66. IEEE.

Xing Shi, Inkit Padhi, and Kevin Knight. 2016. Does string-based neural mt learn source syntax? In *Proceedings of the 2016 Conference on Empirical Methods in Natural Language Processing*, pages 1526–1534.

Aaron Van Oord, Nal Kalchbrenner, and Koray Kavukcuoglu. 2016. Pixel recurrent neural networks. In *International Conference on Machine Learning*, pages 1747–1756.

Eric Wallace, Yizhong Wang, Sujian Li, Sameer Singh, and Matt Gardner. 2019. Do NLP models know numbers? probing numeracy in embeddings. In *Proceedings of the 2019 Conference on Empirical Methods in Natural Language Processing and the 9th International Joint Conference on Natural Language Processing (EMNLP-IJCNLP)*, pages 5306–5314, Hong Kong, China. Association for Computational Linguistics.

Yiben Yang, Larry Birnbaum, Ji-Ping Wang, and Doug Downey. 2018. Extracting commonsense properties from embeddings with limited human guidance. In *Proceedings of the 56th Annual Meeting of the Association for Computational Linguistics (Volume 2: Short Papers)*, pages 644–649, Melbourne, Australia. Association for Computational Linguistics.

Ben Zhou, Qiang Ning, Daniel Khashabi, and Dan Roth. 2020. Temporal common sense acquisition with minimal supervision. In *Association for Computational Linguistics*.

A Model Hyperparameters

Here we provide the model hyperparameters we use for reproducibility.

A.1 Probing Layer of the Scalar Probing Model

For the regression model, we use a ridge regression with regularization strength of 1. For the multiclass classification model, we use a linear classifier with a softmax activation function and regularization strength of 0.01.

Task	Metric	BERT Base	NumBERT
CoLA	Dev Acc	.745	.742
MNLI	Dev Matched Acc	.791	.789
	Dev Mismatched Acc	.795	.798
MRPC	Dev Acc	.816	.802
Squad v1	F1	.799	.789
Squad v2	Best F1	.669	.673
STS-B	Dev Pearson's r	.866	.871

Table 4: NumBERT vs BERT-base on a suite of standard NLP benchmarks.

Dataset	Subset	#Data Samples
DoQ	all masses	76,424
	all prices	212,277
	all lengths	244,517
	animal masses	519
	product category prices	1,789
Product Price	-	1,888
F&C Cleaned	train	172
	dev	1,267
	test	1,522

Table 5: Statistics of Datasets/Resources used in our paper

For experiments on the narrow domains with smaller datasets, we first use PCA to reduce embeddings down to 150 dimensions before training the probing model.

A.2 NumBERT

NumBERT is pretrained on the Wikipedia and Books corpora used by the original BERT paper (Devlin et al., 2018). The BERT configuration is the same as BERT-Base (L=12, H=768, A=12, Total Parameters=110M). The language model masking is applied after WordPiece tokenization with a uniform masking rate of 15%. Maximum sequence length (number of tokens) is 128. We train with batch size of 64 sequences for 1,000,000 steps, which is approximately 40 epochs over the 3.3 billion word corpus. All the other hyperparameters and implementation details (optimizer, warm-up steps, etc.) are the same as the original BERT implementation. Table 4 shows a comparison of NumBERT vs a re-implementation of BERT-base with identical settings as above, on a suite of standard NLP benchmarks, and we conclude that the two models reach similar performance on these tasks.

B   Data Statistics

Table 5 shows the statistics of 3 datasets/resources we use in this paper. For DoQ, we take the original resource and get each subset by filtering using the corresponding dimensions and/or object types (e.g. all objects, animals, product categories, etc.). Also, only objects with more than 100 values collected in the resource are used. For F&C Cleaned dataset, we use the data and the train/dev/test splits from (Elazar et al., 2019).

C   Complete Experimental Results

We model the distributions of those scalar attributes as categorical distributions over 12 categories. We first take the base-10 logarithm of all the values and then round them to the nearest integer (between -2 and 9 for all scales). We treat each integer as a bucket and use the normalized counts in each bucket as the true distribution for that scalar attribute of the object.

To explore the effect of ambiguity, we divide all the data in DoQ for each scale into 2 sets, **Unimodal** where the distribution has one well-defined peak and **Multimodal**, where multiple peaks are present. The number of peaks were identified by a simple hill-climbing algorithm.

As words often have more than one meaning in different contexts or even modifiers, their corresponding distribution from DoQ should reflect the different senses if they appeared enough in the data. When the objects are different enough (e.g. an ice-cream have mainly one meaning and its size doesn't vary much, as opposed to a truck which can be a toy truck, which is very small, or an actual vehicle, which is very big), they may have different modalities. In order to better understand our results, we wish to separate between objects of different modalities to objects with a single modality.

In order to estimate a multi-modal function, we take the bucketed DoQ distribution and smooth it into a probability density function. Then, by finding local maxima over the fitted density function, we estimate a distribution to be multi-modal if we find more than one maximum, otherwise we determine it to be a single-modal distribution.

The complete experiment results including the mutlimodal experiments are in Table 6.

			Accuracy			MSE			EMD		
			All	Multi.	Uni.	All	Multi.	Uni.	All	Multi.	Uni.
Lengths	mcc	Aggregate	.240	.250	.230	.027	.028	.025	.077	.078	.075
		word2vec	.300	.310	.280	.026	.022	.031	.079	.074	.087
		ELMo	.430	.420	.440	.019	.020	.017	.055	.056	.053
		BERT	.420	.410	.420	.020	.021	.018	.056	.058	.054
		NumBERT	.400	.400	.410	.021	.022	.019	.052	.053	.049
	rgr	Aggregate	.240	.250	.230	.027	.028	.025	.077	.078	.075
		word2vec	.120	.120	.130	.099	.100	.097	.072	.070	.074
		ELMo	.230	.230	.240	.084	.085	.082	.072	.070	.074
		BERT	.240	.230	.240	.084	.085	.081	.072	.070	.074
		NumBERT	.220	.210	.220	.086	.088	.084	.072	.070	.074
Masses	mcc	Aggregate	.150	.150	.150	.026	.027	.024	.076	.077	.074
		word2vec	.260	.260	.260	.025	.026	.023	.082	.083	.080
		ELMo	.360	.360	.360	.021	.021	.019	.061	.062	.059
		BERT	.330	.330	.330	.021	.022	.019	.062	.063	.060
		NumBERT	.320	.320	.330	.021	.022	.019	.057	.058	.055
	rgr	Aggregate	.150	.150	.150	.026	.027	.024	.076	.077	.074
		word2vec	.200	.190	.200	.088	.090	.086	.077	.076	.080
		ELMo	.210	.200	.210	.087	.088	.085	.077	.076	.080
		BERT	.220	.210	.220	.085	.086	.084	.077	.076	.080
		NumBERT	.200	.190	.200	.088	.089	.086	.077	.076	.080
Prices	mcc	Aggregate	.240	.240	.250	.019	.021	.016	.057	.060	.054
		word2vec	.260	.250	.280	.019	.014	.024	.063	.055	.072
		ELMo	.370	.360	.380	.016	.018	.013	.051	.053	.047
		BERT	.330	.320	.330	.017	.019	.014	.054	.055	.051
		NumBERT	.320	.320	.330	.017	.019	.014	.051	.053	.048
	rgr	Aggregate	.240	.240	.250	.019	.021	.016	.057	.060	.054
		word2vec	.140	.130	.150	.090	.093	.085	.087	.084	.092
		ELMo	.210	.210	.220	.081	.083	.078	.087	.084	.092
		BERT	.190	.190	.190	.083	.085	.081	.087	.084	.092
		NumBERT	.170	.180	.170	.085	.087	.083	.087	.084	.092
Animals Masses	mcc	Aggregate	.300	.280	.330	.022	.021	.024	.059	.055	.064
		word2vec	.330	.320	.350	.021	.020	.023	.069	.066	.075
		ELMo	.430	.440	.420	.016	.015	.019	.057	.056	.059
		BERT	.410	.390	.450	.017	.016	.019	.058	.057	.060
		NumBERT	.420	.430	.410	.018	.016	.020	.053	.052	.055
	rgr	Aggregate	.300	.280	.330	.022	.021	.024	.059	.055	.064
		word2vec	.350	.350	.360	.069	.069	.069	.077	.081	.070
		ELMo	.280	.250	.330	.079	.080	.077	.077	.081	.070
		BERT	.260	.260	.240	.079	.076	.085	.077	.081	.070
		NumBERT	.230	.230	.240	.083	.081	.086	.077	.081	.070
Household Product Prices	mcc	Aggregate	.470	-	-	.010	-	-	.046	-	-
		word2vec	.510	.490	.540	.008	.008	.008	.041	.041	.041
		ELMo	.540	.520	.570	.007	.007	.007	.038	.038	.039
		BERT	.570	.560	.580	.007	.007	.007	.038	.038	.039
		NumBERT	.550	.530	.570	.007	.007	.007	.038	.038	.039
	rgr	Aggregate	.470	-	-	.010	-	-	.046	-	-
		word2vec	.450	.430	.480	.056	.058	.055	.092	.094	.090
		ELMo	.420	.400	.460	.058	.059	.057	.092	.094	.090
		BERT	.440	.420	.460	.057	.059	.055	.092	.094	.090
		NumBERT	.420	.390	.460	.060	.062	.057	.092	.094	.090

Table 6: Evaluation on all datasets.

Evaluating Attribution Methods using White-Box LSTMs

Yiding Hao
Yale University
New Haven, CT, USA
`yiding.hao@yale.edu`

Abstract

Interpretability methods for neural networks are difficult to evaluate because we do not understand the black-box models typically used to test them. This paper proposes a framework in which interpretability methods are evaluated using manually constructed networks, which we call *white-box networks*, whose behavior is understood *a priori*. We evaluate five methods for producing attribution heatmaps by applying them to white-box LSTM classifiers for tasks based on formal languages. Although our white-box classifiers solve their tasks perfectly and transparently, we find that all five attribution methods fail to produce the expected model explanations.

1 Introduction

Attribution methods are a family of interpretability techniques for individual neural network predictions that attempt to measure the importance of input features for determining the model's output. Given an input, an attribution method produces a vector of *attribution* or *relevance scores*, which is typically visualized as a heatmap that highlights portions of the input that contribute to model behavior. In the context of NLP, attribution scores are usually computed at the token level, so that each score represents the importance of a token within an input sequence. These heatmaps can be used to identify keywords upon which networks base their decisions (Li et al., 2016; Sundararajan et al., 2017; Arras et al., 2017a,b; Murdoch et al., 2018, *inter alia*).

One of the main challenges facing the evaluation of attribution methods is that it is difficult to assess the quality of a heatmap when the network in question is not understood in the first place. If a word is deemed relevant by an attribution method, we do not know whether the model actually considers that word relevant, or whether the attribu-

tion method has erroneously estimated its importance. Indeed, previous studies have argued that attribution methods are sensitive to features unrelated to model behavior in some cases (e.g., Kindermans et al., 2019), and altogether insensitive to model behavior in others (Adebayo et al., 2018).

To tease the evaluation of attribution methods apart from the interpretation of models, this paper proposes an evaluation framework for attribution methods in NLP that uses only models that are fully understood *a priori*. Instead of testing attribution methods on black-box models obtained through training, we construct *white-box* models for testing by directly setting network parameters by hand. Our focus is on white-box LSTMs that implement intuitive strategies for solving simple classification tasks based on formal languages with deterministic solutions. We apply our framework to five attribution methods: *occlusion* (Zeiler and Fergus, 2014), *saliency* (Simonyan et al., 2014; Li et al., 2016), *gradient × input*, (G × I, Shrikumar et al., 2017), *integrated gradients* (IG, Sundararajan et al., 2017), and *layer-wise relevance propagation* (LRP, Bach et al., 2015). In doing so, we make the following contributions.

- We construct four white-box LSTMs that can be used to test attribution methods. We provide a complete description of our model weights in Appendix A.[1] Beyond the five methods considered here, our white-box networks can be used to test any attribution method compatible with LSTMs.

- Empirically, we show that all five attribution methods produce erroneous heatmaps for our white-box networks, despite the models' transparent behavior. As a preview of our re-

---

[1]We also provide code for our models at `https://github.com/yidinghao/whitebox-lstm`.

300

Proceedings of the Third BlackboxNLP Workshop on Analyzing and Interpreting Neural Networks for NLP, pages 300–313
Online, November 20, 2020. ©2020 Association for Computational Linguistics

Task: Determine whether the input contains one of the following subsequences: ab, bc, cd, or dc.
Output: *True*, since the input aacb contains two (non-contiguous) instances of ab.

Occlusion	Saliency	G × I	IG	LRP
aac**b**	aac**b**	aac**b**	aacb	aac**b**
a**a c b**	aac**b**	aac**b**	aacb	aac**b**

Table 1: Sample heatmaps for two white-box networks: a "counter-based" network (top) and an "FSA-based" network (bottom). The features relevant to the output are the two as and the b.

sults, Table 1 shows sample heatmaps computed for two models designed to identify the non-contiguous subsequence ab in the input aacb. Even though both models' outputs are determined by the presence of the two as and the b, all four methods either incorrectly highlight the c or fail to highlight at least one of the as in at least one case.

- We identify two general ways in which four of the five methods do not behave as intended. Firstly, while saliency, G × I and IG are theoretically invariant to differences in model implementation (Sundararajan et al., 2017), in practice we find that these methods can still produce qualitatively different heatmaps for nearly identical models. Secondly, we find that LRP is susceptible to numerical issues, which cause heatmaps to be zeroed out when values are rounded to zero.

2 Related Work

Several approaches have been taken in the literature for understanding how to evaluate attribution methods. On a theoretical level, *axiomatic* approaches propose formal desiderata that attribution methods should satisfy, such as implementation invariance (Sundararajan et al., 2017), input translation invariance (Kindermans et al., 2019), continuity with respect to inputs (Montavon et al., 2018; Ghorbani et al., 2019), or the existence of relationships between attribution scores and logit or softmax scores (Sundararajan et al., 2017; Ancona et al., 2018; Montavon, 2019). The degree to which attribution methods fulfill these criteria can be determined either mathematically or empirically.

Other approaches, which are more experimental in nature, attempt to directly assess the relationship between attribution scores and model behav-ior. A common test, due to Bach et al. (2015) and Samek et al. (2017) and applied to sequence modeling by Arras et al. (2017a), involves ablating or perturbing parts of the input, from those with the highest attribution scores to those with the lowest, and counting the number of features that need to be ablated in order to change the model's prediction. Another test, proposed by Adebayo et al. (2018), tracks how heatmaps change as layers of a network are incrementally randomized.

A third kind of approach evaluates the extent to which heatmaps identify salient input features. For example, Zhang et al. (2018) propose the *pointing game task*, in which the highest-relevance pixel for an image classifier input must belong to the object described by the target output class. Within this framework, Kim et al. (2018), Poerner et al. (2018), Arras et al. (2019), and Yang and Kim (2019) construct datasets in which input features exhibit experimentally controlled notions of importance, yielding "ground truth" attributions against which heatmaps can be evaluated.

Our paper incorporates elements of the ground-truth approaches, since it is straightforward to determine which input features are important for our formal language tasks. We enhance these approaches by using white-box models that are guaranteed to be sensitive to those features.

3 Formal Language Tasks

Formal languages are often used to evaluate the expressive power of RNNs. Here, we focus on formal languages that have been recently used to probe LSTMs' ability to capture three kinds of dependencies: *counting*, *long-distance*, and *hierarchical* dependencies. We define a classification task based on each of these formal languages.

3.1 Counting Dependencies

Counter languages (Fischer, 1966; Fischer et al., 1968) are languages recognized by automata equipped with counters. Weiss et al. (2018) demonstrate using an acceptance task for the languages $a^n b^n$ and $a^n b^n c^n$ that LSTMs naturally learn to use cell state units as counters. Merrill's (2019) asymptotic analysis shows that LSTM acceptors accept only counter languages when their weights are fully saturated. Thus, counter languages may be viewed as a characterization of the expressive power of LSTMs.

We define the *counting task* based on a simple

301

example of a counting language.

Task 1 (Counting Task). Given a string in $x \in \{a, b\}^*$, determine whether or not x has strictly more as than bs.

Example 2. The counting task classifies aaab as *True*, ab as *False*, and bbbba as *False*.

A counter automaton can solve the counting task by incrementing its counter whenever an a is encountered and decrementing it whenever a b is encountered. It outputs *True* if and only if its counter is at least 1. We expect attribution scores for all input symbols to have roughly the same magnitude, but that scores assigned to a will have the opposite sign to those assigned to b.

3.2 Long-Distance Dependencies

Strictly piecewise (SP, Heinz, 2007) languages were used by Avcu et al. (2017) and Mahalunkar and Kelleher (2018, 2019a,b) to test the propensity of LSTMs to learn long-distance dependencies, compared to Elman's (1990) simple recurrent networks. SP languages are regular languages whose membership is defined by the presence or absence of certain *subsequences*, which may or may not be contiguous. For example, ad is a subsequence of abcde, since both letters of ad occur in abcde, in the same order. Based on these ideas, we define the *SP task* as follows.

Task 3 (SP Task). Given $x \in \{a, b, c, d\}^*$, determine whether or not x contains at least one of the following subsequences: ab, bc, cd, dc.

Example 4. In the SP task, aab is classified as *True*, since it contains the subsequence ab. Similarly, acb is classified as *True*, since it contains ab non-contiguously. The string aaa is classified as *False*.

The choice of SP languages as a test for long-distance dependencies is motivated by the fact that symbols in a non-contiguous subsequence may occur arbitrarily far from one another. The SP task yields a variant of the pointing game task in the sense that the input string may or may not contain an "object" (one of the four subsequences) that the network must identify. Therefore, we expect an input symbol to receive a nonzero attribution score if and only if it comprises a subsequence.

3.3 Hierarchical Dependencies

The *Dyck language* is the language D generated by the following context-free grammar, where ε is the empty string.

$$S \to SS \mid (S) \mid [S] \mid \varepsilon$$

D contains all balanced strings of parentheses and square brackets. Since D is often viewed as a canonical example of a context-free language (Chomsky and Schützenberger, 1959), several recent studies, including Sennhauser and Berwick (2018), Bernardy (2018), Skachkova et al. (2018), and Yu et al. (2019), have used D to evaluate whether LSTMs can learn hierarchical dependencies implemented by pushdown automata. Here, we consider the *bracket prediction task* proposed by Sennhauser and Berwick (2018).

Task 5 (Bracket Prediction Task). Given a prefix p of some string in D, identify the next valid closing bracket for p.

Example 6. The string [([ ] requires a prediction of) , since the (is the last unclosed bracket. Similarly, (( ) [requires a prediction of] . Strings with no unclosed brackets, such as [( )] , require a prediction of *None*.

In heatmaps for the bracket prediction task, we expect the last unclosed bracket to receive the highest-magnitude relevance score.

4 White-Box Networks

We use two approaches to construct white-box networks for our tasks. In the *counter-based* approach, the cell state contains a set of counters, which are incremented or decremented throughout the computation. The network's final output is based on the values of the counters. In the *automaton-based* approach, we use the LSTM to simulate an automaton, with the cell state containing a representation of the automaton's state. We use a counter-based network to solve the counter task and an automaton-based network to solve the bracket prediction task. We use both kinds of networks to solve the SP task. All networks perfectly solve the tasks they were designed for. This section describes our white-box networks at a high level; a detailed description is given in Appendix A.

In the rest of this paper, we identify the alphabet symbols a, b, c, and d with the one-hot vectors for indices 1, 2, 3, and 4, respectively. The vectors $\boldsymbol{f}^{(t)}$, $\boldsymbol{i}^{(t)}$, and $\boldsymbol{o}^{(t)}$ represent the forget, input, and output gates, respectively. $\boldsymbol{g}^{(t)}$ is the value added to the cell state at each time step, and σ represents the sigmoid function. We assume that the hidden state $h^{(t)}$ and cell state $c^{(t)}$ are updated as follows.

$$c^{(t)} = f^{(t)} \odot c^{(t-1)} + i^{(t)} \odot g^{(t)}$$

$$h^{(t)} = o^{(t)} \odot \tanh\left(c^{(t)}\right)$$

4.1 Counter-Based Networks

In the counter-based approach, each position of the cell state contains the value of a counter. To adjust the counter in position j by some value $v \in (-1, 1)$, we set $g_j^{(t)} = v$, and we saturate the gates by setting them to $\sigma(m) \approx 1$, where $m \gg 0$ is a large constant. For example, our network for the counting task uses a single hidden unit, with the gates always saturated and with $g^{(t)}$ given by

$$g^{(t)} = \tanh\left(u\begin{bmatrix} 1 & -1 \end{bmatrix} x^{(t)}\right),$$

where $u > 0$ is a hyperparameter that scales the counter by a factor of $v = \tanh(u)$.[2] When $x^{(t)} = $ a, we have $g^{(t)} = v$, so the counter is incremented by v. When $x^{(t)} = $ b, we compute $g^{(t)} = -v$, so the counter is decremented by v.

For the SP task, we use seven counters. The first four counters record how many occurrences of each symbol have been observed at time step t. The next three counters record the number of bs, cs, and ds that form one of the four distinguished subsequences with an earlier symbol. For example, after seeing the input aaabbc, the counter-based network for the SP task satisfies

$$c^{(6)} = v\begin{bmatrix} 3 & 2 & 1 & 0 & 2 & 1 & 0 \end{bmatrix}^{\top}.$$

The first four counters represent the fact that the input has 3 as, 2 bs, 1 c, and no ds. Counter #5 is $2v$ because the two bs form a subsequence with the as, and counter #6 is v because the c forms a subsequence with the bs.

The logit scores of our counter-based networks are computed by a linear decoder using the tanh of the counter values. For the counting task, the score of the *True* class is $h^{(t)}$, while the score of the *False* class is fixed to $\tanh(v)/2$. This means that the network outputs *True* if and only if the final counter value is at least v. For the SP task, the score of the *True* class is $h_5^{(t)} + h_6^{(t)} + h_7^{(t)}$, while the score of the *False* class is again $\tanh(v)/2$.

---

[2] We use $u = 0.5$ for the counting task, $u = 0.7$ for the SP task, and $m = 50$ for both tasks.

4.2 Automata-Based Networks

We consider two types of automata-based networks: one that implements a finite-state automaton (FSA) for the SP task, and one that implements a pushdown automaton (PDA) for the bracket prediction task.

Our FSA construction is similar to Korsky and Berwick's (2019) FSA construction for simple recurrent networks. Consider a deterministic FSA $\mathcal{A}$ with states Q and alphabet Σ. To simulate $\mathcal{A}$ using an LSTM, we use $|Q| \cdot |\Sigma|$ hidden units, with the following interpretation. Suppose that $\mathcal{A}$ transitions to state q after reading input $x^{(1)}, x^{(2)}, \ldots, x^{(t)}$. The hidden state $h^{(t)}$ is a one-hot representation of the pair $\langle q, x^{(t)} \rangle$, which encodes both the current state of $\mathcal{A}$ and the most recent input symbol. Since the FSA undergoes a state transition with each input symbol, the forget gate always clears $c^{(t)}$, so that information written to the cell state does not persist beyond a single time step. The output layer simply detects whether or not the FSA is in an accepting state. Details are provided in Appendix A.3.

Next, we describe how to implement a PDA for the bracket prediction task. We use a stack containing all unclosed brackets observed in the input string, and make predictions based on the top item of the stack. We represent a bounded stack of size k using $2k + 1$ hidden units. The first $k - 1$ positions contain all stack items except the top item, with (represented by the value 1, [represented by -1, and empty positions represented by 0. The kth position contains the top item of the stack. The next k positions contain the height of the stack in unary notation, and the last position contains a bit indicating whether or not the stack is empty. For example, after reading the input ([(( ) with a stack of size 4, the stack contents ([(are represented by

$$c^{(5)} = \begin{bmatrix} 1 & -1 & 0 & 1 & 1 & 1 & 1 & 0 & 0 \end{bmatrix}^{\top}.$$

The 1 in position 4 indicates that the top item of the stack is (, and the 1, -1, and 0 in positions 1–3 indicate that the remainder of the stack is ([. The three 1s in positions 5–8 indicate that the stack height is 3, and the 0 in position 9 indicates that the stack is not empty.

When $x^{(t)}$ is (or [, it is copied to $c_k^{(t)}$, and $c_k^{(t)}$ is copied to the highest empty position in $c_{:k-1}^{(t)}$, pushing the opening bracket to the stack. The empty stack bit is then set to 0, marking the stack

Name	Formula
Saliency	$R_{t,i}^{(c)}(\boldsymbol{X}) = \dfrac{\partial \hat{y}_c}{\partial x_i^{(t)}}\Big|_{x_i^{(t)}=X_{t,i}}$
G × I	$R_{t,i}^{(c)}(\boldsymbol{X}) = X_{t,i}\dfrac{\partial \hat{y}_c}{\partial x_i^{(t)}}\Big|_{x_i^{(t)}=X_{t,i}}$
IG	$R_{t,i}^{(c)}(\boldsymbol{X}) = X_{t,i}\displaystyle\int_0^1 \dfrac{\partial \hat{y}_c}{\partial x_i^{(t)}}\Big|_{x_i^{(t)}=\alpha X_{t,i}}\,d\alpha$

Table 2: Definitions of the gradient-based methods.

as non-empty. When the current input symbol is a closing bracket, the highest item of positions 1 through $k-1$ is deleted and copied to position k, popping the top item from the stack. Because the PDA network is quite complex, we focus here on describing how the top stack item in position k is determined, and leave other details for Appendix A.4. Let $\alpha^{(t)}$ be 1 if $x^{(t)} = ($, -1 if $x^{(t)} = [$, and 0 otherwise. At each time step, $g_k^{(t)} = \tanh\left(m \cdot u^{(t)}\right)$, where $m \gg 0$ and

$$u^{(t)} = 2^k \alpha^{(t)} + \sum_{j=1}^{k-1} 2^{j-1} h_j^{(t-1)}. \tag{1}$$

Observe that $m \cdot u^{(t)} \gg 0$ when $\alpha^{(t)} = 1$, and $m \cdot u^{(t)} \ll 0$ when $\alpha^{(t)} = -1$. Thus, $g_k^{(t)}$ contains the stack encoding of the current input symbol if it is an opening bracket. If the current input symbol is a closing bracket, then $\alpha^{(t)} = 0$, so the sign of $u^{(t)}$ is determined by the highest item of $h_{:k-1}^{(t-1)}$.

5 Attribution Methods

Let $\boldsymbol{X}$ be a matrix of input vectors, such that the input at time t is the row vector $\boldsymbol{X}_{t,:} = \left(x^{(t)}\right)^{\top}$. Given $\boldsymbol{X}$, an LSTM classifier produces a vector $\hat{\boldsymbol{y}}$ of logit scores. Based on $\boldsymbol{X}$, $\hat{\boldsymbol{y}}$, and possibly a *baseline input* $\overline{\boldsymbol{X}}$, an attribution method assigns an attribution score $R_{t,i}^{(c)}(\boldsymbol{X})$ to input feature $X_{t,i}$ for each output class c. These feature-level scores are then aggregated to produce token-level scores:

$$R_t^{(c)}(\boldsymbol{X}) = \sum_i R_{t,i}^{(c)}(\boldsymbol{X}).$$

Broadly speaking, our five attribution methods are grouped into three types: one *perturbation-based*, three *gradient-based*, and one *decomposition-based*. The following subsections describe how each method computes $R_{t,i}^{(c)}(\boldsymbol{X})$.

5.1 Perturbation- and Gradient-Based Methods

Perturbation-based methods are premised on the idea that if $X_{t,i}$ is an important input feature, then changing the value of $X_{t,i}$ would cause $\hat{\boldsymbol{y}}$ to change. The one perturbation method we consider is occlusion. In this method, $R_{t,i}^{(c)}(\boldsymbol{X})$ is the change in $\hat{y}_c$ observed when $\boldsymbol{X}_{t,:}$ is replaced by 0.

Gradient-based methods rely on the same intuition as perturbation-based methods, but use automatic differentiation to simulate infinitesimal perturbations. The definitions of our three gradient-based methods are given in Table 2. The most basic of these is saliency, which simply measures relevance by the derivative of the logit score with respect to each input feature. G × I attempts to improve upon saliency by using the first-order terms in a Taylor-series approximation of the model instead of the gradients on their own. IG is designed to address the issue of small gradients found in saturated units by integrating G × I along the line connecting $\boldsymbol{X}$ to a baseline input $\overline{\boldsymbol{X}}$, here taken to be the zero matrix.

5.2 Decomposition-Based Methods

Decomposition-based methods are methods that satisfy the relation

$$\hat{y}_c = R_{\text{bias}}^{(c)} + \sum_{t,i} R_{t,i}^{(c)}(\boldsymbol{X}), \tag{2}$$

where $R_{\text{bias}}^{(c)}$ is a relevance score assigned to the bias units of the network. The interpretation of equation (2) is that the logit score $\hat{y}_c$ is "distributed" among the input features and the bias units, so that the relevance scores form a "decomposition" of $\hat{y}_c$.

The one decomposition-based method we consider is LRP, which computes scores using a backpropagation algorithm that distributes scores layer by layer. The scores of the output layer are initialized to

$$r_i^{(c,\text{output})} = \begin{cases} \hat{y}_i, & i = c \\ 0, & \text{otherwise.} \end{cases}$$

For each layer l with activation $\boldsymbol{z}^{(l)}$, activation function $f^{(l)}$, and output $\boldsymbol{a}^{(l)} = f^{(l)}\left(\boldsymbol{z}^{(l)}\right)$, the relevance $\boldsymbol{r}^{(c,l)}$ of $\boldsymbol{a}^{(l)}$ is determined by the following *propagation rule*:

$$r_i^{(c,l)} = \sum_{l'}\sum_j r_j^{(c,l')} \frac{W_{j,i}^{(l'\leftarrow l)} a_i^{(l)}}{z_j^{(l')} + \text{sign}\left(z_j^{(l')}\right)\varepsilon},$$

where l' ranges over all layers to which l has a forward connection via $\boldsymbol{W}^{(l'\leftarrow l)}$ and $\varepsilon > 0$ is a stabilizing constant.[3] For the LSTM gate interactions, we follow Arras et al. (2017b) in treating multiplicative connections of the form $\boldsymbol{a}^{(l_1)} \odot \boldsymbol{a}^{(l_2)}$ as activation functions of the form $\boldsymbol{a}^{(l_1)} \odot f^{(l_2)}(\cdot)$, where $\boldsymbol{a}^{(l_1)}$ is $\boldsymbol{f}^{(t)}$, $\boldsymbol{i}^{(t)}$, or $\boldsymbol{o}^{(t)}$. The final attribution scores are given by the values propagated to the input layer:

$$R_{t,i}^{(c)}(\boldsymbol{X}) = r_i^{(c,\text{input}_t)}.$$

6 Qualitative Evaluation

To evaluate attribution methods under our framework, we begin with a qualitative description of the heatmaps that are computed for our white-box networks, based on the illustrative sample of heatmaps appearing in Table 3.

6.1 Counting Task

Occlusion, G $\times$ I, and IG are well-behaved for the counting task. As expected, these methods assign a a positive value and b a negative value when the output class for attribution is $c = True$. When the number of as is different from the number of bs, occlusion assigns a lower-magnitude score to the symbol with fewer instances. When $c = False$, all relevance scores are 0. This is because $\hat{y}_{False}$ is fixed to a constant value supplied by a bias term, so input features cannot affect its value.

Saliency and LRP both fail to produce nonzero scores, at least in some cases. Saliency scores satisfy $R_{t,1}^{(True)}(\boldsymbol{X}) = -R_{t,2}^{(True)}(\boldsymbol{X})$, resulting in token-level scores of 0 for all inputs. Heatmaps #3 and #4 show that LRP assigns scores of 0 to prefixes containing equal numbers of as and bs. We will see in Subsection 7.1 that this phenomenon appears to be related to the fact that the LSTM gates are saturated.

6.2 SP Task

We obtain radically different heatmaps for the two SP task networks, despite the fact that they produce the same classifications for all inputs.

For the counter-based network, all methods except for saliency assign positive scores for $c = True$ to symbols constituting one of the four subsequences, and scores of zero elsewhere. The saliency heatmaps do not adhere to this pattern, and instead generally assign higher scores

to tokens occurring near the end of the input. Heatmaps #7–10 show that LRP fails to assign positive scores to the first symbol of each subsequence, while the other methods generally do not.[4] The LRP behavior reflects the fact that the initial a does not increment the subsequence counters, which determine the final logit score. In contrast, the behavior of occlusion, G $\times$ I, and IG is explained by the fact that removing either the a or the b destroys the subsequence. Note that the as in heatmap #9 receive scores of 0 from occlusion and G $\times$ I, since removing only one of the two as does not destroy the subsequence.

For the FSA-based network, saliency, G $\times$ I, and LRP assign only the last symbol a nonzero score when the relevance output class c matches the network's predicted class. IG appears to produce erratic heatmaps, exhibiting no immediately obvious pattern. Although occlusion appears to be erratic at first glance, its behavior can be explained by the fact that changing $\mathbf{x}^{(t)}$ to $\mathbf{0}$ causes $\mathbf{h}^{(t)}$ to be $\mathbf{0}$, which the LSTM interprets as the initial state of the FSA; thus, $R_t^{(c)}(\mathbf{X}) \neq 0$ precisely when $\mathbf{X}_{t+1:,:}$ is classified differently from $\mathbf{X}$. In all cases, the heatmaps for the FSA-based network diverge significantly from the expected heatmaps.

6.3 Bracket Prediction Task

The heatmaps for the PDA-based network also differ strikingly from those of the other networks, in that the gradient-based methods never assign nonzero scores. This is because equation (1) causes $g^{(t)}$ to be highly saturated, resulting in zero gradients. In the case of LRP, the matching bracket is highlighted when $c \neq None$. When the matching bracket is not the last symbol of the input, the other unclosed brackets are also highlighted, with progressively smaller magnitudes, and with brackets of the opposite type from c receiving negative scores. This pattern reflects the mechanism of (1), in which progressively larger powers of 2 are used to determine the content copied to $c_k^{(t)}$. When the relevance output class is $c = None$, LRP assigns opening brackets a negative score, revealing the fact that those input symbols set the bit $c_{2k+1}^{(t)}$ to indicate that the stack is not empty. Although occlusion sometimes highlights the matching bracket, it does not appear to be consistent in doing so. For example, it fails to highlight the matching bracket

---

[3]We use $\varepsilon = 0.001$.

[4]Although it is difficult to see, IG assigns a small positive score to the bs in heatmaps #7 and #8.

305

Network	#	c	Target	Occlusion	Saliency	$G \times I$	IG	LRP
Counting	1	True	True	aaabb	aaabb	aaabb	aaabb	aaabb
	2	True	False	bbbaa	bbbaa	bbbaa	bbbaa	bbbaa
	3	True	False	aaabbb	aaabbb	aaabbb	aaabbb	aaabbb
	4	True	False	aabbb	aabbb	aabbb	aabbb	aabbb
	5	False	True	aaabb	aaabb	aaabb	aaabb	aaabb
	6	False	False	aabbb	aabbb	aabbb	aabbb	aabbb
SP (Counter)	7	True	True	acb	acb	acb	acb	acb
	8	True	True	acbb	acbb	acbb	acbb	acbb
	9	True	True	aacb	aacb	aacb	aacb	aacb
	10	True	True	abcab	abcab	abcab	abcab	abcab
	11	True	False	aacc	aacc	aacc	aacc	aacc
	12	False	True	acb	acb	acb	acb	acb
	13	False	False	aacc	aacc	aacc	aacc	aacc
SP (FSA)	14	True	True	acb	acb	acb	acb	acb
	15	True	True	acbb	acbb	acbb	acbb	acbb
	16	True	True	aacb	aacb	aacb	aacb	aacb
	17	True	True	abcab	abcab	abcab	abcab	abcab
	18	True	False	aacc	aacc	aacc	aacc	aacc
	19	False	True	acb	acb	acb	acb	acb
	20	False	False	aacc	aacc	aacc	aacc	aacc
Bracket (PDA)	21	]	]	([[([	([[([	([[([	([[([	([[([
	22	)	)	([[([]	([[([]	([[([]	([[([]	([[([]
	23	None	None	([[]])	([[]])	([[]])	([[]])	([[]])
	24	]	]	[([][()	[([][()	[([][()	[([][()	[([][()
	25	)	]	[([][()	[([][()	[([][()	[([][()	[([][()

Table 3: Selected heatmaps based on $R_t^{(c)}(\boldsymbol{X})$. **Red** represents positive values and **blue** represents negative values. Heatmaps with all values within the range of $\pm 1 \times 10^{-5}$ are shown as all 0s.

u	v	$\hat{y}_{True}$	Saliency	$G \times I$	IG
0.6	0.537	0.151	accb	accb	accb
0.7	0.604	0.533	accb	accb	accb
0.8	0.664	0.581	accb	accb	accb
1	0.762	0.642	accb	accb	accb
4	0.999	0.761	accb	accb	accb
8	1.000	0.762	accb	accb	accb
16	1.000	0.762	accb	accb	accb
64	1.000	0.762	accb	accb	accb

Table 4: Gradient-based heatmaps of $R_t^{(True)}(\texttt{accb})$ for the counter-based SP network, with $0.6 \leq u \leq 64$.

m	$\sigma(m)$	$c^{(t)}$	Accuracy	% Blank
4	0.982	-8.74×10^{-3}	90.1	0.2
5	0.993	-3.48×10^{-3}	96.1	2.2
6	0.998	-1.32×10^{-3}	99.8	6.5
7	0.999	-4.91×10^{-4}	100.0	22.0
8	1.000	-1.81×10^{-4}	100.0	42.1
9	1.000	-6.68×10^{-5}	100.0	69.9
10	1.000	-2.46×10^{-5}	100.0	92.3
11	1.000	-9.05×10^{-6}	100.0	98.7
12	1.000	-3.33×10^{-6}	100.0	99.8

Table 5: The results of the LRP saturation test, including the value of m, the average value of $c^{(t)}$ when the counter reaches 0, the network's testing accuracy, and the percentage of examples with blank heatmaps for prefixes with equal numbers of as and bs.

in heatmap #21, and highlights one other bracket in heatmaps #23–24.

7 Detailed Evaluations

We now turn to focused investigations of particular phenomena that attribution methods exhibit when applied to white-box networks. Subsection 7.1 begins by discussing the effect of network saturation on the gradient-based methods and LRP. In Subsection 7.2 we apply Bach et al.'s (2015) ablation test to our attribution methods for the SP task.

7.1 Saturation

As mentioned in the previous section, network saturation causes gradients to be approximately 0 when using sigmoid or tanh activation functions. To test how attribution methods are affected by saturation, Table 4 shows heatmaps for the input $\texttt{accb}$ generated by gradient-based methods for different instantiations of the counter-based SP network with varying degrees of saturation. Recall from Section 4 that counter values for this network are expressed in multiples of the scaling factor v. We control the saturation of the network via the parameter $u = \tanh^{-1}(v)$. For all three gradient-based methods, scores for a decrease and scores for b increase as u increases. Additionally, saliency scores for the first c decrease when u increases. When $u = 8$, v is almost completely saturated, causing $G \times I$ to produce all-zero heatmaps.

On the other hand, IG is still able to produce nonzero heatmaps even at $u = 64$. Thus, IG is much more resistant to the effects of saturation than G × I.

According to Sundararajan et al. (2017), gradient-based methods satisfy the axiom of *implementation invariance*: they produce the same heatmaps for any two networks that compute the same function. This formal property is seemingly at odds with the diverse array of heatmaps appearing in Table 4, which are produced for networks that all yield identical classifiers. In particular, the networks with $u = 8$, 16, and 64 yield qualitatively different heatmaps, despite the fact that the three networks are distinguished only by differences in v of less than 0.001. Because the three functions are technically not equal, implementation invariance is not violated in theory; but the fact that IG produces different heatmaps for three nearly identical networks shows that the intuition described by implementation invariance is not borne out in practice.

Besides the gradient-based methods, LRP is also susceptible to problems arising from saturation. Recall from heatmaps #3 and #4 of Table 3 that for the counting task network, LRP assigns scores of 0 to prefixes with equal numbers of as and bs. We hypothesize that this phenomenon is related to the fact $c^{(t)} = 0$ after reading such prefixes, since the counter has been incremented and decremented in equal amounts. Accordingly, we test whether this phenomenon can be mitigated by desaturating the gates so that $c^{(t)}$ does not exactly reach 0. Recall that the white-box LSTM gates approximate $1 \approx \sigma(m)$ using a constant $m \gg 0$. We construct networks with varying values of m and compute LRP scores on a randomly generated testing set of 1000 strings, each of which contains at least one prefix with equal numbers of as and bs. In Table 5 we report the percentage of examples for which such prefixes receive LRP scores of 0, along with the network's accuracy on this testing set and the average value of $c^{(t)}$ when the counter reaches 0. Indeed, the percentage of prefixes receiving scores of 0 increases as the approximation $c^{(t)} \approx 0$ becomes more exact.

7.2 Ablation Test

So far, we have primarily compared attribution methods via visual inspection of individual examples. To compare the five methods quantitatively,

Method	SP (Counter)	SP (FSA)
Occlusion	$61.8_{\pm 12.2}$	$\mathbf{52.6}_{\pm 11.7}$
Saliency	$97.8_{\pm 1.1}$	$96.0_{\pm 2.5}$
G × I	$65.7_{\pm 14.4}$	$96.0_{\pm 2.5}$
IG	$\mathbf{47.5}_{\pm 7.6}$	$94.9_{\pm 2.9}$
LRP	$64.3_{\pm 12.7}$	$96.0_{\pm 2.5}$
Random		$96.1_{\pm 2.5}$
Optimal		$\mathbf{42.7}_{\pm 3.8}$

Table 6: Mean and standard deviation results of the ablation test, normalized by string length and expressed as a percentage. "Optimal" is the best possible score.

we apply the ablation test of Bach et al. (2015) to our two white-box networks for the SP task.[5] Given an input string classified as *True*, we iteratively remove the symbol with the highest relevance score, recomputing heatmaps at each iteration, until the string no longer contains any of the four subsequences. We apply the ablation test to 100 randomly generated input strings, and report the average percentage of each string that is ablated in Table 6. A peculiar property of the SP task is that removing a symbol preserves the validity of input strings. This means that, unlike in NLP settings, our ablation test does not suffer from the issue that ablation produces invalid inputs.

Saliency, G × I, and LRP perform close to the random baseline on the FSA network; this is unsurprising, since these methods only assign nonzero scores to the last input symbol. While Table 3 shows some variation in the IG heatmaps, IG also performs close to the random baseline. Only occlusion performs considerably better, since it is able to identify symbols whose ablation would destroy subsequences.

On the counter-based SP network, IG performs remarkably close to the optimal benchmark, which represents the best possible performance on this task. Occlusion, G × I, and LRP achieve a similar level of performance to one another, while saliency performs worse than the random baseline.

8   Conclusion

Of all the heatmaps considered in this paper, only those computed by G × I and IG for the counting task fully matched our expectations. In other cases, all attribution methods fail to identify at least some of the input features that should be considered relevant, or assign relevance to input features that do

---

[5]We do not consider the counting task because its heatmaps are already easy to understand, and we do not consider the PDA network because the gradient-based methods fail to produce nonzero heatmaps for that network.

not affect the model's behavior. Among the five methods, saliency achieves the worst performance: it never assigns nonzero scores for the counting and bracket prediction tasks, and it does not identify the relevant symbols for either of the two SP networks. Saliency also achieves the worst performance on the ablation test for both the counter-based and the FSA-based SP networks. Among the four white-box networks, the two automata-based networks proved to be much more challenging for the attribution methods than the counter-based networks. While the LRP heatmaps for the PDA network correctly identify the matching bracket when available, no other method produces reasonable heatmaps for the PDA network, and all five methods fail to interpret the FSA network.

Taken together, our results suggest that attribution heatmaps should be viewed with skepticism. This paper has identified cases in which heatmaps fail to highlight relevant features, as well as cases in which heatmaps incorrectly highlight irrelevant features. Although most of the methods perform better for the counter-based networks than the automaton-based networks, in practical settings we do not know what kinds of computations are implemented by a trained network, making it impossible to determine whether the network under analysis is compatible with the attribution method being used.

In future work, we encourage the use of our four white-box models as qualitative benchmarks for evaluating interpretability methods. For example, the style of evaluation we have developed can be replicated for attribution methods not covered in this paper, including DeepLIFT (Shrikumar et al., 2017) and contextual decomposition (Murdoch et al., 2018). We believe that insights gleaned from white-box analysis can help researchers choose between different attribution methods and identify areas of improvement in current techniques.

Acknowledgments

I would like to thank Dana Angluin and Robert Frank for their advice and mentorship on this project. I would also like to thank Yoav Goldberg, John Lafferty, Tal Linzen, R. Thomas Mc-Coy, Aaron Mueller, Karl Mulligan, Shauli Ravfogel, Jason Shaw, and the reviewers for their helpful feedback and discussion.

References

Julius Adebayo, Justin Gilmer, Michael Muelly, Ian Goodfellow, Moritz Hardt, and Been Kim. 2018. Sanity Checks for Saliency Maps. In *Advances in Neural Information Processing Systems 31*, volume 31, pages 9505–9515, Montreal, Canada. Curran Associates, Inc.

Marco Ancona, Enea Ceolini, Cengiz Öztireli, and Markus Gross. 2018. Towards better understanding of gradient-based attribution methods for Deep Neural Networks. In *ICLR 2018 Conference Track*, Vancouver, Canada. OpenReview.

Leila Arras, Franziska Horn, Grégoire Montavon, Klaus-Robert Müller, and Wojciech Samek. 2017a. "What is relevant in a text document?": An interpretable machine learning approach. *PLOS ONE*, 12(8):e0181142.

Leila Arras, Grégoire Montavon, Klaus-Robert Müller, and Wojciech Samek. 2017b. Explaining Recurrent Neural Network Predictions in Sentiment Analysis. In *Proceedings of the 8th Workshop on Computational Approaches to Subjectivity, Sentiment and Social Media Analysis*, pages 159–168, Copenhagen, Denmark. Association for Computational Linguistics.

Leila Arras, Ahmed Osman, Klaus-Robert Müller, and Wojciech Samek. 2019. Evaluating Recurrent Neural Network Explanations. In *Proceedings of the 2019 ACL Workshop BlackboxNLP: Analyzing and Interpreting Neural Networks for NLP*, pages 113–126, Florence, Italy. Association for Computational Linguistics.

Enes Avcu, Chihiro Shibata, and Jeffrey Heinz. 2017. Subregular Complexity and Deep Learning. In *Proceedings of the Conference on Logic and Machine Learning in Natural Language (LaML 2017), Gothenburg, 12–13 June 2017*, volume 1 of *CLASP Papers in Computational Linguistics*, pages 20–33, Gothenburg, Sweden. Centre for Linguistic Theory and Studies in Probability (CLASP), University of Gothenburg.

Sebastian Bach, Alexander Binder, Grégoire Montavon, Frederick Klauschen, Klaus-Robert Müller, and Wojciech Samek. 2015. On Pixel-Wise Explanations for Non-Linear Classifier Decisions by Layer-Wise Relevance Propagation. *PLOS ONE*, 10(7):e0130140.

Jean-Philippe Bernardy. 2018. Can Recurrent Neural Networks Learn Nested Recursion? *Linguistic Issues in Language Technology*, 16(1):1–20.

N. Chomsky and M. P. Schützenberger. 1959. The Algebraic Theory of Context-Free Languages. In P. Braffort and D. Hirschberg, editors, *Studies in Logic and the Foundations of Mathematics*, volume 26 of *Computer Programming and Formal Systems*, pages 118–161. North-Holland Publishing Company, Amsterdam, Netherlands.

Jeffrey L. Elman. 1990. Finding Structure in Time. *Cognitive Science*, 14(2):179–211.

Patrick C. Fischer. 1966. Turing Machines with Restricted Memory Access. *Information and Control*, 9(4):364–379.

Patrick C. Fischer, Albert R. Meyer, and Arnold L. Rosenberg. 1968. Counter Machines and Counter Languages. *Mathematical systems theory*, 2(3):265–283.

Amirata Ghorbani, Abubakar Abid, and James Zou. 2019. Interpretation of Neural Networks Is Fragile. *Proceedings of the AAAI Conference on Artificial Intelligence*, 33(01):3681–3688.

Jeffrey Nicholas Heinz. 2007. *Inductive Learning of Phonotactic Patterns*. PhD Dissertation, University of California, Los Angeles, Los Angeles, CA, USA.

Been Kim, Martin Wattenberg, Justin Gilmer, Carrie Cai, James Wexler, Fernanda Viegas, and Rory Sayres. 2018. Interpretability Beyond Feature Attribution: Quantitative Testing with Concept Activation Vectors (TCAV). In *International Conference on Machine Learning, 10–15 July 2018, Stockholmsmässan, Stockholm Sweden*, volume 80 of *Proceedings of Machine Learning Research*, pages 2668–2677, Stockholm, Sweden. PMLR.

Pieter-Jan Kindermans, Sara Hooker, Julius Adebayo, Maximilian Alber, Kristof T. Schütt, Sven Dähne, Dumitru Erhan, and Been Kim. 2019. The (Un)reliability of Saliency Methods. In Wojciech Samek, Grégoire Montavon, Andrea Vedaldi, Lars Kai Hansen, and Klaus-Robert Müller, editors, *Explainable AI: Interpreting, Explaining and Visualizing Deep Learning*, number 11700 in Lecture Notes in Computer Science, pages 267–280. Springer International Publishing, Cham, Switzerland.

Samuel A. Korsky and Robert C. Berwick. 2019. On the Computational Power of RNNs. *Computing Research Repository*, arXiv:1906.06349.

Jiwei Li, Xinlei Chen, Eduard Hovy, and Dan Jurafsky. 2016. Visualizing and Understanding Neural Models in NLP. In *Proceedings of the 2016 Conference of the North American Chapter of the Association for Computational Linguistics: Human Language Technologies*, pages 681–691, San Diego, CA, USA. Association for Computational Linguistics.

Abhijit Mahalunkar and John Kelleher. 2019a. Multi-Element Long Distance Dependencies: Using SP_k Languages to Explore the Characteristics of Long-Distance Dependencies. In *Proceedings of the Workshop on Deep Learning and Formal Languages: Building Bridges*, pages 34–43, Florence, Italy. Association for Computational Linguistics.

Abhijit Mahalunkar and John D. Kelleher. 2018. Using Regular Languages to Explore the Representational Capacity of Recurrent Neural Architectures.

In *Artificial Neural Networks and Machine Learning – ICANN 2018*, volume 11141 of *Lecture Notes in Computer Science*, pages 189–198, Rhodes, Greece. Springer International Publishing.

Abhijit Mahalunkar and John D. Kelleher. 2019b. Understanding Recurrent Neural Architectures by Analyzing and Synthesizing Long Distance Dependencies in Benchmark Sequential Datasets. *Computing Research Repository*, arXiv:1810.02966v3.

William Merrill. 2019. Sequential Neural Networks as Automata. In *Proceedings of the Workshop on Deep Learning and Formal Languages: Building Bridges*, pages 1–13, Florence, Italy. Association for Computational Linguistics.

Grégoire Montavon. 2019. Gradient-Based Vs. Propagation-Based Explanations: An Axiomatic Comparison. In Wojciech Samek, Grégoire Montavon, Andrea Vedaldi, Lars Kai Hansen, and Klaus-Robert Müller, editors, *Explainable AI: Interpreting, Explaining and Visualizing Deep Learning*, number 11700 in Lecture Notes in Computer Science, pages 253–265. Springer International Publishing, Cham, Switzerland.

Grégoire Montavon, Wojciech Samek, and Klaus-Robert Müller. 2018. Methods for interpreting and understanding deep neural networks. *Digital Signal Processing*, 73:1–15.

W. James Murdoch, Peter J. Liu, and Bin Yu. 2018. Beyond Word Importance: Contextual Decomposition to Extract Interactions from LSTMs. In *ICLR 2018 Conference Track*, Vancouver, Canada. OpenReview.

Nina Poerner, Hinrich Schütze, and Benjamin Roth. 2018. Evaluating neural network explanation methods using hybrid documents and morphosyntactic agreement. In *Proceedings of the 56th Annual Meeting of the Association for Computational Linguistics*, volume 1: Long Papers, pages 340–350, Melbourne, Australia. Association for Computational Linguistics.

Wojciech Samek, Alexander Binder, Grégoire Montavon, Sebastian Lapuschkin, and Klaus-Robert Müller. 2017. Evaluating the Visualization of What a Deep Neural Network Has Learned. *IEEE Transactions on Neural Networks and Learning Systems*, 28(11):2660–2673.

Luzi Sennhauser and Robert Berwick. 2018. Evaluating the Ability of LSTMs to Learn Context-Free Grammars. In *Proceedings of the 2018 EMNLP Workshop BlackboxNLP: Analyzing and Interpreting Neural Networks for NLP*, pages 115–124, Brussels, Belgium. Association for Computational Linguistics.

Avanti Shrikumar, Peyton Greenside, Anna Shcherbina, and Anshul Kundaje. 2017. Not Just a Black Box: Learning Important Features Through Propagating

Activation Differences. *Computing Research Repository*, arXiv:1605.01713.

Karen Simonyan, Andrea Vedaldi, and Andrew Zisserman. 2014. Deep Inside Convolutional Networks: Visualising Image Classification Models and Saliency Maps. In *ICLR 2014 Workshop Proceedings*, Banff, Canada. arXiv.

Natalia Skachkova, Thomas Trost, and Dietrich Klakow. 2018. Closing Brackets with Recurrent Neural Networks. In *Proceedings of the 2018 EMNLP Workshop BlackboxNLP: Analyzing and Interpreting Neural Networks for NLP*, pages 232–239, Brussels, Belgium. Association for Computational Linguistics.

Mukund Sundararajan, Ankur Taly, and Qiqi Yan. 2017. Axiomatic Attribution for Deep Networks. In *Proceedings of the 34th International Conference on Machine Learning*, volume 70 of *Proceedings of Machine Learning Research*, pages 3319–3328, Sydney, Australia. PMLR.

Gail Weiss, Yoav Goldberg, and Eran Yahav. 2018. On the Practical Computational Power of Finite Precision RNNs for Language Recognition. In *Proceedings of the 56th Annual Meeting of the Association for Computational Linguistics*, volume 2: Short Papers, pages 740–745, Melbourne, Australia. Association for Computational Linguistics.

Mengjiao Yang and Been Kim. 2019. Benchmarking Attribution Methods with Relative Feature Importance. *Computing Research Repository*, arXiv:1907.09701.

Xiang Yu, Ngoc Thang Vu, and Jonas Kuhn. 2019. Learning the Dyck Language with Attention-based Seq2Seq Models. In *Proceedings of the 2019 ACL Workshop BlackboxNLP: Analyzing and Interpreting Neural Networks for NLP*, pages 138–146, Florence, Italy. Association for Computational Linguistics.

Matthew D. Zeiler and Rob Fergus. 2014. Visualizing and Understanding Convolutional Networks. In *Computer Vision – ECCV 2014*, volume 8689 of *Lecture Notes in Computer Science*, pages 818–833, Zurich, Switzerland. Springer International Publishing.

Jianming Zhang, Sarah Adel Bargal, Zhe Lin, Jonathan Brandt, Xiaohui Shen, and Stan Sclaroff. 2018. Top-Down Neural Attention by Excitation Backprop. *International Journal of Computer Vision*, 126(10):1084–1102.

A   Detailed Descriptions of White-Box Networks

This appendix provides detailed descriptions of our four white-box networks.

A.1   Counting Task Network

As described in Subsection 4.1, the network for the counting task simply sets $g^{(t)}$ to $v = \tanh(u)$ when $x^{(t)} = $ a and $-v$ when $x^{(t)} = $ b. All gates are fixed to 1. The output layer uses $h^{(t)} = \tanh\left(c^{(t)}\right)$ as the score for the *True* class and $v/2$ as the score for the *False* class.

$$g^{(t)} = \tanh\left(u \begin{bmatrix} 1 & -1 \end{bmatrix} x^{(t)}\right)$$

$$f^{(t)} = \sigma(m)$$

$$i^{(t)} = \sigma(m)$$

$$o^{(t)} = \sigma(m)$$

$$\hat{y}^{(t)} = \begin{bmatrix} 1 \\ 0 \end{bmatrix} h^{(t)} + \begin{bmatrix} 0 \\ v/2 \end{bmatrix}$$

A.2   SP Task Network (Counter-Based)

The seven counters for the SP task are implemented as follows. First, we compute $g^{(t)}$ under the assumption that one of the first four counters is always incremented, and one of the last three counters is always incremented as long as $x^{(t)} \neq $ a.

$$g^{(t)} = \tanh\left(u \begin{bmatrix} & & I_4 & \\ \hdashline 0 & 1 & 0 & 0 \\ 0 & 0 & 1 & 0 \\ 0 & 0 & 0 & 1 \end{bmatrix} x^{(t)}\right)$$

Then, we use the input gate to condition the last three counters on the value of the first four counters. For example, if $h_1^{(t-1)} = 0$, then no as have been encountered in the input string before time t. In that case, the input gate for counter #5, which represents subsequences ending with b, is set to $i_5^{(t)} = \sigma(-m) \approx 0$. This is because a b encountered at time t would not form part of a subsequence if no as have been encountered so far, so counter #5 should not be incremented.

$$i^{(t)} = \sigma\left(2m \begin{bmatrix} & & 0 & & & 0 \\ \hdashline 1 & 0 & 0 & 0 & & \\ 0 & 1 & 0 & 1 & & 0 \\ 0 & 0 & 1 & 0 & & \end{bmatrix} h^{(t-1)} \right.$$
$$\left. + m \begin{bmatrix} 1 & 1 & 1 & 1 & -1 & -1 & -1 \end{bmatrix}^\top \right)$$

All other gates are fixed to **1**. The output layer sets the score of the *True* class to $h_5^{(t)} + h_6^{(t)} + h_7^{(t)}$ and the score of the *False* class to $v/2$.

$$f^{(t)} = \sigma(m\mathbf{1})$$

$$o^{(t)} = \sigma(m\mathbf{1})$$

$$\hat{y}^{(t)} = \begin{bmatrix} \mathbf{0} & 1 & 1 & 1 \\ \mathbf{0} & 0 & 0 & 0 \end{bmatrix} h^{(t)} + \begin{bmatrix} 0 \\ v/2 \end{bmatrix}$$

A.3 FSA Network

Here we describe a general construction of an LSTM simulating an FSA with states Q, accepting states $Q_F \subseteq Q$, alphabet Σ, and transition function $\delta : Q \times \Sigma \to Q$. Recall that $h^{(t)}$ contains a one-hot representation of pairs in $Q \times \Sigma$ encoding the current state of the FSA and the most recent input symbol. The initial state $h^{(0)} = \mathbf{0}$ represents the starting configuration of the FSA.

At a high level, the state transition system works as follows. First, $g^{(t)}$ first marks all the positions corresponding to the current input $x^{(t)}$.[6]

$$
g^{(t)}_{\langle q,x\rangle} = \begin{cases} v, & x = x^{(t)} \\ 0, & \text{otherwise} \end{cases}
$$

The input gate then filters out any positions that do not represent valid transitions from the previous state q', which is recovered from $h^{(t-1)}$.

$$
i^{(t)}_{\langle q,x\rangle} = \begin{cases} 1, & \delta(q',x) = q \\ 0, & \text{otherwise} \end{cases}
$$

Now, we describe how this behavior is implemented in our LSTM.

The cell state update is straightforwardly implemented as follows:

$$
g^{(t)} = \tanh\left(u \mathbf{W}^{(c,x)} x^{(t)} \right),
$$

where

$$
W^{(c,x)}_{\langle q,x\rangle,j} = \begin{cases} 1, & j \text{ is the index for } x \\ 0, & \text{otherwise.} \end{cases}
$$

Observe that the matrix $\mathbf{W}^{(c,x)}$ essentially contains a copy of I_4 for each state, such that each copy is distributed across the different cell state units designated for that state.

The input gate is more complex. First, the bias term handles the case where the current case is the starting state q_0. This is necessary because the initial configuration of the network is represented by $h^{(0)} = \mathbf{0}$.

$$
b^{(i)}_{\langle q,x\rangle} = \begin{cases} m, & \delta(q_0,x) = q \\ -m, & \text{otherwise} \end{cases}
$$

The bias vector sets $i^{(t)}_{\langle q,x\rangle}$ to be 1 if the FSA transitions from q_0 to q after reading x, and 0 otherwise. We replicate this behavior for other values

---

[6]We use $v = \tanh(1) \approx 0.762$.

of $h^{(t-1)}$ by using the weight matrix $\mathbf{W}^{(i,h)}$, taking the bias vector into account:

$$
i^{(t)} = \sigma\left(\mathbf{W}^{(i,h)} h^{(t-1)} + b^{(i)} \right),
$$

where

$$
W^{(i)}_{\langle q,x\rangle,\langle q',x'\rangle} = \begin{cases} m - b^{(i)}_{\langle q,x\rangle}, & \delta(q',x) = q \\ -m - b^{(i)}_{\langle q,x\rangle}, & \text{otherwise.} \end{cases}
$$

The forget gate is fixed to -1, since the state needs to be updated at every time step. The output gate is fixed to $\mathbf{1}$.

$$
f^{(t)} = \sigma(-m\mathbf{1})
$$
$$
o^{(t)} = \sigma(m\mathbf{1})
$$

The output layer simply selects hidden units that represent accepting and rejecting states:

$$
\hat{y}^{(t)} = \mathbf{W} h^{(t)},
$$

where

$$
W_{c,\langle q,x\rangle} = \begin{cases} 1, & c = \textit{True} \text{ and } q \in Q_F \\ 1, & c = \textit{False} \text{ and } q \notin Q_F \\ 0, & \text{otherwise.} \end{cases}
$$

A.4 PDA Network

Finally, we describe how the PDA network for the bracket prediction task is implemented. Of the four networks, this one is the most intricate. Recall from Subsection 4.2 that we implement a bounded stack of size k using $2k + 1$ hidden units, with the following interpretation:

- $c^{(t)}_{:k-1}$ contains the stack, except for the top item

- $c^{(t)}_{k}$ contains the top item of the stack

- $c^{(t)}_{k+1:2k}$ contains the height of the stack in unary notation

- c_{2k+1} is a bit, which is set to be positive if the stack is empty and nonpositive otherwise.

We represent the brackets (, [,), and] in one-hot encoding with the indices 1, 2, 3, and 4, respectively. The opening brackets (and [are represented on the stack by 1 and -1, respectively. T

We begin by describing $g^{(t)}$. Due to the complexity of the network, we describe the weights and biases individually, which are combined as follows.

$$g^{(t)} = \tanh\left(m\left(z^{(g,t)}\right)\right), \text{ where}$$
$$z^{(g,t)} = W^{(c,x)}x^{(t)} + W^{(c,h)}h^{(t-1)} + b^{(c)}$$

First, the bias vector sets $c_{2k+1}^{(t)}$ to be 1, indicating that the stack is empty. This ensures that the initial hidden state $h^{(t)} = 0$ is treated as an empty stack.

$$b^{(c)} = \begin{bmatrix} 0 \\ \hline 2 \end{bmatrix}$$

$W^{(c,x)}$ serves three functions when $x^{(t)}$ is an open bracket, and does nothing when $x^{(t)}$ is a closing bracket. First, it pushes $x^{(t)}$ to the top of the stack, represented by $c_k^{(t)}$. The values $\pm 2^k$ are determined by equation (1) in Subsection 4.2. Second, it sets $g_{k+1:2k}^{(t)}$ to 1 in order to increment the unary counter for the height of the stack. Later, we will see that the input gate filters out all positions except for the top of the stack. Finally, $W^{(c,x)}$ sets the empty stack indicator to -1, indicating that the stack is not empty.

$$W^{(c,x)} = \begin{bmatrix} 0 & 0 & 0 & 0 \\ \hline 2^k & -2^k & 0 & 0 \\ \hline 1 & 1 & 0 & 0 \\ \hline -2 & -2 & 0 & 0 \end{bmatrix}$$

$W^{(c,h)}$ performs two functions. First, it completes equation (1) for $c_k^{(t)}$, setting it to be the second-highest stack item from the previous time step. Second, it copies the top of the stack to the first $k-1$ positions, with the input gate filtering out all but the highest position.

$$W^{(c,h)} = \begin{bmatrix} 0 & & & 1 & 0 & 0 \\ \hline 2 & 4 & \cdots & 2^{k-1} & 0 & 0 & 0 \\ \hline 0 & & & 0 & 0 & 0 \\ \hline 0 & & & 0 & -1 & 0 \end{bmatrix}$$

Finally, the -1s serve to decrease the empty stack indicator by an amount proportional to the stack height at time $t-1$. Observe that if $x^{(t)}$ is a closing bracket and $h^{(t-1)}$ represents a stack with only one item, then

$$W_{2k+1,:}^{(c,x)}x^{(t)} + W_{2k+1,:}^{(c,h)}h^{(t-1)} + b_{2k+1}^{(c)}$$
$$= -1 + 2 = 1,$$

so the empty stack indicator is set to 1, indicating that the stack is empty. Otherwise,

$$W_{2k+1,:}^{(c,x)}x^{(t)} + W_{2k+1,:}^{(c,h)}h^{(t-1)} \leq -2,$$

so the empty stack indicator is nonpositive.

Now, we describe the input gate, given by the following.

$$i^{(t)} = \sigma\left(m\left(z^{(i,t)}\right)\right)$$
$$z^{(i,t)} = W^{(i,x)}x^{(t)} + W^{(i,h)}h^{(t-1)} + b^{(i)}$$

$W^{(i,x)}$ sets the input gate for the first $k-1$ positions to 0 when $x^{(t)}$ is a closing bracket. In that case, an item needs to be popped from the stack, so nothing can be copied to these hidden units. When $x^{(t)}$ is an opening bracket, $W^{(i,x)}$ sets $i_k^{(t)} = 1$, so that the bracket can be copied to the top of the stack.

$$W^{(i,x)} = 2 \begin{bmatrix} 0 & 0 & -1 & -1 \\ \hline 1 & 1 & 0 & 0 \\ \hline & & 0 & \end{bmatrix}$$

$W^{(i,h)}$ uses a matrix $T_n \in \mathbb{R}^{n \times n}$, defined below.

$$T_n = \begin{bmatrix} 1 & -1 & 0 & \cdots & 0 & 0 \\ 0 & 1 & -1 & \cdots & 0 & 0 \\ \vdots & \vdots & \vdots & \ddots & \vdots & \vdots \\ 0 & 0 & 0 & \cdots & 1 & -1 \\ 0 & 0 & 0 & \cdots & 0 & 1 \end{bmatrix}$$

Suppose v represents the number s in unary notation: v_j is 1 if $j \leq s$ and 0 otherwise. T_n has the special property that $T_n v$ is a one-hot vector for s. Based on this, $W^{(i,h)}$ is defined as follows.

$$W^{(i,h)} = 2 \begin{bmatrix} 0 & \begin{array}{c} (T_k)_{:k-1,:} \\ \hline 0 \\ \hline (T_k)_{:k-1,:} \\ \hline 0 \end{array} & 0 \end{bmatrix}$$

$W_{:k-1,k+1:2k}^{(i,h)}$ contains T_k, with the last row truncated. This portion of the matrix converts $h_{k+1:2k}^{(t-1)}$, which contains a unary encoding of the stack height, to a one-hot vector marking the position of the top of the stack. This ensures that, when pushing to the stack, the top stack item from time $t-1$ is only copied to the appropriate position of $h_{:k-1}^{(t)}$. The other copy of T_k, again with the last row omitted, occurs in $W_{k+2:2k,k+1:2k}^{(i,h)}$. This copy of T_k ensures that when the unary counter for the stack height is incremented, only the appropriate position is updated. Finally, the bias vector ensures that the top stack item and the empty stack indicator are always updated.

$$\boldsymbol{b}^{(i)} = \begin{bmatrix} -\mathbf{1} \\ \hline \mathbf{1} \\ \hline -\mathbf{1} \\ \hline \mathbf{1} \end{bmatrix}$$

The forget gate is responsible for deleting portions of memory when stack items are popped.

$$\boldsymbol{f}^{(t)} = \sigma \left(m \left(\boldsymbol{z}^{(f,t)} \right) \right)$$
$$\boldsymbol{z}^{(f,t)} = \boldsymbol{W}^{(f,x)} \boldsymbol{x}^{(t)} + \boldsymbol{W}^{(f,h)} \boldsymbol{h}^{(t-1)} + \boldsymbol{b}^{(f)}$$

$\boldsymbol{W}^{(f,x)}$ first ensures that no stack items are deleted when an item is pushed to the stack.

$$\boldsymbol{W}^{(f,x)} = 2 \begin{bmatrix} \mathbf{1} & \mathbf{1} & \mathbf{0} & \mathbf{0} \\ \hline \mathbf{0} & \mathbf{0} & \mathbf{0} & \mathbf{0} \\ \hline \mathbf{1} & \mathbf{1} & \mathbf{0} & \mathbf{0} \\ \hline \mathbf{0} & \mathbf{0} & \mathbf{0} & \mathbf{0} \end{bmatrix}$$

Next, $\boldsymbol{W}^{(f,h)}$ marks the second highest stack position and the top of the unary counter for deletion, in case an item needs to be popped.

$$\boldsymbol{W}^{(f,h)} = 2 \begin{bmatrix} \mathbf{0} & \begin{matrix} -(\boldsymbol{T}_k)_{2:,:} \\ \hline \mathbf{0} \\ \hline -\boldsymbol{T}_k \\ \hline \mathbf{0} \end{matrix} & \mathbf{0} \end{bmatrix}$$

Finally, the bias term ensures that the top stack item and empty stack indicator are always cleared.

$$\boldsymbol{b}^{(i)} = \begin{bmatrix} \mathbf{1} \\ \hline -\mathbf{1} \\ \hline \mathbf{1} \\ \hline -\mathbf{1} \end{bmatrix}$$

To complete the construction, we fix the output gate to $\mathbf{1}$, and have the output layer read the top stack position:

$$\boldsymbol{o}^{(t)} = \sigma(m\mathbf{1})$$
$$\hat{\boldsymbol{y}}^{(t)} = \boldsymbol{W}\boldsymbol{h}^{(t)},$$

where

$$W_{c,j} = \begin{cases} 1, & c = \text{)} \text{ and } j = k \\ -1, & c = \text{]} \text{ and } j = k \\ 1, & c = None \text{ and } j = 2k + 1 \\ 0, & \text{otherwise.} \end{cases}$$

Defining Explanation in an AI Context

Tejaswani Verma

Mercedes-Benz Innovation Lab, Berlin, Germany
Saarbrücken Graduate School of Computer Science, Saarland University
`tejaswani.verma@daimler.com`

Christoph Lingenfelder

Mercedes-Benz Innovation Lab, Berlin, Germany
`christoph.lingenfelder@daimler.com`

Dietrich Klakow

Saarland University, Saarbrücken, Germany
`dietrich.klakow@lsv.uni-saarland.de`

Abstract

With the increase in the use of AI systems, a need for explanation systems arises. Building an explanation system requires a definition of *explanation*. However, the natural language term *explanation* is difficult to define formally as it includes multiple perspectives from different domains such as psychology, philosophy, and cognitive sciences. We study multiple perspectives and aspects of explainability of recommendations or predictions made by AI systems, and provide a generic definition of *explanation*. The proposed definition is ambitious and challenging to apply. With the intention to bridge the gap between theory and application, we also propose a possible architecture of an automated explanation system based on our definition of *explanation*.

1 Introduction

Definitions of explanation have been proposed by many researchers from the perspective of various fields of science, however the scope of our research is focused on computer science and cognitive science perspectives, as we are looking for automatically generated explanations for people affected by recommendations or predictions made by AI systems. Explanation is often described as a phenomenon which enables transfer of specific information. Philosophically, acceptance of a statement as an explanation is subject to acceptance by the recipient (Gilpin et al., 2018). However, according to computer scientists explanations must be *complete*, i.e. encapsulate all factors of complex internal workings, and *accurate*, i.e. hold high fidelity to the AI model in question (Gilpin et al., 2018).

We can find many definitions in different domains, often conflicting. Some choose to focus only on selected aspects of explanation. For generating explanations automatically, a strong understanding of how people define, generate, select, evaluate, and present explanations is essential. In order to design and implement intelligent agents that are truly capable of providing appropriate explanations to people, analyzing how humans explain decisions and behavior to each other is a good starting point.

In the past, researchers have defined models and conducted social experiments, many of which uncovered novel and essential aspects of human explanations (Harman, 1965; Hanson, 1958; Hesslow, 1988). Specifically social experiments help us understand the impact of unquantifiable attributes of human behavior which include belief, desire, social norms, intention to understand, emotions, personality traits, etc. These attributes are aptly defined by folk psychology, or commonsense psychology (Heider and Simmel, 1944; Malle, 2006). Folk psychology does not describe our thought process or behavior but our expected thought process or behavior, which makes it an important aspect of explanation.

As mentioned earlier, most of the past research is focused on selective aspects of explanation. This is because building a generic explanation system is a tedious task. With the intention to take a step towards realization of this task, we assume the AI system to be a *black-box* i.e. all internal structure and/or processes are hidden and only input-output pairs are perceivable. No restriction is imposed on inputs and outputs.

Proceedings of the Third BlackboxNLP Workshop on Analyzing and Interpreting Neural Networks for NLP, pages 314–322
Online, November 20, 2020. ©2020 Association for Computational Linguistics

In this paper we will review cognitive and social models, experiments and definitions which may assist us in writing a more generic definition of explanation. In the background section we will discuss the need for explanation in detail, which will enable us to define necessary conditions and possible quality measures. We will also highlight important models, theories and conflicting definitions. In later sections, we argue which aspects of explanation are most important and propose a generic definition of explanation. Lastly, we introduce a possible architecture of a generic automated explanation system based on our proposed definition.

2 Background

In this section, we will discuss why explanation is required, the theoretical advances made towards building explanation models and insights about conflicts in the definitions proposed so far.

2.1 Need for Explanation

Many AI systems are complex and hard to understand. Even though AI systems possess potential to address plethora of problems, their applications may be limited due to our inability to comprehend their results and reasoning process. A definition of explanation would be beneficial for multiple groups, the most prominent of which is receivers of a prediction or recommendation made by any AI system. Other groups include researchers, AI developers, users of the system, etc. We refer to all these groups together as *recipients* and a *recipient* can be any individual from this group.

We reviewed the significance of explanation covered by several authors. Here, we reiterate the reasons majorly presented in Doshi-Velez and Kim (2017), Samek et al. (2017), and Lipton (2018). The reasons presented below depict the importance of explanation:

- Enhancement of scientific understanding: Most AI systems are quite powerful, they can process data faster and can find patterns which may go unperceived by humans. Understanding the reasons which contribute to the prediction of a *black-box* offers a great opportunity for learning and extending our scientific understanding. (Doshi-Velez and Kim, 2017; Samek et al., 2017)

- Verification of the system: Explanations can enable us to examine if the system is working as intended and abides by the user's and the recipient's objectives. The workings of the overall system and its objectives are important as the user of an AI system and the recipient of the prediction might have different objectives. (Doshi-Velez and Kim, 2017; Samek et al., 2017)

- Understanding multi-objective trade-offs: In case of multiple objectives an explanation provides information to the recipient regarding which features outweigh others, their magnitude and their collaborative impact on the output. (Doshi-Velez and Kim, 2017)

- Improvement of system:An explanation can also help developers detect fallacies within the system, which allows further improvement of the system. (Samek et al., 2017)

- Inculcating Trust in user: AI system predictions can be confusing at times, explanations will give users an insight of why a certain prediction was made. This makes it easier for users to accept the prediction. It also provides a rough estimate to the user regarding how often the system is right and also what makes it right. (Lipton, 2018)

- Inferring Causal relations in data: Inferring causal relations in data is not trivial, researchers wish to discover such relations which can help them in generating hypotheses about the natural world. Explanations can play a crucial part in deepening our knowledge of the universe. (Doshi-Velez and Kim, 2017; Lipton, 2018)

- Enabling Transferability: Humans possess great abilities such as generalizing and transferring learned skills. Artificial neural networks were inspired by the ability of the human brain to execute multiple tasks given the correct data and processing power, however their capabilities are still limited due to their inability to learn and transfer skills like humans. Explanation might bring us one step closer to understand, how to enable the ability to transfer learned skills. (Lipton, 2018)

- Fair and Ethical Decision-Making: Automated decision making is embedded in our daily lives from social media platforms, to stock market, to process of approving loans and much more. It has become essential to ensure fair and ethical decision making. This requires transparency in the decision making process which can be enabled by explanations even though the system may not be originally transparent. (Doshi-Velez and Kim, 2017)

- Ensuring safety to use AI models: Although prediction and recommendation systems might not seem dangerous, in certain sensitive scenarios the results can be catastrophic. There is a risk factor involved with every automated decision making system however with some AI models, which might be used for medical diagnosis or self-driving cars, the risk factor is much higher. In order to ensure safety while using these systems we need to understand the system's actions or predictions, measure the risk factors and take appropriate steps. (Doshi-Velez and Kim, 2017)

- Compliance to Legislation: In 2016, European Union GDPR enabled the "Right to Explanation" act[1], making it a legal necessity for all automated systems to provide explanations.

2.2 Explanation vs Interpretation

Explanation definitions can be controversial. The difference between *explainability* and *interpretability* is frequently debated in the computer science community. In the process of distinguishing between explainability and interpretability, the essence of human understandability is often lost.
Technically, an *explanation* is considered to be complete and often complex, whereas an *interpretation* defines internal workings of a system in an abstract human understandable way (Gilpin et al., 2018). Intuitively, the term *explanation* used by humans is much closer to the technical term *interpretation*. This is a subject of debate in the research community, however considering the objective explanations, many researchers use these terms interchangeably. From this point onwards we will use the term explanation for the technical term interpretation.

---

[1]"Right to Explanation" in EU Legislation (Last accessed on: 2020-10-06): `https://www.privacy-regulation.eu/en/r71.html`

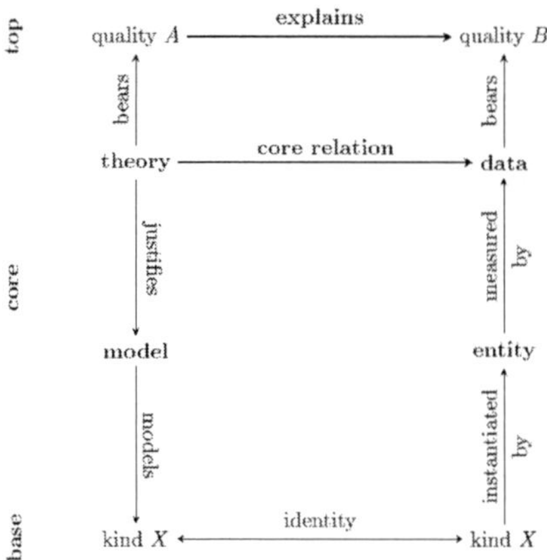

Figure 1: A general structure of a theory-data explanation proposed by Overton.(Overton, 2012)

2.3 Models for generating explanation

Many tried to model explanations and explanation systems for different types of questions (why, why not, how, etc.), Aristotle's four causes model, also known as the Modes of explanation model (Hankinson, 2001), offers an analytical solution to the why questions by classifying them into four different elements:

- Material- The substance or material of which something is made. For example, rubber is a material cause for a car tire.

- Formal- The form or properties of something that make it what it is. For example, being round is a formal cause of a car tire. These are sometimes referred to as categorical explanations.

- Efficient- The main mechanism which cause something to change. For example, a tire manufacturer is an efficient cause for a car tire. These are sometimes referred to as mechanistic explanations.

- Final- The end or goal of something. Moving a vehicle is an efficient cause of a car tire. These are sometimes referred to as functional or teleological explanations.

It is important to note that although all the elements are individually necessary for an explanation, they are not individually sufficient.

Overton defines the structure of explanations with five categories of properties or objects that are explained in science: theories, models, kinds, entities and data (Overton, 2012, 2013). To explain this concept further, let's look at the example of a billard ball hitting another ball at rest in a billard game. According to the example, the components of the model in Figure 1 will be as follows:

- Theory: Newton's third law to motion

- Model: $F_A = -F_B$.

- Kind X: If A exerts force upon B, B must exert force of equal and opposite magnitude.

- Entities A and B: Ball A and Ball B respectively.

- Data/Observation: A moving ball A hits ball B (initially at rest). The momentum of ball B increases and the momentum of ball A decreases due to equal and opposite forces exerted by each ball upon the other.

Extending Overton's Work, Malle argued social explanation has three layers: base, core and top (Malle, 2006).

- Base: Encapsulates underlying assumptions about human behaviour and explanation.

- Core: Psychological processes used to construct explanation.

- Top: Responsible for linguistic realization of the explanation.

Malle also proposed a theory of explanation (Malle, 2006, 2011), which breaks down the psychological processes used to offer explanations into two distinct groups information processes (for devising and assembling explanations), and impression management processes (for governing the social interactions of explanations). These two dimensions are divided into two further dimensions, which refer to the tools for constructing and giving explanations, and the explainer's perspective or knowledge about the explanation. This particular model is quite insightful due to its proximity with computer science domain. As presented in Figure 2, there are four dimensions:

- Information requirements - What information is required to provide an appropriate explanation?

- Information access - What information is accessible to the explainer to convey as an explanation?

- Pragmatic goals - What is the objective of the explanation?

- Functional capacities - What are the functional capacities or limitations of the given explanatory tools?

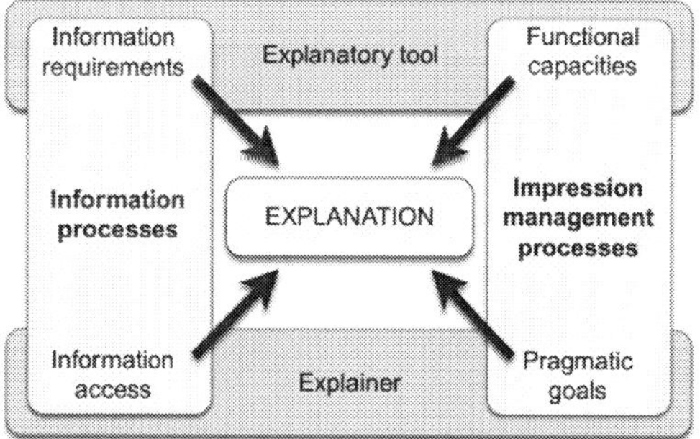

Figure 2: Malle's process model for explanation (Malle, 2011)

Some researchers portray explanations as representations of underlying causes which led to a system's output and which reflects the system's decision-making process. Other researchers assert that explanations are much more, for example when humans explain something they prioritize information, give examples and counter examples, select important details, etc. One of the most important factor of human explanations is the social component, explanations are almost always tailored for a specific audience or recipient. In Miller (2019), the author shares four important findings for explainable AI:

- Explanations are contrastive: In many scenarios, contrastive explanations are chosen by people due to their ease of comprehension.

- Explanations are selected: Humans usually don't analyze all causes of an event. They generally select a few main causes which are deemed "sufficient" as an explanation. The selected causes can be simple or complex, even global or local.

- Explanations are social: Explanation can be taken as transfer of knowledge, which includes many social aspects such as the receiver's cognitive and comprehension ability, the explainer's and receiver's beliefs, knowledge and presumptions, etc. Explainer's presumption Recipient's prior knowledge comprehension capacities

- Probabilities probably don't matter: "The most likely explanation is not always the best explanation for a person, and importantly, using statistical generalizations to explain why events occur is unsatisfying, unless accompanied by an underlying causal explanation for the generalization itself." (Miller, 2019)

3 Aspects of Explanation

As mentioned earlier, explanation has multiple aspects. Philosophically acceptance of a statement as an explanation is subject to acceptance by the recipient. Although this is intuitive, this definition of explanation is vague and incomplete. We argue that important aspects of explanation include *the posed question*, *the type of explanation*, *the explainer* and *the recipient*. We discuss each of them in this section.

3.1 The Posed Question

The posed question defines the objective of the explanation and provides direction for selecting an abstract, comparatively simple, reasoning of a complex state. Much emphasis is put into researching explanation models with the assumption that the posed question is either a "why" or "why not" question. Even though the assumption is intuitive and holds true for most cases, in some cases the posed question could also be of the following type: "how", "what", "what if", etc.

Aristotle's Modes of explanation model mentioned in section 2.3, only caters to the why-questions. Miller (Miller, 2019) proposed a simple model for explanatory questions based on Pearl and Mackenzie's Ladder of Causation (Pearl and Mackenzie, 2018). This model places explanatory questions into three classes:

- What-questions, such as "What event happened?" – Requires associative reasoning to determine which unobserved events occurred based on the occurrence of observed events.

- How-questions, such as "How did that event happen?" – Requires interventionist reasoning to determine necessary and sufficient causes of the given event. This may also require associative reasoning.

- Why-questions, such as "Why did that event happen?" – Requires counterfactual reasoning to undo events and introduce hypothetical events. This also requires associative and interventionist reasoning.

3.2 The Type of Explanation

There is a wide spectrum from which an explanation can be produced. It is important to understand that there are numerous accurate possible explanation for each scenario. Mills argued that causal connection and explanation selection are essentially arbitrary and the scientifically/philosophically it is "wrong" to select one explanation over another (Mill, 1973).

Based on Lipton (2018), Mittelstadt et al. (2019) and Pedreschi et al. (2019), we deduce that an explanation can be of many types. It can be example-based or statistical, generalized or specialized, technical or in layman terms. We argue that the choice between the latter two may be deduced by the information available about the posed question and the recipient. However, Adhikari (2018) shows via experiments that in most cases example-based explanations are preferred.

3.3 The Explainer

As mentioned in the introduction, the impact of unquantifiable attributes of human behavior, which includes belief, desire, social norms, intention to understand, emotions, personality traits, etc., can affect explanation. Even though the explainer's intention to explain and her beliefs about the recipient(s) may be important, we argue that there are other aspects which can be just as important (if not more). These aspects include the knowledge of the explainer herself, her ability to explain and the availability of information about the recipient's knowledge. This argument becomes stronger when we remove the pre-assumption of the explainer being a human. If the explainer is a machine then the importance of social aspects reduces.

3.4 The Recipient

The recipient is arguably the most important aspect for any explanation as many other aspects are manipulated by the recipient. Similar to the explainer, even though the social aspects such as intention to understand and her belief system are important, we argue that recipient's knowledge and ability to comprehend is also important. Although for building an explanation system, we would not relax the pre-assumption of human recipient(s).

4 Proposed Definition

In this section we present a generic definition, break down its components which can be interpreted differently depending on perspectives and discuss them from the AI perspective. Here, if an explanation is requested for a certain prediction/recommendation made via a particular black-box, we will represent the combination of input to the black-box, the black-box itself and the prediction/recommendation as a *scenario*. We argue that explanation requires pre-existing information about three major aspects: *the posed question*, *the recipient's knowledge*, and *the given scenario*. With respect to the aforementioned three aspects, we propose the following definition of explanation:

An explanation is a representation of fair and accurate assessments made by an explainer to transfer relevant knowledge (about a given scenario) from the explainer to a recipient.

In AI perspective, each component of the definition can be translated as follows:

- Assessments: It can be plain observations or analysis of observations. In AI, these observations tend to be about internal workings of a system and about factors which are important for a given input-output pair.

- Fair and accurate assessments: Here, *fair and accurate* depicts unbiased observations which hold high fidelity w.r.t the given AI model.

- Representation: It must be an appropriate depiction of assessments made by the explainer and acceptable by the recipient. It can be in the form of text, image, dialogue, etc. or a combination thereof.

- Explainer: It is an entity, human or machine, that mediates information. In AI, the explainer is a machine which reduces the impact of social aspects.

- Recipient: It is an entity to which clarification of a subject matter is presented. This clarifi-

cation may be in the form of a statement or a response to a posed question.

- Transfer of Relevant Knowledge: The concepts of explainability (complete and complex) and interpretability (abstract and comprehensible) of an explanation can be generalized by using "transfer of relevant knowledge" as a function of information gained by the recipient. This transfer of relevant knowledge can be active or passive.

Explanation as a statement represents a passive form of knowledge transfer based on only the given scenario. On the other hand, explanation as a response to a question posed by a recipient represents an active form of knowledge transfer based on the posed question, the recipient's knowledge, and the given scenario.

4.1 Examples

Here we consider three different scenarios in which the same underlying logic is conveyed in different ways to the recipient according to their knowledge and experience, when a particular question is asked. Please note that these examples only provide naïve insights into possible explanations. In reality the recipient's knowledge might be a complicated model which cannot be allotted one of the basic groups such as novice, intermediate or expert. The question "How do we model a recipient's knowledge?" is one of many difficult questions which need to be answered in order to build such complex explanation systems.

In Table 1, Scenario (1) and (2) offers contrast in generated explanations for the same type of recipient's knowledge. In Scenario (1), the explanation for a novice in the medical domain is kept very simple but the expert explanation has a lot of medical details, which might be burdensome for most patients. On the other hand, in Scenario (2) the banking domain novice explanation gives reasons of a loan rejection in a detailed yet simple manner, while the explanation for an expert is short. This uncovers the possibility of having different types of explanation depending on not only the scenario but also the domain of the scenario. Since it is not feasible to create different models for every scenario or domain of scenario, we need a generalized explanation system which can adapt and learn.

Scenario	Question	Logic Found	Recipient's Knowledge	Explanation
(1) A medical treatment X was recommended for a patient with symptoms Y.	Why was treatment X recommended to me?	Treatment X worked for other patients with symptoms Y	Novice	This treatment has worked before.
			Intermediate	Similar symptoms were healed with treatment X before.
			Expert	This treatment has a high probability of success as the similarity between the current patients and a past patient, who responded to treatment X, is above 70% due to the following underlying facts ….
(2) A bank loan request was rejected.	Why was my loan request rejected?	Risk factors were found too high due to already existing loans.	Novice	Since there is a lot of money already loaned to the applicant, the return of the requested amount to the bank becomes improbable.
			Intermediate	The amount loaned already is high which makes this a risky request for the bank to approve
			Expert	Due to high risk implied by multiple prior loans.
(3) A certain movie was recommended.	Why was this movie recommended to me?	98% match with other movies in user profile	Novice	You watched similar movies.
			Intermediate	There is 98% match with similar movies that you have watched before.
			Expert	You will probably like this movie as there is a 98% match with similar movies that you have watched before, due to the following reasons…

Table 1: Here we present three examples of a scenario with three possible types recipients each i.e. novice, intermediate and expert.

4.2 Proposed Architecture for Definition

The need for a generalized explanation system which can adapt and learn has been discussed in the previous sections. Application of the presented definition from the perspective of computer science is complicated and ambitious, it has multiple factors to be considered. In order to take another step towards building explanation systems, we take inspiration from classic *Natural Language Generation* (NLG) Model to propose an architecture for generation of user understandable explanations for desired scenarios (Dale and Reiter, 1997; Reiter and Dale, 2000).The functionality of each component of the architecture is provided below.

In Figure 3, the classical NLG pipeline of Content Determination – Content Refining – Content Lexicalization – Text Generation consists of several components. The initial input of the pipeline is black box's input-output pair which is fed to the first component (Content Determination). Following which each component takes as input the output of the previous component, together producing the following sequence of outputs: Logical Content – Structured Content – Lexicalized Content – Generated Text/Explanation. This entire setup can be placed in an environment responsible for learning models about the individual recipients' preferences. For each query, multiple explanations will be generated and ranked by the learning environment. Based on recipient's choice, the corresponding model will be refined for future queries.

Each component of this architecture brings forward a different challenge. The most intriguing ones are from the section of content determination and the learning environment. Feature Importance Extraction has been researched vividly in recent years with black box solutions such as LIME (Ribeiro et al., 2016a), LEAFAGE (Adhikari,

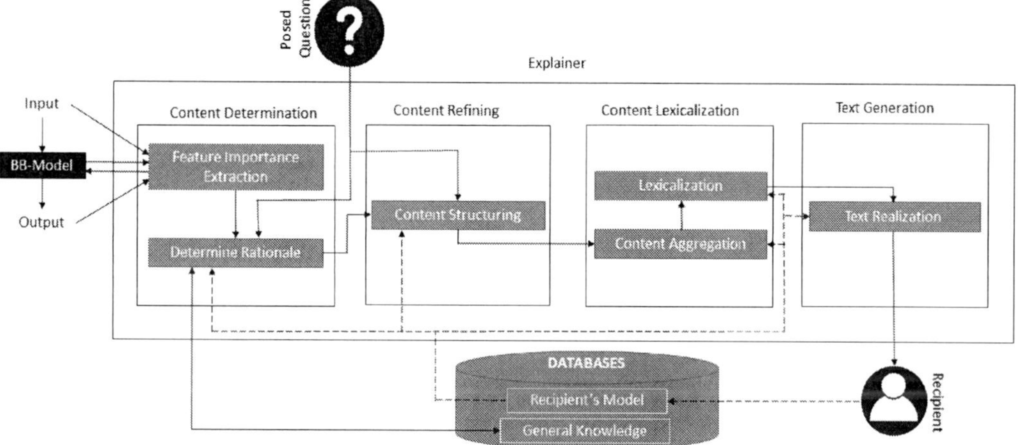

Figure 3: A possible architecture of a generic explanation system based on the proposed definition. This is a slightly modified setup of the classical NLG pipeline. This setup will be placed in an iterative learning environment for refining individual recipients' models.

2018), XEMP [2], etc. However, very little attention has been given to bridging the gap between black box inputs and human interpretable features in a generic way.

The suggested architecture enables us to partly mimic Overton's structure of explanations and Malle's structure of social explanations (section 2.3) via the NLG pipeline and the learning environment. In reference to Overton's structure of explanations, the NLG pipeline receives an *input-output pair* as *data/observation* and extracts the *model* as *Logical Content*. Similarly, the learning environment will capture the recipient's underlying behavior as described in Malle's structure of social explanation.

Also, by generating multiple explanations we acknowledge Miller's four important findings for explainable AI (section 2.3) and Mill's theory of selection of an explanation (section 3.2). We argue that there exists multiple possible explanations for each query. Each explanation generated by following the suggested procedure and supported by factual data cannot be "wrong". However, the system must be iteratively trained based on the recipients' acceptance of explanations and gain of information. This makes the learning environment a crucial part of the system.

---

5 Conclusion

In this paper, we review multiple perspectives and aspects of explanation. Based on this, we summarize the most important aspects of explanation and propose a generic definition. The definition and examples of explanation in different scenarios guide us towards building an explanation system. We propose an architecture for one such generic explanation system based on the proposed definition of explanation. It is capable of producing multiple explanations depending on the given recipient, the posed question and a given scenario. We hope that this paper paves the way to build generic explanation systems.

6 Future Work

Each of the components of the proposed architecture is challenging in a different way. The challenges include the process of creating a recipient model, refining the recipient's model based on their preferences, making the explanation system generic, etc. The learning environment will also bring forth a cold-start problem. These are some of the many ambitious topics which need to be researched, analyzed and applied. We intend to start by creating a prototype of a content determination module from the proposed architecture of a generic explanation system.

[2]XEMP White Paper (Last accessed on: 2020-10-06): `www.datarobot.com/resource/xemp-prediction-explanations/`

References

Ajaya Adhikari. 2018. Example and feature importance-based explanations for black-box machine learning models.

Or Biran and Courtenay Cotton. 2017. Explanation and justification in machine learning: A survey. In *IJCAI-17 workshop on explainable AI (XAI)*, volume 8, pages 8–13.

Robert Dale and Ehud Reiter. 1997. Tutorial on building applied natural language generation systems. In *ANLP-97*.

Finale Doshi-Velez and Been Kim. 2017. Towards a rigorous science of interpretable machine learning. *arXiv preprint arXiv:1702.08608*.

Leilani H Gilpin, David Bau, Ben Z Yuan, Ayesha Bajwa, Michael Specter, and Lalana Kagal. 2018. Explaining explanations: An overview of interpretability of machine learning. In *2018 IEEE 5th International Conference on data science and advanced analytics (DSAA)*, pages 80–89. IEEE.

Riccardo Guidotti, Anna Monreale, Salvatore Ruggieri, Franco Turini, Fosca Giannotti, and Dino Pedreschi. 2018. A survey of methods for explaining black box models. *ACM computing surveys (CSUR)*, 51(5):1–42.

Robert James Hankinson. 2001. *Cause and explanation in ancient Greek thought*. Oxford University Press.

Norwood Russell Hanson. 1958. *Patterns of discovery: An inquiry into the conceptual foundations of science*, volume 251. CUP Archive.

Gilbert H Harman. 1965. The inference to the best explanation. *The philosophical review*, 74(1):88–95.

Fritz Heider and Marianne Simmel. 1944. An experimental study of apparent behavior. *The American journal of psychology*, 57(2):243–259.

Germund Hesslow. 1988. The problem of causal selection. *Contemporary science and natural explanation: Commonsense conceptions of causality*, pages 11–32.

Denis J Hilton. 1990. Conversational processes and causal explanation. *Psychological Bulletin*, 107(1):65.

John R Josephson and Susan G Josephson. 1996. *Abductive inference: Computation, philosophy, technology*. Cambridge University Press.

Sebastian Lapuschkin, Stephan Wäldchen, Alexander Binder, Grégoire Montavon, Wojciech Samek, and Klaus-Robert Müller. 2019. Unmasking clever hans predictors and assessing what machines really learn. *Nature communications*, 10(1):1–8.

David Lewis. 1986. Causal explanation, in his philosophical papers, vol. 2.

Peter Lipton. 1990. Contrastive explanation. *Royal Institute of Philosophy Supplement*, 27:247–266.

Zachary C Lipton. 2018. The mythos of model interpretability. *Queue*, 16(3):31–57.

Bertram F Malle. 2006. *How the mind explains behavior: Folk explanations, meaning, and social interaction*. Mit Press.

Bertram F Malle. 2011. Time to give up the dogmas of attribution: An alternative theory of behavior explanation. In *Advances in experimental social psychology*, volume 44, pages 297–352. Elsevier.

John Stuart Mill. 1973. A system of logic, books i-iii, volume vii of collected works.

Tim Miller. 2019. Explanation in artificial intelligence: Insights from the social sciences. *Artificial Intelligence*, 267:1–38.

Brent Mittelstadt, Chris Russell, and Sandra Wachter. 2019. Explaining explanations in ai. In *Proceedings of the conference on fairness, accountability, and transparency*, pages 279–288.

James A Overton. 2012. *Explanation in Science*. Electronic Thesis and Dissertation Repository.

James A Overton. 2013. "explain" in scientific discourse. *Synthese*, 190(8):1383–1405.

Judea Pearl and Dana Mackenzie. 2018. *The book of why: the new science of cause and effect*. Basic Books.

Dino Pedreschi, Fosca Giannotti, Riccardo Guidotti, Anna Monreale, Salvatore Ruggieri, and Franco Turini. 2019. Meaningful explanations of black box ai decision systems. In *Proceedings of the AAAI Conference on Artificial Intelligence*, volume 33, pages 9780–9784.

Ehud Reiter and Robert Dale. 2000. *Building natural language generation systems*. Cambridge university press.

Marco Tulio Ribeiro, Sameer Singh, and Carlos Guestrin. 2016a. " why should i trust you?" explaining the predictions of any classifier. In *Proceedings of the 22nd ACM SIGKDD international conference on knowledge discovery and data mining*, pages 1135–1144.

Marco Tulio Ribeiro, Sameer Singh, and Carlos Guestrin. 2016b. Model-agnostic interpretability of machine learning. *arXiv preprint arXiv:1606.05386*.

Wojciech Samek, Thomas Wiegand, and Klaus-Robert Müller. 2017. Explainable artificial intelligence: Understanding, visualizing and interpreting deep learning models. *arXiv preprint arXiv:1708.08296*.

Searching for a Search Method: Benchmarking Search Algorithms for Generating NLP Adversarial Examples

Jin Yong Yoo,[*] **John X. Morris**,[*] **Eli Lifland** **Yanjun Qi**
Department of Computer Science, University of Virginia
{jy2ma, yq2h}@virginia.edu

Abstract

We study the behavior of several black box search algorithms used for generating adversarial examples for natural language processing (NLP) tasks. We perform a fine-grained analysis of three elements relevant to search: search algorithm, search space, and search budget. When new search algorithms are proposed in past work, the attack search space is often modified alongside the search algorithm. Without ablation studies benchmarking the search algorithm change with the search space held constant, one cannot tell if an increase in attack success rate is a result of an improved search algorithm or a less restrictive search space. Additionally, many previous studies fail to properly consider the search algorithms' run-time cost, which is essential for downstream tasks like adversarial training. Our experiments provide a reproducible benchmark of search algorithms across a variety of search spaces and query budgets to guide future research in adversarial NLP. Based on our experiments, we recommend greedy attacks with word importance ranking when under a time constraint or attacking long inputs, and either beam search or particle swarm optimization otherwise.

1 Introduction

Research has shown that current deep neural network models lack the ability to make correct predictions on adversarial examples (Szegedy et al., 2013). The field of investigating the adversarial robustness of NLP models has seen growing interest, both in contributing new attack methods [1] for generating adversarial examples (Ebrahimi et al., 2017; Gao et al., 2018; Alzantot et al., 2018; Jin

et al., 2019; Ren et al., 2019; Zang et al., 2020) and better training strategies to make models resistant to adversaries (Jia et al., 2019; Goodfellow et al., 2014).

Recent studies formulate NLP adversarial attacks as a combinatorial search task and feature the specific search algorithm they use as the key contribution (Zhang et al., 2019b). The search algorithm aims to perturb a text input with language transformations such as misspellings or synonym substitutions in order to fool a target NLP model when the perturbation adheres to some linguistic constraints (e.g., edit distance, grammar constraint, semantic similarity constraint) (Morris et al., 2020a). Many search algorithms have been proposed for this process, including varieties of greedy search, beam search, and population-based search.

The literature includes a mixture of incomparable and unclear results when comparing search strategies since studies often fail to consider the other two necessary primitives in the search process: the search space (choice of transformation and constraints) and the search budget (in queries to the victim model). The lack of a consistent benchmark on search algorithms has hindered the use of adversarial examples to understand and to improve NLP models. In this work, we attempt to clear the air by answering the following question: *Which search algorithm should NLP researchers pick for generating NLP adversarial examples?*

We focus on black-box search algorithms due to their practicality and prevalence in the NLP attack literature. Our goal is to understand to what extent the choice of search algorithms matter in generating text adversarial examples and how different search algorithms compare when we hold the search space constant or when we standardize the search cost. We select three families of search algorithms proposed from literature and benchmark

---

[*] Equal contribution. Code implementation shared via `https://github.com/QData/TextAttack`

[1] In this work, we use "adversarial example generation methods" and "adversarial attacks" interchangeably.

Proceedings of the Third BlackboxNLP Workshop on Analyzing and Interpreting Neural Networks for NLP, pages 323–332
Online, November 20, 2020. ©2020 Association for Computational Linguistics

their performance on generating adversarial examples for sentiment classification and textual entailment tasks. Our main findings can be summarized as the following:

- Across three datasets and three search spaces, we found that beam search and particle swarm optimization are the best algorithms in terms of attack success rate.
- When under a time constraint or when the input text is long, greedy with word importance ranking is preferred and offers sufficient performance.
- Complex algorithms such as PWWS (Ren et al., 2019) and genetic algorithm (Alzantot et al., 2018) are often less performant than simple greedy methods both in terms of attack success rate and speed.

2 Background

2.1 Components of an NLP Attack

Morris et al. (2020b) formulated the process of generating natural language adversarial examples as a system of four components: a goal function, a set of constraints, a transformation, and a search algorithm.

Such a system searches for a perturbation from x to x' that fools a predictive NLP model by both achieving some goal (like fooling the model into predicting the wrong classification label) and fulfilling certain constraints. The search algorithm attempts to find a sequence of transformations that results in a successful perturbation.

2.2 Elements of a Search Process

Search Algorithm: Recent methods proposed for generating adversarial examples in NLP frame their approach as a combinatorial search problem. This is necessary because of the exponential nature of the search space. Consider the search space for an adversarial attack that replaces words with synonyms: If a given sequence of text consists of W words, and each word has T potential substitutions, the total number of perturbed inputs to consider is $(T + 1)^W - 1$. Thus, the graph of all potential adversarial examples for a given input is far too large for an exhaustive search.

While heuristic search algorithms cannot guarantee an optimal solution, they can be employed to efficiently search this space for a valid adversarial example. Studies on NLP attacks have explored various heuristic search algorithms, including beam search (Ebrahimi et al., 2017), genetic algorithm (Alzantot et al., 2018), and greedy method with word importance ranking (Gao et al., 2018; Jin et al., 2019; Ren et al., 2019).

Search Space: In addition to its search method, an NLP attack is defined by how it chooses its search space. The search space is mainly determined by two things: a transformation, which defines how the original text is perturbed (e.g. word substitution, word deletion) and the set of linguistic constraints (e.g minimum semantic similarity, correct grammar) enforced to ensure that the perturbed text is a valid adversarial example. A larger search space corresponds to a looser definition of a valid adversarial example. With a looser definition, the search space includes more candidate adversarial examples. The more candidates there are, the more likely the search is to find an example that fools the victim model – thereby achieving a higher attack success rate (Morris et al., 2020b).

Search Cost/Budget: Furthermore, most works do not consider the runtime of the search algorithms. This has created a large, previously unspoken disparity in runtimes of proposed works. Population-based algorithms like Alzantot et al. (2018) and Zang et al. (2020) are significantly more expensive than greedy algorithms like Jin et al. (2019) and Ren et al. (2019). Additionally, greedy algorithms with word importance ranking are linear with respect to input length, while beam search algorithms are quadratic. In tasks such as adversarial training, adversarial examples must be generated quickly, and a more efficient algorithm may preferable– even at the expense of a lower attack success rate.

2.3 Evaluating Novel Search Algorithms

Past studies on NLP attacks that propose new search algorithms often also propose a slightly altered search space, by proposing either new transformations or new constraints. When new search algorithms are benchmarked in a new search space, they cannot be easily compared with search algorithms from other attacks.

To show improvements over a search method from previous work, a new search method must be benchmarked in the search space of the original method. However, many works fail to set the search space to be consistent when comparing their method to baseline methods. For example, Jin et al. (2019) compares its `TextFooler` method against Alzantot et al. (2018)'s method without accounting for the fact that `TextFooler` uses the Universal Sentence Encoder (Cer et al., 2018) to filter perturbed text while Alzantot et al. (2018) uses Google 1 billion words language model (Chelba et al., 2013). A more severe case is Zhang et al. (2019a)[2], which claims that its Metropolis-Hastings sampling method is superior to Alzantot et al. (2018) without setting any constraints – like Alzantot et al. (2018) does – that ensure that the perturbed text preserves the original semantics of the text.

We do note that Ren et al. (2019) and Zang et al. (2020) do provide comparisons where the search spaces are consistent. However, these works consider a small number of search algorithms as baseline methods, and fail to provide a comprehensive comparison of methods proposed in the literature.

3 Benchmarking Setup

3.1 Defining Search Spaces

As defined in Section 2.1, each NLP adversarial attack includes four components: a goal function, constraints, a transformation, and a search algorithm. We define the *attack search space* as the set of perturbed text $\mathbf{x}'$ that are generated for an original input $\mathbf{x}$ via valid transformations and satisfy a set of linguistic constraints. The goal of a search algorithm is to find those $\mathbf{x}'$ that achieves the attack goal function (i.e. fooling a victim model) as fast as it can.

Word-swap transformations: Assuming $\mathbf{x} = (x_1, \ldots, x_i, \ldots, x_n)$, a perturbed text $\mathbf{x}'$ can be generated by swapping x_i with altered x_i'. The swap can occur at word, character, or sentence level, depending on the granularity of x_i. Most works in literature choose to swap out words; therefore, we choose to focus on word-swap transformations for our experiments.

Constraints: Morris et al. (2020b) proposed a set of linguistic constraints to enforce that $\mathbf{x}$ and perturbed $\mathbf{x}'$ should be similar in both meaning and fluency to make $\mathbf{x}'$ a valid *potential adversarial* example. This indicates that the search space should ensure $\mathbf{x}$ and $\mathbf{x}'$ are close in semantic embedding space. Multiple automatic constraint ensuring strategies have been proposed in the literature. For

example, when swapping word $\mathbf{x}_i$ with $\mathbf{x}_i'$, we can require that the cosine similarity between word embedding vectors $e_{\mathbf{x}_i}$ and $e_{\mathbf{x}_i'}$ meet certain minimum threshold. More details on the specific constraints we use are in Section A.1.

Now we use notation $T(\mathbf{x}) = \mathbf{x}'$ to denote transformations perturbing $\mathbf{x}$ to $\mathbf{x}'$, and assume the $j - th$ constraints as Boolean functions $C_j(\mathbf{x}, \mathbf{x}')$ indicating whether $\mathbf{x}'$ satisfies the constraint C_j. Then, we can define the search space S mathematically as:

$$S(\mathbf{x}) = \{T(\mathbf{x}) | C_j(\mathbf{x}, T(\mathbf{x})) \ \forall j \in [m]\} \quad (1)$$

The goal of a search algorithm is to find $\mathbf{x}' \in S(x)$ such that $\mathbf{x}'$ succeeds in fooling the victim model. Table 1 describes three search spaces we use to benchmark the search algorithms. Details of transformations and constraints used in defining these search spaces are in Appendix Section A.1.

	Transformation	Constraints
1	Counter-fitted GLOVE Word Embedding	Word embedding similarity, BERTScore, POS consistency
2	HowNet	BERTScore, POS consistency
3	WordNet	USE similarity, POS consistency

Table 1: The three search spaces in our benchmarking.

3.2 Heuristic Scoring Function

Search algorithms evaluate potential perturbations before branching out to other solutions. In the case of an untargeted attack against a classifer, the adversary aims to find examples that make the classifier predict the wrong class (label) for $\mathbf{x}'$. Here the assumption is that the ground truth label of $\mathbf{x}'$ is the same as that of the original $\mathbf{x}$.

Naturally, we use a heuristic scoring function *score* defined as:

$$score(\mathbf{x}') = 1 - F_y(\mathbf{x}') \quad (2)$$

where $F_y(\mathbf{x})$ is the probability of class y predicted by the model and y is the ground truth output of original text $\mathbf{x}$.

3.3 Search Algorithms

We select the following five search algorithms proposed for generating adversarial examples, summarized in Table 2. All search algorithms are limited to modifying each word at most once.

---

[2]Zhang et al. (2019a) is not considered in this paper due to failure to replicate its results.

Search Algorithm	Deterministic?	Hyperparameters	Num. Queries
Beam Search (Ebrahimi et al., 2017)	✓	b (beam width)	$\mathcal{O}(b * W^2 * T)$
Greedy [Beam Search with b=1]	✓	–	$\mathcal{O}(W^2 * T)$
Greedy w. Word Importance Ranking (Gao et al., 2018; Jin et al., 2019; Ren et al., 2019)	✓	–	$\mathcal{O}(W * T)$
Genetic Algorithm (Alzantot et al., 2018)	✗	p (population size), g (number of iterations)	$\mathcal{O}(g * p * T)$
Particle Swarm Optimization (Zang et al., 2020)	✗	p (population size), g (number of iterations)	$\mathcal{O}(g * p * W * T)$

Table 2: Different search algorithms proposed for NLP attacks. W indicates the number of words in the input. T is the maximum number of transformation options for a given input.

Beam Search For given text $\mathbf{x}$, all the possible perturbed texts $\mathbf{x}'$ generated by substituting each word $\mathbf{x}_i$ are scored using the heuristic scoring function, and the top b texts are kept (b is called the "beam width"). Then, the process repeats by further perturbing each of the top b perturbed texts to generate the next set of candidates.

Greedy Search Like beam search, each $\mathbf{x}_i$ are considered for subsitution. We take the best perturbation across all possible perturbations, and repeat until we succeed or run out of possible perturbations. It equals to a beam search with b set to 1.

Greedy with Word Importance Ranking (WIR) Words of the given input $\mathbf{x}$ are ranked according to some importance function. Then, in order of descending importance, word $\mathbf{x}_i$ is substituted with $\mathbf{x}'_i$ that maximizes the scoring function until the goal is achieved, or all words have been perturbed. We experiment with four different ways to determine word importance:

- **UNK**: Each word's importance is determined by how much the heuristic score changes when the word is substituted with an UNK token (Gao et al., 2018).
- **DEL**: Each word's importance is determined by how much the heuristic score changes when the word is deleted from the original input (Jin et al., 2019).
- **PWWS**: Each word's importance is determined by multiplying the change in score when the word is substituted with an UNK token with the maximum score gained by perturbing the word (Ren et al., 2019).
- **Gradient**: Similar to how Wallace et al. (2019) visualize saliency of words, each word's importance is determined by calculating the gradient of the loss with respect to the word[3] and taking its norm.

We test an additional scheme, which we call RAND, as an ablation study. Instead of perturbing words in order of their importance, RAND perturbs words in a random order.

Genetic Algorithm. We implement the genetic algorithm of Alzantot et al. (2018). At each iteration, each member of the population is perturbed by randomly choosing one word and picking the best $\mathbf{x}'$ gained by perturbing it. Then, crossover occurs between members of the population, with preference given to the more successful members. The algorithm is run for a fixed number of iterations unless it succeeds in the middle. Following Alzantot et al. (2018), the population size was 60 and the algorithm was run for at maximum 20 iterations.

Particle Swarm Optimization We implement the particle swarm optimization (PSO) algorithm of Zang et al. (2020). At each iteration, each member of the population is perturbed by first generating all potential $\mathbf{x}'$ obtained by substituting each $\mathbf{x}_i$ and then sampling one $\mathbf{x}'$. Each member is also crossovered with the best perturb text previously found for the member (i.e. local optimum) and the best perturb text found among all members (i.e. global optimum). Following Zang et al. (2020), the population size is set to 60 and the algorithm was run for a maximum of 20 iterations.

Our genetic algorithm and PSO implementations have one small difference from the original implementations. The original implementations contain crossover operations that further perturb the text without considering whether the resulting text meets the defined constraints. In our implementation, we check if the text produced by these subroutines meets our constraints to ensure a consistent search space.

3.4 Victim Models

We attack BERT-base (Devlin et al., 2018) and an LSTM fine-tuned on three different datasets:

---

[3] For sub-word tokenization scheme, we take average over all sub-words constituting the word.

- Yelp polarity reviews (Zhang et al., 2015) (sentiment classification)
- Movie Reviews (MR) (Pang and Lee, 2005) (sentiment classification)
- Stanford Natural Language Inference (SNLI) (Bowman et al., 2015) (textual entailment).

For Yelp and SNLI dataset, we attack 1000 samples from the test set, and for MR dataset, we attack 500 samples. Language of all three datasets is English.

3.5 Implementation

We implement all of our attacks using the NLP attack package TextAttack[4] (Morris et al., 2020a). TextAttack provides separate modules for search algorithms, transformations, and constraints, so we can easily compare search algorithms without changing any other part of the attack.

3.6 Evaluation Metrics

We use attack success rate ($\frac{\text{\# of successful attacks}}{\text{\# of total attacks}}$) to measure how successful each search algorithm is for attacking a victim model.

To measure the runtime of each algorithm, we use the average number of queries to the victim model as a proxy.

To measure the quality of adversarial examples generated by each algorithm, we use three metrics:

1. Average percentage of words perturbed
2. Universal Sentence Encoder (Cer et al., 2018) similarity between x and x'
3. Percent change in perplexities of x and x' (using GPT-2 (Radford et al., 2019))

4 Results and Analysis

4.1 Attack Success Rate Comparison

Table 3 shows the results of each attack when each search algorithm is allowed to query the victim model an unlimited number of times. Word importance ranking methods makes far fewer queries than beam or population-based search, while retaining over 60% of their attack success rate in each case. Beam search (b=8) and PSO are the two most successful search algorithms in every model-dataset combination. However, PSO is more query-intensive. On average, PSO requires 6.3 times[6]

more queries than beam search (b=8), but its attack success rate is only on average 1.2% higher than that of beam search (b=8).

4.2 Runtime Analysis

Using number of queries to the victim model as proxy for total runtime, Figure 1 illustrates how the number of words in the input affects runtime for each algorithm. We can empirically confirm that beam and greedy search algorithms scale quadratically with input length, while word importance ranking scales linearly. For shorter datasets, this did not make a significant difference. However, for the longer Yelp dataset, the linear word importance ranking strategies are significantly more query-efficient. These observations match the expected runtimes of the algorithms described in Table 2.

For shorter datasets, genetic and PSO algorithms are significantly more expensive than the other algorithms as the size of population and number of iterations are the dominating factors. Furthermore, PSO is observed to be more expensive than genetic algorithm.

4.3 Performance under Query Budget

In a realistic attack scenario, the attacker must conserve the number of queries made to the model. To see which search method was most query-efficient, we calculated the search methods' attack success rates under a range of query budgets. Figure 2 shows the attack success rate of each search algorithm as the maximum number of queries permitted to perturb a single sample varies from 0 to 20,000 for Yelp dataset and 0 to 3000 for MR and SNLI.

For both Yelp and MR datasets, the linear (word importance ranking) methods show relatively high success rates within just a few queries, but are eventually surpassed by the slower, quadratic methods (greedy and beam search). The genetic algorithm and PSO lag behind. For SNLI, we see exceptions as the initial queries that linear methods make to determine word importance ranking does not pay off as other algorithms appear more efficient with their queries. This shows that the most effective search method depends on both on the attacker's query budget and the victim model. An attacker with a small query budget may prefer a linear method, but an attacker with a larger query budget may aim to choose a quadratic method to make more queries in exchange for a higher success rate.

---

[4]TextAttack is available at `https://github.com/QData/TextAttack`.

[6]This is with one outlier (BERT-SNLI with GLOVE word embedding) ignored. If it is included, the number jumps to 10.8.

Model	Dataset	Search Method	GLOVE Word Embedding		HowNet		WordNet	
			A.S. %	Avg # Queries	A.S. %	Avg # Queries	A.S. %	Avg # Queries
BERT	Yelp	Greedy (b=1)	39.5	810	93.2	3668	63.2	1480
		Beam Search (b=4)	42.0	2857	95.0	10,766	65.9	5033
		Beam Search (b=8)	42.7	5546	95.6	19,810	67.3	9674
		WIR (UNK)	33.2	187	92.3	344	55.3	232
		WIR (DEL)	33.7	189	91.9	364	54.3	238
		WIR (PWWS)	35.3	259	95.1	1300	58.2	395
		WIR (Gradient)	33.2	55	77.6	189	53.7	94
		WIR (RAND)	29.9	61	72.3	279	53.9	118
		Genetic Algorithm	37.6	5098	89.3	11,015	62.1	8257
		PSO	**47.2**	20,279	**96.6**	62,346	**74.9**	28,971
	MR	Greedy (b=1)	20.6	35	78.6	214	59.4	69
		Beam Search (b=4)	21.4	95	80.6	392	64.6	170
		Beam Search (b=8)	**21.8**	175	81.2	632	**65.8**	303
		WIR (UNK)	17.8	28	53.6	58	55.6	40
		WIR (DEL)	17.0	29	53.6	59	54.0	40
		WIR (PWWS)	21.0	41	73.6	205	58.2	71
		WIR (Gradient)	19.8	14	56.6	46	53.4	24
		WIR (RAND)	17.6	12	48.8	49	53.4	24
		Genetic Algorithm	**21.8**	516	80.0	1670	65.6	1063
		PSO	**21.8**	2413	**82.4**	2039	65.4	2078
	SNLI	Greedy (b=1)	19.8	7	87.3	77	49.6	19
		Beam Search (b=4)	**20.1**	12	89.2	97	52.0	33
		Beam Search (b=8)	**20.1**	18	**89.4**	125	**52.6**	49
		WIR (UNK)	19.3	22	85.1	47	47.3	30
		WIR (DEL)	18.5	22	84.8	47	46.7	30
		WIR (PWWS)	19.8	26	86.9	116	49.1	42
		WIR (Gradient)	18.8	5	68.4	25	46.9	10
		WIR (RAND)	18.3	5	82.6	30	46.2	11
		Genetic Algorithm	20.0	78	89.0	477	52.2	250
		PSO	**20.1**	1248	89.1	398	51.9	975
LSTM	Yelp	Greedy (b=1)	53.0	682	98.2	2611	80.0	982
		Beam Search (b=4)	53.2	2313	98.5	7347	81.7	3277
		Beam Search (b=8)	53.5	4516	98.6	13,643	82.3	6240
		WIR (UNK)	49.3	133	95.2	222	75.8	204
		WIR (DEL)	49.1	181	95.2	230	75.3	205
		WIR (PWWS)	51.2	247	97.3	1212	77.8	361
		WIR (Gradient)	49.3	56	90.0	215	75.3	97
		WIR (RAND)	47.4	57	88.3	217	74.6	98
		Genetic Algorithm	51.3	5212	98.3	7408	78.5	7245
		PSO	**54.9**	17,647	**98.8**	34,659	**84.4**	17,145
	MR	Greedy (b=1)	38.4	29	87.6	187	74.2	59
		Beam Search (b=4)	38.6	71	88.6	290	75.6	131
		Beam Search (b=8)	38.6	127	88.8	427	76.0	222
		WIR (UNK)	35.8	27	81.0	51	72.0	36
		WIR (DEL)	36.2	27	80.2	50	72.2	35
		WIR (PWWS)	37.6	40	86.2	203	73.4	68
		WIR (Gradient)	35.4	10	76.6	36	72.8	18
		WIR (RAND)	34.4	11	68.0	40	71.8	22
		Genetic Algorithm	**39.0**	375	88.6	949	76.0	730
		PSO	**39.0**	1592	**89.0**	795	**76.6**	1179

Table 3: Comparison of search methods across three datasets. Models are BERT-base and LSTM fine-tuned for the respective task. "A.S.%" represents attack success rate and "Avg # Queries" represents the average number of queries made to the model per successful attacked sample.[5]

Lastly, we can see that both Gradient and RAND ranking methods are initially more successful than UNK and DEL methods, which is due to the overhead involved in calculating word importance ranking for UNK and DEL – for both methods, each attack makes W queries to determine the importance of each word. Still, UNK and DEL outperform RAND at all but the smallest query budgets, indicating that the order in which words are swapped do matter. Furthermore, in 12 out 15 scenarios, UNK

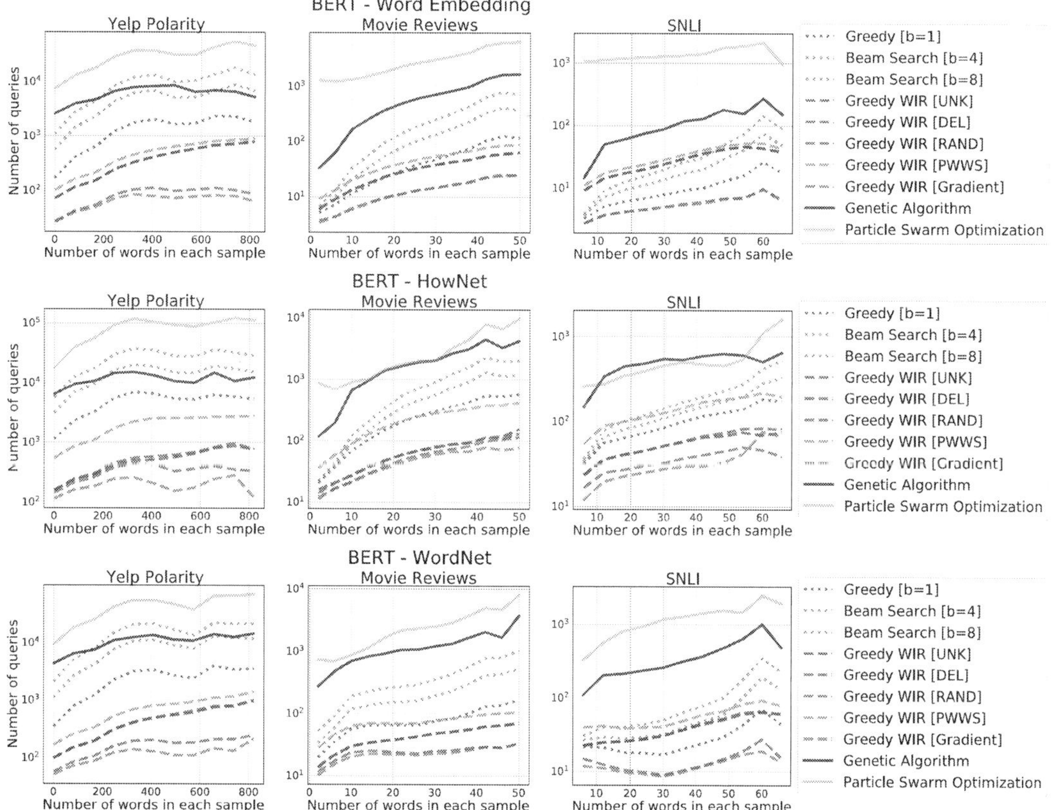

Figure 1: Number of queries vs. length of input text. Similar figure for LSTM models are available in the appendix.

and `DEL` methods perform as well as or even better than `Gradient` method, which shows that they are excellent substitutes to the `Gradient` method for black-box attacks.

4.4 Quality of Adversarial Examples

We selected adversarial examples whose original text $\mathbf{x}$ was successfully attacked by all search algorithms for quality evaluation. Full results of quality evaluation are shown in Table 4 in the appendix. We can see that beam search algorithms consistently perturb the lowest percentage of words. Furthermore, we see that a fewer number of words perturbed generally corresponds with higher average USE similarity between $\mathbf{x}$ and $\mathbf{x}_{adv}$ and a smaller increase in perplexity. This indicates that the beam search algorithms generate higher-quality adversarial examples than other search algorithms.

5 Discussion

5.1 How to Choose A Search Algorithm

Across all nine scenarios, we can see that choice of search algorithm can have a modest impact on the attack success rate. Query-hungry algorithms such as beam search, genetic algorithm, and PSO perform better than fast WIR methods. Out of the WIR methods, `PWWS` performs significantly better than `UNK` and `DEL` methods. In every case, we see a clear trade-off of performance versus speed.

With this in mind, one might wonder about what the best way is to choose a suitable search algorithm. The main factor to consider is the length of the input text. If the input texts are short (e.g. sentence or two), beam search is certainly the appropriate choice: it can achieve a high success rate without sacrificing too much speed. However, when the input text is longer than a few sentences, WIR methods are the most practical choice. If one wishes for the best performance on longer inputs regardless of efficiency, beam search and PSO are the top choices.

5.2 Effectiveness of `PWWS` Word Importance Ranking

Across all tasks, the `UNK` and `DEL` methods perform about equivalently, while `PWWS` performs significantly better than `UNK` and `DEL`. In fact, `PWWS`

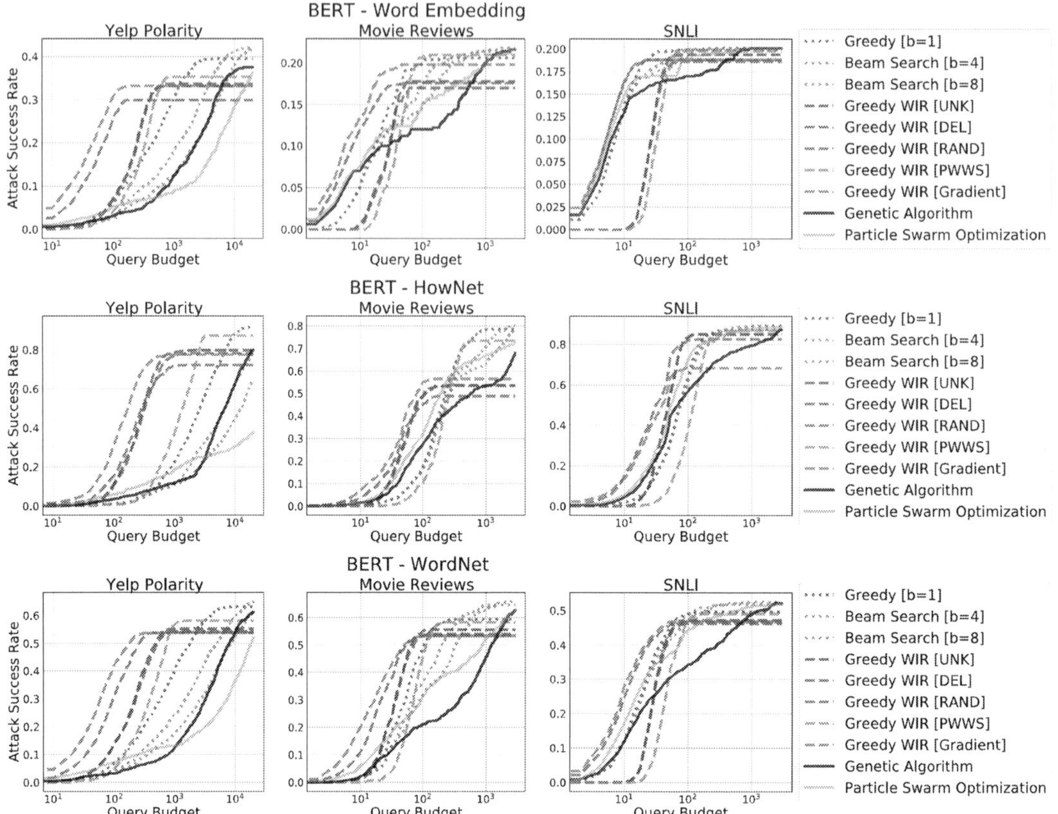

Figure 2: Attack success rate by query budget for each search algorithm and dataset. Similar figure for LSTM models are available in the appendix.

performs better than greedy search in two cases. However, this gain in performance does come at a cost: PWWS makes far larger number of queries to the victim model to determine the word importance ranking. Out of the 15 experiments, PWWS makes more queries than greedy search in 8 of them. Yet, on average, greedy search outperforms PWWS by 2.5%.

Our results question the utility of the PWWS search method. PWWS neither offers the performance that is competitive when compared to greedy search nor the query efficiency that is competitive when compared to UNK or DEL.

5.3 Effectiveness of Genetic Algorithm

The genetic algorithm proposed by Alzantot et al. (2018) uses more queries than the greedy-based beam search (b=8) in 11 of the 15 scenarios, but only achieves a higher attack success rate in 1 scenario. Thus it is generally strictly worse than the simpler beam search (b=8), achieving a lower success rate at a higher cost.

6   Conclusion

The goal of this paper is not to introduce a new method, but to make empirical analysis towards understanding how search algorithms from recent studies contribute in generating natural language adversarial examples. We evaluated six search algorithms on BERT-base and LSTM models fine-tuned on three datasets. Our results show that when runtime is not a concern, the best-performing methods are beam search and particle swarm optimization. If runtime is of concern, greedy with word importance ranking is the preferable method. We hope that our findings will set a new standard for the reproducibility and evaluation of search algorithms for NLP adversarial examples.

Acknowledgements on Funding:

This work was partly supported by the National Science Foundation CCF-1900676. Any Opinions, findings and conclusions or recommendations expressed in this material are those of the author(s) and do not necessarily reflect those of the National Science Foundation.

References

Alan Akbik, Duncan Blythe, and Roland Vollgraf. 2018. Contextual string embeddings for sequence labeling. In *COLING 2018, 27th International Conference on Computational Linguistics*, pages 1638–1649.

Moustafa Alzantot, Yash Sharma, Ahmed Elgohary, Bo-Jhang Ho, Mani Srivastava, and Kai-Wei Chang. 2018. Generating natural language adversarial examples. *arXiv preprint arXiv:1804.07998*.

Samuel R. Bowman, Gabor Angeli, Christopher Potts, and Christopher D Manning. 2015. A large annotated corpus for learning natural language inference. In *Proceedings of the 2015 Conference on Empirical Methods in Natural Language Processing (EMNLP)*. Association for Computational Linguistics.

Daniel Cer, Yinfei Yang, Sheng-yi Kong, Nan Hua, Nicole Limtiaco, Rhomni St. John, Noah Constant, Mario Guajardo-Cespedes, Steve Yuan, Chris Tar, Yun-Hsuan Sung, Brian Strope, and Ray Kurzweil. 2018. Universal sentence encoder. *CoRR*, abs/1803.11175.

Ciprian Chelba, Tomas Mikolov, Mike Schuster, Qi Ge, Thorsten Brants, and Phillipp Koehn. 2013. One billion word benchmark for measuring progress in statistical language modeling. *CoRR*, abs/1312.3005.

Jacob Devlin, Ming-Wei Chang, Kenton Lee, and Kristina Toutanova. 2018. BERT: pre-training of deep bidirectional transformers for language understanding. *CoRR*, abs/1810.04805.

Zhendong Dong, Qiang Dong, and Changling Hao. 2010. Hownet and its computation of meaning. In *Proceedings of the 23rd International Conference on Computational Linguistics: Demonstrations*, COLING '10, page 53–56, USA. Association for Computational Linguistics.

Javid Ebrahimi, Anyi Rao, Daniel Lowd, and Dejing Dou. 2017. Hotflip: White-box adversarial examples for text classification. In *ACL*.

Ji Gao, Jack Lanchantin, Mary Lou Soffa, and Yanjun Qi. 2018. Black-box generation of adversarial text sequences to evade deep learning classifiers. *2018 IEEE Security and Privacy Workshops (SPW)*, pages 50–56.

Ian J Goodfellow, Jonathon Shlens, and Christian Szegedy. 2014. Explaining and harnessing adversarial examples. *arXiv preprint arXiv:1412.6572*.

Mohit Iyyer, John Wieting, Kevin Gimpel, and Luke Zettlemoyer. 2018. Adversarial example generation with syntactically controlled paraphrase networks.

Robin Jia, Aditi Raghunathan, Kerem Göksel, and Percy Liang. 2019. Certified robustness to adversarial word substitutions. *arXiv preprint arXiv:1909.00986*.

Di Jin, Zhijing Jin, Joey Tianyi Zhou, and Peter Szolovits. 2019. Is bert really robust? natural language attack on text classification and entailment. *ArXiv*, abs/1907.11932.

Qi Lei, Lingfei Wu, Pin-Yu Chen, Alex Dimakis, Inderjit S. Dhillon, and Michael J Witbrock. 2019. Discrete adversarial attacks and submodular optimization with applications to text classification. In *Proceedings of Machine Learning and Systems 2019*, pages 146–165.

George A. Miller. 1995. Wordnet: A lexical database for english. *Commun. ACM*, 38(11):39–41.

Seungyong Moon, Gaon An, and Hyun Oh Song. 2019. Parsimonious Black-Box adversarial attacks via efficient combinatorial optimization.

John Morris, Eli Lifland, Jin Yong Yoo, and Yanjun Qi. 2020a. TextAttack: A framework for adversarial attacks in natural language processing. *ArXiv*, abs/2005.05909.

John X. Morris, Eli Lifland, Jack Lanchantin, Yangfeng Ji, and Yanjun Qi. 2020b. Reevaluating adversarial examples in natural language.

Nikola Mrksic, Diarmuid Ó Séaghdha, Blaise Thomson, Milica Gasic, Lina Maria Rojas-Barahona, Pei hao Su, David Vandyke, Tsung-Hsien Wen, and Steve J. Young. 2016. Counter-fitting word vectors to linguistic constraints. In *HLT-NAACL*.

Bo Pang and Lillian Lee. 2005. Seeing stars: Exploiting class relationships for sentiment categorization with respect to rating scales. In *Proceedings of the 43rd Annual Meeting of the Association for Computational Linguistics (ACL'05)*, pages 115–124, Ann Arbor, Michigan. Association for Computational Linguistics.

Alec Radford, Jeff Wu, Rewon Child, David Luan, Dario Amodei, and Ilya Sutskever. 2019. Language models are unsupervised multitask learners.

Shuhuai Ren, Yihe Deng, Kun He, and Wanxiang Che. 2019. Generating natural language adversarial examples through probability weighted word saliency. In *Proceedings of the 57th Annual Meeting of the Association for Computational Linguistics*, pages 1085–1097, Florence, Italy. Association for Computational Linguistics.

Marco Tulio Ribeiro, Sameer Singh, and Carlos Guestrin. 2018. Semantically equivalent adversarial rules for debugging NLP models. pages 856–865.

Christian Szegedy, Wojciech Zaremba, Ilya Sutskever, Joan Bruna, Dumitru Erhan, Ian Goodfellow, and Rob Fergus. 2013. Intriguing properties of neural networks. *arXiv preprint arXiv:1312.6199*.

Eric Wallace, Jens Tuyls, Junlin Wang, Sanjay Subramanian, Matt Gardner, and Sameer Singh. 2019. AllenNLP Interpret: A framework for explaining predictions of NLP models. In *Empirical Methods in Natural Language Processing*.

Yuan Zang, Fanchao Qi, Chenghao Yang, Zhiyuan Liu, Meng Zhang, Qun Liu, and Maosong Sun. 2020. Word-level textual adversarial attacking as combinatorial optimization. In *Proceedings of the 58th Annual Meeting of the Association for Computational Linguistics*, pages 6066–6080, Online. Association for Computational Linguistics.

Huangzhao Zhang, Hao Zhou, Ning Miao, and Lei Li. 2019a. Generating fluent adversarial examples for natural languages. In *Proceedings of the 57th Annual Meeting of the Association for Computational Linguistics*, pages 5564–5569, Florence, Italy. Association for Computational Linguistics.

Tianyi Zhang*, Varsha Kishore*, Felix Wu*, Kilian Q. Weinberger, and Yoav Artzi. 2020. Bertscore: Evaluating text generation with bert. In *International Conference on Learning Representations*.

Wei Emma Zhang, Quan Z. Sheng, and Ahoud Abdulrahmn F. Alhazmi. 2019b. Generating textual adversarial examples for deep learning models: A survey. *CoRR*, abs/1901.06796.

Xiang Zhang, Junbo Zhao, and Yann LeCun. 2015. Character-level convolutional networks for text classification. In C. Cortes, N. D. Lawrence, D. D. Lee, M. Sugiyama, and R. Garnett, editors, *Advances in Neural Information Processing Systems 28*, pages 649–657. Curran Associates, Inc.

This is a BERT. Now there are several of them.
Can they generalize to novel words?

Coleman Haley
Department of Cognitive Science
Johns Hopkins University
chaley7@jhu.edu

Abstract

Recently, large-scale pre-trained neural network models such as BERT have achieved many state-of-the-art results in natural language processing. Recent work has explored the linguistic capacities of these models. However, no work has focused on the ability of these models to generalize these capacities to novel words. This type of generalization is exhibited by humans (Berko, 1958), and is intimately related to morphology–humans are in many cases able to identify inflections of novel words in the appropriate context. This type of morphological capacity has not been previously tested in BERT models, and is important for morphologically-rich languages, which are under-studied in the literature regarding BERT's linguistic capacities. In this work, we investigate this by considering monolingual and multilingual BERT models' abilities to agree in number with novel plural words in English, French, German, Spanish, and Dutch. We find that many models are not able to reliably determine plurality of novel words, suggesting potential deficiencies in the morphological capacities of BERT models.

1 Introduction

In recent years, large-scale pre-trained neural network models have transformed the landscape of natural language processing (NLP) research. This approach to NLP became prominent after several models such as BERT (Devlin et al., 2019) achieved new state of the art performance on a wide range of NLP tasks such as natural language inference. The successful performance of BERT and other models like it on natural language understanding tasks suggests that they may be learning valuable general linguistic competencies. However, it is not clear whether these models are able to generalize these competencies to unseen words. With the large training sets of these models (3.3 billion

tokens in Devlin et al. (2019)), their state-of-the-art-establishing performance may feasibly have been achieved without ever being tested on a word that was not in the training set.

Nevertheless, BERT may need be concerned about unseen words. Increasingly, there is an interest in creating BERT and BERT-like models trained on large corpora of languages other than English. In comparison to English, many of the world's languages exhibit a much greater amount of inflectional morphology. However, most of the results motivating this explosion of BERT models are in English NLP. It is unclear, then, how well BERT will generalize to languages with complex morphology. While BERT models are being developed for other languages, many of these models have been less comprehensively evaluated than English BERT. For instance, the publicly available Turkish (Schweter, 2020) BERT model (one of the most morphologically complex languages for which a BERT model is available) has only been evaluated on named entity recognition and part-of-speech tagging. It is unclear, then, how well the model would fare on more complex NLP tasks.

In this work, we investigate BERT's ability to capture this type of information by studying its ability to identify the correct plural form of novel words in English, French, Spanish, Dutch, and German. We find that BERT is able to distinguish plural and singular forms to perform number agreement significantly above chance in all languages. However, many BERT models perform substantially worse on novel words than on words in the training set, even when prompted with an example that shows the singular form, a task which humans are known to be capable of (Berko, 1958). This indicates that even simple morphological capacities are not reliably acquired in a human-like way in the BERT training paradigm, showing room for improvement in future models.

333

Proceedings of the Third BlackboxNLP Workshop on Analyzing and Interpreting Neural Networks for NLP, pages 333–341
Online, November 20, 2020. ©2020 Association for Computational Linguistics

2 Background

BERT is part of a growing research direction of pre-training deep learning models, often a variant of a "Transformer" architecture (Vaswani et al., 2017), on large amounts of natural language data using some variant of a language modelling objective. This line of research includes other such successful models as ELMo (Peters et al., 2018) and XLNet (Yang et al., 2019). All of these models are trained on very large corpora, with ELMo being the smallest (trained on 1 billion tokens in Peters et al. (2018) – in contrast to BERT's 4 billion tokens in Devlin et al. (2019)). All of these models are also highly computationally intensive to train, so it is desirable to avoid training new BERT models.

BERT uses a transformer-based architecture, making it bidirectionally sensitive. It is trained on a masked language modelling objective, meaning that it takes in as input a sequence with some words replaced with a [MASK] token, and is expected to output the original sequence. To enable this, a final fully connected layer and softmax is added after the transformer encoder to produce the desired output. This means BERT is "out of the box" capable of answering exactly those questions that can be posed as replacing [MASK] tokens.

BERT-like models are also generally so-called *open-vocabulary* language models, meaning they can assign a probability to any string. This enables them to give probabilities to novel words and novel forms of known words, giving BERT the capacity to learn morphological generalizations. This is achieved through the use of subword segmentation, in which a strategy such as byte-pair encoding (BPE) (Sennrich et al., 2016) or Unigram LM segmentation (such as WordPiece (Kudo, 2018) and the related SentencePiece) is used to turn words into a sequence of multi-character tokens.

These segmentation strategies use statistical methods to determine which multi-character tokens are added to their vocabularies, meaning that high-frequency sub-word strings will more likely be added as tokens. These tokens may or may not correspond to morpheme boundaries. If they do not, then models that rely on them will encounter the same morpheme expressed in many distinct tokens, requiring the model to learn agreement for *all* tokens which may contain, e.g., the plural affix. This may mean that uncommon segments containing inflectional affixes will be less reliable in agreement, since they have no relation in representation to frequently-occurring subwords containing the same inflection.

2.1 BERT and linguistic competence

Previous work has explored the types of generalizations predicted by linguistic and psycholinguistic theory that have been learned by the English BERT models. This work has focused primarily on syntactic generalizations. Initial work by Goldberg found that BERT models showed promise at modelling short- and long-distance subject-verb agreement as well as reflexive anaphora phenomena (Goldberg, 2019). van Schijndel et al. (2019) revisited these results without giving a bidirectional context to BERT and found it performed at best no better than existing LSTM models (contrasting with Goldberg's work). Ettinger (2020) differentiates her work from these works by noting their primarily syntactic focus, and promises to test more diverse linguistic capacities, but focuses on semantic and pragmatic capacities, showing among other things that BERT fails to fully model the meaning of negation. Recently, Mueller et al. (2020) presented cross-linguistic targeted syntactic evaluation of BERT, but only considered multilingual BERT. Most of the work on the formal linguistic capacities has not considered monolingual BERT models for languages other than English (one recent exception being Edmiston (2020)).

Very recently, a few works have considered the morphological aspects of BERT. Bostrom and Durrett (2020) argue that byte-pair encoding less faithfully expresses English morphology than Unigram segmentation, and show a performance improvement in downstream tasks with a unigram-segmentation-based BERT model. Hofmann et al. (2020) show that BERT can be fine-tuned with a classification layer to complete a derivational morphology cloze task, finding that imposing morpheme boundaries with hyphenation on the input side ultimately improved BERT's performance at this task. Finally, Edmiston (2020) investigates several monolingual BERT models for representations of morphological information. Edmiston shows that many morphological features can be extracted by training a simple classifier on a BERT layer. He also identifies a small number of attention heads in each model that seem to pay attention to the morphologically marked words in agreement phenomena over other words. However, this agreement experiment makes no attempt to isolate the morphological information from words which BERT has seen, allowing for the possibility of morphological "memorization" rather than true human-like generalization.

Previous work in psycholinguistics has investigated the human capacity for morphological generalization, and it is this work we intend to build on to explore BERT's morphological capacity. Specifically, Berko (1958) presents the Wug test, a simple test for productive morphology in which speakers are prompted with a sentence containing one form of an unknown word and prompted to complete a sentence with another form. We present a task inspired by this one in which the ability to *recognize* an unseen form of a word is probed through the ability to correctly *agree* with that word's form. In this work, we specifically investigate subject-verb number agreement.

3 Methods

This work focuses on BERT's ability to recognize novel words as singular or plural. This construction was chosen for its testability (through number agreement on verbs) and its disparity in complexity between languages. In English, French, Dutch and Spanish, a large majority of plurals are derived according to rules that can be expressed simply in terms of adding a suffix corresponding to the suffix of the base noun. Further, in French and Spanish, the plurality of a noun is unambiguous if it is preceded by a determiner.

3.1 Plural formations of the languages

In written English, the plural of most nouns is formed by one of three strategies: either 1. -*s* is added to the end of the noun, 2. -*es* is added to the end, or 3. a copy of the final letter followed by -*es* is added to the end. Strategy 2 is used after sibilant sounds, and Strategy 3 is generally used after sibilant sounds which are preceded by a lax vowel. Strategy 1 is used in all other cases (except known irregulars). The words selected for this study were chosen such that their spelling indicates an obvious phonetic realization, and that they are distributed across these 3 strategies.

The French and Spanish plural constructions are arguably simpler than in English. In French, plural nouns are generally formed by adding -*s* to the end; unless the noun ends in *s*, *z*, or *x*, in which case nothing is added, in *eau*, in which case -*x* is added, or in -*al* or -*ail* in which case the suffix

may be removed and -*aux* added. In addition to inflecting the word, French marks plurality in its definite determiner, making it unambiguous from the determiner whether a noun is singular or plural.

On the other hand, the German plural construction is significantly more complex than in English. Like French and Spanish, German marks for plurality in the determiner, but the determiner used to indicate plurality in the nominative case is shared with that used to mark feminine noun gender, meaning that noun gender cannot be determined purely from the determiner. Consider for example *the woman→the women*, which in Spanish is *la mujer→las mujeres*, but in German is *die Frau→die Frauen*. Further, German uses several different strategies to form the plural, including adding nothing to the word (-∅), adding -*e*, adding -*(e)r*, adding -*(e)n*, and adding -*s*. These strategies (with the exception of -*(e)n*) may also be combined with "umlautification" of the stressed vowel in the noun, yielding a total of 7 possible plural markers, none of which consitute a majority of examples (Köpcke, 1988; Wiese, 2000).

Singular form	Plural form
das Fett	die Fette
das Brett	die Bretter
das Bett	die Betten
der Sohn	die Söhne
der Thron	die Throne

Table 1: The German plural cannot be predicted from the form of the singular word. Here, we see similar singular words that form the plural in different ways.

The literature on the German plural generally considers it to be a phenomenon over lexical classes which are not phonologically predictable. Several tendencies can be observed in German plural formation, though few are universal. For example, nouns ending in -*e* typically form their plural by adding -*n* (Trommer, 2020). Nevertheless, even near-minimal pairs of nouns may form their plural in distinct ways (see Table 1). Indeed, adult German speakers often vary widely in their choices for novel words (Zaretsky et al., 2013; McCurdy et al., 2020). Accordingly, substantial prior work has suggested the German plural may be a challenging pattern for neural networks to learn (Feldman, 2005; Marcus et al., 1995; McCurdy et al., 2020).

The Dutch plural represents an interesting intermediate case. As in German, the determiner gives

Condition	Stimulus	Candidates
No prime, real words	The author knows many different foreign languages and [MASK] playing tennis with colleagues.	enjoy/**enjoys**
Prime, real words	This is a pilot. the pilots [MASK].	**laugh**/laughs
Prime, non-words	This is a bik. the biks [MASK].	**laugh**/laughs

Table 2: Sample agreement stimuli in representative conditions in English. Correct completion is in **bold**.

Model	Language	Parameters	Training tokens	Tokenization
$\text{BERT}_{\text{BASE}}$ (Devlin et al., 2019)	English	110M	3.3B	WordPiece 30k
CamemBERT (Martin et al., 2020)	French	110M	32.7B	SentencePiece 32k
FlauBERT (Le et al., 2020)	French	138M	12.8B	BPE 50k
BETO (Cañete et al., 2020)	Spanish	110M	3B	BPE 32k
BERTje (Vries et al., 2019)	Dutch	110M	2.4B	SentencePiece 30k
Deepset [1]	German	110M	1.8B	SentencePiece 30k
dbmdz[2]	German	110M	2.4B	SentencePiece 30k
mBERT[3]	All	110M	–	WordPiece 110k

Table 3: The models used in this work and associated statistics. Note that the SentencePiece and WordPiece segmentation methods are different implementations of the same algorithm, described in Kudo (2018).

some ambiguous information about plurality, with the determiners *het* and *de* both being used for singular nouns, but only *de* used with plural nouns. The plural in Dutch is constructed using either the ending *-en* or *-s*. Generally, *-en* is used to form the plural of nouns ending with a stressed syllable, and *-s* is used with nouns ending in an unstressed syllable, although this generalization is not perfect (van der Hulst and Kooij, 1998).

3.2 Experimental setup

This experiment probes the ability of BERT to *recognize* the plurals of novel words as such. We probe this indirectly, though a number agreement task following the setup in van Schijndel et al. (2019). As in that study, We use the challenge set from Marvin and Linzen (2018) as a starting point. Number agreement was chosen as a task because it is not fully understood how to treat BERT as a generative model. Therefore, we probe plural recognition as an auxiliary task which BERT has been shown to succeed at (Goldberg, 2019). This task is formulated as a forced choice between a plural verb form or singular verb form.

The Marvin and Linzen (2018) challenge set was translated into English, German, Dutch, Spanish,

and French by fluent speakers with an elementary background in formal linguistics. These languages each have a singular-plural distinction and subject-verb number agreement. Syntactic constructions not possible in all five languages were omitted. Some verbs in each dataset were changed to ensure each verb was a single token for all models in that language. The datasets in each language were then modified to replace the subject of the targeted verb with a non-word. For each language, 24 non-words were used. English, French, Spanish, and Dutch non-words were manually created by fluent speakers, while the 24 German non-words were taken from McCurdy et al. (2020), to account for the fact that the German plural of non-words is known to be inconsistent across speakers. The plural formation chosen by a plurality of German speakers in McCurdy et al. (2020) for each German non-word was used; genders were chosen to be distributed uniformly.

The BERT models were evaluated on number agreement on the original datasets and the non-word datasets. Models were evaluated bidirectionally, as in Goldberg (2019), to provide a maximally-charitable estimate of BERT's morphological capacity in each language.

Finally, models were reevaluated on the non-word data with a "prime" for the non-word. In English, the prime takes the form of the sentence

---

336

		Real words		Non-words	
Language	Model	No prime	Prime	No prime	Prime
English	BERT$_\text{BASE}$	1.00	1.00	0.87	0.90
French	CamemBERT	0.99	0.98	0.98	0.99
	FlauBERT	0.92	0.97	0.89	0.98
	mBERT	0.97	0.98	0.99	0.99
Spanish	BETO	0.98	0.87	0.90	0.80
	mBERT	0.89	0.89	0.81	0.84
Dutch	BERTje	1.00	0.98	0.85	0.79
	mBERT	0.93	0.93	0.77	0.81
German	deepset	1.00	1.00	0.70	0.72
	dbmdz	1.00	0.99	0.75	0.79
	mBERT	1.00	1.00	0.80	0.75

Table 4: Agreement accuracy on simple sentences (e.g. "The author laughs.").

"This is a _____", where the blank was replaced with the singular form of the novel noun in the target sentence and the appropriate determiner for the noun's gender was selected. This construction was translated into each language.

While it may seem unintuitive that BERT could benefit from the use of this prime at test time, since it is unable to adjust its weights, with self-attention it is theoretically possible to encode a simple "rule" for using the number of a noun seen for the first time (as disambiguated via subject-verb agreement) to influence number agreement for a noun with a similar form. It is this possibility, as well as the human capacity for this type of generalization, that motivates this condition. Examples of stimuli in each condition for English are presented in Table 2.

We consider several cased BERT models, both monolingual and multilingual. The BERT$_\text{BASE}$ size was used for all languages for comparability between models, as not all languages have a BERT$_\text{LARGE}$ model available. The models used are summarized in Table 3 Experiments were run on a single Nvidia GeForce GTX 1080 Ti, and take under an hour to run.[4]

4   Results

Table 4 presents the results for the simple agreement tests with bidirectional context. Here, "simple" refers to sentences consisting of a subject immediately followed by an intransitive verb (e.g., "The man laughed."). The number of singular sen-

tences ranged between 212-672 depending on language and non-word condition. As in Goldberg (2019), ceiling performance is found on the original dataset in English. CamemBERT also performed near ceiling. Since the task is a forced choice between 2 verb forms (singular or plural), and there are an equal number of singular and plural subjects, chance performance is 0.5. Agreement performance on the non-word sentences was much better than chance, even without the inclusion of a prime for the non-word ($p < 0.001$). This indicates the model is often able to guess whether an noun not seen in training is likely to be singular or plural. Notably, not all models across languages succeeded completely at subject-verb agreement even with real words on simple sentences–FlauBERT for French and mBERT for Dutch and Spanish achieved less than 0.95 accuracy in this simple task.

Cross-linguistically, there is no consistent trend in whether the model is able to use the prime to achieve better performance. While FlauBERT was the only model to achieve statistically significant gains ($p < 0.01$) in the non-word case with the addition of the prime, this gain was also significant ($p < 0.05$) in the real word case, suggesting deeper issues with this model's agreement capabilities generally. Many models were slightly hurt by the inclusion of the prime, suggesting that they may be spuriously agreeing with the prime, even across a sentence boundary.

As one might expect, the German BERT models had the lowest average performance on the non-word conditions, with no model surpassing 0.80

---

[4]Code for generating the dataset and replicating the experiments is available at https://github.com/ColemanHaley/BERT-novel-morphology.

accuracy. However, only French models achieved an accuracy of greater than 0.90 in any non-word case. Given that the correct form for French and Spanish agreement can be determined from the noun's article alone, it is surprising that the Spanish models do not fully utilize this heuristic; this heuristic may explain the high French performance.

mBERT performs about as well as the monolingual BERT models in French and German, but performs worse in Dutch and Spanish. In no case did it significantly out-perform a monolingual model ($p > 0.1$).

5 Discussion

To investigate whether the lower novel-word performance was related to the segmentations of the novel words, we measured how often each non-word was associated with an error. We found inconsistent results across models. BERTje was found to perform especially poorly on 4 out of 24 non-words, incorrectly choosing a singular verb for a plural form of the word 93% of the time. On investigating the segmentations, these words were found to be segmented to "[UNK]" by the tokenizer. This model uses the standard SentencePiece Unigram tokenizer[5], ostensibly the same as many of these other models. Typically, this tokenizer is considered to be open-vocabulary, yet it fails to segment these subwords, indicating that this is not strictly true for this very popular implementation. If these 4 words are disregarded, in the no-prime case this model achieves an accuracy of 0.93, the highest of all non-French models across languages. While this error is of substantial concern, it affects only the Dutch BERTje results, as no other models were found to have this behavior.

Other models were found to frequently fail on the plural or singular forms of some words, such as BETO, which 50% of the time identified "co-manas" as a singular word form. Some models, such as the English model and FlauBERT, instead seemed to be uncertain about the plurality of all forms, making a moderate amount errors at roughly equal rates across non-words. In the case of the English model, the model has a bias towards plurality, with plural accuracy 0.19 greater than singular accuracy; however, FlauBERT makes agreement errors at roughly equal rates regardless of whether the subject is singular or plural.

With the German models, accuracy was > 0.88 for singular non-words, many of which are disambiguated by their determiner. Accordingly, most errors are plural word forms which the model identified as singular. Both monolingual German models showed a pattern of having many plural forms that were identified as singular $> 70\%$ of the time. Most of the remaining forms in each model were correctly identified as plural $> 70\%$ of the time, indicating that these models are relatively certain in their predictions. Unfortunately, no clear relationship to how closely the segmentation pattern matches the morphology was found with whether the correct verb is selected for a given non-word. However, it is possible that the *frequency* of the final subword segment occurring as a plural affix in a German corpus would be more predictive of which segments are likely to result in errors.

5.1 Non-linguistic factors

Although these results are largely consistent with the linguistic hypotheses discussed in Section 3.1, there is an uneven amount of training data across the models and languages. Notably, the French monolingual models used the most data, with German models using the least. However, this relationship is different within the mBERT model itself. This model, being trained on the Wikipedia dumps of each language, has the most data for English, followed by German, then French, then Spanish, then Dutch. While this does not completely disentangle the effects of training size (e.g., for the low Dutch performance), it does indicate that the disparity between model performances in, e.g., French and German cannot be explained solely by this factor. Further, almost all models use the same vocabulary size and number of parameters, with only FlauBERT being substantially larger, so this is also likely not a major factor. Therefore, it seems plausible that a primary driver of the differences in model performance between languages reported here is the language's plural construction.[6]

5.2 Implications for BERTology

While this study is primarily focused on the morphological and novel-word generalization capacities of BERT, it also investigates more models and languages than prior work on BERT's linguistic capacities–no previous work has looked at

---

[5] https://github.com/google/sentencepiece

[6] Additional architectural differences between the models are described in Appendix A.

more than one monolingual model for a single non-English language. The results here strongly suggest that the field of "BERTology" needs to consider the generality of their claims across not just different languages, but even across different BERT models developed on the same language. Even models based on the same architecture and within the same language, such as the German deepset and dbmdz models show different results on this simple task. While French subject-verb agreement can be determined solely from the subject determiner, FlauBERT achieved only 0.92 accuracy on even simple French sentences, while both mBERT and CamemBERT achieve accuracies higher than 0.95. This suggests that even in languages where subject-verb agreement is relatively simple, the BERT training objective alone cannot guarantee total generalization, even when the model performs well on downstream tasks. This suggests a need for greater scruitiny of claims of BERT's linguistic capacity that evaluate only one or two models.

5.3 Potential practical implications

Finally, To consider the relation of these theoretical findings to real-world performance, we ran the German experiments on real nouns again without capitalizing nouns. While all nouns are capitalized in formal German, this case serves as an example of a simple typo that might occur in real data. Agreement accuracy dropped from 1.00 in all 3 German models to 0.90, 0.79, and 0.89 in the mBERT, deepset, and dbmdz models respectively. This indicates that BERT's agreement faculty is highly sensitive to noise, failing to generalize even to highly plausible "non-words" (in this case, uncased nouns). This casts substantial doubt on the generality of BERT's extensively studied agreement competencies.

6 Conclusion

These results suggest that BERT models have some understanding of morphology when applied to novel words (or at least the plurals in a few Germanic and Romance languages). Performance is much significantly better than chance in simple agreement cases, even when no prime is given. This shows that the BERT models have learned something about what plural and singular forms "look like." However, non-word performance is not helped especially by the inclusion of a priming sentence, indicating that the BERT models in ques-

tion may not have learned to recognize new words and apply rules to them, as humans might. Further work should investigate what types of primes affect the performance and how.

The model performance here represents a *best case* for BERT's morphological capacity on novel words. The plural construction is extremely common in text and is connected to phenomena like agreement which additionally pressures it to be learned on a non-semantic level. Further, the simple sentences studied here allow for the potential of n-gram-level agreement heuristics which are not possible in the general case.

That BERT struggles to capture morphology in this way is likely not due to a lack of training data. There are two potential culprits: the tokenization method and the training objective. The FlauBERT results especially indicate that the masked language modeling objective may not sufficiently encourage agreement. Cross-linguistically, the models seem not to have picked up on how to use the information in the prime. In addition, the subword tokenization methods used by BERT and BERT-like models make the morphology learning problem significantly more complicated. This is because the plural morpheme is connected to some number of final characters of a word as a single token, meaning even plurals formed in the same way may be represented differently. This work points to a need for subword segmentation strategies that more closely mirror a language's morphology than current approaches like Unigram segmentation or byte pair encoding. In this aspect of language, there remains a large gap between BERT's behavior and human performance.

Acknowledgments

The author would like to thank Paul Schauenburg for his grammaticality judgements and extensive help with preparing the plural non-word data. I would also like to thank Tom McCoy, Tal Linzen, and Colin Wilson for their helpful and clarifying comments. This work was supported in part by a Provost's Undergraduate Research Award from Johns Hopkins University.

References

Jean Berko. 1958. The child's learning of english morphology. *Word*, 14:150–177.

Kaj Bostrom and Greg Durrett. 2020. Byte pair encoding is suboptimal for language model pretraining. *Computing Research Repository*, arXiv:2004.03720. To appear in *Findings of ACL: EMNLP 2020*.

José Cañete, Gabriel Chaperon, Rodrigo Fuentes, and Jorge Pérez. 2020. Spanish pre-trained BERT model and evaluation data. To appear in PML4DC at ICLR 2020.

Jacob Devlin, Ming-Wei Chang, Kenton Lee, and Kristina Toutanova. 2019. BERT: Pre-training of deep bidirectional transformers for language understanding. In *Proceedings of the 2019 Conference of the North American Chapter of the Association for Computational Linguistics: Human Language Technologies, Volume 1 (Long and Short Papers)*, pages 4171–4186, Minneapolis, Minnesota. Association for Computational Linguistics.

Daniel Edmiston. 2020. A systematic analysis of morphological content in bert models for multiple languages. *Computing Research Repository*, arXiv:2004.03032.

Allyson Ettinger. 2020. What BERT is not: Lessons from a new suite of psycholinguistic diagnostics for language models. *Transactions of the Association for Computational Linguistics*, 8:34–48.

Naomi Feldman. 2005. Learning and overgeneralization patterns in a connectionist model of the German plural. Master's thesis, University of Vienna.

Yoav Goldberg. 2019. Assessing BERT's syntactic abilities. *Computing Research Repository*, arXiv:1901.05287.

Valentin Hofmann, Janet B. Pierrehumbert, and Hinrich Schütze. 2020. DagoBERT: Generating derivational morphology with a pretrained language model. *Computing Research Repository*, arXiv:2005.00672.

H. G. van der Hulst and J. Kooij. 1998. Prosodic choices in plural formation in Dutch. In W. Kehrein and R. Wiese, editors, *Phonology and morphology of the Germanic languages*, pages 187–198. Niemeyer, Tübingen.

Taku Kudo. 2018. Subword regularization: Improving neural network translation models with multiple subword candidates. In *Proceedings of the 56th Annual Meeting of the Association for Computational Linguistics (Volume 1: Long Papers)*, pages 66–75, Melbourne, Australia. Association for Computational Linguistics.

Klaus-Michael Köpcke. 1988. Schemas in German plural formation. *Lingua*, 74(4):303 – 335.

Hang Le, Loïc Vial, Jibril Frej, Vincent Segonne, Maximin Coavoux, Benjamin Lecouteux, Alexandre Allauzen, Benoît Crabbé, Laurent Besacier, and Didier Schwab. 2020. FlauBERT: Unsupervised language model pre-training for french. In *Proceedings of The 12th Language Resources and Evaluation Conference*, pages 2479–2490, Marseille, France. European Language Resources Association.

Yinhan Liu, Myle Ott, Naman Goyal, Jingfei Du, Mandar Joshi, Danqi Chen, Omer Levy, Mike Lewis, Luke Zettlemoyer, and Veselin Stoyanov. 2019. RoBERTa: A robustly optimized BERT pre-training approach. *Computing Research Repository*, arXiv:1907.11692.

G. F. Marcus, U. Brinkmann, H. Clahsen, R. Wiese, and S. Pinker. 1995. German inflection: the exception that proves the rule. *Cogn Psychol*, 29(3):189–256.

Louis Martin, Benjamin Muller, Pedro Javier Ortiz Suárez, Yoann Dupont, Laurent Romary, Éric de la Clergerie, Djamé Seddah, and Benoît Sagot. 2020. CamemBERT: a tasty French language model. In *Proceedings of the 58th Annual Meeting of the Association for Computational Linguistics*, pages 7203–7219, Online. Association for Computational Linguistics.

Rebecca Marvin and Tal Linzen. 2018. Targeted syntactic evaluation of language models. In *Proceedings of the 2018 Conference on Empirical Methods in Natural Language Processing*, pages 1192–1202, Brussels, Belgium. Association for Computational Linguistics.

Kate McCurdy, Sharon Goldwater, and Adam Lopez. 2020. Inflecting when there's no majority: Limitations of encoder-decoder neural networks as cognitive models for German plurals. In *Proceedings of the 58th Annual Meeting of the Association for Computational Linguistics*, pages 1745–1756, Online. Association for Computational Linguistics.

Aaron Mueller, Garrett Nicolai, Panayiota Petrou-Zeniou, Natalia Talmina, and Tal Linzen. 2020. Cross-linguistic syntactic evaluation of word prediction models. In *Proceedings of the 58th Annual Meeting of the Association for Computational Linguistics*, pages 5523–5539, Online. Association for Computational Linguistics.

Matthew Peters, Mark Neumann, Mohit Iyyer, Matt Gardner, Christopher Clark, Kenton Lee, and Luke Zettlemoyer. 2018. Deep contextualized word representations. In *Proceedings of the 2018 Conference of the North American Chapter of the Association for Computational Linguistics: Human Language Technologies, Volume 1 (Long Papers)*, pages 2227–2237, New Orleans, Louisiana. Association for Computational Linguistics.

Marten van Schijndel, Aaron Mueller, and Tal Linzen. 2019. Quantity doesn't buy quality syntax with neural language models. In *Proceedings of the 2019 Conference on Empirical Methods in Natural Language Processing and the 9th International Joint Conference on Natural Language Processing (EMNLP-IJCNLP)*, pages 5831–5837, Hong Kong, China. Association for Computational Linguistics.

Stefan Schweter. 2020. *BERTurk - BERT models for Turkish*. Zenodo.

Rico Sennrich, Barry Haddow, and Alexandra Birch. 2016. Neural machine translation of rare words with subword units. In *Proceedings of the 54th Annual Meeting of the Association for Computational Linguistics (Volume 1: Long Papers)*, pages 1715–1725, Berlin, Germany. Association for Computational Linguistics.

Jochen Trommer. 2020. The subsegmental structure of German plural allomorphy. *Natural Language & Linguistic Theory*.

Ashish Vaswani, Noam Shazeer, Niki Parmar, Jakob Uszkoreit, Llion Jones, Aidan N Gomez, Ł ukasz Kaiser, and Illia Polosukhin. 2017. Attention is all you need. In I. Guyon, U. V. Luxburg, S. Bengio, H. Wallach, R. Fergus, S. Vishwanathan, and R. Garnett, editors, *Advances in Neural Information Processing Systems 30*, pages 5998–6008. Curran Associates, Inc.

Wietse de Vries, Andreas van Cranenburgh, Arianna Bisazza, Tommaso Caselli, Gertjan van Noord, and Malvina Nissim. 2019. BERTje: A Dutch BERT Model. *Computing Research Repository*, arXiv:1912.09582.

R. Wiese. 2000. *The Phonology of German*. Oxford Linguistics. Oxford University Press.

Zhilin Yang, Zihang Dai, Yiming Yang, Jaime Carbonell, Russ R Salakhutdinov, and Quoc V Le. 2019. Xlnet: Generalized autoregressive pretraining for language understanding. In H. Wallach, H. Larochelle, A. Beygelzimer, F. d'Alché Buc, E. Fox, and R. Garnett, editors, *Advances in Neural Information Processing Systems 32*, pages 5753–5763. Curran Associates, Inc.

Eugen Zaretsky, Benjamin P. Lange, Harald A. Euler, and Katrin Neumann. 2013. Differences in plural forms of monolingual German preschoolers and adults. *Lingue e Linguaggi*, 10:169–180.

A Additional model details

This appendix summarizes some additional differences between the models. It is not clear to the author that these would be related to the pattern of results presented here, but they are included so that interested readers need not hunt them down.

The models vary in whether they use an auxiliary task in addition to the masked language modelling (MLM) task described in the background. Some models use next-sentence prediction (NSP), in which the BERT model sees two sentences and must determine whether the second one follows the first. The initial BERT study indicated this improved performance, but subsequent work (Liu et al., 2019) found the opposite to be true, and many subsequent BERT models omit this objective.

BERTje instead includes a sentence order prediction (SOP) task, in which the model is presented with two consecutive sentences which may be in their original order or may be swapped, and must predict if they are in the correct order. (Vries et al., 2019) claim the addition of this objective improves their performance on downstream tasks.

Another attribute of the models that vary is how they handle the masking in MLM. The original BERT model masked out a portion of its training data before training, so every time a sentence is encountered the masked segments are the same. Subsequent works such as Liu et al. (2019) utilize *dynamic masking*, where different segments are masked in different training epochs. This is often achieved by masking the training data a fixed number of times and cycling through them during training. Finally, some models utilize sub-word masking (SWM), in which individual subwords are masked independently, while other models use whole-word masking (WWM), where all subwords of a single word are always masked together.

Model	Objective(s)	Masking Strategy
BERT$_{BASE}$	MLM, NSP	Static, SWM
CamemBERT	MLM	Dynamic, WWM
FlauBERT	MLM	Dynamic, WWM
BETO	MLM	Dynamic, WWM
BERTje	MLM, SOP	Static, WWM
Deepset	MLM, NSP	Static, SWM
dbmdz	MLM, NSP	Static, SWM
mBERT	MLM, NSP	Static, SWM

Table 5: Additional details of models. MLM = masked language modeling, NSP = next sentence prediction, SOP = sentence order prediction, SWM = sub-word masking, WWM = whole-word masking .

diagNNose: A Library for Neural Activation Analysis

Jaap Jumelet

Institute for Logic, Language and Computation, University of Amsterdam
j.w.d.jumelet@uva.nl

Abstract

In this paper we introduce diagNNose, an open source library for analysing the activations of deep neural networks. diagNNose contains a wide array of interpretability techniques that provide fundamental insights into the inner workings of neural networks. We demonstrate the functionality of diagNNose with a case study on subject-verb agreement within language models. diagNNose is available at https://github.com/i-machine-think/diagnnose.

1 Introduction

We introduce diagNNose, an open source library for analysing deep neural networks. The diagNNose library allows researchers to gain better insights into the internal representations of such networks, providing a broad set of tools of state-of-the-art analysis techniques. The library supports a wide range of model types, with a main focus on NLP architectures based on LSTMs (Hochreiter and Schmidhuber, 1997) and Transformers (Vaswani et al., 2017).

Open-source libraries have been quintessential in the progress and democratisation of NLP. Popular packages include HuggingFace's transformers (Wolf et al., 2019) – allowing easy access to pre-trained Transformer models; jiant (Pruksachatkun et al., 2020) – focusing on multitask and transfer learning within NLP; Captum (Kokhlikyan et al., 2020) – providing a range of feature attribution methods; and LIT (Tenney et al., 2020) – a platform for visualising and understanding model behaviour. We contribute to the open-source community by incorporating several **interpretability** techniques that have not been present in these packages.

Recent years have seen a considerable interest in improving the understanding of how deep neural networks operate (Linzen et al., 2019). The high-dimensional nature of these models makes it notoriously challenging to untangle their inner dynamics. This has given rise to a novel subfield within AI that focuses on interpretability, providing us a peak inside the black box. diagNNose aims to unify several of these techniques into one library, allowing interpretability research to be conducted in a more streamlined and accessible manner.

diagNNose's main focus lies on techniques that aid in uncovering linguistic knowledge that is encoded within a model's representations. The library provides abstractions that allow recurrent models to be investigated in the same way as Transformer models, in a modular fashion. It contains an extensive **activation extraction** module that allows for the extraction of (intermediate) model activations on a corpus. The analysis techniques that are currently implemented include:

- **Targeted syntactic evaluation tasks**, such as those of Linzen et al. (2016) and Marvin and Linzen (2018).

- **Probing** with **diagnostic classifiers** (Hupkes et al., 2018; Adi et al., 2016), and **control tasks** (Hewitt and Liang, 2019).

- **Feature attributions** that retrieve a feature's contribution to a model prediction (Lundberg and Lee, 2017; Murdoch et al., 2018). Our implementation is model-agnostic, which means that any type of model architecture can be explained by it.

In this paper we present both an overview of the library, as well as a case study on subject-verb agreement within language models. We first present a brief overview of interpretability within NLP and a background to the analysis techniques that are part of the library (Section 2). We then provide an overview of diagNNose and expand briefly on its individual modules (Section 3). We

Proceedings of the Third BlackboxNLP Workshop on Analyzing and Interpreting Neural Networks for NLP, pages 342–350
Online, November 20, 2020. ©2020 Association for Computational Linguistics

conclude with a case study on subject-verb agreement, demonstrating several of diagNNose's features in an experimental setup (Section 4).

2 Background

The increasing capacities of language models (and deep learning in general) have led to a rich field of research that aims to gain a better understanding of how these models operate. Approaches in this research area are often interdisciplinary in nature, borrowing concepts from fields such as psycholinguistics, information theory, and game theory. diagNNose provides support for several influential analysis techniques, for which we provide a brief background here.

2.1 Targeted syntactic evaluations

Language models have stood at the basis of many successes within NLP in recent years (Peters et al., 2018; Devlin et al., 2019). These models are trained on the objective of predicting the probability of an upcoming (or masked) token. In order to succeed in this task, these models need to possess a notion of many different linguistic aspects, such as syntax, semantics, and general domain knowledge. One popular line of research that tries to uncover a model's linguistic capacities does this via so-called targeted syntactic evaluations (Linzen et al., 2016; Gulordava et al., 2018; Marvin and Linzen, 2018; Jumelet and Hupkes, 2018). This type of analysis compares a model's output on minimally different pairs of grammatical and ungrammatical constructions. If it assigns a higher probability to the grammatical construction, the model is said to possess a notion of the underlying linguistic principles, such as subject-verb agreement or NPI licensing:

(1)   a.   The **ladies** near <u>John</u> **walk**.

       b.   * The **ladies** near <u>John</u> <u>walks</u>.

(2)   a.   **Nobody** has **ever** been there.

       b.   * Someone has **ever** been there.

diagNNose supports a wide range of syntactic tasks, as well as an interface that allows new tasks to be added without effort.

2.2 Diagnostic Classifiers

A second line of work tries to assess a model's understanding of linguistic properties – such as part-of-speech tags or number information – by directly training **diagnostic classifiers** on top of its representations (Hupkes et al., 2018; Adi et al., 2016; Belinkov et al., 2017). This type of analysis, also referred to as **probing**, has led to numerous insights into the inner workings of language models (Liu et al., 2019a; Tenney et al., 2019). The activations diagnostic classifiers are trained on are not restricted to just the hidden states of a language model at their top layer: this can, for instance, also be done on the individual gate activations to reveal patterns at the cell-level of a model (Giulianelli et al., 2018; Lakretz et al., 2019).

Recently, it has been a topic of discussion to what extent a high accuracy of a diagnostic classifier signifies that that property is actively being encoded by the model. Several solutions to assess this have been proposed, such as training a diagnostic classifier on a baseline of random labels (called a *control task* (Hewitt and Liang, 2019)), or based on the minimum description length of the classifier, a concept from information theory (Voita and Titov, 2020; Pimentel et al., 2020). diagNNose currently facilitates the training of diagnostic classifiers, as well as training control tasks alongside them.

2.3 Feature Attributions

Although probing allows us to uncover specific properties that are embedded within the model representations, it is unable to explain *how* a model transforms its input features into a successful prediction. This question can be addressed by computing the input **feature contributions** to a subsequent output. This is a challenging task, as the high-dimensional, non-linear nature of deep learning models prevents us from expressing these contributions directly on the basis of the model parameters.

Feature attributions can be computed in different ways. One common approach to this task is based on a concept that stems from cooperative game theory, called the Shapley value (Shapley, 1953). A Shapley value expresses the contribution of a player (in our case an input feature) to the outcome of game (in our the case a model prediction). Computing Shapley values is computationally expensive, and several approximation algorithms have therefore been proposed, such as SHAP (Lundberg and Lee, 2017), and Integrated Gradients (Sundararajan et al., 2017). diagNNose currently facilitates the computation of feature attributions using a technique called Contextual Decomposition (Murdoch et al., 2018), and its generalisation as proposed by Jumelet et al. (2019).

3 Library Overview

3.1 Modules

The library is structured into several modules that can be used as building blocks for an experimental pipeline. We provide an overview of a possible experimental pipeline in Figure 1.

3.1.1 Core modules

The following core modules stand at the basis of the different pipelines that can be build on top of diagNNose.

models We provide an abstraction over language models, enabling recurrent and Transformer models to derive from the same interface. Importing pre-trained Transformer models is done via the `transformers` library. For recurrent models we provide a wrapper that enables access to intermediate activations, including gate activations. We also provide functionality that allows to set the initial hidden states of recurrent LMs, based on a sentence or corpus.[1]

corpus Corpora are imported as a `Dataset` from the `torchtext` package. A Corpus can be transformed into an iterator for processing. Tokenization is done using the `transformers` tokenizers, allowing tokenization to be done in both a traditional token-per-token fashion, or based on subword units, such as byte pair encodings (Sennrich et al., 2016).

extract Central to most of the analysis modules is the extraction of activations. We provide an Extractor class that can extract the activations of a model given a corpus. Thanks to our model wrappers activation extraction is not restricted to just the top layer of a model; intermediate (gate) activations can be extracted as well. To facilitate the extraction of larger corpora with limited computational resources, activations can be dumped dynamically to disk.

activations Extracted activations can easily be retrieved using a `ActivationReader`, providing access to activations that correspond to a specific subset of corpus sentences. We also provide functionality for extracting only a specific subset of activations, based on sentence and token information. This way it is possible, for instance, to only

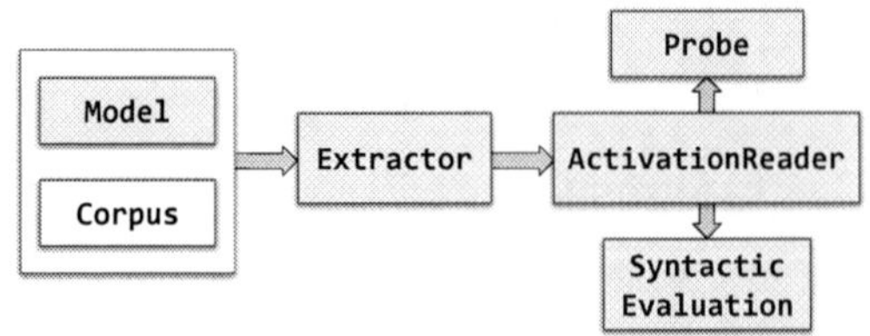

Figure 1: Pipeline stages for conducting syntactic evaluation and probing experiments. Note the modular nature of the pipeline: activations need only to be extracted once, after which the setup of the analysis experiments can be fine-tuned effortlessly.

extract the activations at the position of tokens of particular interest.

config The pipeline of diagNNose is configuration-driven. Configuration is defined in JSON format, but individual attributes can also be set from the command line directly.

3.1.2 Analysis modules

We currently support three main types of experimental modules. We provide a graphical overview of these modules in Figure 2.

syntax The library provides functionality for a large suite of targeted syntactic evaluation tasks. Currently we provide support for the following tasks:

- The subject-verb agreement corpus of Linzen et al. (2016), for which we also provide more fine-grained attractor conditions;
- The wide range of linguistic expressions of Marvin and Linzen (2018);
- The subject-verb agreement tasks of Lakretz et al. (2019);
- The NPI corpus of Warstadt et al. (2019);
- The stereotypically gendered anaphora resolution corpus of Jumelet et al. (2019), based on the original WinoBias corpus of Zhao et al. (2018).

Furthermore, the current implementation permits similar types of tasks to be easily added, and we plan on incorporating a larger set of tasks in the near future.

probe We provide easy tooling for training diagnostic classifiers (Hupkes et al., 2018; Adi et al., 2016) on top of extracted activations, to probe for linguistic information that might be embedded within them. Our extraction module facilitates

---

[1] As has been noted by Jumelet et al. (2019), LSTM LMs perform better when initialised with the phrase ". <eos>", instead of zero-valued vectors.

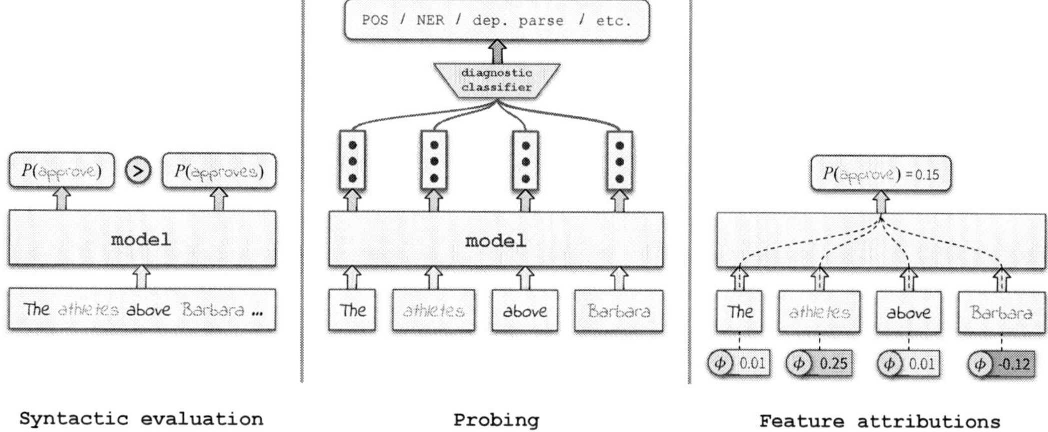

Figure 2: Schematic overview of three different types of experiments that are supported by diagNNose.

training diagnostic classifiers on top of intermediate activations as well, including gate activations. In recent years it has been pointed out that a high probing accuracy does not necessarily imply that linguistic information is actively being encoded by a model. To address this we have incorporated functionality for Control Tasks (Hewitt and Liang, 2019), providing more qualitative insights.

attribute We provide functionality for model-agnostic feature attributions, that allow the output of a model to be decomposed into a sum of contributions. This is achieved by implementing a wrapper over the operations of PyTorch[2], allowing intermediate feature contributions to be propagated during a forward pass in the model. Our implementation provides a basis for many Shapley-based attribution methods, as it allows different approximation methods to be tested easily. We currently facilitate the approximation procedure of (Generalised) Contextual Decomposition (Murdoch et al., 2018; Jumelet et al., 2019), Shapley sampling values (Castro et al., 2009), and the exact computation of propagated Shapley values. Our implementation is the first model-agnostic implementation of Contextual Decomposition: previous implementations were dependent on a fixed model structure.

3.2 Requirements

diagNNose is released on pip and can be installed using pip install diagnnose, or directly cloned from the GitHub repository: https://github.com/i-machine-think/diagnnose. The

library supports Python 3.6 or later, and its core dependencies are PyTorch (Paszke et al., 2019) (v1.5+), torchtext[3], and HuggingFace's transformers (Wolf et al., 2019). diagNNose is released under the MIT License (Open Source Initiative, 2020). diagNNose runs both on CPUs and GPUs, and has especially been optimised for smaller consumer setups, due to limited computational resources during development.

The diagNNose code base is fully typed using Python type hints. The code is formatted using *Black*.[4] All methods and classes are documented, and an overview of this documentation can be found on https://diagnnose.readthedocs.io.

4 Case Study: Subject-Verb Agreement

To demonstrate the functionality of diagNNose we will consider the subject-verb agreement corpora of Lakretz et al. (2019) on a set of language models. For our experiments we consider the following models: BERT (Devlin et al., 2019), RoBERTa (Liu et al., 2019b), DistilRoBERTa (Sanh et al., 2019), and the LSTM language model of Gulordava et al. (2018).

4.1 Corpora

The corpora of Lakretz et al. (2019) are formed by seven tasks of template-based syntactic constructions. These constructions contain an "agreement attractor" in between the subject and the verb, which might trick a language model into predicting the incorrect number of the verb. A model thus

---

[2]The wrapper is defined based on the __torch_function__ functionality that has been introduced in PyTorch 1.5.

[3]https://pytorch.org/text/
[4]https://github.com/psf/black

needs to possess a strong notion of the structure of a sentence: nouns within a prepositional phrase, for instance, should have no impact on the number of the main verb in a sentence.

The seven tasks are defined by the following templates:

SIMPLE
The **athletes approve**

ADV
The **uncle** probably **avoids**

2ADV
The **athlete** most probably **understands**

COADV
The **farmer** overtly and deliberately **knows**

NAMEPP
The **women** near John **remember**

NOUNPP
The **athlete** beside the tables **approves**

NOUNPPADV
The **aunt** behind the bikes certainly **knows**

Each task contains 600 to 900 distinct sentences. Sentences are split up into multiple conditions based on the number of the subject, and the number of the intervening noun phrase. The NOUNPP corpus, for instance, is split up into 4 conditions:

SS: The **athlete** beside the table **approves**

SP: The **athlete** beside the tables **approves**

PS: The **athletes** beside the table **approves**

PP: The **athletes** beside the tables **approves**

To test these corpora on a recurrent model, we first compute the model's hidden state at the position of the verb by feeding it the sub-sentence up till that position. Based on this hidden state we compute the output probabilities of the verb of the correct number ($v^{\checkmark}$), and the incorrect number ($v^{\times}$), and compare these:

$$P(v^{\checkmark} \mid h_t) > P(v^{\times} \mid h_t)$$

For bi-directional masked language models, such as BERT, we can not compute a model's intermediate hidden state by passing it a sub-sentence, because these models also incorporate the input of future tokens. To solve this, we replace the verb in each sentence with a `<mask>` token, and assess the model's probabilities at the position of this token.

```
# distilroberta_syntax.json
{
  "model": {
    "model_name": "distilroberta-base",
    "mode": "language_modeling"
  },
  "syntax": {
    "config": {
      "lakretz": {
        "path": "path_to_corpora/"
      }
    }
  }
}


# syntax.py
from diagnnose.config import create_config_dict
from diagnnose.syntax import SyntacticEvaluator
from diagnnose.models import import_model
from diagnnose.tokenizer import create_tokenizer

config_dict = create_config_dict()

model = import_model(config_dict)

tokenizer = create_tokenizer(config_dict)

suite = SyntacticEvaluator(
  model, tokenizer, **config_dict["syntax"]
)

suite.run()
```

(3a) Example setup for running the targeted syntactic evaluation tasks of Lakretz et al. (2019) on DistilRoBERTa.

```
# distilroberta_attribute.json
{
  "model": {
    "model_name": "distilroberta-base",
    "mode": "language_modeling"
  }
}


# attribute.py
from diagnnose.attribute import (
  Explainer, ShapleyDecomposer
)
from diagnnose.config import create_config_dict
from diagnnose.models import import_model
from diagnnose.tokenizer import create_tokenizer

config_dict = create_config_dict()

model = import_model(config_dict)

tokenizer = create_tokenizer(config_dict)

decomposer = ShapleyDecomposer(model)
explainer = Explainer(decomposer, tokenizer)

explainer.explain(
  ["The athletes above Barbara <mask>."],
  ["approve", "approves"]
)
```

(3b) Example setup for creating the feature attributions of DistilRoBERTa on a sentence from the NAMEPP corpus of Lakretz et al. (2019).

Corpus	Condition	BERT	RoBERTa	DistilRoBERTa	LSTM
SIMPLE	S	**100**	**100**	**100**	**100**
	P	**100**	**100**	**100**	**100**
ADV	S	**100**	**100**	**100**	**100**
	P	**100**	**100**	**100**	99.6
2ADV	S	**100**	**100**	**100**	99.2
	P	**100**	**100**	**100**	99.3
COADV	S	**100**	**100**	**100**	98.7
	P	**100**	**100**	**100**	99.3
NAMEPP	SS	93.0	75.7	81.5	**99.3**
	PS	**88.4**	65.9	32.4	68.9
NOUNPP	SS	95.7	88.9	98.1	**99.2**
	SP	**93.3**	84.7	91.1	87.2
	PS	**96.7**	90.6	85.3	92.0
	PP	**100**	**100**	**100**	99.0
NOUNPPADV	SS	99.6	**100**	**100**	99.5
	SP	99.2	99.8	**100**	91.2
	PS	**100**	**100**	**100**	99.2
	PP	**100**	**100**	**100**	99.8

Table 1: Results of the targeted syntactic evaluation tasks of Lakretz et al. (2019).

Modern language models often make use of BPE tokenization that might split a word into multiple sub-words. In our experiments we therefore only compare verb forms for which both the plural and singular form are split into a single token.[5]

4.2 Targeted syntactic evaluations

We run the targeted syntactic evaluation suite on all the 7 templates. An example configuration and script of this experiment in provided in Figure 3a. To run the experiment on a different model, the only configuration that needs to be changed is the `model_name`. The results of the experiment are shown in Table 1.

It can be seen that the Transformer language models generally achieve higher scores than the LSTM model. Interestingly, the NAMEPP task poses a challenge for all models, and both RoBERTa and DistilRoBERTa score lower on this task than the LSTM. A second point of interest is the difference in performance between RoBERTa and DistilRoBERTa on the NAMEPP and NOUNPP tasks. Even though DistilRoBERTa has been trained to emulate the behaviour of RoBERTa, its performance on a downstream task like this differs significantly. These results can provide a starting point for a more fine-grained analysis, such as creating the feature attributions of a model on a specific template.

4.3 Feature attributions

To gain a better insight into why the language models struggle so strongly with the NAMEPP corpus, we run the feature attribution module on these constructions. An example configuration of this experimental setup is provided in Figure 3b. The results for the experiment are shown in Figure 4.

We show the attributions for DistilRoBERTa on an example sentence from the corpus, which highlights the difference in impact of the intervening attractor on the number of the verb. The results should be interpreted as follows: the score at the top of the attribution denotes the *full logit* of the model for that class, these are the logits that are transformed into probabilities using SoftMax. This logit is *decomposed* in a sum of contributions, which we denote at the bottom of each token. It can be validated that the contributions sum up together to the logit. This is an important property of feature attribution methods – called *efficiency* – that warrants a certain degree of faithfulness of an explanation to the model. A negative value indicates a negative feature contribution to an output class: the impact of that feature led to a decreased preference for the class. Feature attributions also

---

[5]The RoBERTa tokenizer, for example, splits "confuses" into "conf" + "uses", and "confuse" into "confuse". Comparing the model probabilities for these two forms directly is hence not possible.

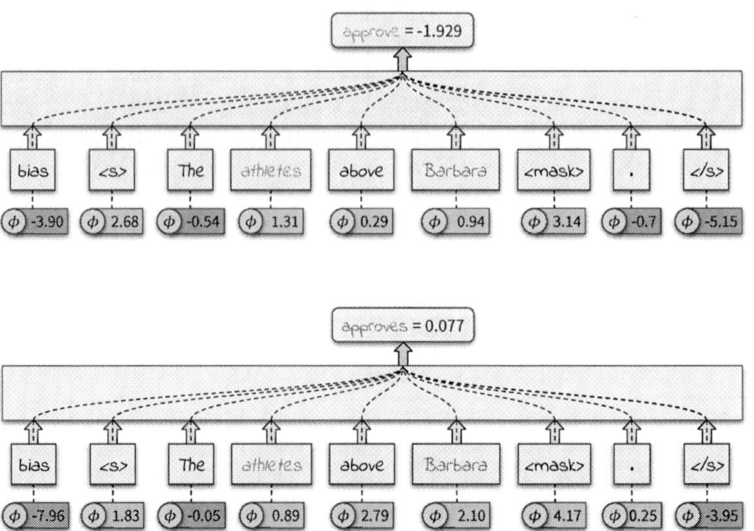

Figure 4: The feature attributions for DistilRoBERTa on an example sentence from the NAMEPP task of Lakretz et al. (2019). The logits of two output tokens, '*approve*' and '*approves*', are decomposed into a sum of contributions.

include the influence of model biases: an aggregate of all information that is statically present within the network such as weight intercepts.

On the presented example sentence, Distil-RoBERTa makes an incorrect prediction: the logit of the incorrect singular form '*approves*' is larger than that of the plural '*approve*'. The model's misstep in predicting the correct verb form arrives from the fact that the subject '*athletes*' provided not enough contribution to overrule the negative contributions stemming from other input features. A model that has a thorough understanding of subject-verb agreement should assign a larger contribution to the subject when predicting the main verb: the number signal provided by the subject should be propagated strongly enough to overrule other interfering signals.

The `attribute` module is still in active development. The exponential nature of computing Shapley values makes creating these explanations a challenging task, and we look forward to incorporate other techniques that aim to alleviate the computing costs.

5   Conclusion

diagNNose provides essential tools for conducting interpretability research, providing cutting edge analysis techniques such as diagnostic classifiers and feature attributions. The modular design of the library allows complex hypotheses to be tested rapidly, and provides a solid basis for the development of novel interpretability techniques. The library code is open source and welcomes others to contribute: we are eagerly looking forward to collaborate on adding new features to the library.

Acknowledgments

The author gratefully acknowledges the feedback received from Dieuwke Hupkes during the development of the library.

References

Yossi Adi, Einat Kermany, Yonatan Belinkov, Ofer Lavi, and Yoav Goldberg. 2016. Fine-grained analysis of sentence embeddings using auxiliary prediction tasks. *arXiv preprint arXiv:1608.04207*.

Yonatan Belinkov, Nadir Durrani, Fahim Dalvi, Hassan Sajjad, and James Glass. 2017. What do neural machine translation models learn about morphology? In *Proceedings of the 55th Annual Meeting of the Association for Computational Linguistics (Volume 1: Long Papers)*, pages 861–872.

Javier Castro, Daniel Gómez, and Juan Tejada. 2009. Polynomial calculation of the shapley value based on sampling. *Computers Operations Research*, 36(5):1726 – 1730. Selected papers presented at the

Tenth International Symposium on Locational Decisions (ISOLDE X).

Jacob Devlin, Ming-Wei Chang, Kenton Lee, and Kristina Toutanova. 2019. Bert: Pre-training of deep bidirectional transformers for language understanding. In *Proceedings of the 2019 Conference of the North American Chapter of the Association for Computational Linguistics: Human Language Technologies, Volume 1 (Long and Short Papers)*, pages 4171–4186.

Mario Giulianelli, Jack Harding, Florian Mohnert, Dieuwke Hupkes, and Willem Zuidema. 2018. Under the hood: Using diagnostic classifiers to investigate and improve how language models track agreement information. In *Proceedings of the 2018 EMNLP Workshop BlackboxNLP: Analyzing and Interpreting Neural Networks for NLP*, pages 240–248.

Kristina Gulordava, Piotr Bojanowski, Édouard Grave, Tal Linzen, and Marco Baroni. 2018. Colorless green recurrent networks dream hierarchically. In *Proceedings of the 2018 Conference of the North American Chapter of the Association for Computational Linguistics: Human Language Technologies, Volume 1 (Long Papers)*, pages 1195–1205.

John Hewitt and Percy Liang. 2019. Designing and interpreting probes with control tasks. In *Proceedings of the 2019 Conference on Empirical Methods in Natural Language Processing and the 9th International Joint Conference on Natural Language Processing (EMNLP-IJCNLP)*, pages 2733–2743.

Sepp Hochreiter and Jürgen Schmidhuber. 1997. Long short-term memory. *Neural computation*, 9(8):1735–1780.

Dieuwke Hupkes, Sara Veldhoen, and Willem Zuidema. 2018. Visualisation and'diagnostic classifiers' reveal how recurrent and recursive neural networks process hierarchical structure. *Journal of Artificial Intelligence Research*, 61:907–926.

Jaap Jumelet and Dieuwke Hupkes. 2018. Do language models understand anything? on the ability of lstms to understand negative polarity items. In *Proceedings of the 2018 EMNLP Workshop BlackboxNLP: Analyzing and Interpreting Neural Networks for NLP*, pages 222–231.

Jaap Jumelet, Willem Zuidema, and Dieuwke Hupkes. 2019. Analysing neural language models: Contextual decomposition reveals default reasoning in number and gender assignment. In *Proceedings of the 23rd Conference on Computational Natural Language Learning (CoNLL)*, pages 1–11, Hong Kong, China. Association for Computational Linguistics.

Narine Kokhlikyan, Vivek Miglani, Miguel Martin, Edward Wang, Bilal Alsallakh, Jonathan Reynolds, Alexander Melnikov, Natalia Kliushkina, Carlos Araya, Siqi Yan, and Orion Reblitz-Richardson. 2020. Captum: A unified and generic model interpretability library for pytorch. *CoRR*, abs/2009.07896.

Yair Lakretz, German Kruszewski, Theo Desbordes, Dieuwke Hupkes, Stanislas Dehaene, and Marco Baroni. 2019. The emergence of number and syntax units in LSTM language models. In *Proceedings of the 2019 Conference of the North American Chapter of the Association for Computational Linguistics: Human Language Technologies, Volume 1 (Long and Short Papers)*, pages 11–20, Minneapolis, Minnesota. Association for Computational Linguistics.

Tal Linzen, Grzegorz Chrupała, Yonatan Belinkov, and Dieuwke Hupkes. 2019. Proceedings of the 2019 acl workshop blackboxnlp: Analyzing and interpreting neural networks for nlp. In *Proceedings of the 2019 ACL Workshop BlackboxNLP: Analyzing and Interpreting Neural Networks for NLP*.

Tal Linzen, Emmanuel Dupoux, and Yoav Goldberg. 2016. Assessing the ability of LSTMs to learn syntax-sensitive dependencies. *Transactions of the Association for Computational Linguistics*, 4:521–535.

Nelson F Liu, Matt Gardner, Yonatan Belinkov, Matthew E Peters, and Noah A Smith. 2019a. Linguistic knowledge and transferability of contextual representations. In *Proceedings of the 2019 Conference of the North American Chapter of the Association for Computational Linguistics: Human Language Technologies, Volume 1 (Long and Short Papers)*, pages 1073–1094.

Yinhan Liu, Myle Ott, Naman Goyal, Jingfei Du, Mandar Joshi, Danqi Chen, Omer Levy, Mike Lewis, Luke Zettlemoyer, and Veselin Stoyanov. 2019b. Roberta: A robustly optimized bert pretraining approach. *arXiv preprint arXiv:1907.11692*.

Scott M Lundberg and Su-In Lee. 2017. A unified approach to interpreting model predictions. In *Advances in neural information processing systems*, pages 4765–4774.

Rebecca Marvin and Tal Linzen. 2018. Targeted syntactic evaluation of language models. In *Proceedings of the 2018 Conference on Empirical Methods in Natural Language Processing*, pages 1192–1202, Brussels, Belgium. Association for Computational Linguistics.

W. James Murdoch, Peter J. Liu, and Bin Yu. 2018. Beyond word importance: Contextual decomposition to extract interactions from lstms. In *6th International Conference on Learning Representations, ICLR 2018, Vancouver, BC, Canada, April 30 - May 3, 2018, Conference Track Proceedings*.

Open Source Initiative. 2020. The mit license.

Adam Paszke, Sam Gross, Francisco Massa, Adam Lerer, James Bradbury, Gregory Chanan, Trevor Killeen, Zeming Lin, Natalia Gimelshein, Luca

Antiga, et al. 2019. Pytorch: An imperative style, high-performance deep learning library. In *Advances in neural information processing systems*, pages 8026–8037.

Matthew Peters, Mark Neumann, Mohit Iyyer, Matt Gardner, Christopher Clark, Kenton Lee, and Luke Zettlemoyer. 2018. Deep contextualized word representations. In *Proceedings of the 2018 Conference of the North American Chapter of the Association for Computational Linguistics: Human Language Technologies, Volume 1 (Long Papers)*, pages 2227–2237.

Tiago Pimentel, Josef Valvoda, Rowan Hall Maudslay, Ran Zmigrod, Adina Williams, and Ryan Cotterell. 2020. Information-theoretic probing for linguistic structure. *arXiv preprint arXiv:2004.03061*.

Yada Pruksachatkun, Phil Yeres, Haokun Liu, Jason Phang, Phu Mon Htut, Alex Wang, Ian Tenney, and Samuel R Bowman. 2020. jiant: A software toolkit for research on general-purpose text understanding models. *arXiv preprint arXiv:2003.02249*.

Victor Sanh, Lysandre Debut, Julien Chaumond, and Thomas Wolf. 2019. Distilbert, a distilled version of bert: smaller, faster, cheaper and lighter. *arXiv preprint arXiv:1910.01108*.

Rico Sennrich, Barry Haddow, and Alexandra Birch. 2016. Neural machine translation of rare words with subword units. In *Proceedings of the 54th Annual Meeting of the Association for Computational Linguistics (Volume 1: Long Papers)*, pages 1715–1725.

Lloyd S. Shapley. 1953. A value for n-person games. *Contributions to the Theory of Games*, (28):307–317.

Mukund Sundararajan, Ankur Taly, and Qiqi Yan. 2017. Axiomatic attribution for deep networks. In *Proceedings of the 34th International Conference on Machine Learning, ICML 2017, Sydney, NSW, Australia, 6-11 August 2017*, pages 3319–3328.

Ian Tenney, Dipanjan Das, and Ellie Pavlick. 2019. Bert rediscovers the classical nlp pipeline. In *Proceedings of the 57th Annual Meeting of the Association for Computational Linguistics*, pages 4593–4601.

Ian Tenney, James Wexler, Jasmijn Bastings, Tolga Bolukbasi, Andy Coenen, Sebastian Gehrmann, Ellen Jiang, Mahima Pushkarna, Carey Radebaugh, Emily Reif, and Ann Yuan. 2020. The language interpretability tool: Extensible, interactive visualizations and analysis for NLP models. *CoRR*, abs/2008.05122.

Ashish Vaswani, Noam Shazeer, Niki Parmar, Jakob Uszkoreit, Llion Jones, Aidan N Gomez, Łukasz Kaiser, and Illia Polosukhin. 2017. Attention is all you need. In *Advances in neural information processing systems*, pages 5998–6008.

Elena Voita and Ivan Titov. 2020. Information-theoretic probing with minimum description length. *arXiv preprint arXiv:2003.12298*.

Alex Warstadt, Yu Cao, Ioana Grosu, Wei Peng, Hagen Blix, Yining Nie, Anna Alsop, Shikha Bordia, Haokun Liu, Alicia Parrish, Sheng-Fu Wang, Jason Phang, Anhad Mohananey, Phu Mon Htut, Paloma Jeretic, and Samuel R. Bowman. 2019. Investigating BERT's knowledge of language: Five analysis methods with NPIs. In *Proceedings of the 2019 Conference on Empirical Methods in Natural Language Processing and the 9th International Joint Conference on Natural Language Processing (EMNLP-IJCNLP)*, pages 2877–2887, Hong Kong, China. Association for Computational Linguistics.

Thomas Wolf, Lysandre Debut, Victor Sanh, Julien Chaumond, Clement Delangue, Anthony Moi, Pierric Cistac, Tim Rault, Rémi Louf, Morgan Funtowicz, Joe Davison, Sam Shleifer, Patrick von Platen, Clara Ma, Yacine Jernite, Julien Plu, Canwen Xu, Teven Le Scao, Sylvain Gugger, Mariama Drame, Quentin Lhoest, and Alexander M. Rush. 2019. Huggingface's transformers: State-of-the-art natural language processing. *ArXiv*, abs/1910.03771.

Jieyu Zhao, Tianlu Wang, Mark Yatskar, Vicente Ordonez, and Kai-Wei Chang. 2018. Gender bias in coreference resolution: Evaluation and debiasing methods. In *Proceedings of the 2018 Conference of the North American Chapter of the Association for Computational Linguistics: Human Language Technologies, Volume 2 (Short Papers)*, pages 15–20.

Association for Computational Linguistics
209 N. Eighth Street
Stroudsburg, Pennsylvania 18360

ISBN 978-1-7138-1988-2